수능특강

영어영역 **영어듣기**

KB214064

기획 및 개발	감수	책임 편집
김유진(EBS 교과위원)	한국교육과정평가원	권경희
양성심(EBS 교과위원)		
김현경(EBS 교과위원)		

듣기 MP3 파일
바로듣기 & 다운로드

본 교재의 듣기 MP3 및 정답과 해설은 EBS*i* 사이트(www.ebsi.co.kr)에서 다운로드 받으실 수 있습니다.

교재 내용 문의
교재 및 강의 내용 문의는
EBS*i* 사이트(www.ebsi.co.kr)의 학습 Q&A 서비스를
활용하시기 바랍니다.

교재 정오표 공지
발행 이후 발견된 정오 사항을
EBS*i* 사이트 정오표 코너에서 알려 드립니다.
교재 → 교재 자료실 → 교재 정오표

교재 정정 신청
공지된 정오 내용 외에 발견된 정오 사항이 있다면
EBS*i* 사이트를 통해 알려 주세요.
교재 → 교재 정정 신청

항공·보건·조리 특성화대학

초당대학교

2025학년도 신입생 모집

대학기본역량진단 일반재정지원대학
재정지원수혜 2022~2024
(교육부 2021년)

광주 전남 4년제 사립대학 취업률 2위 73.4%
전국 평균 취업률 64.2%
(2022년 대학알리미 공시 기준)

대학 평생교육체제 지원사업 선정
(LiFE 2.0)

콘도르비행교육원 / 항공기술교육원 / 초당드론교육원 운영
- 국토교통부, 항공종사자 전문교육기관 및 무인헬기 조종사 양성 교육기관 지정

수시모집: 2024년 9월 9일(월) ~ 13일(금)
정시모집: 2024년 12월 31일(화) ~ 2025년 1월 3일(금)

초당대학교

58530 전라남도 무안군 무안읍 무안로 380

입학문의: 1577-2859

▶ 바로가기

 유튜브 초당대학교
 페이스북 초당대학교
 인스타그램 @chodang.univ
 카카오톡채널 초당대학교입학상담

수능특강

영어영역 영어듣기

이 책의 **구성과 특징** Structure

Part I 유형편

수능과 모의평가에 빈번하게 출제되는 듣기 유형을 학습합니다. 예제를 통해 유형별 특징 및 듣기 전략을 파악한 다음, 〈Exercises〉와 〈Dictations〉를 통해 듣기에 친숙해진 후, 〈유형 심화〉를 풀며 듣기 능력을 강화한다면 수능 영어듣기의 모든 유형을 마스터할 수 있을 것입니다.

유형 소개
유형에 대한 특징 및 출제 경향 소개

기출 예제
해당 유형으로 출제된 최신 수능 및 모의평가 문제

단계별 듣기 전략
제대로 듣고 정답을 맞히기 위한 3단계 듣기 전략

Dictations
예제를 다시 들으며 빈칸에 들어갈 말을 적어 봄으로써 학습 효과 UP

Communicative Functions
듣기 및 말하기 상황에 유용한 의사소통 기능 학습

Useful Expressions, Idioms and Phrases
기출 숙어 및 관용어 학습

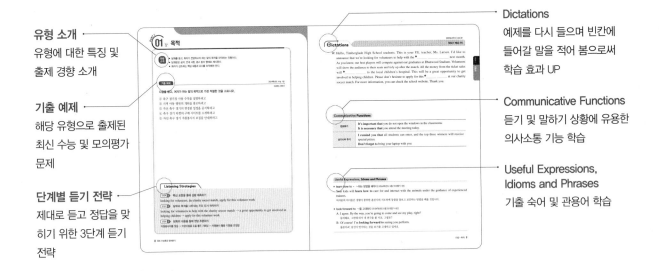

Exercises
연습문제를 통한 듣기 유형별 집중 학습

Dictations
Exercises에서 풀어 본 문제를 다시 듣고 받아쓰는 연습을 하면서 중요한 표현 확인

유형 심화 I, II
이전 강에서 학습한 유형들을 심화 문제로 다지면서 유형 완벽 마스터

Part **II** 소재편

최신 수능과 모의평가 영어듣기에 자주 등장하는 소재들을 학습합니다. 다양한 상황 안에서 이루어지는 대화 및 담화를 들으며 다양한 소재에 익숙해지고 소재와 관련된 여러 가지 어휘와 표현을 익힘으로써 수능과 모의평가에 출제될 가능성이 큰 소재에 대비할 수 있습니다.

소재 소개 ·
소재에 대한 특징 및
출제 경향 소개

기출 예제 ·
소재와 관련된 수능 및
모의평가 문제

문항 속의 소재 ·
기출문제의 토막
대본에서 연관된
소재 확인

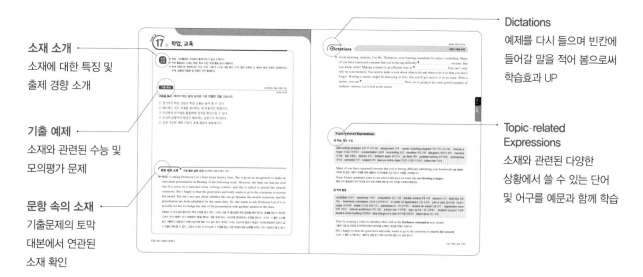

Dictations
예제를 다시 들으며 빈칸에
들어갈 말을 적어 봄으로써
학습효과 UP

Topic-related Expressions
소재와 관련된 다양한
상황에서 쓸 수 있는 단어
및 어구를 예문과 함께 학습

Exercises
연습문제를 통한 집중 학습

Dictations
Exercises에서 풀어 본 문제를 다시 듣고
받아 쓰는 연습을 하면서 중요 표현 확인

Part **III** 실전편

최신 모의평가와 수능 영어듣기 문항의 경향을 반영하여 구성한 실전 모의고사 6회분이 제공됩니다. 유형편과 소재편에서 키운 영어듣기 능력을 바탕으로 실전 모의고사를 풀어봄으로써 수능 실전 감각을 기르고 영어듣기에 대한 자신감을 키울 수 있습니다.

이 책의 **차례** Contents

Part **I** 유형편

학생

인공지능 DANCHOQ
푸리봇 문|제|검|색

EBS*i* 사이트와 EBS*i* 고교강의 APP 하단의 **AI 학습도우미 푸리봇**을 통해 문항코드를 검색하면 푸리봇이 해당 문제의 해설과 해설 강의를 찾아 줍니다. **사진 촬영으로도 검색**할 수 있습니다.

문제별 문항코드 확인   문항코드 검색

[24006-0001]
1. 아래 그래프를 이해한 내용으로 가장 적절한 것은?

→ 24006-0001

[24006-0001]
사진 촬영 검색

선생님

EBS 교사지원센터
교재 관련 자|료|제|공

교재의 문항 한글(HWP) 파일과 교재이미지, 강의자료를 무료로 제공합니다.

한글다운로드   교재이미지   강의자료

• 교사지원센터(teacher.ebsi.co.kr)에서 '교사인증' 이후 이용하실 수 있습니다.
• 교사지원센터에서 제공하는 자료는 교재별로 다를 수 있습니다.

Part

I

유형편

PART I

01강 목적

유형 소개
- 담화를 듣고, 화자가 전달하고자 하는 말의 목적을 파악하는 유형이다.
- 담화문은 공지, 안내 사항, 광고 등의 형태로 제시된다.
- 화자가 강조하는 핵심 내용과 요지를 파악해야 한다.

기출 예제

2024학년도 수능 1번

24006-0001

다음을 듣고, 여자가 하는 말의 목적으로 가장 적절한 것을 고르시오.

① 축구 경기장 사용 수칙을 설명하려고
② 지역 아동 병원의 개원을 홍보하려고
③ 자선 축구 경기의 변경된 일정을 공지하려고
④ 축구 경기 티켓의 구매 사이트를 소개하려고
⑤ 자선 축구 경기 자원봉사자 모집을 안내하려고

Listening Strategies

STEP 1 핵심 표현을 통해 상황 예측하기

looking for volunteers, the charity soccer match, apply for this volunteer work

STEP 2 담화의 목적을 나타내는 주요 단서 파악하기

looking for volunteers to help with the charity soccer match → a great opportunity to get involved in helping children → apply for this volunteer work

STEP 3 담화의 내용을 통해 정답 추론하기

자원봉사자를 찾음 → 어린이들을 도울 좋은 기회임 → 자원봉사 활동 지원을 요청함

Dictations

W: Hello, Timberglade High School students. This is your P.E. teacher, Ms. Larsen. I'd like to announce that we're looking for volunteers to help with the ❶_____ _____ _____ next month. As you know, our best players will compete against our graduates at Ebanwood Stadium. Volunteers will show the audience to their seats and tidy up after the match. All the money from the ticket sales will ❷_____ _____ to the local children's hospital. This will be a great opportunity to get involved in helping children. Please don't hesitate to apply for this ❸_____ _____ at our charity soccer match. For more information, you can check the school website. Thank you.

Communicative Functions

강조하기	**It's important that** you do not open the windows in the classrooms. **It is necessary that** you attend the meeting today.
상기시켜 주기	**I remind you that** all students can enter, and the top three winners will receive special prizes. **Don't forget to** bring your laptop with you.

Useful Expressions, Idioms and Phrases

■ **learn how to ~** ～하는 방법을 배우다 (2024학년도 9월 모의평가 1번)

Your kids will **learn how to** care for and interact with the animals under the guidance of experienced trainers.

여러분의 아이들은 경험이 풍부한 훈련사의 지도하에 동물을 돌보고 교감하는 방법을 배울 것입니다.

■ **look forward to** ～을 고대하다 (2024학년도 6월 모의평가 4번)

A: I agree. By the way, you're going to come and see my play, right?

동의해요. 그런데 와서 내 연극을 볼 거죠, 그렇죠?

B: Of course! I'm **looking forward to** seeing you perform.

물론이죠! 당신이 연기하는 것을 보기를 고대하고 있어요.

01 다음을 듣고, 남자가 하는 말의 목적으로 가장 적절한 것을 고르시오.   24006-0002

① 축구 클럽 운영 방식을 설명하려고
② 경기 관람 시 유의 사항을 안내하려고
③ 축구 리그 우승 축하 행사를 공지하려고
④ 행사장 입장 시 질서 유지를 당부하려고
⑤ 리그 결승전 입장권 구매 방법을 알리려고

02 다음을 듣고, 여자가 하는 말의 목적으로 가장 적절한 것을 고르시오.   24006-0003

① 과제 제출 기한 준수를 당부하려고
② 대회 신청 조기 마감을 공지하려고
③ 지리 현장 체험 학습을 홍보하려고
④ 여행 글쓰기 대회 참가를 독려하려고
⑤ 여행지 선택 시 고려 사항을 설명하려고

03 다음을 듣고, 남자가 하는 말의 목적으로 가장 적절한 것을 고르시오.   24006-0004

① 학교 간 배구 경기 일정을 공지하려고
② 교내 배구팀 선수 간의 협업을 독려하려고
③ 체육관 공사로 인한 수업 시간 변경을 알리려고
④ 배구 경기에서 우승하기 위한 전술을 설명하려고
⑤ 교내 배구팀의 신규 선수 선발 테스트를 안내하려고

04 다음을 듣고, 여자가 하는 말의 목적으로 가장 적절한 것을 고르시오. 24006-0005

① 새로 열린 문어 전시회를 홍보하려고
② 해양 탐사를 위한 준비물을 안내하려고
③ 문어의 독특한 학습 방법을 설명하려고
④ 관람객을 위한 특별 할인 행사를 소개하려고
⑤ 전시관 수리로 인한 관람 시간 변경을 공지하려고

05 다음을 듣고, 남자가 하는 말의 목적으로 가장 적절한 것을 고르시오. 24006-0006

① 학교 환기 시스템 교체를 건의하려고
② 교실 창문 교체 공사 시기를 안내하려고
③ 미세 먼지의 발생 원인과 유해성에 대해 알리려고
④ 교실 공기 질 개선을 위한 아이디어를 요청하려고
⑤ 나쁜 공기 유입을 막기 위한 창문 닫기를 당부하려고

06 다음을 듣고, 여자가 하는 말의 목적으로 가장 적절한 것을 고르시오. 24006-0007

① 지하 주차장 내 계단 보수 공사를 공지하려고
② 지하 주차장 사용에 관한 주민 의견을 요청하려고
③ 지하 주차장 내 엘리베이터 고장 원인을 설명하려고
④ 지하 주차장 내 계단 낙상 사고의 위험을 경고하려고
⑤ 지하 주차장 내 노후 설비의 보수 및 개선을 촉구하려고

Dictations

01

M: Good afternoon, listeners! This is Eric Moore, manager of the football league champion, Kingston Football Club. This past season was our first championship in our 17-year history. We'd like to ❶_____ _____ _____ of our club's historic victory with as many of you as possible. To celebrate our victory, we're going to hold a celebration full of colorful events. It will take place at Kingston Stadium at 2 p.m. next Saturday, and all of our players will enjoy ❷_____ _____ _____ together with participants. Additionally, we will provide participants with some cool Kingston Football Club souvenirs. Anyone can enjoy the celebration for free ❸_____ _____ _____ on our website. I can't wait to see you at the event!

02

W: Hello, Deerland High School students! This is your geography teacher, Ms. Barkley. Since I ❶_____ _____ _____ _____ for the Travel Writing Contest, which is April 6th, next Friday, only a few students have applied. ❷_____ _____ _____ _____ will be a great opportunity for you, not only to understand your travel destination better but also to utilize what you've learned in school. I remind you that all students can enter, and the top three winners will ❸_____ _____ _____. So don't hesitate and sign up for the contest if you're considering it. Check the school website for more information on the contest. I hope many of you will join this great educational event. Thank you.

03

M: Hello, students! This is your physical education teacher, Mr. Nickelson. As you know, next semester is volleyball season. So this Friday, we're ❶_____ _____ for new players to join the school volleyball team. The tryouts will take place from 3:00 p.m. to 5:00 p.m. in the school gym. No prior sign-up is required. Be sure to wear comfortable clothes and shoes. Also, ❷_____ _____ _____ _____ to stay refreshed during the tryouts. We're looking forward to seeing some fresh faces for the upcoming season! If you have any questions, please ❸_____ _____ _____ _____ my office anytime. See you at the gym!

04

W: Attention, visitors. I'm Taylor Gibson, the general manager of Garland Aquarium, with exciting news for you. Our brand-new octopus exhibit is now open! ❶ _____ _____ _____ _____ and observe these incredible creatures' graceful movements and fascinating behaviors up close. The exhibit showcases an accurately recreated underwater ecosystem, including rocks, seaweed, and ❷_____ _____ _____ _____ that resemble the natural surroundings of octopuses. It's a unique opportunity to learn about these intelligent beings and appreciate the wonders of their world. Enjoy ❸_____ _____ _____ that brings you closer to the marvels of the ocean!

05

M: Good morning, students. This is your principal, Mr. Kim. I want to inform you that due to the really ❶ _____ _____ _____ _____, it's important that you do not open the windows in the classrooms. Bad air containing fine dust particles can enter the classrooms through open windows and ❷_____ _____ _____ _____, especially for those who have breathing difficulties. To maintain the health and safety of all students and faculty members, we're working hard to improve the air quality inside the classrooms. Opening the windows and letting bad air inside works against these efforts. So please do not open them ❸_____ _____ _____ _____ your health. Thank you for your cooperation.

06

W: Hello, residents! I'm Sarah Hawkins representing the Cozy Apartment Management Office. Recently, residents have told us that the stairs leading to the elevators in the underground parking lot are ❶_____ _____ _____ _____. At the last general meeting, some residents shared that they had fallen on the stairs. So, we're ❷_____ _____ _____ _____ in the underground parking lot next week. They will be renovated one by one from Monday to Thursday. We request that, during this period, you use one of the stairways that are not under renovation when accessing the underground parking area. We're sorry ❸_____ _____ _____ and genuinely appreciate your cooperation.

02강 의견

> **유형 소개**
> - 대화를 듣고, 화자의 의견이 무엇인지 파악하는 유형이다.
> - 대화에서 논의되고 있는 문제나 상황의 내용을 정확하게 이해하는 것이 중요하다.
> - 의견을 나타내는 표현들에 주목하여 화자가 주장하는 의견을 정확하게 분석해야 한다.

기출 예제

2024학년도 수능 2번
24006-0008

대화를 듣고, 남자의 의견으로 가장 적절한 것을 고르시오.

① 상대방이 말할 때는 말을 끊지 말아야 한다.
② 회의 발언은 주제에서 벗어나지 않아야 한다.
③ 적절한 제스처는 대화의 전달력을 높일 수 있다.
④ 회의를 진행할 때는 개인적인 감정을 배제해야 한다.
⑤ 자신의 의견을 주장할 때는 충분한 근거를 들어야 한다.

Listening Strategies

STEP 1 대화의 첫 부분을 통해 문제 상황 파악하기

[주요 단서] got into an argument, jump in to finish her sentence

STEP 2 남자의 의견에 해당하는 주요 단서 파악하기

shouldn't interrupt someone when they're in the middle of speaking (M) → she kept talking (W) → not polite (M) → when somebody's talking, you shouldn't cut them off (M)

STEP 3 대화에서 드러난 문제 상황과 주요 단서를 종합하여 의견 추론하기

(여자) 친구의 말을 끝내기 위해 끼어듦 → (남자) 누군가가 한창 말하고 있을 때 방해해서는 안 됨 → (여자) 그 친구가 계속 말했음 → (남자) 예의가 아님 → (남자) 누군가가 말하고 있을 때 말을 끊으면 안 됨

M: Ellie, you seem down. What's on your mind?

W: Well, Dad, Tiffany and I ❶_____ _____ _____ _____ at school.

M: You two are so close. What happened?

W: During our student council meeting, she was taking too long to make her point, so I had to jump in to finish her sentence.

M: Oh, no. You shouldn't interrupt someone when they're in the middle of speaking.

W: I know. But she kept talking ❷_____ _____ _____ _____.

M: Still, that's not polite. How would you feel if you were her?

W: I'd probably be upset.

M: Exactly. That's why when somebody's talking, you shouldn't cut them off.

W: You're right. I guess I didn't see things from her point of view.

M: So, how about ❸_____ _____ _____ what they're saying next time?

W: Okay. Thanks, Dad. I'll apologize to her tomorrow.

Communicative Functions

요청하기	Dad, **could you** help me enroll in a class to take next semester? Honey. **Can you** come help me make some bread?
모르고 있음 표현하기	Oh, **I didn't know that**. I only thought it was important in hot weather. Thanks! **I had no idea**. I'll pack my water bottle right away.

Useful Expressions, Idioms and Phrases

- **I find that ~.** 나는 ～을 알게 되다. (2024학년도 9월 모의평가 2번)

  A: **I find that** exercising at lunch time boosts my energy.
  저는 점심시간에 운동하면 저의 활력을 높인다는 것을 알게 되었어요.

  B: Really? I think it would make me more tired.
  정말요? 저는 그게 저를 더 피곤하게 만들 거로 생각해요.

- **as far as I know** 내가 알기로는 (2024학년도 6월 모의평가 2번)

  A: **As far as I know**, wearing a hat helps maintain babies' body temperature.
  내가 알기로는, 모자를 쓰는 것이 아기의 체온을 유지하는 데 도움을 줘.

  B: It's the beginning of summer, though.
  하지만, 지금은 여름의 시작이야.

01 대화를 듣고, 여자의 의견으로 가장 적절한 것을 고르시오. 24006-0009

① 지나친 햇빛 노출은 피부 건강에 해롭다.
② 자외선 차단제는 자주 덧바르는 것이 좋다.
③ 추운 날씨에도 충분한 수분 섭취가 중요하다.
④ 겨울철 야외 활동 시 피부 보습에 유의해야 한다.
⑤ 더운 날씨에 차가운 물을 많이 마시면 건강에 좋지 않다.

02 대화를 듣고, 남자의 의견으로 가장 적절한 것을 고르시오. 24006-0010

① 신체 활동은 자신감 향상에 도움이 된다.
② 경쟁보다는 협력을 통해 자신감을 기르도록 해야 한다.
③ 신체 활동 선택 시 흥미와 성취를 균형 있게 고려해야 한다.
④ 개인 운동보다는 단체 운동이 운동에 대한 흥미를 높일 수 있다.
⑤ 가벼운 운동보다는 강도 높은 운동이 스트레스 해소에 더 효과적이다.

03 대화를 듣고, 여자의 의견으로 가장 적절한 것을 고르시오. 24006-0011

① 공원에 반려견을 위한 별도의 산책로가 필요하다.
② 반려견을 키우면 아이의 사회성 발달에 도움이 된다.
③ 주인의 허락 없이 반려견을 함부로 만져서는 안 된다.
④ 반려견을 산책시킬 때는 항상 목줄을 착용시켜야 한다.
⑤ 반려견이 돌발 행동을 하지 못하도록 평소에 교육해야 한다.

04 대화를 듣고, 남자의 의견으로 가장 적절한 것을 고르시오.   24006-0012

① 힘든 과목의 수강이 개인의 성장에 도움이 된다.
② 다양한 분야의 과목을 골고루 수강하는 것이 중요하다.
③ 높은 학업 성취도를 이루려면 학습 전략을 잘 세워야 한다.
④ 학업과 휴식을 적절히 안배하여 좋은 컨디션을 유지해야 한다.
⑤ 심화 과목 선택 시 담당 교사에게 조언을 구하는 것이 필요하다.

05 대화를 듣고, 여자의 의견으로 가장 적절한 것을 고르시오.   24006-0013

① 따뜻한 물에 발을 담그면 피로 해소에 도움이 된다.
② 용도에 따라 적당한 양말을 선택하는 것이 중요하다.
③ 양말을 신고 자면 발을 따뜻하게 하여 더 잘 잘 수 있다.
④ 활동이 많은 낮에 수면 양말을 신으면 발 건강에 좋지 않다.
⑤ 잠을 잘 자는 것은 면역력을 높이는 손쉬운 방법 중 하나이다.

06 대화를 듣고, 남자의 의견으로 가장 적절한 것을 고르시오.   24006-0014

① 제빵 반죽 과정에서 정확한 순서대로 재료를 넣어야 한다.
② 별도의 계량 도구 없이 재료를 간편하게 계량할 수 있다.
③ 레시피를 활용하면 누구나 제빵을 쉽게 할 수 있다.
④ 홈베이킹은 아이와 함께할 수 있는 좋은 놀이이다.
⑤ 제빵을 할 때 정확한 계량이 중요하다.

Dictations

01

M: Mom, I'm so excited about our upcoming trip to Mt. Everfrost! I can't wait to enjoy the thrill of outdoor winter adventures.

W: Me neither! The snowy landscapes there will be absolutely breathtaking. Have you started packing yet?

M: Yes. I've got ❶_____ _____ _____ _____.

W: Good for you! How about sunscreen?

M: Yes, I packed some. Even though it's cold, it's going to be really sunny.

W: What about your water bottle?

M: I don't think I'll need it. When it's cold, I don't usually feel thirsty.

W: You know, cold air can ❷_____ _____ _____ _____. It's crucial to drink lots of water even in the cold.

M: Oh, I didn't know that. I only thought it was important in hot weather.

W: Most people think that way. It's easy to forget to drink water when it's cold, but our bodies need water to maintain our fluid levels.

M: Thanks! I had no idea. I'll ❸_____ _____ _____ _____ right away.

W: Of course. I'm glad I could help.

02

M: Hey, Olivia, is something wrong? You look worried.

W: Hi, Charles. I'm concerned about my son. ❶_____ _____ _____ and is even afraid to participate in class discussions.

M: Have you tried helping him?

W: I want to, but I'm not sure how.

M: How about getting him involved in physical activities? It can help him to enhance his self-esteem.

W: Really?

M: Yes, physical activity causes the release of endorphins and enhances overall well-being, which can lead to a boost in confidence.

W: Those are good points, but he's ❷_____ _____ _____ _____.

M: That's fine. It could be as simple as going for a walk, bike ride, or dancing.

W: That's a good idea. I'll try to encourage him to be more active.

M: Great! Just give it a try. It's surprising ❸_____ _____ _____ can boost people's confidence.

W: Thanks for the suggestion.

03

W: Paul, where are you going with Max?

M: I'm taking him out to a nearby park for a walk, Mom.

W: Good, but make sure to ❶_____ _____ _____ _____ _____ while you walk him.

M: Oh, can't I just let him walk alongside me without a leash?

W: It's best to use a leash on walks outside, Paul.

M: Why is that?

W: Using a leash is ❷_____ _____ _____ _____ _____. It prevents our dog from jumping up on people we encounter.

M: Max just gets excited around people. That's all.

W: Not everyone feels comfortable around our dog, Paul. Using a leash keeps Max under control and ❸_____ _____ _____ for others on the street.

M: I see your point, Mom.

W: Additionally, it's the law that dogs must be leashed at all times in public areas, so it's important to follow the rules.

M: I understand now. I'll make sure to put a leash on him before we head out.

04

W: Dad, could you help me enroll in a class to take next semester?

M: Sure, honey. What are you considering?

W: I'm thinking about enrolling in Advanced Calculus. I'm interested in it, but I've heard it's ❶_____ _____ _____ _____.

M: Well, it's true that it's a tough course. However, I believe taking on such challenges can lead to personal growth.

W: Do you really think so?

M: Yes. You can learn a lot about yourself by doing something that is challenging. That's why I think you should ❷_____ _____ _____ _____.

W: But what if I get a bad grade?

M: Grades aren't everything. If you don't give up and try, you can succeed in many areas of your life in the long run.

W: I hadn't thought about it that way.

M: It can also boost your self-confidence and provide a ❸_____ _____ _____, ultimately helping you become a better person.

W: Okay, Dad. Thanks for your support.

05

W: Aiden, you look pretty tired. You've got dark circles under your eyes.

M: Hey, Claire. I've been ❶_____ _____ _____ lately.

W: Sorry to hear that. Do you know why?

M: No. I'm not sure. It started happening recently.

W: Maybe it's due to the recent cold weather. It's hard to sleep when ❷_____ _____ _____ _____.

M: Hmm. You may be right. My feet have been uncomfortably cold at night.

W: It's possible. These days, I ❸_____ _____ _____ _____, and it helps me sleep better.

M: I'm just used to sleeping barefoot.

W: I understand, but try wearing socks. It can warm your feet and improve your sleep.

M: Thanks, I'll give it a shot.

W: I'm sure it will make a difference.

06

M: Honey. Can you come help me make some bread?

W: Sure. How can I help?

M: Can you ❶_____ _____ _____ _____? Everything you need is over there.

W: I can, but is it really necessary to measure? I usually just roughly estimate how much to add by sight.

M: Please measure. It's ❷_____ _____ _____ _____ to bake properly.

W: Is baking bread really different from cooking other dishes? I never measure when I make soup, and it turns out fine.

M: Yes, it can be quite different. With baking, if you're off by even a little bit, it can affect ❸_____ _____ _____ _____ of the bread.

W: Oh, I had no idea. So, how would you like me to measure?

M: Use the kitchen scale for the dry ingredients and measuring cups and spoons for the liquids.

W: Okay, I got it.

M: Baking is like chemistry, and ❹_____ _____ are the key to success.

03강 관계

기출 예제 2023학년도 9월 모의평가 3번

24006-0015

대화를 듣고, 두 사람의 관계를 가장 잘 나타낸 것을 고르시오.

① 건축가 – 건물 주인
② 코딩 강사 – 수강생
③ 영양사 – 과일 도매상
④ 음식 평론가 – 요리사
⑤ 홍보 회사 직원– 과일 농장 주인

Listening Strategies

STEP 1 대화자의 직업 또는 대화가 이루어지는 상황 예측하기

[주요 단서] begun packaging the summer fruits for sale, promote my fruit farm more actively on the Internet, Our advertisements will definitely help you attract new customers, ask my boss

STEP 2 대화자의 관계를 추론할 수 있는 단서 파악하기

Josh Gordon from Gordon's Fresh Fruits (M) → begun packaging the summer fruits for sale (M) → display it on personal blogs and social networking sites (W) → Our advertisements will definitely help you attract new customers and increase your fruit sales. (W)

STEP 3 대화 내용의 정확한 파악을 통해서 정답 추론하기

(남자) Gordon's Fresh Fruits에서 일하고 있음 → (남자) 판매용 여름 과일을 포장하기 시작함 → (남자) 자신의 과일 농장을 인터넷에서 홍보하고 싶어 함 → (여자) 디지털 배너를 만들어 개인 블로그와 소셜 네트워킹에 게시할 수 있다고 말해 줌 → (여자) 자신의 광고가 손님을 유치하고 과일 판매를 늘리는데 도움이 될 것이라고 말함

Ⓓictations

[Telephone rings.]

W: Good morning. Cathy Sullivan speaking.

M: Hello, Ms. Sullivan. This is Josh Gordon from Gordon's Fresh Fruits.

W: Hi, Mr. Gordon! How's ❶_____ _____ _____ _____?

M: This has been the best year since I started my farm. I've already begun packaging the summer fruits for sale.

W: That's good to hear. How may I help you today?

M: Well, I'd like to ❷_____ _____ _____ _____ more actively on the Internet.

W: In that case, we can make a digital banner and display it on personal blogs and social networking sites.

M: That sounds like a good idea.

W: Our advertisements will definitely help you ❸_____ _____ _____ and increase your fruit sales.

M: Sounds wonderful. When can you start promoting my farm?

W: I'll ❹_____ _____ _____ and call you back.

M: Great. Thank you.

Communicative Functions

제안하기	Then, **how about** going with me? **Why don't you** have lunch together?
기대, 희망 표현하기	**I really wish** I could go with you. **I'm looking forward to** the trip to Bangkok.

Useful Expressions, Idioms and Phrases

■ **Is there anything I can help you with?** 제가 뭐 도와드릴 게 있을까요? (2023학년도 6월 모의평가 13번)

A: **Is there anything I can help you with?**
제가 뭐 도와드릴 게 있을까요?

B: That'd be lovely. Can you get the butter from the refrigerator?
그러면 좋겠네요. 냉장고에서 버터를 갖다 줄 수 있어요?

■ **I'd like to ~.** 나는 ~하고 싶다. (2023학년도 9월 모의평가 3번)

A: How may I help you today?
오늘은 어떻게 도와드릴까요?

B: Well, **I'd like to** promote my fruit farm more actively on the Internet.
음, 저는 제 과일 농장을 인터넷에 더 적극적으로 홍보하고 싶어요.

01 대화를 듣고, 두 사람의 관계를 가장 잘 나타낸 것을 고르시오. 24006-0016

① 미술품 경매사 – 화가
② 미술 교사 – 자선 경매 관계자
③ 자선 기관 직원 – 자원봉사 참가자
④ 미술 재료 도매상 – 미술 전공 학생
⑤ 미술 전시회 기획자 – 행사 포스터 제작자

02 대화를 듣고, 두 사람의 관계를 가장 잘 나타낸 것을 고르시오. 24006-0017

① 교장 – 수학 교사
② 학생 기자 – 수학자
③ 학교 보안관 – 학부모
④ 회의 진행자 – 참석자
⑤ 동아리 담당 교사 – 강연자

03 대화를 듣고, 두 사람의 관계를 가장 잘 나타낸 것을 고르시오. 24006-0018

① 고객 – 서점 주인
② 기술자 – 기계 판매원
③ 기업가 – 출판사 직원
④ 영화감독 – 시나리오 작가
⑤ 마케팅 담당자 – 광고업자

04 대화를 듣고, 두 사람의 관계를 가장 잘 나타낸 것을 고르시오. 24006-0019

① 귀농인 – 농업 기술 전수자
② 농장 주인 – 비료 판매업자
③ 공장 관리인 – 비료 공장 직원
④ 수리 의뢰인 – 농기계 수리 기사
⑤ 식료품점 주인 – 농산품 도매 상인

05 대화를 듣고, 두 사람의 관계를 가장 잘 나타낸 것을 고르시오. 24006-0020

① 의료기 수리 기사 – 고객
② 보석 세공사 – 판매업자
③ 보안 검색 요원 – 승객
④ 방사선사 – 간호사
⑤ 치과 의사 – 환자

06 대화를 듣고, 두 사람의 관계를 가장 잘 나타낸 것을 고르시오. 24006-0021

① 소방관 – 실습생
② 코치 – 체조 선수
③ 공군 조종사 – 관제사
④ 놀이기구 안전요원 – 이용객
⑤ 스카이다이빙 강사 – 체험객

Dictations

01

W: Thank you for taking the time to visit, Mr. Brooks, especially with your busy schedule for ❶_____ _____ _____.

M: My pleasure, Mrs. Kristy. *[Pause]* Wow! This is such a lovely art classroom!

W: Thank you.

M: I also want to express my gratitude for your generous offer to ❷_____ _____ _____ _____ _____.

W: I'm so happy to help. These are the paintings I mentioned over the phone.

M: Oh, they are really nice.

W: My art students are excited to offer them to your charity.

M: Please thank them for me. Their paintings are going to be popular at the auction.

W: I'm pleased to hear that. By the way, some of my fellow teachers are interested in volunteering.

M: That would be greatly appreciated.

W: Could you provide me with a poster for the auction? I'll post it on the ❸_____ _____ _____.

M: Sure. I'll get one from the car.

02

W: Welcome to Newton High School, Mr. Moore. I'm Ms. Johnson, who called you.

M: Nice to meet you, and thank you for inviting me.

W: Thank you for coming. Shall we go to the conference room?

M: Sure. Is that where I'm going to ❶_____ _____ _____ today?

W: Yes. Our school math club students are waiting for you there.

M: Okay. So are you ❷_____ _____ _____ the club?

W: Yes. I'm managing the club students.

M: I see. I hope my lecture can inspire the students today.

W: Definitely. Many of my students you'll speak to want to be mathematicians in the future.

M: Great to hear that. I'm so happy to ❸_____ _____ _____ as a mathematician with the enthusiastic students.

W: I'm sure that they're going to greatly appreciate hearing your story.

03

W: Hello, Mr. Collins. It's great to talk with you in person.

M: Same here, Ms. Douglas.

W: As I said on the phone, I'm excited to have the company you work for ❶_____ _____ _____.

M: It's an honor. I was in awe while reading the manuscript you sent me. You opened a small store 30 years ago and have grown it into a big international company today.

W: Thank you. I'm hoping my experiences in my company can ❷_____ _____ _____.

M: Your autobiography will certainly help many people.

W: I hope so. And I'm not a writer, so my manuscript will need work.

M: Don't worry. My co-workers have a lot of experience ❸_____ _____ _____.

W: Great. I've read a few autobiographies your company has published. All the best-sellers. And I've enjoyed them all.

M: Glad to hear. Your autobiography will also be a best-seller.

W: That'd be amazing.

04

[Cell phone rings.]

W: Hello, Henry.

M: Hello, Katie. Did you see the message I sent you this morning?

W: No, I didn't. I've been busy all day trying ❶_____ _____ _____ _____.

M: Oh, no! What's wrong with it?

W: It doesn't start. I couldn't fix it, so I called a mechanic to have it fixed.

M: I hope it'll be a cheap and easy fix. In fact, I messaged to tell you the ❷_____ _____ _____ _____ last week arrived at my store from the factory. I'll bring it over to you today.

W: Oh, good. I need it for the crops in my fields.

M: I know. The fertilizer you ordered at my store will make your crops grow better.

W: Right. When will you come by?

M: I should ❸_____ _____ _____ _____ around three o'clock.

W: Okay. I'll be at the farm at that time.

M: All right. I'll call you if I'm running late.

W: Okay. See you then.

05

W: All right, Mr. Hawkins. Your examination is complete.

M: Great. Were you able to figure out what's wrong?

W: Yes. Look at this X-ray. Can you see how these two are ❶_____ _____?

M: Oh. Will they need to be pulled?

W: No. I'll remove the decayed areas by drilling and then ❷_____ _____ _____ _____.

M: Okay. What will you fill the holes with?

W: You have the option of getting an amalgam filling or a composite filling.

M: ❸_____ _____ _____ _____?

W: I recommend a composite filling since they're ❹_____ _____ _____. It'll be less visible because it's about the same color as your teeth.

M: Oh, that's great. Then I'll get a composite filling.

06

M: Hello. Are you ready?

W: Yes, but I'm nervous. I can't believe I'm going to ❶_____ _____ _____ _____.

M: Don't worry. You'll be fine. First, let me explain the gear. Here's your jumpsuit and safety belt.

W: Okay. How do I wear the belt?

M: Let me show you. Like this.

W: All right. And is there anything I need to do when we're ❷_____ _____ _____ _____?

M: Just relax and enjoy the view! It's truly amazing. And after we jump, we'll free-fall for about a minute before I ❸_____ _____ _____.

W: Got it. I'm still worried it might not open.

M: Trust me. It will. I take safety extremely seriously.

W: Okay, I trust you. Let's do it!

M: Great! Let's ❹_____ _____ _____ _____ _____ _____ before we board the plane. You're going to have a fantastic experience today.

04강 그림 내용 일치

유형
소개
- 대화를 듣고 그림에서 두 사람이 말하는 내용과 일치하지 않는 부분을 찾는 유형이다.
- 사진, 그림, 포스터, 특정한 장소 등이 그림으로 제시되고 그림에 대해 묘사하는 방식으로 대화가 진행되므로 그림의 세부 사항을 언급하는 부분에 집중하여 듣는다.
- 사람, 동물, 사물의 외형적인 특징, 위치, 개수, 무늬 등에 주목하여 이를 나타내는 표현을 중심으로 그림과 대화 간의 불일치를 파악해야 한다.

기출 예제   2024학년도 수능 4번
24006-0022

대화를 듣고, 그림에서 대화의 내용과 일치하지 <u>않는</u> 것을 고르시오.

Listening Strategies

STEP 1 선택지와 관련된 표현 예측하기

[주요 단서] banner, tent, backpack, chairs, tablecloth

STEP 2 선택지에 해당하는 대화 내용 파악하기

that banner on the wall (W) → the cone-shaped tent (M) → the backpack next to the box (M) → those two chairs (W) → that striped tablecloth (M)

STEP 3 대화의 내용과 일치하지 않는 부분 찾기

(남자) 상자 옆에 있는 배낭이 현재 가장 잘 팔리는 상품이라고 말함 → 그림에는 상자 위에 배낭이 있음

Dictations

M: Ms. Blake, I've finished decorating the camping gear section to ❶_____ _____ _____ _____.

W: Thanks, Chris. It's much nicer than what's represented in our sales plan. I like that banner on the wall.

M: I think it'll attract our customers' attention. And I set up the cone-shaped tent ❷_____ _____ _____ _____.

W: Good. That Native American-style tent is quite popular these days.

M: Yes, it is. Also, the backpack next to the box is currently our best-selling item.

W: That's true. I love its design. Oh, those two chairs look comfortable. I'd like to sit on one of them and ❸_____ _____ _____ _____.

M: Me, too. And isn't that striped tablecloth really eye-catching?

W: It certainly is. Everything looks really good. You did an excellent job!

Communicative **Functions**

진술하기와 보고하기	**They hung a *Lucky Night* banner from the ceiling.** Look, **here's a picture I took there the other day**.
(정체) 확인하기와 상술하기	**The woman reading a book near the tent must be your mother**, right? **That's my friend**, Matilda. She often walks her dog there.

Useful Expressions, **Idioms and Phrases**

■ **fit the setting well** 배경에 잘 어울리다 (2024학년도 6월 모의평가 4번)

A: I also got the flower-patterned rug at the market.
    꽃무늬 깔개도 그 시장에서 샀어요.

B: They all **fit the setting well**.
    모두 배경에 잘 어울려요.

■ **give ~ a professional look** ~을 전문적으로 보이게 하다 (2023학년도 6월 모의평가 4번)

A: Oh, there are three cameras. They **give** the studio **a professional look**.
    아, 카메라가 세 대 있네요. 그게 있어서 방송실이 전문적으로 보여요.

B: I know. I can't wait to start broadcasting the school news.
    알아요. 학교 소식을 빨리 방송하고 싶어요.

01   대화를 듣고, 그림에서 대화의 내용과 일치하지 <u>않는</u> 것을 고르시오.   24006-0023

02   대화를 듣고, 그림에서 대화의 내용과 일치하지 <u>않는</u> 것을 고르시오.   24006-0024

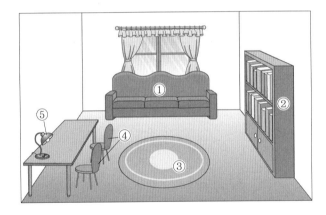

03   대화를 듣고, 그림에서 대화의 내용과 일치하지 <u>않는</u> 것을 고르시오.   24006-0025

04 대화를 듣고, 그림에서 대화의 내용과 일치하지 <u>않는</u> 것을 고르시오.   24006-0026

05 대화를 듣고, 그림에서 대화의 내용과 일치하지 <u>않는</u> 것을 고르시오.   24006-0027

06 대화를 듣고, 그림에서 대화의 내용과 일치하지 <u>않는</u> 것을 고르시오.   24006-0028

Dictations

01

M: Emma, I went to the first public showing of the movie *Lucky Night* last week. Check it out. I took a picture before it started.

W: Cool! They hung a *Lucky Night* banner ❶_____ _____ _____.

M: Right. And look at the curtains.

W: Oh, they have star prints. Were they to match the movie title?

M: Yeah. Pretty creative, right? And see this balloon archway on the stage?

W: Yes. Were the actors ❷_____ _____ _____ _____ _____ onto the stage?

M: That's right.

W: Wow! The crowd must've loved that.

M: For sure. Everybody was cheering so loudly.

W: So what was this ❸_____ _____ on the table for?

M: The actors got it for the director. It was really touching.

W: That's nice. And what about these boxes under the table?

M: Those were gifts for the actors from a few fans in the crowd.

W: I see. What an amazing experience!

M: Definitely.

02

W: Hey, Mike. How was your weekend?

M: Hi, Sonia. I ❶_____ _____ _____ my family's study room. Do you want to see a picture of it?

W: Sure. *[Pause]* Um. You put the sofa in front of the window.

M: Yeah. I can enjoy the sunshine on the sofa on sunny days.

W: Good. Why is the bookshelf on the right completely empty?

M: Oh, I took this picture ❷_____ _____ _____ _____ on the bookshelf.

W: I see. Is the round rug on the floor new? I like the design.

M: Yeah. I recently bought it online for only $50!

W: What a deal! Did you buy the two chairs on the left, too?

M: No, I brought them with the dining table from the kitchen.

W: Oh, you're going to use ❸_____ _____ _____ _____ _____, aren't you?

M: Right. That's why I put a desk lamp on it.

W: It seems like your remodeling went really well.

03

M: Honey, did you finish making Natalie's birthday party invitation card?

W: Almost. Look at the monitor.

M: Oh, let's see. I like how you put a castle in the middle.

W: And I put the phrase "Happy Birthday" above the castle.

M: Good. I also like the balloons ❶_____ _____ _____ of it.

W: What about Natalie's picture in the heart?

M: She's really cute!

W: Can you guess why I put five stars below Natalie's picture?

M: Sure! They mean Natalie's age, don't they?

W: That's right. I can't believe she's already turning 5.

M: Me, neither. By the way, why is ❷_____ _____ _____ _____ _____?

W: I'll type in the party information such as time and place.

M: I got it. I think you did a really good job.

04

W: John, how was your family camping trip last weekend?

M: It couldn't have been better. This is a picture that I took during the trip.

W: Cool. Did you ❶_____ _____ _____ _____ under the big tree?

M: Yes, I did. It was the perfect spot with a cool breeze.

W: Awesome. The woman reading a book near the tent must be your mother, right?

M: Yes. She really enjoys reading. And the man ❷_____ _____ _____ on the table is my father.

W: You resemble your father a lot. Oh, the dog under the table is really cute.

M: Can you guess what's ❸_____ _____ _____ _____?

W: Um... dog food?

M: Right. That's why our dog is staying near the basket.

W: I can tell by the picture you had a great time.

05

W: Hey, Danny, long time no see! Your hair has gotten really long.

M: That's why I came to get it cut. Oh, I see you've remodeled the beauty shop a little bit.

W: Right, I did that recently. Do you like the new look?

M: Yeah, it's nice! ❶_____ _____ _____ _____ _____ look good.

W: Thanks. I think they make the shop feel warmer.

M: I agree they do. And I like those two round mirrors on the wall.

W: The old mirrors ❷_____ _____ _____ in them. What do you think of the clock inside the head?

M: It's perfect! And I don't remember seeing the plant stand on the right.

W: Right. I ❸_____ _____ _____ last weekend. I like how it displays the plants.

M: Yeah, me, too.

W: Feel free to read one of the books which are on the cushioned bench. I just need a few minutes to clean up.

M: Okay, sounds good.

06

W: Joshua, have you ever been to Evergreen Park?

M: No. How about you?

W: I go jogging there every day. It's really nice. Look, here's a picture I took there the other day.

M: Wow, the bench under the tree is a perfect place to relax.

W: I know. I like to sit there and ❶_____ _____ _____ _____. Well, what do you think of the two hands holding a book?

M: That's unique. I bet a lot of people come to see it.

W: Yes. It's a popular place to take pictures.

M: I also like ❷_____ _____ _____ _____ _____ in the word 'LOVE'. They replaced the 'O' with this heart there.

W: It's cool, right? And see these three ducks in the pond. They swim there every day.

M: Cute! Who's the girl holding a dog in her arms?

W: That's my friend, Matilda. She often ❸_____ _____ _____ there.

PART I

05강 할 일

유형 소개
- 대화를 듣고 남자 또는 여자가 할 일을 파악하는 유형이다.
- 대화를 듣기 전에 선택지를 읽고, 이를 통해 대화의 내용을 대략 짐작해 본다.
- 대화의 초반부에서 상황을 파악하고, 남자 또는 여자가 해야 할 일과 관련하여 언급하는 내용에 집중하여 듣는다.
- 대화에서 언급된 내용으로 선택지가 구성되며, 일반적으로 대화의 후반부에 정답과 관련된 결정적인 내용이 언급된다.

기출 예제

2024학년도 수능 5번

24006-0029

대화를 듣고, 여자가 할 일로 가장 적절한 것을 고르시오.

① 신입 회원 선물 준비하기
② 대회 일정 인쇄하기
③ 음악 재생 목록 만들기
④ 식당 예약하기
⑤ 문자 메시지 보내기

Listening Strategies

STEP 1 도입부에서 두 사람이 놓여 있는 상황 파악하기

the party for the new members of our tennis club this Friday

STEP 2 두 사람의 대화에서 한 일 또는 할 일 파악하기

go through the to-do list (M) → reserve the Mexican restaurant (W) → prepared gifts for the new members (W) → sent a text message to everyone (W) → printed it out (M) → do it tonight (W)

STEP 3 여자가 앞으로 할 일 파악하기

테니스 대회 일정 인쇄하기

Ⓓictations

W: Oliver, I'm so excited about the party for the new members of our tennis club this Friday.

M: Me, too. Let's go through the to-do list. I ❶_____ _____ _____ _____ _____.

W: Agreed. Did you reserve the Mexican restaurant downtown for the party?

M: Yes, I did. The restaurant is spacious, so it's perfect for a party like ours.

W: Plus, the food there is terrific. And you ❷_____ _____ _____ the new members, right?

M: Yeah, they're in my car. Did you remind the members about the party?

W: I've just sent a text message to everyone.

M: Great. What about ❸_____ _____ _____ _____? Have you printed it out?

W: Oh, I almost forgot. I'll do it tonight. Um, is the music ready?

M: Uh-huh. I made a playlist last night.

W: That's great. I think we're good to go!

Communicative Functions

예정 계획 표현하기	I **was** just **about to** call you for that favor. My train **is supposed to** get there at 4 p.m.
걱정, 두려움 표현하기	I wish I could, but I'**m scared to** disappoint him. **Are you concerned about** your child's sleep habits?

Useful Expressions, Idioms and Phrases

- **sign up for** ~을 신청[가입]하다 (2024학년도 6월 모의평가 5번)

  A: Did you **sign up for** the Internet at our new place?

  우리 새집에 인터넷 신청을 했어요?

  B: Yes, I did. It should be connected by the move-in date.

  네, 했어요. 입주일까지는 연결되어 있어야 해요.

- **check if everything's ready** 모든 것이 준비되었는지 확인해 보다 (2024학년도 9월 모의평가 5번)

  A: Shall we **check if everything's ready**?

  모든 것이 준비되었는지 확인해 볼까요?

  B: Sure. Let's see.... Did you reserve the school gym?

  물론이죠. 어디 봅시다…. 학교 체육관은 예약하셨나요?

01   대화를 듣고, 남자가 할 일로 가장 적절한 것을 고르시오.   24006-0030

① 창문 닫기
② 커피 준비하기
③ 손전등 사 오기
④ 휴대폰 충전하기
⑤ 구급상자 가져오기

02   대화를 듣고, 여자가 할 일로 가장 적절한 것을 고르시오.   24006-0031

① 저녁 준비하기
② 집 안 청소하기
③ 보고서 검토하기
④ 세탁물 찾아오기
⑤ 발표 주제 제안하기

03   대화를 듣고, 남자가 할 일로 가장 적절한 것을 고르시오.   24006-0032

① 발표 자료 만들기
② 프로젝트 기획하기
③ 동료에게 전화하기
④ 이메일로 자료 보내기
⑤ 새로운 팀원 모집하기

04 대화를 듣고, 여자가 할 일로 가장 적절한 것을 고르시오. 24006-0033

① 프라이팬 닦기
② 튀김 기름 주문하기
③ 감자 재고량 확인하기
④ 화장실 전구 교체하기
⑤ 음식물 쓰레기 버리기

05 대화를 듣고, 남자가 할 일로 가장 적절한 것을 고르시오. 24006-0034

① 과일 사 오기
② 쓰레기 내놓기
③ 귀중품 포장하기
④ 이사 업체에 전화하기
⑤ 차고에 상자 갖다 놓기

06 대화를 듣고, 여자가 대화 직후에 할 일로 가장 적절한 것을 고르시오. 24006-0035

① 문자 메시지 보내기
② 자동차에 연료 넣기
③ 자동차 타이어 주문하기
④ 자동차 설명서 가져다주기
⑤ 가장 가까운 정비소 찾아보기

01

M: Honey, it seems like we have everything ready for our camping trip.

W: Yeah. I can't wait to sleep in the tent tonight!

M: Me neither. You ❶_____ _____ _____ I bought yesterday, right?

W: Yes. And I got the small first-aid kit just in case.

M: Good thinking! Let's head out!

W: We can't leave just yet. My cell phone's charging. It'll take about 20 more minutes ❷_____ _____ _____.

M: Then shall I make some coffee to take with us in the car while you're waiting?

W: Sounds great. Actually, I'm feeling a little sleepy.

M: I understand. It's still early in the morning. I'll prepare the coffee ❸_____ _____ _____ _____.

W: Thanks, honey. I'm going to make sure all of the windows in the house are closed.

M: Good idea. It might rain while we're gone.

W: I'll be right back.

02

M: I'm home, honey. I picked up the laundry on my way home.

W: Good! I was just about to call you for that favor. I was a little busy cleaning the house.

M: Wow, the house looks nice and clean!

W: Thanks. So how was your day at work?

M: Actually, our team project ❶_____ _____ _____ and we'll present it in front of the whole staff.

W: Wow, congratulations! So who's going to present?

M: Me. I was the one who first proposed the idea for our project.

W: That's great! When is the presentation?

M: It's tomorrow. I need to ❷_____ _____ _____ for the presentation, so I have to do some work at home tonight.

W: Oh, my. Is there anything I can help you with?

M: Well, it's my turn to prepare dinner tonight, but could you do it for me?

W: Don't worry. I'll ❸_____ _____ _____ _____. Just focus on preparing for the presentation.

M: Thank you, honey. That means a lot to me.

W: You're welcome.

03

M: Hey, Sharon. Do you have a minute?

W: Hi, Michael. Sure, what's up?

M: My team has been working on a project for a few months, and we're ❶_____ _____ _____ _____.

W: Oh, nice. It'll feel great when it's finally done.

M: Definitely. I'm actually looking for someone who can look over our project with a fresh perspective.

W: So, you want me to be that person?

M: Right. Would you be able to review the materials we've made and ❷_____ _____ _____ _____?

W: Of course. When do you need it by?

M: Ideally by the end of this week, but I understand if you're busy and need more time.

W: No problem. I can do it.

M: Thanks so much. I'll email you the materials right away.

W: Okay. I'll give you a call when I ❸_____ _____ _____.

04

M: Samantha, today was a long day, wasn't it?

W: It sure was, Mr. Peterson. I think we sold the most French fries we've ever sold in a day.

M: Yeah. Let's quickly ❶_____ _____ _____ _____ for tomorrow and head home.

W: Okay.

M: Do we have enough potatoes and oil in the storage room?

W: We have three boxes of potatoes and ten liters of oil.

M: Then we don't have to order potatoes and oil until next Monday.

W: Oh, I forgot to tell you that a light bulb in the restroom is out.

M: Okay. I'll ❷_____ _____ _____ a new one before I leave.

W: Now I'll go clean the frying pans.

M: Don't worry. I've already done that.

W: Thank you. Then, I'll ❸_____ _____ _____ _____ _____.

M: All right. You can leave after that. I'll take care of the rest.

05

M: Honey, can you believe that tomorrow is our moving day?

W: I know. It's our last night in this house. It's kind of emotional.

M: Yeah. I ❶_____ _____ _____ to confirm that they'll be here by 8 a.m.

W: Thanks for doing that. So we'll have to have a quick breakfast tomorrow. What do you want to eat?

M: How about just yogurt and fruit? There's yogurt in the fridge.

W: Good idea. Then I'll go buy some bananas at the store now.

M: Okay. Can you ❷_____ _____ _____ _____ on your way out?

W: Sure. And let's not forget to gather all our small valuables and pack them.

M: Oh, right. We need to ❸_____ _____ _____ not to lose them.

W: We can do it together when I get back home.

M: Don't worry about it. There's not much. I'll do it while you're out.

W: Thanks. You can use the small boxes in the garage to put them in.

M: All right.

06

W: Sweetie, there's something wrong with the car.

M: Oh, you're right. The warning lights on the dashboard are on.

W: I'll pull over. *[Pause]* I'm not sure what this sign means.

M: It's not the low fuel light, is it?

W: No. I ❶_____ _____ _____ _____ yesterday.

M: Hmm.... I'll check the car owner's manual. Where is it?

W: Just a second. *[Pause]* Here it is.

M: Let me see.... The sign means there's ❷_____ _____ _____ in the tires.

W: Really? We should go to the nearest car repair shop now to get them fixed.

M: Then we're going to be late picking up Jimmy.

W: ❸_____ _____ _____. I'll send him a text asking him to wait for about 15 minutes.

M: Okay. Then leave it to me to search for the nearest repair shop.

W: Good.

06강 숫자 정보

- 대화를 듣고, 구매자가 지불해야 하는 금액을 파악하는 유형이다.
- 대화문은 상점에서 물건을 사는 상황의 형태로 제시된다.
- 구매자가 무엇을 몇 개 사려고 하는지를 파악해야 한다.
- 구매자가 사용하는 쿠폰이나 할인 조건 등을 고려해서 계산해야 한다.

기출 예제

2024학년도 수능 6번

24006-0036

대화를 듣고, 남자가 지불할 금액을 고르시오.

① $63
② $70
③ $72
④ $78
⑤ $80

Listening Strategies

STEP 1 대화 장소 파악하기

Jamie's Gift Shop

STEP 2 사려는 물건의 가격과 수량 파악하기

photo tumbler, $30 (W) → two of them (M) → These Christmas key chains look cute. Oh, they're $5 each., take four (M) → 10% off the total cost (W)

STEP 3 정보를 이용하여 가격 계산하기

(여자) 사진 텀블러 한 개에 30달러임 → (남자) 사진 텀블러 2개를 구입함 → (남자) 개당 5달러인 열쇠고리를 4개 구입함 → (여자) 총 비용에서 10% 할인 제공함

Ⓓictations

W: Welcome to Jamie's Gift Shop! What can I do for you?

M: Hi. I need to get Christmas gifts for my friends. Is there anything you can recommend?

W: Sure. How about this ❶_____ _____? You can insert a picture of your friends into the tumbler to decorate it.

M: Ooh, my friends will love it. How much is it?

W: It's $30.

M: It seems a bit pricey, but I like it. I'll take ❷_____ _____ _____.

W: Okay. Anything else?

M: These Christmas ❸_____ _____ look cute. Oh, they're $5 each.

W: Yes. They're only available this month.

M: Are they? I'll take four then. I think that's all.

W: So, that's two tumblers and four key chains.

M: That's right.

W: And you get 10% ❹_____ _____ _____ _____ for our Christmas promotion.

M: Great. Here's my credit card.

Communicative Functions

추가 구매 여부 묻기	**Anything else (for you)?** **Is there anything missing** that you need?
할인 받기	You **get a** 10% **discount off the total**. They're originally $20 a pair, but **they're on sale for** 50% **off**.

Useful Expressions, Idioms and Phrases

■ **What would you recommend?** 무엇을 추천해 주시겠어요? (2023학년도 6월 모의평가 6번)

　A: Welcome to Spring Road Garden. May I help you?

　　Spring Road Garden에 오신 것을 환영합니다. 도와드릴까요?

　B: Hi. I'm thinking of putting some flowers in the living room. **What would you recommend?**

　　안녕하세요. 저는 거실에 꽃을 좀 두는 것을 생각하고 있습니다. 무엇을 추천해 주시겠어요?

■ **That's a good deal.** 좋은 거래네요. (2022학년도 9월 모의평가 6번)

　A: Well, if you buy the lighter one, I can give you a dozen shuttlecocks worth $10 for free. You'll need shuttlecocks anyway.

　　음, 만약 더 가벼운 것을 사시면, 10달러 상당의 12개의 셔틀콕을 공짜로 드릴 수 있습니다. 어차피 셔틀콕은 필요하실 거예요.

　B: **That's a good deal.** Then I'll get the lighter one.

　　좋은 거래네요. 그럼 더 가벼운 것으로 할게요.

01 대화를 듣고, 여자가 지불할 금액을 고르시오. 24006-0037

① $36
② $60
③ $63
④ $70
⑤ $77

02 대화를 듣고, 남자가 지불할 금액을 고르시오. 24006-0038

① $21
② $24
③ $28
④ $31
⑤ $33

03 대화를 듣고, 여자가 지불할 금액을 고르시오. 24006-0039

① $90
② $100
③ $110
④ $120
⑤ $130

04 대화를 듣고, 남자가 지불할 금액을 고르시오. 24006-0040

① $50
② $57
③ $60
④ $75
⑤ $80

05 대화를 듣고, 여자가 지불할 금액을 고르시오. 24006-0041

① $30
② $31
③ $37
④ $44
⑤ $45

06 대화를 듣고, 남자가 지불할 금액을 고르시오. 24006-0042

① $33
② $35
③ $36
④ $38
⑤ $41

Dictations

01

M: Welcome to Blue Marine Aquarium. How may I help you?

W: Hi. I'd like ❶_____ _____ _____ _____ along with the penguin feeding experience.

M: Okay. General admission tickets to the aquarium are $10 for adults and $5 for children.

W: I need two adult tickets and two child tickets.

M: All right. And you said you also want the penguin feeding experience, right?

W: Yes, all four of us want to ❷_____ _____ _____.

M: That's an additional $10 per person.

W: Sounds good. It's not ❸_____ _____ _____ _____ _____ it'd be.

M: So, you'll be paying for general admission tickets for two adults and two children with the penguin feeding experience for all four people, right?

W: Yes. And I have this coupon.

M: Okay. You get a 10% discount off the total.

W: Thanks. Here's my credit card.

02

W: Honey, it's already lunchtime. Should we order some food for delivery?

M: Sure. Let's see if there are ❶_____ _____ _____ on my food delivery app.

W: Okay. *[Pause]* How about these hot beef noodles?

M: They look delicious. And $7 for one is a good deal. Let's get two noodles.

W: Okay. And let's get some side dishes, too.

M: Good idea. I'm hungry. They have shrimp rolls for $4 each and vegetable rolls for $3 each.

W: Then, why don't we ❷_____ _____ _____ _____ and eat them together?

M: Sounds good.

W: By the way, there's a $3 delivery fee.

M: Don't worry. I have a coupon for free delivery.

W: Great. Let's order now. Do you want me to get you the credit card?

M: No, I'll ❸_____ _____ _____ _____.

03

M: Welcome to Ocean Tower Resort. How may I help you?

W: Hello. I'm staying in Room 807. I'd like to buy tickets for the ❶_____ _____ _____ tonight.

M: Okay. They're $30 for adults and $20 for children.

W: All right. I need ❷_____ _____ _____ and two child tickets.

M: Okay. And since you're staying in the resort, you get 10% off the tickets.

W: That's great.

M: We're ❸_____ _____ _____ _____ for the firefly watching event now. Would you like to buy some?

W: Oh, they look really nice. How much are they?

M: They're $10 each.

W: My kids will love them. I'll buy 2 bracelets. Are these bracelets 10% off, too?

M: No, they're not sale items. Would you buy them?

W: Sure. Here's my credit card.

04

W: Hey, Sam. Are you surfing the Internet?

M: Hi, Emma. Actually, I'm shopping for ❶_____ _____ _____ _____ _____. She's graduating this Friday.

W: That's cool. Is she going to college?

M: Yeah. I can't decide between the fountain pen set or the ballpoint pen set. Which do you think I should get her?

W: Hmm, I'd go with the ballpoint pen set. I think ❷_____ _____ _____ _____, it's more useful than a fountain pen set.

M: I agree. And the ballpoint pen set is $30 and the fountain pen set is $50.

W: Look here! The ballpoint pen set is even 10% off.

M: Oh, nice! I'll buy her the set. I'm getting her this flower bouquet, too.

W: She'll love it. How much is it?

M: The bouquet is $30. So I'll ❸_____ _____ _____ because I'm spending over $50.

W: That's good.

M: I'm going to place my order now.

05

M: Welcome to Wonderful Home Living. Can I help you find something?

W: Yes. Where are place mats?

M: I'll show you. [Pause] Here they are. We sell them ❶_____ _____ _____ _____.

W: I like both this rectangular set and this round set. How much are they?

M: The rectangular set is $22, and the round one is $15.

W: Both are reasonable. What colors does the rectangular set come in?

M: It comes in three colors: pink, gray, and light blue.

W: Great. I'll ❷_____ _____ _____ _____, one pink and one light blue.

M: Okay. Is there anything else I can help you find?

W: No. That's all, thanks. And ❸_____ _____ _____ _____ for me? They're a gift.

M: Sure. Gift-wrapping is free, and if you'd like to add a card, it's ❹_____ _____ _____.

W: Please give me a card as well. Here's my credit card.

06

W: Welcome to Pop & Soda. How may I help you?

M: Hi. How much is cherry-flavored soda?

W: It's $3 for a small one and $5 for a large one.

M: Okay. I'll ❶_____ _____ _____ _____ _____ _____. And I also want some popcorn. How much is it?

W: It's $6 ❷_____ _____ _____. We also have ❸_____ _____ _____ _____.

M: Oh, that's cool! The bucket is the elephant character in the movie, *Bingbo*. My daughter loves that character.

W: The bucket is $24, and it comes filled with popcorn. And it's $3 ❹_____ _____ _____ _____.

M: Great. I'll take one box of popcorn and one refillable popcorn bucket.

W: Okay. How will you be paying?

M: By credit card. Here it is.

07강 이유

> **유형소개**
> - 대화를 듣고 대화자가 어떤 행동을 하거나 할 수 없는 이유를 파악하는 유형이다.
> - 실생활과 관련된 소재가 주로 출제되며 먼저 대화의 주제를 파악하는 것이 중요하다.
> - 대화를 나누고 있는 대화자가 처해 있는 구체적인 상황을 파악하는 것이 중요하다.

기출 예제

2024학년도 수능 7번
24006-0043

대화를 듣고, 여자가 산책을 할 수 <u>없는</u> 이유를 고르시오.

① 얇은 재킷을 입어서
② 회의 준비를 해야 해서
③ 알레르기 증상이 심해서
④ 경찰서에 방문해야 해서
⑤ 병원 진료를 받아야 해서

Listening Strategies

STEP 1 제안과 거절 파악하기

Shall we take a walk as usual before going back to the office? (M) → I'd love to, but I can't today. (W)

STEP 2 이유를 묻고 답하는 대화의 흐름 이해하기

Your jacket does look thin. (M) → No, I'm okay. (W) → Then, are your allergy symptoms bothering you again? (M) → Not really. (W) → So, why not today? (M) → Actually, I need to visit the police station. (W)

STEP 3 여자의 응답을 통해 이유 파악하기

(남자) 재킷이 얇아 보인다고 말함 → (여자) 괜찮다고 답함 → (남자) 알레르기 증상 때문에 또 괴롭냐고 물음 → (여자) 그런 건 아니라고 답함 → (남자) 그럼, 오늘은 왜 안되는지 물음 → (여자) 경찰서에 방문해야 한다고 답함

Dictations

W: It was nice having lunch outside the office.

M: Yes. It feels so good now that fall is in the air. Shall we take a walk as usual before going back to the office?

W: I'd love to, but I can't today.

M: Is it too cold? Your jacket does ❶_____ _____.

W: No, I'm okay. This jacket is warmer than it looks.

M: Then, are your ❷_____ _____ bothering you again?

W: Not really. I had a runny nose, but I've already seen a doctor. It's okay now.

M: So, why not today?

W: Actually, I need to visit the ❸_____ _____. I got a text message saying that my new driver's license is ready.

M: I see. Then I'll just go back to prepare for the afternoon meeting.

W: Okay. See you at the office.

Communicative Functions

제안 거절하기	**I'd love to, but I can't** today. **I'm sorry but I can't** right now.
의무 표현하기	Actually, **I need to** visit the police station. **I need to** print out the final script. What **should I** do?

Useful Expressions, Idioms and Phrases

- **go (on) well** 잘 되(어 가)다 (2024학년도 6월 모의평가 7번)

  A: I was worried about you. I hope everything **went well**.
  당신이 걱정되었어요. 모든 일이 잘되있기를 바라요.

  B: Yes, it did. Thanks for asking.
  네, 그랬어요. 물어봐 줘서 고마워요.

- **keep one's fingers crossed** 행운을 빌다 (2024학년도 9월 모의평가 7번)

  A: Science debate competition? That's amazing! I'll **keep my fingers crossed**.
  과학 토론 대회라고? 굉장하구나! 행운을 빌게.

  B: Thanks.
  고마워.

01 대화를 듣고, 남자가 탄산음료를 마시지 <u>않는</u> 이유를 고르시오.   24006-0044

① 살이 찔까 봐
② 두통이 생겨서
③ 배가 아플까 봐
④ 치아가 상할까 봐
⑤ 화장실을 자주 가서

02 대화를 듣고, 여자가 이번 주말에 서커스를 보러 갈 수 <u>없는</u> 이유를 고르시오.   24006-0045

① 다친 딸을 돌봐야 해서
② 관람권을 예매하지 못해서
③ 친구와 하이킹을 가기로 해서
④ 판매 보고서를 작성해야 해서
⑤ 아이의 축구 시합에 가야 해서

03 대화를 듣고, 남자가 Patrick의 대본을 영화로 제작하지 <u>않기로</u> 한 이유를 고르시오.   24006-0046

① 제작비가 많이 들어서
② 특수 효과 기술이 좋지 않아서
③ 다른 영화 제작과 일정이 겹쳐서
④ 전쟁 영화를 사람들이 좋아하지 않아서
⑤ 영화감독이 대본을 마음에 들어 하지 않아서

04 대화를 듣고, 여자가 토요일 저녁에 재즈 콘서트에 갈 수 <u>없는</u> 이유를 고르시오. 24006-0047

① 구직 면접을 봐야 해서
② 화학 보고서를 써야 해서
③ 식당에서 일을 해야 해서
④ 입장권을 구입하지 못해서
⑤ 다른 친구들과 선약이 있어서

05 대화를 듣고, 남자가 직장에 점심을 싸 오는 이유를 고르시오. 24006-0048

① 식사량을 줄여야 해서
② 단백질 섭취를 늘려야 해서
③ 회사 구내식당 음식 가격이 올라서
④ 회사 구내식당 음식을 좋아하지 않아서
⑤ 회사 구내식당에서 식사하는 게 불편해서

06 대화를 듣고, 여자가 남자의 댄스 대회를 보러 갈 수 <u>없는</u> 이유를 고르시오. 24006-0049

① 무릎이 아파서
② 노인 센터에 가야 해서
③ 건강 검진을 받아야 해서
④ 날씨가 안 좋다고 예보되어서
⑤ 친구들과의 소풍 계획이 잡혀 있어서

Dictations

01

W: Hey, Brian. While you were in the restroom, I was checking out the menu. How about getting pepperoni pizza?

M: Sounds good to me. Anything to drink?

W: How about soda? It goes perfectly with pizza.

M: I know. But I ❶_____ _____ _____ _____.

W: Why not? Is it because you're worried ❷_____ _____ _____ _____?

M: No. If that were the reason, I wouldn't be eating pizza!

W: True. Then why on earth don't you drink soda? Are you worried ❸_____ _____ _____?

M: No. I take good care of my teeth. And besides, I've never been a heavy soda drinker. It's just that drinking soda ❹_____ _____ _____ _____.

W: Oh, I see. Sometimes I get headaches from drinking soda. So what do you want to drink?

M: Iced tea would be great for me.

02

W: Tom, it's already Friday! Do you have weekend plans?

M: Hey, Rachel. Yeah. I'm going hiking with my friends. You're going to ❶_____ _____ _____ with your family, right?

W: That was our plan, but we had to cancel it.

M: Why's that? You've finished your sales report due Monday, right?

W: Yeah, I finished it yesterday.

M: I'm surprised you're not going to the circus. You said your children were ❷_____ _____ _____ _____.

W: Right. They really wanted to see it.

M: Did you fail to reserve the tickets?

W: No. In fact, the tickets weren't even sold out. Actually, my daughter ❸_____ _____ _____ pretty badly while playing soccer yesterday.

M: Oh, my. I'm sorry to hear that. So it sounds like you need to take care of her this weekend.

W: Right. But I think we can go next weekend.

03

W: Jason, have you finished reading Patrick's movie script?

M: Yeah. It was really good.

W: So are you going to ❶_____ _____ _____ _____ _____?

M: I thought about it, but then I decided not to.

W: Why's that? Didn't your production team ❷_____ _____ _____?

M: Yes. They also loved the script.

W: Then why did you decide not to make it into a movie?

M: Well, you know that ❸_____ _____ _____ _____ during two wars in medieval Europe, right?

W: Ah, I see what you're hinting at. You're worried about the production cost, right?

M: Yeah. It's just so costly to have all the special effects we need for these war scenes.

W: Definitely. And the movie market is not that good nowadays.

M: Precisely. I don't want to take the risk of making a movie with a high production cost ❹_____ _____ _____ _____.

W: I understand.

04

M: Hey, Nicole. I've finally finished my chemistry report. How about you?

W: So have I. At last, ❶_____ _____ _____.

M: Me, too. You know, I'm going to the Midtown Jazz Concert on Saturday evening.

W: Really? I'm ❷_____ _____ _____ _____.

M: Then, how about going with me? I have an extra ticket.

W: I'd love to go, but I can't.

M: Why? Do you have plans with other friends?

W: No, but that evening I ❸_____ _____ _____ for a part-time job at a seafood restaurant on Lexington Street.

M: Really? I didn't know that. I'll ❹_____ _____ _____ _____ for you.

W: Thanks. I really wish I could go with you.

M: There will be another opportunity.

05

W: Hey, Matthew. I haven't seen you in the company cafeteria recently. Have you been skipping lunch?

M: No, Mia. I've been ❶_____ _____ _____ _____ to work.

W: Any particular reason? I thought you liked the cafeteria food.

M: I do like it.

W: Oh, then maybe it's because the prices have gone up recently.

M: That's not the reason. The food there is still reasonably priced.

W: So are you just ❷_____ _____ _____ _____?

M: No, my doctor told me to eat more protein. So I make and bring my own meals to make sure I get enough.

W: I see. What kind of meals are you making?

M: I usually make chicken and fish dishes.

W: Nice! Bringing your own lunch can also help save some money, right?

M: Not really, considering the cost of the foods I prepare. But sometimes I ❸_____ _____ _____ of the cafeteria.

W: I can understand that.

06

M: Hi, Grandma. How are you feeling? Is your knee better?

W: Hello, dear. It's healed now. Thanks for asking.

M: Great! My dance competition is this Saturday. Could you ❶_____ _____ _____ _____?

W: I'd love to, but I won't be able to make it.

M: I'm sorry that you can't come. Do you have to go to the senior center then?

W: No, not this weekend. It's closed for maintenance.

M: I see. Oh, you mentioned going on a picnic with friends? Is it this Saturday?

W: We wanted to, but we canceled ❷_____ _____ _____ _____ _____. It'll be rainy and windy this weekend.

M: Really? Then it won't be easy for you to come see the contest.

W: No worries, dear. Actually, I have a health checkup on Saturday, ❸_____ _____ _____ _____.

M: I understand. I'll show you the dance video later.

W: That'd be great. I'm sure you'll do great.

M: Thank you.

08강 유형 심화 I

01 다음을 듣고, 여자가 하는 말의 목적으로 가장 적절한 것을 고르시오.

24006-0050

① 화재 진압 요령을 소개하려고
② 화재 발생 시 대피 순서를 안내하려고
③ 산불 발생의 주요 원인에 대해 설명하려고
④ 숲속 안전사고 방지를 위한 주의 사항을 알리려고
⑤ 산불 확산을 막기 위해 신속한 화재 신고를 당부하려고

02 대화를 듣고, 남자의 의견으로 가장 적절한 것을 고르시오.

24006-0051

① 스포츠 시설이 Green 공원 내 설치되어야 한다.
② Green 공원에 더 많은 녹지가 조성되어야 한다.
③ 가족과 함께 보내는 시간이 가장 보람 있는 순간이다.
④ Green 공원은 가족과 함께 시간을 보내기에 좋은 장소이다.
⑤ 가족 여행은 가족의 사랑을 키울 수 있는 좋은 계기가 될 수 있다.

03 대화를 듣고, 여자의 의견으로 가장 적절한 것을 고르시오.

24006-0052

① 꾸준히 노력하는 사람이 외국어를 잘할 수 있다.
② 외국어에 능숙한 사람이 해외 지사에 근무해야 한다.
③ 정보를 많이 가진 사람일수록 구직 경쟁에서 성공한다.
④ 유창한 외국어 실력은 일자리를 구하는 데 큰 도움이 된다.
⑤ 해외 지사에서 근무하기 위해서는 현지 생활에 빨리 적응해야 한다.

04 대화를 듣고, 두 사람의 관계를 가장 잘 나타낸 것을 고르시오.   24006-0053

① 미술관장 – 화가
② 잡지 기자 – 모델
③ 사진작가 – 건축가
④ 인테리어업자 – 의뢰인
⑤ 건축 자재 납품업자 – 집주인

05 대화를 듣고, 그림에서 대화의 내용과 일치하지 <u>않는</u> 것을 고르시오.   24006-0054

06 대화를 듣고, 그림에서 대화의 내용과 일치하지 <u>않는</u> 것을 고르시오.   24006-0055

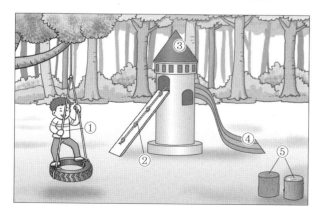

07 대화를 듣고, 여자가 할 일로 가장 적절한 것을 고르시오.   24006-0056

① 졸업 앨범 수령하기
② 강당 배치 도와주기
③ 포토존 장식품 구매하기
④ 졸업식 현수막 찾아오기
⑤ 졸업식 수상자 상품 포장하기

08 대화를 듣고, 남자가 할 일로 가장 적절한 것을 고르시오.   24006-0057

① 간식 주문하기
② 플래카드 만들기
③ 배송 상황 확인하기
④ 간식 개별 포장하기
⑤ 문자 메시지 보내기

09 대화를 듣고, 여자가 지불할 금액을 고르시오.   24006-0058

① $530
② $550
③ $580
④ $600
⑤ $650

10 대화를 듣고, 남자가 지불할 금액을 고르시오.　　　　　　24006-0059

① $240
② $250
③ $270
④ $330
⑤ $340

11 대화를 듣고, 여자가 피자를 주문하지 <u>않으려는</u> 이유를 고르시오.　　　　24006-0060

① 배달비가 비싸서
② 배달 시간이 오래 걸려서
③ 배달 도중에 식을까 봐서
④ 냉동 피자가 집에 있어서
⑤ 원하는 재료로 피자를 만들고 싶어서

12 대화를 듣고, 남자가 교사 독서 토론 모임에 참석할 수 <u>없는</u> 이유를 고르시오.　　24006-0061

① 병원 진료가 있어서
② 자녀를 돌봐야 해서
③ 다른 모임이 있어서
④ 초과 근무를 해야 해서
⑤ 아내를 마중 나가야 해서

09강 언급 유무

■ 대화를 듣고, 특정한 소재에 관해 언급되지 않은 것을 고르는 유형이다.

■ 발문을 읽고 대화의 소재를 파악한 뒤, 세부적인 내용에 집중해서 들어야 한다.

■ 소재에 관해 언급되는 순서대로 선택지가 배열되어 있으므로 선택지의 내용과 비교하면서 들어야 한다.

기출 예제

대화를 듣고, 남자가 예약할 연극 공연에 관해 언급되지 <u>않은</u> 것을 고르시오.

① 제목
② 날짜
③ 출연자
④ 입장료
⑤ 시작 시각

Listening Strategies

STEP 1 발문을 읽고 대화의 소재 파악 후, 대화의 전반부에서 이를 확인하기

연극 공연, to see the play

STEP 2 선택지와 대화의 내용을 비교하면서 듣기

The Shiny Moments (M) → on December 27th (M) → $30 each (M) → starts at 3 p.m. (W)

STEP 3 대화에서 언급되지 않은 내용 파악하기

(남자) 연극의 제목이 *The Shiny Moments*인지 재확인 → (남자) 12월 27일에 예약하기를 원함 → (남자) 입장권은 장당 30달러임을 확인 → (여자) 연극은 오후 3시에 시작함 → (언급되지 않은 것) 예약할 연극의 '출연자'에 관해서는 언급되지 않음

[Telephone rings.]

W: Jason Theater. How may I help you?

M: Hi, this is William Parker from Breezeville Senior Center.

W: Oh, Mr. Parker. You called yesterday about bringing your seniors to see the play.

M: Yes. Before I book, I'd like to ❶_____ _____ _____ _____. It's *The Shiny Moments*, right?

W: That's right. Have you decided on the date?

M: Yes. Could I ❷_____ _____ _____ 25 people on December 27th?

W: Absolutely. But in that case, you'll need to pay today.

M: Okay. You said ❸_____ _____ _____ _____ are $30 each.

W: That's correct. I'll send you the link for the payment.

M: Thank you. I'll pay tonight.

W: That'll be fine. The play starts at 3 p.m., but please come 30 minutes early.

M: No problem. See you then.

Communicative **Functions**

궁금증 표현하기	**I wonder** what kind of cake we'll make in the class. **May I ask you a few questions about** the child swimming classes?
사실 재확인하기	It's pretty cheap, **isn't it?** You were able to book the conference room at Brahms Hotel, **right?**

Useful Expressions, **Idioms and Phrases**

■ **had better** ～하는 것이 좋을 거야 (2024학년도 9월 모의평가 8번)

  A: Thanks. I'll do it today.
    고마워. 오늘 그것을 할게.

  B: You**'d better** hurry! It's limited to only 100 people.
    서두르는 것이 좋을 거야! 100명 한정이야.

■ **be held** 열리다, 개최되다 (2024학년도 6월 모의평가 8번)

  A: Do you remember where it's going to **be held**?
    어디서 열리는지 기억나세요?

  B: Yes, at Golden Maples Field Stadium.
    네, Golden Maples Field Stadium에서입니다.

01 대화를 듣고, Upcycled Art Gallery에 관해 언급되지 <u>않은</u> 것을 고르시오.   24006-0063

① 전시 작품
② 위치
③ 교통편
④ 입장료
⑤ 개관 시간

02 대화를 듣고, 사진 강좌에 관해 언급되지 <u>않은</u> 것을 고르시오.   24006-0064

① 개설 기관
② 수업 요일
③ 수강료
④ 신청 방법
⑤ 강사

03 대화를 듣고, GET 2024 행사에 관해 언급되지 <u>않은</u> 것을 고르시오.   24006-0065

① 참가 대상
② 활동 내용
③ 담당 교수
④ 참가 비용
⑤ 신청 방법

04 대화를 듣고, Jane's Cake Baking Class에 관해 언급되지 <u>않은</u> 것을 고르시오.   24006-0066

① 수강 대상
② 강좌 내용
③ 강좌 요일
④ 수강료
⑤ 소요 시간

05 대화를 듣고, Eco-Vision Workshop에 관해 언급되지 <u>않은</u> 것을 고르시오.   24006-0067

① 개최 장소
② 참가 인원
③ 강연자
④ 진행 시간
⑤ 주최 기관

06 대화를 듣고, Forevi Sports Center 어린이 수영 수업에 관해 언급되지 <u>않은</u> 것을 고르시오.   24006-0068

① 참가 연령
② 수업 레벨
③ 제한 인원
④ 월 등록비
⑤ 수업 시간

Dictations

01

W: Eddie, have you heard about the newly opened Upcycled Art Gallery?

M: No. It sounds interesting, though. Have you been there?

W: No. I've just read about it. They exhibit artworks such as images ❶_____ _____ _____ _____ _____ or sculptures made of pieces of cardboard.

M: Cool. I'd like to go there with my kids. Where is it located?

W: It's right next to City Hall.

M: Good. That's very near to here. Do you know how much ❷_____ _____ _____ _____?

W: Just a second. I'm checking out their website. [pause] Oh, it's $10 for adults and $5 for kids.

M: That's reasonable. Could you check the opening hours?

W: It's open from 10 a.m. to 5 p.m.

M: Okay. I hope it's ❸_____ _____ _____.

W: It is.

M: Great. I think I'll go there this Saturday. Would you like to go too?

W: Sure. Let's do it!

02

M: Alice, are you still interested in ❶_____ _____?

W: Yeah. Why do you ask?

M: I heard that the Landon Community Center is holding a photo class. How about taking it together?

W: Sounds good! When is the class?

M: It's on Friday afternoons in May. There are a total of four lessons.

W: All right. Do you know ❷_____ _____ _____ _____ _____?

M: Yeah. It's $40 per person. It's pretty cheap, isn't it?

W: Not bad. Do you know who teaches it?

M: That's the cool part. ❸_____ _____ _____ _____ by a different teacher, who is a professional photographer.

W: Awesome! Let's ❹_____ _____.

M: Okay. I think it's going to be a really fun class.

03

W: Mark, have you heard about the GET 2024 event?

M: No, what is it, Jenny?

W: GET stands for Geography Exploration Tour. It's for first-year geography majors like us.

M: That sounds fun. What exactly will we do if we join?

W: We will visit a region down south and ❶_____ _____ _____ _____ _____.

M: Wow, that's an excellent way to get hands-on experience.

W: Right. We'll also visit its local markets for shopping.

M: Awesome. Who's ❷_____ _____ _____ _____?

W: Professor Richard is the supervisor.

M: Great! How can we sign up for it?

W: You need to ❸_____ _____ _____ _____ in the department office. I'm going there after lunch.

M: Cool. I'll go with you.

04

M: Kayla, Mom's birthday is next month. Do you still want to bake a cake for her?

W: Definitely. I've ❶_____ _____ _____ of Jane's Cake Baking Class. Here it is.

M: Let me see.... Oh, this is a class for beginners!

W: Yeah. That's good for us.

M: I wonder what kind of cake we'll make in the class.

W: It says they'll teach us to bake chocolate cake, which is Mom's favorite.

M: Perfect! When is the class?

W: It's held every Saturday. ❷_____ _____ _____ this Saturday?

M: Sure, in the morning. But I'm busy in the afternoon. How long is the class?

W: Four hours. It's offered twice a day, so we can take the morning class.

M: Great. Let's ❸_____ _____ _____ _____ .

W: Okay. Mom will be so surprised!

05

W: Steve, we should go over the preparations for next month's Eco-Vision Workshop.

M: Sounds good, Lisa. You were able to ❶_____ _____ _____ _____ at Brahms Hotel, right?

W: Yeah. I booked it last week.

M: Good. I remember the conference room was very nice last year.

W: Right. It holds up to 100 people, and we're expecting around 80 people this year.

M: Great. And Professor Schilt emailed me, and confirmed he'd be the main speaker.

W: Oh, that's wonderful.

M: Yeah. He's an amazing speaker.

W: No doubt. So the plan is ❷_____ _____ _____ _____ for about 2 hours from 10 a.m., right?

M: Yes. Then the attendees will have a discussion about the speech after lunch.

W: Perfect. So the workshop ❸_____ _____ _____ _____ _____ and finishes at 2 p.m.

M: That's the plan. I think it'll work out.

W: All right. It sounds good.

06

[Telephone rings.]

W: Hello. Forevi Sports Center. How may I help you?

M: Hello. May I ask you a few questions about the child swimming classes? I'm thinking about signing up my son.

W: Sure. What would you like to know?

M: What's the age limit?

W: The child swimming class is ❶_____ _____ _____ between the ages of 6 to 12.

M: I see. Are there different levels for the child swimming classes?

W: Yes. There are three levels. They are beginner, intermediate, and advanced.

M: Okay. My son should be a beginner. How many kids can ❷_____ _____ _____ _____ _____ ?

W: A maximum of ten kids per class.

M: I see. And what time do the Saturday classes start?

W: There are two Saturday classes for child beginners. One starts at 10 a.m., and the other at 2 p.m.

M: Sounds good. I'll ❸_____ _____ _____ _____ _____ to sign up my son for one of the classes.

W: All right.

10 강 담화 내용 일치

유형 소개
- 담화의 세부적인 내용과 선택지의 일치 여부를 파악하는 유형이다.
- 담화 내용의 순서에 따라 선택지가 구성되어 있으므로 선택지를 미리 읽어 두어야 한다.
- 담화에서 선택지의 내용에 해당하는 정보에 유의하여 듣고 일치 여부를 파악해야 한다.

기출 예제

2024학년도 수능 9번
24006-0069

Golden Palette Walking Tour에 관한 다음 내용을 듣고, 일치하지 <u>않는</u> 것을 고르시오.

① 11월에 매일 진행된다.
② 안내 책자가 무료로 제공된다.
③ 오전 10시 30분에 시작한다.
④ 출발 지점은 Central Studio의 남쪽 문이다.
⑤ 참가자 전원은 선물을 받을 것이다.

Listening Strategies

STEP 1 선택지를 통해 담화의 주요 내용을 미리 예측하기

[주요 단서] 11월에 매일 진행, 안내 책자 무료 제공, 오전 10시 30분에 시작, Central Studio 남쪽 문에서 출발, 참가자 전원 선물 받기

STEP 2 선택지 표현과 관련된 내용 파악하기

runs every day in November → brochures, for free → begins at 10:30 a.m. → The starting point, the north gate of Central Studio → All participants, receive a postcard as a gift

STEP 3 일치하지 않는 정보를 확인하고 정답 찾기

11월에 매일 진행됨 → 무료로 안내 책자 제공 → 오전 10시 30분에 시작 → 출발 지점은 Central Studio의 북쪽 문 → 참가자 전원 선물 받음

ⒹΙictations

M: Hello, viewers. Are you looking for an interesting experience? How about joining the *Golden Palette* Walking Tour? You'll get the chance to see some of the famous filming sites from the movie *Golden Palette*. This tour runs every day in November. It's a three-hour walking tour with one of our professional guides. Also, brochures ❶_____ _____ _____ _____, and you can find additional information about the filming sites there. The tour begins at 10:30 a.m. and takes you to six locations from the movie. The starting point is ❷_____ _____ _____ _____ of Central Studio. The price for this tour is $40 per person. All participants will receive ❸_____ _____ _____ _____ _____. Book it now on our website!

Communicative **Functions**

이의 제기하기	I **don't think** it's safe for kids. I think I get too emotional when people **disagree with** me.
선호 표현하기	Which day would you **prefer to** meet up? I think black would be **better than** white.

Useful Expressions, **Idioms and Phrases**

- **no longer than** 최대한 ~인, ~보다 길지 않은 (2022학년도 6월 모의평가 9번)

  Don't forget your essay should be **no longer than** three pages.

  당신의 에세이는 최대한 3페이지를 넘지 않아야 한다는 것을 잊지 마세요.

- **pick up** ~을 치우다[정리정돈하다] (2024학년도 9월 모의평가 9번)

  In this event, participants will **pick up** trash in pairs.

  이번 행사에서는 참가자들이 2인 1조로 쓰레기를 치울 것입니다.

01　The 5th Spotlight Drama Camp에 관한 다음 내용을 듣고, 일치하지 <u>않는</u> 것을 고르시오. 　24006-0070

① 일주일간 진행된다.
② 새로 단장한 Rainbow Theater에서 열린다.
③ 최종 공연 비용은 참가비와 별도로 지불한다.
④ 이전의 연기 경험이 요구되지 않는다.
⑤ 웹사이트에서 등록해야 한다.

02　Lockwood Snow Festival에 관한 다음 내용을 듣고, 일치하지 <u>않는</u> 것을 고르시오. 　24006-0071

① 매년 1월에 개최된다.
② 전 세계의 예술가들이 참가하는 얼음 조각 대회가 열린다.
③ 방문객들은 야간 활동을 즐길 수 있다.
④ 일부 활동은 유료이다.
⑤ 간식과 음료를 판매한다.

03　2024 Summer Hiking Trip에 관한 다음 내용을 듣고, 일치하지 <u>않는</u> 것을 고르시오. 　24006-0072

① 사흘 동안 진행될 것이다.
② 다섯 명의 전문 안내원과 함께할 것이다.
③ 첫째 날에 산 정상까지 오를 것이다.
④ 둘째 날에 종일 강을 따라 걸을 것이다.
⑤ 모든 활동은 조별로 이루어질 것이다.

04 Happy Dog Photo Contest에 관한 다음 내용을 듣고, 일치하지 <u>않는</u> 것을 고르시오.   24006-0073

① 친구의 반려견을 찍은 사진으로 참가할 수 있다.
② 학교 로비에 있는 게시판에 사진을 게시할 것이다.
③ 사진 제출 마감일은 4월 19일이다.
④ 학생들이 3일간 마음에 드는 사진에 투표할 것이다.
⑤ 우승자는 반려견 사료를 받을 것이다.

05 Global Policy Debate Contest에 관한 다음 내용을 듣고, 일치하지 <u>않는</u> 것을 고르시오.   24006-0074

① 8월 1일부터 3일까지 개최될 것이다.
② 토론 경험과 관계없이 참여할 수 있다.
③ 정책 토론의 전문가들이 토론을 평가할 것이다.
④ 상위 다섯 팀이 장학금과 상을 받을 것이다.
⑤ 등록은 7월 말까지 가능하다.

06 Sunshine Beach Yoga Class에 관한 다음 내용을 듣고, 일치하지 <u>않는</u> 것을 고르시오.   24006-0075

① 매일 오전 10시에서 오전 11시까지 진행된다.
② 초보자를 위한 수업이다.
③ 호텔 바로 뒤에 있는 해변에서 진행된다.
④ 호텔 투숙객의 참가비는 수업 당 10달러이다.
⑤ 녹화된 수업이 호텔 웹사이트에서 방송될 것이다.

Dictations

01

M: Attention, young actors and actresses. ❶_____ _____ _____ _____ on stage this summer! The 5th Spotlight Drama Camp is here and better than ever! This camp will last for one week and offer exciting activities filled with learning, creativity, and fun. It'll be at ❷_____ _____ _____ _____ _____ downtown. Experienced camp staff will teach you everything from acting basics to developing your characters. The participation fee is $200 per person and covers all materials, costumes, and a final performance. ❸_____ _____ _____ _____ is required. However, spaces are limited, so you should register on our website as soon as possible. Don't miss this chance to showcase your talent on stage this summer!

02

W: Good morning, listeners! Are you looking for a place to go with your family this winter? Then ❶_____ _____ _____ going to the Lockwood Snow Festival? It takes place in January every year and features a wide range of winter activities. One of the main attractions is the "Ice Sculpture Contest," in which artists from all over the world participate by ❷_____ _____ _____ out of ice. Visitors can enjoy sledding, snow tubing, and nighttime activities like ice skating under the stars. And remember all of these activities are free. The festival also has a lot of food trucks selling snacks and drinks. So if you're ❸_____ _____ _____ _____ _____ to enjoy the winter, you can't miss the Lockwood Snow Festival!

03

M: Hello, students! Guess what's just around the corner. It's our school's 2024 Summer Hiking Trip! It'll be from August 11 to August 13. This year, we're hiking Donovan Mountain with five professional guides and ❶_____ _____ _____ in Donovan Mountain National Park all together. On the first day, we'll hike to the ❷_____ _____ _____ _____ and enjoy the beautiful view there. On the second day, we'll walk to the Donovan River in the morning and enjoy rafting for about two hours. It's going to be so much fun! And then we'll return home on the last day. All activities will ❸_____ _____ _____ _____. For more details, check the school website. Don't miss out on this great event!

04

W: Hello, everyone. This is Katie Jones, the head of the school photography club. I'm pleased to announce our club's most fun contest of the year, the Happy Dog Photo Contest. The contest gives you a chance to share ❶_____ _____ _____ _____ _____ _____ with other students. And if you don't have a dog, no problem. You can enter the contest with a photo you take of a friend or relative's dog. Just ❷_____ _____ _____ of your or their dog with your name, and we'll ❸_____ _____ _____ _____ _____ in the school lobby. The submission deadline is Friday, April 19th. Students will ❹_____ _____ their favorite photos ❺_____ _____ _____ starting April 22nd. And the winner will receive an organic pet shampoo and conditioner set. So hurry up and tell your furry friend to say "Cheese!"

05

M: Attention, students! Are you interested in discussing global issues and ❶_____ _____ _____ _____ with your peers worldwide? If so, we invite you to join the upcoming Global Policy Debate Contest. The contest will take place online from August 1st to 3rd. It is open to students of all age groups, ❷_____ _____ _____ _____ _____. The topic of this year's debates is global health challenges. Experts in policy debates will evaluate the discussions and provide you with valuable feedback to enhance your debating skills. Additionally, the top five teams will receive scholarships and prizes. Registration is currently open online until the end of June, and ❸_____ _____ _____ _____ _____. For more details, please visit www.gpfdebate.org. Don't miss out on this fantastic opportunity.

06

W: Hi, everyone. I'm Jessica Kim, the manager at Sunshine Hotel. I'd like to tell you about our Sunshine Beach Yoga Class, which takes place daily from 10 a.m. to 11 a.m. As one of the most popular programs in our hotel, the class is for ❶_____ _____ who have never done yoga before. So, no prior yoga experience is ❷_____ _____ _____ in this class. It takes place on the beach right behind the hotel, which is just a 5-minute walk from the hotel lobby. Hotel guests can join for free. Non-guests can join for a $10 fee per class. Please be aware that this class will ❸_____ _____ _____ _____ on our hotel website. Stop by the front desk if you have any questions. Thank you for your attention.

11 강 도표

유형 소개
- 제시된 표를 보면서 대화를 듣고, 대화자가 구매[주문]하거나 예약[수강]하기 위해 선택하는 대상을 고르는 유형이다.
- 대화를 듣기 전, 제시된 표의 항목과 내용을 미리 살펴보면서 대화의 내용을 예측해 보는 것이 필요하다.
- 대화를 들으면서 대화자가 제외하는 내용을 차례로 지워 나가면서 최종적으로 선택하는 것을 찾는다.

기출 예제   2024학년도 수능 10번

24006-0076

다음 표를 보면서 대화를 듣고, 남자가 주문할 접이식 카트를 고르시오.

Foldable Carts

	Model	Price	Weight Limit	Color	Handle Material
①	A	$38	30 kg	Black	Silicone
②	B	$42	40 kg	Green	Silicone
③	C	$44	45 kg	Blue	Metal
④	D	$48	50 kg	White	Metal
⑤	E	$53	45 kg	Red	Rubber

Listening Strategies

STEP 1 주요 단서가 되는 표에 제시된 항목 파악하기

Price, Weight Limit, Color, Handle Material

STEP 2 각 항목에 관해 묻고 답하는 대화의 흐름 이해하기

let's not spend more than $50 (M) → How about the weight limit? (W) → that wasn't strong enough (M) → Do you have any color preference? (M) → Why don't we get a different color this time? (W) → Which handle material do you like better? (M) → metal gets too cold in winter (W) → Then, let's get the other model. (M)

STEP 3 각 항목에 관한 두 사람의 선택을 파악하여 남자가 주문할 물건 고르기

(남자) 50달러 넘게 쓰지 말자고 함 → (여자) 무게 한도를 물음 → (남자) 30kg은 충분히 강하지 않다고 함 → (남자) 선호하는 색을 물음 → (여자) 이번엔 (파란색이 아닌) 다른 색으로 하기를 권유함 → (남자) 손잡이 재질을 물음 → (여자) 금속은 겨울에 너무 차가워진다고 말함 → (남자) 금속이 아닌 다른 모델을 주문

W: Honey, what are you doing on your laptop?

M: I'm trying to choose one of these foldable carts. You know our cart broke yesterday.

W: Oh, that's right. Let me see the ones you're looking at.

M: Sure. There are these five. They all look good, but ❶_____ _____ _____ more than $50.

W: All right. How about the weight limit? Our last one was 30 kilograms.

M: Hmm, that wasn't strong enough.

W: Okay. Then, this one won't be any good.

M: Yeah. Do you have any color preference?

W: The old one was blue. Why don't we ❷_____ _____ _____ _____ this time?

M: Good idea. Now, there are two options left. Which handle material do you like better?

W: Well, metal gets too cold in winter.

M: Good point. Then, let's ❸_____ _____ _____ _____. I'll order it now.

Communicative Functions

동의하기	Oh, **that's a good idea**. **Same here**.
권유하기	**Why don't we** get a different color this time? **Why don't you** try a digital detox?

Useful Expressions, Idioms and Phrases

- **have ~ in mind** ~을 염두에 두다[생각하다] (2024학년도 6월 모의평가 10번)

  A: There are many shapes to choose from. Do you **have** one **in mind**?

  선택할 수 있는 모양이 많네. 염두에 두고 있는 게 있어?

  B: The star-shaped cutters look cool.

  별 모양의 커터가 멋져 보여.

- **anything but ~** ~ 외에는 무엇이나, ~이 결코 아닌 (2024학년도 9월 모의평가 10번)

  A: Which sports do you like?

  어떤 스포츠를 좋아하니?

  B: **Anything but** baseball. I don't like baseball that much.

  야구 외에는 뭐든지. 난 야구를 별로 안 좋아해.

01 다음 표를 보면서 대화를 듣고, 여자가 구매할 전동칫솔을 고르시오. 24006-0077

Electric Toothbrushes

	Model	Price	Brushing Modes	Pressure Sensor	Color
①	A	$35	5	×	black
②	B	$48	3	×	blue
③	C	$78	6	○	white
④	D	$99	5	○	black
⑤	E	$107	6	○	white

02 다음 표를 보면서 대화를 듣고, 두 사람이 주문할 디지털 주방 저울을 고르시오. 24006-0078

Digital Kitchen Scales

	Model	Price	Surface Material	Number of Measuring Units	Color
①	A	$13	stainless steel	5	white
②	B	$14	plastic	3	pink
③	C	$18	stainless steel	5	silver
④	D	$25	glass	3	white
⑤	E	$32	glass	5	silver

03 다음 표를 보면서 대화를 듣고, 남자가 구입할 온습도계를 고르시오. 24006-0079

Temperature & Humidity Sensors

	Model	Type	Waterproof	Power Source	Size (inches)
①	A	Tabletop	○	USB	2×3
②	B	Tabletop	○	Battery	3×4
③	C	Wall	×	USB	3×4
④	D	Tabletop & Wall	○	USB	4×5
⑤	E	Tabletop & Wall	×	Battery	5×6

04 다음 표를 보면서 대화를 듣고, 두 사람이 예약할 투어를 고르시오.　24006-0080

Tora Tora Island Tours

	Tour	Price	Transportation	Stops	Activities
①	A	$100	Cruise	Khai Beach	Fishing & Swimming
②	B	$130	Cruise	Coral Bay	Fishing & Snorkeling
③	C	$150	Speed Boat	Maya Bay	Swimming & Snorkeling
④	D	$180	Cruise	Maya Bay & Khai Beach	Swimming & Snorkeling
⑤	E	$220	Speed Boat	Maya Bay & Khai Beach	Fishing & Snorkeling

05 다음 표를 보면서 대화를 듣고, 두 사람이 대여할 커피 메이커를 고르시오.　24006-0081

Star Coffee Makers

	Model	Monthly Rental Fee	Milk Foam Attachment	Minimum Rental Period (years)	Free Gift
①	A	$17	×	4	mug
②	B	$24	○	2	mug
③	C	$24	○	2	coffee beans (200 g)
④	D	$27	○	3	coffee beans (200 g)
⑤	E	$35	×	2	mug, coffee beans (200 g)

06 다음 표를 보면서 대화를 듣고, 여자가 보러 가기로 선택한 아파트를 고르시오.　24006-0082

Studio Apartments for Rent

	Studio Apartment	Monthly Rental Cost	Furnished	Walking Distance from Pacifica University	Floor
①	A	$800	×	20 minutes	2nd
②	B	$850	×	10 minutes	3rd
③	C	$900	○	10 minutes	2nd
④	D	$950	×	5 minutes	4th
⑤	E	$1,100	○	5 minutes	5th

01

M: Welcome to J's Electronics. What can I do for you?

W: Hi. I'm looking for an electric toothbrush.

M: Okay. *[Pause]* These are the ones we have. Do you have a particular brand in mind?

W: No, but I do have a budget. I'd like to ❶_____ _____ _____ _____.

M: Got it. So if you take a look here, they have different brushing modes. It's nice to have a variety of them.

W: Right. I'd like to get one ❷_____ _____ _____ _____ _____.

M: Okay. That leaves a few great options.

W: Oh, these have a pressure sensor. I really ❸_____ _____ _____ _____.

M: That's a useful function to protect your gums. So these two seem to fit what you'd like. Do you have a color preference?

W: Everything in my bathroom is bright, so I don't want black. I'll ❹_____ _____ _____ _____.

M: Okay. Sounds good.

02

W: Honey, are you checking your social media?

M: No, I'm looking at a site that sells baking supplies. We should get a digital kitchen scale.

W: Great idea. Since we got the new oven, we'll be baking more.

M: Right. *[Pause]* Here are the site's five best-selling models. This one is pretty expensive.

W: Yeah. Let's ❶_____ _____ _____ _____.

M: Okay. I'd prefer to buy one that's ❷_____ _____ _____ _____ _____ _____. Germs don't stick as much, so they're cleaner.

W: That makes sense. And how many measuring units do you think we need?

M: Hmm. I think we'll need ❸_____ _____ _____ different units such as gram, ounce, and pound.

W: Okay. Then we should get one of these two. Which color do you prefer?

M: I think ❹_____ _____ _____ _____ in our kitchen.

W: I agree. So let's order this one.

03

M: Mom, I'm trying to find a good temperature and humidity sensor to buy online. I'd like ❶_____ _____ _____ _____. Can you help me?

W: Sure. Have you found a website?

M: Yes. This website has these five models. I'm not sure which one to get though.

W: Hmm. Let me see. Where do you plan on placing it?

M: I was thinking of putting it on the table.

W: Okay, let's rule out this one then. Oh, and make sure you ❷_____ _____ _____ _____.

M: That narrows it down to these three models. Do you think I should get a USB-powered one?

W: Most of the time, a USB-powered one would be more convenient. However, for travel purposes, a battery-powered one might be more suitable.

M: I won't be ❸_____ _____ _____, so I'll go for a USB-powered option.

W: So now you need to choose between these two. What about this one?

M: It looks good, but it's quite big. I'll buy the other one.

W: Good choice.

04

M: Darling, I brought this brochure from Tora Tora Island Tours. They ❶_____ _____ _____ _____.

W: Wonderful! We're planning to visit there next month. Let me have a look. *[Flipping sound]* These all sound fun.

M: Absolutely. I personally like this one the most, but I'm afraid it might ❷_____ _____ _____.

W: Right. Let's keep it under $200. Also, this tour won't work for me. I can't be on a speed boat.

M: Really? I find it quite thrilling.

W: I know, but I would definitely get seasick.

M: I see. So we need to choose one of these three options. Do you have any preference regarding the stops?

W: Well, I've heard that Coral Bay tends to ❸_____ _____ _____. Let's skip that one.

M: Agreed. That leaves us with these two choices. I love snorkeling.

W: Me, too! Let's go ahead and book this one.

M: Perfect! I can't wait to go.

05

W: Sweetie, since our ❶_____ _____ _____ _____, I was thinking we should rent one.

M: Okay. Do you know where we can do that?

W: Yeah. Check out this website. They have several models ❷_____ _____ _____.

M: All right. *[Pause]* These all look good, but I think this one over $30 per month is too expensive for us.

W: I agree. Let's choose one which costs less than $30.

M: They don't all come ❸_____ _____ _____ _____. We definitely want that for café lattes.

W: Right. Look. The remaining three have different minimum rental periods.

M: Well, 3 years seems too long. I think 2 years is better.

W: Me, too. So then between these two, how about this one? It comes with coffee beans as a free gift.

M: Sounds good. Besides, we already have ❹_____ _____ _____ _____.

W: Right. Then let's rent this one.

M: Okay!

06

M: Hi. Welcome to Maple Grove Townhomes.

W: Hi, I'm looking to ❶_____ _____ _____ _____ near Pacifica University. Are there any available?

M: Sure. What's your rental budget?

W: I can only ❷_____ _____ _____ of $1,000 per month.

M: Okay. Do you need a furnished apartment?

W: No, I don't. I have my own furniture.

M: All right. How close do you want to be to the university?

W: Well, I'd like to be within a 15-minute walk.

M: Okay. We have a couple available. This one's on the 4th floor. Is that okay?

W: Actually, I prefer a lower floor.

M: No problem. Then how about this one?

W: It seems perfect. Can I ❸_____ _____ _____ _____ this Saturday at noon?

M: Absolutely. Just write down your name and phone number here.

짧은 대화의 응답

유형
소개
- 짧은 대화를 듣고, 마지막 말에 대한 적절한 응답을 찾는 유형이다.
- 마지막 말까지 잘 듣고 대화의 정확한 내용을 파악하는 것이 중요하다.
- 마지막 말이 질문으로 제시되는 경우, 그에 대한 답을 찾아야 한다.
- 마지막 말이 질문이 아닌 경우, 상황을 고려한 적절한 응답을 찾아야 한다.

기출 예제

2024학년도 수능 11번

24006-0083

대화를 듣고, 여자의 마지막 말에 대한 남자의 응답으로 가장 적절한 것을 고르시오.

① Right. We should've watched them.
② Why not? Just put the mat on the shelf.
③ Great. We can store some snacks at home.
④ I'm sorry. I can't find the parking lot.
⑤ No problem. I'll take care of it.

Listening Strategies

STEP 1 **대화의 소재나 상황 파악하기**

we also need the picnic mat to sit on

STEP 2 **대화의 흐름 이해하기**

I think I put it on one of the shelves in the storage room (M) → Then, could you find the mat (W)

STEP 3 **문맥을 고려하여 적절한 응답 찾기**

(남자) 돗자리를 어디에 두었는지 확실하지 않음 → (여자) 간식과 음료수를 챙기는 동안 돗자리를 찾도록 부탁

Dictations

W: Dad, we should leave soon to watch the fireworks in the park. Shall we bring something to eat?

M: Yeah, we might get hungry. Oh, we also need the ❶_____ _____ to sit on. I think I put it on one of the shelves in the storage room, but I'm not sure.

W: Then, ❷_____ _____ _____ the mat while I pack some snacks and soft drinks?

Communicative Functions

도움 요청하기	I have **a favor to ask**. It's my turn to prepare dinner tonight, but **could you do it for me**?
가능성 정도 표현하기	But this one won't be any good since our equipment weighs **at least 60 kilograms**. I think we need **at least five** considering our recent use.

Useful Expressions, Idioms and Phrases

- **We're going to ~ as scheduled.** 우리는 예정대로 ~할 것입니다. (2024학년도 6월 모의평가 12번)

  A: **We're going to** go **as scheduled.** Is there anything wrong?
  우리는 예정대로 갈 것입니다. 무슨 문제라도 있습니까?

  B: Actually, Kevin has a fever, so I don't think he can go tomorrow.
  사실 Kevin이 열이 나서 그가 내일 갈 수 없을 것 같습니다.

- **be about to** 곧 ~할 것이다 (2021학년도 수능 12번)

  A: You cannot park here because we**'re about to** close off this section of the parking lot.
  주차장의 이 구역을 곧 폐쇄할 것이기 때문에 이곳에 주차할 수 없습니다.

  B: Why? What's going on here?
  왜요? 여기에 무슨 일이 있습니까?

01 대화를 듣고, 여자의 마지막 말에 대한 남자의 응답으로 가장 적절한 것을 고르시오.

24006-0084

① I agree. We need to reschedule the audition.
② I'm trying. But it exceeds the maximum number.
③ Right. One person should play more than one role.
④ At least seven. But only five have signed up so far.
⑤ Two more applicants came today. That's enough now.

02 대화를 듣고, 남자의 마지막 말에 대한 여자의 응답으로 가장 적절한 것을 고르시오.

24006-0085

① Oh, you have different types of tea. Can I try some?
② No problem. I know a good coffee shop around here.
③ Definitely. Drinking coffee also helps you keep in shape.
④ No, thanks. I already had a cup of coffee this morning.
⑤ Right. If I drink coffee, I'm not able to sleep well.

03 대화를 듣고, 여자의 마지막 말에 대한 남자의 응답으로 가장 적절한 것을 고르시오.

24006-0086

① I see. When do I have to move out?
② Good for you. How did you find the apartment?
③ That's great news. Can you introduce me to her?
④ Sorry to hear that. Why is she moving out so soon?
⑤ I'm surprised. When did you decide to move there?

04 대화를 듣고, 남자의 마지막 말에 대한 여자의 응답으로 가장 적절한 것을 고르시오. 24006-0087

① Good idea. I'll drop you off here.
② I agree. We'd better find another table.
③ I'm sorry. There are no tables available.
④ No worries. The restaurant will be open soon.
⑤ Thanks. This parking spot is good for all day.

05 대화를 듣고, 여자의 마지막 말에 대한 남자의 응답으로 가장 적절한 것을 고르시오. 24006-0088

① Okay. What shall we cook for dinner this evening?
② Don't worry. I'll prescribe you stronger medicines.
③ I see. Could you please go buy some medicine for me?
④ Absolutely. You shouldn't have eaten the leftover food.
⑤ Sure. Why don't we go for a walk after we have dinner?

06 대화를 듣고, 남자의 마지막 말에 대한 여자의 응답으로 가장 적절한 것을 고르시오. 24006-0089

① Sounds great. Please tell me the name of the app.
② Of course. I use the app whenever I take pictures.
③ Thanks. I handed in my report on time with your help.
④ No, I won't. I'll use my tablet PC for a few more years.
⑤ Okay. I'm glad it doesn't cost a lot to repair my tablet PC.

07 대화를 듣고, 여자의 마지막 말에 대한 남자의 응답으로 가장 적절한 것을 고르시오. 24006-0090

① Really? I completely forgot about the staff dinner.
② Thanks. I'll try to get this done as soon as possible.
③ Not at all. I received the email you sent this morning.
④ Right. The restaurant is already fully booked that day.
⑤ All right. I'll order our food to be delivered right now.

08 대화를 듣고, 남자의 마지막 말에 대한 여자의 응답으로 가장 적절한 것을 고르시오. 24006-0091

① I learned about doing it online.
② I'll mark the date on my calendar.
③ I don't know how to reuse old calendars.
④ I've marked all the critical parts in the book.
⑤ It was easy to make this calendar on a website.

09 대화를 듣고, 여자의 마지막 말에 대한 남자의 응답으로 가장 적절한 것을 고르시오. 24006-0092

① Yes. It doesn't take long to get a haircut.
② I think so. I'll pick a hairstyle from a magazine.
③ Sure. I made an appointment for a haircut today.
④ Never mind. You can part my hair on either side.
⑤ Exactly. Just give the hair on the sides a slight cut.

10 대화를 듣고, 남자의 마지막 말에 대한 여자의 응답으로 가장 적절한 것을 고르시오. 24006-0093

① I brought my lunch. I don't have to wait in line.
② I'm sorry I'm late. The traffic was really terrible.
③ Okay. Let's go somewhere nearby without a wait.
④ Oh, wow! These are the best noodles I've ever had.
⑤ Excuse me. This isn't the noodle dish that I ordered.

11 대화를 듣고, 여자의 마지막 말에 대한 남자의 응답으로 가장 적절한 것을 고르시오. 24006-0094

① Right. Turn off your laptop when you don't use it.
② Sure. Your laptop is old, so I'll buy you a new one.
③ I know. That looks like a nice protective laptop cover.
④ Okay. Let's go and find a suitable cover for your laptop.
⑤ I understand. But your old cover is good enough for protection.

12 대화를 듣고, 남자의 마지막 말에 대한 여자의 응답으로 가장 적절한 것을 고르시오. 24006-0095

① We'd better get more houseplants to freshen the air.
② We can save the plant if we start watering it regularly.
③ Why don't we go out for a walk to get some fresh air?
④ Let's move it outside to get more fresh air and sunlight.
⑤ How about making an indoor garden with various plants?

01

W: Jake, how is ❶_____ _____ _____ _____ your school film club going?

M: Not so good, Mom. I'm worried I may not be able to get the minimum number of members.

W: Oh, really? ❷_____ _____ _____ do you need?

02

M: Louise, you've had a lot more energy the past few days. Did you finally ❶_____ _____ _____ _____?

W: Hey, Mark. Yes, I did. I've started drinking decaffeinated tea instead of coffee, and it has helped.

M: Glad to hear that. Actually, I noticed you haven't had a single cup of coffee this week, ❷_____ _____.

03

W: Hey, Mike. I heard you were looking for a new apartment. Have you found one?

M: Not yet. I want to move closer to work, but there are not ❶_____ _____ _____.

W: Well, my co-worker who sits next to me is ❷_____ _____ _____ _____ for her apartment. It's really close to our office.

04

M: Wow, the restaurant parking lot is packed. I hope we can find an open spot.

W: Then it's ❶_____ _____ inside the restaurant, too. I wonder if there are any tables available.

M: Shall I ❷_____ _____ _____ _____ while you park the car?

05

W: Honey, are you sick or something? You ❶_____ _____ _____ _____.

M: Yeah. I have had an upset stomach since dinner. Do we have ❷_____ _____ _____ _____ _____?

W: No, we don't have any, but I can buy some at the drugstore.

06

M: Emma, I see you're working hard on your tablet PC. Is everything okay?

W: Hi, Brian. I need to ❶_____ _____ _____ for my geography report. But I don't know how to do it.

M: I see. I know a ❷_____ _____ _____ _____ _____. Why don't you install it?

07

W: Andy, are you almost finished with your work? All of the other co-workers are ❶_____ _____ _____ _____ for our dinner meeting.

M: I know. I'm almost done. I just need to quickly finish writing this email.

W: All right. Then I'll ❷_____ _____ _____ _____ _____ a few minutes.

08

M: Hey, Amy. Cool bookmark. Where did you get it?

W: I ❶_____ _____ _____ using an old calendar.

M: Wow. What a cool way to make something useful out of an old calendar! I'm wondering ❷_____ _____ _____ _____.

09

W: So, ❶_____ _____ _____ _____ your hair cut?

M: Well, can you style the sides and the top like this picture?

W: Hmm, so ❷_____ _____ _____ _____ take some off the sides and leave it longer on top, right?

10

M: Oh, honey, I know you want to get noodles from this restaurant. But look at ❶ _____ _____ _____ _____ _____!

W: It's because the noodles are so good. My friend said it's a famous restaurant.

M: But I'm starving. I don't feel like ❷ _____ _____ _____ for an hour.

11

W: Dad, can we go shopping this afternoon? I want to ❶ _____ _____ _____ for my laptop.

M: Why do you need a new one? Don't you already have a cover?

W: No, I don't and I need one. I want to ❷ _____ _____ _____ when I take it to school or to the library.

12

M: Honey, could you come to the living room and take a look at this plant? It seems like it's ❶ _____ _____ _____.

W: Sure. Oh, poor thing! We do water it regularly, but it might be lacking fresh air or sunlight.

M: What do you think we should do? I don't ❷ _____ _____ _____ _____.

PART I
13강 긴 대화의 응답

유형소개

- 긴 대화를 듣고, 남자[여자]의 마지막 말에 대한 여자[남자]의 적절한 응답을 찾는 유형이다.
- 대화의 전체 흐름을 파악하여, 여자[남자]가 할 적절한 응답을 추론해야 한다.
- 마지막에 언급되는 남자[여자]의 말이 정답을 추론하는 직접적인 근거가 될 수 있으므로, 마지막 말에 주의해서 듣는 전략이 필요하다.

기출 예제

2024학년도 수능 13번

24006-0096

대화를 듣고, 여자의 마지막 말에 대한 남자의 응답으로 가장 적절한 것을 고르시오.

Man: _____

① Don't give up! You've inspired me to be a painter.
② Cheer up! The fashion market is open to everybody.
③ You have a point. I don't have any fashion sense at all.
④ I agree. You should make a balance between work and life.
⑤ Be positive. You can start pursuing your dream at any time.

Listening Strategies

STEP 1 대화 첫 부분의 핵심 어구를 통해서 대화의 소재나 상황 예측하기

a senior fashion model

STEP 2 대화의 전체적인 흐름 파악하기

be an inspiration to many people our age (W) → so flattered (M) → you successfully switched careers (W) → My dream has finally come true. (M) → realize your dream in your 60s (W) → age was never an issue (M) → my old passion to be a painter (W) → Now is the time (M) → I think it's too late (W)

STEP 3 마지막 말에 대한 적절한 응답 찾기

(여자) 남자가 같은 또래의 많은 사람에게 자극을 줬다고 함 → (남자) 과찬이라고 함 → (여자) 남자가 성공적으로 직업을 바꾼 것에 놀람 → (남자) 자신의 꿈이 이루어짐 → (여자) 60대에 꿈을 실현하는 것의 어려움 → (남자) 나이는 전혀 문제가 되지 않음 → (여자) 화가가 되고 싶었던 옛 열정 → (남자) 지금이 바로 그것을 시도해 볼 때임 → (여자) 그러기에 너무 늦었다고 생각 → (남자의 응답 추론) 꿈을 추구하는 것은 언제든 시작할 수 있다고 여자를 독려

Dictations

W: Shaun, you really rocked the runway as a senior fashion model yesterday!

M: Thanks for coming to my first show, Grace.

W: My pleasure. You'll ❶_____ _____ _____ _____ many people our age.

M: I'm so flattered.

W: It's amazing that you successfully switched careers.

M: Thank you. My dream has ❷_____ _____ _____.

W: It couldn't have been easy to realize your dream in your 60s.

M: It wasn't. But I've always believed in myself, and age was ❸_____ _____ _____ for me.

W: You make me think of my old passion to be a painter, but I put it off for too long.

M: Now is the time to give it a try.

W: I think it's too late for that.

Communicative Functions

확실성 정도 표현하기	But **I'm still not sure** I'll be able to wake up so early in the morning. **I bet** your students had a really good experience.
놀람 표현하기	**It's amazing that** you speak four languages! **I can't believe** you finished that work so quickly!

Useful Expressions, Idioms and Phrases

- **It seems like ~** ～인 것 같아요. (2024학년도 9월 모의평가 14번)

  A: **It seems like** barefoot walking will be good for both body and mind.
  맨발 걷기가 몸과 마음 둘 다에 좋은 것 같군요.

  B: Exactly. I think we should do it.
  맞아요. 우리도 그것을 해 봐야겠어요.

- **drop ~ off** (어디로 가는 길에) ～를 내려 주다 (2024학년도 6월 모의평가 14번)

  A: Are you going to **drop** him **off** at my house tomorrow?
  내일 그를 저희 집에 내려 주실 건가요?

  B: Sorry, I can't. I have a few things to do before the trip.
  미안하지만, 그럴 수 없어요. 출장 전에 해야 할 일이 몇 가지 있거든요.

01 대화를 듣고, 남자의 마지막 말에 대한 여자의 응답으로 가장 적절한 것을 고르시오.   24006-0097

Woman: _____

① You can search the Internet for a good place to party.
② I'll ask her to come over to discuss our science project.
③ I don't know how much birthday cakes cost at that shop.
④ She'll probably agree with my idea about the surprise party.
⑤ We need to check how many people are coming to the party.

02 대화를 듣고, 여자의 마지막 말에 대한 남자의 응답으로 가장 적절한 것을 고르시오.   24006-0098

Man: _____

① I'm sorry, but you'll receive the bag within a week.
② Too bad. You should've called the company earlier.
③ Thanks. I finally received the bag I ordered last week.
④ Well, they ended up losing your package during delivery.
⑤ I see. I'll check if the package was sent to the wrong address.

03 대화를 듣고, 남자의 마지막 말에 대한 여자의 응답으로 가장 적절한 것을 고르시오.   24006-0099

Woman: _____

① I see. Then I'll give you a wake-up call.
② Oh, no! The alarm went off, but I didn't wake up.
③ I can't believe it. I didn't expect her to win a medal.
④ I'm so sorry that I couldn't watch her final this morning.
⑤ It was so fun to wake up early and watch the final together.

04 대화를 듣고, 여자의 마지막 말에 대한 남자의 응답으로 가장 적절한 것을 고르시오.　　　24006-0100

Man: _____

① I see. I'll visit the website to sign up for the program right now.
② For sure. I recommend that you participate in the program.
③ I know. We need to prepare a lot for next month's program.
④ Great. I'm glad our students went together to the program.
⑤ Right. My students found the program really informative.

05 대화를 듣고, 남자의 마지막 말에 대한 여자의 응답으로 가장 적절한 것을 고르시오.　　　24006-0101

Woman: _____

① Sorry. I'll exchange it right away for you.
② Oh. I didn't realize the sale ended last week.
③ Sure. Here's the credit card I used to buy the vest.
④ Right. A white T-shirt will go well with your sweater vest.
⑤ Okay. I'll look around for something to buy with the credit.

06 대화를 듣고, 여자의 마지막 말에 대한 남자의 응답으로 가장 적절한 것을 고르시오.　　　24006-0102

Man: _____

① I don't mind. Any type of seafood is good for me.
② We should set up a volleyball net so we can play.
③ I'm not really in the mood to go to the beach.
④ Right. I think we'll stay home this weekend.
⑤ I feel the same way. Let's make it happen!

07 대화를 듣고, 남자의 마지막 말에 대한 여자의 응답으로 가장 적절한 것을 고르시오.   24006-0103

Woman: _____

① Sorry, but you must be able to speak French.
② Believe it or not, I can't speak a foreign language.
③ I agree. You don't have to speak French like a native.
④ It's like that at first, but practice and patience make a big difference.
⑤ Now I understand how you're able to learn foreign languages quickly.

08 대화를 듣고, 여자의 마지막 말에 대한 남자의 응답으로 가장 적절한 것을 고르시오.   24006-0104

Man: _____

① But I won't be free then. Why don't we meet up on another day?
② I'm afraid the café will be noisy. How about going somewhere else?
③ Great! I'm glad you can make it on time for the book club meeting.
④ Perfect! I'll call the café and check if a study room will be available.
⑤ Cool! It's great that we'll be able to work on the project together at the library.

09 대화를 듣고, 남자의 마지막 말에 대한 여자의 응답으로 가장 적절한 것을 고르시오.   24006-0105

Woman: _____

① I couldn't agree more. That's why I always shop at online stores.
② Okay. I'll reduce my online shopping and prioritize shopping offline.
③ Terrific! It's a great idea for us to open up an eco-friendly local store.
④ You're right. I should pay more attention to recycling for the environment.
⑤ Good idea. I'll provide constructive feedback to local businesses to help them.

10 대화를 듣고, 여자의 마지막 말에 대한 남자의 응답으로 가장 적절한 것을 고르시오.   24006-0106

Man: _____

① You don't have to. I know all about the badminton club.
② Sounds good. I'll buy a racket right away so I can join the club.
③ Awesome. I can't wait to play badminton and make new friends.
④ Okay. I'll sign up for the badminton competition online right now.
⑤ Thanks for the information. I'll do my best to win the competition.

11 대화를 듣고, 남자의 마지막 말에 대한 여자의 응답으로 가장 적절한 것을 고르시오.   24006-0107

Woman: _____

① Let's find ways he can make new friends.
② It's not a good idea to force him to go outside.
③ Don't disturb him when he's playing board games.
④ Then let's try taking a family walk in the evenings.
⑤ Reading books together is the best activity for him.

12 대화를 듣고, 여자의 마지막 말에 대한 남자의 응답으로 가장 적절한 것을 고르시오.   24006-0108

Man: _____

① That's not true. Zoos are losing popularity these days.
② You're right. Zoo animals are forced to live there for us.
③ Sorry. I disagree. Each person has a different view of zoos.
④ Really? Zoo animals are actually well cared for by zookeepers.
⑤ It makes sense. Zoos contribute to preserving endangered species.

Dictations

01

W: Hi, Paul. What's up?

M: Hi, Lisa. I'm planning to throw a surprise birthday party for Susan.

W: Oh, right. Her birthday is next Saturday, isn't it?

M: It is. How did you know?

W: She told me last week at science class. We are on the same team for a science project. We ❶_____ _____ _____ _____.

M: Oh, really? Great. Then could you help me get the party ready?

W: Of course. So how many people are you inviting?

M: I was hoping to invite eight, but I still don't know ❷_____ _____ _____ _____ _____.

W: How about at my house? I can even put up some really cool decorations.

M: Really? That'd be perfect.

W: Now we ❸_____ _____ _____ _____ to invite Susan to my house without telling her it's her birthday party.

M: Hmm.... You said you are on the same team at science class. Do you have any good ideas?

02

W: Jack, have you received the new bag you ordered online?

M: No, I haven't, Mom.

W: Wow. It's ❶_____ _____ _____ than I expected.

M: I know. It was supposed to be delivered by last Thursday.

W: It's already been ten days since you ordered it, right?

M: Yes. I wonder what could have happened.

W: Well, maybe it ❷_____ _____ _____ _____. That happened to me a while ago.

M: Really? So what did you do?

W: I called the company and asked where the product was.

M: What did they do for you?

W: They ❸_____ _____ _____ and found out that it was delivered to the wrong address. The same may have happened to your package.

03

M: Jenny, you're a big fan of Judy Anderson, right?

W: Yes, Kevin. She's my favorite figure skater.

M: She's mine too! She's so amazing.

W: Right. I was so happy when she ❶_____ _____ _____ _____ at the international figure skating competition last year.

M: Me, too. She seems to be in her prime.

W: I think you're right. And do you know she advanced to this year's final in Italy?

M: Yes, I heard about it. The final is being broadcast tomorrow morning, right?

W: Yes. It starts at 3 a.m. here in Korea, and I'm going to ❷_____ _____ _____ _____ _____.

M: Well, I also want to see it live, but I'm not sure I'll be able to wake up so early.

W: Try going to bed early tonight, and you should be able to wake up on time. Plus, it's Saturday tomorrow, so you can go back to sleep after watching it.

M: True. But I'm still not sure I'll be able to ❸_____ _____ _____ _____ in the morning.

04

W: Hello, Mr. Wilson.

M: Hello, Ms. Brown. How was the ❶_____ _____ _____ _____ _____ yesterday?

W: It was great. We visited the Ministry of Foreign Affairs for a student program they have.

M: I bet your students had a really good experience.

W: Yes, they did. They had a chance to listen to a lecture and ❷_____ _____ _____ _____.

M: Wow, that's a special experience. How did you find out about the program?

W: I saw it on their website last month, and so I signed up for it.

M: I see. I should take the political science club this time.

W: That's a great idea. I guarantee they'll like it, but you should ❸_____ _____ _____ _____ _____ for the program at the website of the Ministry of Foreign Affairs.

M: Why? Is it very popular?

W: Yes, it is. They told me that recently a lot of schools want the program.

05

M: Hi. Can I help you with something?

W: Yes. I ❶_____ _____ _____ _____ here a couple of days ago.

M: Okay. Is there something wrong with it?

W: No, it just didn't look good on me. Could I ❷_____ _____ _____?

M: Sure. As long as it has the original price tag and there's nothing wrong with it.

W: Great. It still has the tag, and all I did was try it on once. Here it is.

M: Yeah, it looks good. Do you ❸_____ _____ _____?

W: Yes. Here it is.

M: Okay. *[Pause]* Oh, you bought this vest on sale. I'm sorry, but we don't ❹_____ _____ _____ _____ _____.

W: Really? So I can't get my money back?

M: No, you can't. But I can give you credit that you can use in the store.

06

M: Joy. I was thinking we ❶_____ _____ _____ _____ _____ this weekend.

W: You know I won't say no to that! What beach are you thinking of?

M: I was thinking of Bonny Island Beach.

W: That'd be cool. I love it there!

M: I knew you'd like it there. There's ❷_____ _____ _____ _____ _____ _____. The beach has volleyball nets, so I'll bring a ball.

W: Awesome.

M: Paddleboards are ❸_____ _____ _____ _____.

W: We ❹_____ _____ _____ _____ _____.

M: For sure. And there are food trucks on the beach, so we can have lunch there.

W: Perfect! I can't wait for the weekend.

07

M: Amy, were you just talking on the phone in French?

W: Yeah. I was talking to a college friend.

M: Wow. I didn't know you spoke French. How many languages can you speak?

W: I can speak four, including English.

M: It's amazing that you speak four languages!

W: Well, it's not like I speak them all perfectly. My French ❶_____ _____ _____ _____ _____ _____, but I haven't used it for a while.

M: Are you saying that it's important to keep using a foreign language not to forget it?

W: Yes, exactly. Learning a foreign language ❷_____ _____ _____.

M: That makes sense.

W: Not only does it take a lot of practice, but it ❸_____ _____ _____ _____ _____, too. Didn't you start learning Chinese recently?

M: Yes, I did, but it's not easy ❹_____ _____ _____ _____.

08

W: Hi, Lucas, would you like to ❶_____ _____ _____ _____ _____ together this weekend?

M: Hi, Isabella. Sure, that sounds like a good idea.

W: Which day would you prefer to meet up?

M: I'm available all weekend. How about you?

W: I have a book club meeting on Saturday, so Sunday would be better. How about 2 p.m.?

M: Okay. Where should we meet?

W: The library is definitely the best place for us to study. They have ❷_____ _____ _____ _____, and it's usually quiet.

M: That's a bit far. What about the café down the street? They offer good foods, and their chairs are really comfortable.

W: That's true, but I'm concerned about the noise level there. It can get quite loud at times.

M: It shouldn't be a problem. They have quiet study rooms now. I can ❸_____ _____ _____ for our project.

W: That's great! Let's meet up there then.

09

W: Dad, I got a notice that my package just arrived.

M: Oh, what did you order this time?

W: I got some clothes and shoes.

M: It seems like you've been doing ❶_____ _____ _____ _____ _____ lately.

W: Yes, online shopping is just so convenient and often offers better prices.

M: True, but have you thought about the environmental impact of ❷_____ _____ _____?

W: Honestly, it never crossed my mind. But you're right. Excessive packaging can harm the environment.

M: Exactly. It's also important to support local businesses.

W: Yeah, I haven't been shopping locally much.

M: You should consider shopping more at local stores. It ❸_____ _____ _____ _____.

10

W: Jeremy, I was wondering if you'd be interested in joining the badminton club I'm in.

M: Hmm. That sounds like fun. I'm not good at badminton though. I've only played a few times.

W: No problem. The club ❶_____ _____ _____ _____, including beginners.

M: How often does it meet?

W: Twice a week.

M: That's good. Will I have to buy a racket?

W: No. The club has a bunch of rackets you can use. All you really need are ❷_____ _____ _____ _____.

M: That sounds great! I'm in. It'll be also nice to meet new people.

W: Absolutely. Everybody's really nice. You're going to have a great time with us.

M: Thanks for inviting me. What should I do now?

W: The pleasure is mine. Just come with me, and I'll ❸_____ _____ _____ _____ to the club's social media page later.

11

W: Honey, I'm home.

M: Hi, sweetie. Did you have a good day?

W: Yes. How was your day with our little guy?

M: Great. Kevin and I had a lot of fun.

W: Awesome. What did you do?

M: We baked cookies, played board games, and then read books.

W: Sounds fun. By the way, it seems like ❶_____ _____ _____ all day long.

M: Right. I asked him if he wanted to go to the park and kick a soccer ball, but he didn't.

W: He usually prefers staying home. I want to get him outside more for exercise.

M: Me, too. Do you have any good ideas?

W: How about we all ❷_____ _____ _____ _____ or bike rides together?

M: He might find it hard to ride a bike. I'm sure he'd like ❸_____ _____ _____ _____ if we do it together.

12

M: Wendy, what are you watching ❶_____ _____ _____?

W: It's a documentary about zoo animals, Dad. It deals with an issue about them.

M: Why? Is there anything wrong with zoo animals?

W: Yeah. Some of them behave abnormally.

M: How?

W: They repeatedly move ❷_____ _____ _____ _____ or in circles in the same spot.

M: Hmm, it's probably because they feel stuck and stressed out in the zoo cages.

W: Well, it would be better for animals to live in zoos ❸_____ _____ _____ _____, right?

M: No. Zoo animals don't live in cages because they want to.

W: Now I see. They could feel ❹_____ _____ _____ _____ _____ our needs.

유형
소개
- 특정 상황에 대한 설명을 듣고, 그 상황에서 해야 할 말을 추론하는 유형이다.
- 언급되는 상황에 대한 정확한 파악을 기반으로 등장인물 사이의 관계를 이해해야 한다.
- 담화의 마지막 부분에 해야 할 말에 대한 결정적인 정보가 언급되므로, 이 부분을 특히 유의한다.

기출 예제

2024학년도 수능 15번
24006-0109

다음 상황 설명을 듣고, Jake가 Yuna에게 할 말로 가장 적절한 것을 고르시오.

Jake: _____

① Could you please take my picture again with the rock in it?
② I'd appreciate it if you could come to the mountain with me.
③ You shouldn't take any photos while climbing the rock.
④ I'm wondering if you can pose in front of the rock.
⑤ Why don't you take a selfie in the national park?

Listening Strategies

STEP 1 등장인물에 대해 알 수 있는 구체적인 단서 찾기

[주요 단서] members of a climbing club, taking selfies with it, finds a great spot to take a photo with the rock, include the rock

STEP 2 등장인물이 처해 있는 전체적인 상황 파악하기

(Jake & Yuna) visiting a national park → (Jake) taking selfies with it → (Yuna) offers to take photos for him → (Jake) the rock is not in them → (Jake) get another shot of him and this time include the rock

STEP 3 전체적인 상황과 구체적인 단서를 조합하여 정답 추론하기

Jake는 Yuna와 함께 국립공원을 방문함 → Jake는 바위 배경으로 사진을 찍을 수 있는 멋진 장소를 발견함 → Yuna가 Jake의 사진을 찍음 → Yuna가 찍은 사진에 바위가 보이지 않는다는 것을 Jake가 파악함 → Jake가 Yuna에게 바위를 넣어서 다시 사진을 찍어줄 것을 요청하고 싶어 함

M: Jake and Yuna are members of a climbing club. Today, they're ❶_____ _____ _____ _____ with other club members. At the top of the mountain, Jake sees a beautiful rock. He starts ❷_____ _____ with it. When Yuna sees Jake, she offers to take photos for him. Jake finds ❸_____ _____ _____ to take a photo with the rock and gives Yuna his smartphone. After Yuna takes some photos of him, Jake looks at the photos and notices that the rock is not in them. So Jake wants to ask Yuna to ❹_____ _____ _____ of him and this time include the rock. In this situation, what would Jake most likely say to Yuna?

Communicative **Functions**

관심에 대해 묻기	Alice, **are you** still **interested in** learning photography? **What are you interested in?**
의견 표현하기	**I think** it's going to be a really fun class. **In my opinion**, the blue bag is too expensive.

Useful Expressions, **Idioms and Phrases**

- **have nothing to do with** ~와 관계가 없다 (2023학년도 9월 모의평가 7번)
  A: Really? Why not? Did you have to do something with your family?
  정말? 왜 안 갔어? 가족과 함께 무언가를 해야만 했니?
  B: Not at all. It **had nothing to do with** my family.
  전혀 아니야. 가족과는 아무 상관도 없었어.

- **adjust to** ~에 적응하다 (2023학년도 9월 모의평가 15번)
  She has **adjusted to** life at the new school and has made many new friends.
  그녀는 새 학교에서의 생활에 적응했고 새 친구를 많이 사귀었습니다.

01 다음 상황 설명을 듣고, Jason이 Angela에게 할 말로 가장 적절한 것을 고르시오.

24006-0110

Jason: _____

① If you go there, you should try surfing.
② Thanks to you, I'm able to surf by myself.
③ Sure. You're much better at surfing than I am.
④ Okay. I'll sign up for your private surfing lesson.
⑤ That's right. Our surfing lessons are the best in the area.

02 다음 상황 설명을 듣고, Laura가 Hank에게 할 말로 가장 적절한 것을 고르시오.

24006-0111

Laura: _____

① Don't worry about it. I have a spare lab coat.
② I'm sorry. They don't sell this lab coat anymore.
③ Amazing! Good luck with your drama performance.
④ Wow, I can't believe you have an extra role as a doctor!
⑤ Oh, my! You should have the lab coat washed at a dry cleaner's.

03 다음 상황 설명을 듣고, Alex가 Sandra에게 할 말로 가장 적절한 것을 고르시오.

24006-0112

Alex: _____

① Why don't you read different genres of web novels?
② How about using a screen filter to protect your eyes?
③ Are you planning on getting an eye examination soon?
④ You had better increase your distance from your monitor.
⑤ A screen filter really helps to protect the monitor from scratches.

04 다음 상황 설명을 듣고, Paul이 Olivia에게 할 말로 가장 적절한 것을 고르시오. 24006-0113

Paul: _____

① You shouldn't be hard on yourself like that.
② Regular exercise can help you release stress.
③ I'm sure you can get a better score next time.
④ No matter how many times you fail, keep trying.
⑤ I don't think it's a good idea to drop English class.

05 다음 상황 설명을 듣고, Mindy가 Jason에게 할 말로 가장 적절한 것을 고르시오. 24006-0114

Mindy: _____

① It's no use if we cannot find a place to practice our routine.
② Let's practice four times a week to improve our performance.
③ I think it'd be better for our team to stick to the original music.
④ Our performance needs some new steps to better match the music.
⑤ You need to move faster and more energetically in the performance.

06 다음 상황 설명을 듣고, Thomas가 Shelly에게 할 말로 가장 적절한 것을 고르시오. 24006-0115

Thomas: _____

① You can tell facts from opinions if you read more reviews.
② Do you think robot vacuum cleaners are worth the high price?
③ You must apply for membership to read more detailed reviews.
④ You should find a website that has various robot vacuum cleaners.
⑤ You should first establish your standards to be more time-efficient.

Dictations

01

W: Jason is ❶_____ _____ _____ _____ from his friend, Angela, who is very good at surfing. Angela first tells Jason the basics of surfing on the beach, and then they go into the water. Whenever Jason tries ❷_____ _____ _____ _____ _____, he falls down right away. However, Angela kindly continues encouraging him to keep trying, and Jason finally succeeds. Now he thinks he is able to stand and stay up on the surfboard alone. Angela tells him to try surfing alone, and she ❸_____ _____ _____ _____ _____. After surfing for about half an hour, Jason comes out of the water and goes to Angela. He wants to ❹_____ _____ _____ to her for helping him surf alone. In this situation, what would Jason most likely say to Angela?

02

M: In their second year of high school, Laura and Hank are ❶_____ _____ _____ _____ different school clubs. Laura belongs to the school science club, while Hank is in the school drama club. For his club performance at the school festival last Friday, Hank borrowed a white lab coat from Laura for ❷_____ _____ _____ _____ _____. Before returning the lab coat to Laura, he washes and dries it. However, while folding it, he notices ❸_____ _____ _____ _____. Feeling sorry, Hank informs Laura about the tear and offers to buy her a new lab coat. But Laura wants to tell Hank that he doesn't need to do that because she has an extra one. In this situation, what would Laura most likely say to Hank?

03

W: Sandra reads web novels on her computer every day to become a web novel writer. Recently, she read an article on eye health risks associated with electromagnetic waves. ❶_____ _____ _____ _____ to electromagnetic waves, Sandra discusses this issue with her friend Alex, a computer programmer. He tells Sandra that he sits away from his monitor and ❷_____ _____ _____ while using the computer. He advises her to do the same. But Sandra says she believes she should do more to protect herself. Alex thinks she should ❸_____ _____ _____ _____ that blocks blue light emissions from the monitor. So he wants to suggest that she apply a screen filter for her eyes. In this situation, what would Alex most likely say to Sandra?

96 EBS 수능특강 영어듣기

04

M: Paul and Olivia are high school classmates who have been friends since elementary school. One day, Olivia complains to Paul about her English mid-term exam score. She ❶_____ _____ _____ _____, but she received a lower score than she expected. Paul thinks it's unnecessary for her to get so upset about her score. Paul thinks Olivia is ❷_____ _____ _____ _____ on herself and that she should look on the bright side of her achievement. So he wants to say that she should be ❸_____ _____ _____ _____. In this situation, what would Paul most likely say to Olivia?

05

W: Mindy and Jason are both members of the school hip-hop dance team. Recently, their team has been ❶_____ _____ _____ _____ _____ at a local festival, which is next week. They've been practicing their dance routine together three times a week. However, Jason tells Mindy that he doesn't ❷_____ _____ _____ _____ because he thinks it's too slow. He suggests that they change the music to something that has a faster beat. But Mindy thinks it's too late to change the music now because they have ❸_____ _____ _____ _____ before the festival. So Mindy wants to tell Jason that she prefers they not change their music. In this situation, what would Mindy most likely say to Jason?

06

M: Shelly is considering buying a robot vacuum cleaner for her mother, who has ❶_____ _____ _____ _____. So, Shelly searches for reliable online user reviews of robot vacuum cleaners. She visits various websites and reads reviews for days. Thomas, Shelly's husband, notices she spends too much time ❷_____ _____ _____ _____ _____, and he asks her why she hasn't decided which robot vacuum cleaner to buy yet. She tells him there are so many reviews that it's hard to choose which review to follow. Thomas wants to tell her that she first needs to ❸_____ _____ _____ _____ based on her preference not to waste time. In this situation, what would Thomas most likely say to Shelly?

15강 복합 이해

유형
소개
- 긴 담화를 듣고 두 개의 문항(대의와 세부내용 파악)을 푸는 유형이다.
- 담화문은 강의, 안내 등 다양한 형태로 제시된다.
- 첫 번째 문항은 대의를 파악하는 유형으로, 주로 담화의 주제를 묻는 방식으로 출제된다.
- 두 번째 문항은 세부 정보를 묻는 유형으로, 주로 언급 여부를 묻는 방식으로 출제된다.

기출 예제

2024학년도 수능 16번~17번

[01~02] 다음을 듣고, 물음에 답하시오.

01 여자가 하는 말의 주제로 가장 적절한 것은?   24006-0116

① various natural materials as a source of building supplies
② how upcycling is used in architecture across the globe
③ strategic use of upcycled plastics in different countries
④ impact of architectural waste on the global environment
⑤ why nations should employ eco-friendly shipping methods

02 언급된 나라가 아닌 것은?   24006-0117

① Singapore   ② Mexico   ③ Australia
④ Indonesia   ⑤ France

Listening Strategies

STEP 1 담화 앞부분의 핵심 어구를 통해서 담화의 주제 파악하기
선택지와 발문에 나라(countries)가 등장하고, 담화의 초반부(Today, I'll focus on how this eco-friendly practice is employed in architecture around the world.)에서 주제를 확인할 수 있음

STEP 2 담화의 주제와 관련하여 언급된 구체적 내용 확인하기
how this eco-friendly practice is employed in architecture around the world
Singapore (Enabling Village) → old shipping containers
Mexico (Tubohotel) → huge upcycled concrete pipes
Indonesia (Microlibrary Bima) → 2,000 plastic ice cream buckets
France (the Circular Pavilion) → 180 reused wooden doors

STEP 3 언급된 나라가 아닌 것 파악하기
업사이클링이 나라마다 어떻게 이용되고 있는지를 싱가포르, 멕시코, 인도네시아, 프랑스의 예를 언급하면서 설명함

Dictations

W: Hello, students. Last week, we learned about upcycling, the process of ❶_____ _____ _____ to make a new object more valuable than the original pieces. Today, I'll focus on how this eco-friendly practice is employed in architecture around the world. Our first example is a community center in Singapore, called Enabling Village. Its buildings are famous for being made from ❷_____ _____ _____. Second, we have a hotel in Mexico, called Tubohotel. The capsule-style rooms of this hotel were built using huge upcycled concrete pipes. Next, Microlibrary Bima is a ❸_____ _____ _____ located in Indonesia. The building was constructed by arranging 2,000 plastic ice cream buckets. Finally, there's the Circular Pavilion in France. It is known for its ❹_____ _____ which consists of 180 reused wooden doors. Each of these examples shows how upcycling is applied in architecture globally to minimize our environmental footprint. Now, let's watch a video showing how these buildings were made.

Communicative Functions

주제 소개하기	Today, **we'll explore** the flowers that great artists liked to paint as subjects. I want to turn away from the wild and **talk about** companion animals.
청자의 관심 끌기	**Have you noticed that** AI is finding its way into virtually everything nowadays? **Have you heard about** the wish-granting animals?

Useful Expressions, Idioms and Phrases

- **I've been waiting so long to** ~ 오랫동안 ~하기를 기다렸어요. (2024학년도 9월 모의평가 7번)

  A: **I've been waiting so long to** see them perform. When is the concert?
  오랫동안 그들이 공연하는 것을 보기를 기다렸어요. 콘서트는 언제인가요?

  B: It's on October 6th.
  10월 6일이에요.

- **I couldn't make it.** (모임 등에) 갈 수 없다[참석할 수 없다] (2024학년도 6월 모의평가 6번)

  A: Sandra, I didn't see you at the company book club meeting yesterday.
  Sandra, 어제 회사 독서 모임에서 당신을 못 봤어요.

  B: Yeah, I really wanted to go, but **I couldn't make it**.
  네, 정말 가고 싶었지만 저는 갈 수가 없었어요.

[01~02] 다음을 듣고, 물음에 답하시오.

01 남자가 하는 말의 주제로 가장 적절한 것은?   24006-0118

① predictions on how AI will change sports
② cases of AI applications in different sports
③ ethical issues in sports caused by using AI
④ AI-driven marketing strategies of sports clubs
⑤ improvements of athletic performance through AI

02 언급된 스포츠가 <u>아닌</u> 것은?   24006-0119

① football　　② basketball　　③ rugby
④ tennis　　⑤ baseball

[03~04] 다음을 듣고, 물음에 답하시오.

03 여자가 하는 말의 주제로 가장 적절한 것은?   24006-0120

① cultures that have their own unique calendar systems
② how to wish a happy New Year in different languages
③ the world's best New Year's celebration spots to explore
④ why countries celebrate New Year on different days
⑤ unusual New Year's customs around the world

04 언급된 나라가 <u>아닌</u> 것은?   24006-0121

① Spain　　② Denmark　　③ Brazil
④ Greece　　⑤ Colombia

[05～06] 다음을 듣고, 물음에 답하시오.

05 남자가 하는 말의 주제로 가장 적절한 것은? 24006-0122

① tips for appreciating classical flower paintings
② the historical evolution of depicting flowers in art
③ reasons Impressionists painted flowers in different ways
④ flower painting techniques passed down through generations
⑤ the flowers that served as beloved subjects for famous painters

06 언급된 꽃이 아닌 것은? 24006-0123

① sunflowers　　② water lilies　　③ roses
④ poppies　　⑤ daisies

[07～08] 다음을 듣고, 물음에 답하시오.

07 여자가 하는 말의 주제로 가장 적절한 것은? 24006-0124

① important reasons to protect wild animals
② considerations for raising companion animals
③ different ways wild animals are domesticated
④ various benefits of raising companion animals
⑤ differences between wild animals and companion animals

08 언급된 동물이 아닌 것은? 24006-0125

① cats　　② dogs　　③ parrots
④ rabbits　　⑤ hamsters

Dictations

[01~02]

M: Hello, students. Have you noticed that AI is finding its way ❶_____ _____ _____ nowadays? It's even used in the sports industry. Let me share with you some examples of how AI is being integrated into various sports. First, AI is making its way into football. For example, one Spanish football club has implemented an AI system named Zone7. It uses medical data collected during training to ❷_____ _____ _____ _____ during a game. Another AI is in rugby. It's difficult for referees to see everything that happens during a rugby match. So if there's any confusion, referees use highly complex AI video analysis tools to make the right judgment. Also, a lot of tennis players use a range of apps built by AI experts. Using the apps enables them to get automated analyses of shot speed and accuracy and analyze their games ❸_____ _____ _____. Lastly, to combat inaccurate decisions made during a game, AI robots have been tested in baseball. They sit above home plate and accurately read pitches. There's no doubt that AI is already having a significant impact on sports.

[03~04]

W: Good afternoon, students. The year is coming to an end. Some of you probably have ❶_____ _____ _____ _____. This is also true for various cultures around the world, which welcome the change of the calendar with unique traditions. Here are some more unconventional traditions ❷_____ _____ _____ _____ _____. In Spain, it's customary to eat 12 grapes. Each grape represents ❸_____ _____ _____ _____ of the coming year. Residents of Denmark greet the new year by ❹_____ _____ _____ _____ _____ against the doors of family and friends to chase away evil spirits. In Brazil, wearing special underwear on New Year's Eve is thought to bring good luck for the next year. The most popular colors are red and yellow. And citizens of Colombia walk around ❺_____ _____ _____ _____ on New Year's Eve to bring good fortune for their upcoming travels. Now, let's watch some videos on this topic.

[05~06]

M: Good afternoon, everyone! Welcome to our art lecture. Today, we'll talk about the fascinating flowers that great artists liked to ❶_____ _____ _____. Vincent van Gogh's sunflowers stand out as one of the most famous examples. His use of vivid colors and bold brushstrokes in these paintings is truly ❷_____ _____ _____. Claude Monet is famous for his beautiful paintings of water lilies. He painted these flowers in various colors and with an impressionistic style. Henri Matisse, on the other hand, loved painting roses. Throughout his career, he created numerous paintings of these flowers using bright colors and simplified forms that ❸_____ _____ _____ _____. And of course, poppies, those bright red or orange flowers, have always been popular among artists. Claude Monet's *Field of Poppies* is a fantastic example. The painting features loose, impressionistic brushstrokes and bold, vivid colors that ❹_____ _____ _____ of these beautiful flowers. Now, let's take a look at these great paintings online.

[07~08]

W: Hello, animal-loving viewers! Welcome to my online channel, Animal World. I'm Alice Brown. I'm going to ❶_____ _____ _____ _____. If you're thinking about raising one, there are some important things to consider. First, you should know their personality. If you know cats are ❷_____ _____ _____ _____, it'll help you coexist with them. Second, you have to think about time. For example, dogs are active and enjoy playing. So, if you don't have a lot of free time, it's not a good idea to ❸_____ _____. Next, consider the cost. Parrots can be expensive to raise, just like other pets. Think about your economic situation before ❹_____ _____ _____. Lastly, listen to what your family members think. For example, if you want to raise a hamster, but someone in your family doesn't like hamsters, it'll be difficult to keep one. ❺_____ _____ _____ _____ _____ and leave any questions you have in the comments below.

16강 유형 심화Ⅱ

01 대화를 듣고, Sun Farms delivery service에 관해 언급되지 <u>않은</u> 것을 고르시오.   24006-0126

① 배송 품목
② 배송 주기
③ 배송 지역
④ 이용료
⑤ 신청 방법

02 Special Belt-Making Class에 관한 다음 내용을 듣고, 일치하지 <u>않는</u> 것을 고르시오.   24006-0127

① 6월 13일 목요일에 열린다.
② 가죽 공예를 소개하는 초급 수업이다.
③ 재봉틀로 가죽 벨트를 만드는 체험을 제공한다.
④ 오전 9시에 시작하여 오후 5시에 마친다.
⑤ 참가를 원하면 안내대에서 미리 등록을 해야 한다.

03 다음 표를 보면서 대화를 듣고, 두 사람이 주문할 책상을 고르시오.   24006-0128

Children's Desks

	Model	Price	LED Light	Adjustable Table	Drawers
①	A	$150	fixed	height only	○
②	B	$150	detachable	height only	×
③	C	$200	detachable	height and table angle	×
④	D	$230	detachable	height and table angle	○
⑤	E	$270	fixed	height and table angle	○

04 다음 표를 보면서 대화를 듣고, 두 사람이 주문할 구강 청결제를 고르시오.

24006-0129

Mouthwashes

	Model	Volume (ml)	Price	Flavor	Alcohol
①	A	120	$4	Mint	×
②	B	380	$7	Bubble Gum	○
③	C	500	$9	Pineapple	×
④	D	820	$15	Mint	○
⑤	E	1000	$22	Watermelon	×

05 대화를 듣고, 여자의 마지막 말에 대한 남자의 응답으로 가장 적절한 것을 고르시오.

24006-0130

① Thanks to you, I had a great camping trip.
② If I were you, I wouldn't buy the tent there.
③ I'm afraid I have something to do this weekend.
④ Good idea. Let's go camping at Grand Forest Park.
⑤ Don't worry. Just come to my house and take my tent.

06 대화를 듣고, 남자의 마지막 말에 대한 여자의 응답으로 가장 적절한 것을 고르시오.

24006-0131

① No. I haven't booked the tickets yet.
② Sorry. I'm not interested in Chagall's works.
③ Sure. Working at this art center is quite good.
④ Okay. Let's go to the exhibition this Saturday.
⑤ No. I've never seen any of Chagall's works before.

07 대화를 듣고, 여자의 마지막 말에 대한 남자의 응답으로 가장 적절한 것을 고르시오.　24006-0132

Man: _____

① Okay. I'm sure she'll accept our suggestion.
② Sure. Let's decide which country to go to.
③ No worries. She really enjoyed the trip.
④ Good idea. Let's join her if she lets us.
⑤ Sorry. She's too busy to travel with us.

08 대화를 듣고, 남자의 마지막 말에 대한 여자의 응답으로 가장 적절한 것을 고르시오.　24006-0133

Woman: _____

① Why bother? We can send your item by parcel for free.
② Just a moment, please. I'm looking for your record now.
③ My goodness! I suggest you come back as soon as possible.
④ My pleasure. I'll contact you after checking for your lost item.
⑤ Trust me. We keep all of our guest information safe and secure.

09 다음 상황 설명을 듣고, Cindy가 Greg에게 할 말로 가장 적절한 것을 고르시오.　24006-0134

Cindy: _____

① Focusing on every basic step in detail is a waste of time.
② We should focus on math first before we go on to literature.
③ Why don't we ask our math teacher to explain it step by step?
④ Can you please explain thoroughly without skipping basic steps?
⑤ I think you will find math much easier if you first learn the basics.

10 다음 상황 설명을 듣고, Mr. Winston이 Elena에게 할 말로 가장 적절한 것을 고르시오.　24006-0135

Mr. Winston: _____

① Believe me. I won't miss the next singing practice.
② Keep on practicing. You'll definitely win the competition.
③ You did a great job! I'm so happy you participated in the competition!
④ It'll be fine. There are still a few days left before the competition.
⑤ Don't worry. Just participating will be a valuable experience.

[11~12] 다음을 듣고, 물음에 답하시오.

11 여자가 하는 말의 주제로 가장 적절한 것은?　24006-0136

① influence of emotional changes on the body
② diverse cultural interpretations of body language
③ nonverbal communication that describes bodily functions
④ similarities of sayings across different languages and cultures
⑤ reasons for using body-related expressions in communication

12 언급된 신체 부위가 아닌 것은?　24006-0137

① stomach　② chin　③ leg
④ back　⑤ hand

Part

II

소재편

PART II
17강 학업, 교육

소재 소개	■ 학업·교육활동은 수능에서 출제 빈도가 높은 소재이다. ■ 주로 활용되는 소재는 학습, 학교 수업, 학생 활동 등의 내용이다. ■ 문제 유형으로 대화에서는 의견, 주장, 그림이나 도표 내용 일치, 이유, 짧은 대화와 긴 대화의 응답 유형이, 담화에서는 주제, 상황에 적절한 말 유형이 자주 출제된다.

기출 예제   2024학년도 9월 모의평가 3번

24006-0138

다음을 듣고, 여자가 하는 말의 요지로 가장 적절한 것을 고르시오.

① 정기적인 학습 상담은 학습 능률을 높여 줄 수 있다.
② 메모하는 것은 과제를 관리하는 데 효율적인 방법이다.
③ 자신만의 암기법을 활용하면 성적을 향상시킬 수 있다.
④ 두뇌의 균형적인 발달은 메모하는 습관으로 촉진된다.
⑤ 실천 가능한 계획 수립이 과제 해결의 출발점이다.

문항 속의 소재 **수업 발표 날짜 조정** (2024학년도 6월 모의평가 15번)

M: Kate is taking Professor Lee's East Asian history class. She is given an assignment to make an individual presentation on Monday of the following week. However, she finds out that she won the first prize in a national essay writing contest, and she is asked to attend the awards ceremony. She's happy to hear the good news and really wants to go to the ceremony to receive her award. But she's not sure about whether she can go because the awards ceremony and the presentation are both scheduled for the same time. So, she wants to ask Professor Lee if it is possible for her to change the date of the presentation with another student in the class.

Kate는 이 교수님의 동아시아 역사 수업을 듣고 있다. 그녀는 다음 주 월요일에 개인 발표를 해야 한다는 과제를 받는다. 하지만 그녀는 전국 에세이 쓰기 대회에서 1등을 했다는 것을 알게 되고, 시상식에 참석하라는 요청을 받는다. 그녀는 그 좋은 소식을 듣고 기뻐하고 상을 받기 위해 시상식에 정말 가고 싶어 한다. 하지만 그녀는 시상식과 발표가 똑같은 시간에 예정되어 있어서 갈 수 있을지 확신할 수 없다. 그래서 그녀는 이 교수님께 그 수업을 듣는 다른 학생과 발표 날짜를 바꾸는 것이 가능한지 묻고 싶다.

W: Good morning, students. I'm Ms. Thompson, your learning consultant for today's workshop. Many of you have expressed concerns that you're having difficulty ❶_____ _____ _____ on time. But you know what? Making a memo is an efficient way to ❷_____ _____ _____. You can't only rely on your memory. You need to make a note about what to do and when to do it so that you don't forget. Writing a memo might be annoying at first, but you'll get used to it in no time. With a memo, you can ❸_____ _____ _____ _____. Now, we're going to see some good examples of students' memos. Let's look at the screen.

Topic-related Expressions

▶ 학습, 학교 수업

after-school program 방과 후 프로그램   assignment 과제   career coaching program 진로 코칭 프로그램   choose a major 전공을 선택하다   concentration 집중력   counseling 상담   deadline 마감 시한   discipline (학문의) 분야   handout 유인물   lab 실험실   lecture 강의   midterm exam 중간고사   on time 제때   problem-solving 문제 해결   scholarship 장학금   semester 학기   subject 과목   take an online class 온라인 수업을 수강하다   tuition fee 수업료

Many of you have expressed concerns that you're having difficulty submitting your homework **on time**.
여러분 중 많은 사람이 과제를 제때 제출하는 데 어려움을 겪고 있다고 걱정을 나타냈습니다.

Some former graduates came to our school and gave us some tips on **choosing a major**.
몇몇 이전 졸업생이 우리 학교에 와서 전공 선택에 대한 몇 가지 조언을 우리에게 해줬어요.

▶ 학생 활동

candidate 후보자   ceremony 시상식   competition 경기, 시합   debate contest 토론 대회   election 선거   field trip 현장 학습   freshmen orientation 신입생 오리엔테이션   in order of application 신청 순으로   join a club 동아리에 가입하다   judge 심사위원   make it (모임 등에) 가다   participate in ~에 참가하다   receive an award 상을 받다   registration form 등록 신청서   school auditorium 학교 강당   school trip 수학여행   sign up for ~을 신청하다   student council 학생회   student union building 학생회관   take charge of a club 동아리를 담당하다   talent show 장기 자랑

They're creating a video to introduce their club at the **freshmen orientation** next month.
그들은 다음 달 신입생 오리엔테이션에서 동아리를 소개하는 영상을 만들고 있습니다.

She's happy to hear the good news and really wants to go to the ceremony to **receive her award**.
그녀는 그 좋은 소식을 듣고 기뻐하고 상을 받기 위해 시상식에 정말 가고 싶어 합니다.

01 다음을 듣고, 남자가 하는 말의 목적으로 가장 적절한 것을 고르시오. 24006-0139

① 개교 기념행사에 초대하려고
② 기념식 홍보 대사를 모집하려고
③ 학교 슬로건의 의미를 설명하려고
④ 학교 슬로건 공모전을 공지하려고
⑤ 홈페이지가 개편되었음을 알리려고

02 대화를 듣고, 여자의 의견으로 가장 적절한 것을 고르시오. 24006-0140

① 학생들이 고전 문학을 읽게 하는 것이 필요하다.
② 학생들이 원하는 다양한 동아리를 개설해야 한다.
③ 좋은 문학 작품을 선별하는 비판적인 안목을 키워야 한다.
④ 문학 작품은 시대적 이념과 당시의 사회상을 반영해야 한다.
⑤ 학생들이 고전 문학을 이해하는 데 교사의 지도가 중요하다.

03 대화를 듣고, 그림에서 대화의 내용과 일치하지 않는 것을 고르시오. 24006-0141

04 대화를 듣고, 남자가 할 일로 가장 적절한 것을 고르시오. 24006-0142

① 버스 예약하기
② 리조트에 전화하기
③ 수학여행 계획 짜기
④ 학부모 허가서 발송하기
⑤ 국립공원 웹사이트 검색하기

05 대화를 듣고, 남자가 지불할 금액을 고르시오. 24006-0143

① $50
② $55
③ $63
④ $68
⑤ $75

06 대화를 듣고, 여자가 Westfield Mall에 갈 수 없는 이유를 고르시오. 24006-0144

① 자매학교를 방문해야 해서
② 피아노 수업을 받아야 해서
③ 힙합 댄스 공연을 해야 해서
④ 과학 실험대회에 참가해야 해서
⑤ 동아리 캠페인에 참여해야 해서

07 대화를 듣고, Korean Proficiency Test에 관해 언급되지 <u>않은</u> 것을 고르시오. 24006-0145

① 응시 대상
② 연간 시행 횟수
③ 시험 종류
④ 평가 영역
⑤ 주관 기관

08 다음 표를 보면서 대화를 듣고, 두 사람이 수강할 강좌를 고르시오. 24006-0146

Summer School Science Classes

	Class	Day	Time	Class Size (Number of Students)
①	Biology	Monday	8:00–11:00	8
②	Biology	Wednesday	8:00–11:00	20
③	Earth Science	Wednesday	13:00–16:00	8
④	Physics	Saturday	8:00–11:00	15
⑤	Chemistry	Thursday	10:00–13:00	15

09 대화를 듣고, 남자의 마지막 말에 대한 여자의 응답으로 가장 적절한 것을 고르시오. 24006-0147

① No problem. I'll make sure you're up early enough.
② I know. That's why the study group changed its schedule.
③ Don't worry. I'll help you improve your health more than before.
④ Come on. You'll have to wake up early to do morning exercises.
⑤ I understand. It was a wise choice you joined the evening study group.

10 대화를 듣고, 여자의 마지막 말에 대한 남자의 응답으로 가장 적절한 것을 고르시오. 24006-0148

① The problem is that you are overconfident.
② Right. I think the A is the result of my effort.
③ I'd like to take the same biology class as you.
④ Sorry, but I don't have time to study with you.
⑤ Yeah. You shouldn't have taken the biology class.

PART II

소재편

11 대화를 듣고, 남자의 마지막 말에 대한 여자의 응답으로 가장 적절한 것을 고르시오. 24006-0149

Woman: _____

① Right. You can be distracted when working with others.
② Great. I'm glad to hear that the group likes your opinions.
③ Good. It takes practice, but I'm sure you'll make progress.
④ Sorry. I'm looking for someone good at working on a team.
⑤ Sure. I'll try not to hurt your feelings while we work together.

12 다음 상황 설명을 듣고, Oliver가 Katie에게 할 말로 가장 적절한 것을 고르시오. 24006-0150

Oliver: _____

① How did you find such an excellent study group?
② Thanks for encouraging me to join the study group.
③ My math has improved a lot through the study group.
④ Do you think we should allow another member to join us?
⑤ I need to ask my group members if you can join the study group.

Dictations

01

M: Hello, Stewart High School students. This is your principal, Mr. Ballen. This year marks our school's 30th anniversary. ❶_____ _____ _____ this anniversary, I'm pleased to announce a school slogan contest to replace the current one. We're seeking a new slogan that powerfully reflects the mission and vision of our school. You can ❷_____ _____ _____ for the school slogan from March 18th to the 22nd on the school website. The winning slogan will be used in ❸_____ _____ _____ and materials. Plus, awards will be given to the winning slogan and the second- and third-place slogans. I can't wait to see your creative ideas. For more details, visit the school website. Thank you.

02

M: What school club are you planning on running this semester, Ms. Kim?

W: I thought maybe I'd start a club for students to read classics.

M: Do you think students will find that interesting?

W: I think some will. I just feel it's important for students to read ❶_____ _____ _____ _____ and understanding of the world.

M: But can't other types of literature achieve the same goal?

W: Sure, but classics have ❷_____ _____ _____ _____ _____.

M: I know, but wouldn't it be difficult for students to connect their lives with characters or settings from different time periods?

W: Well, I think they ❸_____ _____ _____ and broaden their understanding of various perspectives by exploring different eras and cultures through classics.

M: I see your point.

W: It's important to expose students to classics across various cultures and eras.

M: I agree.

03

M: Emily, how was your visit to the Science Museum with your friends?

W: Dad, it was really fun. Look at this picture I took there.

M: Wow, cool! Look at you. You're wearing star-shaped sunglasses. Where did you get them?

W: I bought them ❶_____ _____ _____ _____ in the museum.

M: What is this round one next to you? Is it a wheel?

W: Yes, it is. It's one of the ❷_____ _____ _____.

M: I see. Why do they have a hot air balloon next to the left wall?

W: Oh, it's an exhibit that explains how hot air balloons work.

M: Ah, I get it. And is that a whale behind you?

W: That's right. It's a model whale in a glass case.

M: It looks very big and nice! And a butterfly is ❸_____ _____ _____ _____ next to the right wall.

W: Yes. It's a model of a beautiful butterfly.

M: Well, I'm so glad you had a great time there, honey.

04

W: Hello, Mr. Sanders. You look busy today.

M: Yeah, Ms. Wallace. I've been busy getting ready for the school trip to Oleta National Park.

W: I ❶_____ _____ _____ _____ that last year.

M: And I remember you told me how much work it was.

W: Right. So, have you sent out the permission letters to the students' parents and booked everything?

M: Yes, I sent them out last week. And I've reserved the buses, but I've had some difficulty ❷_____ _____ _____.

W: Oh, is it already fully booked?

M: Yes. They said there aren't enough rooms.

W: Oh, I see. Well, I know another nice resort in the area. It's called Oleta Palace Resort. I'm sure they ❸_____ _____ _____. Why don't you call them?

M: Oh, really? Then I'll do that right now.

W: Sounds good. I hope that works out for you.

M: Thank you, Ms. Wallace.

05

M: Hi, I'd like to ❶_____ _____ an evening Korean conversation course for beginners.

W: Alright. We offer two classes for beginners.

M: What are they?

W: One is a basic class with a tuition of $50 per month, and the other is an intensive class with a tuition of $70 per month.

M: Um.... I ❷_____ _____ _____ every day. Does the basic class have daily lessons?

W: No, only the intensive class has daily lessons.

M: Okay, I'll take ❸_____ _____ _____ _____ _____ for a month. Do I need to purchase a textbook?

W: Yes, you do. The textbook costs $5.

M: Got it. I'll buy the textbook as well. Is it true that Green University students get a 10% discount ❹_____ _____ _____?

W: Yes, that's correct. Please show me your student ID card.

M: Alright. Here are my ID card and credit card.

06

M: Hey, Jenny, I heard you won the science competition. Congratulations!

W: Thanks. It feels so good. I guess ❶_____ _____ _____ _____ _____.

M: I bet! So are you free these days?

W: Yeah. What's up?

M: You know our sister school from Singapore is visiting next week, right?

W: Yes. We're having ❷_____ _____ _____.

M: Yeah. Well, actually, I'm performing a hip-hop dance routine at the ceremony.

W: Wow, that's really cool!

M: So I'm planning to go to the Westfield Mall this Friday after school to buy some clothes for it. Would you mind going with me and helping me pick something out?

W: Oh, I'd love to, but I'm afraid I can't. I have to participate in the science club's ECO Challenge Campaign on that day. Sorry about that.

M: No worries. I'll ask Tom if he can come with me after his piano lesson.

W: Okay. I hope you ❸_____ _____ _____ _____.

07

M: Hey, Natalie. What's that you're studying?

W: Hi, Jacob. I'm preparing for a Korean Proficiency Test.

M: Oh. I knew you liked Korean TV shows, but I didn't know you were studying Korean. Is the test for foreigners?

W: Yes. And that includes ❶_____ _____ _____ whose native language isn't Korean.

M: I see. ❷_____ _____ _____ for the test?

W: Yes. I registered for the April test. It's offered ❸_____ _____ _____ _____.

M: It's almost April. Do you feel ready?

W: I feel pretty good. I'm taking the beginner-level test. There's an advanced-level test, too.

M: I assume that the advanced one is for people who ❹_____ _____ _____ _____ in Korea, right?

W: Yes. The beginner level test has only a listening and a reading part. But the advanced one has a writing part, too.

M: Maybe in the future, you'll take the advanced one. Keep up the studying!

08

M: Nari, do you have any plans for summer vacation?

W: I'm thinking about taking a summer school science class at school. Here are the ones available.

M: Oh, I was planning on doing that too. We should take one together!

W: Great idea! What class are you interested in?

M: I've ❶_____ _____ _____, so I'd like something different.

W: Me, too. What day works for you?

M: Any weekday is fine. I work on weekends.

W: Actually, I prefer weekdays, too. Also, I'd like to take a morning class to ❷_____ _____ _____ during summer break.

M: I agree. Then we'll have time to do other things in the afternoon.

W: Great. Then we have only two options left. They have different class sizes.

M: Do you prefer a larger class?

W: Not really. I like smaller classes because I tend to be ❸_____ _____ _____ in a smaller group.

M: Me, too. Then let's enroll in this class together.

W: All right.

09

M: Mom, I ❶_____ _____ _____ _____ _____. So I have to go to school early from tomorrow.

W: That's fantastic! What time do you need to be at school?

M: We meet at 7:30, so I'll have to leave home around 7. But I'm worried that I won't be able to ❷_____ _____ _____ _____.

10

W: Shaun, have you received your biology exam results?

M: Yeah, I did. All my time and energy ❶_____ _____. I got an A in the exam.

W: Wow! That's great. You ❷_____ _____ _____ really hard to prepare for the exam.

11

M: Hi, Ms. Jefferson.

W: Hi, Brian! It's been a while!

M: Yeah. I can't believe it's been a year ❶_____ _____ _____.

W: I know. How's your college life?

M: It's a lot busier than my high school life.

W: I'm sure it is. Do you like your major? It's business, right?

M: Right. Yeah, I like it. But sometimes it can be ❷_____ _____ _____.

W: Do you mean the content is difficult to understand?

M: It's not about the content.

W: What do you mean by that? Can you tell me more?

M: It's the group assignments that I find challenging. I'm not used to working with others.

W: Ah, so working together can be a little uncomfortable?

M: Yes. I think ❸_____ _____ _____ _____ when people disagree with me.

W: Oh, I understand. It's not easy to separate personal feelings from a heated discussion when that happens.

M: Yes, and I'm trying to get better at controlling my feelings in those situations, hoping I'll improve.

12

W: Katie and Oliver are college freshmen majoring in economics. These days, Katie has been thinking she should ❶_____ _____ _____ to understand economics better. When she tells this to Oliver, he tells her it's a good idea and that he's already in a mathematical economics study group that ❷_____ _____ _____ _____. Katie thinks that's a great way to study mathematical economics, so she tells Oliver that she wants to be a member of the study group. Thinking it's good to study with her, Oliver wants to tell Katie he should ❸_____ _____ _____ _____ _____ if she can join the study group. In this situation, what would Oliver most likely say to Katie?

PART Ⅱ 18강 건강, 안전, 봉사, 환경 보호

소재 소개
- 건강·안전, 봉사, 환경 보호 활동은 수능에서 빈출되는 소재들이다.
- 주로 체육 활동, 건강 관리, 미용, 안전 수칙, 자원봉사 및 기부, 환경 보호, 반려 동물 예절, 생물 다양성 등을 소재로 다룬다.
- 문제 유형으로 대화에서는 의견, 주제, 할 일, 이유, 짧은 대화의 응답 유형 등이, 담화에서는 목적, 상황에 적절한 말, 복합 이해 유형 등이 자주 출제된다.

기출 예제

2024학년도 9월 모의평가 2번

24006-0151

대화를 듣고, 남자의 의견으로 가장 적절한 것을 고르시오.

① 점심시간에 운동하는 것은 활력과 집중력을 높인다.
② 개인의 건강 상태에 따라 운동 강도를 조절해야 한다.
③ 부상 방지를 위해 올바른 자세로 운동하는 것이 중요하다.
④ 규칙적인 운동은 정서 안정에 도움을 줄 수 있다.
⑤ 과도한 아침 운동은 업무에 방해가 될 수 있다.

문항 속의 소재 **숲속에서 맨발로 걷기** (2024학년도 9월 모의평가 14번)

W: Barefoot walking in the woods. Have you heard of it?
숲속에서 맨발로 걷기에요. 들어봤어요?

M: You mean walking without shoes? That doesn't sound comfortable. Why would people want to do that?
신발 없이 걷는 것 말이지요? 별로 편하지 않을 것 같은데요. 사람들은 왜 그걸 하기를 원할까요?

W: According to the brochure, it's effective for relieving foot pain.
홍보 책자에 따르면, 그것이 발 통증을 완화하는 데 효과적이래요.

M: Really? My feet have been a little bit sore these days. How does it work?
정말요? 내가 요즘 발이 좀 아팠어요. 그건 어떻게 효과가 있나요?

Dictations

W: Hey, Kevin! Where are you going?

M: I'm going to take the staff ❶_____ _____.

W: Oh, is it the 25-minute lunch break workout that the company is offering?

M: That's right. I find that exercising at lunch time ❷_____ _____ _____ and helps me focus on my work.

W: Really? I think it would make me more tired. I usually just want to take a rest.

M: I did, too. But I actually feel more energized after the ❸_____ _____ _____. It even improves my concentration.

W: You mean you have more energy and can focus better when you get back to your desk?

M: Exactly. It's been very helpful for me.

W: Okay. Maybe I'll join. Thanks for the information.

M: My pleasure.

Topic-related Expressions

▶ 건강 관리, 미용, 스포츠

ankle 발목   chronic 만성의   content 함유량, 함량   foam 거품   germ 세균, 미생물   humidity 습도   joint 관절   organic 유기농의   pill 알약   posture 자세   prescribe 처방하다   sprain 삐다   strain (근육의) 긴장   supplement 보충제   upset stomach 배탈   veggie 채소, 채식주의자

Actually, my daughter **sprained** her **ankle** pretty badly while playing soccer yesterday.
사실, 제 딸이 어제 축구를 하다가 발목을 꽤 심하게 삐었어요.

I'd like to talk about low-impact exercises which place less stress and **strain** on the **joints**.
제가 관절에 스트레스와 긴장을 덜 주는, 충격이 적은 운동에 관해 이야기하려고 합니다.

▶ 안전 관리, 봉사

charity 자선 행위; 자선 단체   dedicated 헌신적인, 전념하는   dispose of ~을 처리하다   donate 기부하다, 기증하다   generous 후한, 관대한   inconvenience 불편   maintenance 유지보수   renovate 보수하다   rewarding 보람 있는   slippery 미끄러운 vulnerable 취약한   worn out 낡은, 마모된

The stairs leading laboratory are **worn out** and **slippery**. 실험실로 통하는 계단이 낡고 미끄럽습니다.

Thanks to these **dedicated** volunteers, our library has become a more inviting space for us.
이러한 헌신적인 자원봉사자들 덕분에, 우리 도서관은 우리에게 더 매력적인 공간이 되었습니다.

▶ 환경 보호, 동물 보호

companion animal 반려동물   crop 농작물   diminish 줄이다   feed 먹이를 주다   fertilizer 비료   independent 독립적인 leash (동물 등을 매는) 목줄, 가죽끈   metal straw 금속 빨대   preserve 보존하다   region 지역   resource 자원   soil 토양, 흙 sustainable 지속 가능한   trap 가두다

Using a **leash** is basic etiquette for dog owners. 목줄을 사용하는 것은 반려견 주인으로서 지켜야 할 기본 예절입니다.

So, let's choose reusable alternatives like **metal straws** instead of single-use plastics.
따라서, 일회용의 플라스틱 대신 금속 빨대와 같은 재사용 가능한 대안을 선택합시다.

01 다음을 듣고, 여자가 하는 말의 목적으로 가장 적절한 것을 고르시오.   24006-0152

① 안전한 자동차 여행에 대해 조언하려고
② 휴가철에 유용한 필수 앱을 홍보하려고
③ 고속도로 휴게소의 활용 팁을 알려주려고
④ 여행을 떠나기 전 자동차 점검을 권고하려고
⑤ 자동차 여행에 좋은 드라이브 코스를 소개하려고

02 다음을 듣고, 남자가 하는 말의 요지로 가장 적절한 것을 고르시오.   24006-0153

① 환경 개선을 위해 플라스틱 사용을 줄이자.
② 인간과 야생동물이 공존하는 환경을 조성하자.
③ 친환경 소재로 만들어진 플라스틱을 사용하자.
④ 환경 보호는 우리 모두가 져야 할 공동의 책임이다.
⑤ 지속 가능한 발전을 전제로 자원이 개발되어야 한다.

03 대화를 듣고, 그림에서 대화의 내용과 일치하지 <u>않는</u> 것을 고르시오.   24006-0154

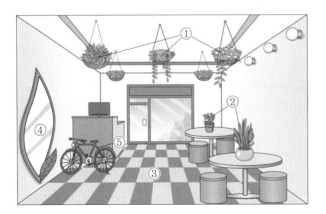

04 대화를 듣고, 여자가 할 일로 가장 적절한 것을 고르시오. 24006-0155

① 슬로건 만들기
② 참가자 확인하기
③ 예산액 알아보기
④ 현수막 디자인하기
⑤ 병에 든 물 주문하기

05 대화를 듣고, 남자가 지불할 금액을 고르시오. 24006-0156

① $130
② $135
③ $140
④ $150
⑤ $250

06 대화를 듣고, 여자가 Glendale Avenue로 우회하려는 이유를 고르시오. 24006-0157

① 교통사고가 발생해서
② 폭우로 도로에 물이 차서
③ 도심의 도로 공사 때문에
④ 직장 동료를 태우러 가야 해서
⑤ 마라톤 행사로 인한 교통 혼잡 때문에

07 대화를 듣고, Jefferson Fire Expo에 관해 언급되지 <u>않은</u> 것을 고르시오. 24006-0158

① 전시업체 수
② 개최 장소
③ 어린이 프로그램
④ 입장료
⑤ 개최 기간

08 Rural Wildlife Caretaker Project에 관한 다음 내용을 듣고, 일치하지 <u>않는</u> 것을 고르시오. 24006-0159

① 부상당한 야생 동물들을 구조하고 돕는 역할을 한다.
② 총 12주 동안 진행될 것이다.
③ 실습생들은 첫 주에 7일간 훈련을 받는다.
④ 실습 동안 동물들에 대해 기록을 한다.
⑤ 무료 셔틀버스 서비스가 제공된다.

09 대화를 듣고, 남자의 마지막 말에 대한 여자의 응답으로 가장 적절한 것을 고르시오. 24006-0160

① I'm eating more protein, but I don't like meat that much.
② Be careful! Focusing too much on your health can be harmful.
③ For sure. Vegetable-based diets are actually not always healthy.
④ The calorie content of a dish can differ depending on the recipe.
⑤ Well, you could try adding veggies to your favorite foods, like omelet.

10   대화를 듣고, 여자의 마지막 말에 대한 남자의 응답으로 가장 적절한 것을 고르시오.   24006-0161

Man: _____

① I'm sorry. But I had no choice but to leave the club.
② It's already been two months since I joined this club.
③ Don't worry. Let me donate some money to the club.
④ Okay! I'll join you in cleaning the beaches every Saturday.
⑤ Right. You should have picked up trash before leaving the beach.

[11~12] 다음을 듣고, 물음에 답하시오.

11   남자가 하는 말의 주제로 가장 적절한 것은?   24006-0162

① advantages of various types of low-impact exercises
② how to prevent injuries when doing low-impact exercises
③ effects of low-impact exercises on reducing mental stress
④ the most optimal place and time to do low-impact exercises
⑤ importance of doing low-impact exercises on a regular basis

12   언급된 운동이 아닌 것은?   24006-0163

① swimming   ② cycling   ③ walking
④ rowing   ⑤ hiking

01

W: Hello, listeners. This is Ellie Williams with Everyday Travel. It's summer, which means it's vacation time! For some people, ❶_____ _____ _____ _____. So, let me give you some tips for things you can do ❷_____ _____ _____ _____ _____ while on the road. First, if you're traveling in a group with multiple people who can drive, try to ❸_____ _____ _____. Also, remember to stop frequently to get out, walk around, and stretch. Now, here are the things not to do. Don't ever drive when you feel sleepy. Driving while tired can be dangerous. And don't drive when it's dark if you ❹_____ _____ _____ _____. Unlit highways can be especially dark. Keep these tips in mind. I'll be back right after a commercial break. Stay tuned!

02

M: Hi, everyone. I'm Kevin Brown, the host of One-Minute Environment. Yesterday, I watched a documentary on TV highlighting the challenging conditions ❶_____ _____ _____. The documentary emphasized that the primary cause of environmental destruction is the widespread use of plastic. It means that the more we ❷_____ _____ _____ _____, the greater the improvement in our environment. So, let's reduce use of single-use plastics and instead choose reusable alternatives like metal straws. Additionally, let's be mindful of our purchases by selecting products with minimal plastic packaging and choosing items ❸_____ _____ _____ _____ such as glass. Remember, by diminishing our plastic usage, we can significantly contribute to a cleaner and healthier planet. That's all. See you next time.

03

M: Susan, where did you get the salad you were eating for lunch? It looked delicious.

W: It indeed was delicious. I bought it from a café near my house. Let me show you a picture of it.

M: Wow, the plants ❶_____ _____ _____ _____ make the café look like a garden.

W: It feels like that when you're there. They also ❷_____ _____ _____ _____ on each table.

M: I see that. It makes sense that they serve salads.

W: Right. The café has a nice eco-friendly interior design.

M: That's a nice touch. And I like ❸_____ _____ _____. It's really modern.

W: Yeah. Do you see ❹_____ _____ _____?

M: Oh, that's so pretty! It would be cool to take a picture in front of it.

W: Many people do that. And there's a bicycle in front of the counter. It matches the eco-friendly concept of the café.

M: That makes sense. I'd love to go there too.

04

M: Hello, Ms. Henderson.

W: Hi, David. How's everything going for the club campaign? Friday is the big day!

M: We've already gathered a lot of participants and made ❶_____ _____ _____.

W: That's great. How many students are participating in the campaign?

M: Twenty five students in total.

W: Okay, that's good. So have you made the campaign banner yet?

M: Not yet. I'm going to design it tomorrow.

W: Sounds great. Is there anything else left to do?

M: We're hoping to get some ❷_____ _____ _____ _____ to drink. Could you help us with that?

W: No problem. There's enough money for that in the budget. I'll order ❸_____ _____ _____ right away.

M: Thank you, Ms. Henderson.

W: My pleasure. I'll see you on Friday.

05

W: Hi, may I help you?

M: Yes. I'm looking for Star Medicine vitamin D supplements. Do you ❶_____ _____ _____ _____?

W: Sure. We carry all the Star Medicine supplements. They're right over here.

M: Oh, great. I'm glad you carry them.

W: Here's the vitamin D. ❷_____ _____ _____ has 180 pills, and it's $30.

M: I'd like the yellow one with 360 pills.

W: Okay. It's $50.

M: All right. I'll take three of these yellow bottles.

W: That's quite a lot of vitamin D. You ❸_____ _____ _____ for other people, too.

M: Right. I'm shopping for the whole family.

W: I got it. Oh, and because you're spending over $100, you can get 10% ❹_____ _____ _____.

M: That's nice. Here's my credit card.

06

M: Hi, Martha. Thank you for ❶_____ _____ _____ _____ _____.

W: No problem, James. How was your weekend? Did the heavy rain cause any trouble for you?

M: Actually, yes. The heavy downpour damaged the road near my house.

W: That's too bad.

M: Yeah, but it's getting repaired now.

W: That's good. By the way, this road is ❷_____ _____ _____ _____ for this time of day. Do you think there might have been an accident?

M: Well, let me check on my smartphone if any accidents happened nearby. [Pause] Oh, there's a marathon beginning at 10 o'clock.

W: I heard about that on the news.

M: So traffic is being redirected this way because some roads near City Hall are closed.

W: I see. Then I'm going to ❸_____ _____ _____ Glendale Avenue to get out of this bad traffic.

M: Good idea. I don't think we'll be late for the meeting, fortunately.

07

M: Jennifer, I **❶**_____ _____ _____ for the Jefferson Fire Expo on the radio. Have you?

W: No, I haven't. What's it all about?

M: It's a fire expo, where they exhibit fire equipment and technology.

W: Oh, I see. I'm curious, how many exhibitors will be there?

M: They said there will be over 400 exhibitors.

W: That's quite impressive! Where is it being held?

M: It's taking place at the Kinster Expo Center.

W: Oh, that's convenient. Are you planning to go?

M: Yes, I'm actually **❷**_____ _____ _____ _____. They also have many interesting programs for children, like the junior firefighter challenges.

W: That sounds exciting! I'd love to take my kids too. Do you know the dates?

M: Sure. It's happening on May 25th and 26th, and I'm considering going on the 25th.

W: All right, thanks for sharing. I'll make **❸**_____ _____ _____ _____.

08

W: Hello, everybody! I'm Judy Smith, manager of the Rural Wildlife Caretaker Project. It's a pleasure to have student trainees in the animal resources department. This project **❶**_____ _____ _____ _____ _____ wounded wild animals. And it provides opportunities to **❷**_____ _____ _____ _____ _____ in your major subjects. The whole project will last for twelve weeks. During the first week, you will have a five-day training and follow and watch instructors working **❸**_____ _____ _____ _____. During your practice, you will prepare food, feed animals, clean cages, and keep animal records. Free shuttle bus services will be provided **❹**_____ _____ _____. If you have any questions, see me at the management office. Thank you.

09

M: Susan, I want to **❶**_____ _____ _____, but I'm not sure where to begin.

W: Why not include more vegetables in your diet?

M: That is a good idea, but I'm not **❷**_____ _____ _____ _____ _____. Do you have any tips on how to get more in my diet?

10

M: Cindy, I heard you recently joined a volunteer club.

W: Yes, I did. I love it. We ❶_____ _____ _____ _____ _____ for the environment.

M: Do you? What exactly do you do?

W: We go to different beaches and spend a few hours ❷_____ _____ _____.

M: Cool. That must be really rewarding.

W: Yeah, it is. Would you like to join? I know ❸_____ _____ _____ _____ about the environment.

M: I'm interested in the club. How often does your club meet up?

W: Once a week. Every Saturday, we normally meet at the beach around 9 a.m.

M: Oh, I'm available at that time. How do you like everyone in the club?

W: They're all really nice. Just like you, everybody is really concerned about ❹_____ _____ _____.

[11~12]

M: Good afternoon, everyone. Last class, we learned about common injuries that happen in different sports. Today, I'd like to talk about low-impact exercises which place less stress and strain on the joints, and therefore have ❶_____ _____ _____ _____. Here are several examples. First, swimming is a great low-impact exercise that is gentle on your joints. It provides a full-body workout and can help build muscle and improve flexibility. Cycling is another exercise that is ❷_____ _____ _____ _____. It provides a great workout for your heart and can help build lower-body strength. Another example is walking, a low-impact exercise that can be done almost anywhere. It can help reduce mental stress, strengthen the legs, and promote weight loss. Lastly, hiking is a low-impact exercise that can help improve strength and balance of your body without putting too much stress on your joints and muscles. Overall, there are various types of low-impact exercises, which can provide ❸_____ _____ _____ _____ _____ as I've just mentioned. Now let's work in pairs to talk about our experiences with them.

PART II

19 강 여행, 체험 활동

소재 소개

- 주로 여행 계획, 행선지 정보, 대중교통, 숙박 관광 등 여행 관련이나 캠핑, 현장 학습, 만들기 등의 체험 활동에 관련된 내용들을 소재로 활용한다.
- 여행, 체험 활동 소재는 대부분 대화 형식에서 다루어지지만 최근에는 안내 방송이나 광고와 같은 담화 형식에서 다루어 출제되는 경우가 많다.
- 문제 유형으로 대화에서는 지불할 금액, 대화자의 관계, 할 일, 언급 유무, 마지막 말에 이어질 응답 등을 묻는 문제가 출제되며 담화에서는 목적, 담화 내용 일치, 상황에 적절한 말, 복합 이해 유형 등이 출제된다.

기출 예제

2024학년도 9월 모의평가 1번
24006-0164

다음을 듣고, 여자가 하는 말의 목적으로 가장 적절한 것을 고르시오.

① 멸종 위기 동물을 소개하려고
② 동물원 관람 예절을 안내하려고
③ 어린이 동물 캠프를 홍보하려고
④ 신입 동물 훈련사를 모집하려고
⑤ 야생 동물 보호를 독려하려고

문항 속의 소재 학교 **수학여행** (2024학년도 9월 모의평가 12번)

W: Dad, I'm so excited. It's my first time to go on a school trip to the mountains in the fall.

아빠, 저 너무 신나요. 가을에 산으로 수학여행을 가는 건 처음이에요.

M: Right. It'll be especially great to look at the stars outside. Maybe you'll need something to keep yourself warm because it's getting colder at night.

그래. 밖에서 별을 보면 특히 좋을 것 같아. 밤에는 날씨가 점점 더 추워지고 있으니까 아마도 따뜻하게 해줄 것이 필요할 거야.

W: So, do you think I should bring my little blanket?

그러면, 제가 작은 담요를 가져가야 한다고 생각하세요?

M: That's a good idea. You'd better take it.

좋은 생각이야. 그걸 가져가는 게 좋을 거야.

Dictations

정답과 해설 104쪽
www.ebsi.co.kr

W: Hello, viewers! Are you looking for a fun activity for your kids to enjoy on the weekend? Then, come and join our ❶_____ _____ _____ _____. Happy Animal Friends Camp will be held every weekend in September. We'll provide hands-on activities with a wide variety of animals such as rabbits, turtles, and parrots. Your kids will learn how to care for and interact with the animals ❷_____ _____ _____ of experienced trainers. If your children like spending time with animals, sign them up for the Happy Animal Friends Camp! You can find more information on our website. Don't miss this great opportunity!

Topic-related Expressions

▸ 여행 준비, 교통편 이용

board ~에 타다 camper 캠핑카 car owner's manual 차 사용자 설명서 destination 목적지 fee 수수료, 요금 head to ~로 가다 insurance 보험 international driver's license 국제 운전 면허증 rent 빌리다 reschedule 일정을 변경하다 stop 경유지 suitcase 여행 가방

I'm thinking about getting my **international driver's license** and **renting** a car.
나는 국제 운전 면허증을 발급받아서 차를 빌릴까 생각 중이야.

Do you have any preference regarding the **stops**? 당신은 경유지에 대해 선호하는 것이 있어요?

▸ 관광, 숙박

accommodation 숙박 book 예약하다 booth 칸막이가 있는 자리 check in 호텔에 투숙하다 complimentary 무료의 confirm 확인하다 lounge 휴게실 reservation 예약 resort 리조트 souvenir 기념품 vending machine 자판기 walking trail 산책로

I hope we can secure our **booking**. 우리가 예약을 확보할 수 있기를 바라요.

There's a playground for kids, cycling paths, **walking trails**, sports facilities, and more.
어린이를 위한 놀이터, 사이클 도로, 산책로, 스포츠 시설, 그리고 더 많은 것이 있어.

▸ 취미, 체험 활동

antique 골동품의, 고대의 aquarium 수족관 be held 열리다, 개최되다 enroll 등록하다 exhibition 전시회, 전시 explore 알아보다, 탐험하다 feeding experience 먹이 주기 체험 gear 장비 participant 참가자 registration form 신청서 set up 설치하다 snorkeling 스노클링

First, let me explain the **gear**. Here's your jumpsuit and safety belt.
먼저 장비에 관해 설명해드릴게요. 여기 점프 슈트와 안전벨트가 있습니다.

The class provides **participants** with an experience in making leather belts totally by hand without a sewing machine. 그 수업은 참가자에게 재봉틀 없이 온전히 손으로만 가죽 벨트를 만드는 체험을 제공합니다.

19강 • 여행, 체험 활동 **131**

01 다음을 듣고, 남자가 하는 말의 목적으로 가장 적절한 것을 고르시오. 24006-0165

① 돌아가는 항공편 일정 변경을 안내하려고
② 여행 방문지 변경에 대한 양해를 구하려고
③ 폭설로 인해 여행이 취소되었음을 공지하려고
④ 항공기 착륙이 지연되는 것에 대해 사과하려고
⑤ 겨울철 여행 시 지켜야 할 안전 수칙을 설명하려고

02 대화를 듣고, 여자의 의견으로 가장 적절한 것을 고르시오. 24006-0166

① 여행 시 최대한 짐을 가볍게 꾸려야 한다.
② 여행 갈 때 예산 외에 추가 경비를 준비해야 한다.
③ 여행 짐은 여러 개의 가방에 나누어서 넣어야 한다.
④ 여행 시 한 지갑에 모든 현금을 보관해서는 안 된다.
⑤ 여행 가방이 분실되지 않도록 눈에 띄는 표식을 해야 한다.

03 대화를 듣고, 그림에서 대화의 내용과 일치하지 <u>않는</u> 것을 고르시오. 24006-0167

04 대화를 듣고, 남자가 할 일로 가장 적절한 것을 고르시오.   24006-0168

① 버스 예약하기
② 구급함 가져다주기
③ 해변 출입 허가증 받기
④ 샌드위치와 물 주문하기
⑤ 해변 도보 여행 경로 짜기

05 대화를 듣고, 여자가 지불할 금액을 고르시오.   24006-0169

① $75
② $81
③ $83
④ $88
⑤ $90

06 대화를 듣고, 남자가 자선 달리기 행사에 참가하지 <u>못하는</u> 이유를 고르시오.   24006-0170

① 몸 상태가 좋지 않아서
② 대회 장소가 너무 멀어서
③ 평소에 달리기를 하지 않아서
④ 정기 건강 검진을 받아야 해서
⑤ 딸의 장기 자랑에 참석해야 해서

07 대화를 듣고, Skyline Broadcasting Conference에 관해 언급되지 <u>않은</u> 것을 고르시오. 24006-0171

① 주제
② 개최 기간
③ 등록비
④ 참가 가능 인원
⑤ 참가 신청 마감일

08 다음 표를 보면서 대화를 듣고, 두 사람이 선택할 물놀이 활동을 고르시오. 24006-0172

Water Activities

	Activities	Price (per person)	Age Restriction	Days Offered	Guide Accompanied
①	Snorkeling	$50	6 and Over	Mon. & Wed.	×
②	Stand-up Paddle Boarding	$80	11 and Over	Tues. & Fri.	○
③	Banana Boat Riding	$100	13 and Over	Mon. & Thurs.	○
④	Fishing	$100	Adults Only	Tues. & Thurs.	×
⑤	Sunset Sailing	$160	13 and Over	Wed. & Fri.	○

09 대화를 듣고, 여자의 마지막 말에 대한 남자의 응답으로 가장 적절한 것을 고르시오. 24006-0173

① Sounds amazing! Give me more details.
② Sorry. That's more expensive than I expected.
③ That's too bad! When did the special deal end?
④ Why don't you try something safer than bungee jumping?
⑤ Well, I don't feel like bungee jumping on Tiwi Island again.

10 대화를 듣고, 남자의 마지막 말에 대한 여자의 응답으로 가장 적절한 것을 고르시오.   24006-0174

① This restaurant is the best one I've been to recently.
② You should download the restaurant app and give it a try!
③ Well, I don't think we can always rely on customer reviews.
④ It's helpful to check customer reviews before visiting a new place.
⑤ I'd like to know if you can recommend a good restaurant near here.

11 대화를 듣고, 여자의 마지막 말에 대한 남자의 응답으로 가장 적절한 것을 고르시오.   24006-0175

Man: _____

① My bike trip cost more than your camping trip.
② I really appreciate your parents taking care of me.
③ I understand why you said you had a terrible weekend.
④ You're the one who insisted on going on the trip with Alice.
⑤ I should have joined you on your camping trip last weekend.

12 다음 상황 설명을 듣고, Lena가 Alex에게 할 말로 가장 적절한 것을 고르시오.   24006-0176

Lena: _____

① You'd better choose the right type of bag for the trip.
② Size is an important factor when buying a new suitcase.
③ If you need more space in your suitcase, roll up your clothes.
④ How about renting a four-wheel drive car to get around the island?
⑤ Instead of buying a new suitcase, why don't you change the wheel?

Dictations

01

M: Good morning, everyone! I hope you're all feeling excited and ready for another day of adventure. Before we set off, I have some important news to share ❶_____ _____ _____ _____. Unfortunately, due to heavy snowfall at our destination, we've had to reschedule our return flight to December 13th, one day later ❷_____ _____ _____ _____. I truly apologize for any inconvenience this may cause and any disruption to your personal plans. Our staff is currently working on arranging your future schedule ❸_____ _____ _____ _____. I'll be sharing all the details with you soon. Thank you for your understanding and cooperation.

02

W: Ted, have you finished packing?

M: Yes, Mom. I'm all set. I'm super excited for my trip!

W: That's great to hear! Actually, I wanted to talk to you about ❶_____ _____ _____ _____ while you're traveling.

M: Okay. What should I do?

W: Well, don't keep all of your cash in your wallet. That way, if something happens and you lose your wallet, you'll still have some money.

M: Oh, that makes sense. How much do you think I should keep out of it?

W: I ❷_____ _____ _____ _____ _____ just one or two days' expenses.

M: Yes, Mom. I'll do that. Where should I keep the separate cash?

W: It's best to keep it in a different bag that's ❸_____ _____ _____ _____ _____ to others.

M: I got it. Thanks for the advice, Mom.

W: You're welcome, dear.

03

W: Honey. Look at this picture of a camper. I'd like to rent it for our camping trip next month.

M: Oh, let me see. Wow, it's nice! I love the large square ceiling light.

W: Yeah. It's ❶_____ _____ _____ in an actual house.

M: Look, the blinds on the windows are just like our living room blinds.

W: Right! Maybe they're the same brand.

M: If we ❷_____ _____ _____ _____, where would we eat?

W: We could eat on the table next to the sink, which has the laptop computer on it in this picture.

M: Yeah, that should work.

W: And I love the striped rug on the floor.

M: Yeah, it's cool. And we can use the sofa on the left as a bed.

W: Right. And the ❸_____ _____ _____ _____ can be our pillows.

M: Great. Let's call now to rent it.

04

M: Hi, Ms. Taylor. Has it been a busy day for you?

W: Yes, Mr. Wilson. I'm getting ready for a beach trekking field trip with my students this weekend.

M: Sounds exciting! How's it going?

W: Almost done. I've planned ❶_____ _____ _____ _____ _____. We'll be heading to Ocean Vista Beach.

M: Great choice! Did you receive the access permit from the local department of natural resources?

W: Yes, everything's set. I've also made a bus reservation for transportation.

M: Perfect. Will the students need to bring their own lunch?

W: No, I've already ❷_____ _____ _____ _____ for everyone.

M: Impressive! Just make sure not to forget a first aid kit.

W: Thanks for reminding me. I'll ask the school nurse for one later.

M: No problem. In fact, I'm on my way to see the school nurse now. Let me get it for you.

W: Wow, thanks a lot! I ❸_____ _____ _____.

05

M: Welcome to Galaxy Fun Park! How may I assist you today?

W: Hi, there. I ❶_____ _____ _____ _____ _____ for two adults and two children, please. How much are they?

M: Adult tickets are $25 each, and child tickets are $10 each.

W: Okay, got it. Do you offer any discounts if I use a credit card?

M: Actually, we do. If you use a Rainbow credit card, you can ❷_____ _____ _____.

W: Great! I have one. Oh, and I'm interested in ❸_____ _____ _____ _____. How much is that?

M: It's an additional $5 per person. And just so you know, the credit card discount doesn't apply to the magic show.

W: No problem. I'd like to buy four tickets for that too. And what time does the magic show start?

M: It starts at 2 p.m.

W: Perfect! Here's my card.

06

W: Hi, Edward. Have you received the results of your health check-up from last week?

M: Hi, Jane. Yes, I have. And the results were good. Thanks for asking.

W: Glad to hear! I think your running every day ❶_____ _____ _____ _____ _____.

M: I think so too.

W: Actually, there's a charity run to raise money ❷_____ _____ _____ this weekend. How about joining together?

M: That sounds fun. Where is it held?

W: At Eastwood Park. It's close to your house.

M: Great. Oh, wait. Is it on Saturday or Sunday?

W: It's on Saturday.

M: Then, I'm afraid I can't go.

W: Why not?

M: My daughter ❸_____ _____ _____ _____ at her kindergarten on that day. I must be there to support her.

W: Oh, okay. You're such a lovely father!

07

M: Lucy, check out this Skyline Broadcasting Conference leaflet.

W: Okay. Oh, it's for high school students ❶_____ _____ _____.

M: Yeah, the theme is "Broadcasting Futures: Nurturing Young Voices in Media." Doesn't it sound fascinating?

W: It does. We should go.

M: Sure! It's from July 15th to 17th at the Skyline Convention Center. Can you make it on the 16th?

W: Yes, I'm available then. I guess we ❷_____ _____ _____.

M: You're right. Look at the registration fee. Early bird fee is $75, but after June 30th, it's $90. So let's register before July.

W: Good idea. Oh, look here! It says the conference is limited to 300 attendees.

M: That's important to know. Let's go to their website and sign up right now.

W: Okay. I'm really excited to ❸_____ _____ _____ _____ of broadcasting!

M: Absolutely! It's going to be awesome.

08

M: Honey, don't you love staying at this resort?

W: Yeah. It's so nice! And our boys are having so much fun.

M: Yeah, they are. Hey, how about ❶_____ _____ _____ _____ later today?

W: Great idea. I'll look up the water activities they offer on my cell phone. Here they are.

M: Hmm.... Oh, this one's over $100 per person. That's too much.

W: I agree. And this other one is only for adults. We need one that our boys can do.

M: Right. So we have ❷_____ _____ _____ _____, then.

W: How about this one? It sounds fun.

M: But they're not offering it today. Today's Monday.

W: Oh, that's right. So then let's choose one of these two activities.

M: I think we should choose this one. It has a guide, so it'll ❸_____ _____ _____ _____.

W: I was thinking the same thing. Let's choose that.

09

W: Hey, Ethan. You've always wanted to try bungee jumping on Tiwi Island, right?

M: Yeah, that's ❶_____ _____ _____ _____. Are you interested in that, too?

W: Absolutely! I found a ❷_____ _____ _____ _____ for bungee jumping there. How do you feel about giving it a try?

10

M: Mom, what do you think of the food here? This restaurant is ❶_____ _____ _____ _____ in this area.

W: Honestly, I don't think the food is that great. Who recommended this restaurant to you?

M: I found it on the Internet. It had ❷_____ _____ _____.

12

W: Lena and her husband, Alex, are going to Hawaii. They're both excited to spend time together in the sun, on the beach. ❶_____ _____ _____, they notice that one of the wheels on Alex's suitcase is broken. Alex says that he should ❷_____ _____ _____ _____ because they will be pulling their suitcases a lot on the trip. But Lena knows they could ❸_____ _____ _____ _____ quickly and easily since they know the suitcase's brand and wheel type. And she thinks they could save money by replacing the wheel. So, Lena wants to suggest to Alex that he replace the wheel ❹_____ _____ _____ a new suitcase. In this situation, what would Lena most likely say to Alex?

11

W: Brian, how was your bike trip with Alice last weekend?

M: It was awesome! Next time we go, you should come with us. You'd love it. How was your weekend?

W: The opposite of yours. It was terrible.

M: Really? What happened?

W: My family went camping near the Ace River, but the weather was really bad. It even rained at times.

M: That's too bad. Rain can ❶_____ _____ a camping experience.

W: That wasn't even the worse part. The campground was really ❷_____ _____ _____.

M: Oh, no. I'm sorry to hear that.

W: So basically, the entire time we were there, we didn't have a relaxing moment.

20강 정보 통신, 방송, 사교 활동

소재
소개

- 주된 소재는 정보 통신이나 방송활동에서는 스마트폰, 인터넷이 사용되고, 사교 활동에서는 동아리 활동이나 친구들 사이의 다양한 활동이 활용된다.
- 정보 통신과 방송의 경우에는 담화 형식으로 출제되는 경향이 있고, 사교 활동의 경우는 일반적으로 대화 형식으로 출제된다.
- 목적 추론, 할 일 추론, 짧은 대화와 긴 대화의 응답, 이유 추론 등 거의 모든 유형의 문제가 출제된다.

기출 예제

2024학년도 6월 모의평가 9번
24006-0177

Found 211에 관한 다음 내용을 듣고, 일치하지 <u>않는</u> 것을 고르시오.

① H-rail 기차에서 분실한 물건에 대한 정보를 제공한다.
② 웹사이트 회원이 아니어도 사용할 수 있다.
③ 분실한 물건 발견 시 문자 메시지로 통지한다.
④ 다양한 언어로 외국어 서비스가 제공된다.
⑤ 모바일 앱에서도 사용할 수 있다.

문항 속의 소재 (2024학년도 9월 모의평가 15번)

M: Jack and Amy are members of their high school orchestra club. They're creating a video to introduce their club at the freshmen orientation next month. Jack records the orchestra during practice and interviews some members. Amy says she'll edit the video clips so they can review them in their meeting tomorrow.

Jack과 Amy는 그들의 고등학교 오케스트라 동아리의 회원입니다. 그들은 다음 달 신입생 오리엔테이션에서 동아리를 소개하는 영상을 만들고 있습니다. Jack은 연습 중에 오케스트라를 녹화하고 몇몇 회원을 인터뷰합니다. Amy는 내일 회의에서 영상을 검토할 수 있도록 편집하겠다고 말합니다.

Dictations

W: Attention, H-rail train passengers. We would like to introduce a new website called Found 211 to help you ❶_____ _____ _____ _____. Found 211 provides information about items you've lost on H-rail trains. To use Found 211, you first have to be a member of the website. Then, you need to ❷_____ _____ _____ of your lost items to the website. If your lost items are found, Found 211 will inform you by a text message. In addition, foreign language services are provided in various languages, including French, Spanish and Chinese. You can also use Found 211 ❸_____ _____ _____ _____. We hope you have a pleasant trip to your destination. Thank you.

Topic-related Expressions

▶ 정보 통신, 방송

commercial break 광고 방송 시간   dub 더빙하다   easy-to-use program 사용하기 쉬운 프로그램   email account 이메일 계정   log-in 로그인, 접속하기   online shopping mall 온라인 쇼핑몰   stay tuned 채널을 고정하다   subtitle 자막   text 문자 메시지를 보내다   website address 웹사이트 주소

Can you **text** me the **website address** where you downloaded this song?
네가 이 노래를 내려받은 웹사이트 주소를 문자 메시지로 보내줄 수 있어?

I want to buy a desk from the **online shopping mall** you mentioned.
네가 말한 온라인 쇼핑몰에서 책상을 사고 싶어.

▶ 사교활동

alumni association 동창회   be a member of the club 동아리의 회원이 되다   campsite 야영지, 캠프장   club activity 동아리 활동   farewell party 송별 파티   go camping 캠핑 가다   host an event 행사를 주최하다   recruit new members 새로운 회원을 모집하다   social outing 사교적 야유회   school reunion 학교 동창회   welcome 환영하다

To use our service, you first have to **be a member of the club**.
저희 서비스를 이용하기 위해서는, 먼저 동아리의 회원이어야 합니다.

Why don't we **go camping** next week at a **campsite** near the Colorado River?
다음 주에 Colorado 강 근처에 있는 캠프장으로 캠핑 가는 게 어때?

01 다음을 듣고, 남자가 하는 말의 목적으로 가장 적절한 것을 고르시오.   24006-0178

① 온라인 학습 자료를 공유하려고
② 온라인 상담 전문 사이트를 홍보하려고
③ 온라인 범죄의 심각성에 대해 경고하려고
④ 온라인 상담 카페에 가입할 것을 권유하려고
⑤ 온라인 의사소통 시 유의 사항을 알려주려고

02 다음을 듣고, 여자가 하는 말의 요지로 가장 적절한 것을 고르시오.   24006-0179

① 아이의 성취를 축하할 때 재능보다 노력을 칭찬해야 한다.
② 디지털 도구의 활용은 자녀와의 관계 강화에 도움이 된다.
③ 자녀의 스마트폰 중독에 대한 정확한 원인 분석이 필요하다.
④ 가정 내 디지털 환경을 조성하는 데 가족 간 합의가 중요하다.
⑤ 지나친 디지털 기기 의존으로 아동의 정서적 문제가 발생한다.

03 대화를 듣고, 그림에서 대화의 내용과 일치하지 <u>않는</u> 것을 고르시오.   24006-0180

04 대화를 듣고, 여자가 할 일로 가장 적절한 것을 고르시오. 24006-0181

① 초대장 보내기
② 스피커 설치하기
③ 음식 메뉴 정하기
④ 무도회장 장식하기
⑤ 음악 밴드 섭외하기

05 대화를 듣고, 남자가 지불할 금액을 고르시오. 24006-0182

① $64
② $90
③ $94
④ $100
⑤ $104

06 대화를 듣고, 여자가 어제 온라인 수업에 결석한 이유를 고르시오. 24006-0183

① 몸이 아파서
② 노트북이 고장 나서
③ 인터넷 연결이 끊겨서
④ 수업 일정을 혼동해서
⑤ 수업 안내 메시지를 못 받아서

07 대화를 듣고, *Amazing World*에 관해 언급되지 <u>않은</u> 것을 고르시오.

24006-0184

① 프로그램 유형
② 진행자
③ 방영 시간
④ 방영 예정 도시
⑤ 총 방영 횟수

08 Lanyard Museum of Broadcasting에 관한 다음 내용을 듣고, 일치하지 <u>않는</u> 것을 고르시오.

24006-0185

① 5월 24일에 공식 개관한다.
② 라디오와 텔레비전 장비를 전시한다.
③ 1950년 이전에 만들어진 텔레비전을 소장하고 있다.
④ 미디어 엔지니어인 가이드가 방문객을 안내한다.
⑤ 매주 토요일과 일요일에만 문을 연다.

09 대화를 듣고, 여자의 마지막 말에 대한 남자의 응답으로 가장 적절한 것을 고르시오.

24006-0186

① Oh, no! I forgot to attach the file with it.
② That's right. I've finished my presentation.
③ No problem. I'll check my email right away.
④ Don't worry. You can use my laptop computer.
⑤ Of course. Please let me know your email address.

10 대화를 듣고, 남자의 마지막 말에 대한 여자의 응답으로 가장 적절한 것을 고르시오.

24006-0187

Woman: _____

① That's okay. It's all a matter of personal taste.
② Well, I get your point, but I still don't like them.
③ I'm sorry. I can't go to the photo exhibit with you.
④ When it comes to art, I love coming to art museums.
⑤ That's why young people are indifferent to his exhibit.

[11~12] 다음을 듣고, 물음에 답하시오.

11 여자가 하는 말의 목적으로 가장 적절한 것은?

24006-0188

① 노인 사교 활동 제공 장소들을 공지하려고
② 노인들의 여가 활동 선호도 순위를 알려주려고
③ 노인들에게 건강에 이로운 사교 활동들을 소개하려고
④ 노인들에게 여가 활동 별 주의 사항을 당부하려고
⑤ 노인 사교 활동의 신청 절차를 안내하려고

12 언급된 활동이 아닌 것은?

24006-0189

① 산책하기
② 정원 가꾸기
③ 노래 부르기
④ 그림 그리기
⑤ 춤추기

Dictations

01

M: Hi, everyone! Welcome back to my online channel, *Digital World.* I'm happy to see you again. Today, I'd like to talk to you about two important things to keep in mind when ❶_____ _____. First, do not give out your personal information, such as your address or phone number, because it can ❷_____ _____ _____. Second, always follow basic communication manners, just like when talking in person. For example, say hello and goodbye when you start and end a chat, and ❸_____ _____ _____ that can hurt other people's feelings. Please keep watching the monitor. I'll show you further examples of good online communication.

02

W: Hello, parents! As an expert in child education, I know your concerns about the amount of time your kids spend on screen. While digital devices can be distracting, they ❶_____ _____ _____ to bring your family closer. So make time each week for video calls with your child to discuss their day, listen to their thoughts, and ❷_____ _____. Use messaging apps to share funny photos and inspiring quotes, or to simply say "I love you." Social media can also be a platform to celebrate your child's achievements and share significant family events. By ❸_____ _____ _____ _____, you can develop a deeper connection with your child. Thank you for your attention!

03

M: Hi, Lisa. How was your weekend?

W: Hi, Ryan. It was super fun. I went to the filming site of the TV show *Love in Heaven*. Look at this picture.

M: Wow, it looks cool. There's a standing signboard showing a picture of the ❶_____ _____ _____ on the beach.

W: Right. That's the exact spot where the opening scene of the show was shot.

M: I remember! And look, there is a piano on the round stage!

W: Yeah. It's the actual piano the actors used in the show. And do you remember the bicycle in front of the house?

M: Sure! The main characters ❷_____ _____ _____ together in the show, right?

W: Right. I think the parasol and the chairs next to the house look nice.

M: So do I. The boat ❸_____ _____ _____ _____ also makes the scenery look romantic.

W: I agree. Visitors can take a boat ride there.

M: Sounds nice! After seeing this picture, I need to go there sometime.

W: I highly recommend it.

04

W: Hey, Rogan, how's the preparation for the community dance night coming along?

M: We're making good progress. The place has been booked, and the invitations have been sent out.

W: That's great to hear. Have you ❶_____ _____ _____?

M: Yes, we've settled on serving sandwiches and chips.

W: Sounds like a delicious and convenient choice. What about the music?

M: We've hired a country band for some lively tunes.

W: That's fantastic! And how is the dance hall setup going?

M: It's currently underway. The volunteers are ❷_____ _____ _____ _____, and I'll be checking on their progress later.

W: If you need any extra hands, I'm here to help.

M: Actually, since you have experience with sound systems, we could really ❸_____ _____ _____ in setting up the speakers.

W: I can handle that. I'll head over now to take care of it.

M: Thank you so much for offering your help. We truly appreciate it!

05

W: Hi, how may I help you?

M: Hi. I need to send two packages to Miami, one containing clothes and ❶_____ _____ _____ _____.

W: All right. Let me weigh them. [Pause] One is 5 kg and the other 15 kg. Which shipping service would you like?

M: I need them to arrive in 3 days, so I think ❷_____ _____ _____ would be suitable.

W: Okay. The lighter package will be $25, and the heavier one will be $35. Would you like to add any insurance to the packages?

M: No, thanks. But I'd like to purchase four sets of large bubble envelopes.

W: Okay. They're $10 per set.

M: All right. And I've heard that there's a card that offers ❸_____ _____ _____ _____.

W: Right. If you pay with an ABC card, you can receive a 10% discount on the postage, but not on the bubble envelopes.

M: Sounds great! Here's my ABC card.

06

[Telephone rings.]

M: Hello. Is this Jenny Park? This is your math teacher.

W: Oh, hi, Mr. Kim.

M: Hi, Jenny. I was surprised that you ❶_____ _____ _____ _____ _____ yesterday.

W: I'm sorry, Mr. Kim. I just got confused.

M: Oh! It can be hard ❷_____ _____ _____ _____. Do you need help with your computer?

W: No, it's okay. I know how to log on to online classes.

M: Oh? Then what happened?

W: Well, I received the text message you sent about class, but I thought the first class was on Friday.

M: Oh, I see. I guess you know now that yesterday was our first class.

W: Yes, I'm sorry. I promise I won't ❸_____ _____ _____ _____ again.

M: Okay, Jenny. Be sure to be present next time.

07

M: Alice, have you heard about the new program, *Amazing World*, starting on WBS next week?

W: No, I haven't. What type of program is it?

M: It's a reality program about ❶_____ _____ _____.

W: Oh, I like reality programs about traveling. Who hosts the program?

M: Olivia Jackson!

W: Really? She's my favorite comedian. What time is the program ❷_____ _____?

M: It starts at 7 p.m. every Friday from next week.

W: Cool. Do you know which travel destinations the program visits?

M: I heard that some Asian cities, such as Seoul and Bangkok, will appear in the first episode.

W: Sounds interesting. I'm sure it'll ❸_____ _____ _____, including me.

M: I think so, too. It's going to be a popular show.

08

W: Hello, listeners. I'm Sharon Parker, CEO of the Lanyard Broadcasting Company. I'm happy to announce the official opening of the Lanyard Museum of Broadcasting on May 24th. Our museum displays all sorts of radio and television technology from ❶_____ _____ _____, which is sure to delight the young and old alike. We even have quite a few vintage radios and televisions made before 1950 ❷_____ _____ _____ _____. Also, our guides are media engineers who can't wait to take visitors around and demonstrate how broadcasting devices work. We're only open on Fridays and Saturdays, so ❸_____ _____ _____ _____. Plus, on the grand opening day only, admission is free for all visitors. So come and enjoy a wonderful display of broadcasting history! Thanks for listening.

09

W: David, I sent you an email ❶_____ _____ _____ _____ our upcoming presentation. Did you get it?

M: I checked my email last night, but I didn't see it. When did you send it?

W: I sent it this morning. I'm sorry I sent it a little late. Can you ❷_____ _____ _____ _____ _____?

10

M: Ms. Hoffman, how do you feel about the art museum?

W: I love it. It's wonderful. I love seeing all the different forms of art.

M: Me, too. I'm surprised to see so many people here. I didn't expect it to be so popular.

W: I know! More and more people seem to be ❶_____ _____ _____ _____ art these days.

M: Yes. I noticed young people are especially interested in the Jeremy Cooper exhibit.

W: He's really popular on social media nowadays.

M: Oh, really? What do you think of his paintings then?

W: I think they're really creative. I like the way he uses shadows. How about you?

M: To be honest, they're ❷_____ _____ _____ _____ _____ to me.

W: I can understand that. They're pretty abstract, which some people don't like.

M: Oh, is that so? Maybe that's why I'm ❸_____ _____ _____ _____ _____.

[11~12]

W: Hello, everybody. I'm Kerry McDonnell, the activity director here at Greenville Senior Center. We really enjoy providing our community's seniors with fun activities, but today I'd like to ❶_____ _____ _____ _____ to help you ❷_____ _____. Just going for a walk with friends is one of the best activities. With only a pair of walking shoes, you can combine fitness and socializing at the same time. ❸_____ with others is also an enjoyable social activity. Digging, planting and weeding with someone while you talk about plants provide you with not only exercise but also opportunities for ❹_____ _____. Or if you love to sing, singing regularly in a group a few times a week is perfect. Singing with others helps improve mental health and boosts self-confidence. Dancing is another social activity since it normally ❺_____ _____ _____. It's not only a lot of fun, but it's also a great mind and body workout. If you're interested in these activities, why don't you get started today?

PART Ⅱ

21강 가사, 쇼핑, 직장 업무

소재 소개
- 가사, 쇼핑, 직장 업무는 일상에서 친숙한 소재로서 수능에서도 자주 출제된다.
- 가사와 관련하여 가족 행사나 기념일, 의식주 관리, 쇼핑과 관련하여 온라인이나 상점에서 물건을 주문 또는 구매, 직장 업무와 관련하여 회사 업무, 취업 등이 소재로 등장한다.
- 문제 유형으로 대화 형식으로 할 일, 숫자 정보, 도표, 짧은 대화나 긴 대화의 응답 유형 등이, 담화 형식으로 상황에 적절한 말을 묻는 유형이 출제될 수 있다.

기출 예제

2024학년도 6월 모의평가 5번

24006-0190

대화를 듣고, 여자가 할 일로 가장 적절한 것을 고르시오.

① 청소 업체 예약하기
② 인터넷 설치 신청하기
③ 아들의 새 학교에 연락하기
④ 버릴 의자에 스티커 붙이기
⑤ 이사 업체에 이사 날짜 확인하기

문항 속의 소재 **쿠키 커터 세트 구입** (2024학년도 6월 모의평가 10번)

M: Ellie, what are you looking at on your tablet PC?

Ellie, 네 태블릿 PC에서 뭘 보고 있어?

W: I'm looking for a set of new cookie cutters. Can you help me pick a new set out from among these five?

새 쿠키 커터 세트를 찾고 있어. 이 다섯 가지 중에서 새 쿠키 커터 세트를 고르는 걸 도와줄 수 있니?

M: Sure. There are many shapes to choose from. Do you have one in mind?

물론이지. 선택할 수 있는 모양이 많네. 마음에 드는 게 있어?

W: The star-shaped cutters look cool.

별 모양의 커터가 멋져 보여.

Dictations

W: Honey, our moving day is coming up in two weeks.

M: Yeah. I think we need to check our to-do list again.

W: Okay. We ❶_____ _____ _____ from the moving company for the date, right?

M: Yes, we did. Did you sign up for the Internet at our new place?

W: Uh-huh, I did. It should be connected by the move-in date. And I already put stickers on the chairs we will ❷_____ _____.

M: Great. Oh, I still have to wrap the crystal vases.

W: That's okay. You have time. Did you call our son's new school? Did they tell you what he needs to take with him on his first day?

M: Yes, he has to bring the uniform for his gym class. Oh, we forgot to ❸_____ _____ _____ with the cleaning company.

W: No worries. I'll do it right now.

M: Thanks.

Topic-related Expressions

◉ 가사, 쇼핑

food waste 음식물 쓰레기　recycling 재활용　refrigerator 냉장고　tidy up 정리하다　to-do list 할 일 목록　vacuum cleaner 진공청소기　washing machine 세탁기
budget 예산　delivery 배달　department store 백화점　flyer 전단, 광고지　membership 회원 자격, 멤버십　pay by credit card 신용 카드로 지불하다　shipping 배송

Let's **tidy up** the messy room.
지저분한 방을 정리하자.

I buy some cheese with overnight **delivery** service.
야간 배달 서비스로 치즈를 좀 살게요.

◉ 직장 업무

anniversary (창립) 기념일　business trip 출장　deadline 마감일　meeting 회의　overtime 초과 근무　presentation 프레젠테이션, 발표　sales report 판매 보고서

I was late for the **meeting** this morning.
저는 오늘 아침 회의에 늦었어요.

The **sales report** is due next Monday.
판매 보고서는 다음 월요일이 마감이에요.

Exercises

01 대화를 듣고, 남자의 의견으로 가장 적절한 것을 고르시오. 24006-0191

① 정기적인 가계부 작성은 계획적인 소비 생활에 도움을 준다.
② 식품 구매 시 원산지와 유통 기한을 꼼꼼하게 살펴봐야 한다.
③ 합리적 쇼핑을 위해 충분한 시간을 두고 구매를 결정해야 한다.
④ 냉장고의 위생 상태 유지를 위해서는 내부 청소를 자주 해야 한다.
⑤ 쇼핑 전 구매 목록을 작성하면 불필요한 물건의 구매를 막을 수 있다.

02 다음을 듣고, 여자가 하는 말의 요지로 가장 적절한 것을 고르시오. 24006-0192

① 공공 와이파이에 접속하여 온라인 쇼핑을 하는 것은 안전하지 않다.
② 온라인으로 물품 구매 시 결제는 신용 카드로 하는 것이 안전하다.
③ 온라인 쇼핑은 오프라인 쇼핑에 비해 시간적 제약을 받지 않는다.
④ 온라인 쇼핑몰의 아이디와 비밀번호는 수시로 바꾸는 것이 좋다.
⑤ 무료 인터넷 접속 환경을 갖춘 공공장소가 확대되어야 한다.

03 대화를 듣고, 그림에서 대화의 내용과 일치하지 <u>않는</u> 것을 고르시오. 24006-0193

04 대화를 듣고, 남자가 할 일로 가장 적절한 것을 고르시오.   24006-0194

① 기자 초대하기
② 회의실 정리하기
③ 행사 장소 예약하기
④ 무선 이어폰 구입하기
⑤ 마이크 상태 점검하기

05 대화를 듣고, 남자가 지불할 금액을 고르시오.   24006-0195

① $81
② $90
③ $99
④ $100
⑤ $110

06 대화를 듣고, 여자가 오늘 늦게 귀가하는 이유를 고르시오.   24006-0196

① 부모님 댁에 들러야 해서
② 서점에서 책을 구매해야 해서
③ 도서관에서 책을 대출해야 해서
④ 아들의 담임 교사를 만나야 해서
⑤ 체육관으로 아들을 데리러 가야 해서

07 대화를 듣고, Golden Plaza Shopping Mall에 관해 언급되지 <u>않은</u> 것을 고르시오.   24006-0197

① 개장일
② 위치
③ 개장 행사
④ 영업 시간
⑤ 푸드코트 시설

08 다음 표를 보면서 대화를 듣고, 남자가 주문할 플래너 보드를 고르시오.   24006-0198

Planner Boards

		Width/Height (cm)	Price	Period	Color
①	A	80×50	$47	monthly	white
②	B	100×60	$60	weekly	white
③	C	110×60	$53	monthly	black
④	D	115×75	$75	weekly	black
⑤	E	125×70	$67	monthly	black

09 대화를 듣고, 여자의 마지막 말에 대한 남자의 응답으로 가장 적절한 것을 고르시오.   24006-0199

① The printer hasn't been working since last week.
② I'm afraid the office manager is not at work today.
③ We definitely need a larger budget for office supplies.
④ There's a box on the bottom shelf in the supply room.
⑤ I think we need at least five considering our recent use.

10 대화를 듣고, 남자의 마지막 말에 대한 여자의 응답으로 가장 적절한 것을 고르시오.   24006-0200

① I agree. I also thought that the map was too confusing.
② Oh, it's really close. It's right over there next to the bank.
③ Not at all. Feel free to ask as many questions as you want.
④ Thanks, but I'm okay. I already finished shopping yesterday.
⑤ Right. The Central Shopping Mall is 5 minutes' walk from here.

11 대화를 듣고, 여자의 마지막 말에 대한 남자의 응답으로 가장 적절한 것을 고르시오.   24006-0201

Man: _____

① Thanks for understanding. Let's each pay half.
② Well, I think the repair cost might be inaccurate.
③ Sorry. I lent the grass cutter to my neighbor last week.
④ Great! I'll be really careful when I use your grass cutter.
⑤ Definitely. You'd better take the grass cutter to a repair shop.

12 다음 상황 설명을 듣고, Paul이 할머니에게 할 말로 가장 적절한 것을 고르시오.   24006-0202

Paul: _____

① It's very nice of you to praise my cooking skills.
② I'm so happy that you like my pumpkin soup recipe.
③ I'd appreciate it if you could make me a pumpkin soup.
④ Thanks a lot for teaching me how to make this amazing soup.
⑤ I'm really grateful that you gifted me this wonderful recipe book.

Dictations

01

W: Honey, I think we need to clean out the fridge. There are so many things that we're never going to eat.

M: Totally. I'm sure there are also ❶_____ _____ _____ _____ that are expired.

W: For sure there are.

M: We always buy more than we need, which is a waste of food and money. Let's try to stop doing that from now on.

W: Okay. How should we try to do that?

M: I think we should make a list before we go shopping.

W: What do you mean?

M: We can ❷_____ _____ _____ _____ and see what we're running out of, and then write down what we need.

W: So, you mean keep a grocery list?

M: Exactly. If we ❸_____ _____ _____ _____, we won't buy things that we don't really need just because they're on sale.

W: Sounds like a good plan. Let's start doing that.

M: I'm sure that'll help us control our spending.

02

W: Hello, Bargain Hunter listeners! There is one thing you ❶_____ _____ _____ _____ to keep your money and your data secure when shopping online. While buying something online comfortably at your favorite coffee shop may seem appealing, it comes with ❷_____ _____ _____ _____.
Public Wi-Fi networks are vulnerable to abuse, allowing hackers to steal all kinds of personal data, including your searching history, and access to your email and your passwords. What's more, if you decide to shop online while using a public Wi-Fi connection, you ❸_____ _____ _____ your credit card details and your name. So next time you want to do online shopping, make sure to do it safely by using a secure Internet connection rather than public Wi-Fi networks.

03

M: What are you looking at, honey?

W: A picture of my sister Anna's baby's room she sent me. Take a look.

M: Oh, yeah. Anna has a baby on the way. She said it's a boy, right?

W: Yes. Don't you love ❶_____ _____ _____ _____ _____ _____ _____ on the floor?

M: Yeah. The baby's room has an outer space theme. Look at ❷_____ _____ _____ _____ _____.

W: Oh, you're right! Maybe she wants her boy to grow up to be an astronaut!

M: Haha! And ❸_____ _____ _____ on the wall is really cool.

W: Yeah. The plant in the corner of the room is really nice, too.

M: And it should help purify the air.

W: Right. And she installed blinds ❹_____ _____ _____ because she can clean them frequently. She told me she was doing that.

M: That's a good idea. I can't wait to meet her baby boy.

W: Me, too!

04

W: Eric, is the conference room all ready? Our promotional event for the new wireless earphones ❶ _____ _____ _____ _____ _____ now.

M: Right. Only three days left now.

W: I can't overstress how important this is. We're targeting reporters.

M: About that... I now have 60 reporters confirmed as attending the event.

W: That's great. I can't wait to see their reactions to the new earphones.

M: I'm sure they'll be extremely ❷ _____ _____ _____.

W: I hope so. Ah, have you checked the audio system in the conference room? I heard that ❸ _____ _____ _____ _____ _____ at a meeting yesterday.

M: Really? I'll go there now and check it.

W: Sounds good. It would be a disaster if the microphone didn't work during the event.

M: Definitely. All our hard work would be wasted.

W: Let's do our best to ❹ _____ _____ _____.

05

W: Welcome to Clear View Optics. How can I help you?

M: Hi, I'd like to get ❶ _____ _____ _____ _____ _____.

W: All right. Do you have a prescription?

M: Yes, here it is. Could you help me choose the frames and lenses?

W: I'd be glad to help. Here are our newest frames.

M: Hmm.... Ooh, I really ❷ _____ _____ _____

_____. How much is it?

W: It's $50.

M: Wow, that's cheap. I'll take it.

W: All right. Now let's look at the lenses. Do you need any special type of lens?

M: No. Just regular ones.

W: Okay. Then the lenses you need are $20 each, so $40 for your glasses. Would you like ❸ _____ _____ _____ ? It's an extra $10 for the pair.

M: Yeah. I definitely need the coating. Oh, by the way, I have this 10%-off coupon. Can I use it?

W: Sure. You can get a 10 percent discount off the total price.

M: Great. Here's my credit card.

06

[Cell phone rings.]

M: Hi, honey.

W: Hi, honey. Did you ❶ _____ _____ _____ _____ _____ _____ ?

M: I'm on my way now. Where are you?

W: I just finished meeting Jason's homeroom teacher. Oh, and I'll be home late today.

M: Do you have to stop by your parents' house?

W: No. I need to go to the bookstore downtown.

M: Why is that?

W: Do you remember Jason said he needs a book ❷ _____ _____ _____ _____ ?

M: Yeah. Didn't he check it out from the library?

W: No, he said there aren't any available copies at the library right now. So he asked me to buy it for him.

M: I see. Are you sure the bookstore downtown has it?

W: Yes. I called, and they told me they ❸ _____ _____ _____ _____. So, I'm going to get it and head straight home.

M: Okay. Then I'll make dinner when I get home.

07

W: Hey, Nick, have you heard about the Golden Plaza Shopping Mall opening next month?

M: I think I ❶_____ _____ _____ about it, but I'm not sure. When does it open?

W: It opens on August 31st, the last Saturday of the month.

M: Oh, yes. Isn't it located downtown?

W: Yes, it is. The shopping mall is right ❷_____ _____ _____ _____ _____, close to the subway station.

M: That's cool!

W: I heard they're having a special opening event with live music performances.

M: That sounds like fun. Do you know what stores or facilities it will have?

W: Well, it'll have popular fashion brands, electronics shops, and a large food court with various dining options.

M: Sounds like a one-stop destination for shopping and dining. I ❸_____ _____ _____ _____ it out.

W: Me, neither. Let's go together on the opening day.

M: Okay!

08

W: Daniel, it's lunchtime.

M: Sorry, Rachel. I just need a few more minutes. I need to ❶_____ _____ _____ _____ _____ for the office wall. I'm trying to choose one of these from this online store.

W: Oh, let me help. Do you know how large the space is?

M: Yes. It's 120 cm wide and 80 cm high.

W: Then we can't buy this one because it's too wide. Is there a price limit?

M: Yes. I can spend up to $70. Oh, then that means this one is out, too.

W: Right. And I assume that it should be a monthly planner, not a weekly one.

M: Yeah, you're right. We need it so we can easily see ❷_____ _____ _____ _____ for the month.

W: Then we should get one of these two monthly ones.

M: How about the board color? I think black would be better than white.

W: I agree. It ❸_____ _____ _____ _____ if we use bright-colored markers. Then order this one, Daniel.

M: Okay, I will. Thanks, Rachel. Let's go to lunch right after this.

09

W: Mr. Thompson. The printer is ❶_____ _____ _____. Should I bring some from the supply room?

M: I'm afraid there's no paper left in the supply room, either. Could you call the office manager and ❷_____ _____ _____ _____ right away?

W: Okay. How many boxes do you think we need?

10

M: Excuse me, do you know ❶_____ _____ _____ _____ _____ the Central Shopping Mall?

W: I'm sorry, but I'm ❷_____ _____ _____, too. Why don't you ask the information center?

M: Oh, thank you. But I can't see the information center.

11

M: Hi, Ms. Baker. Can we talk about my grass cutter you borrowed last week?

W: Of course. Is there something wrong?

M: Well, after you returned it, the engine was making strange noises, like it ❶_____ _____ _____ _____ _____.

W: Really? I'm so sorry.

M: Did you notice anything wrong with the grass cutter when you used it?

W: No, it was working fine. I didn't notice any problems with it.

M: Hmm… maybe something happened while you ❷_____ _____ _____ _____.

W: Yeah, I guess so, too.

M: I actually had to ❸_____ _____ _____, and it cost me $80. I hope you can share some of the repair costs.

W: Of course I can. I'm so sorry about that.

12

W: Paul walks into his grandmother's house while she is about to cook pumpkin soup. He asks her to teach him ❶_____ _____ _____ _____ _____. His grandmother smiles and says she would be happy to teach him. She begins to explain the recipe step by step. She shows Paul how to chop the pumpkin and cook it in butter, and how to ❷_____ _____ _____ to create a smooth, creamy soup. After making the soup, they sit down and enjoy it together. Paul is proud that he learned how to make such a delicious food. He wants ❸_____ _____ _____ _____ to his grandmother. In this situation, what would Paul most likely say to his grandmother?

Part

III

실전편

01　다음을 듣고, 여자가 하는 말의 목적으로 가장 적절한 것을 고르시오.　　24006-0203

① 학교 구내식당 실내 공사 계획을 알리려고
② 학교 구내식당에서 질서 유지를 당부하려고
③ 주방에서 스토브 사용 시 유의 사항을 설명하려고
④ 학교 급식 만족도 조사에 참여할 것을 요청하려고
⑤ 예정된 음식 대신 다른 음식이 제공됨을 공지하려고

02　대화를 듣고, 남자의 의견으로 가장 적절한 것을 고르시오.　　24006-0204

① 규칙적인 생활 습관을 만들면 만성 피로를 없앨 수 있다.
② 스마트 전자 기기를 활용하면 효과적으로 운동할 수 있다.
③ 건강한 신체가 바탕이 되어야 건전한 정신을 기를 수 있다.
④ 수면 부족은 집중력과 정서적 건강에 악영향을 끼칠 수 있다.
⑤ 건강을 위해 전자 기기 화면에 노출되는 시간을 조절해야 한다.

03　다음을 듣고, 여자가 하는 말의 요지로 가장 적절한 것을 고르시오.　　24006-0205

① 사람들과 대화할 때 모두에게 친숙한 주제로 말하는 것이 좋다.
② 다른 사람이 이야기할 때 끼어들어 끊지 않도록 해야 한다.
③ 상대방의 마음을 상하지 않게 말하려고 노력해야 한다.
④ 다른 사람의 말에 주의를 기울여 끝까지 들어야 한다.
⑤ 말을 장황하게 해서 대화를 독차지하지 않아야 한다.

04 대화를 듣고, 그림에서 대화의 내용과 일치하지 <u>않는</u> 것을 고르시오.   24006-0206

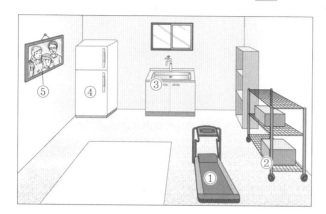

05 대화를 듣고, 남자가 할 일로 가장 적절한 것을 고르시오.   24006-0207

① 식당 예약하기
② 케이크 주문하기
③ 은퇴식 참여하기
④ 선생님 모셔 오기
⑤ 문자 메시지 보내기

06 대화를 듣고, 여자가 지불할 금액을 고르시오. [3점]   24006-0208

① $25
② $27
③ $30
④ $35
⑤ $40

07 대화를 듣고, 남자가 오늘 배드민턴을 그만 치려는 이유를 고르시오. 24006-0209

① 몸이 너무 많이 지쳐서
② 저녁 식사 약속이 있어서
③ 팔꿈치가 아프기 시작해서
④ 새 라켓을 사러 가기로 해서
⑤ 내일 경기에 대비하기 위해서

08 대화를 듣고, Green Energy Festival에 관해 언급되지 <u>않은</u> 것을 고르시오. 24006-0210

① 주요 행사
② 축제 기간
③ 주최 기관
④ 참여 단체의 수
⑤ 신청 방법

09 *Future Science Brain*에 관한 다음 내용을 듣고, 일치하지 <u>않는</u> 것을 고르시오. 24006-0211

① 다양한 과학 분야를 다룬다.
② 처음 세 편이 방송되었다.
③ 인기 있는 어린이 배우들이 출연한다.
④ 구독료를 따로 낼 필요는 없다.
⑤ 매주 금요일 저녁에 방송된다.

10 다음 표를 보면서 대화를 듣고, 여자가 신청할 그룹 테니스 수업을 고르시오.

24006-0212

Beginner Group Tennis Lessons

	Lesson	Day	Time	Court	Current Number of People
①	A	Mon./Wed.	7:00 p.m. – 7:30 p.m.	indoor	2
②	B	Tue./Thu.	6:30 p.m. – 7:00 p.m.	indoor	3
③	C	Wed./Fri.	7:30 p.m. – 8:00 p.m.	indoor	4
④	D	Thu./Sat.	9:00 p.m. – 9:30 p.m.	outdoor	2
⑤	E	Thu./Sat.	8:00 p.m. – 8:30 p.m.	outdoor	3

11 대화를 듣고, 남자의 마지막 말에 대한 여자의 응답으로 가장 적절한 것을 고르시오.

24006-0213

① Thank you for saying that, but I can do it myself.

② You're right. She really likes to play soccer with us.

③ That'd be good! I'm so glad that she got her cast off.

④ That's great. She got home safely thanks to your help.

⑤ Good idea. Let's offer to carry her bag when she goes home.

12 대화를 듣고, 여자의 마지막 말에 대한 남자의 응답으로 가장 적절한 것을 고르시오.

24006-0214

① I see. I'll call to reserve a table for us right now.

② Don't worry. I'll make sure to get home on time.

③ Oh, no! I feel bad that they're already going home.

④ I understand. I'll try not to be late for school again.

⑤ Of course. Dinner with my grandparents was really nice.

13 대화를 듣고, 남자의 마지막 말에 대한 여자의 응답으로 가장 적절한 것을 고르시오. [3점]

24006-0215

Woman: _____

① All right. I'll print out your assignment while I wait.
② I'm afraid I can't go to the movies after school today.
③ I think you'd better finish your assignment before we leave.
④ That's nice. I'll collect the data for the literature assignment.
⑤ Sure. I can finish the assignment before we go to the movies.

14 대화를 듣고, 여자의 마지막 말에 대한 남자의 응답으로 가장 적절한 것을 고르시오. [3점]

24006-0216

Man: _____

① Sure. I checked the tent myself and bought it.
② Okay. I'll ask the seller if I can see the tent first.
③ You're right. I think we've used our tent too long.
④ No problem. I'll take the used tent to him by myself.
⑤ I don't think so. He promised to be on time with the tent.

15 다음 상황 설명을 듣고, Mr. Wilson이 여자아이에게 할 말로 가장 적절한 것을 고르시오.

24006-0217

Mr. Wilson: _____

① Please don't stand on the swings in the playground.
② Do you need to have good balance to swing on swings?
③ This swing is not safe to ride, so please use another one.
④ Can you let the other kids waiting have a turn on the swing?
⑤ I'd like you to hold the chains tight while you're on the swing.

[16～17] 다음을 듣고, 물음에 답하시오.

16 남자가 하는 말의 주제로 가장 적절한 것은?   24006-0218

① basic principles of VR technology
② new jobs related to VR technology
③ various modern uses of VR technology
④ social problems caused by VR technology
⑤ economic benefits of using VR technology

17 언급된 분야가 <u>아닌</u> 것은?   24006-0219

① gaming
② education
③ healthcare
④ architecture
⑤ tourism

01 다음을 듣고, 여자가 하는 말의 목적으로 가장 적절한 것을 고르시오.

24006-0220

① 스노클을 사용하는 방법을 알려 주려고
② 수영 입문자에게 호흡 연습을 권장하려고
③ 오리발의 올바른 착용 방법을 설명하려고
④ 초보자를 위한 스노클링 장비를 광고하려고
⑤ 스노클링을 하기 전 준비 운동의 중요성을 강조하려고

02 대화를 듣고, 남자의 의견으로 가장 적절한 것을 고르시오.

24006-0221

① 양초를 켜 두면 음식 냄새를 없애는 데 도움이 된다.
② 라벤더 향은 심신을 안정시키고 불면증을 완화할 수 있다.
③ 미세 먼지 농도가 높은 날은 야외 활동을 자제하는 것이 좋다.
④ 양초로 인한 화재의 원인은 일상생활 속 부주의로 인한 경우가 많다.
⑤ 좁은 공간에서 양초를 켜면 실내 공기가 오염돼 건강에 해로울 수 있다.

03 다음을 듣고, 여자가 하는 말의 요지로 가장 적절한 것을 고르시오.

24006-0222

① 여행은 특별한 경험이 아닌 일상의 연장이다.
② 매일 오후 산책을 통해 행복감을 충전해 보자.
③ 일상의 작은 즐거움에 감사하며 행복을 느끼자.
④ 다른 사람과 함께 운동하는 행복감이 기대 수명을 늘린다.
⑤ 원만하고 성숙한 인간관계는 행복한 삶의 중요한 요소이다.

04 대화를 듣고, 그림에서 대화의 내용과 일치하지 <u>않는</u> 것을 고르시오.

24006-0223

05 대화를 듣고, 여자가 할 일로 가장 적절한 것을 고르시오.

24006-0224

① 간식 주문하기
② 모임 장소 정하기
③ 공지 문자 보내기
④ 물품 배송 추적하기
⑤ 전광판 문구 수정하기

06 대화를 듣고, 남자가 지불할 금액을 고르시오. [3점]

24006-0225

① $22
② $27
③ $30
④ $33
⑤ $35

07 대화를 듣고, 여자가 체육관을 옮긴 이유를 고르시오.   24006-0226

① 운동 기구가 많아서
② 사무실에서 가까워서
③ 야간에 이용할 수 있어서
④ 식단 관리 프로그램이 있어서
⑤ 새로운 개인 트레이너를 추천받아서

08 대화를 듣고, Hara Hot Springs에 관해 언급되지 <u>않은</u> 것을 고르시오.   24006-0227

① 위치
② 영업시간
③ 수영장 종류
④ 예약 방법
⑤ 식당

09 Tasabay Winery Tour에 관한 다음 내용을 듣고, 일치하지 <u>않는</u> 것을 고르시오.   24006-0228

① 대략 한 시간 정도 소요된다.
② 와인 제조 과정에 대해 배운다.
③ 발리 와인 생산 구역을 들를 것이다.
④ 가이드가 시음실까지 동행할 것이다.
⑤ 다섯 가지 와인을 시음할 것이다.

10 다음 표를 보면서 대화를 듣고, 여자가 주문할 USB 허브를 고르시오.   24006-0229

USB Hubs

	Model	Number of Ports	Price	Cable Length (cm)	Color
①	A	5	$22	21	black
②	B	5	$18	20	gray
③	C	4	$17	27	black
④	D	4	$16	18	black
⑤	E	3	$19	19	gray

11 대화를 듣고, 남자의 마지막 말에 대한 여자의 응답으로 가장 적절한 것을 고르시오.   24006-0230

① He told us all to study abroad in Italy.
② He forces us to do the exercises in the textbook.
③ He is one of the best students I taught Italian to.
④ He uses interactive activities like games and role plays.
⑤ He suggested I take an Italian class at the language school.

12 대화를 듣고, 여자의 마지막 말에 대한 남자의 응답으로 가장 적절한 것을 고르시오.   24006-0231

① You can count on us for complete maintenance service.
② There's an escalator over there you can use to arrive there.
③ Fill out this form. I can finish repairing your shoes in six days.
④ If you're looking for the shoe department, it's on the sixth floor.
⑤ You can get off on this floor. The shoe department is to the right.

13 대화를 듣고, 남자의 마지막 말에 대한 여자의 응답으로 가장 적절한 것을 고르시오. 24006-0232

Woman: _____

① Why not? I'm really glad you like durian.
② Right. It sounds like you've got a stuffy nose.
③ I'm not sure. But it tastes exactly the same as durian.
④ It's easy. You can tell if food has gone bad by its smell.
⑤ Just try it! I think you'll be pleasantly surprised by the taste.

14 대화를 듣고, 여자의 마지막 말에 대한 남자의 응답으로 가장 적절한 것을 고르시오. [3점] 24006-0233

Man: _____

① I remember I broke my leg playing soccer in high school.
② Don't worry! It's all about having fun and staying active.
③ You should see a doctor if the bruise doesn't go away.
④ I'm not really into team sports, but I do enjoy yoga.
⑤ You're not alone. I'm not really into sports, either.

15 다음 상황 설명을 듣고, Max가 Maria에게 할 말로 가장 적절한 것을 고르시오. [3점] 24006-0234

Max: _____

① We should not share prescription medications with each other.
② We need to remove any personal information from the containers.
③ Let's locate a nearby pharmacy that will take our old medications.
④ How about consulting with your pharmacist about your medication?
⑤ Why don't we buy over-the-counter medicine at a pharmacy nearby?

[16~17] 다음을 듣고, 물음에 답하시오.

16 여자가 하는 말의 주제로 가장 적절한 것은? 24006-0235

① several methods of classifying musical instruments
② the most challenging stringed instruments to play
③ different ways string instruments produce sound
④ sound range levels of various string instruments
⑤ the most popular instruments in modern music

17 언급된 악기가 <u>아닌</u> 것은? 24006-0236

① violin
② cello
③ guitar
④ harp
⑤ piano

01 다음을 듣고, 여자가 하는 말의 목적으로 가장 적절한 것을 고르시오.   24006-0237

① 도서관 자원봉사 활동 참여를 독려하려고
② 도서관 시설 이용 시 주의할 사항을 당부하려고
③ 자원봉사자들의 도서관 개선 작업 결과를 홍보하려고
④ 도서관 보수 공사로 인한 이용 시간 변경을 안내하려고
⑤ 도서관 공간 디자인을 위한 아이디어 제출을 부탁하려고

02 대화를 듣고, 남자의 의견으로 가장 적절한 것을 고르시오.   24006-0238

① 시를 읽음으로써 문학적 감수성과 사고력을 키울 수 있다.
② 시를 감상할 때는 비유적인 의미를 이해하는 것이 중요하다.
③ 시대상이 잘 반영된 시는 소설보다 더 큰 통찰력을 제공한다.
④ 시를 잘 쓰려면 다양한 문화적 배경의 시를 읽어 보는 것이 좋다.
⑤ 시인의 문화적 배경을 아는 것은 시를 더 잘 이해하는 데 도움이 된다.

03 다음을 듣고, 여자가 하는 말의 요지로 가장 적절한 것을 고르시오.   24006-0239

① 숙면을 위해 쾌적한 취침 환경을 조성해야 한다.
② 취침 전 과도한 운동과 활동은 숙면에 방해가 된다.
③ 자녀의 건강한 수면을 위해 일관된 잠자리 준비 습관을 형성해야 한다.
④ 잠자리에서 책을 읽어 주는 것은 자녀의 독서 습관 형성에 효과적이다.
⑤ 자녀의 정신적 안정감을 위해 취침 시간을 일정하게 유지하는 것이 좋다.

04 대화를 듣고, 그림에서 대화의 내용과 일치하지 <u>않는</u> 것을 고르시오. 24006-0240

05 대화를 듣고, 남자가 할 일로 가장 적절한 것을 고르시오. 24006-0241

① 출력물 가져다주기
② 회의 간식 준비하기
③ 통계 자료 출력하기
④ 발표 자료 파일 제작하기
⑤ 부모님께 점심 식사 대접하기

06 대화를 듣고, 여자가 지불할 금액을 고르시오. [3점] 24006-0242

① $26
② $36
③ $45
④ $46
⑤ $55

07 대화를 듣고, 남자가 지금 수업 자료 파일을 줄 수 <u>없는</u> 이유를 고르시오.

24006-0243

① 영어 말하기 대회 준비로 바빠서
② 수업 자료를 아직 만들지 못해서
③ 바이러스 때문에 파일이 열리지 않아서
④ 파일이 들어 있는 컴퓨터가 고장이 나서
⑤ 파일이 들어 있는 노트북을 형에게 빌려 줘서

08 대화를 듣고, Moonlight Walk에 관해 언급되지 <u>않은</u> 것을 고르시오.

24006-0244

① 개최 일시
② 출발 장소
③ 소요 시간
④ 신청 마감일
⑤ 참가비

09 Bottle Terrarium Workshop에 관한 다음 내용을 듣고, 일치하지 <u>않는</u> 것을 고르시오.

24006-0245

① 유리병 안에 미니 정원을 만드는 법을 배운다.
② 5월 4일 토요일에 개최된다.
③ 참가비 외에 재료비를 별도로 내야 한다.
④ 18세 이상만 참가할 수 있다.
⑤ 수강 인원에 제한이 있다.

10 다음 표를 보면서 대화를 듣고, 남자가 구입할 옷걸이 세트를 고르시오.   24006-0246

Clothing Hanger Sets

	Set	Material	Price	Non-Slip	Number of Hangers
①	A	Plastic	$43	×	50
②	B	Wood	$38	○	25
③	C	Copper	$28	○	35
④	D	Velvet	$25	○	20
⑤	E	Metal Wire	$25	×	30

11 대화를 듣고, 남자의 마지막 말에 대한 여자의 응답으로 가장 적절한 것을 고르시오.   24006-0247

① I think next weekend would be ideal.
② Let's start doing it now with the new paint.
③ I don't remember when we painted the fence.
④ I'm not sure if we should paint the fence again.
⑤ We should sign up for painting classes right away.

12 대화를 듣고, 여자의 마지막 말에 대한 남자의 응답으로 가장 적절한 것을 고르시오.   24006-0248

① Exactly, the issue was just with the battery running out of power.
② Right, the screen and the battery should be replaced right now.
③ Actually, the brightness setting was simply set too low.
④ Yeah, you need to reduce the amount of time you use your phone.
⑤ Okay, I'll take it to the repair center to address the brightness problem.

13 대화를 듣고, 남자의 마지막 말에 대한 여자의 응답으로 가장 적절한 것을 고르시오. [3점]　　24006-0249

Woman: _____

① Cool! Thanks for finding such a nice eco-friendly resort to stay at.
② Me, too. It'll be wonderful to enjoy an eco-friendly summer vacation.
③ Don't worry. I already called and made a reservation with the resort.
④ Yeah. I'm happy to do volunteer work with you to save the environment.
⑤ Sure. But I have no idea where to go to experience sustainable tourism.

14 대화를 듣고, 여자의 마지막 말에 대한 남자의 응답으로 가장 적절한 것을 고르시오. [3점]　　24006-0250

Man: _____

① That'd be great. I really appreciate you creating the model for me.
② Really? I'm really grateful that you want to buy me the science journals.
③ Good idea! I'll check out the websites to order the science journals now.
④ You're a life saver! Now I think I can start working on the science project.
⑤ Thanks. But I don't need them because I already finished the science project.

15 다음 상황 설명을 듣고, Emma가 Jack에게 할 말로 가장 적절한 것을 고르시오.　　24006-0251

Emma: _____

① I want to compliment you for following my suggestion.
② I appreciate you sending me beautiful flowers and a gift.
③ I'm grateful that you recommended me to wear the floral dress.
④ It's thoughtful of you to advise me to bring flowers to the concert.
⑤ Thank you for getting me these lovely floral accessories for the dress.

[16~17] 다음을 듣고, 물음에 답하시오.

16 남자가 하는 말의 주제로 가장 적절한 것은? 24006-0252

① tips for relieving aging stress
② things that can get better as we age
③ crucial aspects for a happier senior life
④ adopting lifestyle changes for graceful aging
⑤ why seniors need physical and mental balance

17 언급된 것이 <u>아닌</u> 것은? 24006-0253

① relationships
② expertise
③ emotional intelligence
④ self-confidence
⑤ enjoyment

01 다음을 듣고, 남자가 하는 말의 목적으로 가장 적절한 것을 고르시오.   24006-0254

① 요리 대회 수상자를 축하하려고
② 백화점에서 일할 직원을 모집하려고
③ 요리 대회에 참가할 것을 권유하려고
④ 문화 센터의 잘못된 운영을 비판하려고
⑤ 새로 개설된 백화점 웹사이트를 홍보하려고

02 대화를 듣고, 여자의 의견으로 가장 적절한 것을 고르시오.   24006-0255

① 국제 운전 면허증은 호주 여행에서 꼭 필요하다.
② 호주는 혼자서 배낭여행을 하기에 좋은 나라이다.
③ 여행을 하면서 현지인과 친구가 되는 것은 쉽지 않다.
④ 호주 버스 여행은 여행자에게 다양한 이점을 제공한다.
⑤ 여행지 교통편 선택 시 개인의 여행 성향을 고려해야 한다.

03 다음을 듣고, 남자가 하는 말의 요지로 가장 적절한 것을 고르시오.   24006-0256

① 규칙적인 생활 습관이 건강한 삶을 이끈다.
② 자신의 삶에 충실한 사람이 일기를 꾸준히 쓴다.
③ 일기 쓰기는 글쓰기 실력 향상에 큰 도움이 된다.
④ 논리적으로 사고하는 사람이 논리적인 글을 쓴다.
⑤ 모든 사람에게 동일하게 적용되는 글쓰기 실력 향상 방법은 없다.

04 대화를 듣고, 그림에서 대화의 내용과 일치하지 <u>않는</u> 것을 고르시오. 24006-0257

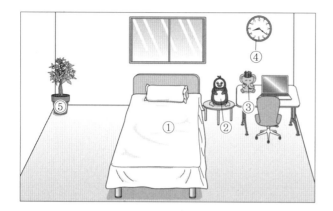

05 대화를 듣고, 여자가 할 일로 가장 적절한 것을 고르시오. 24006-0258

① 전단 복사하기
② 공연 순서 짜기
③ 인쇄소 방문하기
④ 공연 포스터 디자인하기
⑤ 공연 초대장 나누어 주기

06 대화를 듣고, 남자가 지불할 금액을 고르시오. [3점] 24006-0259

① $39
② $48
③ $52
④ $56
⑤ $66

07 대화를 듣고, 여자가 Tata View Hotel에 투숙하기를 원하지 <u>않는</u> 이유를 고르시오.　　24006-0260

① 객실료가 비싸서
② 조식 서비스가 없어서
③ 호텔의 편의 시설이 낡아서
④ 수영장을 사용할 수 없어서
⑤ 해변에서 멀리 떨어져 있어서

08 대화를 듣고, Green Auto Show에 관해 언급되지 <u>않은</u> 것을 고르시오.　　24006-0261

① 개최 기간
② 티켓 가격
③ 전시 모델 수
④ 주관 단체
⑤ 예상 방문객 수

09 한국어 말하기 대회에 관한 다음 내용을 듣고, 일치하지 <u>않는</u> 것을 고르시오.　　24006-0262

① 한국 방문의 해를 기념하기 위해 열린다.
② 주제는 '한국의 전통문화'이다.
③ 원고는 800 단어에서 1,000 단어 사이로 작성되어야 한다.
④ 1등 수상자는 무선 이어폰을 받을 것이다.
⑤ 등록은 센터의 웹사이트에서 이루어진다.

10 다음 표를 보면서 대화를 듣고, 남자가 대여할 복사기를 고르시오.

24006-0263

Copy Machine Rental Service

	Model	Monthly Rental Fee	Rental Period (months)	Wi-Fi (connectivity)	Color Copy
①	A	$89	18	○	○
②	B	$77	12	○	○
③	C	$75	18	×	○
④	D	$65	12	○	×
⑤	E	$60	12	×	×

11 대화를 듣고, 남자의 마지막 말에 대한 여자의 응답으로 가장 적절한 것을 고르시오.

24006-0264

① That's good. Let's read over the report together.
② Sure. I'll text you the website address right now.
③ Me, too. I also want to correct my grammar errors.
④ Okay. Let me tell you how to remove the program.
⑤ Definitely. Writing the report was quite demanding.

12 대화를 듣고, 여자의 마지막 말에 대한 남자의 응답으로 가장 적절한 것을 고르시오.

24006-0265

① I got it. Let me clean the fridge right now.
② Okay. I'll teach you how to make pizza now.
③ Don't worry. Just heat it up in the microwave.
④ Oh, I'm so full. There's no way I can eat anything else.
⑤ It tastes so good. Your pizza is better than restaurant pizza.

13 대화를 듣고, 남자의 마지막 말에 대한 여자의 응답으로 가장 적절한 것을 고르시오. [3점]

24006-0266

Woman: _____

① Don't worry. I'll book our tickets online right now.
② Right. I should have seen the championship in real time.
③ Don't worry. From now on, let me teach you how to skate.
④ Then as you said, Lucy Kim is most likely to win the competition.
⑤ Sure! Jennifer Brown's moves were way more artistic than the others'.

14 대화를 듣고, 여자의 마지막 말에 대한 남자의 응답으로 가장 적절한 것을 고르시오.

24006-0267

Man: _____

① Yes, I can lend you money to buy the computer.
② Yes, you can use my laptop anytime you want.
③ No, I can't go to the computer store right now.
④ No, you can't receive the repair free of charge.
⑤ Sure. As soon as the repair is done, I'll let you know.

15 다음 상황 설명을 듣고, Kate가 Daniel에게 할 말로 가장 적절한 것을 고르시오. [3점]

24006-0268

Kate: _____

① You're right. What I want is to become a casting director.
② Sure. Picking the right actors for a movie is not that easy.
③ I'm sorry, but you're not exactly what I want for this film.
④ That was good, so I'd like to give you a follow-up audition.
⑤ Thanks for the recommendation because that was a great movie.

[16~17] 다음을 듣고, 물음에 답하시오.

16 여자가 하는 말의 주제로 가장 적절한 것은?   24006-0269

① techniques predators use to catch their prey
② difficulties wild animals may face in the wild
③ ways animals protect themselves from predators
④ biological differences between plants and animals
⑤ effects of environmental destruction on animal habitats

17 언급되지 <u>않은</u> 동물은?   24006-0270

① octopuses
② kangaroos
③ parrots
④ skunks
⑤ dolphins

01 다음을 듣고, 남자가 하는 말의 목적으로 가장 적절한 것을 고르시오.

24006-0271

① 중간고사 일정 연기를 공지하려고
② 폭우로 인한 침수 피해를 경고하려고
③ 효과적인 시험공부 요령을 설명하려고
④ 새로 바뀐 시험 응시 방법을 안내하려고
⑤ 안전사고 예방을 위한 주의를 당부하려고

02 대화를 듣고, 남자의 의견으로 가장 적절한 것을 고르시오.

24006-0272

① 언어와 문화는 상호 영향을 주고받으며 발전한다.
② 영상 자막의 활용이 외국어 어휘 학습에 도움이 된다.
③ 외국어 학습에서 정확한 어법과 표현을 익히는 것이 중요하다.
④ TV 드라마 시청을 통해 외국어 의사소통 능력을 향상할 수 있다.
⑤ 문화 이해를 위해 좋은 TV 드라마를 선별하는 안목을 키워야 한다.

03 다음을 듣고, 남자가 하는 말의 요지로 가장 적절한 것을 고르시오.

24006-0273

① 양육에 어려움을 겪고 있는 부모를 도와주어야 한다.
② 아이들이 요청한 도움에 대해 적절한 지원이 요구된다.
③ 신발끈 매기 활동은 아이의 소근육 발달에 매우 효과적이다.
④ 아이들이 할 수 있는 일을 스스로 하게 하는 것이 성장에 중요하다.
⑤ 아이들의 성취감을 높이기 위해 구체적인 활동 목표를 설정해야 한다.

04 대화를 듣고, 그림에서 대화의 내용과 일치하지 <u>않는</u> 것을 고르시오.   24006-0274

05 대화를 듣고, 남자가 할 일로 가장 적절한 것을 고르시오.   24006-0275

① 포스터 붙이기
② 강사에게 연락하기
③ 간식과 음료 더 사 오기
④ 강당에 테이블 설치하기
⑤ 인쇄실에서 일정표 가져오기

06 대화를 듣고, 여자가 지불할 금액을 고르시오. [3점]   24006-0276

① $48
② $54
③ $56
④ $60
⑤ $62

07 대화를 듣고, 남자가 기차역으로 마중 나갈 수 <u>없는</u> 이유를 고르시오. 24006-0277

① 고객과 회의가 있어서
② 학회에 참석해야 해서
③ 수영 강습을 받아야 해서
④ 로봇 센터를 방문해야 해서
⑤ 교수님과 점심 약속이 있어서

08 대화를 듣고, 2024 Vision Scholarship에 관해 언급되지 <u>않은</u> 것을 고르시오. 24006-0278

① 신청 자격 요건
② 신청 방법
③ 신청 마감일
④ 추천서 필요 여부
⑤ 장학금 액수

09 2024 Winter Family Fun Day에 관한 다음 내용을 듣고, 일치하지 <u>않는</u> 것을 고르시오. 24006-0279

① 오전 11시부터 오후 4시까지 열린다.
② 지역 사회가 주최하는 행사이다.
③ 5세 미만의 어린이는 무료이다.
④ 간식을 위해 별도의 비용을 지불해야 한다.
⑤ 온라인에서 입장권을 구입할 수 있다.

10 다음 표를 보면서, 대화를 듣고, 남자가 구입할 담요를 고르시오.

24006-0280

Summer Blankets

	Blanket	Material	Size	Price	Color
①	A	Silk	Twin	$70	Green
②	B	Silk	Double	$85	Brown
③	C	Cotton	Twin	$90	Blue
④	D	Linen	Double	$105	Brown
⑤	E	Linen	Queen	$110	Green

11 대화를 듣고, 남자의 마지막 말에 대한 여자의 응답으로 가장 적절한 것을 고르시오.

24006-0281

① Same with me. I couldn't live in that temperature.
② A heater is not warm enough in this cold weather.
③ Don't worry. It's not so bad once you get used to it.
④ It's better to keep the temperature above 18 degrees.
⑤ My heating bill this month is much higher than usual.

12 대화를 듣고, 여자의 마지막 말에 대한 남자의 응답으로 가장 적절한 것을 고르시오.

24006-0282

① I'll say. I think you need to give it some fertilizer.
② Oh, my! You shouldn't water it more than twice a week.
③ Sure. I researched the best soil mix to use for the plant.
④ Okay. It'd be a good idea to get a larger pot for the plant.
⑤ Why not? Let's quickly move the plant to the living room.

13 대화를 듣고, 여자의 마지막 말에 대한 남자의 응답으로 가장 적절한 것을 고르시오. [3점]   24006-0283

Man: _____

① Great! You can arrive there before the closing time.
② I'm not sure. But I know you can't use that service at night.
③ Oh, no! The self-checkout machine seems to be out of order.
④ Definitely. It might be beneficial to get ideas for my business.
⑤ Hurry! You need to reserve your book before the library closes.

14 대화를 듣고, 남자의 마지막 말에 대한 여자의 응답으로 가장 적절한 것을 고르시오. [3점]   24006-0284

Woman: _____

① Sure. I'll try to live up to my father's expectations.
② Unfortunately, I don't have the aptitude to become an artist.
③ Never mind. There's nothing else to try to convince my dad.
④ Be brave. Try to have a heartfelt conversation with your father.
⑤ Right. He'll probably finally stop pressuring me to study business.

15 다음 상황 설명을 듣고, Roger가 Chloe에게 할 말로 가장 적절한 것을 고르시오.   24006-0285

Roger: _____

① I'd like to know about donating hair to sick children.
② I hope to see you more often at the high school reunion.
③ You have changed so much since graduating high school.
④ A long hairstyle could be a great option for you to consider.
⑤ Thank you for inspiring me to donate my hair for sick children.

[16~17] 다음을 듣고, 물음에 답하시오.

16 남자가 하는 말의 주제로 가장 적절한 것은?　　　　　　　24006-0286

① challenges when designing an eco-friendly building
② how amazingly designed structures aid environmental protection
③ roles of technological innovations in recreating natural environments
④ tips for maintaining a consistent temperature in a building year-round
⑤ changes eco-friendly buildings are making to the future of architecture

17 언급된 나라가 <u>아닌</u> 것은?　　　　　　　24006-0287

① Italy
② Spain
③ France
④ Tanzania
⑤ the US

01 다음을 듣고, 남자가 하는 말의 목적으로 가장 적절한 것을 고르시오.

24006-0288

① 쓰레기 분리수거일 변경을 공지하려고
② 재활용품 수거 서비스 이용 방법을 안내하려고
③ 건물 내 쓰레기 배출 장소와 배출 요일을 알려 주려고
④ 쓰레기를 종류에 따라 지정된 용기에 버리도록 요청하려고
⑤ 깨끗한 골목 조성을 위한 집 앞 청소하기 캠페인을 홍보하려고

02 대화를 듣고, 여자의 의견으로 가장 적절한 것을 고르시오.

24006-0289

① 커피 찌꺼기는 말려서 사용하는 것이 좋다.
② 신발장을 건조하게 하면 악취를 제거할 수 있다.
③ 커피 찌꺼기는 일상에서 유용하게 쓰일 수 있다.
④ 적당한 커피 섭취는 건강 유지에 도움을 줄 수 있다.
⑤ 악취의 원인에 따라 제거 방법을 다르게 해야 한다.

03 다음을 듣고, 남자가 하는 말의 요지로 가장 적절한 것을 고르시오.

24006-0290

① 건강을 위해 휴대 전화를 정기적으로 소독할 필요가 있다.
② 세균 감염을 막기 위해 자주 얼굴과 입을 씻어야 한다.
③ 휴대 전화의 모든 기능을 제대로 알아야 한다.
④ 지나친 휴대 전화 사용은 건강에 나쁜 영향을 끼친다.
⑤ 휴대 전화의 음량을 너무 높이면 청력에 손상을 줄 수 있다.

04 대화를 듣고, 그림에서 대화의 내용과 일치하지 <u>않는</u> 것을 고르시오.　　　24006-0291

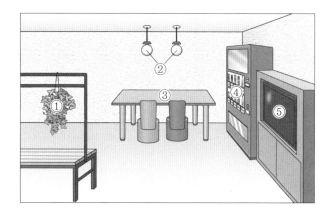

05 대화를 듣고, 여자가 할 일로 가장 적절한 것을 고르시오.　　　24006-0292

① 학부모에게 연락하기
② 확인 목록 작성하기
③ 참석자 명찰 만들기
④ 유인물 출력하기
⑤ 연필 사 오기

06 대화를 듣고, 남자가 지불할 금액을 고르시오. [3점]　　　24006-0293

① $40
② $45
③ $60
④ $70
⑤ $80

07 대화를 듣고, 여자가 지난주 금요일 요가 수업을 빠진 이유를 고르시오. 24006-0294

① 허리를 다쳐서
② 지방으로 출장을 가서
③ 휴대 전화를 수리해야 해서
④ 아들을 병원에 데려가야 해서
⑤ 수업이 있다는 것을 잊어버려서

08 대화를 듣고, 아이스 링크에 관해 언급되지 않은 것을 고르시오. 24006-0295

① 위치
② 개장 시간
③ 교통편
④ 입장료
⑤ 입장 제한 인원

09 Whale Festival에 관한 다음 내용을 듣고, 일치하지 않는 것을 고르시오. 24006-0296

① 해안가 마을 Greenville에서 개최된다.
② 보통 10월 말이나 11월 초에 주말 동안 열린다.
③ 절벽을 따라 걸으며 고래를 구경할 수 있다.
④ 지역 노점상에서 다양한 종류의 음식과 음료를 판매한다.
⑤ 환경 문제에 대한 워크숍이 포함되어 있다.

10 다음 표를 보면서 대화를 듣고, 여자가 구입할 스케이트보드를 고르시오.   24006-0297

Skateboards

	Model	Deck Width (inches)	Deck Material	Wheels	Price
①	A	7.4	wood	soft	$50
②	B	7.6	wood	hard	$35
③	C	7.8	plastic	soft	$45
④	D	7.9	wood	soft	$40
⑤	E	8.2	plastic	hard	$38

11 대화를 듣고, 남자의 마지막 말에 대한 여자의 응답으로 가장 적절한 것을 고르시오.   24006-0298

① Is it possible to get my watch fixed by next week?
② Have you seen my watch anywhere near the table?
③ Would you like me to clean up the room right now?
④ How long do you think it will take to find your watch?
⑤ Why don't you look on the dining table in the kitchen?

12 대화를 듣고, 여자의 마지막 말에 대한 남자의 응답으로 가장 적절한 것을 고르시오.   24006-0299

① Well, I think my computer is working fine.
② No problem. I don't need to use it for a while.
③ I'm sorry, but I can't connect to the Internet right now.
④ That's okay. I already asked for technical support yesterday.
⑤ Never mind. I'll just send your computer to the repair shop.

13 대화를 듣고, 남자의 마지막 말에 대한 여자의 응답으로 가장 적절한 것을 고르시오. [3점]

24006-0300

Woman: _____

① Thank you for letting us sit in a booth.
② That's why I want to cancel the reservation.
③ I'm so excited to have dinner with you here.
④ In that case, sitting near the window sounds great.
⑤ It seems like we won't be able to make it at that time.

14 대화를 듣고, 여자의 마지막 말에 대한 남자의 응답으로 가장 적절한 것을 고르시오.

24006-0301

Man: _____

① Cheer up! You'll get a better score next time.
② Don't worry. It's never too late to say sorry.
③ That's right. She'll be happy to meet you.
④ No problem. I'm glad I could be of help.
⑤ I agree. You should be angry with her.

15 다음 상황 설명을 듣고, Amy가 Peter에게 할 말로 가장 적절한 것을 고르시오. [3점]

24006-0302

Amy: _____

① I can't believe you can cook like a professional chef.
② Thank you for planning such a wonderful date for me.
③ It'll be fun to go on a trip together with all of our friends.
④ Both sound good to me, but let's try the cooking class first.
⑤ You'll definitely love camping because you like outdoor activities.

[16~17] 다음을 듣고, 물음에 답하시오.

16 여자가 하는 말의 주제로 가장 적절한 것은?   24006-0303

① importance of eating a healthy balanced diet
② best ways to buy seasonal fruit at local markets
③ how eating seasonal fruit can help us stay healthy
④ difficulties in finding fresh fruit in different seasons
⑤ different types of vitamins commonly found in fruits

17 언급된 과일이 <u>아닌</u> 것은?   24006-0304

① strawberries
② watermelons
③ grapes
④ apples
⑤ oranges

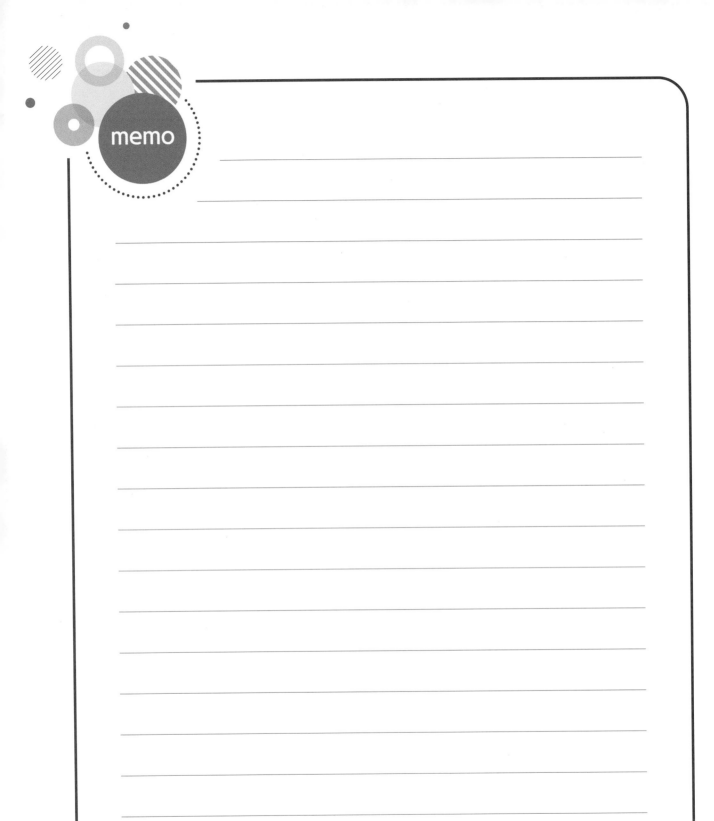

memo

한눈에 보는 정답

Part I 유형편

기출예제	01	02	03	04	05	06	07	08	09	10	11	12
01 ⑤	③	④	⑤	①	⑤	①						
02 ①	③	①	④	①	③	⑤						
03 ⑤	②	⑤	③	②	⑤	⑤						
04 ③	④	②	⑤	③	⑤	⑤						
05 ②	②	①	④	⑤	③	①						
06 ③	③	③	③	②	⑤	④						
07 ④	③	①	①	①	②	③						
08	⑤	④	④	③	②	⑤	④	④	③	③	⑤	②
09 ③	③	④	④	④	⑤	④						
10 ④	③	④	④	⑤	⑤	④						
11 ②	③	③	①	④	③	②						
12 ⑤	④	⑤	③	①	③	①	②	①	⑤	③	④	④
13 ⑤	②	⑤	①	①	⑤	⑤	④	④	②	③	④	②
14 ①	②	①	②	①	③	⑤						
15 ②,③	②	②	⑤	④	⑤	⑤	②	④				
16	③	③	③	③	⑤	④	①	④	④	⑤	⑤	③

Part II 소재편

기출예제	01	02	03	04	05	06	07	08	09	10	11	12
17 ②	④	①	⑤	②	④	⑤	⑤	①	①	②	③	⑤
18 ①	①	①	③	⑤	②	⑤	④	③	⑤	④	①	④
19 ③	①	④	⑤	③	③	⑤	⑤	③	①	③	⑤	⑤
20 ②	⑤	②	⑤	②	④	⑤	⑤	③	①	③	④	④
21 ①	⑤	①	⑤	②	⑤	②	④	③	⑤	②	①	④

Part III 실전편

01	02	03	04	05	06	07	08	09	10	11	12	13	14	15	16	17
22 ⑤	⑤	①	⑤	⑤	④	②	④	④	①	⑤	②	①	②	③	③	④
23 ①	⑤	③	④	④	②	⑤	④	⑤	④	④	②	⑤	②	③	③	④
24 ③	⑤	③	⑤	①	④	⑤	④	③	④	①	③	②	④	③	②	④
25 ③	④	③	④	②	②	①	④	④	②	②	③	④	⑤	③	③	⑤
26 ①	④	④	③	③	②	①	④	④	⑤	③	④	⑤	⑤	⑤	②	③
27 ④	③	①	③	⑤	⑤	④	③	②	①	⑤	②	④	②	④	③	③

고2~N수 수능 집중 로드맵

로드맵 흐름도

수능 입문	→	기출 / 연습	→	연계+연계 보완	→	심화 / 발전	→	모의고사

수능 입문
- 윤혜정의 개념/패턴의 나비효과
- 하루 6개 1등급 영어독해
- 수능 감(感)잡기
- 수능특강 Light
- 강의노트 수능개념

기출 / 연습
- 윤혜정의 기출의 나비효과
- 수능 기출의 미래
- 수능 기출의 미래 미니모의고사
- 수능특강Q 미니모의고사

연계+연계 보완
- 수능연계교재의 VOCA 1800
- 수능연계 기출 Vaccine VOCA 2200
- 연계
  - 강수 수능특강
  - 강수 수능완성
- 수능특강 사용설명서
- 수능특강 연계 기출
- 수능 영어 간접연계 서치라이트
- 수능완성 사용설명서

심화 / 발전
- 수능연계완성 3주 특강
- 박봄의 사회·문화 표 분석의 패턴

모의고사
- FINAL 실전모의고사
- 만점마무리 봉투모의고사
- 만점마무리 봉투모의고사 시즌2

시리즈 상세

구분	시리즈명	특징	수준	영역
수능 입문	윤혜정의 개념/패턴의 나비효과	윤혜정 선생님과 함께하는 수능 국어 개념/패턴 학습		국어
	하루 6개 1등급 영어독해	매일 꾸준한 기출문제 학습으로 완성하는 1등급 영어 독해		영어
	수능 감(感) 잡기	동일 소재·유형의 내신과 수능 문항 비교로 수능 입문		국/수/영
	수능특강 Light	수능 연계교재 학습 전 연계교재 입문서		영어
	수능개념	EBSi 대표 강사들과 함께하는 수능 개념 다지기		전 영역
기출/연습	윤혜정의 기출의 나비효과	윤혜정 선생님과 함께하는 까다로운 국어 기출 완전 정복		국어
	수능 기출의 미래	올해 수능에 딱 필요한 문제만 선별한 기출문제집		전 영역
	수능 기출의 미래 미니모의고사	부담없는 실전 훈련, 고품질 기출 미니모의고사		국/수/영
	수능특강Q 미니모의고사	매일 15분으로 연습하는 고품격 미니모의고사		전 영역
연계 + 연계 보완	수능특강	최신 수능 경향과 기출 유형을 분석한 종합 개념서		전 영역
	수능특강 사용설명서	수능 연계교재 수능특강의 지문·자료·문항 분석		국/영
	수능특강 연계 기출	수능특강 수록 작품·지문과 연결된 기출문제 학습		국어
	수능완성	유형 분석과 실전모의고사로 단련하는 문항 연습		전 영역
	수능완성 사용설명서	수능 연계교재 수능완성의 국어·영어 지문 분석		국/영
	수능 영어 간접연계 서치라이트	출제 가능성이 높은 핵심만 모아 구성한 간접연계 대비 교재		영어
	수능연계교재의 VOCA 1800	수능특강과 수능완성의 필수 중요 어휘 1800개 수록		영어
	수능연계 기출 Vaccine VOCA 2200	수능-EBS 연계 및 평가원 최다 빈출 어휘 선별 수록		영어
심화/발전	수능연계완성 3주 특강	단기간에 끝내는 수능 1등급 변별 문항 대비서		국/수/영
	박봄의 사회·문화 표 분석의 패턴	박봄 선생님과 사회·문화 표 분석 문항의 패턴 연습		사회탐구
모의고사	FINAL 실전모의고사	EBS 모의고사 중 최다 분량, 최다 과목 모의고사		전 영역
	만점마무리 봉투모의고사	실제 시험지 형태와 OMR 카드로 실전 훈련 모의고사		전 영역
	만점마무리 봉투모의고사 시즌2	수능 완벽대비 최종 봉투모의고사		국/수/영

나는 꿈꾸고 우리는 이룹니다.

서울여자대학교

세상을 이끌어갈 우리,

실천적 교육으로 키워낸 전문성과

바른 교육으로 길러낸 인성으로

미래를 선도합니다.

현재의 우리가 미래를 만들어 나갑니다.
Learn to Share, Share to Learn!

글로벌ICT인문융합학부 신설   사회수요에 맞춘 실무형 집중교육과정 마이크로전공 운영

2025학년도 신·편입학 모집

서울여자대학교
SEOUL WOMEN'S UNIVERSITY

입학처 http://admission.swu.ac.kr   입학상담 및 문의 02-970-5051~4

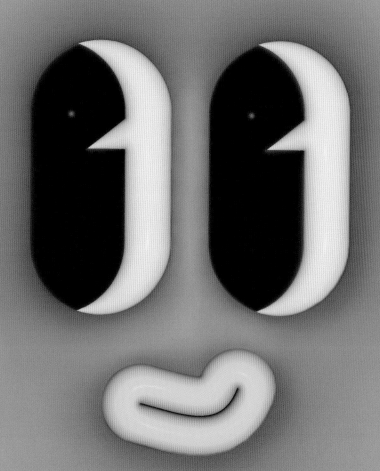

정답과 해설

수능특강

영어영역

영어듣기

2025학년도 수능 연계교재

본 교재는 대학수학능력시험을 준비하는 데 도움을 드리고자 영어과 교육과정을 토대로 제작된 교재입니다.
학교에서 선생님과 함께 교과서의 기본 개념을 충분히 익힌 후 활용하시면 더 큰 학습 효과를 얻을 수 있습니다.

EBS와 **교보문고**가 함께하는 듄듄한 스터디메이트!

듄듄한 할인 혜택을 담은 **학습용품**과 **참고서**를 한 번에!

기프트/도서/음반 추가 할인 쿠폰팩

COUPON
PACK

+QR코드를 스캔하시면 듄듄문고 쿠폰팩을 다운받을 수 있는 이벤트 페이지로 연결됩니다+

수능특강

영어영역 **영어듣기**

01강 목적

본문 8~11쪽

기출예제 ⑤

Exercises 01 ③ 02 ④ 03 ⑤ 04 ① 05 ⑤ 06 ①

기출 예제

본문 8쪽

정답 | ⑤

| Script & Translation |

W: Hello, Timberglade High School students. This is your P.E. teacher, Ms. Larsen. I'd like to announce that we're looking for volunteers to help with the charity soccer match next month. As you know, our best players will compete against our graduates at Ebanwood Stadium. Volunteers will show the audience to their seats and tidy up after the match. All the money from the ticket sales will get donated to the local children's hospital. This will be a great opportunity to get involved in helping children. Please don't hesitate to apply for this volunteer work at our charity soccer match. For more information, you can check the school website. Thank you.

여: 안녕하세요, Timberglade 고등학교 학생 여러분. 저는 여러분의 체육 교사인 Larsen 선생님입니다. 저는 우리가 다음 달에 있을 자선 축구 경기를 도울 자원봉사자를 찾고 있다는 것을 알려 드리고자 합니다. 여러분도 알고 있듯이, 우리의 최고의 선수들이 Ebanwood 경기장에서 우리 졸업생들과 겨룰 것입니다. 자원봉사자들은 관중들을 그들의 자리로 안내하고 경기 후에 정리 정돈을 할 것입니다. 티켓 판매로 얻은 모든 돈은 지역 어린이 병원에 기부될 것입니다. 이것은 어린이들을 돕는 일에 참여할 좋은 기회가 될 것입니다. 우리의 자선 축구 경기에서의 이 자원봉사 활동에 망설이지 말고 지원하세요. 더 많은 정보를 원하시면, 학교 웹사이트에서 확인할 수 있습니다. 감사합니다.

◐ Topic & Situation 자선 축구 경기 자원봉사자 모집

◐ Solution
다음 달에 있을 재학생 대표와 졸업생 간의 자선 축구 경기 행사에서 활동할 자원봉사자를 모집하고 있다는 것을 학생들에게 안내하고 있으므로, 여자가 하는 말의 목적으로 가장 적절한 것은 ⑤ '자선 축구 경기 자원봉사자 모집을 안내하려고'이다.

◐ Words & Phrases

P.E. 체육(physical education)   announce 알리다, 발표하다 charity 자선   compete 겨루다, 경쟁하다   graduate 졸업생   tidy up ~을 정리 정돈하다   donate 기부하다   hesitate 망설이다

Exercises

본문 10~11쪽

01

정답 | ③

| Script & Translation |

M: Good afternoon, listeners! This is Eric Moore, manager of the football league champion, Kingston Football Club. This past season was our first championship in our 17-year history. We'd like to share the joy of our club's historic victory with as many of you as possible. To celebrate our victory, we're going to hold a celebration full of colorful events. It will take place at Kingston Stadium at 2 p.m. next Saturday, and all of our players will enjoy various exciting events together with participants. Additionally, we will provide participants with some cool Kingston Football Club souvenirs. Anyone can enjoy the celebration for free by signing up on our website. I can't wait to see you at the event!

남: 안녕하세요, 청취자 여러분! 저는 축구 리그 챔피언 Kingston Football Club의 감독 Eric Moore입니다. 지난 시즌은 저희의 17년 역사상 첫 번째 우승이었습니다. 저희 클럽의 역사적인 승리의 기쁨을 가능한 한 많은 여러분과 나누고 싶습니다. 승리를 축하하기 위해, 저희는 다채로운 행사로 가득 찬 축하 행사를 열 것입니다. 그것은 다음 주 토요일 오후 2시에 Kingston Stadium에서 개최될 것이며, 저희 모든 선수들은 참가자들과 함께 다양하고 신나는 행사를 즐길 것입니다. 게다가, 저희는 참가하신 분들에게 몇 가지 멋진 Kingston Football Club 기념품을 드릴 것입니다. 저희 웹사이트에서 신청하시면 누구든지 축하 행사를 무료로 즐기실 수 있습니다. 저는 그 행사에서 여러분을 빨리 뵙고 싶습니다!

◐ Topic & Situation 축구 리그 우승 축하 행사 공지

◐ Solution
남자는 자신이 감독으로 있는 축구 클럽이 17년 역사상 처음으로 리그 우승을 차지한 것을 축하하기 위한 축하 행사의 일시와 장

소, 행사 내용과 신청 방법 등을 알리고 있으므로, 남자가 하는 말의 목적으로 가장 적절한 것은 ③ '축구 리그 우승 축하 행사를 공지하려고'이다.

◐ Words & Phrases

historic 역사적인　　celebrate 축하하다　　colorful 다채로운
participant 참가자　　souvenir 기념품

자가 하는 말의 목적으로 가장 적절한 것은 ④ '여행 글쓰기 대회 참가를 독려하려고'이다.

◐ Words & Phrases

geography 지리(학)　application 신청(서), 지원(서)　participate in ~에 참가하다　destination (여행 등의) 목적지　utilize 활용하다, 사용하다　hesitate 망설이다　sign up for ~에 등록[신청]하다

02 　　　　　　　　　　　정답 | ④

| Script & Translation |

W: Hello, Deerland High School students! This is your geography teacher, Ms. Barkley. Since I announced the application deadline for the Travel Writing Contest, which is April 6th, next Friday, only a few students have applied. Participating in the contest will be a great opportunity for you, not only to understand your travel destination better but also to utilize what you've learned in school. I remind you that all students can enter, and the top three winners will receive special prizes. So don't hesitate and sign up for the contest if you're considering it. Check the school website for more information on the contest. I hope many of you will join this great educational event. Thank you.

여: 안녕하세요, Deerland 고등학교 학생 여러분! 저는 여러분의 지리 교사, Barkley 선생님입니다. 4월 6일, 다음 주 금요일인 여행 글쓰기 대회의 신청 마감일을 제가 발표한 이후, 몇 명 안 되는 학생만이 신청했습니다. 대회에 참가하는 것은 여러분의 여행지를 더 잘 이해할 수 있을 뿐만 아니라 학교에서 배운 것을 활용할 수 있는 좋은 기회가 될 것입니다. 모든 학생이 참가할 수 있고, 상위 3명의 우승자들은 특별한 상을 받을 것임을 다시 한 번 알려 드립니다. 그러니 그것에 대해 생각하고 있다면 망설이지 말고 그 대회에 등록하세요. 대회에 대한 더 많은 정보를 얻으려면 학교 웹사이트를 확인하세요. 많은 학생들이 이 좋은 교육 행사에 참여하기를 바랍니다. 감사합니다.

◐ Topic & Situation 여행 글쓰기 대회 참가 독려

◐ Solution

여자는 여행 글쓰기 대회에 아직 몇 명 안 되는 학생만이 신청했다고 말하면서 망설이지 말고 대회에 등록하라고 했다. 따라서 여

03 　　　　　　　　　　　정답 | ⑤

| Script & Translation |

M: Hello, students! This is your physical education teacher, Mr. Nickelson. As you know, next semester is volleyball season. So this Friday, we're holding tryouts for new players to join the school volleyball team. The tryouts will take place from 3:00 p.m. to 5:00 p.m. in the school gym. No prior sign-up is required. Be sure to wear comfortable clothes and shoes. Also, bring a water bottle to stay refreshed during the tryouts. We're looking forward to seeing some fresh faces for the upcoming season! If you have any questions, please feel free to visit my office anytime. See you at the gym!

남: 안녕하세요, 학생 여러분! 저는 체육 교사 Nickelson 선생님입니다. 여러분이 아시다시피, 다음 학기는 배구 시즌입니다. 그래서 이번 주 금요일에, 우리는 학교 배구팀에 합류할 새로운 선수들을 뽑기 위해 선발 테스트를 개최할 것입니다. 선발 테스트는 학교 체육관에서 오후 3시부터 5시까지 열릴 것입니다. 사전 등록은 필요하지 않습니다. 반드시 편한 옷과 신발을 착용하세요. 또한, 선발 테스트 동안 상쾌함을 유지할 수 있도록 물병을 가져오세요. 우리는 다가오는 시즌에 일부 새로운 얼굴들을 볼 수 있기를 고대하고 있습니다! 어떠한 질문이라도 있으면, 언제든지 자유롭게 제 사무실을 방문해 주세요. 체육관에서 만나요!

◐ Topic & Situation 교내 배구팀 신규 선수 선발 테스트 안내

◐ Solution

남자는 다음 학기가 배구 시즌이고, 학교 배구팀에 합류할 새로운 선수들을 뽑기 위해 선발 테스트를 개최할 것이라고 하면서, 선발 테스트 일정과 참가 복장 및 준비물 등에 대해 안내하고 있다. 따라서 남자가 하는 말의 목적으로 가장 적절한 것은 ⑤ '교내 배구팀의 신규 선수 선발 테스트를 안내하려고'이다.

Words & Phrases

physical education 체육   semester 학기   volleyball 배구
tryout 선발 테스트   look forward to ~을 고대하다   feel free to
do 자유롭게 ~하다

Words & Phrases

aquarium 수족관   brand-new 아주 새로운   octopus 문어
observe 관찰하다   graceful 우아한   fascinating 매력적인
behavior 행동   showcase 보여 주다, 전시하다   accurately 정확
하게   recreate 재현하다, 되살리다   seaweed 해초, 해조류
resemble 닮다, 비슷하다   surroundings 환경   opportunity 기회
intelligent 지적인, 똑똑한   marvel 경이로움

04
정답 | ①

| Script & Translation |

W: Attention, visitors. I'm Taylor Gibson, the general manager of Garland Aquarium, with exciting news for you. Our brand-new octopus exhibit is now open! Make sure to visit and observe these incredible creatures' graceful movements and fascinating behaviors up close. The exhibit showcases an accurately recreated underwater ecosystem, including rocks, seaweed, and carefully designed hiding spots that resemble the natural surroundings of octopuses. It's a unique opportunity to learn about these intelligent beings and appreciate the wonders of their world. Enjoy this extraordinary experience that brings you closer to the marvels of the ocean!

여: 주목해 주세요, 방문객 여러분. 저는 Garland Aquarium의 총괄 매니저인 Taylor Gibson으로 여러분에게 신나는 소식을 전합니다. 우리의 아주 새로운 문어 전시회가 이제 문을 열었습니다! 꼭 방문하셔서 이 놀라운 생물들의 우아한 움직임과 매력적인 행동을 바로 가까이서 관찰하세요. 전시회는 암석, 해초, 그리고 문어의 자연환경을 닮은 세심하게 설계된 은신처를 포함하여 정확하게 재현된 수중 생태계를 보여 줍니다. 그것은 이 지적인 존재들에 대해 배우고 그들 세계의 경이로움을 감상할 수 있는 아주 특별한 기회입니다. 여러분을 바다의 경이로움에 더 가깝게 데려가 주는 이 놀라운 경험을 즐기세요!

● Topic & Situation 문어 전시회 홍보

● Solution

여자는 새로운 문어 전시회 개최를 알리면서, 이 놀라운 생물들의 우아한 움직임과 매력적인 행동을 가까이서 관찰하라고 권유하고 있고, 전시회의 특징에 대한 설명과 더불어 이 전시회가 지적인 존재들에 대해 배우고 그들 세계의 경이로움을 감상할 수 있는 아주 특별한 기회라고 말하고 있다. 따라서 여자가 하는 말의 목적으로 가장 적절한 것은 ① '새로 열린 문어 전시회를 홍보하려고'이다.

05
정답 | ⑤

| Script & Translation |

M: Good morning, students. This is your principal, Mr. Kim. I want to inform you that due to the really bad air quality outside, it's important that you do not open the windows in the classrooms. Bad air containing fine dust particles can enter the classrooms through open windows and cause serious health problems, especially for those who have breathing difficulties. To maintain the health and safety of all students and faculty members, we're working hard to improve the air quality inside the classrooms. Opening the windows and letting bad air inside works against these efforts. So please do not open them for the sake of your health. Thank you for your cooperation.

남: 좋은 아침입니다, 학생 여러분. 여러분의 교장인 Kim 선생님입니다. 바깥 공기의 질이 매우 나쁘기 때문에, 저는 여러분들에게 교실 창문을 열지 않는 것이 중요하다는 것을 알려 드리고 싶습니다. 미세 먼지 입자가 포함된 나쁜 공기가 열린 창문을 통해 교실로 들어올 수 있고 특히 호흡 곤란을 겪는 사람들에게 심각한 건강 문제를 일으킬 수 있습니다. 모든 학생과 교직원의 건강과 안전을 지키기 위해, 우리는 교실 안 공기의 질을 향상시키려고 열심히 노력하고 있습니다. 창문을 열어 나쁜 공기가 실내로 들어오게 하는 것은 이런 노력에 역행하는 것입니다. 그러니 여러분의 건강을 위해서 창문을 열지 마세요. 여러분의 협조에 감사합니다.

● Topic & Situation 나쁜 공기의 유입을 막기 위한 교실 창문 닫기

● Solution

남자는 바깥 공기의 질이 매우 나쁘고, 미세 먼지 입자가 창문을 통해 교실로 들어와 건강을 해칠 수 있으므로, 교실 창문을 닫아

외부 공기가 들어오지 않도록 해 달라고 당부하고 있다. 따라서 남자가 하는 말의 목적으로 가장 적절한 것은 ⑤ '나쁜 공기 유입을 막기 위한 창문 닫기를 당부하려고'이다.

◑ Words & Phrases

principal 교장 quality 질 fine dust 미세 먼지 particle 입자 breathing 호흡, 숨쉬기 faculty member 교직원 for the sake of ~을 위해서

---

06 정답 | ①

| Script & Translation |

W: Hello, residents! I'm Sarah Hawkins representing the Cozy Apartment Management Office. Recently, residents have told us that the stairs leading to the elevators in the underground parking lot are worn out and slippery. At the last general meeting, some residents shared that they had fallen on the stairs. So, we're renovating all the stairways in the underground parking lot next week. They will be renovated one by one from Monday to Thursday. We request that, during this period, you use one of the stairways that are not under renovation when accessing the underground parking area. We're sorry for any inconvenience and genuinely appreciate your cooperation.

여: 안녕하세요, 입주민 여러분! 저는 Cozy 아파트 관리 사무소를 대표하는 Sarah Hawkins입니다. 최근 주민들께서 지하 주차장 내 엘리베이터로 통하는 계단이 낡고 미끄럽다고 저희에게 말씀해 주셨습니다. 지난 총회에서 일부 주민들은 계단에서 넘어지셨다는 사실을 전해 주셨습니다. 그래서 다음 주에 지하 주차장의 모든 계단들을 보수할 것입니다. 계단들은 월요일부터 목요일까지 하나씩 차례차례 보수될 것입니다. 이 기간 동안 지하 주차장에 접근하실 때 보수 공사를 진행하지 않는 계단들 중 하나를 이용해 주시기를 요청합니다. 불편을 끼쳐 드려 죄송하고 협조에 진심으로 감사드립니다.

◑ Topic & Situation 아파트 지하 주차장 내 계단 보수 공사 공지

◑ Solution

여자는 아파트 지하 주차장의 계단이 낡고 미끄럽다는 주민들의 민원과 일부 주민의 낙상 사고 제보로 인해 지하 주차장 내 계단 보수 공사가 진행될 예정이라고 말하며 그와 관련된 일정 및 요청

사항을 공지하고 있다. 따라서 여기서 하는 말의 목적으로 가장 적절한 것은 ① '지하 주차장 내 계단 보수 공사를 공지하려고'이다.

◑ Words & Phrases

resident 입주민, 거주민 represent 대표하다 stair 계단 worn out 닳은, 마모된 slippery 미끄러운 renovate 보수하다 access 접근하다 genuinely 진심으로

Dictations 본문 9, 12~13쪽

기출 예제
❶ charity soccer match
❷ get donated
❸ volunteer work

01 ❶ share the joy
❷ various exciting events
❸ by signing up

02 ❶ announced the application deadline
❷ Participating in the contest
❸ receive special prizes

03 ❶ holding tryouts
❷ bring a water bottle
❸ feel free to visit

04 ❶ Make sure to visit
❷ carefully designed hiding spots
❸ this extraordinary experience

05 ❶ bad air quality outside
❷ cause serious health problems
❸ for the sake of

06 ❶ worn out and slippery
❷ renovating all the stairways
❸ for any inconvenience

02강 의견

본문 14~17쪽

기출예제 ①

Exercises 01 ③ 02 ① 03 ④ 04 ① 05 ③ 06 ⑤

기출 예제

본문 14쪽

정답 | ①

| Script & Translation |

M: Ellie, you seem down. What's on your mind?

W: Well, Dad, Tiffany and I got into an argument at school.

M: You two are so close. What happened?

W: During our student council meeting, she was taking too long to make her point, so I had to jump in to finish her sentence.

M: Oh, no. You shouldn't interrupt someone when they're in the middle of speaking.

W: I know. But she kept talking about so many details.

M: Still, that's not polite. How would you feel if you were her?

W: I'd probably be upset.

M: Exactly. That's why when somebody's talking, you shouldn't cut them off.

W: You're right. I guess I didn't see things from her point of view.

M: So, how about letting others finish what they're saying next time?

W: Okay. Thanks, Dad. I'll apologize to her tomorrow.

남: Ellie, 기분이 안 좋아 보이는구나. 무슨 일이야?

여: 저, 아빠, Tiffany와 제가 학교에서 말다툼했어요.

남: 너희 둘은 아주 친하잖아. 무슨 일이 있었던 거니?

여: 우리 학생회 회의 중에, 그녀가 자신의 주장을 말하는 데 너무 오래 걸려서, 제가 그녀의 말을 끝내기 위해 끼어들어야 했어요.

남: 오, 안 돼. 누군가가 한창 말하는 중에 방해해서는 안 돼.

여: 알아요. 하지만 그녀는 너무 많은 세세한 부분에 대해 계속 얘기했어요.

남: 그래도 그건 예의가 아니야. 네가 그 애라면 기분이 어떨 것 같니?

여: 아마 화가 날 거예요.

남: 맞아. 그래서 누군가가 말하고 있을 때 말을 끊으면 안 돼.

여: 아빠 말씀이 맞아요. 제가 그녀의 입장에서 생각하지 못했던 것 같아요.

남: 그럼, 다음에는 다른 사람들이 하고 있는 말을 끝마치도록 하는 게 어떨까?

여: 알겠어요. 고마워요, 아빠. 내일 그녀에게 사과할게요.

○ Topic & Situation 상대방이 말하고 있을 때 방해하지 않기

○ Solution

학생회 회의 중에 너무 오래 얘기하는 친구의 말을 도중에 끊어서 그 친구와 말다툼했다는 여자의 말을 듣고 남자는 누군가가 말하고 있을 때 끼어들어 중단시키는 것은 예의가 아니므로 하지 말아야 한다고 말하고 있다. 따라서 남자의 의견으로 가장 적절한 것은 ① '상대방이 말할 때는 말을 끊지 말아야 한다.'이다.

○ Words & Phrases

argument 말다툼 student council 학생회 point 주장, 의견
jump in (대화에 불쑥) 끼어들다 interrupt 방해하다 in the middle of 한창 ~하는 중에 cut ~ off ~의 말을 끊다 point of view 입장, 관점 apologize 사과하다

Exercises

본문 16~17쪽

01

정답 | ③

| Script & Translation |

M: Mom, I'm so excited about our upcoming trip to Mt. Everfrost! I can't wait to enjoy the thrill of outdoor winter adventures.

W: Me neither! The snowy landscapes there will be absolutely breathtaking. Have you started packing yet?

M: Yes. I've got all my clothes packed.

W: Good for you! How about sunscreen?

M: Yes, I packed some. Even though it's cold, it's going to be really sunny.

W: What about your water bottle?

M: I don't think I'll need it. When it's cold, I don't usually feel thirsty.

W: You know, cold air can dry you out quickly. It's crucial to drink lots of water even in the cold.

M: Oh, I didn't know that. I only thought it was important in hot weather.

W: Most people think that way. It's easy to forget to drink water when it's cold, but our bodies need water to maintain our fluid levels.

M: Thanks! I had no idea. I'll pack my water bottle right away.

W: Of course. I'm glad I could help.

남: 엄마, 저는 다가오는 Everfrost산 여행에 너무 설레요! 빨리 겨울 야외 모험의 짜릿함을 즐기고 싶어요.

여: 나도 그래! 그곳의 눈 덮인 풍경은 정말 숨 막히게 아름다울 거야. 벌써 짐을 싸기 시작했니?

남: 네. 옷은 다 쌌어요.

여: 잘했네! 자외선 차단제는?

남: 네, 좀 쌌어요. 날씨는 춥지만, 정말 화창할 거예요.

여: 네 물병은?

남: 그건 필요 없을 것 같아요. 추울 때, 저는 보통 목마르지 않아요.

여: 있잖아, 차가운 공기는 빠르게 몸을 건조하게 만들 수 있어. 추운 날씨에도 물을 많이 마시는 게 중요하단다.

남: 아, 그건 몰랐어요. 저는 그것이 더운 날씨에서만 중요하다고 생각했어요.

여: 대부분의 사람들이 그렇게 생각해. 추울 때 물 마시는 걸 잊기 쉬운데, 우리의 몸은 수분 수준을 유지하기 위해 물이 필요해.

남: 고마워요! 저는 전혀 몰랐어요. 지금 바로 제 물병을 쌀게요.

여: 당연히 그래야지. 도울 수 있어서 기쁘구나.

◐ Topic & Situation 추운 날씨에 수분 섭취의 중요성

◐ Solution

남자는 겨울 야외 모험을 할 수 있는 Everfrost산 여행을 위해 짐을 싸면서 추운 날씨에는 목마르지 않으니 물병은 필요 없을 거라고 말하고, 여자는 차가운 공기가 빨리 몸을 건조하게 만들 수 있으므로 추운 날씨에도 물을 많이 마시는 것이 중요하다고 설명하고 있다. 따라서 여자의 의견으로 가장 적절한 것은 ③ '추운 날씨에도 충분한 수분 섭취가 중요하다.'이다.

◐ Words & Phrases

upcoming 다가오는 thrill 짜릿함, 전율 landscape 풍경, 경치 breathtaking 숨 막히게 아름다운 pack 싸다, 꾸리다 dry ~ out ~을 건조하게 만들다 crucial 중요한 maintain 유지하다 fluid 수분, 액체

02

정답 | ①

| Script & Translation |

M: Hey, Olivia, is something wrong? You look worried.

W: Hi, Charles. I'm concerned about my son. He lacks confidence and is even afraid to participate in class discussions.

M: Have you tried helping him?

W: I want to, but I'm not sure how.

M: How about getting him involved in physical activities? It can help him to enhance his self-esteem.

W: Really?

M: Yes, physical activity causes the release of endorphins and enhances overall well-being, which can lead to a boost in confidence.

W: Those are good points, but he's not really into sports.

M: That's fine. It could be as simple as going for a walk, bike ride, or dancing.

W: That's a good idea. I'll try to encourage him to be more active.

M: Great! Just give it a try. It's surprising how much exercise can boost people's confidence.

W: Thanks for the suggestion.

남: 안녕, Olivia, 무슨 일 있니? 걱정이 있어 보여.

여: 안녕, Charles. 내 아들 때문에 걱정이야. 그는 자신감이 부족하고 학급 토론에 참여하는 것조차 두려워해.

남: 그를 도와주려고 노력해 봤니?

여: 그러고 싶지만, 어떻게 해야 할지 잘 모르겠어.

남: 그를 신체 활동에 참여시켜 보는 건 어때? 그것은 그가 자존감을 높이는 데 도움이 될 수 있어.

여: 정말?

남: 응, 신체 활동은 엔도르핀을 분출시키고 전반적인 행복감을 높여서, 자신감 향상으로 이어질 수 있어.

여: 좋은 의견이기는 한데, 그는 스포츠에 별로 관심이 없어.

남: 괜찮아. 산책하러 가기, 자전거 타기, 또는 춤추기와 같이 간단한 것이어도 돼.

여: 좋은 생각이야. 그가 더 활동적으로 되도록 격려해 봐야겠어.

남: 좋아! 그냥 한 번 시도해 봐. 운동이 사람들의 자신감을 얼마나 많이 높일 수 있는지는 놀라워.

여: 제안해 줘서 고마워.

◐ Topic & Situation 자신감과 신체 활동의 관계

◐ Solution

남자는 자신감이 부족한 아들 때문에 걱정이 된다는 여자에게 아들을 신체 활동에 참여시켜 보기를 권하면서, 신체 활동은 엔도르핀을 분출시키고 전반적인 행복감을 높여서 자신감 향상으로 이어질 수 있다고 설명하고 있다. 따라서 남자의 의견으로 가장 적

절한 것은 ① '신체 활동은 자신감 향상에 도움이 된다.'이다.

▶ **Words & Phrases**

concerned 걱정스러운   lack ~이 부족하다   confidence 자신감
participate in ~에 참여하다   involve 참여시키다   enhance 높이
다, 향상하다   self-esteem 자존감   release 분출   endorphin 엔도
르핀   lead to ~로 이어지다   boost 향상, 증진; 높이다   suggestion
제안

03

정답 | ④

| Script & Translation |

W: Paul, where are you going with Max?

M: I'm taking him out to a nearby park for a walk, Mom.

W: Good, but make sure to put a leash on him while you
walk him.

M: Oh, can't I just let him walk alongside me without a
leash?

W: It's best to use a leash on walks outside, Paul.

M: Why is that?

W: Using a leash is basic etiquette for dog owners. It
prevents our dog from jumping up on people we
encounter.

M: Max just gets excited around people. That's all.

W: Not everyone feels comfortable around our dog,
Paul. Using a leash keeps Max under control and
prevents any surprises for others on the street.

M: I see your point, Mom.

W: Additionally, it's the law that dogs must be leashed at
all times in public areas, so it's important to follow
the rules.

M: I understand now. I'll make sure to put a leash on
him before we head out.

여: Paul, Max랑 어디에 가니?

남: 그를 데리고 근처 공원에 산책하러 나가요, 엄마.

여: 좋아, 하지만 산책시킬 때 그에게 목줄을 착용시키렴.

남: 아, 그냥 목줄 없이 제 곁에서 걷도록 두면 안 될까요?

여: 바깥에서 산책시킬 때는 목줄을 사용하는 것이 최선이야,
Paul.

남: 왜 그렇죠?

여: 목줄을 사용하는 것은 반려견 주인의 기본 예절이야. 그것은
우리 반려견이 맞닥뜨리는 사람들에게 달려 드는 것을 막아 준
단다.

남: Max는 그저 사람들이 주변에 있을 때 신이 나는 거예요. 그
것뿐이에요.

여: 모든 사람이 주변에 우리 반려견이 있는 것을 편하게 느끼지는
않아, Paul. 목줄을 사용하면 Max를 통제하고 길에서 다른
사람들을 놀라게 하는 것을 막을 수 있어.

남: 무슨 말씀인지 알겠어요, 엄마.

여: 게다가, 공공장소에서는 반려견이 항상 목줄을 매고 있어야
하는 것이 법이어서, 규칙을 따르는 것이 중요해.

남: 이제 알겠어요. 나가기 전에 꼭 그에게 목줄을 착용시킬게요.

▶ **Topic & Situation** 반려견 산책 시 목줄 착용의 중요성

▶ **Solution**

남자가 반려견을 산책시키러 공원에 간다고 하자, 여자는 반드시
목줄을 착용시키라고 당부한다. 남자가 꼭 그래야 하냐고 되묻자,
여자는 반려견이 다른 사람에게 달려 드는 것을 막기 위해 목줄을
착용시켜야 하며, 그것은 법으로도 정해진 규칙이라고 말한다. 따
라서 여자의 의견으로 가장 적절한 것은 ④ '반려견을 산책시킬
때는 항상 목줄을 착용시켜야 한다.'이다.

▶ **Words & Phrases**

walk 산책; (동물을) 산책시키다   leash (동물 등을 매는) 목줄, 가죽끈;
(특히 개를) 줄에 매어 두다   encounter 맞닥뜨리다

04

정답 | ①

| Script & Translation |

W: Dad, could you help me enroll in a class to take next
semester?

M: Sure, honey. What are you considering?

W: I'm thinking about enrolling in Advanced Calculus.
I'm interested in it, but I've heard it's a really
challenging course.

M: Well, it's true that it's a tough course. However, I
believe taking on such challenges can lead to
personal growth.

W: Do you really think so?

M: Yes. You can learn a lot about yourself by doing
something that is challenging. That's why I think you
should take the advanced course.

W: But what if I get a bad grade?

M: Grades aren't everything. If you don't give up and
try, you can succeed in many areas of your life in the
long run.

W: I hadn't thought about it that way.

M: It can also boost your self-confidence and provide a sense of accomplishment, ultimately helping you become a better person.

W: Okay, Dad. Thanks for your support.

여: 아빠, 다음 학기에 제가 수강할 수업에 등록하는 데 도움을 주시겠어요?

남: 물론이지, 얘야. 무엇을 고려 중이니?

여: 심화 미적분학에 등록하는 것에 대해 생각 중이에요. 저는 그것에 관심이 있지만, 그것은 정말로 힘든 과목이라고 들었어요.

남: 음, 그것이 힘든 과목인 것은 사실이야. 하지만 그런 도전을 하는 것이 개인적 성장으로 이어질 수 있다고 난 믿어.

여: 정말로 그렇게 생각하세요?

남: 그럼. 도전적인 일을 함으로써 너 자신에 대해 많이 배울 수 있어. 그렇기 때문에 네가 그 심화 과목을 들어야 한다고 생각해.

여: 하지만 나쁜 성적을 받으면 어떡해요?

남: 성적이 전부는 아니야. 포기하지 않고 시도한다면, 너는 결국 네 인생의 다양한 영역에서 성공할 수 있어.

여: 전 그것에 대해 그런 식으로 생각해 본 적은 없어요.

남: 그것은 또한 너의 자신감을 북돋아 주고 성취감을 제공해 주어서, 결국 네가 더 나은 사람이 되는 데 도움이 될 수 있을 거야.

여: 알았어요, 아빠. 도움에 감사드려요.

● **Topic & Situation** 힘든 과목 수강으로 얻을 수 있는 것

● **Solution**
여자가 남자에게 다음 학기 과목 수강에 대해 조언을 구하며, 심화 미적분학이라는 힘든 과목을 등록해야 할지 고민이 된다고 하자, 남자는 여자에게 힘든 과목의 수강에 도전하면 결국 개인의 성장으로 이어질 수 있다고 말한다. 따라서 남자의 의견으로 가장 적절한 것은 ① '힘든 과목의 수강이 개인의 성장에 도움이 된다.'이다.

● **Words & Phrases**
semester 학기 Advanced Calculus 심화 미적분학 challenging 힘든, 도전적인 tough 어려운 in the long run 결국 boost 북돋아 주다 self-confidence 자신감 accomplishment 성취 ultimately 결국

05 정답 | ③

| Script & Translation |

W: Aiden, you look pretty tired. You've got dark circles under your eyes.

M: Hey, Claire. I've been having trouble sleeping lately.

W: Sorry to hear that. Do you know why?

M: No. I'm not sure. It started happening recently.

W: Maybe it's due to the recent cold weather. It's hard to sleep when your feet are cold.

M: Hmm. You may be right. My feet have been uncomfortably cold at night.

W: It's possible. These days, I wear socks to bed, and it helps me sleep better.

M: I'm just used to sleeping barefoot.

W: I understand, but try wearing socks. It can warm your feet and improve your sleep.

M: Thanks, I'll give it a shot.

W: I'm sure it will make a difference.

여: Aiden, 꽤 피곤해 보이네. 눈 밑에 다크서클이 생겼어.

남: 어, Claire. 내가 요즘 잠을 잘 자지 못해.

여: 안됐네. 왜 그런지 알아?

남: 아니. 잘 모르겠어. 최근에 그런 일이 일어나기 시작했어.

여: 어쩌면 최근 추운 날씨 때문인지도 몰라. 발이 차가우면 잠을 자기가 힘들어.

남: 흠. 네 말이 맞을지도 몰라. 밤에 내 발이 불편할 정도로 차가웠어.

여: 그럴 수 있어. 요즘 나는 양말을 신고 자는데, 그것이 내가 잠을 더 잘 자게 도와줘.

남: 나는 그냥 맨발로 자는 게 익숙해.

여: 이해하지만, 양말을 신어 봐. 그러면 발을 따뜻하게 해서 수면을 개선할 수 있어.

남: 고마워, 한번 해 볼게.

여: 분명 그것이 변화를 가져올 거야.

● **Topic & Situation** 양말 신고 자기

● **Solution**
남자가 요즘 잠을 잘 자지 못한다고 하자, 여자는 최근의 추운 날씨 때문일 수 있다며 양말을 신고 자면 발을 따뜻하게 해 주어 잠을 더 잘 잘 수 있을 거라고 말한다. 따라서 여자의 의견으로 가장 적절한 것은 ③ '양말을 신고 자면 발을 따뜻하게 하여 더 잘 잘 수 있다.'이다.

● **Words & Phrases**
due to ~ 때문에 uncomfortably 불편하게 be used to ~에 익숙하다 barefoot 맨발로 give ~ a shot ~을 한번 해 보다 make a difference 변화를 가져오다

06

| Script & Translation |

M: Honey. Can you come help me make some bread?

W: Sure. How can I help?

M: Can you measure out the ingredients? Everything you need is over there.

W: I can, but is it really necessary to measure? I usually just roughly estimate how much to add by sight.

M: Please measure. It's more accurate and better to bake properly.

W: Is baking bread really different from cooking other dishes? I never measure when I make soup, and it turns out fine.

M: Yes, it can be quite different. With baking, if you're off by even a little bit, it can affect the texture and flavor of the bread.

W: Oh, I had no idea. So, how would you like me to measure?

M: Use the kitchen scale for the dry ingredients and measuring cups and spoons for the liquids.

W: Okay, I got it.

M: Baking is like chemistry, and accurate measurements are the key to success.

남: 여보. 와서 제가 빵 만드는 것 좀 도와줄래요?

여: 물론이죠. 어떻게 도와줄까요?

남: 재료를 좀 계량해 줄래요? 필요한 모든 것이 저기 있어요.

여: 네, 그런데 꼭 계량해야 할까요? 저는 보통 눈으로 얼마를 넣어야 할지 그냥 대강 어림하거든요.

남: 계량해 주세요. 그게 제대로 제빵을 하는 데 더 정확하고 더 좋아요.

여: 빵을 굽는 것이 다른 음식을 요리하는 것과 정말 다른가요? 저는 수프를 만들 때 계량하지 않는데 괜찮던데요.

남: 네, 꽤 다를 수 있어요. 제빵은 조금이라도 어긋나면 빵의 질감과 풍미에 영향을 줄 수 있거든요.

여: 아, 전혀 몰랐어요. 그럼, 어떻게 계량할까요?

남: 마른 재료는 주방 저울을 사용하고 액체는 계량컵과 스푼을 사용하세요.

여: 네, 알겠어요.

남: 제빵은 화학과 같아서 정확한 계량이 성공의 비결이에요.

◐ Topic & Situation 제빵과 정확한 계량

◐ Solution

여자가 재료를 계량하지 않고 보통 눈으로 양을 어림한다고 하자, 남자는 계량하는 것이 제대로 제빵을 하는 데 더 정확하고 더 좋다고 말하며 정확한 계량이 제빵 성공의 비결이라고 강조한다. 따라서 남자의 의견으로 가장 적절한 것은 ⑤ '제빵을 할 때 정확한 계량이 중요하다.'이다.

◐ Words & Phrases

measure 계량하다   ingredient 재료   roughly 대강, 대략
estimate 어림하다, 추정하다   texture 질감, 식감   flavor 풍미
kitchen scale 주방 저울   liquid 액체   chemistry 화학

> **Dictations**
> 본문 15, 18~19쪽
>
> 기출 ❶ got into an argument
> 예제 ❷ about so many details
> ❸ letting others finish
> 01 ❶ all my clothes packed
> ❷ dry you out quickly
> ❸ pack my water bottle
> 02 ❶ He lacks confidence
> ❷ not really into sports
> ❸ how much exercise
> 03 ❶ put a leash on him
> ❷ basic etiquette for dog owners
> ❸ prevents any surprises
> 04 ❶ a really challenging course
> ❷ take the advanced course
> ❸ sense of accomplishment
> 05 ❶ having trouble sleeping
> ❷ your feet are cold
> ❸ wear socks to bed
> 06 ❶ measure out the ingredients
> ❷ more accurate and better
> ❸ the texture and flavor
> ❹ accurate measurements

03강 관계

본문 20~23쪽

기출예제 ⑤

Exercises 01 ② 02 ⑤ 03 ③ 04 ② 05 ⑤ 06 ⑤

기출 예제

본문 20쪽

정답 | ⑤

| Script & Translation |

[Telephone rings.]

W: Good morning. Cathy Sullivan speaking.

M: Hello, Ms. Sullivan. This is Josh Gordon from Gordon's Fresh Fruits.

W: Hi, Mr. Gordon! How's this year's fruit harvest?

M: This has been the best year since I started my farm. I've already begun packaging the summer fruits for sale.

W: That's good to hear. How may I help you today?

M: Well, I'd like to promote my fruit farm more actively on the Internet.

W: In that case, we can make a digital banner and display it on personal blogs and social networking sites.

M: That sounds like a good idea.

W: Our advertisements will definitely help you attract new customers and increase your fruit sales.

M: Sounds wonderful. When can you start promoting my farm?

W: I'll ask my boss and call you back.

M: Great. Thank you.

[전화벨이 울린다.]

여: 안녕하세요. Cathy Sullivan입니다.

남: 안녕하세요, Sullivan 씨. Gordon's Fresh Fruits의 Josh Gordon입니다.

여: 안녕하세요, Gordon 씨! 올해 과일 수확은 어떤가요?

남: 제가 농장을 시작한 이후로 올해가 최고의 해예요. 저는 벌써 판매용 여름 과일을 포장하기 시작했어요.

여: 좋은 소식이네요. 오늘은 어떻게 도와드릴까요?

남: 음, 저는 제 과일 농장을 인터넷에 더 적극적으로 홍보하고 싶어요.

여: 그런 경우라면, 저희가 디지털 배너를 만들어서 그것을 개인 블로그와 소셜 네트워킹 사이트에 게시할 수 있어요.

남: 좋은 생각인 것 같네요.

여: 저희 광고가 틀림없이 새로운 손님을 유치하고 고객님의 과일 판매를 늘리는 데 도움이 될 거예요.

남: 정말 괜찮은 듯하네요. 언제 제 농장을 홍보하는 것을 시작할 수 있나요?

여: 제 상사에게 물어 보고 다시 전화 드릴게요.

남: 좋아요. 감사합니다.

◑ Topic & Situation 과일 농장 홍보

◑ Solution

남자는 농장을 운영하고 있으며, 판매용 여름 과일을 포장하기 시작했고, 자신의 과일 농장을 인터넷에 더 적극적으로 홍보하고 싶어 한다고 말했고, 여자는 디지털 배너를 만들어 개인 블로그와 소셜 네트워킹 사이트에 게시하여 농장을 홍보할 수 있다고 말했다. 따라서 두 사람의 관계를 가장 잘 나타낸 것은 ⑤ '홍보 회사 직원 — 과일 농장 주인'이다.

◑ Words & Phrases

harvest 수확, 작황   package 포장하다   promote 홍보하다
actively 적극적으로   definitely 틀림없이, 분명히

Exercises

본문 22~23쪽

01

정답 | ②

| Script & Translation |

W: Thank you for taking the time to visit, Mr. Brooks, especially with your busy schedule for charity auction preparation.

M: My pleasure, Mrs. Kristy. *[Pause]* Wow! This is such a lovely art classroom!

W: Thank you.

M: I also want to express my gratitude for your generous offer to donate artwork to our charity.

W: I'm so happy to help. These are the paintings I mentioned over the phone.

M: Oh, they are really nice.

W: My art students are excited to offer them to your charity.

M: Please thank them for me. Their paintings are going to be popular at the auction.

W: I'm pleased to hear that. By the way, some of my fellow teachers are interested in volunteering.

M: That would be greatly appreciated.

W: Could you provide me with a poster for the auction? I'll post it on the school bulletin board.

M: Sure. I'll get one from the car.

여: 특히 자선 경매 준비로 바쁘신 일정에도 시간을 내어 방문해 주셔서 감사합니다, Brooks 씨.

남: 저도 기쁩니다, Kristy 선생님. *[잠시 후]* 와! 이곳은 정말 아름다운 미술 교실이에요!

여: 감사합니다.

남: 저희 자선 단체에 미술품을 기증해 주시겠다는 후한 제안에 대해서도 감사의 말씀을 드리고 싶습니다.

여: 도와드리게 되어 정말 기쁩니다. 이것들이 제가 전화로 말씀드린 그림들입니다.

남: 오, 정말 좋은 그림들이에요.

여: 제 미술반 학생들이 그것들을 당신의 자선 단체에 드리게 되어 무척 신이 나 있습니다.

남: 저 대신 그들에게 감사 인사를 부탁드립니다. 그들의 그림은 경매에서 인기를 끌 것입니다.

여: 그렇다고 하시니 기쁩니다. 그런데, 제 동료 선생님 몇 분이 자원하여 일을 맡는 데에 관심이 많으십니다.

남: 그렇게 해주시면 정말 감사하겠습니다.

여: 경매 포스터를 한 부 주시겠어요? 학교 게시판에 게시하겠습니다.

남: 물론입니다. 차에서 하나 가져올게요.

◐ Topic & Situation 자선 경매 행사를 위한 미술반 학생들의 작품 기증

◐ Solution
남자는 자선 경매를 준비하고 있고, 여자는 미술반에서 지도하는 학생들이 그린 그림들을 남자의 자선 단체에 기증하고, 일부 동료 교사들이 경매에 자원봉사자로 참여하기를 원한다고 전하며, 남자에게 학교에 게시할 경매 포스터를 달라고 요청하고 있으므로, 두 사람의 관계를 가장 잘 나타낸 것은 ② '미술 교사 – 자선 경매 관계자'이다.

◐ Words & Phrases
charity 자선 행위, 자선 단체   auction 경매   gratitude 감사
generous 후한, 관대한   donate 기증하다, 기부하다   mention 말하다, 언급하다   post 게시하다

02

| Script & Translation |

W: Welcome to Newton High School, Mr. Moore. I'm Ms. Johnson, who called you.

M: Nice to meet you, and thank you for inviting me.

W: Thank you for coming. Shall we go to the conference room?

M: Sure. Is that where I'm going to give my lecture today?

W: Yes. Our school math club students are waiting for you there.

M: Okay. So are you in charge of the club?

W: Yes. I'm managing the club students.

M: I see. I hope my lecture can inspire the students today.

W: Definitely. Many of my students you'll speak to want to be mathematicians in the future.

M: Great to hear that. I'm so happy to share my experiences as a mathematician with the enthusiastic students.

W: I'm sure that they're going to greatly appreciate hearing your story.

여: Newton 고등학교에 오신 걸 환영합니다, Moore 씨. 제가 전화드렸던 Johnson입니다.

남: 만나서 반갑고, 초대해 주셔서 감사합니다.

여: 와 주셔서 감사합니다. 회의실로 가실까요?

남: 네. 그곳이 오늘 제가 강연할 곳인가요?

여: 네. 저희 학교 수학 동아리 학생들이 거기서 당신을 기다리고 있습니다.

남: 그렇군요. 그럼, 당신이 그 동아리를 담당하고 계시나요?

여: 네. 제가 동아리 학생들을 지도하고 있습니다.

남: 그렇군요. 오늘 제 강연이 학생들에게 영감을 줄 수 있기를 바랍니다.

여: 물론이죠. 당신이 강연할 많은 학생이 장래에 수학자가 되고 싶어 하거든요.

남: 반가운 말씀이네요. 수학자로서의 제 경험을 열정적인 학생들과 공유할 수 있게 되어 정말 기쁩니다.

여: 학생들이 당신의 이야기를 듣고 매우 고마워할 것이라고 확신합니다.

◐ Topic & Situation 동아리 담당 교사가 강연자 안내하기

◐ Solution
여자는 수학 동아리를 담당하는 교사로서 수학 동아리 학생들에

게 강연하러 온 강연자를 강연 장소로 안내하고 있으므로, 두 사람의 관계를 가장 잘 나타낸 것은 ⑤ '동아리 담당 교사 – 강연자'이다.

◐ Words & Phrases

conference room 회의실 lecture 강연 in charge of ~을 담당하고 있는 manage 지도하다 mathematician 수학자 enthusiastic 열정적인 appreciate 고마워하다

03　　　　　　　　　　　　　정답 | ③

| Script & Translation |

W: Hello, Mr. Collins. It's great to talk with you in person.

M: Same here, Ms. Douglas.

W: As I said on the phone, I'm excited to have the company you work for publish my autobiography.

M: It's an honor. I was in awe while reading the manuscript you sent me. You opened a small store 30 years ago and have grown it into a big international company today.

W: Thank you. I'm hoping my experiences in my company can help inspire others.

M: Your autobiography will certainly help many people.

W: I hope so. And I'm not a writer, so my manuscript will need work.

M: Don't worry. My co-workers have a lot of experience proofreading and revising.

W: Great. I've read a few autobiographies your company has published. All the best-sellers. And I've enjoyed them all.

M: Glad to hear. Your autobiography will also be a best-seller.

W: That'd be amazing.

여: 안녕하세요, Collins 씨. 당신과 직접 이야기할 수 있어서 좋아요.

남: 저도 마찬가지예요, Douglas 씨.

여: 전화로 말씀드렸듯이, 당신이 일하는 회사가 제 자서전을 출판하게 되어서 매우 기뻐요.

남: 영광이에요. 저는 당신이 보내 주신 원고를 읽으면서 경외감을 느꼈어요. 당신은 30년 전에 작은 가게를 열었고 오늘날 그것을 큰 국제적인 회사로 성장시켜 오셨잖아요.

여: 감사해요. 제 회사에서의 경험이 다른 사람들에게 영감을 주는 데 도움이 될 수 있기를 바라요.

남: 당신의 자서전은 분명 많은 사람들에게 도움이 될 거예요.

여: 그러길 바라요. 그리고 저는 작가가 아니어서, 제 원고는 작업이 필요할 거예요.

남: 걱정하지 마세요. 제 동료들은 교정과 수정 경험이 많거든요.

여: 좋아요. 당신의 회사에서 출판한 자서전을 몇 권 읽었어요. 모두 베스트셀러들이더군요. 그리고 저는 그것들을 모두 즐겁게 읽었어요.

남: 다행이에요. 당신의 자서전도 베스트셀러가 될 거예요.

여: 그럼 정말 멋질 것 같아요.

◐ Topic & Situation 기업가의 자서전 출판

◐ Solution

여자는 작은 가게를 열었고 그것을 국제적인 회사로 성장시킨 자신의 경험을 담은 자서전을 남자의 회사가 출판하게 되어 기쁘다고 하며, 자신이 전문 작가가 아니기 때문에 추가 작업이 필요할 것이라고 말하고 있고, 남자는 자신의 동료들이 교정과 수정 경험이 많으니 걱정하지 말라고 말했다. 따라서 두 사람의 관계를 가장 잘 나타낸 것은 ③ '기업가 – 출판사 직원'이다.

◐ Words & Phrases

in person 직접 publish 출판하다 autobiography 자서전 awe 경외감 manuscript 원고 inspire 영감을 주다 proofread 교정하다 revise 수정하다

04　　　　　　　　　　　　　정답 | ②

| Script & Translation |

[Cell phone rings.]

W: Hello, Henry.

M: Hello, Katie. Did you see the message I sent you this morning?

W: No, I didn't. I've been busy all day trying to fix my tractor.

M: Oh, no! What's wrong with it?

W: It doesn't start. I couldn't fix it, so I called a mechanic to have it fixed.

M: I hope it'll be a cheap and easy fix. In fact, I messaged to tell you the fertilizer you had ordered last week arrived at my store from the factory. I'll bring it over to you today.

W: Oh, good. I need it for the crops in my fields.

M: I know. The fertilizer you ordered at my store will make your crops grow better.

W: Right. When will you come by?

M: I should arrive at your farm around three o'clock.

W: Okay. I'll be at the farm at that time.

M: All right. I'll call you if I'm running late.

W: Okay. See you then.

[휴대 전화가 울린다.]

여: 안녕하세요, Henry.

남: 안녕하세요, Katie. 제가 오늘 아침에 보낸 메시지 보셨어요?

여: 아니요, 못 봤어요. 트랙터를 고치느라 하루 종일 바빴거든요.

남: 아, 저런! 그것에 무슨 문제가 있나요?

여: 시동이 안 걸려요. 제가 수리할 수 없어서, 정비사를 불러서 수리를 맡겼어요.

남: 그것이 저렴하고 쉬운 수리가 되길 바라요. 사실, 저는 지난주에 주문하신 비료가 공장에서 저희 가게에 도착했다고 전하려고 메시지를 보냈어요. 오늘 그것을 드릴게요.

여: 아, 좋아요. 저는 제 밭에 있는 농작물을 위해 그것이 필요해요.

남: 알아요. 제 가게에 주문했던 그 비료는 당신의 작물을 더 잘 자라게 할 거예요.

여: 맞아요. 언제 들르실 건가요?

남: 저는 3시쯤 당신의 농장에 도착할 거예요.

여: 좋아요. 저는 그 시간에 농장에 있을 거예요.

남: 알겠어요. 제가 만일 늦으면 전화하겠습니다.

여: 좋아요. 그때 봐요.

◉ Topic & Situation 주문받은 비료 배달

◉ Solution

여자는 트랙터를 고치느라 바빴다고 하면서 자신의 밭에 있는 농작물을 위해 주문했던 비료가 필요하다고 말했고, 남자는 주문받았던 비료가 공장에서 자신의 가게로 도착해서 오늘 여자에게 배달을 해 주겠다고 말했다. 따라서 두 사람의 관계를 가장 잘 나타낸 것은 ② '농장 주인 – 비료 판매업자' 이다.

◉ Words & Phrases

fix 수리하다, 고치다; 수리   mechanic 정비사   fertilizer 비료   crop 농작물

05

정답 | ⑤

| Script & Translation |

W: All right, Mr. Hawkins. Your examination is complete.

M: Great. Were you able to figure out what's wrong?

W: Yes. Look at this X-ray. Can you see how these two are partially decayed?

M: Oh. Will they need to be pulled?

W: No. I'll remove the decayed areas by drilling and then fill in the holes.

M: Okay. What will you fill the holes with?

W: You have the option of getting an amalgam filling or a composite filling.

M: Which do you recommend?

W: I recommend a composite filling since they're your front teeth. It'll be less visible because it's about the same color as your teeth.

M: Oh, that's great. Then I'll get a composite filling.

여: 좋습니다, Hawkins 씨. 검사는 완료되었습니다.

남: 잘됐네요. 무엇이 문제인지 알아낼 수 있었나요?

여: 네. 이 엑스레이를 보세요. 이 두 개가 부분적으로 썩어 있는 것이 보이시나요?

남: 오. 그걸 뽑아야 하나요?

여: 아니요. 드릴로 썩은 부분을 제거한 다음 구멍을 메울 겁니다.

남: 알겠습니다. 구멍은 무엇으로 메울 건가요?

여: 아말감 충전재 또는 복합 충전재 중 선택하실 수 있으세요.

남: 어떤 것을 추천하시나요?

여: 앞니이기 때문에 복합 충전재를 추천해 드려요. 당신의 치아와 거의 같은 색이기 때문에, 눈에 덜 띌 겁니다.

남: 오, 잘됐네요. 그럼 복합 충전재로 하겠습니다.

◉ Topic & Situation 치과 진료

◉ Solution

여자가 남자에게 엑스레이를 보여 주며 남자의 썩은 치아를 어떻게 치료할 것인지를 설명하고 남자의 질문에 대답하고 있으므로, 두 사람의 관계를 가장 잘 나타낸 것은 ⑤ '치과 의사 – 환자'이다.

◉ Words & Phrases

examination 검사   complete 완료된   figure out ~을 알아내다   partially 부분적으로   decay 썩게 하다   amalgam 아말감(흔히 치과에서 쓰는 수은과 다른 금속의 합금)   filling 충전재   composite 복합의, 합성의   visible 눈에 띄는, (눈에) 보이는

06

정답 | ⑤

| Script & Translation |

M: Hello. Are you ready?

W: Yes, but I'm nervous. I can't believe I'm going to jump from 10,000 feet.

M: Don't worry. You'll be fine. First, let me explain the gear. Here's your jumpsuit and safety belt.

W: Okay. How do I wear the belt?

M: Let me show you. Like this.

W: All right. And is there anything I need to do when we're falling through the air?

M: Just relax and enjoy the view! It's truly amazing. And after we jump, we'll free-fall for about a minute before I open the parachute.

W: Got it. I'm still worried it might not open.

M: Trust me. It will. I take safety extremely seriously.

W: Okay, I trust you. Let's do it!

M: Great! Let's go over some final safety checks before we board the plane. You're going to have a fantastic experience today.

남: 안녕하세요. 준비됐나요?

여: 네, 하지만 긴장돼요. 제가 10,000피트 상공에서 뛰어내린다는 게 믿기지 않아요.

남: 걱정하지 마세요. 괜찮을 겁니다. 먼저, 장비에 관해 설명해 드릴게요. 여기 점프 슈트와 안전벨트가 있습니다.

여: 네. 벨트는 어떻게 착용하나요?

남: 제가 보여 드릴게요. 이렇게요.

여: 알았어요. 그리고 우리가 공중에서 떨어질 때 제가 해야 할 일이 있나요?

남: 그냥 긴장을 풀고 경치를 즐기세요! 정말 멋지답니다. 그리고 뛰어내린 후 제가 낙하산을 펼치기 전에 1분 정도 자유 낙하를 할 거예요.

여: 알겠어요. 전 여전히 그것이 안 펴질까 봐 걱정되네요.

남: 절 믿으세요. 그건 펴질 겁니다. 저는 안전을 대단히 중대하게 생각하거든요.

여: 네, 믿어요. 해 보죠!

남: 좋아요! 비행기에 탑승하기 전에 몇 가지 최종 안전 점검을 해 봅시다. 오늘 환상적인 경험을 하게 될 거예요.

○ Topic & Situation 스카이다이빙 체험

○ Solution

남자는 여자에게 장비 착용법을 보여 주며 10,000피트 상공에서 뛰어내릴 상황을 걱정하는 여자에게 안전에 대해 걱정하지 말고 그냥 경치를 즐기라며 긴장을 풀어 주며 비행기 탑승 전 몇 가지 최종 안전 점검을 하자는 말을 하고 있으므로, 두 사람의 관계를 가장 잘 나타낸 것은 ⑤ '스카이다이빙 강사 – 체험객'이다.

○ Words & Phrases

gear 장비 jumpsuit 점프 슈트 free-fall (낙하산이 펴질 때까지) 자유 낙하를 하다 parachute 낙하산 extremely 대단히 seriously 중대하게 go over ~을 점검하다 board ~에 탑승하다 fantastic 환상적인, 기막히게 좋은

Dictations 본문 21, 24~25쪽

기출예제
❶ this year's fruit harvest
❷ promote my fruit farm
❸ attract new customers
❹ ask my boss

01 ❶ charity auction preparation
❷ donate artwork to our charity
❸ school bulletin board

02 ❶ give my lecture
❷ in charge of
❸ share my experiences

03 ❶ publish my autobiography
❷ help inspire others
❸ proofreading and revising

04 ❶ to fix my tractor
❷ fertilizer you had ordered
❸ arrive at your farm

05 ❶ partially decayed
❷ fill in the holes
❸ Which do you recommend
❹ your front teeth

06 ❶ jump from 10,000 feet
❷ falling through the air
❸ open the parachute
❹ go over some final safety checks

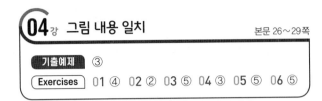

04강 그림 내용 일치

본문 26~29쪽

기출예제 ③

Exercises 01 ④ 02 ② 03 ⑤ 04 ③ 05 ⑤ 06 ⑤

기출 예제

본문 26쪽

정답 | ③

| Script & Translation |

M: Ms. Blake, I've finished decorating the camping gear section to look like a campsite.

W: Thanks, Chris. It's much nicer than what's represented in our sales plan. I like that banner on the wall.

M: I think it'll attract our customers' attention. And I set up the cone-shaped tent as you suggested before.

W: Good. That Native American-style tent is quite popular these days.

M: Yes, it is. Also, the backpack next to the box is currently our best-selling item.

W: That's true. I love its design. Oh, those two chairs look comfortable. I'd like to sit on one of them and make myself some coffee.

M: Me, too. And isn't that striped tablecloth really eye-catching?

W: It certainly is. Everything looks really good. You did an excellent job!

남: Blake 씨, 저는 캠핑 장비 코너를 캠프장처럼 보이도록 꾸미는 것을 마쳤어요.

여: 고마워요, Chris. 우리 판매 계획에 나와 있는 것보다 훨씬 좋군요. 벽에 걸린 저 현수막이 마음에 들어요.

남: 그것이 고객들의 관심을 끌 것으로 생각해요. 그리고 당신이 전에 제안한 대로 원뿔 모양의 텐트를 설치했어요.

여: 좋아요. 저 북미 원주민 스타일 텐트가 요즘 꽤 인기예요.

남: 네, 그렇죠. 그리고 상자 옆에 있는 배낭은 현재 우리의 가장 잘 팔리는 상품이에요.

여: 맞아요. 디자인이 마음에 들어요. 아, 저 의자 두 개는 편해 보이네요. 그중 하나에 앉아서 나를 위해 커피를 내리고 싶네요.

남: 저도요. 그리고 저 줄무늬 식탁보는 정말 눈길을 끌지 않나요?

여: 확실히 그래요. 모든 게 정말 좋아 보이네요. 정말 잘하셨어요!

◑ Topic & Situation 캠핑 장비 코너 꾸미기

◑ Solution

남자가 상자 옆에 있는 배낭이 현재 가장 잘 팔리는 상품이라고 했는데, 그림에서는 상자 위에 배낭이 있으므로, 그림에서 대화의 내용과 일치하지 않는 것은 ③이다.

◑ Words & Phrases

decorate 꾸미다 camping gear 캠핑 장비 cone-shaped 원뿔 모양의 tablecloth 식탁보 eye-catching 눈길을 끄는

Exercises

본문 28~29쪽

01

정답 | ④

| Script & Translation |

M: Emma, I went to the first public showing of the movie *Lucky Night* last week. Check it out. I took a picture before it started.

W: Cool! They hung a *Lucky Night* banner from the ceiling.

M: Right. And look at the curtains.

W: Oh, they have star prints. Were they to match the movie title?

M: Yeah. Pretty creative, right? And see this balloon archway on the stage?

W: Yes. Were the actors supposed to walk through it onto the stage?

M: That's right.

W: Wow! The crowd must've loved that.

M: For sure. Everybody was cheering so loudly.

W: So what was this two-layer cake on the table for?

M: The actors got it for the director. It was really touching.

W: That's nice. And what about these boxes under the table?

M: Those were gifts for the actors from a few fans in the crowd.

W: I see. What an amazing experience!

M: Definitely.

남: Emma, 나는 지난주에 *Lucky Night* 영화의 첫 공개 상영회

에 갔었어. 이것 좀 봐. 그것이 시작하기 전에 내가 사진을 찍었어.
여: 멋지다! 그들은 천장에 *Lucky Night* 현수막을 매달아 놓았구나.
남: 맞아. 그리고 커튼 좀 봐.
여: 오, 별무늬가 있네. 그것은 영화 제목과 어울리게 하려는 것이었을까?
남: 응. 꽤 창의적이야, 그렇지? 그리고 무대에 있는 이 풍선 아치 통로 보이니?
여: 응. 배우들이 그것을 통과해 무대로 걸어 들어가게 되어 있었니?
남: 맞아.
여: 와! 관객들이 정말 좋아했겠다.
남: 당연하지. 모두가 매우 큰 소리로 환호하고 있었어.
여: 그러면 탁자 위의 이 2단 케이크는 무엇을 위한 거였니?
남: 배우들이 감독을 위해 준비한 거야. 정말 감동적이었어.
여: 그거 좋네. 그러면 탁자 밑에 있는 이 상자들은?
남: 관객 중 몇몇 팬들이 배우들을 위해 준비한 선물이었어.
여: 그렇구나. 정말 멋진 경험이다!
남: 정말 그래.

Topic & Situation 영화 공개 상영회 무대 모습

Solution

대화에서 탁자 위에 2단 케이크가 있다고 했는데, 그림의 케이크는 1단이다. 따라서 그림에서 대화의 내용과 일치하지 않는 것은 ④이다.

Words & Phrases

banner 현수막 archway 아치 통로 two-layer 2단의 director 감독 touching 감동을 주는

02

정답 | ②

| Script & Translation |

W: Hey, Mike. How was your weekend?
M: Hi, Sonia. I was busy remodeling my family's study room. Do you want to see a picture of it?
W: Sure. *[Pause]* Um. You put the sofa in front of the window.
M: Yeah. I can enjoy the sunshine on the sofa on sunny days.
W: Good. Why is the bookshelf on the right completely empty?
M: Oh, I took this picture before putting the books on the bookshelf.
W: I see. Is the round rug on the floor new? I like the design.
M: Yeah. I recently bought it online for only $50!
W: What a deal! Did you buy the two chairs on the left, too?
M: No, I brought them with the dining table from the kitchen.
W: Oh, you're going to use the table as a desk, aren't you?
M: Right. That's why I put a desk lamp on it.
W: It seems like your remodeling went really well.

여: 안녕하세요, Mike. 주말은 어떻게 보내셨어요?
남: 안녕하세요, Sonia. 나는 우리 가족의 공부방을 리모델링하느라 바빴어요. 그것의 사진을 볼래요?
여: 물론이죠. *[잠시 후]* 음. 소파를 창문 앞에 놓았군요.
남: 네. 맑은 날에는 소파에서 햇볕을 즐길 수 있어요.
여: 좋네요. 왜 오른쪽에 있는 책꽂이가 완전히 비어 있나요?
남: 아, 책을 책꽂이에 꽂기 전에 이 사진을 찍었어요.
여: 그렇군요. 바닥에 있는 둥근 양탄자는 새것인가요? 디자인이 마음에 들어요.
남: 네. 저는 최근에 그것을 인터넷에서 단돈 50달러에 샀어요!
여: 잘 사셨네요! 왼쪽에 있는 의자 두 개도 사셨나요?
남: 아니요, 전 그 의자들을 부엌에서 식탁과 함께 가져왔어요.
여: 아, 식탁을 책상으로 사용하실 거군요, 그렇지 않나요?
남: 맞아요. 그래서 그것 위에 책상 램프를 올려놓았어요.
여: 리모델링이 정말 잘된 것 같아요.

Topic & Situation 가족 공부방 리모델링

Solution

대화에서 여자는 책꽂이가 완전히 비어 있다고 했는데 그림에서는 책꽂이에 책이 가득 꽂혀 있다. 따라서 그림에서 대화의 내용과 일치하지 않는 것은 ②이다.

Words & Phrases

bookshelf 책꽂이 rug 양탄자 deal 거래

03

정답 | ⑤

| Script & Translation |

M: Honey, did you finish making Natalie's birthday

party invitation card?

W: Almost. Look at the monitor.

M: Oh, let's see. I like how you put a castle in the middle.

W: And I put the phrase "Happy Birthday" above the castle.

M: Good. I also like the balloons on both sides of it.

W: What about Natalie's picture in the heart?

M: She's really cute!

W: Can you guess why I put five stars below Natalie's picture?

M: Sure! They mean Natalie's age, don't they?

W: That's right. I can't believe she's already turning 5.

M: Me, neither. By the way, why is the bottom oval shape blank?

W: I'll type in the party information such as time and place.

M: I got it. I think you did a really good job.

남: 여보, Natalie의 생일 파티 초대장을 다 만들었나요?
여: 거의요. 모니터를 보세요.
남: 오, 한 번 보죠. 당신이 가운데에 성을 넣은 방식이 마음에 들어요.
여: 그리고 성 위에 'Happy Birthday' 문구를 놓았어요.
남: 좋아요. 그것의 양쪽에 있는 풍선들 또한 마음에 들어요.
여: 하트 모양에 있는 Natalie의 사진은 어때요?
남: 정말로 귀여워요!
여: 내가 왜 Natalie의 사진 아래에 다섯 개의 별을 놓았는지 추측해 볼래요?
남: 물론이죠! 그것들은 Natalie의 나이를 의미하잖아요, 그렇지 않나요?
여: 맞아요. 그 애가 벌써 다섯 살이 된다니 믿을 수 없어요.
남: 나도 그래요. 그런데, 아래에 있는 타원 모양은 왜 비어 있나요?
여: 시간과 장소 같은 파티 정보를 타이프 쳐서 넣을 거예요.
남: 알았어요. 당신이 정말로 잘 한 것 같아요.

○ **Topic & Situation** 생일 초대장

○ **Solution**
대화에서 남자가 생일 파티 초대장 아래에 비어 있는 타원 모양이 있다고 했는데 그림에는 직사각형 모양이 배치되어 있다. 따라서 그림에서 대화의 내용과 일치하지 않는 것은 ⑤이다.

○ **Words & Phrases**
invitation 초대, 초대장 oval 타원의 blank 비어 있는, 텅 빈

04

| Script & Translation |

W: John, how was your family camping trip last weekend?

M: It couldn't have been better. This is a picture that I took during the trip.

W: Cool. Did you set up this tent under the big tree?

M: Yes, I did. It was the perfect spot with a cool breeze.

W: Awesome. The woman reading a book near the tent must be your mother, right?

M: Yes. She really enjoys reading. And the man cutting a watermelon on the table is my father.

W: You resemble your father a lot. Oh, the dog under the table is really cute.

M: Can you guess what's inside the rectangular basket?

W: Um... dog food?

M: Right. That's why our dog is staying near the basket.

W: I can tell by the picture you had a great time.

여: John, 지난 주말 가족 캠핑 여행 어땠어?
남: 정말로 좋았어. 이것이 여행 중에 내가 찍은 사진이야.
여: 멋지다. 큰 나무 아래에 이 텐트를 네가 설치했니?
남: 그래, 내가 설치했어. 이곳이 시원한 산들바람을 맞을 수 있는 완벽한 장소였거든.
여: 근사하다. 텐트 근처에서 책을 읽는 여자가 네 어머님임에 틀림없어, 맞지?
남: 그래. 어머니께서는 독서를 정말로 즐기셔. 그리고 식탁에 있는 수박을 자르는 남자가 내 아버지야.
여: 너는 아버지를 많이 닮았구나. 오, 식탁 아래에 있는 개가 정말로 귀여워.
남: 직사각형 바구니 안에 무엇이 들어 있는지 추측해 볼래?
여: 음… 개 먹이?
남: 맞아. 그래서 우리 개가 바구니 근처에 머물러 있는 거야.
여: 사진을 통해서 네가 매우 멋진 시간을 보냈다는 것을 알 수 있어.

○ **Topic & Situation** 캠핑 여행 사진

○ **Solution**
대화의 중반에 남자가 식탁에 있는 수박을 자르고 있다고 했는데 그림에서는 수박을 먹고 있다. 따라서 그림에서 대화의 내용과 일치하지 않는 것은 ③이다.

○ **Words & Phrases**
set up ~을 설치하다 breeze 산들바람 resemble 닮다
rectangular 직사각형의

05

정답 | ⑤

| Script & Translation |

W: Hey, Danny, long time no see! Your hair has gotten really long.

M: That's why I came to get it cut. Oh, I see you've remodeled the beauty shop a little bit.

W: Right, I did that recently. Do you like the new look?

M: Yeah, it's nice! Those curtains on the left look good.

W: Thanks. I think they make the shop feel warmer.

M: I agree they do. And I like those two round mirrors on the wall.

W: The old mirrors started getting cracks in them. What do you think of the clock inside the head?

M: It's perfect! And I don't remember seeing the plant stand on the right.

W: Right. I set it up last weekend. I like how it displays the plants.

M: Yeah, me, too.

W: Feel free to read one of the books which are on the cushioned bench. I just need a few minutes to clean up.

M: Okay, sounds good.

여: 안녕, Danny, 오랜만이에요! 머리가 정말 많이 길었네요.

남: 그래서 머리를 자르려고 왔어요. 아, 미용실을 약간 리모델링하셨네요.

여: 맞아요, 최근에 그것을 리모델링했어요. 새로운 모습이 마음에 드세요?

남: 네, 멋져요! 왼쪽에 있는 커튼이 좋아 보이네요.

여: 고마워요. 그것들이 미용실을 더 따뜻한 느낌이 나게 만들어 주는 것 같아요.

남: 그렇다는 데 저도 동의해요. 그리고 벽에 있는 저 두 개의 둥근 거울도 마음에 들어요.

여: 예전 거울들에 금이 가기 시작했어요. 머리 안의 시계는 어떻게 생각하세요?

남: 완벽해요! 그런데 오른쪽에 식물 진열대를 보았던 기억이 안 나네요.

여: 맞아요. 제가 그것을 지난 주말에 설치했어요. 그것이 식물들을 보여 주는 방식이 마음에 들어요.

남: 네, 저도요.

여: 쿠션을 단 벤치 위에 있는 책 중 하나를 마음껏 읽으세요. 제가 청소할 시간이 몇 분쯤 필요하거든요.

남: 알겠어요, 좋습니다.

◐ Topic & Situation 리모델링한 미용실

◐ Solution

여자는 남자에게 쿠션을 단 벤치 위에 있는 책 중 하나를 마음껏 읽으라고 했는데, 책은 벤치 옆 탁자 위에 있다. 따라서 그림에서 대화의 내용과 일치하지 않는 것은 ⑤이다.

◐ Words & Phrases

beauty shop 미용실   mirror 거울   crack 금; 갈라지다   plant stand 식물 진열대

06

정답 | ⑤

| Script & Translation |

W: Joshua, have you ever been to Evergreen Park?

M: No. How about you?

W: I go jogging there every day. It's really nice. Look, here's a picture I took there the other day.

M: Wow, the bench under the tree is a perfect place to relax.

W: I know. I like to sit there and watch people go by. Well, what do you think of the two hands holding a book?

M: That's unique. I bet a lot of people come to see it.

W: Yes. It's a popular place to take pictures.

M: I also like the heart with an arrow in the word 'LOVE'. They replaced the 'O' with this heart there.

W: It's cool, right? And see these three ducks in the pond. They swim there every day.

M: Cute! Who's the girl holding a dog in her arms?

W: That's my friend, Matilda. She often walks her dog there.

여: Joshua, 너 Evergreen 공원에 가 본 적 있니?

남: 아니. 너는 어때?

여: 나는 매일 거기에 조깅하러 가. 정말 좋아. 봐봐, 여기 내가 며칠 전에 거기서 찍은 사진이 있어.

남: 와, 나무 아래에 있는 벤치는 휴식을 취하기에 완벽한 장소구나.

여: 맞아. 나는 거기에 앉아서 사람들이 지나가는 것을 구경하는 것을 좋아해. 음, 책을 잡고 있는 두 손은 어떻게 생각해?

남: 그건 독특하구나. 장담컨대 많은 사람이 그것을 보러 올 거야.

여: 그렇지. 사진 찍기에 인기 있는 장소야.

남: 나는 'LOVE'라는 단어에서 화살이 꽂힌 하트도 마음에 들어. 그들은 거기에서 'O'를 이 하트로 대체했네.

여: 멋져, 그렇지? 그리고 연못에 있는 이 오리 세 마리를 보렴. 그것들은 매일 거기서 헤엄을 쳐.

남: 귀여워! 개를 품에 안고 있는 소녀는 누구야?

여: 개는 내 친구, Matilda야. 그녀는 자주 그곳에서 개를 산책시켜.

◐ **Topic & Situation** Evergreen 공원

◐ **Solution**

남자는 여자에게 개를 품에 안고 있는 소녀가 누구인지 물었는데, 그림에서는 소녀가 개의 목줄을 잡고 달리고 있다. 따라서 그림에서 대화의 내용과 일치하지 않는 것은 ⑤이다.

◐ **Words & Phrases**

the other day 며칠 전에, 일전에   arrow 화살   replace 대체하다, 대신하다

Dictations   본문 27, 30~31쪽

기출
예제
❶ look like a campsite
❷ as you suggested before
❸ make myself some coffee

01 ❶ from the ceiling
❷ supposed to walk through it
❸ two-layer cake

02 ❶ was busy remodeling
❷ before putting the books
❸ the table as a desk

03 ❶ on both sides
❷ the bottom oval shape blank

04 ❶ set up this tent
❷ cutting a watermelon
❸ inside the rectangular basket

05 ❶ Those curtains on the left
❷ started getting cracks
❸ set it up

06 ❶ watch people go by
❷ the heart with an arrow
❸ walks her dog

05강 할 일   본문 32~35쪽

기출예제   ②

Exercises   01 ② 02 ① 03 ④ 04 ⑤ 05 ③ 06 ①

기출 예제   본문 32쪽

정답 | ②

| **Script & Translation** |

W: Oliver, I'm so excited about the party for the new members of our tennis club this Friday.

M: Me, too. Let's go through the to-do list. I want it to be perfect.

W: Agreed. Did you reserve the Mexican restaurant downtown for the party?

M: Yes, I did. The restaurant is spacious, so it's perfect for a party like ours.

W: Plus, the food there is terrific. And you prepared gifts for the new members, right?

M: Yeah, they're in my car. Did you remind the members about the party?

W: I've just sent a text message to everyone.

M: Great. What about the tennis competition schedule? Have you printed it out?

W: Oh, I almost forgot. I'll do it tonight. Um, is the music ready?

M: Uh-huh. I made a playlist last night.

W: That's great. I think we're good to go!

여: Oliver, 나는 이번 주 금요일 우리 테니스 클럽 신입 회원을 위한 파티로 무척 신나.

남: 나도 그래. 할 일 목록을 살펴보자. 나는 그것(파티)이 완벽하길 원해.

여: 동의해. 너는 파티를 위해 시내에 있는 멕시코 식당을 예약했니?

남: 응, 했어. 식당이 넓어서, 우리 파티와 같은 파티에 더할 나위 없이 좋아.

여: 게다가, 거기 음식도 훌륭해. 그리고 너는 신입 회원을 위한 선물을 준비했지, 그렇지?

남: 응, 그것들은 내 차에 있어. 회원들에게 파티에 대해 다시 한 번 알려 줬니?

여: 방금 모두에게 문자 메시지를 보냈어.

남: 좋아. 테니스 대회 일정은 어떻게 되었어? 그것을 인쇄했니?

여: 아, 잊을 뻔했어. 내가 오늘 밤에 그것을 할게. 음, 음악은 준비되었니?

남: 응. 어젯밤에 재생 목록을 만들었어.

여: 잘됐다. 준비가 다 된 것 같아!

○ **Topic & Situation** 테니스 클럽 신입 회원을 위한 파티 준비

○ **Solution**

두 사람은 테니스 클럽의 신입 회원을 위한 파티를 위해 할 일을 점검하고 있는데, 남자가 테니스 대회 일정을 인쇄했는지 묻자, 여자가 잊을 뻔했는데 자신이 오늘 밤에 인쇄하겠다고 말했으므로, 여자가 할 일로 가장 적절한 것은 ② '대회 일정 인쇄하기'이다.

○ **Words & Phrases**

go through ~을 살펴보다 reserve 예약하다 spacious 넓은
terrific 훌륭한, 멋진 remind (기억하도록) 다시 한번 알려 주다
good to go 준비가 다 된

Exercises   본문 34~35쪽

01   정답 | ②

| Script & Translation |

M: Honey, it seems like we have everything ready for our camping trip.

W: Yeah. I can't wait to sleep in the tent tonight!

M: Me neither. You packed the flashlight I bought yesterday, right?

W: Yes. And I got the small first-aid kit just in case.

M: Good thinking! Let's head out!

W: We can't leave just yet. My cell phone's charging. It'll take about 20 more minutes to fully charge.

M: Then shall I make some coffee to take with us in the car while you're waiting?

W: Sounds great. Actually, I'm feeling a little sleepy.

M: I understand. It's still early in the morning. I'll prepare the coffee using the coffee machine.

W: Thanks, honey. I'm going to make sure all of the windows in the house are closed.

M: Good idea. It might rain while we're gone.

W: I'll be right back.

남: 여보, 우리 캠핑 여행을 갈 모든 준비가 다 된 것 같아요.

여: 네. 오늘 밤 텐트에서 빨리 자고 싶어요!

남: 나도 그래요. 어제 내가 산 손전등은 챙겼지요, 그렇지요?

여: 네. 그리고 만약을 위해 작은 구급상자를 넣었어요.

남: 좋은 생각이에요! 출발합시다!

여: 우리는 아직 떠날 수 없어요. 내 휴대 전화가 충전 중이거든요. 완전히 충전되려면 약 20분이 더 걸릴 거예요.

남: 그럼 당신이 기다리는 동안, 나는 우리가 차에 가지고 탈 커피를 좀 내릴까요?

여: 좋아요. 실은, 내가 약간 졸리거든요.

남: 알겠어요. 아직 이른 아침이니까요. 내가 커피 머신을 사용해서 커피를 준비할게요.

여: 고마워요, 여보. 내가 집 안의 모든 창문이 닫혔는지 확인할게요.

남: 좋은 생각이에요. 우리가 없는 동안 비가 올지도 몰라요.

여: 금방 올게요.

○ **Topic & Situation** 캠핑 여행 준비

○ **Solution**

휴대 전화가 충전 중이어서 아직 떠날 수 없다고 말하는 여자에게 남자가 기다리는 동안 자신이 차에 가지고 탈 커피를 내려 줄지 물어 보자 여자가 좋다고 하고는 약간 졸리다고 말했다. 이에 대해 남자가 알겠다고 하면서 커피 머신을 사용해 커피를 준비하겠다고 했으므로, 남자가 할 일로 가장 적절한 것은 ② '커피 준비하기'이다.

○ **Words & Phrases**

can't wait to *do* 빨리 ~하고 싶다, 몹시 바라다 pack (짐을) 챙기다
[꾸리다] first-aid kit 구급상자 head out 출발하다 charge 충전하다

02   정답 | ①

| Script & Translation |

M: I'm home, honey. I picked up the laundry on my way home.

W: Good! I was just about to call you for that favor. I was a little busy cleaning the house.

M: Wow, the house looks nice and clean!

W: Thanks. So how was your day at work?

M: Actually, our team project has been approved and we'll present it in front of the whole staff.

W: Wow, congratulations! So who's going to present?

M: Me. I was the one who first proposed the idea for our project.

W: That's great! When is the presentation?

M: It's tomorrow. I need to review some reports for the presentation, so I have to do some work at home tonight.

W: Oh, my. Is there anything I can help you with?

M: Well, it's my turn to prepare dinner tonight, but could you do it for me?

W: Don't worry. I'll take care of dinner. Just focus on preparing for the presentation.

M: Thank you, honey. That means a lot to me.

W: You're welcome.

남: 나 왔어요, 여보. 집에 오는 길에 세탁물을 찾아 왔어요.

여: 좋아요! 그 부탁을 하려고 당신에게 막 전화하려던 참이었어요. 집을 청소하느라 조금 바빴어요.

남: 와, 집이 멋지고 깔끔해 보여요!

여: 고마워요. 직장에서 당신 하루는 어땠나요?

남: 사실, 우리 팀 프로젝트가 승인돼서, 우리가 전체 직원들 앞에서 그것을 발표할 예정이에요.

여: 와, 축하해요! 그래서 누가 발표를 할 건가요?

남: 나예요. 우리 프로젝트를 위한 아이디어를 처음으로 제안한 사람이 나였어요.

여: 그거 굉장하네요! 발표는 언제예요?

남: 그게 내일이에요. 발표를 위해 몇몇 보고서를 검토할 필요가 있어서, 나는 오늘밤 집에서 일을 좀 해야 해요.

여: 오, 저런. 내가 도와줄 일이 있나요?

남: 그게, 오늘 내가 저녁을 준비할 차례인데, 나 대신 그것을 해 줄 수 있을까요?

여: 걱정 마요. 내가 저녁을 맡을게요. 당신은 발표 준비하는 것에만 집중하세요.

남: 고마워요, 여보. 그건 나한테 정말 큰 힘이 돼요.

여: 천만에요.

● Topic & Situation 남편의 발표 준비를 위해 저녁 준비를 대신해 주는 아내

● Solution

남자는 내일 발표를 앞두고 오늘밤 집에서 일을 좀 해야 한다고 말하고, 이에 여자가 도와줄 일이 있냐고 묻자, 남자는 자신이 저녁을 준비해야 할 차례인데, 그것을 대신해 줄 수 있는지 물었고, 이에 여자는 그렇게 하겠다고 말한다. 따라서 여자가 할 일로 가장 적절한 것은 ① '저녁 준비하기'이다.

● Words & Phrases

laundry 세탁물 approve 승인하다 staff 직원 propose 제안하다

03
정답 | ④

| Script & Translation |

M: Hey, Sharon. Do you have a minute?

W: Hi, Michael. Sure, what's up?

M: My team has been working on a project for a few months, and we're getting close to finishing.

W: Oh, nice. It'll feel great when it's finally done.

M: Definitely. I'm actually looking for someone who can look over our project with a fresh perspective.

W: So, you want me to be that person?

M: Right. Would you be able to review the materials we've made and give us some feedback?

W: Of course. When do you need it by?

M: Ideally by the end of this week, but I understand if you're busy and need more time.

W: No problem. I can do it.

M: Thanks so much. I'll email you the materials right away.

W: Okay. I'll give you a call when I finish reviewing them.

남: 저기, Sharon. 잠시 시간 있나요?

여: 안녕하세요, Michael. 물론이죠, 무슨 일인가요?

남: 저희 팀이 몇 달간 프로젝트에 노력을 들이고 있는데, 마무리에 가까워지고 있어요.

여: 오, 좋네요. 마침내 끝나면 기분이 아주 좋을 거예요.

남: 물론이죠. 사실 저는 우리 프로젝트를 새로운 관점에서 검토해 줄 누군가를 찾고 있어요.

여: 그래서, 제가 그 사람이 되기를 원하시는 건가요?

남: 맞아요. 저희가 만든 자료들을 검토해 보시고 저희에게 피드백을 좀 주실 수 있을까요?

여: 물론이죠. 언제까지 그것이 필요하신가요?

남: 이상적으로는 이번 주말까지이지만, 당신이 바빠서 시간이 더 필요하다고 해도 이해합니다.

여: 문제없어요. 할 수 있습니다.

남: 정말 감사해요. 제가 자료들을 곧바로 이메일로 보내 드리겠습니다.

여: 알겠어요. 검토를 끝내면 전화를 드리겠습니다.

Topic & Situation 프로젝트 자료에 대한 피드백 요청하기

Solution

남자가 자기 팀이 진행 중인 프로젝트를 새로운 관점에서 검토해줄 사람을 찾고 있으며, 여자에게 그러한 역할을 해 줄 수 있는지물었고, 여자가 기꺼이 그렇게 해 주겠다고 대답하자, 남자는 고마움을 표시하며 곧바로 자료를 이메일로 보내겠다고 한다. 따라서 남자가 할 일로 가장 적절한 것은 ④ '이메일로 자료 보내기'이다.

Words & Phrases

look over ~을 검토하다   perspective 관점   review 검토하다
material 자료   ideally 이상적으로는. 원칙상으로는

04
정답 | ⑤

| Script & Translation |

M: Samantha, today was a long day, wasn't it?

W: It sure was, Mr. Peterson. I think we sold the most French fries we've ever sold in a day.

M: Yeah. Let's quickly check what we need for tomorrow and head home.

W: Okay.

M: Do we have enough potatoes and oil in the storage room?

W: We have three boxes of potatoes and ten liters of oil.

M: Then we don't have to order potatoes and oil until next Monday.

W: Oh, I forgot to tell you that a light bulb in the restroom is out.

M: Okay. I'll replace it with a new one before I leave.

W: Now I'll go clean the frying pans.

M: Don't worry. I've already done that.

W: Thank you. Then, I'll throw away the food waste.

M: All right. You can leave after that. I'll take care of the rest.

남: Samantha, 오늘은 긴 하루였네요, 그렇지 않나요?

여: 확실히 그랬어요, Peterson 씨. 제 생각에 지금껏 우리가 팔았던 것 중 하루 동안에 가장 많은 감자튀김을 판 것 같아요.

남: 그래요. 내일 우리가 필요한 것들을 빨리 확인하고 집에 갑시다.

여: 네.

남: 저장고에 감자랑 기름이 충분한가요?

여: 감자 세 상자랑 기름 10리터가 있어요.

남: 그러면 다음 주 월요일까지는 감자와 기름을 주문하지 않아도되겠네요.

여: 아, 화장실의 전구 한 개가 나갔다고 말씀드리는 걸 깜빡했어요.

남: 괜찮아요. 내가 퇴근하기 전에 새 것으로 교체할게요.

여: 이제 저는 프라이팬을 닦으러 갈게요.

남: 걱정 말아요. 내가 이미 했어요.

여: 감사합니다. 그럼 음식물 쓰레기를 버리도록 할게요.

남: 좋아요. 그것이 끝난 후에 퇴근해도 돼요. 나머지는 내가 처리할게요.

Topic & Situation 음식점 업무 마무리

Solution

여자가 프라이팬을 닦으러 간다고 말하자 남자는 자신이 이미 다해 놓았다고 말하고, 이에 여자는 퇴근하기 전에 음식물 쓰레기를버리겠다고 이야기했으므로 여자가 할 일로 가장 적절한 것은⑤ '음식물 쓰레기 버리기'이다.

Words & Phrases

head 가다. 향하다   storage room 저장고   light bulb 전구
replace 교체하다   throw away ~을 버리다   rest 나머지

05
정답 | ③

| Script & Translation |

M: Honey, can you believe that tomorrow is our moving day?

W: I know. It's our last night in this house. It's kind of emotional.

M: Yeah. I called the movers to confirm that they'll be here by 8 a.m.

W: Thanks for doing that. So we'll have to have a quick breakfast tomorrow. What do you want to eat?

M: How about just yogurt and fruit? There's yogurt in the fridge.

W: Good idea. Then I'll go buy some bananas at the store now.

M: Okay. Can you take out the trash on your way out?

W: Sure. And let's not forget to gather all our small valuables and pack them.

M: Oh, right. We need to take special care not to lose them.

W: We can do it together when I get back home.

M: Don't worry about it. There's not much. I'll do it

while you're out.

W: Thanks. You can use the small boxes in the garage to put them in.

M: All right.

남: 여보, 내일이 우리 이삿날이라는 게 믿어지나요?

여: 그러게요. 이 집에서 보내는 우리의 마지막 밤이네요. 뭔가 감정적이 되게 하네요.

남: 맞아요. 내가 이삿짐 운반 직원에게 전화해서 그들이 오전 8시까지 여기에 올 것이라는 것을 확인했어요.

여: 그렇게 해 줘서 고마워요. 그러면 내일 아침은 빨리 먹어야겠네요. 무엇을 먹고 싶어요?

남: 요구르트와 과일 정도면 어때요? 냉장고에 요구르트가 있어요.

여: 좋은 생각이에요. 그러면 지금 가게에 가서 바나나를 좀 사 올게요.

남: 알았어요. 나가는 길에 쓰레기 좀 버려 줄래요?

여: 물론이죠. 그리고 작은 귀중품은 모두 모아서 포장하는 것도 잊지 말자고요.

남: 아, 맞아요. 그것들을 잃어버리지 않도록 특히 주의해야 해요.

여: 내가 집에 돌아오면 그 일을 같이할 수 있어요.

남: 걱정하지 마세요. 별로 많지 않아요. 당신이 외출한 동안 내가 할게요.

여: 고마워요. 그것들을 넣기 위해 차고에 있는 작은 상자들을 사용하면 돼요.

남: 알겠어요.

○ **Topic & Situation** 이사 준비하기

○ **Solution**

여자가 이사를 앞두고 귀중품을 모두 모아서 포장하자고 말하면서 자신이 외출 후 돌아오면 같이 할 수 있다고 하자, 남자는 여자가 외출한 동안 자신이 하겠다고 말하고 있다. 따라서 남자가 할 일로 가장 적절한 것은 ③ '귀중품 포장하기'이다.

○ **Words & Phrases**

mover 이삿짐 운반 직원   confirm 확인하다   fridge 냉장고
gather 모으다   valuables 귀중품   garage 차고

06   정답 | ①

| Script & Translation |

W: Sweetie, there's something wrong with the car.

M: Oh, you're right. The warning lights on the dashboard are on.

W: I'll pull over. *[Pause]* I'm not sure what this sign means.

M: It's not the low fuel light, is it?

W: No. I filled up the car yesterday.

M: Hmm.... I'll check the car owner's manual. Where is it?

W: Just a second. *[Pause]* Here it is.

M: Let me see.... The sign means there's low air pressure in the tires.

W: Really? We should go to the nearest car repair shop now to get them fixed.

M: Then we're going to be late picking up Jimmy.

W: Safety comes first. I'll send him a text asking him to wait for about 15 minutes.

M: Okay. Then leave it to me to search for the nearest repair shop.

W: Good.

여: 여보, 차에 문제가 생겼어요.

남: 아, 그러네요. 계기판에 경고등이 켜졌어요.

여: 내가 차를 세울게요. *[잠시 후]* 이 표시가 무슨 뜻인지 잘 모르겠어요.

남: 연료 부족 표시등은 아니죠, 그렇죠?

여: 네. 어제 차에 연료를 가득 채웠어요.

남: 음…. 내가 차 사용자 설명서를 확인해 볼게요. 그게 어디 있죠?

여: 잠깐만요. *[잠시 후]* 여기 있어요.

남: 어디 보자…. 그 표시는 타이어의 공기압이 낮다는 뜻이에요.

여: 정말요? 지금 바로 가까운 자동차 정비소에 가서 그것을 고쳐야겠네요.

남: 그러면 우리가 Jimmy를 데리러 가는 데 늦을 거예요.

여: 안전이 제일 중요해요. 제가 그에게 15분 정도 기다려 달라는 문자를 보낼게요.

남: 알았어요. 그러면 가장 가까운 정비소를 찾는 건 저에게 맡겨요.

여: 좋아요.

○ **Topic & Situation** 자동차 수리로 인해 늦는다는 문자 메시지 보내기

○ **Solution**

차 계기판에 타이어 공기압이 낮다는 경고등이 켜져서 여자가 그것을 고치러 자동차 정비소로 바로 가자고 말하자 남자는 Jimmy를 데리러 가는 데 늦겠다고 말한다. 이에 여자가 안전이 제일 중요하다고 하며 자신이 Jimmy에게 기다려 달라는 문자를 보내겠

다고 말한다. 따라서 여자가 대화 직후에 할 일로 가장 적절한 것은 ① '문자 메시지 보내기'이다.

● Words & Phrases

warning light 경고등 dashboard 계기판 pull over (길 한 쪽으로) 차를 세우다[대다] fill up ~을 가득 채우다 manual 설명서 air pressure 공기압 car repair shop 자동차 정비소

Dictations
본문 33, 36~37쪽

기출
예제
❶ want it to be perfect
❷ prepared gifts for
❸ the tennis competition schedule
01 ❶ packed the flashlight
❷ to fully charge
❸ using the coffee machine
02 ❶ has been approved
❷ review some reports
❸ take care of dinner
03 ❶ getting close to finishing
❷ give us some feedback
❸ finish reviewing them
04 ❶ check what we need
❷ replace it with
❸ throw away the food waste
05 ❶ called the movers
❷ take out the trash
❸ take special care
06 ❶ filled up the car
❷ low air pressure
❸ Safety comes first

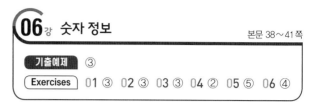

06강 숫자 정보
본문 38~41쪽

기출예제 ③

Exercises 01 ③ 02 ③ 03 ③ 04 ② 05 ⑤ 06 ④

기출 예제
본문 38쪽

정답 | ③

| Script & Translation |

W: Welcome to Jamie's Gift Shop! What can I do for you?

M: Hi. I need to get Christmas gifts for my friends. Is there anything you can recommend?

W: Sure. How about this photo tumbler? You can insert a picture of your friends into the tumbler to decorate it.

M: Ooh, my friends will love it. How much is it?

W: It's $30.

M: It seems a bit pricey, but I like it. I'll take two of them.

W: Okay. Anything else?

M: These Christmas key chains look cute. Oh, they're $5 each.

W: Yes. They're only available this month.

M: Are they? I'll take four then. I think that's all.

W: So, that's two tumblers and four key chains.

M: That's right.

W: And you get 10% off the total cost for our Christmas promotion.

M: Great. Here's my credit card.

여: Jamie의 선물 가게에 오신 것을 환영합니다! 무엇을 도와드릴까요?

남: 안녕하세요. 친구들에게 줄 크리스마스 선물을 사야 해요. 추천해 주실 수 있는 것이 있나요?

여: 물론입니다. 이 사진 텀블러는 어떠세요? 텀블러에 친구들의 사진을 넣어 그것을 장식할 수 있어요.

남: 오오, 제 친구들이 아주 좋아할 거예요. 얼마죠?

여: 30달러입니다.

남: 약간 비싼 것 같지만, 그것이 마음에 들어요. 두 개 살게요.

여: 알겠습니다. 필요하신 다른 것이 있으신가요?

남: 이 크리스마스 열쇠고리가 귀여워 보이네요. 오, 하나에 5달러군요.

여: 네. 그것들은 이번 달에만 살 수 있습니다.

남: 그래요? 그러면 네 개 사겠습니다. 그게 다인 것 같습니다.

여: 그럼, 텀블러 두 개와 열쇠고리 네 개이군요.

남: 맞습니다.

여: 그리고 크리스마스 판촉으로 총비용의 10%를 할인받으십니다.

남: 매우 좋군요. 여기 제 신용 카드가 있습니다.

● **Topic & Situation** 사진 텀블러와 열쇠고리 구입

● **Solution**

남자는 하나에 30달러인 사진 텀블러 두 개와 5달러짜리 열쇠고리 네 개를 구입했는데, 총비용의 10%를 할인받았으므로, 남자가 지불할 금액은 ③ '$72'이다.

● **Words & Phrases**

decorate 장식하다   pricey 비싼   promotion 판촉[홍보] (활동)

Exercises

본문 40~41쪽

01

정답 | ③

| **Script & Translation** |

M: Welcome to Blue Marine Aquarium. How may I help you?

W: Hi. I'd like tickets for the aquarium along with the penguin feeding experience.

M: Okay. General admission tickets to the aquarium are $10 for adults and $5 for children.

W: I need two adult tickets and two child tickets.

M: All right. And you said you also want the penguin feeding experience, right?

W: Yes, all four of us want to participate in it.

M: That's an additional $10 per person.

W: Sounds good. It's not as much as I thought it'd be.

M: So, you'll be paying for general admission tickets for two adults and two children with the penguin feeding experience for all four people, right?

W: Yes. And I have this coupon.

M: Okay. You get a 10% discount off the total.

W: Thanks. Here's my credit card.

남: Blue Marine Aquarium에 오신 것을 환영합니다. 어떻게 도와드릴까요?

여: 안녕하세요. 펭귄 먹이 주기 체험과 함께 수족관 입장권을 구매하고 싶습니다.

남: 알겠습니다. 수족관 일반 입장권은 성인 10달러이고, 어린이 5달러입니다.

여: 성인 입장권 두 장과 어린이 입장권 두 장이 필요합니다.

남: 알겠습니다. 그리고 펭귄 먹이 주기 체험도 하고 싶다고 하셨죠, 맞나요?

여: 네, 저희 네 명 모두 거기에 참여하고 싶어요.

남: 그것은 1인당 10달러가 추가됩니다.

여: 좋아요. 생각했던 것만큼 많지는 않네요.

남: 그러면 성인 두 명과 어린이 두 명의 일반 입장권과 네 명 모두의 펭귄 먹이 주기 체험 비용을 지불하실 거죠, 그렇죠?

여: 네. 그리고 이 쿠폰이 있어요.

남: 알겠습니다. 손님께서는 총액에서 10% 할인을 받으십니다.

여: 고맙습니다. 여기 제 신용 카드예요.

● **Topic & Situation** 수족관 입장권과 펭귄 먹이 주기 체험 비용

● **Solution**

수족관 입장권은 성인용 한 장에 10달러인데 여자가 두 장이 필요하다고 했으므로 20달러이고, 어린이용은 한 장에 5달러인데 두 장이 필요하다고 했으므로 10달러이다. 펭귄 먹이 주기 체험은 1인당 10달러인데 네 명이 참여를 원한다고 했으므로 40달러이다. 쿠폰으로 총액에서 10% 할인을 받는다고 했으므로, 여자가 지불할 금액은 ③ '$63'이다.

● **Words & Phrases**

aquarium 수족관   along with ~과 함께   feeding experience 먹이 주기 체험   additional 추가의

02

정답 | ③

| **Script & Translation** |

W: Honey, it's already lunchtime. Should we order some food for delivery?

M: Sure. Let's see if there are any good deals on my food delivery app.

W: Okay. *[Pause]* How about these hot beef noodles?

M: They look delicious. And $7 for one is a good deal. Let's get two noodles.

W: Okay. And let's get some side dishes, too.

M: Good idea. I'm hungry. They have shrimp rolls for $4 each and vegetable rolls for $3 each.

W: Then, why don't we order two of each and eat them together?

M: Sounds good.

W: By the way, there's a $3 delivery fee.

M: Don't worry. I have a coupon for free delivery.

W: Great. Let's order now. Do you want me to get you the credit card?

M: No, I'll pay through the app.

여: 여보, 벌써 점심시간이에요. 우리 배달 음식을 시켜 먹을까요?

남: 그래요. 내 음식 배달 앱에 괜찮은 가격의 음식이 있는지 알아보죠.

여: 네. [잠시 후] 이 소고기 온면 어때요?

남: 맛있어 보이네요. 그리고 한 그릇에 7달러면 괜찮은 가격이네요. 두 그릇 주문해요.

여: 네. 그리고 곁들임 요리도 좀 사요.

남: 좋은 생각이에요. 배가 고프네요. 하나에 4달러짜리 새우 롤과 하나에 3달러짜리 채소 롤이 있네요.

여: 그러면, 각각 두 개씩 주문해서 같이 먹는 게 어때요?

남: 좋은 생각이에요.

여: 그런데 배달비 3달러가 있어요.

남: 걱정하지 말아요. 나한테 무료 배달 쿠폰이 있어요.

여: 좋아요. 이제 주문해요. 신용 카드 줄까요?

남: 아니요, 앱으로 결제할게요.

◑ Topic & Situation 배달 앱을 통한 음식 주문

◑ Solution

남자는 여자와 함께 배달 음식을 주문하면서 7달러인 소고기 온면 두 그릇과 4달러인 새우 롤 두 개, 3달러인 채소 롤 두 개를 주문했는데, 3달러의 배달료에 대해서는 무료 배달 쿠폰을 사용한다고 했으므로, 남자가 지불할 금액은 ③ '$28'이다.

◑ Words & Phrases

delivery 배달 side dish 곁들임 요리 fee 수수료, 요금

03   정답 | ③

| Script & Translation |

M: Welcome to Ocean Tower Resort. How may I help you?

W: Hello. I'm staying in Room 807. I'd like to buy tickets for the firefly watching event tonight.

M: Okay. They're $30 for adults and $20 for children.

W: All right. I need two adult tickets and two child tickets.

M: Okay. And since you're staying in the resort, you get 10% off the tickets.

W: That's great.

M: We're selling these LED bracelets for the firefly watching event now. Would you like to buy some?

W: Oh, they look really nice. How much are they?

M: They're $10 each.

W: My kids will love them. I'll buy 2 bracelets. Are these bracelets 10% off, too?

M: No, they're not sale items. Would you buy them?

W: Sure. Here's my credit card.

남: Ocean Tower Resort에 오신 것을 환영합니다. 어떻게 도와드릴까요?

여: 안녕하세요. 저는 807호실에 묵고 있어요. 저는 오늘 밤 반딧불이 관람 행사 표를 사고 싶어요.

남: 알겠습니다. 어른은 30달러이고, 어린이는 20달러입니다.

여: 좋아요. 저는 어른 표 두 장과 어린이 표 두 장이 필요해요.

남: 알겠습니다. 그리고 손님은 리조트에 투숙하고 계시기 때문에 표를 10% 할인 받으실 수 있습니다.

여: 그거 잘됐네요.

남: 저희는 그 반딧불이 관람 행사를 위해 이 LED 팔찌들을 판매하고 있습니다. 그것들을 좀 사시겠습니까?

여: 아, 그것들은 정말 멋져 보이네요. 얼마예요?

남: 각각 10달러예요.

여: 제 아이들이 그것들을 좋아할 거예요. 그 팔찌 두 개를 살게요. 이것들도 10% 할인을 하나요?

남: 아니요, 그것은 할인 품목이 아니에요. 그것들을 사시겠어요?

여: 네. 여기 제 신용 카드가 있어요.

◑ Topic & Situation 반딧불이 관람 행사 표와 LED 팔찌 구입

◑ Solution

여자는 반딧불이 관람 행사를 위한 30달러짜리 어른 표 두 장과 20달러짜리 어린이 표 두 장을 10% 할인 받으면서 사고, 10달러짜리 LED 팔찌를 두 개 사겠다고 했으므로, 여자가 지불할 금액은 ③ '$110'이다.

◑ Words & Phrases

firefly 반딧불이 bracelet 팔찌

04

정답 | ②

| Script & Translation |

W: Hey, Sam. Are you surfing the Internet?

M: Hi, Emma. Actually, I'm shopping for a gift for my sister. She's graduating this Friday.

W: That's cool. Is she going to college?

M: Yeah. I can't decide between the fountain pen set or the ballpoint pen set. Which do you think I should get her?

W: Hmm, I'd go with the ballpoint pen set. I think for a college student, it's more useful than a fountain pen set.

M: I agree. And the ballpoint pen set is $30, and the fountain pen set is $50.

W: Look here! The ballpoint pen set is even 10% off.

M: Oh, nice! I'll buy her the set. I'm getting her this flower bouquet, too.

W: She'll love it. How much is it?

M: The bouquet is $30. So I'll get free shipping because I'm spending over $50.

W: That's good.

M: I'm going to place my order now.

여: 안녕, Sam. 인터넷 서핑하고 있니?

남: 안녕, Emma. 사실, 나는 내 여동생을 위한 선물을 사려고 쇼핑 중이야. 그 애는 이번 주 금요일에 졸업하거든.

여: 그거 멋지다. 그 애는 대학에 가니?

남: 응. 만년필 세트랑 볼펜 세트 중에서 결정을 못하겠어. 내가 그녀에게 어떤 것을 사 줘야 할까?

여: 음, 나라면 볼펜 세트를 선택하겠어. 대학생에게는 만년필 세트보다 그게 더 쓸모 있다고 생각해.

남: 동의해. 그리고 볼펜 세트는 30달러이고 만년필 세트는 50달러야.

여: 여기 봐! 그 볼펜 세트는 심지어 10% 할인이 돼.

남: 아, 좋아! 그 애에게 그 세트를 사 줄 거야. 나는 이 꽃다발도 그 애에게 줄 거야.

여: 그 애가 그것을 좋아할 거야. 그건 얼마야?

남: 그 꽃다발은 30달러야. 그래서 내가 50달러 넘게 쓰고 있기 때문에 무료 배송을 받을 거야.

여: 그거 좋구나.

남: 내가 지금 주문할게.

◑ Topic & Situation 여동생 졸업 선물 주문

◑ Solution

남자는 여동생을 위한 졸업 선물로, 30달러인 볼펜 세트를 10% 할인 받아서 산다고 했으며, 30달러인 꽃다발을 추가로 사면서, 무료 배송을 받을 거라고 했으므로, 남자가 지불할 금액은 ② '$57'이다.

◑ Words & Phrases

fountain pen 만년필 ballpoint pen 볼펜 flower bouquet 꽃다발 shipping 배송

05

정답 | ⑤

| Script & Translation |

M: Welcome to Wonderful Home Living. Can I help you find something?

W: Yes. Where are place mats?

M: I'll show you. *[Pause]* Here they are. We sell them in sets of six.

W: I like both this rectangular set and this round set. How much are they?

M: The rectangular set is $22, and the round one is $15.

W: Both are reasonable. What colors does the rectangular set come in?

M: It comes in three colors: pink, gray, and light blue.

W: Great. I'll take two rectangular sets, one pink and one light blue.

M: Okay. Is there anything else I can help you find?

W: No. That's all, thanks. And could you wrap them for me? They're a gift.

M: Sure. Gift-wrapping is free, and if you'd like to add a card, it's an extra dollar.

W: Please give me a card as well. Here's my credit card.

남: Wonderful Home Living에 오신 것을 환영합니다. 뭐 찾으시는 거 제가 도와드릴까요?

여: 네. 식탁용 식기 받침은 어디에 있나요?

남: 보여 드릴게요. *[잠시 후]* 여기 있습니다. 여섯 개씩 든 세트로 판매하고 있습니다.

여: 이 직사각형 세트와 이 원형 세트 모두 마음에 듭니다. 얼마인가요?

남: 직사각형 세트는 22달러이고, 원형 세트는 15달러입니다.

여: 둘 다 가격은 적정하네요. 직사각형 세트는 어떤 색상으로 나오나요?

남: 그것은 분홍색, 회색, 연한 파란색의 세 가지 색상으로 나옵니다.

여: 좋네요. 분홍색 하나와 연한 파란색 하나로 직사각형 세트 두 개를 사겠습니다.

남: 알겠습니다. 제가 찾는 걸 도와드릴 게 더 있을까요?

여: 아니요. 그게 다예요. 감사합니다. 그리고 그것들을 포장해 주시겠어요? 선물이거든요.

남: 물론입니다. 선물 포장은 무료이며, 카드를 추가하고 싶으시면 1달러를 더 내시면 됩니다.

여: 카드도 한 장 주세요. 여기 제 신용 카드입니다.

◐ Topic & Situation 식탁용 식기 받침 구입

◐ Solution

여자는 여섯 개씩 든 세트로 판매하는 식탁용 식기 받침 세트 중 직사각형 세트로 두 개(22×2=44달러)를 구입하기로 한다. 선물 포장은 무료이고, 카드는 추가로 1달러를 내야 하는데 여자는 카드 한 장을 달라고 말한다. 따라서 여자가 지불할 금액은 ⑤ '$45'이다.

◐ Words & Phrases

place mat 식탁용 식기 받침, 플레이스 매트(식탁에서 각자의 식기 밑에 까는 깔개)   rectangular 직사각형의   reasonable (가격이) 적정한, 너무 비싸지 않은   come (물품, 상품 등이) 나오다, 공급되다

06

정답 | ④

| Script & Translation |

W: Welcome to Pop & Soda. How may I help you?

M: Hi. How much is cherry-flavored soda?

W: It's $3 for a small one and $5 for a large one.

M: Okay. I'll take one small and one large. And I also want some popcorn. How much is it?

W: It's $6 for a box. We also have a refillable popcorn bucket.

M: Oh, that's cool! The bucket is the elephant character in the movie, *Bingbo*. My daughter loves that character.

W: The bucket is $24, and it comes filled with popcorn. And it's $3 to get it refilled.

M: Great. I'll take one box of popcorn and one refillable popcorn bucket.

W: Okay. How will you be paying?

M: By credit card. Here it is.

여: Pop & Soda에 오신 것을 환영합니다. 어떻게 도와드릴까요?

남: 안녕하세요. 체리 맛 탄산음료는 얼마인가요?

여: 작은 것은 3달러이고 큰 것은 5달러입니다.

남: 네. 작은 것 하나와 큰 것 하나로 하겠습니다. 그리고 팝콘도 좀 주세요. 얼마인가요?

여: 한 상자에 6달러입니다. 리필할 수 있는 팝콘 통도 있습니다.

남: 오, 멋지네요! 그 통은 영화 *Bingbo*에 나오는 코끼리 캐릭터 군요. 제 딸이 그 캐릭터를 정말 좋아해요.

여: 그 통은 24달러이고, 팝콘이 가득 들어 있습니다. 그리고 그것을 리필하는 데 3달러입니다.

남: 좋네요. 팝콘 한 상자와 리필할 수 있는 팝콘 통 하나 주세요.

여: 알겠습니다. 계산은 어떻게 하시겠어요?

남: 신용 카드로요. 여기 있습니다.

◐ Topic & Situation 음료와 팝콘 구입

◐ Solution

남자는 체리 맛 탄산음료 작은 것 하나와 큰 것 하나, 팝콘 한 상자와 리필할 수 있는 팝콘 통 하나를 구입하고자 한다. 체리 맛 탄산음료는 작은 것이 3달러, 큰 것이 5달러, 팝콘은 한 상자에 6달러, 리필할 수 있는 팝콘 통은 24달러이므로, 남자가 지불할 금액은 ④ '$38'이다.

◐ Words & Phrases

refillable 리필할 수 있는, 다시 채울 수 있는   bucket 통, 양동이   character (만화의) 캐릭터, 등장인물

Dictations   본문 39, 42~43쪽

기출
예제
- ❶ photo tumbler
- ❷ two of them
- ❸ key chains
- ❹ off the total cost

01
- ❶ tickets for the aquarium
- ❷ participate in it
- ❸ as much as I thought

02
- ❶ any good deals
- ❷ order two of each
- ❸ pay through the app

03
- ❶ firefly watching event
- ❷ two adult tickets
- ❸ selling these LED bracelets

04 ❶ a gift for my sister
   ❷ for a college student
   ❸ get free shipping
05 ❶ in sets of six
   ❷ take two rectangular sets
   ❸ could you wrap them
   ❹ an extra dollar
06 ❶ take one small and one large
   ❷ for a box
   ❸ a refillable popcorn bucket
   ❹ to get it refilled

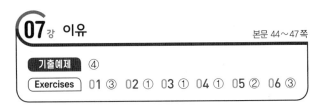

07강 이유

본문 44~47쪽

기출예제 ④

Exercises 01 ③ 02 ① 03 ① 04 ① 05 ② 06 ③

기출 예제

본문 44쪽

정답 | ④

| Script & Translation |

W: It was nice having lunch outside the office.

M: Yes. It feels so good now that fall is in the air. Shall we take a walk as usual before going back to the office?

W: I'd love to, but I can't today.

M: Is it too cold? Your jacket does look thin.

W: No, I'm okay. This jacket is warmer than it looks.

M: Then, are your allergy symptoms bothering you again?

W: Not really. I had a runny nose, but I've already seen a doctor. It's okay now.

M: So, why not today?

W: Actually, I need to visit the police station. I got a text message saying that my new driver's license is ready.

M: I see. Then I'll just go back to prepare for the afternoon meeting.

W: Okay. See you at the office.

여: 사무실 밖에서 점심을 먹어서 좋았어요.

남: 네. 공기 중에 가을이 느껴지니 기분이 너무 좋아요. 사무실로 돌아가기 전에 평소처럼 산책할까요?

여: 그러고 싶지만, 오늘은 안 돼요.

남: 너무 추워요? 재킷이 정말 얇아 보이네요.

여: 아뇨, 전 괜찮아요. 이 재킷은 보기보다 더 따뜻해요.

남: 그럼 알레르기 증상 때문에 또 괴롭나요?

여: 그런 건 아니에요. 콧물이 났지만, 이미 의사의 진찰을 받았어요. 지금은 괜찮아요.

남: 그럼, 오늘은 왜 안 되나요?

여: 사실 제가 경찰서에 방문해야 해요. 새 운전면허증이 준비되었다는 문자 메시지를 받았어요.

남: 그렇군요. 그럼 전 그냥 오후 회의 준비하러 돌아갈게요.

여: 알겠어요. 사무실에서 봐요.

● **Topic & Situation** 산책을 할 수 없는 이유

◐ Solution

점심 식사를 같이한 후, 평소처럼 산책하러 갈 것을 제안한 남자에게 여자는 산책하러 갈 수 없다고 말하고, 이유를 묻는 남자에게 여자는 새 운전면허증이 준비되어 경찰서에 방문해야 한다고 말하고 있다. 따라서 여자가 산책을 할 수 없는 이유는 ④ '경찰서에 방문해야 해서'이다.

◐ Words & Phrases

allergy 알레르기   symptom 증상   driver's license 운전면허증

Exercises

본문 46~47쪽

01

정답 | ③

| Script & Translation |

W: Hey, Brian. While you were in the restroom, I was checking out the menu. How about getting pepperoni pizza?

M: Sounds good to me. Anything to drink?

W: How about soda? It goes perfectly with pizza.

M: I know. But I don't drink soda anymore.

W: Why not? Is it because you're worried about the extra calories?

M: No. If that were the reason, I wouldn't be eating pizza!

W: True. Then why on earth don't you drink soda? Are you worried about your teeth?

M: No. I take good care of my teeth. And besides, I've never been a heavy soda drinker. It's just that drinking soda gives me a stomachache.

W: Oh, I see. Sometimes I get headaches from drinking soda. So what do you want to drink?

M: Iced tea would be great for me.

여: 있잖아. Brian. 네가 화장실에 있는 동안, 나는 메뉴를 살펴보고 있었어. 페퍼로니 피자 어때?

남: 좋아. 마실 것은?

여: 탄산음료 어때? 피자와 아주 잘 어울리잖아.

남: 알아. 하지만 나는 더 이상 탄산음료를 마시지 않아.

여: 왜 안 마시는 건데? 필요 이상의 열량이 걱정돼서 그래?

남: 아니. 그게 이유라면, 나는 피자를 먹지 않았을 거야!

여: 맞아. 그럼 너는 도대체 왜 탄산음료를 마시지 않아? 치아가 걱정되는 거야?

남: 아니. 나는 치아 관리를 잘해. 게다가 난 탄산음료를 많이 마신 적이 없어. 그냥 탄산음료를 마시면 배가 아플 뿐이야.

여: 아, 그렇구나. 가끔 나도 탄산음료를 마시면 머리가 아파. 그럼 너는 뭐 마시고 싶어?

남: 나는 아이스티가 좋을 것 같아.

◐ Topic & Situation   탄산음료를 마시지 않는 이유

◐ Solution

여자가 마실 것으로 피자와 아주 잘 어울리는 탄산음료를 권하자, 남자는 탄산음료를 마시면 배가 아파서 이제 탄산음료를 마시지 않는다고 말한다. 따라서 남자가 탄산음료를 마시지 않는 이유는 ③ '배가 아플까 봐'이다.

◐ Words & Phrases

check out ~을 살펴보다. ~을 확인하다   pepperoni 페퍼로니(소시지의 일종)   soda 탄산음료   why on earth 도대체 왜   stomachache 복통   headache 두통

02

정답 | ①

| Script & Translation |

W: Tom, it's already Friday! Do you have weekend plans?

M: Hey, Rachel. Yeah. I'm going hiking with my friends. You're going to see the circus with your family, right?

W: That was our plan, but we had to cancel it.

M: Why's that? You've finished your sales report due Monday, right?

W: Yeah, I finished it yesterday.

M: I'm surprised you're not going to the circus. You said your children were looking forward to it.

W: Right. They really wanted to see it.

M: Did you fail to reserve the tickets?

W: No. In fact, the tickets weren't even sold out. Actually, my daughter sprained her ankle pretty badly while playing soccer yesterday.

M: Oh, my. I'm sorry to hear that. So it sounds like you need to take care of her this weekend.

W: Right. But I think we can go next weekend.

여: Tom, 벌써 금요일이에요! 주말 계획이 있어요?

남: 안녕하세요, Rachel. 네. 제 친구들과 하이킹을 갈 거예요. 당신은 가족과 함께 서커스를 보러 갈 예정이죠, 맞죠?

여: 그게 저희 계획이었는데 취소해야 했어요.

남: 그건 왜죠? 월요일까지 제출해야 할 판매 보고서는 다 작성하셨잖아요, 맞죠?

여: 네, 어제 그것을 마쳤어요.

남: 서커스에 안 가신다니 놀랍군요. 당신의 아이들이 그것을 고대하고 있다고 말했잖아요.

여: 맞아요. 애들은 그것을 정말 보고 싶어 했어요.

남: 관람권을 예매하지 못했나요?

여: 아니에요. 사실, 관람권은 매진되지도 않았어요. 실은, 제 딸이 어제 축구를 하다가 발목을 꽤 심하게 삐었어요.

남: 오, 저런. 그런 말을 들으니 안타까워요. 그럼 이번 주말에 당신이 그 애를 돌봐야 할 것 같군요.

여: 맞아요. 하지만 우리는 다음 주말에는 갈 수 있을 것 같아요.

● **Topic & Situation** 서커스를 보러 갈 수 없는 이유

● **Solution**

서커스를 보러 가기로 했던 계획을 취소했다는 여자에게 남자가 그 이유를 묻자, 여자는 자신의 딸이 축구를 하다가 발목을 심하게 삐어서 주말에 아이를 돌봐야 한다고 했다. 따라서 여자가 이번 주말에 서커스를 보러 갈 수 없는 이유는 ① '다친 딸을 돌봐야 해서'이다.

● **Words & Phrases**

cancel 취소하다   look forward to ~을 고대하다   sprain 삐다
ankle 발목   take care of ~을 돌보다

03   정답 | ①

| Script & Translation |

W: Jason, have you finished reading Patrick's movie script?

M: Yeah. It was really good.

W: So are you going to make it into a movie?

M: I thought about it, but then I decided not to.

W: Why's that? Didn't your production team like the script?

M: Yes. They also loved the script.

W: Then why did you decide not to make it into a movie?

M: Well, you know that the story takes place during two wars in medieval Europe, right?

W: Ah, I see what you're hinting at. You're worried about the production cost, right?

M: Yeah. It's just so costly to have all the special effects we need for these war scenes.

W: Definitely. And the movie market is not that good nowadays.

M: Precisely. I don't want to take the risk of making a movie with a high production cost in this tough market.

W: I understand.

여: Jason, Patrick의 영화 대본을 다 읽었나요?

남: 네. 정말로 좋더라고요.

여: 그러면 그것을 영화로 만들 건가요?

남: 그것에 대해 생각했지만, 그러지 않기로 결정했어요.

여: 그건 왜죠? 당신의 제작팀이 대본을 좋아하지 않았나요?

남: 아니요. 그들 또한 대본을 아주 좋아했어요.

여: 그러면 왜 그것을 영화로 만들지 않기로 결정한 거죠?

남: 그게, 당신은 그 이야기가 중세 유럽의 두 개의 전쟁 동안에 일어나는 것을 알고 있죠, 맞죠?

여: 아, 당신이 무엇을 암시하는지 알겠어요. 당신은 제작비를 걱정하는 거죠, 맞죠?

남: 맞아요. 이런 전쟁 장면을 위해서 필요한 모든 특수 효과를 만드는 것은 비용이 정말 많이 들잖아요.

여: 물론이죠. 그리고 영화 시장이 현재 그렇게 좋지도 않고요.

남: 맞아요. 이렇게 힘든 시장에서 많은 제작비가 드는 영화를 만드는 모험을 하고 싶지는 않아요.

여: 이해해요.

● **Topic & Situation** 영화 제작을 하지 않기로 한 이유

● **Solution**

남자는 전쟁 장면을 구현하는 것이 비용이 많이 들 거라고 하면서 힘든 영화 시장에서 많은 제작비를 들여 영화를 만드는 모험을 하고 싶지 않다고 말했으므로, 남자가 Patrick의 대본을 영화로 제작하지 않기로 한 이유는 ① '제작비가 많이 들어서'이다.

● **Words & Phrases**

script 대본   medieval 중세의   hint at ~을 암시하다   production cost 제작비   special effects 특수 효과   take the risk of ~하는 모험을 하다

04

| Script & Translation |

M: Hey, Nicole. I've finally finished my chemistry report. How about you?

W: So have I. At last, I can relax.

M: Me, too. You know, I'm going to the Midtown Jazz Concert on Saturday evening.

W: Really? I'm so envious of you.

M: Then, how about going with me? I have an extra ticket.

W: I'd love to go, but I can't.

M: Why? Do you have plans with other friends?

W: No, but that evening I have an interview for a part-time job at a seafood restaurant on Lexington Street.

M: Really? I didn't know that. I'll keep my fingers crossed for you.

W: Thanks. I really wish I could go with you.

M: There will be another opportunity.

남: 야, Nicole. 드디어 내 화학 보고서를 다 썼어. 넌 어때?

여: 나도 그래. 마침내, 쉴 수 있어.

남: 나도 그래. 있잖아, 나는 토요일 저녁에 Midtown 재즈 콘서트에 갈 거야.

여: 정말? 네가 정말로 부러워.

남: 그럼, 나랑 같이 가는 게 어때? 나에게 여분의 입장권이 있어.

여: 가고 싶지만, 갈 수 없어.

남: 왜? 다른 친구들과 계획이 있니?

여: 아니, 하지만 그날 저녁 Lexington 거리에 있는 해산물 식당에서 시간제 일자리 면접이 있어.

남: 정말? 몰랐어. 너의 행운을 빌게.

여: 고마워. 너와 같이 갈 수 있으면 정말로 좋을 텐데 말이야.

남: 다른 기회가 있을 거야.

▶ Topic & Situation 재즈 콘서트에 갈 수 없는 이유

▶ Solution

토요일 저녁에 Midtown 재즈 콘서트에 가자는 남자의 제안에 여자는 토요일에 구직 면접을 봐야 해서 같이 갈 수 없다고 말했으므로, 여자가 토요일 저녁에 재즈 콘서트에 갈 수 없는 이유는 ① '구직 면접을 봐야 해서'이다.

▶ Words & Phrases

extra 여분의, 남는   keep one's fingers crossed 행운을 빌다

05

| Script & Translation |

W: Hey, Matthew. I haven't seen you in the company cafeteria recently. Have you been skipping lunch?

M: No, Mia. I've been bringing my own lunch to work.

W: Any particular reason? I thought you liked the cafeteria food.

M: I do like it.

W: Oh, then maybe it's because the prices have gone up recently.

M: That's not the reason. The food there is still reasonably priced.

W: So are you just trying to eat less?

M: No, my doctor told me to eat more protein. So I make and bring my own meals to make sure I get enough.

W: I see. What kind of meals are you making?

M: I usually make chicken and fish dishes.

W: Nice! Bringing your own lunch can also help save some money, right?

M: Not really, considering the cost of the foods I prepare. But sometimes I miss the convenience of the cafeteria.

W: I can understand that.

여: 안녕하세요, Matthew. 최근에 회사 구내식당에서 당신을 보지 못했어요. 점심을 거르고 있었던 거예요?

남: 아니에요, Mia. 저는 직장에 제 점심을 싸 오고 있었어요.

여: 어떤 특별한 이유가 있나요? 저는 당신이 구내식당 음식을 좋아하는 줄 알았어요.

남: 정말 좋아해요.

여: 아, 그럼 최근 가격이 올라서 그런가 봐요.

남: 그래서가 아니에요. 그곳의 음식은 여전히 합리적으로 가격이 매겨져 있어요.

여: 그렇다면 그냥 덜 먹으려고 하는 건가요?

남: 아니에요, 제 의사가 단백질을 더 섭취하라고 했어요. 그래서 저는 반드시 충분히 섭취할 수 있도록 식사를 직접 만들어서 가지고 와요.

여: 그렇군요. 어떤 종류의 식사를 만드세요?

남: 대개 닭고기와 생선 요리를 만들어요.

여: 좋네요! 직접 점심을 가져오는 것은 돈을 절약하는 데도 도움이 될 수 있죠, 맞죠?

남: 제가 준비하는 음식의 비용을 고려하면, 별로 그렇지 않아요. 하지만 저는 가끔 구내식당의 편리함이 그리워요.

여: 그건 이해할 수 있어요.

● **Topic & Situation** 직장에 점심을 싸 오는 이유

● **Solution**

여자는 최근에 회사 구내식당에서 남자를 보지 못했다면서 이유를 묻고, 남자는 점심을 싸 오고 있다면서 단백질을 더 섭취하라는 의사의 말에 따라 식사를 직접 만들어 가지고 온다고 설명하고 있다. 따라서 남자가 직장에 점심을 싸 오는 이유는 ② '단백질 섭취를 늘려야 해서'이다.

● **Words & Phrases**

recently 최근에 **skip** 거르다, 건너뛰다, 빠뜨리다 **price** 가격; 가격을 매기다 **reasonably** 합리적으로 **protein** 단백질 **meal** 식사 **miss** 그리워하다 **convenience** 편리(함), 편의

06

정답 | ③

| **Script & Translation** |

M: Hi, Grandma. How are you feeling? Is your knee better?

W: Hello, dear. It's healed now. Thanks for asking.

M: Great! My dance competition is this Saturday. Could you come see me dance?

W: I'd love to, but I won't be able to make it.

M: I'm sorry that you can't come. Do you have to go to the senior center then?

W: No, not this weekend. It's closed for maintenance.

M: I see. Oh, you mentioned going on a picnic with friends? Is it this Saturday?

W: We wanted to, but we canceled because of the weather forecast. It'll be rainy and windy this weekend.

M: Really? Then it won't be easy for you to come see the contest.

W: No worries, dear. Actually, I have a health checkup on Saturday, which I can't reschedule.

M: I understand. I'll show you the dance video later.

W: That'd be great. I'm sure you'll do great.

M: Thank you.

남: 안녕하세요, 할머니. 몸은 어떠세요? 무릎은 나아지셨어요?

여: 안녕, 얘야. 이제 다 나았어. 물어봐 줘서 고맙구나.

남: 잘됐네요! 제 댄스 대회가 이번 주 토요일에 있어요. 제가 춤추는 것을 보러 오실 수 있으세요?

여: 그러고 싶지만, 갈 수 없을 것 같구나.

남: 오실 수 없다니 유감이에요. 그때 노인 센터에 가셔야 하는 건가요?

여: 아니, 이번 주말은 아니야. 그곳은 유지 보수 때문에 문을 닫아.

남: 그렇군요. 아, 친구분들과 소풍을 가신다고 하셨죠? 그게 이번 주 토요일이에요?

여: 우리는 그러고 싶었지만, 일기예보 때문에 취소했어. 이번 주말에 비가 내리고 바람이 불 거야.

남: 정말이요? 그렇다면 할머니가 대회를 보러 오시는 것은 쉽지 않겠네요.

여: 걱정하지 마, 얘야. 사실, 내가 토요일에 건강 검진이 있는데, 일정을 변경할 수 없단다.

남: 이해해요. 제가 나중에 댄스 영상을 보여 드릴게요.

여: 그거 좋겠구나. 나는 네가 잘할 거라고 확신해.

남: 감사합니다.

● **Topic & Situation** 손자의 댄스 대회를 보러 갈 수 없는 이유

● **Solution**

이번 주 토요일에 댄스 대회가 있으니 보러 오라는 남자의 말에 여자는 일정을 변경할 수 없는 건강 검진이 있어서 갈 수 없다고 말하고 있다. 따라서 여자가 남자의 댄스 대회를 보러 갈 수 없는 이유는 ③ '건강 검진을 받아야 해서'이다.

● **Words & Phrases**

maintenance 유지 보수 health checkup 건강 검진 reschedule 일정을 변경하다

Dictations

본문 45, 48~49쪽

기출 ❶ look thin

예제 ❷ allergy symptoms

❸ police station

01 ❶ don't drink soda anymore

❷ about the extra calories

❸ about your teeth

❹ gives me a stomachache

02 ❶ see the circus

❷ looking forward to it

❸ sprained her ankle

03 ❶ make it into a movie
   ❷ like the script
   ❸ the story takes place
   ❹ in this tough market
04 ❶ I can relax
   ❷ so envious of you
   ❸ have an interview
   ❹ keep my fingers crossed
05 ❶ bringing my own lunch
   ❷ trying to eat less
   ❸ miss the convenience
06 ❶ come see me dance
   ❷ because of the weather forecast
   ❸ which I can't reschedule

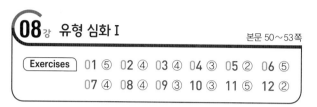

08강 유형 심화 Ⅰ

본문 50~53쪽

Exercises 01 ⑤ 02 ④ 03 ④ 04 ③ 05 ② 06 ⑤
          07 ④ 08 ④ 09 ③ 10 ③ 11 ⑤ 12 ②

Exercises

본문 50~53쪽

01

정답 | ⑤

| Script & Translation |

W: Attention, everyone. I'm Jessica Mccallahan, the Chief of the Landsberg Fire Department. Today, I'd like to share with you some important information on how to prevent forest fires from spreading, which can cause extensive damage to homes, businesses, and the environment. As we approach the drier months, it's important to be aware of the potential risks of forest fires. To prevent forest fires from spreading, please quickly report any signs of fire around you. If you see smoke or fire, call emergency services immediately. The sooner a fire is reported, the faster it can be kept from spreading and put out. Let's work together to keep our communities and environment safe.

여: 주목해 주세요, 여러분. 저는 Landsberg 소방서장 Jessica Mccallahan입니다. 오늘 저는 여러분과 주택, 사업체 및 환경에 광범위한 피해를 줄 수 있는 산불 확산을 막는 방법에 관한 몇 가지 중요한 정보를 공유하고자 합니다. 더 건조한 달이 다가옴에 따라 산불의 잠재적인 위험성을 인식하는 것이 중요합니다. 산불 확산을 막기 위해, 여러분의 주변에서 화재의 징후가 있으면 빠르게 신고해 주세요. 연기나 불이 보이면 즉시 응급 구조대에 전화하세요. 화재 신고가 빠를수록, 화재의 확산을 더 빠르게 막아 화재가 진화될 수 있습니다. 우리 지역 사회와 환경을 안전하게 유지하기 위해 함께 노력합시다.

◑ **Topic & Situation** 신속한 화재 신고 당부하기

◑ **Solution**
산불 확산의 위험성을 인식하는 것의 중요성을 언급하며, 화재의 징후가 보이면 즉시 응급 구조대에 전화하여 빠른 신고를 할 것을 당부하고 있으므로, 여자가 하는 말의 목적으로 가장 적절한 것은 ⑤ '산불 확산을 막기 위해 신속한 화재 신고를 당부하려고'이다.

◎ Words & Phrases

fire department 소방서 forest fire 산불 extensive 광범위한

potential 잠재적인 immediately 즉시

02

정답 | ④

| Script & Translation |

W: Sam, you live near Green Park, don't you?

M: Yeah. Why? Are you planning to go there?

W: Yes. I'm thinking of going there with my family to hang out this weekend. Do you think Green Park would be a good place for that?

M: Absolutely! Green Park is extremely family-friendly.

W: That's good to hear. What does it have?

M: It has a variety of facilities that everyone in the family can enjoy.

W: What kind of facilities are there?

M: There are a playground for kids, cycling paths, walking trails, sports facilities, and more. It has something for everyone.

W: Wow, it sounds like my family will really like the park.

M: Definitely. Green Park is the perfect place to spend time with family.

W: Now I'm really looking forward to going there. I can't wait to tell my family about it.

여: Sam, 너는 Green 공원 근처에 살지, 그렇지 않니?

남: 그래. 왜? 거기에 갈 계획이야?

여: 맞아. 이번 주말에 가족과 함께 거기에 놀러 갈까 생각 중이야. Green 공원이 그렇게 하기에 좋은 장소라고 생각하니?

남: 당연하지! Green 공원은 대단히 가족 친화적이거든.

여: 좋은데. 그 공원에는 무엇이 있니?

남: 가족 모두가 즐길 수 있는 다양한 시설이 있어.

여: 어떤 종류의 시설이 있는데?

남: 어린이를 위한 놀이터, 사이클 도로, 산책로, 스포츠 시설, 그리고 더 많은 것이 있어. 그곳에는 모두를 위한 무언가가 있어.

여: 와, 우리 가족이 그 공원을 정말로 마음에 들어 할 것 같은데.

남: 물론이지. Green 공원은 가족과 함께 시간을 보내기에 완벽한 장소야.

여: 이제 그곳에 가는 것이 정말로 기대가 돼. 우리 가족에게 그곳에 대해 빨리 말해 주고 싶어.

◎ Topic & Situation 가족 친화적인 Green 공원

◎ Solution

Green 공원 근처에 살고 있는 남자는 Green 공원에 가족 모두가 즐길 수 있는 시설이 있다고 하면서 Green 공원이 가족과 함께 시간을 보내기에 완벽한 장소라고 말했으므로, 남자의 의견으로 가장 적절한 것은 ④ 'Green 공원은 가족과 함께 시간을 보내기에 좋은 장소이다.'이다.

◎ Words & Phrases

hang out 놀다, 어울리다 family-friendly 가족 친화적인 a variety of 다양한 path 도로, 길 walking trail 산책로

03

정답 | ④

| Script & Translation |

W: Hi, Robert. Did you hear about the job opening at Star Electronics?

M: No. What's the job?

W: It's a marketing position for their international sales division.

M: A marketing position? That sounds interesting.

W: They're looking for someone to work at their Korean and Chinese branches. Since you speak both Korean and Chinese fluently, you should apply.

M: Oh, perfect! I will. Thanks for letting me know.

W: My pleasure. I think speaking foreign languages fluently like you is really helpful for getting a job.

M: Well, I just learned the languages because I like them, but hearing you saying it, maybe you're right.

W: Sure. My roommate recently got a job at a trading company because she speaks fluent Spanish.

M: Why don't you start learning a foreign language? It's never too late to get started.

W: You're right. I'll look into it.

여: 안녕, Robert. Star Electronics의 채용 일자리에 대해 들었니?

남: 아니. 어떤 일인데?

여: 해외 영업부의 마케팅 직책이야.

남: 마케팅 직책이라고? 흥미로운걸.

여: 그들은 한국과 중국 지사에서 일할 사람을 찾고 있어. 네가 한국어와 중국어를 둘 다 유창하게 하니까, 지원해 봐.

남: 오, 완벽해! 그럴게. 알려 줘서 고마워.

여: 천만에. 나는 너처럼 외국어를 유창하게 말하는 것이 일자리를 얻는 데 큰 도움이 될 수 있다고 생각해.

남: 음, 나는 그저 외국어가 좋아서 그것을 공부했지만, 네가 말하는 것을 들어 보니 네 말이 맞는 것 같아.

여: 당연하지. 내 룸메이트는 스페인어를 유창하게 구사해서 최근에 무역 회사에 취직했어.

남: 외국어 공부를 시작하는 게 어때? 시작하기에 너무 늦은 때란 없어.

여: 맞아. 외국어 공부를 알아볼 거야.

◉ Topic & Situation 외국어 실력이 구직에 미치는 영향

◉ Solution
한국어와 중국어를 유창하게 할 수 있어서 Star Electronics에 지원할 수 있게 된 남자를 보면서 여자는 외국어를 유창하게 말하는 것이 일자리를 얻는 데 큰 도움이 될 수 있다고 말했으므로, 여자의 의견으로 가장 적절한 것은 ④ '유창한 외국어 실력은 일자리를 구하는 데 큰 도움이 된다.'이다.

◉ Words & Phrases
division (조직의) 부, 국   branch 지사   fluently 유창하게   apply 지원하다, 신청하다   trading company 무역 회사

04
정답 | ③

| Script & Translation |

M: Good morning, Ms. Miller. I'm Gavin Swift.

W: Good morning, Mr. Swift. It's a pleasure to meet you.

M: The pleasure is mine. I'm truly impressed with your work. Your creations are remarkable.

W: Thank you. I appreciate your kind words.

M: I'm thrilled to have the opportunity to work with one of your masterpieces. This building looks like a perfect subject for photography.

W: I'm excited to see how you capture its essence.

M: I have some ideas to convey its unique design.

W: Great. I'm looking forward to seeing how you bring out the best in my building through your lens.

M: Well, if it's okay with you, I'd like to start shooting tomorrow.

W: Sure. That works for me.

M: Wonderful. Also, may I explore the building now to determine the best angles for photography?

W: Absolutely. If you have any questions, please feel free to ask me.

남: 안녕하세요, Miller 씨. 저는 Gavin Swift입니다.

여: 안녕하세요, Swift 씨. 만나서 반갑습니다.

남: 저도 반갑습니다. 저는 당신의 작품에 정말로 감명받았습니다. 당신의 창작물은 놀랍습니다.

여: 고맙습니다. 당신의 친절한 말씀에 감사드립니다.

남: 저는 당신의 걸작 중 하나를 대상으로 작업할 기회를 얻게 되어 흥분됩니다. 이 건물은 사진 촬영에 완벽한 대상 같아 보입니다.

여: 당신이 그 정수를 어떻게 정확히 담아낼지 기대됩니다.

남: 그것의 독특한 디자인을 전달할 몇 가지 아이디어가 있습니다.

여: 좋습니다. 당신이 어떻게 당신의 렌즈를 통해 제 건물에서 최상의 부분을 끌어내는지 보길 기대하고 있어요.

남: 음, 만약 괜찮으시다면, 저는 내일부터 촬영을 시작하고 싶습니다.

여: 그래요. 그 시간은 저한테 맞아요.

남: 좋습니다. 또, 사진 촬영에 가장 좋은 각도를 정하기 위해 지금 건물을 탐색해도 될까요?

여: 물론이죠. 질문이 있으시면, 편하게 제게 물어 보십시오.

◉ Topic & Situation 건축가의 작품인 건물 사진 촬영

◉ Solution
남자는 여자의 작품에 감명받았고, 여자의 걸작 중 하나를 가지고 작업할 기회를 얻게 되어 흥분된다고 하면서 여자의 건물이 사진 촬영에 완벽한 대상 같아 보인다고 했으며, 여자는 남자가 렌즈를 통해 자신의 건물에서 최상의 모습을 어떻게 끌어내는지 보길 기대한다고 말했다. 따라서 두 사람의 관계를 가장 잘 나타낸 것은 ③ '사진작가 – 건축가'이다.

◉ Words & Phrases
impressed 감명받은, 감동한   remarkable 놀라운, 훌륭한   appreciate 감사하다   opportunity 기회   masterpiece 걸작   subject 대상, 주제   capture 정확히 담아내다[포착하다], 붙잡다   essence 정수, 본질   convey 전달하다   unique 독특한   bring out ~을 끌어내다[발휘하게 하다]   shooting 촬영   determine 정하다, 결정하다   angle 각도

05
정답 | ②

| Script & Translation |

M: Hi, Jane. What's that you're looking at?

W: It's a picture of the rooftop garden on top of my apartment building. Check it out.

M: Wow! The flowers hanging on the left side wall are so beautiful.

W: I know. They're in full bloom right now. I go here almost every day and read newspapers on this U-shaped bench in the middle.

M: Awesome. I'm sure the parasol next to the bench is great when it's sunny.

W: For sure. Especially when it's about mid-afternoon.

M: Do you ever use the two sunbeds on the right?

W: Yeah, I sometimes use them for tanning. I bring a drink and put it on the round table between the sunbeds.

M: This rooftop garden is super nice! I can't believe it's on top of your building.

W: To me, it's like an oasis in the middle of the city.

남: 안녕, Jane. 네가 보고 있는 것은 무엇이니?

여: 우리 아파트 꼭대기에 있는 옥상 정원 사진이야. 이것 한번 봐 봐.

남: 와! 왼쪽 벽에 걸려 있는 꽃들이 정말 아름답다.

여: 맞아. 지금 꽃이 만발해 있어. 나는 거의 매일 이곳에 가서 가운데에 있는 이 U자 모양의 벤치에서 신문을 읽어.

남: 굉장하네. 햇빛이 비치는 날에는 분명 벤치 옆에 있는 파라솔이 좋을 거야.

여: 물론이지. 오후 중반이면 특히 그래.

남: 오른쪽에 있는 두 개의 선베드를 사용하기도 하니?

여: 응, 나는 가끔 그것들을 태닝할 때 사용해. 나는 음료를 가져와서 선베드 사이의 둥근 탁자 위에 놓아둬.

남: 이 옥상 정원은 정말 멋져! 이곳이 네 건물 위에 있다는 것을 믿을 수가 없어.

여: 나에게는 그곳이 마치 도시 한복판에 있는 오아시스 같아.

● **Topic & Situation** 아파트 옥상 정원

● **Solution**
대화에서 여자가 U자 모양의 벤치에 대해 언급했는데, 그림의 벤치는 일자형이므로, 그림에서 대화의 내용과 일치하지 않는 것은 ②이다.

● **Words & Phrases**
rooftop 옥상 in full bloom (꽃이) 만발하며, 활짝 핀 mid-afternoon 오후 중반 sunbed 선베드(누워서 태양 등을 쬐는 침대) oasis 오아시스

06

| **Script & Translation** |

M: Hi, Jenny. How was your weekend?

W: It was great. My son and I had a really good time at a playground inside a forest at Johnson Creek. Here's a picture of it.

M: Wow, cool. Is this your son on the tire swing on the left?

W: Yes. He played on that for hours.

M: I bet he liked climbing up to the tower on that wooden slope with a rope.

W: Yeah. He said it was like being in an adventure movie!

M: Really? It's interesting how the roof makes the tower in the center look like a castle.

W: That's right. He also enjoyed going down the slide on the right of the tower.

M: Wow, that must have been fun. Look at the three round seats! They all look great.

W: Yeah. I like to sit there and watch my son play.

M: How nice! I should take my kids sometime.

남: 안녕하세요, Jenny. 주말은 어떻게 보내셨나요?

여: 정말 좋았어요. 제 아들과 저는 Johnson Creek에 있는 숲속 놀이터에서 정말 좋은 시간을 보냈답니다. 여기 그곳의 사진이 있어요.

남: 와, 멋지네요. 왼쪽에 있는 타이어 그네에 타고 있는 사람이 당신 아들인가요?

여: 네, 그는 그것을 타며 몇 시간을 놀았어요.

남: 아드님이 하나의 밧줄이 있는 나무로 된 경사로 위에서 탑으로 기어 올라가는 것을 분명 좋아했을 거예요.

여: 맞아요. 마치 모험 영화에 나오는 것 같다고 그가 말했어요!

남: 정말요? 지붕이 중앙의 탑을 성처럼 보이게 하는 것이 흥미롭네요.

여: 맞아요. 그는 또한 탑의 오른쪽에 있는 미끄럼틀을 타고 내려가는 것을 즐겼어요.

남: 와, 그것 정말 재밌었겠네요. 저기 세 개의 둥근 의자들을 보세요! 모두 좋아 보이네요.

여: 네, 저는 거기 앉아 제 아들이 노는 것을 지켜보는 것을 좋아해요.

남: 정말 좋네요! 언젠가 제 아이들을 데려가 봐야겠어요.

● **Topic & Situation** 숲속 놀이터

◐ Solution

남자가 세 개의 둥근 의자들이 있다고 언급했으나, 그림에는 둥근 의자가 두 개이므로, 그림에서 대화의 내용과 일치하지 않는 것은 ⑤이다.

◐ Words & Phrases

playground 놀이터 tire swing 타이어 그네 wooden 나무로 된
slope 경사로 slide 미끄럼틀

07
정답 | ④

| Script & Translation |

W: Mr. White, there are only three days until the graduation ceremony. I think we mostly have everything ready.

M: I think so, too, Ms. Baker. We got the graduation albums, right?

W: Yes. They're ready to be distributed. And I purchased the decoration items for the graduation photo zone yesterday.

M: Good. I received the prizes for the graduation award winners this morning.

W: Well, do you have enough time to wrap them?

M: Yeah. I can wrap them up today.

W: Great. How about the auditorium?

M: I'm planning on helping with the auditorium setup at 9 tomorrow morning. Oh, wait! I just realized I have a problem.

W: Oh, what's the matter?

M: I was supposed to pick up the graduation ceremony banners then. Can you pick them up for me?

W: Of course. I can do that.

M: Thanks so much.

여: White 선생님, 졸업식까지 3일밖에 남지 않았네요. 제 생각에는 거의 다 준비된 것 같아요.

남: 제 생각도 그래요, Baker 선생님. 졸업 앨범을 받았죠, 맞죠?

여: 네. 그것들은 배부될 준비가 되어 있어요. 그리고 저는 졸업식 포토존 장식 물품들을 어제 구매했어요.

남: 좋습니다. 저는 오늘 아침에 졸업식 수상자 상품들을 수령했어요.

여: 음, 그것들을 포장할 충분한 시간이 있으세요?

남: 네. 오늘 포장을 마무리할 수 있습니다.

여: 좋아요. 강당은 어때요?

남: 내일 아침 9시에 강당 배치를 도울 예정입니다. 아, 잠깐만요! 제게 문제가 있다는 것을 막 깨달았어요.

여: 아, 무슨 일이에요?

남: 그때 졸업식 현수막을 찾아오기로 되어 있었어요. 저 대신에 현수막들을 찾아와 줄 수 있나요?

여: 물론이죠. 그건 제가 할 수 있어요.

남: 정말 감사합니다.

◐ Topic & Situation 졸업식 준비

◐ Solution

졸업식의 준비 상황을 확인하는 대화를 나누면서 남자가 내일 아침 9시에 강당 배치를 도울 계획인데, 그 시간에 졸업식 현수막을 찾아오기로 예정되어 있었다며 여자에게 졸업식 현수막을 대신 찾아와 줄 수 있냐고 물었고 여자는 그 일을 할 수 있다고 했다. 따라서 여자가 할 일로 가장 적절한 것은 ④ '졸업식 현수막 찾아오기'이다.

◐ Words & Phrases

graduation ceremony 졸업식 distribute 배부하다, 나누어 주다
decoration 장식, 장식품 award 상 wrap ~ up ~을 포장하다
auditorium 강당, 객석 banner 현수막, 플래카드

08
정답 | ④

| Script & Translation |

W: Jonathan, I'm so excited for the basketball championships tomorrow.

M: Me, too. Everyone from our school has to cheer extra hard!

W: Definitely. This is more than just a regular season game. We need to be super fans!

M: Right. Is the cheer placard ready?

W: Yeah. I finished making it yesterday with some of the student board members.

M: Great. And I ordered snacks online for our school students.

W: When will they arrive?

M: This afternoon. When I get them, I'll divide them into individual packs to distribute them easily.

W: Good idea. I can help you.

M: Don't worry. I can do it by myself.

W: Then I'll send a reminder text message to everybody

about the game tomorrow.

M: Okay. It's going to be so fun.

여: Jonathan, 내일 농구 챔피언 결정전 때문에 너무 흥분돼.

남: 나도 그래. 우리 학교 학생들 모두 정말 열심히 응원해야 해!

여: 당연하지. 이건 단순한 정규 시즌 경기 그 이상이야. 우리는 열렬한 팬이 되어야 해!

남: 맞아. 응원 플래카드는 준비됐니?

여: 응. 어제 학생회 학생들 몇몇과 함께 그것을 만드는 걸 끝냈어.

남: 좋아. 그리고 나는 우리 학교 학생들에게 줄 간식을 온라인으로 주문했어.

여: 그것들은 언제 도착하니?

남: 오늘 오후에. 그것을 받으면 쉽게 나누어 줄 수 있도록 개별 포장으로 나눌 거야.

여: 좋은 생각이야. 도와줄게.

남: 걱정하지 마. 혼자 할 수 있어.

여: 그러면 내가 내일 경기에 대한 안내 문자 메시지를 모두에게 보낼게.

남: 알았어. 정말 재밌을 거야.

● **Topic & Situation** 농구 챔피언 결정전 응원 준비

● **Solution**
학교 학생들에게 나누어 줄 간식이 언제 도착하는지 묻는 여자에게 남자는 오늘 오후에 도착할 것이라고 하며 그것을 받으면 나누어 주기 쉽게 개별 포장을 할 것이라고 말한다. 여자가 도와주겠다고 하자 남자는 혼자 할 수 있다고 했으므로 남자가 할 일로 가장 적절한 것은 ④ '간식 개별 포장하기'이다.

● **Words & Phrases**
placard 플래카드   divide 나누다   individual 개별의

09 정답 | ③

| Script & Translation |

M: Good afternoon, Miranda. How may I help you today?

W: Hi, Jason. I came here today to see if the antique table and chairs set that you had is still available.

M: Yes, we still have it. Are you interested in buying it?

W: Yeah. Glad it hasn't been sold! I believe it was priced at $500. Could you offer a discount?

M: Actually it's already very cheap, but since you're such a loyal customer, I can give you $50 off.

W: That's so generous. Thanks! And do you still have the two stools that matched the set?

M: We sure do! They're $50 each, but if you purchase both, I'll take $20 off the total price.

W: Wow, thanks again! I'll take both of them. Can you deliver everything to my house?

M: We charge $50 for delivery. Is that okay?

W: Sounds good. Here's my credit card.

M: Thank you.

남: 안녕하세요, Miranda. 오늘은 어떻게 도와드릴까요?

여: 안녕하세요, Jason. 오늘 저는 여기 있었던 골동품 식탁과 의자 세트를 아직도 살 수 있는지 알아보려고 왔어요.

남: 네, 아직 있어요. 그것을 사는 데 관심이 있으신가요?

여: 네. 그게 팔리지 않아서 다행이에요! 가격이 500달러였던 것 같은데요. 할인해 주실 수 있을까요?

남: 사실 그건 이미 매우 저렴하지만, 진짜 단골손님이시니까, 50달러 할인해 드릴 수 있습니다.

여: 정말 너그러우시네요. 감사합니다! 그리고 그 세트와 어울렸던 두 개의 스툴이 아직도 있나요?

남: 물론 있습니다! 한 개에 50달러인데, 둘 다 구매하시면 총금액에서 20달러 할인해 드릴게요.

여: 와, 다시 한번 감사합니다! 두 개 다 살게요. 모든 물건을 저의 집으로 배달해 주실 수 있나요?

남: 배달료는 50달러입니다. 괜찮으십니까?

여: 좋아요. 여기 제 신용 카드입니다.

남: 감사합니다.

● **Topic & Situation** 골동품 식탁과 의자 세트와 스툴 구매

● **Solution**
여자는 500달러인 골동품 식탁과 의자 세트를 사면서 50달러를 할인 받고($450), 개당 50달러인 스툴을 2개 사면서 20달러를 할인 받았으며($80), 배달료가 50달러이므로, 여자가 지불할 금액은 ③ '$580'이다.

● **Words & Phrases**
antique 골동품의, 고대의   available 구할 수 있는, 이용할 수 있는
loyal customer 단골손님   generous 너그러운, 관대한   match 어울리다, 맞추다

10 정답 | ③

| Script & Translation |

W: Hello, Joshua, how can I help you today?

M: Hi, Rachel. I'm actually here to renew my Pilates membership.

W: All right, let me check. *[Typing sound]* I see that your membership is expiring next week.

M: Yes, that's correct. There are discounts for long-term memberships, right?

W: Absolutely. The monthly fee is $100, and we offer a 20% discount for a three-month membership and a 30% discount for a six-month membership.

M: Got it. I'd like to go for the three-month membership.

W: Perfect! We also have foam roller classes every Saturday. Are you interested in joining?

M: How much do they cost?

W: They're $10 per class, but you can purchase a package of four classes for $30.

M: Okay, I'll go for a package of four classes. Here's my credit card.

W: Great! Let me handle your membership renewal and the foam roller classes.

여: 안녕하세요, Joshua, 오늘은 어떻게 도와드릴까요?

남: 안녕하세요, Rachel. 저는 사실 필라테스 회원권을 갱신하러 여기 왔어요.

여: 알겠어요, 확인해 볼게요. *[타자 치는 소리]* 회원님의 회원권이 다음 주에 만료된다고 확인됩니다.

남: 네, 맞아요. 장기 회원권 할인이 있죠, 맞죠?

여: 물론이죠. 월 이용료는 100달러인데, 3개월 회원권의 경우 20% 할인, 6개월 회원권의 경우 30% 할인을 제공해요.

남: 알겠어요. 저는 3개월 회원권으로 하고 싶어요.

여: 좋아요! 우리는 또한 매주 토요일에 폼 롤러 강좌가 있어요. 참여하는 데 관심이 있으신가요?

남: 비용은 얼마인가요?

여: 1회 수강은 10달러인데, 4회 수강권 패키지는 30달러에 구입할 수 있습니다.

남: 알겠습니다. 4회 수강권 패키지로 할게요. 여기 제 신용 카드요.

여: 좋습니다! 회원권 갱신과 폼 롤러 강좌를 처리해 드리겠습니다.

◑ Topic & Situation 필라테스 회원권 갱신과 폼 롤러 수강권 구매

◑ Solution
남자는 필라테스 회원권을 월 이용료가 100달러인데 20% 할인이 되는 3개월 회원권($100×3개월-$60)으로 갱신하고, 30달러짜리 폼 롤러 강좌 4회 수강권을 구매하겠다고 했으므로, 남자가 지불할 금액은 ③ '$270'이다.

◑ Words & Phrases

renew 갱신하다   expire 만료되다   long-term 장기의   handle 처리하다

11
정답 | ⑤

| Script & Translation |

W: Wow. Honey, it's already dinner time.

M: Whoa, it is. We have some frozen pizzas from the grocery store in the freezer. Would you like one of them?

W: Pizza sounds good, but I don't feel like a frozen pizza.

M: Oh, I see. Should we order a pizza from the new pizza place then? I have a free delivery coupon.

W: No, I was thinking I could make one from scratch.

M: Well, it's a lot of work and time. Why don't you want delivery pizza? Are you worried it'll be cold by the time it gets here?

W: No. I'm sure they use a pizza delivery bag to keep it hot.

M: Then I wonder why you want to make a pizza instead of getting one delivered.

W: I'd like to make my own pizza with ingredients I want.

M: Like what?

W: I can use the tomatoes and blueberries I picked from the garden this morning.

M: Wow, that sounds delicious.

W: Definitely worth all the work!

여: 와. 여보, 벌써 저녁 식사 시간이에요.

남: 우와, 그렇네요. 냉동실에 식료품점에서 사 온 냉동 피자가 몇 개 있어요. 그중 하나 먹을래요?

여: 피자는 맛있을 것 같은데, 냉동 피자는 먹고 싶지 않아요.

남: 아, 알겠어요. 그러면 새로운 피자 가게에서 피자를 주문할까요? 제게 무료 배달 쿠폰이 있어요.

여: 아니요, 맨 처음부터 하나 만들어 볼까 생각 중이었어요.

남: 음, 그것에는 시간과 노력이 많이 들잖아요. 왜 배달 피자를 원하지 않나요? 그것이 여기 도착할 때쯤이면 식을까 봐 그러나요?

여: 아뇨. 그들은 분명 배달용 가방을 사용해서 피자를 따뜻하게 유지할 거예요.

남: 그러면 당신이 왜 피자를 배달시키지 않고 직접 만들고 싶어 하는지 궁금해요.

여: 제가 원하는 재료로 저만의 피자를 만들고 싶어요.

남: 예를 들면요?

여: 오늘 아침에 제가 텃밭에서 딴 토마토와 블루베리를 활용할 수 있어요.

남: 와, 맛있을 것 같아요.

여: 분명 수고한 가치가 있을 거예요!

● **Topic & Situation** 피자를 주문하지 않으려는 이유

● **Solution**

피자를 주문하지 않고 직접 만들려는 여자에게 남자가 그 이유를 묻자, 여자는 토마토와 블루베리같이 자신이 원하는 재료들을 사용하여 피자를 만들고 싶다고 했으므로, 여자가 피자를 주문하지 않으려는 이유는 ⑤ '원하는 재료로 피자를 만들고 싶어서'이다.

● **Words & Phrases**

freezer 냉동실　from scratch 맨 처음부터　by the time ~할 때 쯤에는　ingredient 재료

12

| Script & Translation |

W: Mr. Pitt, are you okay? You don't look so good.

M: Hi, Ms. Grady. I've had a terrible stomachache since last night.

W: Sorry to hear that. Have you seen a doctor?

M: No, but I took some medicine at home. It's getting a little better.

W: That's good. Can I help you prepare for your classes, like copying and stapling handouts?

M: Thanks, but I've already done that.

W: Okay. By the way, did you hear that the teacher's book discussion meeting was rescheduled?

M: No. I'm afraid I didn't check the notice.

W: It is now next Thursday. I heard about it this morning.

M: Oh, I can't attend it then.

W: Why? Do you have anything else to do?

M: I have to take care of my children on my own because my wife works late on Thursdays.

W: Okay. I'll be sure to grab you a copy of the discussion materials.

M: Oh, I appreciate your kindness.

여: Pitt 선생님, 괜찮으세요? 안색이 그다지 좋아 보이지 않으세요.

남: 안녕하세요, Grady 선생님. 어젯밤부터 배가 많이 아파서요.

여: 그러시다니 안타깝네요. 병원에 가 보셨어요?

남: 아니요, 하지만 집에서 약을 좀 먹었어요. 조금씩 나아지고 있습니다.

여: 다행이네요. 유인물 복사나 스테이플러로 철하기 같은 수업 준비를 도와드릴까요?

남: 감사합니다만, 그건 이미 다 했습니다.

여: 네. 그런데 교사 독서 토론 모임 일정이 변경되었다는 소식 들었어요?

남: 아니요. 전 그 공지를 확인하지 못했어요.

여: 지금은 다음 주 목요일로 되어 있어요. 저는 그 소식을 오늘 아침에 들었어요.

남: 아, 그때는 참석할 수 없는데요.

여: 왜요? 다른 할 일이 있으세요?

남: 아내가 목요일마다 늦게까지 일하기 때문에 아이들을 혼자 돌봐야 해요.

여: 그렇군요. 토론 자료 사본을 꼭 챙겨 드릴게요.

남: 아, 친절에 감사드립니다.

● **Topic & Situation** 교사 독서 토론 모임에 참석할 수 없는 이유

● **Solution**

교사 독서 토론 모임의 일정이 목요일로 변경되었음을 알려주는 여자에게 남자는 아내가 목요일마다 늦게까지 일을 하기 때문에 자기가 아이들을 돌봐야 하므로 모임에 참석할 수 없다고 말하고 있다. 따라서 남자가 교사 독서 토론 모임에 참석할 수 없는 이유는 ② '자녀를 돌봐야 해서'이다.

● **Words & Phrases**

stomachache 복통　staple 스테이플러로 철하다　reschedule 일정을 변경하다　attend 참석하다　take care of ~을 돌보다　grab 챙겨 주다, (붙)잡다, 움켜쥐다　material 자료　appreciate 감사하다, 고마워하다

09강 언급 유무

본문 54~57쪽

기출예제 ③

Exercises 01 ③ 02 ④ 03 ④ 04 ④ 05 ⑤ 06 ④

기출 예제

본문 54쪽

정답 | ③

| Script & Translation |

[Telephone rings.]

W: Jason Theater. How may I help you?

M: Hi, this is William Parker from Breezeville Senior Center.

W: Oh, Mr. Parker. You called yesterday about bringing your seniors to see the play.

M: Yes. Before I book, I'd like to double check the title. It's *The Shiny Moments*, right?

W: That's right. Have you decided on the date?

M: Yes. Could I reserve seats for 25 people on December 27th?

W: Absolutely. But in that case, you'll need to pay today.

M: Okay. You said admission tickets for seniors are $30 each.

W: That's correct. I'll send you the link for the payment.

M: Thank you. I'll pay tonight.

W: That'll be fine. The play starts at 3 p.m., but please come 30 minutes early.

M: No problem. See you then.

[전화벨이 울린다.]

여: Jason 극단입니다. 무엇을 도와드릴까요?

남: 안녕하세요, Breezeville Senior Center의 William Parker입니다.

여: 아, Parker 씨. 노인분들을 모시고 연극을 보러 오는 것에 관해 어제 전화하셨죠.

남: 네. 예약하기 전에 제목을 다시 한번 확인하고 싶습니다. 제목이 *The Shiny Moments*, 맞죠?

여: 맞습니다. 날짜는 정하셨나요?

남: 네. 12월 27일에 25명의 좌석을 예약할 수 있을까요?

여: 물론이죠. 하지만 그 경우 오늘 결제하셔야 합니다.

남: 좋습니다. 노인 입장권은 장당 30달러라고 말씀하셨죠.

여: 맞습니다. 결제 링크를 보내 드리겠습니다.

남: 고맙습니다. 오늘 밤에 결제하겠습니다.

여: 그러면 됩니다. 연극은 오후 3시에 시작하지만, 30분 일찍 와 주십시오.

남: 그럼요. 그때 뵐게요.

◉ Topic & Situation 연극 공연 예약

◉ Solution

남자가 예약할 연극 공연에 관해 제목, 날짜, 입장료, 시작 시각은 언급되었으나, ③ '출연자'는 언급되지 않았다.

◉ Words & Phrases

book 예약하다   double check 다시 한번 확인하다   reserve 예약하다   admission ticket 입장권   payment 결제

Exercises

본문 56~57쪽

01

정답 | ③

| Script & Translation |

W: Eddie, have you heard about the newly opened Upcycled Art Gallery?

M: No. It sounds interesting, though. Have you been there?

W: No. I've just read about it. They exhibit artworks such as images made of used bottle caps or sculptures made of pieces of cardboard.

M: Cool. I'd like to go there with my kids. Where is it located?

W: It's right next to City Hall.

M: Good. That's very near to here. Do you know how much the entrance fee is?

W: Just a second. I'm checking out their website. *[pause]* Oh, it's $10 for adults and $5 for kids.

M: That's reasonable. Could you check the opening hours?

W: It's open from 10 a.m. to 5 p.m.

M: Okay. I hope it's open on weekends.

W: It is.

M: Great. I think I'll go there this Saturday. Would you like to go too?

W: Sure. Let's do it!

여: Eddie, 새로 문을 연 Upcycled Art Gallery에 대해 들어 봤어요?

남: 아니요. 하지만 흥미롭게 들리네요. 당신은 그곳에 가 보셨나요?

여: 아니요. 그저 그곳에 대해 읽어 봤어요. 그곳에서는 사용한 적 있는 병뚜껑으로 만든 이미지들이나 판지로 만든 조각품과 같은 예술작품을 전시하고 있어요.

남: 멋지네요. 우리 아이들과 함께 그곳에 가 보고 싶어요. 어디에 있나요?

여: 시청 바로 옆에 있어요.

남: 좋네요. 여기서 매우 가까워요. 입장료가 얼마인지 아세요?

여: 잠시만요. 제가 그들의 웹사이트를 훑어 보고 있어요. [잠시 후] 오, 어른은 10달러이고, 어린이는 5달러네요.

남: 적당하네요. 개관 시간도 확인해 주실래요?

여: 오전 10시부터 오후 5시까지 열어요.

남: 알겠어요. 주말에도 문을 열었으면 좋겠네요.

여: 열어요.

남: 좋아요. 저는 이번 주 토요일에 그곳에 가 볼 생각이에요. 당신도 갈래요?

여: 물론이죠. 그렇게 하죠!

◉ Topic & Situation Upcycled Art Gallery

◉ Solution
Upcycled Art Gallery에 관해 전시 작품, 위치, 입장료, 개관 시간은 언급되었으나, ③ '교통편'은 언급되지 않았다.

◉ Words & Phrases
upcycled 업사이클링이 된(재활용품에 디자인 또는 활용도를 더해 그 가치를 높인 제품으로 재탄생시킨) exhibit 전시하다 sculpture 조각품 cardboard 판지 entrance fee 입장료 reasonable (가격 등이) 적당한, 비싸지 않은

02

정답 | ④

| Script & Translation |

M: Alice, are you still interested in learning photography?

W: Yeah. Why do you ask?

M: I heard that the Landon Community Center is holding a photo class. How about taking it together?

W: Sounds good! When is the class?

M: It's on Friday afternoons in May. There are a total of four lessons.

W: All right. Do you know how much the tuition is?

M: Yeah. It's $40 per person. It's pretty cheap, isn't it?

W: Not bad. Do you know who teaches it?

M: That's the cool part. Every lesson is taught by a different teacher, who is a professional photographer.

W: Awesome! Let's register today.

M: Okay. I think it's going to be a really fun class.

남: Alice, 너 사진 촬영을 배우는 것에 대해 아직도 관심 있어?

여: 그래. 왜 물어?

남: Landon Community Center가 사진 강좌를 열 거라고 들었어. 그것을 같이 수강하는 게 어때?

여: 좋아! 그 강좌는 언제인데?

남: 5월에 금요일 오후마다 열려. 총 4번의 수업이 있어.

여: 좋아. 수강료가 얼마인지 알고 있어?

남: 그래. 1인당 40달러야. 상당히 저렴해, 그렇지 않아?

여: 나쁘지는 않네. 누가 그것을 가르치는지 알고 있어?

남: 그게 멋진 부분이야. 모든 수업은 각각 다른 강사가 수업을 진행하는데, 강사는 전문 사진작가야.

여: 멋지다! 오늘 등록하자.

남: 좋아. 그것은 정말로 재미있는 수업이 될 것 같아.

◉ Topic & Situation 사진 강좌

◉ Solution
사진 강좌에 관해 두 사람은 개설 기관, 수업 요일, 수강료, 강사에 대해서만 언급되었으나, ④ '신청 방법'은 언급되지 않았다.

◉ Words & Phrases
photography 사진 촬영[찍기], 사진술   hold 열다, 개최하다
awesome 멋진 register 등록하다

03

정답 | ④

| Script & Translation |

W: Mark, have you heard about the GET 2024 event?

M: No, what is it, Jenny?

W: GET stands for Geography Exploration Tour. It's for first-year geography majors like us.

M: That sounds fun. What exactly will we do if we join?

W: We will visit a region down south and examine its soil and rocks.

M: Wow, that's an excellent way to get hands-on experience.

W: Right. We'll also visit its local markets for shopping.

M: Awesome. Who's in charge of it?

W: Professor Richard is the supervisor.

M: Great! How can we sign up for it?

W: You need to fill out a form in the department office. I'm going there after lunch.

M: Cool. I'll go with you.

여: Mark, GET 2024 행사에 대해서 들어 봤어?

남: 아니, 그게 뭐야, Jenny?

여: GET는 지리 답사 투어를 의미해. 우리 같은 지리학과 1학년 학생들을 위한 거야.

남: 재미있겠다. 참가하면 정확히 무엇을 하는데?

여: 우리는 남쪽의 한 지역을 방문해서 그 지역의 토양과 암석을 조사할 거야.

남: 와, 그것은 직접 해 보는 체험을 할 수 있는 훌륭한 방법이네.

여: 맞아. 우리는 또한 그 지역 시장들을 방문해서 쇼핑을 할 거야.

남: 굉장하다. 누가 그것을 담당하셔?

여: Richard 교수님이 지도 교수님이셔.

남: 좋아! 어떻게 그것을 신청할 수 있어?

여: 학과 사무실에서 양식을 작성해야 해. 난 점심 식사 후에 거기에 가려고 해.

남: 좋아. 나도 같이 갈게.

◐ Topic & Situation GET 2024

◐ Solution

GET 2024 행사에 관해 참가 대상, 활동 내용, 담당 교수, 신청 방법은 언급되었으나, ④ '참가 비용'은 언급되지 않았다.

◐ Words & Phrases

stand for ~을 의미하다 geography 지리학 exploration 답사, 탐험 major 전공하는 학생 region 지역 soil 토양, 흙 hands-on 직접 해 보는, 실천하는 in charge of ~을 담당하는 supervisor 지도 교수; 감독관, 관리자 sign up for ~을 신청하다 fill out ~을 작성하다

04

정답 | ④

| Script & Translation |

M: Kayla, Mom's birthday is next month. Do you still want to bake a cake for her?

W: Definitely. I've bookmarked the site of Jane's Cake Baking Class. Here it is.

M: Let me see.... Oh, this is a class for beginners!

W: Yeah. That's good for us.

M: I wonder what kind of cake we'll make in the class.

W: It says they'll teach us to bake chocolate cake, which is Mom's favorite.

M: Perfect! When is the class?

W: It's held every Saturday. Are you available this Saturday?

M: Sure, in the morning. But I'm busy in the afternoon. How long is the class?

W: Four hours. It's offered twice a day, so we can take the morning class.

M: Great. Let's sign up for it.

W: Okay. Mom will be so surprised!

남: Kayla, 엄마 생일이 다음 달이야. 여전히 엄마를 위해 케이크를 만들고 싶니?

여: 당연하지. Jane's Cake Baking Class의 사이트를 즐겨찾기 해 두었어. 여기 있어.

남: 어디 보자…. 오, 이것은 초보자를 위한 강좌구나!

여: 맞아. 우리에게 잘 됐어.

남: 그 강좌에서 우리가 어떤 종류의 케이크를 만들지 궁금해.

여: 초콜릿케이크 만드는 법을 가르쳐 준다고 되어 있는데, 그것은 엄마가 제일 좋아하시는 거잖아.

남: 완벽해! 강좌는 언제 있니?

여: 매주 토요일에 있어. 이번 토요일에 시간 되니?

남: 응, 오전에. 하지만 오후에는 바빠. 강좌 시간은 얼마나 되니?

여: 4시간이야. 하루에 두 번 제공되기 때문에 우리는 오전 강좌를 들을 수 있어.

남: 좋아. 그 강좌에 등록하자.

여: 알았어. 엄마가 정말 놀라실 거야!

◐ Topic & Situation 케이크 만들기 강좌

◐ Solution

Jane's Cake Baking Class에 관해 수강 대상, 강좌 내용, 강좌 요일, 소요 시간은 언급되었으나, ④ '수강료'는 언급되지 않았다.

◐ Words & Phrases

bookmark (인터넷의) 즐겨찾기 해 두다 beginner 초보자 available 시간이 있는 offer 제공하다

05

정답 | ⑤

| Script & Translation |

W: Steve, we should go over the preparations for next month's Eco-Vision Workshop.

M: Sounds good, Lisa. You were able to book the conference room at Brahms Hotel, right?

W: Yeah. I booked it last week.

M: Good. I remember the conference room was very nice last year.

W: Right. It holds up to 100 people, and we're expecting around 80 people this year.

M: Great. And Professor Schilt emailed me, and confirmed he'd be the main speaker.

W: Oh, that's wonderful.

M: Yeah. He's an amazing speaker.

W: No doubt. So the plan is for him to speak for about 2 hours from 10 a.m., right?

M: Yes. Then the attendees will have a discussion about the speech after lunch.

W: Perfect. So the workshop runs for about 4 hours and finishes at 2 p.m.

M: That's the plan. I think it'll work out.

W: All right. It sounds good.

여: Steve, 우리는 다음 달 Eco-Vision Workshop 준비를 검토해야 해요.

남: 좋아요, Lisa. Brahms 호텔의 회의실을 예약할 수 있었죠, 맞죠?

여: 네. 지난주에 그것을 예약했어요.

남: 좋아요. 그 회의실이 작년에 매우 좋았던 것으로 기억해요.

여: 맞아요. 그것은 100명까지 수용할 수 있고, 올해 약 80명이 올 것으로 예상돼요.

남: 좋아요. 그리고 Schilt 교수님이 제게 이메일을 보내셔서 자신이 주요 강연자가 될 것이라고 확인해 주셨어요.

여: 오, 정말 멋지군요.

남: 네. 그는 훌륭한 강연자이시죠.

여: 의심의 여지가 없어요. 그럼 그분은 오전 10시부터 약 두 시간 동안 강연할 계획이죠, 맞죠?

남: 네. 그러면 참석자들은 점심 식사 이후에 그 강연에 대해서 토론을 할 거예요.

여: 완벽해요. 그러니까 그 워크숍은 4시간 동안 운영되고 오후 두 시에 끝나죠.

남: 그게 계획이에요. 그것이 잘 될 것 같아요.

여: 그래요. 좋은 것 같아요.

◯ Topic & Situation Eco-Vision Workshop 준비

◯ Solution

Eco-Vision Workshop에 관해 개최 장소, 참가 인원, 강연자, 진행 시간은 언급되었지만, ⑤ '주최 기관'은 언급되지 않았다.

◯ Words & Phrases

go over ~을 검토하다   book 예약하다   conference room 회의실   confirm 확인하다   attendee 참석자

06

정답 | ④

| Script & Translation |

[Telephone rings.]

W: Hello. Forevi Sports Center. How may I help you?

M: Hello. May I ask you a few questions about the child swimming classes? I'm thinking about signing up my son.

W: Sure. What would you like to know?

M: What's the age limit?

W: The child swimming class is limited to children between the ages of 6 to 12.

M: I see. Are there different levels for the child swimming classes?

W: Yes. There are three levels. They are beginner, intermediate, and advanced.

M: Okay. My son should be a beginner. How many kids can sign up for the class?

W: A maximum of ten kids per class.

M: I see. And what time do the Saturday classes start?

W: There are two Saturday classes for child beginners. One starts at 10 a.m., and the other at 2 p.m.

M: Sounds good. I'll stop by over the weekend to sign up my son for one of the classes.

W: All right.

[전화벨이 울린다.]

여: 안녕하세요. Forevi Sports Center입니다. 어떻게 도와드릴까요?

남: 안녕하세요. 어린이 수영 수업에 대해 몇 가지 질문을 해도 될까요? 제 아들을 등록시킬까 생각 중이거든요.

여: 물론이죠. 무엇을 알고 싶으신가요?

남: 나이 제한이 어떻게 되나요?

여: 어린이 수영 수업은 6세부터 12세까지의 어린이들로 제한되어 있어요.

남: 그렇군요. 어린이 수영 수업에 서로 다른 레벨이 있나요?

여: 네. 세 레벨이 있어요. 그것들은 초급, 중급, 고급이에요.

남: 좋아요. 제 아들은 분명히 초보자예요. 그 수업을 몇 명의 아이들이 등록할 수 있어요?

여: 수업당 최대 10명의 아이요.

남: 그렇군요. 그리고 토요일 수업은 몇 시에 시작하나요?

여: 어린이 초보자들을 위한 두 개의 토요일 수업이 있어요. 하나는 오전 10시에 시작하고, 다른 하나는 오후 2시에 시작해요.

남: 좋아요. 아들을 그 수업들 중 하나에 등록시키기 위해 주말에 들를게요.

여: 알겠습니다.

◉ **Topic & Situation** Forevi Sports Center 어린이 수영 수업

◉ **Solution**

Forevi Sports Center 어린이 수영 수업의 참가 연령, 수업 레벨, 제한 인원, 수업 시간은 언급되었지만, ④ '월 등록비'는 언급되지 않았다.

◉ **Words & Phrases**

intermediate 중급; 중급의   advanced 고급; 고급의   stop by ~에 들르다

05 ❶ book the conference room
   ❷ for him to speak
   ❸ runs for about 4 hours
06 ❶ limited to children
   ❷ sign up for the class
   ❸ stop by over the weekend

Dictations

본문 55, 58~59쪽

기출
예제
❶ double check the title
❷ reserve seats for
❸ admission tickets for seniors
01 ❶ made of used bottle caps
   ❷ the entrance fee is
   ❸ open on weekends
02 ❶ learning photography
   ❷ how much the tuition is
   ❸ Every lesson is taught
   ❹ register today
03 ❶ examine its soil and rocks
   ❷ in charge of it
   ❸ fill out a form
04 ❶ bookmarked the site
   ❷ Are you available
   ❸ sign up for it

additional 추가의   location 장소   participant 참가자

10강 담화 내용 일치
본문 60~63쪽

기출예제 ④

Exercises 01 ③ 02 ④ 03 ④ 04 ⑤ 05 ⑤ 06 ④

기출 예제
본문 60쪽
정답 | ④

| Script & Translation |

M: Hello, viewers. Are you looking for an interesting experience? How about joining the *Golden Palette* Walking Tour? You'll get the chance to see some of the famous filming sites from the movie *Golden Palette*. This tour runs every day in November. It's a three-hour walking tour with one of our professional guides. Also, brochures are provided for free, and you can find additional information about the filming sites there. The tour begins at 10:30 a.m. and takes you to six locations from the movie. The starting point is at the north gate of Central Studio. The price for this tour is $40 per person. All participants will receive a postcard as a gift. Book it now on our website!

남: 안녕하세요, 시청자 여러분. 흥미로운 경험을 찾고 계신가요? *Golden Palette* 걷기 투어에 참여해 보시는 건 어떨까요? 영화 *Golden Palette*의 유명한 촬영지 일부를 둘러볼 기회를 얻을 것입니다. 이 투어는 11월에 매일 진행됩니다. 저희의 전문 안내인 중 한 명과 함께하는 3시간짜리 걷기 투어입니다. 또한, 안내 책자가 무료로 제공되고, 거기서 촬영지에 대한 추가 정보를 찾을 수 있습니다. 투어는 오전 10시 30분에 시작되고 영화에 등장하는 여섯 곳의 장소로 여러분을 데려갑니다. 출발 지점은 Central Studio의 북쪽 문입니다. 이 투어의 가격은 1인당 40달러입니다. 모든 참가자들이 선물로 엽서를 받을 것입니다. 지금 저희 웹사이트에서 예약하세요!

🔹 **Topic & Situation** *Golden Palette* 걷기 투어

🔹 **Solution**
Golden Palette 걷기 투어의 출발 지점은 Central Studio의 북쪽 문이라고 했으므로, 담화의 내용과 일치하지 않는 것은 ④ '출발 지점은 Central Studio의 남쪽 문이다.'이다.

🔹 **Words & Phrases**
filming site 촬영지   brochure 안내 책자   for free 무료로

Exercises
본문 62~63쪽

01
정답 | ③

| Script & Translation |

M: Attention, young actors and actresses. Get ready to shine on stage this summer! The 5th Spotlight Drama Camp is here and better than ever! This camp will last for one week and offer exciting activities filled with learning, creativity, and fun. It'll be at the newly renovated Rainbow Theater downtown. Experienced camp staff will teach you everything from acting basics to developing your characters. The participation fee is $200 per person and covers all materials, costumes, and a final performance. No previous acting experience is required. However, spaces are limited, so you should register on our website as soon as possible. Don't miss this chance to showcase your talent on stage this summer!

남: 주목하세요, 젊은 배우 여러분. 올여름 무대에서 빛날 준비를 하세요! 제5회 Spotlight Drama Camp가 여기에 있고, 이전보다 더욱 훌륭합니다! 이 캠프는 일주일 동안 진행되고, 학습, 창의성, 그리고 재미로 가득한 신나는 활동들을 제공할 것입니다. 그것은 시내에 새로 단장한 Rainbow Theater에서 개최될 것입니다. 경험이 풍부한 캠프 직원들이 연기 기초부터 캐릭터 개발까지 모든 것을 가르쳐 줄 것입니다. 참가비는 1인당 200달러이며, 모든 재료, 의상, 그리고 최종 공연이 포함됩니다. 이전의 연기 경험은 필요하지 않습니다. 하지만 자리가 제한되어 있으니 저희 웹사이트에서 가능한 한 빨리 등록하셔야 합니다. 올여름 무대에서 여러분의 재능을 보여 줄 이 기회를 놓치지 마세요!

🔹 **Topic & Situation** The 5th Spotlight Drama Camp

🔹 **Solution**
참가비는 1인당 200달러이며, 모든 재료, 의상, 그리고 최종 공연이 포함된다고 했으므로, 담화의 내용과 일치하지 않는 것은 ③ '최종 공연 비용은 참가비와 별도로 지불한다.'이다.

Words & Phrases

renovate 새롭게 단장하다, 개조하다   theater 극장   material 재료, 자료   costume 의상, 복장   previous 이전의   register 등록하다

02

정답 | ④

| Script & Translation |

W: Good morning, listeners! Are you looking for a place to go with your family this winter? Then why not consider going to the Lockwood Snow Festival? It takes place in January every year and features a wide range of winter activities. One of the main attractions is the "Ice Sculpture Contest," in which artists from all over the world participate by creating amazing sculptures out of ice. Visitors can enjoy sledding, snow tubing, and nighttime activities like ice skating under the stars. And remember all of these activities are free. The festival also has a lot of food trucks selling snacks and drinks. So if you're looking for a fun way to enjoy the winter, you can't miss the Lockwood Snow Festival!

여: 좋은 아침입니다, 청취자 여러분! 이번 겨울 가족과 함께 갈 곳을 찾고 계신가요? 그렇다면 Lockwood Snow Festival 에 가는 것을 고려해 보는 것은 어떠신가요? 그것은 매년 1월 에 열리고 다양한 겨울 활동을 특징으로 합니다. 주요 볼거리 중 하나는 전 세계의 예술가들이 얼음으로 놀라운 조각품을 만 들어 참가하는 '얼음 조각 대회'입니다. 방문객들은 썰매 타기, 눈썰매, 별 아래에서 스케이트 타기와 같은 야간 활동을 즐길 수 있습니다. 그리고 이 모든 활동은 무료라는 점을 기억하세 요. 축제에는 또한 간식과 음료를 파는 많은 푸드 트럭들도 있 습니다. 그러니 여러분이 겨울을 즐길 재미있는 방법을 찾고 있다면, Lockwood Snow Festival을 놓칠 수는 없습니다!

Topic & Situation   Lockwood Snow Festival

Solution

모든 활동은 무료라고 했으므로, 담화의 내용과 일치하지 않는 것 은 ④ '일부 활동은 유료이다.'이다.

Words & Phrases

feature 특징으로 하다   attraction 볼거리   snow tubing 눈썰매

03

정답 | ④

| Script & Translation |

M: Hello, students! Guess what's just around the corner. It's our school's 2024 Summer Hiking Trip! It'll be from August 11 to August 13. This year, we're hiking Donovan Mountain with five professional guides and enjoy fun activities in Donovan Mountain National Park all together. On the first day, we'll hike to the peak of the mountain and enjoy the beautiful view there. On the second day, we'll walk to the Donovan River in the morning and enjoy rafting for about two hours. It's going to be so much fun! And then we'll return home on the last day. All activities will take place in groups. For more details, check the school website. Don't miss out on this great event!

남: 안녕하세요, 학생 여러분! 무엇이 임박했는지 맞춰 보세요. 그 것은 우리 학교의 2024 Summer Hiking Trip이에요! 그것 은 8월 11일부터 8월 13일까지 진행될 것입니다. 올해, 우리 는 다섯 명의 전문 안내원과 함께 Donovan 산을 하이킹하고 Donovan 산 국립공원에서 함께 즐거운 활동들을 즐길 것입 니다. 첫째 날, 우리는 산 정상까지 하이킹을 가서 그곳에서 아름다운 경치를 즐길 것입니다. 둘째 날, 우리는 아침에 Donovan 강까지 걸어가고 약 두 시간 동안 래프팅을 즐길 것입니다. 그것은 정말 재미있을 거예요! 그런 다음 우리는 마 지막 날에 집으로 돌아올 것입니다. 모든 활동은 조별로 진행 될 것입니다. 더 많은 세부 사항은, 학교 웹사이트를 확인하세 요. 이 멋진 행사를 놓치지 마세요!

Topic & Situation   2024 Summer Hiking Trip

Solution

2024 Summer Hiking Trip의 둘째 날에는 아침에 Donovan 강까지 걸어가고 이후 두 시간 동안 래프팅을 즐길 것이라고 했으 므로, 담화의 내용과 일치하지 않는 것은 ④ '둘째 날에 종일 강을 따라 걸을 것이다.'이다.

Words & Phrases

around the corner 임박하여, 바로 다가와서   peak 정상   detail 세부 사항   miss out on ~을 놓치다

04

정답 | ⑤

| Script & Translation |

W: Hello, everyone. This is Katie Jones, the head of the school photography club. I'm pleased to announce our club's most fun contest of the year, the Happy Dog Photo Contest. The contest gives you a chance to share the joy your dog brings you with other students. And if you don't have a dog, no problem. You can enter the contest with a photo you take of a friend or relative's dog. Just submit one photo of your or their dog with your name, and we'll post it on the bulletin board in the school lobby. The submission deadline is Friday, April 19th. Students will vote for their favorite photos for three days starting April 22nd. And the winner will receive an organic pet shampoo and conditioner set. So hurry up and tell your furry friend to say "Cheese!"

여: 안녕하세요, 여러분. 저는 학교 사진 동아리 회장 Katie Jones입니다. 저희 동아리의 올해 가장 재미있는 대회인 Happy Dog Photo Contest를 알려 드리게 되어 기쁩니다. 이 대회는 반려견이 여러분에게 주는 기쁨을 다른 학생들과 나눌 기회를 제공합니다. 그리고 반려견을 키우지 않더라도 문제 없습니다. 여러분은 친구나 친척의 반려견을 찍은 사진으로 대회에 참가할 수 있습니다. 여러분의 이름과 함께 여러분이나 그들(친구나 친척)의 반려견 사진 한 장만 제출하면 저희가 그것을 학교 로비에 있는 게시판에 게시할 것입니다. 제출 마감일은 4월 19일 금요일입니다. 학생들이 4월 22일부터 3일간 가장 마음에 드는 사진에 투표할 것입니다. 그리고 우승자는 유기농 반려동물 샴푸와 컨디셔너 세트를 받을 것입니다. 그러니 서둘러 여러분의 털북숭이 친구에게 "치즈!" 하라고 말하세요.

◉ Topic & Situation Happy Dog Photo Contest

◉ Solution

대회 우승자는 유기농 반려동물 샴푸와 컨디셔너 세트를 받을 것이라고 했으므로, 담화의 내용과 일치하지 않는 것은 ⑤ '우승자는 반려견 사료를 받을 것이다.'이다.

◉ Words & Phrases

share 나누다, 공유하다   relative 친척   submit 제출하다   post 게시하다   bulletin board 게시판   furry 털로 덮인

05

정답 | ⑤

| Script & Translation |

M: Attention, students! Are you interested in discussing global issues and participating in policy debates with your peers worldwide? If so, we invite you to join the upcoming Global Policy Debate Contest. The contest will take place online from August 1st to 3rd. It is open to students of all age groups, regardless of prior debate experience. The topic of this year's debates is global health challenges. Experts in policy debates will evaluate the discussions and provide you with valuable feedback to enhance your debating skills. Additionally, the top five teams will receive scholarships and prizes. Registration is currently open online until the end of June, and signing up is completely free. For more details, please visit www.gpfdebate.org. Don't miss out on this fantastic opportunity.

남: 주목하세요, 학생 여러분! 전 세계 친구들과 글로벌 이슈를 논의하고 정책 토론에 참여하는 것에 관심이 있습니까? 그렇다면, 다가오는 Global Policy Debate Contest에 참가하라고 여러분을 초대합니다. 그 대회는 8월 1일부터 3일까지 온라인으로 개최될 것입니다. 그것은 이전의 토론 경험에 상관없이 모든 연령 그룹의 학생들에게 개방되어 있습니다. 올해 토론 주제는 세계적인 건강 문제입니다. 정책 토론의 전문가들이 토론을 평가하고, 여러분에게 귀중한 피드백을 제공하여 토론 능력을 향상해 줄 것입니다. 게다가, 상위 다섯 팀은 장학금과 상을 받을 것입니다. 등록은 현재 6월 말까지 온라인으로 가능하며, 참가는 완전히 무료입니다. 더 자세한 내용은 www.gpfdebate.org을 방문하십시오. 이 환상적인 기회를 놓치지 마십시오.

◉ Topic & Situation Global Policy Debate Contest

◉ Solution

등록은 6월 말까지 온라인으로 가능하다고 했으므로, 담화의 내용과 일치하지 않는 것은 ⑤ '등록은 7월 말까지 가능하다.'이다.

◉ Words & Phrases

policy 정책   debate 토론   peer 친구, 동료   upcoming 다가오는   regardless of ~과 상관없이   prior 이전의   expert 전문가   valuable 귀중한   enhance 향상하다   scholarship 장학금   registration 등록   currently 현재   completely 완전히

06

정답 | ④

| Script & Translation |

W: Hi, everyone. I'm Jessica Kim, the manager at Sunshine Hotel. I'd like to tell you about our Sunshine Beach Yoga Class, which takes place daily from 10 a.m. to 11 a.m. As one of the most popular programs in our hotel, the class is for true beginners who have never done yoga before. So, no prior yoga experience is required to participate in this class. It takes place on the beach right behind the hotel, which is just a 5-minute walk from the hotel lobby. Hotel guests can join for free. Non-guests can join for a $10 fee per class. Please be aware that this class will be recorded and broadcast on our hotel website. Stop by the front desk if you have any questions. Thank you for your attention.

여: 안녕하세요, 여러분. 저는 Sunshine 호텔의 매니저 Jessica Kim입니다. 저는 여러분에게 매일 오전 10시에서 11시까지 열리는 Sunshine Beach Yoga Class에 대해 말씀드리고자 합니다. 우리 호텔에서 가장 인기 있는 프로그램의 하나로, 이 수업은 전에 요가를 한 번도 해 본 적 없는 진짜 초보자를 위한 것입니다. 따라서 이 수업에 참여하기 위해서 이전의 요가 경험이 필요하지 않습니다. 이 수업은 호텔 바로 뒤에 있는 해변에서 진행되는데, 이곳은 호텔 로비에서 걸어서 단지 5분 거리에 있습니다. 호텔 투숙객은 무료로 참가하실 수 있습니다. 호텔에 투숙하지 않는 분은 수업 당 10달러의 비용으로 참가할 수 있습니다. 이 수업은 녹화되어서 저희 호텔 웹사이트에서 방송될 것이라는 점을 알아 두세요. 궁금한 점이 있으면 호텔의 프런트 데스크에 들러 주십시오. 관심을 가져 주셔서 감사드립니다.

❍ Topic & Situation Sunshine Beach Yoga Class

❍ Solution

호텔 매니저인 여자는 호텔 투숙객은 Sunshine Beach Yoga Class를 무료로 참여할 수 있다고 했으므로, 담화의 내용과 일치하지 않는 것은 ④ '호텔 투숙객의 참가비는 수업 당 10달러이다.'이다.

❍ Words & Phrases

take place 열리다. 일어나다　participate in ~에 참여하다　aware 알고 있는. 인식하는　broadcast 방송하다　stop by ~에 (잠시) 들르다

Dictations

본문 61, 64~65쪽

기출
예제
❶ are provided for free
❷ at the north gate
❸ a postcard as a gift

01 ❶ Get ready to shine
❷ the newly renovated Rainbow Theater
❸ No previous acting experience

02 ❶ why not consider
❷ creating amazing sculptures
❸ looking for a fun way

03 ❶ enjoy fun activities
❷ peak of the mountain
❸ take place in groups

04 ❶ the joy your dog brings you
❷ submit one photo
❸ post it on the bulletin board
❹ vote for
❺ for three days

05 ❶ participating in policy debates
❷ regardless of prior debate experience
❸ signing up is completely free

06 ❶ true beginners
❷ required to participate
❸ be recorded and broadcast

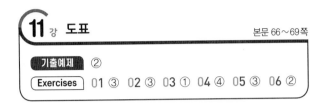

11 강 도표   본문 66~69쪽

기출예제 ②

Exercises 01 ③ 02 ③ 03 ① 04 ④ 05 ③ 06 ②

기출 예제   본문 66쪽

정답 | ②

| Script & Translation |

W: Honey, what are you doing on your laptop?

M: I'm trying to choose one of these foldable carts. You know our cart broke yesterday.

W: Oh, that's right. Let me see the ones you're looking at.

M: Sure. There are these five. They all look good, but let's not spend more than $50.

W: All right. How about the weight limit? Our last one was 30 kilograms.

M: Hmm, that wasn't strong enough.

W: Okay. Then, this one won't be any good.

M: Yeah. Do you have any color preference?

W: The old one was blue. Why don't we get a different color this time?

M: Good idea. Now, there are two options left. Which handle material do you like better?

W: Well, metal gets too cold in winter.

M: Good point. Then, let's get the other model. I'll order it now.

여: 여보, 노트북으로 뭐 하고 있어요?

남: 이 접이식 카트 중 하나를 고르려고요. 어제 우리 카트가 고장 난 거 알잖아요.

여: 오, 맞아요. 당신이 보고 있는 것 좀 보여 줘요.

남: 물론이죠. 이 다섯 가지가 있어요. 그것들 모두 좋아 보이지만, 50달러 넘게는 쓰지 말아요.

여: 좋아요. 무게 한도는 어때요? 지난번 것은 30kg이었어요.

남: 흠, 그건 충분히 강하지 않았어요.

여: 알았어요. 그럼 이건 안 되겠네요.

남: 네. 선호하는 색이 있나요?

여: 예전 것은 파란색이었어요. 이번엔 다른 색으로 사면 어떨까요?

남: 좋은 생각이에요. 이제 두 가지 선택 사항이 남았네요. 어떤 손잡이 재질이 더 마음에 들어요?

여: 글쎄요, 금속은 겨울에 너무 차가워져요.

남: 좋은 지적이네요. 그럼 다른 모델을 사죠. 내가 지금 그것을 주문할게요.

● **Topic & Situation** 접이식 카트 주문

● **Solution**

여자와 남자는 50달러가 넘지 않고, 무게 한도가 30kg이 넘으며, 파란색이 아니고, 손잡이 재질이 금속이 아닌 모델을 선택했고, 남자가 그 모델을 주문하겠다고 했으므로, 남자가 주문할 접이식 카트는 ②이다.

● **Words & Phrases**

foldable 접이식의   weight limit 무게 한도   preference 선호
material 재질, 재료

Exercises   본문 68~69쪽

01   정답 | ③

| Script & Translation |

M: Welcome to J's Electronics. What can I do for you?

W: Hi. I'm looking for an electric toothbrush.

M: Okay. [Pause] These are the ones we have. Do you have a particular brand in mind?

W: No, but I do have a budget. I'd like to keep it under $100.

M: Got it. So if you take a look here, they have different brushing modes. It's nice to have a variety of them.

W: Right. I'd like to get one with at least four modes.

M: Okay. That leaves a few great options.

W: Oh, these have a pressure sensor. I really want to have that.

M: That's a useful function to protect your gums. So these two seem to fit what you'd like. Do you have a color preference?

W: Everything in my bathroom is bright, so I don't want black. I'll buy the other one.

M: Okay. Sounds good.

남: J's Electronics에 오신 것을 환영합니다. 무엇을 도와드릴까요?

여: 안녕하세요. 전동칫솔을 찾고 있는데요.

남: 네. *[잠시 후]* 이것들이 저희가 가지고 있는 것입니다. 염두에 두고 있는 특정 브랜드가 있으신가요?

여: 아니요, 하지만 예산은 정말 있습니다. 100달러 미만으로 하고 싶어요.

남: 알겠습니다. 여기 보시면 칫솔마다 칫솔질 모드가 다릅니다. 여러 가지 모드가 있으면 좋습니다.

여: 맞아요. 최소한 네 가지 모드가 있는 것으로 사고 싶네요.

남: 좋아요. 그러면 선택하실 수 있는 정말 좋은 몇 개가 남습니다.

여: 오, 이것들은 압력 센서가 있네요. 저는 그것을 정말 갖고 싶습니다.

남: 그것은 잇몸을 보호하는 데 유용한 기능입니다. 그렇다면 이 두 가지가 손님이 원하시는 것에 맞는 것 같네요. 선호하는 색상이 있으신가요?

여: 욕실의 모든 것이 밝은 색상이라 검은색은 싫어요. 나머지 하나로 사겠습니다.

남: 네. 좋습니다.

◉ Topic & Situation 전동칫솔 구매

◉ Solution

여자는 100달러 미만의 예산으로, 최소한 네 가지 (칫솔질) 모드와 압력 센서가 있으며, 검은색이 아닌 전동칫솔을 선택했다. 따라서 여자가 구매할 전동칫솔은 ③이다.

◉ Words & Phrases

particular 특정한, 특별한 budget 예산 a variety of 여러 가지의
at least 최소한, 적어도 function 기능 gum 잇몸

02

정답 | ③

| Script & Translation |

W: Honey, are you checking your social media?

M: No, I'm looking at a site that sells baking supplies. We should get a digital kitchen scale.

W: Great idea. Since we got the new oven, we'll be baking more.

M: Right. *[Pause]* Here are the site's five best-selling models. This one is pretty expensive.

W: Yeah. Let's keep it under $30.

M: Okay. I'd prefer to buy one that's made of stainless steel or glass. Germs don't stick as much, so they're cleaner.

W: That makes sense. And how many measuring units do you think we need?

M: Hmm. I think we'll need at least four different units such as gram, ounce, and pound.

W: Okay. Then we should get one of these two. Which color do you prefer?

M: I think silver would look better in our kitchen.

W: I agree. So let's order this one.

여: 여보, 소셜 미디어를 확인하고 있나요?

남: 아니요, 제빵용품을 파는 사이트를 보고 있어요. 우리는 디지털 주방 저울을 사야 해요.

여: 좋은 생각이에요. 새 오븐이 생겼으니, 제빵을 더 많이 할 거예요.

남: 맞아요. *[잠시 후]* 여기 이 사이트에서 가장 많이 팔리는 다섯 가지 모델이 있어요. 이것은 꽤 비싸네요.

여: 네. 30달러 미만으로 해요.

남: 좋아요. 나는 스테인리스 스틸이나 유리로 만든 것을 사고 싶어요. 세균이 잘 달라붙지 않아 더 깨끗하거든요.

여: 일리가 있네요. 그리고 당신은 몇 개의 측정 단위가 필요하다고 생각해요?

남: 흠. 그램, 온스, 파운드 등 적어도 네 개의 다양한 단위가 필요할 것 같아요.

여: 좋아요. 그럼, 이 두 가지 중 하나를 사야겠네요. 어떤 색이 좋아요?

남: 우리 주방에는 은색이 더 잘 어울릴 것 같아요.

여: 동의해요. 그럼 이걸로 주문해요.

◉ Topic & Situation 디지털 주방 저울 주문

◉ Solution

여자와 남자는 가격이 30달러 미만인 스테인리스 스틸이나 유리로 만든 것으로 적어도 네 개의 다양한 단위가 있는 은색 디지털 주방 저울을 선택했다. 따라서 두 사람이 주문할 디지털 주방 저울은 ③이다.

◉ Words & Phrases

supplies 용품, 비품 best-selling 가장 많이 팔리는 germ 세균, 미생물 stick 달라붙다

03

정답 | ①

| Script & Translation |

M: Mom, I'm trying to find a good temperature and humidity sensor to buy online. I'd like one for my room. Can you help me?

W: Sure. Have you found a website?

M: Yes. This website has these five models. I'm not sure which one to get though.

W: Hmm. Let me see. Where do you plan on placing it?

M: I was thinking of putting it on the table.

W: Okay, let's rule out this one then. Oh, and make sure you get a waterproof one.

M: That narrows it down to these three models. Do you think I should get a USB-powered one?

W: Most of the time, a USB-powered one would be more convenient. However, for travel purposes, a battery-powered one might be more suitable.

M: I won't be traveling with it, so I'll go for a USB-powered option.

W: So now you need to choose between these two. What about this one?

M: It looks good, but it's quite big. I'll buy the other one.

W: Good choice.

남: 엄마, 저는 온라인에서 살 만한 좋은 온습도계를 찾고 있어요. 제 방에 하나 두고 싶어요. 도와주실 수 있으세요?

여: 물론이지. 웹사이트를 찾았니?

남: 네. 이 웹사이트에 이 다섯 가지 모델이 있어요. 하지만 어떤 것을 사야 할지 잘 모르겠어요.

여: 음. 어디 보자. 그것을 어디에 둘 계획이니?

남: 탁자 위에 놓을 생각이었어요.

여: 좋아, 그럼 이것은 제외하자꾸나. 아, 그리고 꼭 방수되는 것을 사도록 해.

남: 그러면 이 세 가지 모델로 좁혀져요. USB로 작동하는 것을 사야 할까요?

여: 대부분은, USB로 작동하는 것이 더 편리할 거야. 그러나 여행 목적의 경우 배터리로 작동하는 것이 더 적합할지도 몰라.

남: 저는 그것을 가지고 여행을 가지 않을 거니까, USB로 작동하는 것으로 할래요.

여: 그래서 이제 너는 이 둘 중에서 선택해야 해. 이거 어때?

남: 좋아 보이지만, 꽤 크네요. 나머지 다른 하나를 살게요.

여: 좋은 선택이야.

◐ Topic & Situation 온습도계 구매

◐ Solution

남자는 탁자 위에 둘 수 있고 방수가 되며 USB로 작동하는 두 개의 온습도계 중에서 더 크지 않은 것을 골랐으므로, 남자가 구입할 온습도계는 ①이다.

◑ Words & Phrases

humidity 습도 place 두다, 놓다, 위치하다 rule out ~을 제외하다 waterproof 방수의 narrow ~ down to ... ~을 …으로 좁히다

04

정답 | ④

| Script & Translation |

M: Darling, I brought this brochure from Tora Tora Island Tours. They offer some amazing tours.

W: Wonderful! We're planning to visit there next month. Let me have a look. *[Flipping sound]* These all sound fun.

M: Absolutely. I personally like this one the most, but I'm afraid it might exceed our budget.

W: Right. Let's keep it under $200. Also, this tour won't work for me. I can't be on a speed boat.

M: Really? I find it quite thrilling.

W: I know, but I would definitely get seasick.

M: I see. So we need to choose one of these three options. Do you have any preference regarding the stops?

W: Well, I've heard that Coral Bay tends to get really crowded. Let's skip that one.

M: Agreed. That leaves us with these two choices. I love snorkeling.

W: Me, too! Let's go ahead and book this one.

M: Perfect! I can't wait to go.

남: 여보, 내가 Tora Tora Island Tours에서 이 안내 책자를 가져왔어요. 그들은 놀라운 투어를 제공해요.

여: 멋져요! 우리는 다음 달에 그곳을 방문할 계획이잖아요. 한번 볼게요. *[페이지를 넘기는 소리]* 이것들 모두 재밌을 것 같아요.

남: 정말 그래요. 나는 개인적으로 이것이 가장 마음에 드는데, 우리의 예산을 초과할지도 몰라 걱정돼요.

여: 맞아요. 200달러 미만으로 해요. 또한, 이 투어는 나한테는 맞지 않을 거예요. 나는 고속정을 탈 수 없어요.

남: 정말요? 나는 그것이 꽤 짜릿하다고 생각해요.

여: 알아요, 하지만 나는 분명히 뱃멀미를 느낄 거예요.

남: 그렇군요. 그래서 우리는 이 세 가지 옵션 중 하나를 선택해야 해요. 당신은 경유지에 대해 선호하는 것이 있어요?

여: 글쎄요, Coral Bay는 정말 혼잡해지는 경향이 있다고 들었어요. 그것은 빼요.

남: 동의해요. 그러면 이 두 가지 선택만 남게 되었네요. 나는 스노클링을 좋아해요.
여: 나도요! 어서 이것을 예약해요.
남: 완벽해요! 어서 가고 싶어요.

Topic & Situation 투어 예약하기

Solution

두 사람은 Tora Tora Island Tours의 안내 책자를 보고 가격이 200달러 미만이고 고속정이 아닌 것 중에서 Coral Bay를 경유하지 않고 스노클링을 할 수 있는 것을 선택했으므로, 두 사람이 예약할 투어는 ④이다.

Words & Phrases

brochure 안내 책자, 소책자 personally 개인적으로 exceed 초과하다, 넘어서다 budget 예산 seasick 뱃멀미를 느끼는 preference 선호 crowded 혼잡한, 붐비는 leave 남기다

05

정답 | ③

| Script & Translation |

W: Sweetie, since our coffee maker is broken, I was thinking we should rent one.
M: Okay. Do you know where we can do that?
W: Yeah. Check out this website. They have several models we can rent.
M: All right. *[Pause]* These all look good, but I think this one over $30 per month is too expensive for us.
W: I agree. Let's choose one which costs less than $30.
M: They don't all come with milk foam attachments. We definitely want that for café lattes.
W: Right. Look. The remaining three have different minimum rental periods.
M: Well, 3 years seems too long. I think 2 years is better.
W: Me, too. So then between these two, how about this one? It comes with coffee beans as a free gift.
M: Sounds good. Besides, we already have a lot of mugs.
W: Right. Then let's rent this one.
M: Okay!

여: 여보, 우리 커피 메이커가 고장이 나서, 우리가 한 대를 대여해야 한다고 생각했어요.
남: 좋아요. 우리가 커피 메이커를 빌릴 수 있는 곳을 알고 있어요?
여: 예. 이 웹사이트를 확인해 봐요. 우리가 대여할 수 있는 몇 개의 모델이 있어요.
남: 알았어요. *[잠시 후]* 이것들이 모두 좋아 보이지만, 저는 한 달에 30달러가 넘는 이것은 우리에게 너무 비싼 것 같아요.
여: 동의해요. 30달러보다 비용이 적게 드는 것을 선택해요.
남: 모든 커피 메이커가 우유 거품 첨가 기능이 있는 게 아니네요. 우리는 카페 라떼를 마실 때 그것이 꼭 필요해요.
여: 그래요. 봐요. 남아 있는 세 개의 최소 임대 기간이 달라요.
남: 음, 3년은 너무 긴 것 같아요. 2년이 더 좋은 것 같아요.
여: 나도 그래요. 그러면 이 두 개 중에서, 이것 어때요? 사은품으로 커피콩이 제공되잖아요.
남: 좋은데요. 게다가, 우리는 이미 잔을 많이 가지고 있으니까요.
여: 좋아요. 그러면, 이것을 대여해요.
남: 맞아요!

Topic & Situation 커피 메이커 대여

Solution

여자와 남자는 한 달에 30달러가 넘지 않는 비용으로 우유 거품 첨가 기능이 있으며 최소 임대 기간이 2년인 커피 메이커 중에서 사은품으로 커피콩을 제공하는 커피 메이커를 선택했으므로, 두 사람이 대여할 커피 메이커는 ③이다.

Words & Phrases

be broken 고장 나다 foam 거품 attachment 첨가, 첨부 remaining 남아 있는 mug 잔, 머그

06

정답 | ②

| Script & Translation |

M: Hi. Welcome to Maple Grove Townhomes.
W: Hi, I'm looking to rent a studio apartment near Pacifica University. Are there any available?
M: Sure. What's your rental budget?
W: I can only afford a maximum of $1,000 per month.
M: Okay. Do you need a furnished apartment?
W: No, I don't. I have my own furniture.
M: All right. How close do you want to be to the university?
W: Well, I'd like to be within a 15-minute walk.
M: Okay. We have a couple available. This one's on the 4th floor. Is that okay?
W: Actually, I prefer a lower floor.
M: No problem. Then how about this one?

W: It seems perfect. Can I schedule a viewing for this Saturday at noon?

M: Absolutely. Just write down your name and phone number here.

남: 안녕하세요. Maple Grove Townhomes에 오신 것을 환영합니다.

여: 안녕하세요, 저는 Pacifica 대학 근처에 있는 원룸 아파트를 임차하려고 알아보고 있습니다. 이용 가능한 것이 있나요?

남: 그렇습니다. 임차료 예산이 어떻게 되나요?

여: 한 달에 최대 1,000달러까지만 지불할 수 있어요.

남: 알겠습니다. 가구가 딸린 아파트가 필요하신가요?

여: 아니요, 필요 없습니다. 저는 제 가구를 가지고 있어요.

남: 좋습니다. 대학과 얼마나 가까이 위치하길 원하세요?

여: 음, 걸어서 15분 이내에 있으면 좋겠어요.

남: 알겠습니다. 몇 가지 가능한 것이 있습니다. 이건 4층에 있어요. 괜찮으신가요?

여: 사실, 저는 더 낮은 층을 선호해요.

남: 알겠습니다. 그럼 이건 어떤가요?

여: 완벽해 보여요. 이번 주 토요일 정오에 둘러보기를 예약할 수 있을까요?

남: 물론이죠. 여기에 당신의 이름과 전화번호를 좀 적어 주세요.

◑ Topic & Situation 원룸 아파트 구하기

◑ Solution

여자는 임차료 예산으로 최대 1,000달러까지만 쓸 수 있으며, 가구가 딸리지 않고, 대학까지 걸어서 15분 이내에 위치해 있는 원룸 아파트 중에서, 4층보다 낮은 층을 선호한다고 말했으므로 여자가 보러 가기로 선택한 아파트는 ②이다.

◑ Words & Phrases

studio apartment 원룸 아파트   available 이용할 수 있는   rental 임차료, 임대료   maximum 최대   furnished 가구가 딸린   floor (건물의) 층, 바닥   schedule 일정을 잡다; 일정   absolutely 물론이지; 전적으로, 틀림없이

Dictations 본문 67, 70~71쪽

기출 ❶ let's not spend
예제 ❷ get a different color
❸ get the other model

01 ❶ keep it under $100
❷ with at least four modes
❸ want to have that
❹ buy the other one

02 ❶ keep it under $30
❷ made of stainless steel or glass
❸ at least four
❹ silver would look better

03 ❶ one for my room
❷ get a waterproof one
❸ traveling with it

04 ❶ offer some amazing tours
❷ exceed our budget
❸ get really crowded

05 ❶ coffee maker is broken
❷ we can rent
❸ with milk foam attachments
❹ a lot of mugs

06 ❶ rent a studio apartment
❷ afford a maximum
❸ schedule a viewing for

12강 짧은 대화의 응답

본문 72~77쪽

기출예제 ⑤

Exercises 01 ④ 02 ⑤ 03 ③ 04 ① 05 ③ 06 ①
07 ② 08 ① 09 ⑤ 10 ③ 11 ④ 12 ④

기출 예제

본문 72쪽

정답 | ⑤

| Script & Translation |

W: Dad, we should leave soon to watch the fireworks in the park. Shall we bring something to eat?

M: Yeah, we might get hungry. Oh, we also need the picnic mat to sit on. I think I put it on one of the shelves in the storage room, but I'm not sure.

W: Then, could you find the mat while I pack some snacks and soft drinks?

M: No problem. I'll take care of it.

여: 아빠, 공원에서 열리는 불꽃놀이를 보러 우리는 곧 출발해야 해요. 먹을 것 좀 가져갈까요?

남: 그래, 배고파질 수 있지. 오, 앉을 야외용 돗자리도 필요해. 창고 선반 중 하나에 올려놨던 것 같은데, 잘 모르겠네.

여: 그럼, 제가 간식과 음료수를 좀 챙기는 동안 돗자리를 찾아 주실래요?

남: 물론이지. 내가 그것을 맡을게.

◐ Topic & Situation 불꽃놀이 구경 준비

◐ Solution

남자와 여자가 불꽃놀이를 보러 가는 상황에서, 여자는 자신이 간식과 음료수를 챙기는 동안 남자에게 돗자리를 찾아 달라고 부탁했다. 따라서 여자의 마지막 말에 대한 남자의 응답으로 가장 적절한 것은 ⑤ '물론이지. 내가 그것을 맡을게.'이다.

① 맞아. 우리는 그것을 봤어야 했는데.

② 왜 안 되겠어? 그냥 돗자리를 선반 위에 올려놔.

③ 좋아. 우리는 집에 간식을 좀 보관할 수 있어.

④ 미안해. 주차장을 못 찾겠어.

◐ Words & Phrases

firework 불꽃놀이　mat 돗자리　shelf 선반　snack 간식　soft drink 음료수

Exercises

본문 74~77쪽

01

정답 | ④

| Script & Translation |

W: Jake, how is recruiting members to open your school film club going?

M: Not so good, Mom. I'm worried I may not be able to get the minimum number of members.

W: Oh, really? How many members do you need?

M: At least seven. But only five have signed up so far.

여: Jake, 네 학교 영화 동아리를 개설하기 위한 회원 모집은 잘 되어 가니?

남: 별로 좋지 않아요, 엄마. 저는 최소 회원 수를 확보하지 못할 수도 있어서 걱정이에요.

여: 아, 그래? 몇 명의 회원이 필요한데?

남: 적어도 7명이요. 하지만 지금까지 5명만 가입했어요.

◐ Topic & Situation 학교 영화 동아리 회원 모집

◐ Solution

여자는 남자에게 학교 영화 동아리 회원 모집에 대해 묻고 있고, 남자의 동아리 개설을 위한 최소 인원을 확보하지 못할 것 같아 걱정된다는 응답에 여자는 동아리 개설을 위해 필요한 회원의 수를 묻고 있다. 따라서 여자의 마지막 말에 대한 남자의 응답으로 가장 적절한 것은 ④ '적어도 7명이요. 하지만 지금까지 5명만 가입했어요.'이다.

① 동의해요. 우리는 오디션 일정을 조정해야 해요.

② 노력 중이에요. 하지만 그러면 최대 수를 초과해요.

③ 맞아요. 한 사람이 하나의 역할보다 더 많이 해야 해요.

⑤ 오늘 두 명의 지원자가 더 왔어요. 이제 그거면 충분해요.

◐ Words & Phrases

recruit 모집하다　exceed 초과하다

02

정답 | ⑤

| Script & Translation |

M: Louise, you've had a lot more energy the past few days. Did you finally solve your sleeping problem?

W: Hey, Mark. Yes, I did. I've started drinking decaffeinated tea instead of coffee, and it has helped.

M: Glad to hear that. Actually, I noticed you haven't had a single cup of coffee this week, unlike usual.

W: Right. If I drink coffee, I'm not able to sleep well.

남: Louise, 당신은 지난 며칠 동안 훨씬 더 활력이 있었어요. 마침내 수면 문제를 해결했나요?

여: 안녕하세요, Mark. 네, 그랬어요. 저는 커피 대신 카페인이 없는 차를 마시기 시작했고, 그것이 도움이 되었어요.

남: 다행이에요. 사실, 이번 주에는 평소와 다르게 커피를 한 잔도 안 드셨더군요.

여: 맞아요. 저는 커피를 마시면 잠을 잘 못 자요.

> **Topic & Situation** 수면 문제 해결을 위한 노력

> **Solution**

남자가 여자에게 지난 며칠 동안 훨씬 더 활력이 있었다고 말하며 수면 문제를 해결했냐고 묻자, 여자는 커피 대신 카페인이 없는 차를 마시는 것이 도움이 되었다고 답했다. 뒤이어 남자는 이번 주에는 여자가 평소와 다르게 커피를 마신 적이 없었다고 말했고 이에 대한 여자의 응답으로 가장 적절한 것은 ⑤ '맞아요. 저는 커피를 마시면 잠을 잘 못 자요.'이다.

① 오, 당신은 다른 종류의 차를 가지고 있네요. 마셔 봐도 될까요?

② 문제 없습니다. 저는 이 근처의 좋은 커피숍을 알고 있어요.

③ 물론입니다. 커피를 마시는 것은 또한 당신이 체형을 유지하는 데에 도움이 됩니다.

④ 아뇨, 감사합니다. 저는 오늘 아침에 이미 커피 한 잔을 마셨습니다.

> **Words & Phrases**

the past few days 지난 며칠 동안   decaffeinated 카페인이 없는

03   정답 | ③

| Script & Translation |

W: Hey, Mike. I heard you were looking for a new apartment. Have you found one?

M: Not yet. I want to move closer to work, but there are not many places available.

W: Well, my co-worker who sits next to me is looking for a tenant for her apartment. It's really close to our office.

M: That's great news. Can you introduce me to her?

여: 안녕하세요, Mike. 당신이 새 아파트를 찾고 있다고 들었어요. 찾았나요?

남: 아직요. 회사에서 더 가까운 곳으로 이사하고 싶은데, 구할 수 있는 곳이 많지 않아요.

여: 음, 제 옆에 앉은 동료가 자신의 아파트 세입자를 찾고 있어요. 그 곳은 우리 사무실과 정말 가까워요.

남: 그거 좋은 소식이네요. 저를 그녀에게 소개해 주실 수 있나요?

> **Topic & Situation** 아파트 구하기

> **Solution**

이사할 아파트를 찾았냐는 여자의 질문에 남자가 회사에서 더 가까운 곳으로 이사하고 싶은데 구할 수 있는 곳이 많지 않다고 답하자, 여자는 자신의 옆에 앉은 동료가 사무실 가까운 자신의 아파트 세입자를 구하고 있다고 말하고 있다. 따라서 여자의 마지막 말에 대한 남자의 응답으로 가장 적절한 것은 ③ '그거 좋은 소식이네요. 저를 그녀에게 소개해 주실 수 있나요?'이다.

① 알겠습니다. 제가 언제 이사를 나가야 하나요?

② 잘됐네요. 당신은 그 아파트를 어떻게 구했나요?

④ 유감이네요. 그녀는 왜 벌써 이사를 나가나요?

⑤ 놀랐어요. 당신은 언제 그곳으로 이사하는 것을 결심하셨나요?

> **Words & Phrases**

available 구할 수 있는   co-worker 동료   tenant 세입자

04   정답 | ①

| Script & Translation |

M: Wow, the restaurant parking lot is packed. I hope we can find an open spot.

W: Then it's probably packed inside the restaurant, too. I wonder if there are any tables available.

M: Shall I run in and check while you park the car?

W: Good idea. I'll drop you off here.

남: 와, 식당 주차장이 꽉 찼네요. 빈자리를 찾을 수 있으면 좋겠어요.

여: 그러면 식당 안도 꽉 찼을 거예요. 빈 테이블이 있는지 궁금하네요.

남: 당신이 주차하는 동안 제가 들어가서 확인해 볼까요?

여: 좋은 생각이에요. 여기서 내려 드릴게요.

> **Topic & Situation** 주차하는 동안 자리 확인하기

> **Solution**

식당 주차장이 꽉 찬 것을 보고 여자가 식당 안에 빈 테이블이 있는지 궁금하다고 말하자, 남자는 여자가 주차하는 동안 자신이 먼

저 들어가서 빈 테이블이 있는지 확인해 볼지 묻고 있다. 따라서 남자의 마지막 말에 대한 여자의 응답으로 가장 적절한 것은
① '좋은 생각이에요. 여기서 내려 드릴게요.'이다.
② 동의해요. 우리는 다른 테이블을 찾아보는 게 낫겠어요.
③ 죄송합니다. 이용 가능한 테이블이 없습니다.
④ 걱정하지 마세요. 그 식당은 곧 문을 열 거예요.
⑤ 감사합니다. 이 주차 자리는 온종일 이용하실 수 있습니다.

◐ Words & Phrases

packed 꽉 찬   open 비어 있는   spot 자리

05 　　　　　　　　　　정답 | ③

| Script & Translation |

W: Honey, are you sick or something? You keep holding your stomach.
M: Yeah. I have had an upset stomach since dinner. Do we have any medicine in the cabinet?
W: No, we don't have any, but I can buy some at the drugstore.
M: I see. Could you please go buy some medicine for me?

여: 여보, 어디 아프거나 뭐 그런 거 있어요? 당신은 계속 배를 잡고 있군요.
남: 네. 저녁 식사 후부터 배탈이 났어요. 수납장 안에 약이 있나요?
여: 아니요, 없지만, 내가 약국에서 좀 살 수 있어요.
남: 그렇군요. 나를 위해 약을 좀 사다 줄 수 있어요?

◐ Topic & Situation　배탈약 사 오기

◐ Solution

남자가 배탈이 났다고 하면서 수납장에 약이 있는지 묻자, 여자는 약이 없다고 대답하면서 약국에서 살 수 있다고 말했으므로, 이에 대한 남자의 응답으로 가장 적절한 것은 ③ '그렇군요. 나를 위해 약을 좀 사다 줄 수 있어요?'이다.
① 좋아요. 오늘 저녁에 뭘 요리할까요?
② 걱정하지 마세요. 당신에게 더 강한 약을 처방해 드릴게요.
④ 물론이죠. 당신은 남은 음식을 먹지 말았어야 했어요.
⑤ 그럼요. 저녁 먹고 산책하러 가는 게 어때요?

◐ Words & Phrases

stomach 배, 위   upset stomach 배탈   cabinet 수납장
prescribe 처방하다   leftover 남은

06 　　　　　　　　　　정답 | ①

| Script & Translation |

M: Emma, I see you're working hard on your tablet PC. Is everything okay?
W: Hi, Brian. I need to edit some pictures for my geography report. But I don't know how to do it.
M: I see. I know a convenient app for picture editing. Why don't you install it?
W: Sounds great. Please tell me the name of the app.

남: Emma, 태블릿 PC로 열심히 하고 있구나. 모든 게 괜찮은 거니?
여: 안녕, Brian. 내 지리 보고서를 위한 사진들을 좀 편집해야 해. 그런데 그것을 하는 방법을 모르겠어.
남: 그렇구나. 나는 사진 편집에 편리한 앱을 알고 있어. 그것을 설치해 보는 게 어때?
여: 좋을 것 같아. 그 앱 이름을 내게 말해 줘.

◐ Topic & Situation　사진 편집 앱 설치

◐ Solution

여자가 지리 보고서를 위한 사진들을 편집해야 하는데, 어떻게 해야 할지 모르겠다고 말하자, 남자는 사진 편집에 편리한 앱을 알고 있다고 말하면서 그것을 설치할 것을 권유하고 있으므로, 이에 대한 여자의 응답으로 가장 적절한 것은 ① '좋을 것 같아. 그 앱 이름을 내게 말해 줘.'이다.
② 물론이지. 나는 사진을 찍을 때마다 그 앱을 사용해.
③ 고마워. 네가 도와줘서 내가 보고서를 제때 제출했어.
④ 아니, 안 할 거야. 나는 내 태블릿 PC를 몇 년 더 사용할 거야.
⑤ 좋아. 태블릿 PC 수리 비용이 많이 들지 않아서 다행이야.

◐ Words & Phrases

geography 지리(학)   convenient 편리한   hand in ~을 제출하다
on time 제때, 시간을 어기지 않고

07 　　　　　　　　　　정답 | ②

| Script & Translation |

W: Andy, are you almost finished with your work? All of the other co-workers are ready to head out for our dinner meeting.
M: I know. I'm almost done. I just need to quickly finish writing this email.

W: All right. Then I'll tell the others to wait a few minutes.

M: Thanks. I'll try to get this done as soon as possible.

여: Andy, 일이 거의 끝나가나요? 다른 동료들은 모두 우리의 저녁 식사 모임에 나갈 준비가 되어 있어요.

남: 알아요. 거의 다 했어요. 저는 이 이메일을 빨리 작성해야 해요.

여: 좋아요. 그럼 제가 다른 사람들에게 몇 분 기다리라고 말할게요.

남: 고마워요. 이것을 가능한 한 빨리 끝내도록 노력할게요.

◉ Topic & Situation 동료들과의 저녁 식사 모임

◉ Solution

동료들이 모두 저녁 식사 모임에 나갈 준비가 되어 있다는 여자의 말에, 남자는 이메일을 빨리 작성해야 한다고 대답했고, 이에 여자는 동료들에게 몇 분 기다리라고 말하겠다고 했으므로, 이에 대한 남자의 응답으로 가장 적절한 것은 ② '고마워요. 이것을 가능한 한 빨리 끝내도록 노력할게요.'이다.

① 정말이에요? 저는 그 직원 저녁 식사에 대해 완전히 잊고 있었어요.

③ 전혀 아니에요. 오늘 아침 당신이 보낸 이메일을 받았어요.

④ 맞아요. 그 식당은 그날 이미 예약이 다 되어 있어요.

⑤ 좋아요. 우리 음식이 배달되도록 제가 지금 당장 주문할게요.

◉ Words & Phrases

co-worker 동료   completely 완전히   as soon as possible 가능한 한 빨리   book 예약하다

08
정답 | ①

| Script & Translation |

M: Hey, Amy. Cool bookmark. Where did you get it?

W: I made it myself using an old calendar.

M: Wow. What a cool way to make something useful out of an old calendar! I'm wondering how you made it.

W: I learned about doing it online.

남: 있잖아요, Amy. 책갈피가 멋지네요. 그거 어디서 구했어요?

여: 지난 달력을 이용해서 제가 직접 만들었어요.

남: 와. 지난 달력으로 유용한 무엇인가를 만들다니 정말 멋진 방법이네요! 어떻게 만들었는지 궁금해요.

여: 저는 온라인으로 하는 방법을 배웠어요.

◉ Topic & Situation 지난 달력으로 만든 책갈피

◉ Solution

남자는 여자가 직접 만든 책갈피가 멋지다고 하면서, 어떻게 만들었는지 궁금하다고 말하고 있다. 따라서 남자의 마지막 말에 대한 여자의 응답으로 가장 적절한 것은 ① '저는 온라인으로 하는 방법을 배웠어요.'이다.

② 제 달력에 날짜를 표시해 놓을게요.

③ 저는 지난 달력을 재사용하는 방법을 몰라요.

④ 책에 중요한 부분은 다 표시해 놓았어요.

⑤ 웹사이트에서 이 달력을 만드는 것은 쉬웠어요.

◉ Words & Phrases

bookmark 책갈피   critical 중요한

09
정답 | ⑤

| Script & Translation |

W: So, how would you like your hair cut?

M: Well, can you style the sides and the top like this picture?

W: Hmm, so you want me to take some off the sides and leave it longer on top, right?

M: Exactly. Just give the hair on the sides a slight cut.

여: 그럼, 머리를 어떻게 잘라 드릴까요?

남: 그러니까, 이 사진처럼 옆머리와 윗머리 스타일을 만들어 줄 수 있나요?

여: 흠, 그러니까 옆머리는 좀 자르고 윗머리는 더 길게 남겨달라는 거지요?

남: 맞아요. 옆머리만 약간 잘라 주세요.

◉ Topic & Situation 머리 손질하기

◉ Solution

남자가 사진을 보여 주며 머리 스타일을 만들어 달라고 하자, 여자는 옆머리는 좀 자르고 윗머리는 더 길게 해 달라는 거냐며 스타일을 확인하고 있다. 따라서 여자의 마지막 말에 대한 남자의 응답으로 가장 적절한 것은 ⑤ '맞아요. 옆머리만 약간 잘라 주세요.'이다.

① 네. 이발하는 데 오래 걸리지 않습니다.

② 그런 것 같아요. 제가 잡지에서 헤어스타일을 골라 볼게요.

③ 물론이죠. 오늘 이발 예약을 했습니다.

④ 괜찮아요. 제 머리는 어느 쪽이든 가르마를 타셔도 됩니다.

◉ Words & Phrases

take off (머리를) 자르다[깎다]   make an appointment 예약하다   part 가르마를 타다

10

정답 | ③

| Script & Translation |

M: Oh, honey, I know you want to get noodles from this restaurant. But look at how long the line is!

W: It's because the noodles are so good. My friend said it's a famous restaurant.

M: But I'm starving. I don't feel like standing in line for an hour.

W: Okay. Let's go somewhere nearby without a wait.

남: 오, 여보, 당신이 이 식당에서 국수를 먹고 싶어 하는 건 알겠어요. 그런데 줄이 얼마나 긴지 봐요!

여: 국수가 너무 맛있어서 그래요. 제 친구가 이곳이 유명한 식당이라고 말했어요.

남: 하지만 배고파 죽겠어요. 나는 한 시간 동안 줄을 서고 싶지 않아요.

여: 알았어요. 기다릴 필요 없는 가까운 어디로 가요.

◐ Topic & Situation 줄 서는 식당

◐ Solution

남자는 식당에 길게 늘어선 줄을 보고 배고파 죽겠다며 한 시간 동안 줄을 서고 싶지 않다고 말하고 있다. 따라서 남자의 마지막 말에 대한 여자의 응답으로 가장 적절한 것은 ③ '알았어요. 기다릴 필요 없는 가까운 어디로 가요.'이다.

① 나는 점심을 가져왔어요. 나는 줄을 서서 기다릴 필요가 없어요.

② 늦어서 미안해요. 차가 너무 막혔어요.

④ 오, 와! 이것은 지금까지 먹어본 국수 중 최고예요.

⑤ 실례합니다. 이것은 제가 주문한 국수 요리가 아닙니다.

◐ Words & Phrases

noodles 국수, 면류   stand in line 줄을 서다, 일렬로 서다

11

정답 | ④

| Script & Translation |

W: Dad, can we go shopping this afternoon? I want to get a cover for my laptop.

M: Why do you need a new one? Don't you already have a cover?

W: No, I don't and I need one. I want to protect my laptop when I take it to school or to the library.

M: Okay. Let's go and find a suitable cover for your laptop.

여: 아빠, 오늘 오후에 쇼핑하러 갈 수 있으세요? 제 노트북을 위한 커버를 사고 싶어요.

남: 왜 새것이 필요하니? 이미 커버가 있지 않니?

여: 아니요, 없어서 하나가 필요해요. 학교나 도서관에 노트북을 가지고 갈 때 그것을 보호하고 싶어요.

남: 알겠어. 네 노트북에 알맞은 커버를 찾아보러 가자.

◐ Topic & Situation 노트북 커버 구매

◐ Solution

여자는 남자에게 오늘 오후에 쇼핑하러 가자고 하면서 노트북을 위한 커버를 사고 싶다고 하고, 커버가 이미 있지 않냐는 남자의 말에 없다고 하면서 학교나 도서관에 노트북을 가지고 갈 때 보호하기 위해 커버가 필요하다고 말하고 있다. 따라서 여자의 말에 대한 남자의 응답으로 가장 적절한 것은 ④ '알겠어. 네 노트북에 알맞은 커버를 찾아보러 가자.'이다.

① 맞아. 사용하지 않을 때는 노트북을 끄렴.

② 그래. 네 노트북은 오래됐으니, 네게 새것을 사 줄게.

③ 알아. 그건 좋은 보호용 노트북 커버 같아.

⑤ 이해해. 하지만 네 옛날 커버는 보호용으로 아주 좋아.

◐ Words & Phrases

protect 보호하다   suitable 알맞은, 적합한

12

정답 | ④

| Script & Translation |

M: Honey, could you come to the living room and take a look at this plant? It seems like it's not doing well.

W: Sure. Oh, poor thing! We do water it regularly, but it might be lacking fresh air or sunlight.

M: What do you think we should do? I don't want it to die.

W: Let's move it outside to get more fresh air and sunlight.

남: 여보, 거실로 와서 이 식물 좀 봐 줄래요? 그게 제대로 자라고 있지 않은 것 같아요.

여: 그래요. 오, 가엾게도! 우리는 진짜 정기적으로 물을 주지만, 신선한 공기나 햇빛은 부족할 수도 있어요.

남: 어떻게 해야 할까요? 나는 그것이 죽는 것을 원치 않아요.

여: 그것을 밖으로 옮겨서 더 많은 신선한 공기와 햇빛을 받게 해 봅시다.

● **Topic & Situation** 거실에 있는 식물을 밖으로 옮기기

● **Solution**

여자가 거실에서 제대로 자라고 있지 않은 식물을 보고 정기적으로 물을 주고 있으니 신선한 공기나 햇빛이 부족해서일 수도 있다고 하자, 남자는 여자에게 어떻게 해야 할지 묻고 있다. 따라서 남자의 마지막 말에 대한 여자의 응답으로 가장 적절한 것은 ④ '그것을 밖으로 옮겨서 더 많은 신선한 공기와 햇빛을 받게 해봅시다.'이다.

① 우리는 공기가 상쾌해지도록 더 많은 실내용 식물을 사가는 게 좋을 거예요.

② 우리가 정기적으로 물을 주기 시작하면 이 식물을 살릴 수 있을 거예요.

③ 신선한 공기를 마시러 산책하러 가지 않을래요?

⑤ 다양한 식물로 실내 정원을 만들어 보는 건 어때요?

● **Words & Phrases**

water 물을 주다   regularly 정기적으로   houseplant 실내용 식물

Dictations   본문 73, 78~81쪽

기출 ❶ picnic mat
예제 ❷ could you find

01 ❶ recruiting members to open
   ❷ How many members

02 ❶ solve your sleeping problem
   ❷ unlike usual

03 ❶ many places available
   ❷ looking for a tenant

04 ❶ probably packed
   ❷ run in and check

05 ❶ keep holding your stomach
   ❷ any medicine in the cabinet

06 ❶ edit some pictures
   ❷ convenient app for picture editing

07 ❶ ready to head out
   ❷ tell the others to wait

08 ❶ made it myself
   ❷ how you made it

09 ❶ how would you like
   ❷ you want me to

10 ❶ how long the line is
   ❷ standing in line

11 ❶ get a cover
   ❷ protect my laptop

12 ❶ not doing well
   ❷ want it to die

13강 긴 대화의 응답   본문 82~87쪽

기출예제 ⑤

Exercises 01 ② 02 ⑤ 03 ① 04 ① 05 ⑤ 06 ⑤
07 ④ 08 ④ 09 ② 10 ③ 11 ④ 12 ②

기출 예제   본문 82쪽

정답 | ⑤

| **Script & Translation** |

W: Shaun, you really rocked the runway as a senior fashion model yesterday!

M: Thanks for coming to my first show, Grace.

W: My pleasure. You'll be an inspiration to many people our age.

M: I'm so flattered.

W: It's amazing that you successfully switched careers.

M: Thank you. My dream has finally come true.

W: It couldn't have been easy to realize your dream in your 60s.

M: It wasn't. But I've always believed in myself, and age was never an issue for me.

W: You make me think of my old passion to be a painter, but I put it off for too long.

M: Now is the time to give it a try.

W: I think it's too late for that.

M: Be positive. You can start pursuing your dream at any time.

여: Shaun, 어제 시니어 패션모델로서 무대를 흔들어 놓았어요!

남: 제 첫 쇼에 와 줘서 고마워요, Grace.

여: 천만에요. 당신은 우리 또래의 많은 사람에게 자극을 주는 사람일 거예요.

남: 과찬이십니다.

여: 당신이 성공적으로 직업을 바꿨다니 놀라워요.

남: 고마워요. 제 꿈이 마침내 이루어졌어요.

여: 60대에 꿈을 실현하는 게 쉽지 않았을 것 같은데요.

남: 쉽지 않았죠. 하지만 저는 항상 제 자신을 믿었기에, 나이는 제게 전혀 문제가 되지 않았어요.

여: 당신을 보니 화가가 되고 싶었던 옛 열정이 생각나지만, 너무 오래 그것을 미뤄 두었어요.

남: 지금이 바로 그것을 시도해 볼 때예요.

여: 그러기엔 너무 늦은 것 같아요.

남: 긍정적으로 생각하세요. 당신은 언제든 꿈을 추구하는 것을 시작할 수 있어요.

● **Topic & Situation** 나이와 상관없는 꿈 추구

● **Solution**

60대에 시니어 모델의 꿈을 이룬 남자를 보고 여자는 자신도 화가가 되고 싶었던 옛 열정이 생각나지만, 너무 오래 미뤄 두었다고 하면서 시도하기에는 너무 늦은 것 같다고 말한다. 따라서 이에 대한 남자의 응답으로 가장 적절한 것은 ⑤ '긍정적으로 생각하세요. 당신은 언제든 꿈을 추구하는 것을 시작할 수 있어요.'이다.

① 포기하지 마세요! 당신은 내가 화가가 되도록 자극을 줬어요.
② 힘내세요! 패션 시장은 모두에게 열려 있어요.
③ 당신 말씀이 일리가 있네요. 저는 패션 감각이 전혀 없어요.
④ 동의해요. 당신은 일과 삶 사이에 균형을 맞춰야 해요.

● **Words & Phrases**

inspiration 자극을 주는 존재[것] issue 문제 put off ~을 미루다
give ~ a try ~을 시도하다 positive 긍정적인 pursue 추구하다

(**Exercises**)   본문 84~87쪽

01   정답 | ②

| Script & Translation |

W: Hi, Paul. What's up?
M: Hi, Lisa. I'm planning to throw a surprise birthday party for Susan.
W: Oh, right. Her birthday is next Saturday, isn't it?
M: It is. How did you know?
W: She told me last week at science class. We are on the same team for a science project. We recently became close friends.
M: Oh, really? Great. Then could you help me get the party ready?
W: Of course. So how many people are you inviting?
M: I was hoping to invite eight, but I still don't know where to have the party.
W: How about at my house? I can even put up some really cool decorations.

M: Really? That'd be perfect.
W: Now we need a good excuse to invite Susan to my house without telling her it's her birthday party.
M: Hmm.... You said you are on the same team at science class. Do you have any good ideas?
W: I'll ask her to come over to discuss our science project.

여: 안녕, Paul. 무슨 일이야?
남: 안녕, Lisa. 나는 Susan을 위한 깜짝 생일 파티를 열 계획이야.
여: 아, 맞아. 그녀 생일이 다음 주 토요일이지, 그렇지 않니?
남: 그래. 어떻게 알았어?
여: 지난주 과학 수업시간에 나에게 알려줬어. 우리는 과학 프로젝트에서 같은 팀에 소속되어 있어. 최근에 우리는 가까운 친구가 되었어.
남: 오, 정말? 잘됐다. 그러면 파티 준비를 도와줄 수 있니?
여: 물론이지. 그래서 얼마나 많은 사람을 초대할 거니?
남: 8명을 초대하기를 희망하고 있는데, 아직도 어디서 파티를 열어야 할지 모르겠어.
여: 우리 집에서 하는 것은 어때? 그러면 정말 멋진 장식을 할 수도 있어.
남: 정말? 그러면 완벽할 것 같아.
여: 이제 Susan에게 그녀의 생일 파티라는 것을 알리지 않고 그녀를 우리 집으로 초대할 좋은 핑곗거리가 필요해.
남: 음…. 네가 과학 수업 시간에 같은 팀에 속해 있다고 그랬잖아. 좋은 생각 있니?
여: 그녀에게 우리 과학 프로젝트에 대해 논의하기 위해 오도록 부탁해 볼게.

● **Topic & Situation** 친구의 깜짝 생일 파티 준비하기

● **Solution**

남자가 Susan을 위한 깜짝 생일 파티를 계획 중이라고 여자에게 말하자, 여자가 Susan의 생일 날짜를 이미 알고 있고, 둘은 같은 과학 프로젝트 팀에 소속되어 있어 친하다고 말한다. 남자가 파티 준비를 도와줄 수 있냐고 묻자, 여자는 승낙을 하고, 남자가 아직 파티 장소를 정하지 못했다고 하자, 여자가 자신의 집에서 여는 것을 제안한다. 이어서 여자는 Susan을 초대할 핑곗거리가 필요하다고 했으며, 남자가 여자에게 좋은 생각이 있는지 물어 보고 있으므로, 남자의 마지막 말에 대한 여자의 응답으로 가장 적절한 것은 ② '그녀에게 우리 과학 프로젝트에 대해 논의하기 위해 오도록 부탁해 볼게.'이다.

① 너는 파티하기 좋은 장소를 인터넷에서 검색해 볼 수 있어.
③ 그 가게에서 생일 케이크가 얼마나 하는지 모르겠어.

④ 그녀는 아마 깜짝 파티에 관한 내 아이디어에 동의할 거야.

⑤ 우리는 얼마나 많은 사람이 파티에 올지 확인해 봐야 해.

◉ Words & Phrases

throw a party 파티를 열다   decoration 장식   excuse 핑곗거리,
변명

02

정답 | ⑤

| Script & Translation |

W: Jack, have you received the new bag you ordered online?

M: No, I haven't, Mom.

W: Wow. It's taking much longer than I expected.

M: I know. It was supposed to be delivered by last Thursday.

W: It's already been ten days since you ordered it, right?

M: Yes. I wonder what could have happened.

W: Well, maybe it got lost during delivery. That happened to me a while ago.

M: Really? So what did you do?

W: I called the company and asked where the product was.

M: What did they do for you?

W: They tracked my package and found out that it was delivered to the wrong address. The same may have happened to your package.

M: I see. I'll check if the package was sent to the wrong address.

여: Jack, 네가 온라인으로 주문한 새 가방을 받았니?

남: 아니요, 안 받았어요, 엄마.

여: 와, 그거 예상했던 것보다 훨씬 더 오래 걸리네.

남: 알아요. 원래 지난주 목요일까지 배송되기로 되어 있었어요.

여: 네가 그것을 주문한 지 벌써 열흘이 지났지, 맞지?

남: 네. 무슨 일이 있었는지 궁금해요.

여: 음, 그것이 배송 중에 분실되었는지도 몰라. 얼마 전에 내게 그런 일이 있었거든.

남: 그래요? 그래서 어떻게 하셨어요?

여: 회사에 전화해서 제품이 어디에 있는지 물었어.

남: 그들이 무엇을 해 주었어요?

여: 그들은 내 택배물을 추적해서 그것이 잘못된 주소로 배달되었

다는 것을 알아냈어. 네 택배물에 같은 일이 생겼을지도 몰라.

남: 그렇군요. 그 택배물이 잘못된 주소로 보내졌는지 확인해 볼 게요.

◉ Topic & Situation 제품 배송 상황 확인

◉ Solution

남자가 온라인으로 주문한 가방이 열흘이 지나도록 도착하지 않자, 여자는 그것이 분실되었을지도 모른다고 말하면서 얼마 전에 자신에게도 그런 일이 있어서 회사에 전화해서 자신의 택배물이 잘못된 주소로 배달되었음을 알게 되었다고 말했다. 따라서 이에 대한 남자의 응답으로 가장 적절한 것은 ⑤ '그렇군요. 그 택배물이 잘못된 주소로 보내졌는지 확인해 볼게요.'이다.

① 죄송하지만, 엄마는 일주일 안에 가방을 받으실 거예요.

② 안됐군요. 회사에 더 일찍 전화했어야 했어요.

③ 고마워요. 지난주에 제가 주문한 가방을 드디어 받았어요.

④ 음, 그들은 결국 배달 중에 엄마의 택배물을 잃어버렸군요.

◉ Words & Phrases

be supposed to *do* ~하기로 되어 있다   delivery 배송, 배달   track
추적하다   package 택배물, 소포   end up -ing 결국 ~하다

03

정답 | ①

| Script & Translation |

M: Jenny, you're a big fan of Judy Anderson, right?

W: Yes, Kevin. She's my favorite figure skater.

M: She's mine too! She's so amazing.

W: Right. I was so happy when she won the gold medal at the international figure skating competition last year.

M: Me, too. She seems to be in her prime.

W: I think you're right. And do you know she advanced to this year's final in Italy?

M: Yes, I heard about it. The final is being broadcast tomorrow morning, right?

W: Yes. It starts at 3 a.m. here in Korea, and I'm going to get up and watch it.

M: Well, I also want to see it live, but I'm not sure I'll be able to wake up so early.

W: Try going to bed early tonight, and you should be able to wake up on time. Plus, it's Saturday tomorrow, so you can go back to sleep after watching it.

M: True. But I'm still not sure I'll be able to wake up so early in the morning.

W: I see. Then I'll give you a wake-up call.

남: Jenny, 너 Judy Anderson의 열렬한 팬이지, 맞지?

여: 응, Kevin. 그녀는 내가 가장 좋아하는 피겨 스케이트 선수야.

남: 나에게도 그래! 그녀는 정말 대단해.

여: 맞아. 나는 그녀가 작년에 국제 피겨 스케이팅 대회에서 금메달을 땄을 때 너무 기뻤어.

남: 나도 그랬어. 그녀는 전성기에 있는 것 같아.

여: 네 말이 맞는 것 같아. 그리고 그녀가 올해 이탈리아에서 열리는 결승전에 진출했다는 것을 알고 있니?

남: 응, 그것에 대해 들었어. 결승전이 내일 아침에 방송되지, 맞지?

여: 응, 그것은 여기 한국에서 새벽 세 시에 시작하는데 나는 일어나서 그것을 시청할 거야.

남: 음, 나도 그것을 생방송으로 보고 싶지만, 내가 그렇게 일찍 일어날 수 있을지 모르겠어.

여: 오늘 밤 잠자리에 일찍 들도록 해보렴, 그러면 제시간에 일어날 수 있을 거야. 게다가, 내일은 토요일이니까 그것을 시청하고 나서 다시 자도 되잖아.

남: 맞아. 하지만 나는 여전히 내가 그렇게 이른 아침에 일어날 수 있을지 모르겠어.

여: 알겠어. 그럼 내가 네게 모닝콜을 해줄게.

● **Topic & Situation** 피겨 스케이트 결승전 시청

● **Solution**

여자가 좋아하는 피겨 선수의 결승전이 내일 새벽 세 시에 열리는데, 일찍 일어나서 그것을 시청할 것이라고 말하자, 남자는 자신도 그러고 싶지만, 그 시간에 일어날 수 있을지 모르겠다고 말했다. 이에 여자는 잠을 일찍 잘 것을 권유했지만, 남자는 여전히 그렇게 이른 시간에 일어날 수 있을지 모르겠다고 대답했다. 따라서 이에 대한 여자의 응답으로 가장 적절한 것은 ① '알겠어. 그럼 내가 네게 모닝콜을 해줄게.'이다.

② 오, 안돼! 알람이 울렸지만, 난 일어나지 못했어.

③ 믿을 수가 없어. 나는 그녀가 메달을 딸 것이라고 기대하지 않았어.

④ 나는 오늘 아침에 그녀의 결승전을 보지 못한 것이 매우 아쉬워.

⑤ 일찍 일어나서 같이 결승전을 보는 것이 너무 재미있었어.

● **Words & Phrases**

competition 대회 be in one's prime 전성기에 있다 advance to ~에 진출하다 final 결승전 go off (경보기 등이) 울리다

04

정답 | ①

| Script & Translation |

W: Hello, Mr. Wilson.

M: Hello, Ms. Brown. How was the field trip with your students yesterday?

W: It was great. We visited the Ministry of Foreign Affairs for a student program they have.

M: I bet your students had a really good experience.

W: Yes, they did. They had a chance to listen to a lecture and talk with some diplomats.

M: Wow, that's a special experience. How did you find out about the program?

W: I saw it on their website last month, and so I signed up for it.

M: I see. I should take the political science club this time.

W: That's a great idea. I guarantee they'll like it, but you should hurry up to sign up for the program at the website of the Ministry of Foreign Affairs.

M: Why? Is it very popular?

W: Yes, it is. They told me that recently a lot of schools want the program.

M: I see. I'll visit the website to sign up for the program right now.

여: 안녕하세요, Wilson 선생님.

남: 안녕하세요, Brown 선생님. 어제 학생들과의 현장 학습은 어땠어요?

여: 좋았어요. 저희는 외교부에 있는 학생 프로그램에 참가하려고 그곳을 방문했어요.

남: 학생들이 정말 좋은 경험을 했을 것 같네요.

여: 네, 그랬어요. 그 아이들은 강연을 듣고 몇몇 외교관들과 이야기를 나눌 기회를 가졌어요.

남: 와, 그것은 특별한 경험이네요. 그 프로그램에 대해 어떻게 알게 되었어요?

여: 저는 지난달에 그들의 웹사이트에서 그것을 보았고, 그래서 그것을 신청했어요.

남: 그렇군요. 이번에는 제가 정치학 동아리를 데리고 가야겠어요.

여: 좋은 생각이에요. 그 아이들이 그것을 좋아할 것이라고 장담하지만, 선생님은 서둘러 외교부 웹사이트에서 그 프로그램을 신청해야 해요.

남: 왜죠? 그것이 매우 인기가 있나요?

여: 네, 그래요. 최근에 많은 학교들이 그 프로그램을 원하고 있다고 그들이 제게 말했거든요.

남: 그렇군요. 제가 그 프로그램을 신청하기 위해 지금 당장 그 웹사이트를 방문할게요.

◑ Topic & Situation 외교부 현장 학습 프로그램 신청

◑ Solution

여자가 자신의 학생들과 외교부 현장 학습 프로그램을 신청해서 다녀 온 이야기를 하자, 남자는 자신도 정치학 동아리 학생들을 데리고 가야겠다고 말했다. 이에 여자가 많은 학교들이 그 프로그램을 원하고 있으니 신청을 서둘러야 한다고 말했으므로, 이에 대한 남자의 응답으로 가장 적절한 것은 ① '그렇군요. 제가 그 프로그램을 신청하기 위해 지금 당장 그 웹사이트를 방문할게요.'이다.
② 물론이죠. 저는 선생님이 그 프로그램에 참가하시기를 권해요.
③ 알아요. 우리는 다음 달 프로그램을 위해 많은 준비를 해야 해요.
④ 잘됐군요. 우리 학생들이 그 프로그램에 함께 가서 기뻐요.
⑤ 맞아요. 제 학생들은 그 프로그램이 정말 유익하다는 것을 알았어요.

◑ Words & Phrases

field trip 현장 학습 diplomat 외교관 political science 정치학
guarantee 장담하다. 보장하다 informative 유익한

05
정답 | ⑤

| Script & Translation |

M: Hi. Can I help you with something?

W: Yes. I bought this sweater vest here a couple of days ago.

M: Okay. Is there something wrong with it?

W: No, it just didn't look good on me. Could I get a refund?

M: Sure. As long as it has the original price tag and there's nothing wrong with it.

W: Great. It still has the tag, and all I did was try it on once. Here it is.

M: Yeah, it looks good. Do you have the receipt?

W: Yes. Here it is.

M: Okay. *[Pause]* Oh, you bought this vest on sale. I'm sorry, but we don't give refunds on sale items.

W: Really? So I can't get my money back?

M: No, you can't. But I can give you credit that you can use in the store.

W: Okay. I'll look around for something to buy with the credit.

남: 안녕하세요. 무엇을 도와드릴까요?

여: 네. 며칠 전에 이 스웨터 조끼를 여기서 샀는데요.

남: 네. 무슨 문제라도 있나요?

여: 아니요, 그냥 저한테 안 어울려서요. 환불받을 수 있을까요?

남: 물론입니다. 원래의 가격표가 붙어 있고 그것에 아무 문제가 없다면요.

여: 좋아요. 아직 가격표가 붙어 있고, 한 번 입어 보기만 했어요. 여기 있습니다.

남: 네, 좋아 보이네요. 영수증을 가지고 계시나요?

여: 네, 여기 있어요.

남: 알겠습니다. *[잠시 후]* 아, 이 조끼를 세일할 때 사셨군요. 죄송하지만 세일 품목은 환불해 드리지 않습니다.

여: 정말요? 그럼 돈을 돌려받을 수 없는 건가요?

남: 네, 그럴 수 없습니다. 하지만 매장에서 사용할 수 있는 적립금을 드릴 수 있습니다.

여: 알겠습니다. 그 적립금으로 살 만한 것을 찾아 둘러볼게요.

◑ Topic & Situation 의류 환불 요청

◑ Solution

며칠 전에 구입한 스웨터 조끼를 환불하러 간 여자에게 남자가 그 조끼는 세일 품목으로, 세일 품목은 환불해 줄 수 없다고 한다. 돈을 돌려받을 수 없다는 사실을 확인하는 여자에게 남자는 대신 매장에서 사용할 수 있는 적립금을 줄 수 있다고 말하고 있다. 따라서 남자의 마지막 말에 대한 여자의 응답으로 가장 적절한 것은 ⑤ '알겠습니다. 그 적립금으로 살 만한 것을 찾아 둘러볼게요.'이다.
① 죄송합니다. 손님을 위해 그것을 바로 교환해 드리겠습니다.
② 아, 지난주에 세일이 끝난 줄은 몰랐습니다.
③ 물론이죠. 여기 조끼를 살 때 사용했던 신용 카드가 있습니다.
④ 맞아요. 손님의 스웨터 조끼에는 흰색 티셔츠가 잘 어울릴 것 같아요.

◑ Words & Phrases

look good on ~에게 어울리다 refund 환불(금) price tag 가격표 receipt 영수증

06
정답 | ⑤

| Script & Translation |

M: Joy. I was thinking we should head to the beach this weekend.

W: You know I won't say no to that! What beach are you thinking of?

M: I was thinking of Bonny Island Beach.

W: That'd be cool. I love it there!

M: I knew you'd like it there. There's a lot of stuff to do. The beach has volleyball nets, so I'll bring a ball.

W: Awesome.

M: Paddleboards are also available for rent.

W: We should try that this time.

M: For sure. And there are food trucks on the beach, so we can have lunch there.

W: Perfect! I can't wait for the weekend.

M: I feel the same way. Let's make it happen!

남: Joy. 이번 주말에 우리가 해변에 가야겠다고 생각하고 있었어.

여: 내가 그걸 거절하지 않을 거라는 거 알잖아! 어느 해변을 생각하고 있어?

남: Bonny Island 해변을 생각하고 있었어.

여: 멋질 것 같아. 나 그곳을 좋아해!

남: 네가 그곳을 좋아할 줄 알았어. 할 게 많아. 해변에 배구 네트가 있으니, 내가 공을 가져올게.

여: 멋지다.

남: 패들보드 대여도 가능해.

여: 이번에는 우리도 해 봐야지.

남: 물론이지. 그리고 해변에 푸드트럭이 있어서, 우리는 거기서 점심을 먹을 수 있어.

여: 완벽해! 주말이 너무 기다려진다.

남: 나도 같은 생각이야. 꼭 그렇게 하자!

● **Topic & Situation** 주말 해변 나들이 계획

● **Solution**

이번 주말 해변 나들이를 제안하는 남자의 말에 여자가 전적으로 동의하며 해변에서 할 것과 점심 계획까지 너무 완벽해서 주말이 너무 기다려진다고 말하고 있다. 따라서 여자의 마지막 말에 대한 남자의 응답으로 가장 적절한 것은 ⑤ '나도 같은 생각이야. 꼭 그렇게 하자!'이다.

① 상관없어. 어떤 종류의 해산물이든 좋아.
② 우리가 경기를 할 수 있게 배구 네트를 설치해야 해.
③ 사실 나는 해변에 갈 기분이 아니야.
④ 맞아. 우리는 이번 주말에 집에 있을 것 같아.

● **Words & Phrases**

head to ~로 가다, ~로 향하다   stuff 것, 일   volleyball 배구
paddleboard 패들보드

07
정답 | ④

| **Script & Translation** |

M: Amy, were you just talking on the phone in French?

W: Yeah. I was talking to a college friend.

M: Wow. I didn't know you spoke French. How many languages can you speak?

W: I can speak four, including English.

M: It's amazing that you speak four languages!

W: Well, it's not like I speak them all perfectly. My French used to be a lot better, but I haven't used it for a while.

M: Are you saying that it's important to keep using a foreign language not to forget it?

W: Yes, exactly. Learning a foreign language requires constant practice.

M: That makes sense.

W: Not only does it take a lot of practice, but it takes a lot of patience, too. Didn't you start learning Chinese recently?

M: Yes, I did, but it's not easy to stick with it.

W: It's like that at first, but practice and patience make a big difference.

남: Amy, 너 방금 프랑스어로 전화 통화를 한 거야?

여: 응. 대학 친구와 통화하고 있었어.

남: 와. 네가 프랑스어를 하는 줄 몰랐어. 몇 개 언어를 말할 수 있어?

여: 영어를 포함해서 4개 언어를 말할 수 있어.

남: 4개 언어를 구사한다니 정말 놀랍다!

여: 글쎄, 내가 4개 언어 모두를 완벽하게 구사하는 것은 아니야. 예전에는 프랑스어를 훨씬 더 잘했지만, 한동안 사용하지 않았어.

남: 외국어를 잊지 않으려면 계속 사용하는 것이 중요하다는 말이지?

여: 응, 맞아. 외국어를 배우려면 꾸준한 연습이 필요하거든.

남: 일리 있는 말이야.

여: 많은 연습이 필요할 뿐 아니라 인내심도 많이 필요해. 너 최근에 중국어를 배우기 시작하지 않았어?

남: 응, 그랬는데, 그것을 계속하기가 쉽지 않네.

여: 처음에는 그렇지만, 연습과 인내가 큰 차이를 만들 거야.

● **Topic & Situation** 연습과 인내가 필요한 외국어 학습

● **Solution**

4개 언어를 말할 수 있다는 여자의 말에 남자가 놀라워하자, 여자

는 외국어를 배우려면 꾸준한 연습과 많은 인내심이 필요하다고 말하고 있다. 따라서 요즘 중국어를 배우고 있긴 한데 계속하기가 쉽지 않다는 남자의 마지막 말에 대한 여자의 응답으로 가장 적절한 것은 ④ '처음에는 그렇지만, 연습과 인내가 큰 차이를 만들 거야.'이다.

① 미안하지만, 프랑스어를 할 줄 알아야 해.
② 믿기 힘들겠지만, 나는 외국어를 못해.
③ 동의해. 원어민처럼 프랑스어를 말할 필요는 없어.
⑤ 이제야 네가 어떻게 외국어를 빨리 배울 수 있는지 이해가 되네.

● **Words & Phrases**

require 필요하다   practice 연습   patience 인내, 참을성   stick with ~을 계속하다

08

정답 | ④

| Script & Translation |

W: Hi, Lucas, would you like to work on our history project together this weekend?

M: Hi, Isabella. Sure, that sounds like a good idea.

W: Which day would you prefer to meet up?

M: I'm available all weekend. How about you?

W: I have a book club meeting on Saturday, so Sunday would be better. How about 2 p.m.?

M: Okay. Where should we meet?

W: The library is definitely the best place for us to study. They have plenty of resources available, and it's usually quiet.

M: That's a bit far. What about the café down the street? They offer good foods, and their chairs are really comfortable.

W: That's true, but I'm concerned about the noise level there. It can get quite loud at times.

M: It shouldn't be a problem. They have quiet study rooms now. I can reserve a room for our project.

W: That's great! Let's meet up there then.

M: Perfect! I'll call the café and check if a study room will be available.

여: 안녕, Lucas, 이번 주말에 우리 역사 프로젝트를 함께 할래?

남: 안녕, Isabella. 물론이지, 좋은 생각인 것 같아.

여: 무슨 요일에 만나는 게 좋니?

남: 나는 주말 내내 시간이 있어. 너는 어때?

여: 나는 토요일에 독서 모임이 있어서 일요일이 더 좋을 것 같아. 오후 2시는 어때?

남: 그래. 어디서 만날까?

여: 도서관이 우리가 공부하기에 확실히 최고의 장소야. 이용할 수 있는 자료들이 많이 있고, 보통 조용해.

남: 거기는 좀 멀어. 길 아래쪽에 있는 카페는 어때? 거기서는 좋은 음식을 팔고 의자가 정말 편안해.

여: 맞아, 하지만 나는 거기 소음 수준이 걱정돼. 때때로 꽤 시끄러울 수 있어.

남: 그건 문제가 되지 않을 거야. 현재 거기에는 조용한 스터디 룸이 있어. 내가 우리의 프로젝트를 위해 룸을 예약할 수 있어.

여: 좋아! 그러면 거기서 만나자.

남: 완벽해! 내가 그 카페에 전화를 걸어 스터디 룸이 이용 가능할지 확인해 볼게.

● **Topic & Situation** 카페에서 역사 프로젝트 함께 하기

● **Solution**

두 사람은 이번 주말에 역사 프로젝트를 같이 하기로 했는데, 여자가 토요일에 독서 모임이 있어서 일요일 오후 2시에 만나기로 했다. 길 아래쪽에 있는 카페의 스터디 룸을 예약할 수 있다는 남자의 말에 여자는 거기에서 만나자고 했으므로, 여자의 마지막 말에 대한 남자의 응답으로 가장 적절한 것은 ④ '완벽해! 내가 그 카페에 전화를 걸어 스터디 룸이 이용 가능할지 확인해 볼게.'이다.

① 그런데 내가 그때는 한가하지 않을 거야. 다른 날에 만나는 게 어때?
② 그 카페가 시끄러울 것 같아. 다른 곳으로 가는 게 어때?
③ 좋아! 네가 독서 모임에 시간 맞춰 올 수 있다니 기뻐.
⑤ 멋져! 우리가 도서관에서 함께 프로젝트를 할 수 있다니 정말 좋아.

● **Words & Phrases**

meet up 만나다, 모이다   plenty of 많은, 풍부한   resource 자료, 자원   loud 시끄러운   at times 때때로, 가끔씩

09

정답 | ②

| Script & Translation |

W: Dad, I got a notice that my package just arrived.

M: Oh, what did you order this time?

W: I got some clothes and shoes.

M: It seems like you've been doing a lot of online

shopping lately.

W: Yes, online shopping is just so convenient and often offers better prices.

M: True, but have you thought about the environmental impact of packaging and shipping?

W: Honestly, it never crossed my mind. But you're right. Excessive packaging can harm the environment.

M: Exactly. It's also important to support local businesses.

W: Yeah, I haven't been shopping locally much.

M: You should consider shopping more at local stores. It helps local businesses thrive.

W: Okay. I'll reduce my online shopping and prioritize shopping offline.

여: 아빠, 제 소포가 방금 도착했다는 알림을 받았어요.

남: 아, 이번에는 뭘 주문했니?

여: 옷과 신발을 좀 샀어요.

남: 너는 최근에 온라인 쇼핑을 많이 해온 것 같아.

여: 네, 온라인 쇼핑은 정말 매우 편리하고 흔히 가격이 더 저렴해요.

남: 맞아, 하지만 포장과 배송의 환경적 영향에 대해 생각해 봤니?

여: 솔직히, 그것에 대해 전혀 생각을 해보지 않았어요. 하지만 아빠 말씀이 맞아요. 과도한 포장은 환경에 해를 끼칠 수 있어요.

남: 정확히 그래. 지역 기업을 지원하는 것도 중요하단다.

여: 그래요, 저는 최근에 지역에서 쇼핑을 많이 하지 않았어요.

남: 지역 상점에서 더 많이 쇼핑하는 것을 고려해 봐야 해. 그렇게 하면 지역 기업이 번창하는 데 도움이 돼.

여: 알겠어요. 온라인 쇼핑을 줄이고 오프라인 쇼핑에 우선순위를 두도록 할게요.

◉ **Topic & Situation** 온라인 쇼핑보다 오프라인 쇼핑을 해야 하는 이유

◉ **Solution**

남자는 여자에게 온라인 쇼핑을 많이 하는 것 같다고 하면서 온라인 쇼핑이 매우 편리하고 흔히 가격이 더 저렴하다는 여자의 말에 포장과 배송의 환경적 영향에 대해 생각해봤는지 물었고, 여자는 전혀 생각해 보지 않았지만, 과도한 포장은 환경에 해를 끼칠 수 있다고 말했다. 남자가 지역 상점에서 더 많이 쇼핑하는 것을 고려해 봐야 한다고 하면서 그것이 지역 기업이 번창하는 데 도움이 된다고 했으므로, 남자의 마지막 말에 대한 여자의 응답으로 가장 적절한 것은 ② '알겠어요. 온라인 쇼핑을 줄이고 오프라인 쇼핑에 우선순위를 두도록 할게요.'이다.

① 그 말에 전적으로 동의해요. 그래서 저는 항상 온라인 상점에서 쇼핑해요.

③ 멋져요! 우리가 친환경 지역 상점을 여는 것은 정말 좋은 생각이에요.

④ 맞아요. 저는 환경을 위해 재활용에 더 신경 써야 해요.

⑤ 좋은 생각이에요. 제가 지역 기업들에게 건설적인 피드백을 제공해서 도움을 줄게요.

◉ **Words & Phrases**

lately 최근에, 요즘에   impact 영향   packaging 포장   shipping 배송   cross one's mind ~에게 생각나다   excessive 과도한, 지나친   harm 해를 끼치다   support 지원하다, 응원하다   consider 고려하다, 생각하다   thrive 번창하다   prioritize 우선순위를 두다

10
정답 | ③

| **Script & Translation** |

W: Jeremy, I was wondering if you'd be interested in joining the badminton club I'm in.

M: Hmm. That sounds like fun. I'm not good at badminton though. I've only played a few times.

W: No problem. The club is open to everyone, including beginners.

M: How often does it meet?

W: Twice a week.

M: That's good. Will I have to buy a racket?

W: No. The club has a bunch of rackets you can use. All you really need are comfortable clothes and sneakers.

M: That sounds great! I'm in. It'll be also nice to meet new people.

W: Absolutely. Everybody's really nice. You're going to have a great time with us.

M: Thanks for inviting me. What should I do now?

W: The pleasure is mine. Just come with me, and I'll send you a link to the club's social media page later.

M: Awesome. I can't wait to play badminton and make new friends.

여: Jeremy, 나는 네가 내가 속한 배드민턴 동아리에 가입하는 데 관심이 있을지 궁금했어.

남: 음. 재미있을 것 같아. 하지만 나는 배드민턴을 잘하지 못해. 겨우 몇 번만 해봤어.

여: 괜찮아. 그 동아리는 초보자를 포함하여, 누구에게나 개방되어 있어.

남: 얼마나 자주 만나니?

여: 일주일에 두 번이야.

남: 좋아. 내가 라켓을 사야 할까?

여: 아니. 동아리에는 네가 사용할 수 있는 라켓이 많이 있어. 네가 정말 필요한 건 편한 옷과 운동화뿐이야.

남: 좋아! 들어갈게. 새로운 사람들을 만나는 것도 좋을 거야.

여: 당연하지. 모두가 정말 친절해. 너는 우리와 함께 아주 즐겁게 지낼 거야.

남: 권해 줘서 고마워. 이제 내가 뭘 해야 하지?

여: 내가 기쁘지. 그냥 나랑 같이 가면 되고, 나중에 내가 너에게 동아리 소셜 미디어 페이지 링크를 보내줄게.

남: 정말 좋아. 어서 빨리 배드민턴을 치고 새로운 친구들을 사귀고 싶어.

◉ Topic & Situation 배드민턴 동아리 가입

◉ Solution

여자가 속한 배드민턴 동아리 가입에 관심이 있는 남자는 그 동아리는 초보자에게도 열려 있고, 라켓도 살 필요 없이 편한 옷과 운동화만 있으면 된다는 말을 듣고 가입하겠다고 하면서 새로운 사람을 만나는 것도 좋을 것이라고 말했다. 무엇을 해야 하는지를 묻는 남자에게 여자는 자신과 같이 가기만 하면 된다고 하면서 나중에 동아리 소셜 미디어 페이지 링크를 보내준다고 했으므로, 여자의 마지막 말에 대한 남자의 응답으로 가장 적절한 것은 ③ '정말 좋아. 어서 빨리 배드민턴을 치고 새로운 친구들을 사귀고 싶어.'이다.

① 너는 그럴 필요 없어. 내가 배드민턴 동아리에 대해서 다 알고 있어.

② 좋아. 내가 동아리에 가입할 수 있도록 바로 라켓을 살게.

④ 알겠어. 지금 당장 온라인으로 배드민턴 대회에 참가 신청할게.

⑤ 정보 고마워. 그 대회에서 우승할 수 있도록 최선을 다할게.

◉ Words & Phrases

a bunch of 많은, 다수의   comfortable 편한   sneaker 운동화
awesome 기막히게 좋은, 경탄할 만한, 멋진

11

정답 | ④

| Script & Translation |

W: Honey, I'm home.

M: Hi, sweetie. Did you have a good day?

W: Yes. How was your day with our little guy?

M: Great. Kevin and I had a lot of fun.

W: Awesome. What did you do?

M: We baked cookies, played board games, and then read books.

W: Sounds fun. By the way, it seems like you stayed indoors all day long.

M: Right. I asked him if he wanted to go to the park and kick a soccer ball, but he didn't.

W: He usually prefers staying home. I want to get him outside more for exercise.

M: Me, too. Do you have any good ideas?

W: How about we all go on regular walks or bike rides together?

M: He might find it hard to ride a bike. I'm sure he'd like your other idea better if we do it together.

W: Then let's try taking a family walk in the evenings.

여: 여보, 저 왔어요.

남: 안녕, 여보. 좋은 하루 보냈나요?

여: 네. 우리 아들하고 오늘 어땠어요?

남: 좋았어요. Kevin과 저는 정말 즐거웠어요.

여: 멋지네요. 무엇을 했나요?

남: 쿠키도 굽고, 보드게임도 하고, 그러고 나서 책도 읽었어요.

여: 재밌었겠어요. 그런데 하루 종일 실내에 있었던 것 같네요.

남: 맞아요. 공원에 가서 축구공을 차고 싶은지 그에게 물어 봤는데 원하지 않았어요.

여: 그는 보통 집에 있는 걸 더 좋아하잖아요. 그가 운동하도록 밖에 더 많이 나가게 하고 싶어요.

남: 저도 그래요. 혹시 좋은 생각 있어요?

여: 우리 모두 함께 규칙적으로 산책하거나 자전거를 타러 가는 것은 어때요?

남: 그는 자전거 타기를 힘들어할 것 같아요. 우리가 함께하면 그는 당신의 다른 의견을 더 좋아할 것이라고 확신해요.

여: 그럼 저녁마다 함께 가족 산책을 해봐요.

◉ Topic & Situation 아이가 더 활동적이 되도록 만드는 방법

◉ Solution

아이가 운동하도록 밖에 더 많이 나가게 하고 싶다고 말하는 여자에게 남자가 동의하며 좋은 생각이 있는지 묻자 여자는 함께 규칙적으로 산책을 하거나 자전거 타기를 하는 것이 어떤지 묻고 있다. 남자는 아이가 자전거 타기는 힘들다고 생각할 수 있고 대신 다른 것, 즉 걷기를 더 좋아할 것이라고 말한다. 따라서 남자의 마지막 말에 대한 여자의 응답으로 가장 적절한 것은 ④ '그럼 저녁마다 함께 가족 산책을 해봐요.'이다.

① 그가 새로운 친구를 사귈 수 있는 방법을 함께 찾아봐요.

② 강제로 그를 밖에 나가게 하는 것은 좋은 생각이 아니에요.

③ 그가 보드게임을 할 때 방해하지 마세요.

⑤ 함께 책을 읽는 것이 그에게 가장 좋은 활동이에요.

● Words & Phrases

indoors 실내에   prefer 더 좋아하다   regular 규칙적인   disturb 방해하다

12

정답 | ②

| Script & Translation |

M: Wendy, what are you watching intently on TV?

W: It's a documentary about zoo animals, Dad. It deals with an issue about them.

M: Why? Is there anything wrong with zoo animals?

W: Yeah. Some of them behave abnormally.

M: How?

W: They repeatedly move anxiously back and forth or in circles in the same spot.

M: Hmm, it's probably because they feel stuck and stressed out in the zoo cages.

W: Well, it would be better for animals to live in zoos than in the wild, right?

M: No. Zoo animals don't live in cages because they want to.

W: Now I see. They could feel trapped in cages to satisfy our needs.

M: You're right. Zoo animals are forced to live there for us.

남: Wendy, TV에서 무엇을 몰두해서 보고 있니?

여: 동물원 동물들에 대한 다큐멘터리에요, 아빠. 그것은 그들에 대한 문제를 다루고 있어요.

남: 왜? 동물원 동물들에게 무슨 문제라도 있니?

여: 네. 그들 중 일부는 비정상적으로 행동해요.

남: 어떻게?

여: 그들은 같은 장소에서 초조하게 앞뒤로 왔다 갔다 하거나 원을 그리며 반복적으로 움직여요.

남: 음, 그것은 아마도 그들이 동물원 우리에 갇혀 스트레스를 받아서 그런 것 같아.

여: 글쎄요, 동물들이 야생에서 사는 것보다 동물원에서 사는 것이 더 나을 것 같은데, 그렇죠?

남: 아니야. 동물원 동물들이 원해서 우리에서 사는 건 아니잖니.

여: 이제 알겠어요. 그들은 우리의 욕구를 충족시키기 위해 우리에 갇혀 있다고 느낄 수도 있을 것 같아요.

남: 맞아. 동물원 동물들은 우리를 위해 거기에서 살도록 강요받는 것이지.

● Topic & Situation   동물원 동물들의 이상 행동에 관한 다큐멘터리 시청

● Solution

여자가 다큐멘터리에서 보는 동물원 동물들의 비정상적인 행동에 대해 남자와 대화하는 상황이며, 남자는 동물들이 보이는 이상 행동의 원인이 우리에 갇혀 있어서 생긴 스트레스 때문이고 동물원의 동물들이 원해서 우리에 사는 것은 아니라고 이야기하고 있다. 그에 대해 여자는 동물원의 동물들은 우리의 욕구를 충족시키기 위해 우리에 갇혀 있다고 느낄 거라고 말한다. 이에 대한 남자의 응답으로 가장 적절한 것은 ② '맞아. 동물원 동물들은 우리를 위해 거기에서 살도록 강요받는 것이지.'이다.

① 그건 사실이 아니야. 요즘 동물원은 인기를 잃어 가고 있어.

③ 미안해. 난 동의하지 않아. 각자 동물원에 대해 서로 다른 견해를 가지고 있어.

④ 그래? 사실 동물원 동물들은 사육사들에 의해 보살핌을 잘 받고 있어.

⑤ 일리가 있어. 동물원은 멸종 위기에 처한 종들을 보존하는 데 기여해.

● Words & Phrases

intently 몰두해서   abnormally 비정상적으로   back and forth 앞뒤로   spot 장소, 지점   stuck 갇힌, 빠져나갈 수가 없는   cage 우리   trap 가두다   satisfy 충족시키다   make sense 일리가 있다   contribute to ~에 기여하다   preserve 보존하다

Dictations

본문 83, 88~91쪽

기출   ❶ be an inspiration to
예제   ❷ finally come true

❸ never an issue

01   ❶ recently became close friends

❷ where to have the party

❸ need a good excuse

02   ❶ taking much longer

❷ got lost during delivery

❸ tracked my package

03 ❶ won the gold medal
 ❷ get up and watch it
 ❸ wake up so early
04 ❶ field trip with your students
 ❷ talk with some diplomats
 ❸ hurry up to sign up
05 ❶ bought this sweater vest
 ❷ get a refund
 ❸ have the receipt
 ❹ give refunds on sale items
06 ❶ should head to the beach
 ❷ a lot of stuff to do
 ❸ also available for rent
 ❹ should try that this time
07 ❶ used to be a lot better
 ❷ requires constant practice
 ❸ takes a lot of patience
 ❹ to stick with it
08 ❶ work on our history project
 ❷ plenty of resources available
 ❸ reserve a room
09 ❶ a lot of online shopping
 ❷ packaging and shipping
 ❸ helps local businesses thrive
10 ❶ is open to everyone
 ❷ comfortable clothes and sneakers
 ❸ send you a link
11 ❶ you stayed indoors
 ❷ go on regular walks
 ❸ your other idea better
12 ❶ intently on TV
 ❷ anxiously back and forth
 ❸ than in the wild
 ❹ trapped in cages to satisfy

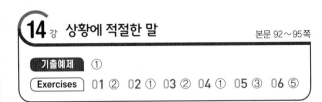

14강 상황에 적절한 말 본문 92~95쪽

기출예제 ①

Exercises 01 ② 02 ① 03 ② 04 ① 05 ③ 06 ⑤

기출 예제 본문 92쪽

정답 | ①

| Script & Translation |

M: Jake and Yuna are members of a climbing club. Today, they're visiting a national park with other club members. At the top of the mountain, Jake sees a beautiful rock. He starts taking selfies with it. When Yuna sees Jake, she offers to take photos for him. Jake finds a great spot to take a photo with the rock and gives Yuna his smartphone. After Yuna takes some photos of him, Jake looks at the photos and notices that the rock is not in them. So Jake wants to ask Yuna to get another shot of him and this time include the rock. In this situation, what would Jake most likely say to Yuna?

Jake: <u>Could you please take my picture again with the rock in it?</u>

남: Jake와 Yuna는 등산 동아리의 회원입니다. 오늘 그들은 동아리의 다른 회원들과 함께 한 국립공원을 찾았습니다. 그 산의 정상에서 Jake는 아름다운 바위를 발견합니다. 그는 그것을 담은 셀피를 찍기 시작합니다. Yuna는 Jake를 보자, 그녀는 그에게 사진을 찍어 주겠다고 제안합니다. Jake는 그 바위를 담은 사진을 찍을 근사한 장소를 발견하고 Yuna에게 자신의 스마트폰을 건넵니다. Yuna가 그의 사진을 몇 장 찍은 후, Jake는 그 사진들을 보고 바위가 사진에 담기지 않은 것을 알아차립니다. 그래서 Jake는 Yuna에게 자신의 사진을 한 장 더 찍어 주되 이번에는 그 바위를 포함하라고 부탁하고 싶습니다. 이러한 상황에서, Jake는 Yuna에게 뭐라고 말하겠습니까?

Jake: 내 사진을 바위를 담아 다시 찍어 줄래?

▶ **Topic & Situation** 바위 배경으로 사진 찍기

▶ **Solution**

Jake는 사진을 찍어 주겠다는 Yuna에게 아름다운 바위를 담은 사진을 찍을 근사한 장소를 찾아 스마트폰을 건넸지만, Yuna가 바위를 담지 않고 사진을 찍은 것을 알고, 바위를 포함하여 사진

을 더 찍어줄 것을 부탁하는 상황이다. 그러므로 Jake가 Yuna에게 할 말로 가장 적절한 것은 ① '내 사진을 바위를 담아 다시 찍어 줄래?'이다.

② 네가 나랑 그 산에 갈 수 있다면 고맙겠어.

③ 그 바위를 오르는 동안에는 사진을 찍으면 안 돼.

④ 네가 그 바위 앞에서 포즈를 취해 줄 수 있는지 궁금해.

⑤ 그 국립공원에서 셀피를 찍지 않을래?

▶ Words & Phrases
national park 국립공원 selfie 셀피(스마트폰으로 찍는 자신의 사진)

Exercises
본문 94~95쪽

01
정답 | ②

| Script & Translation |

W: Jason is taking a surfing lesson from his friend, Angela, who is very good at surfing. Angela first tells Jason the basics of surfing on the beach, and then they go into the water. Whenever Jason tries getting up on the surfboard, he falls down right away. However, Angela kindly continues encouraging him to keep trying, and Jason finally succeeds. Now he thinks he is able to stand and stay up on the surfboard alone. Angela tells him to try surfing alone, and she goes out of the water. After surfing for about half an hour, Jason comes out of the water and goes to Angela. He wants to express his gratitude to her for helping him surf alone. In this situation, what would Jason most likely say to Angela?

Jason: <u>Thanks to you, I'm able to surf by myself.</u>

여: Jason은 서핑을 아주 잘하는 친구 Angela에게서 서핑 강습을 받고 있습니다. Angela가 먼저 해변에서 Jason에게 서핑의 기본에 대해 알려 주고 나서 그들은 물에 들어갑니다. Jason이 서핑보드 위에서 일어서려고 할 때마다, 그는 바로 넘어집니다. 하지만 Angela는 Jason에게 계속 시도하라고 친절하게 계속 격려를 하고, Jason은 마침내 성공합니다. 이제 Jason은 자신이 혼자 서핑보드 위에서 일어서서 계속 서 있을 수 있다고 생각합니다. Angela는 Jason에게 혼자서 서

핑을 해 보라고 말하고 물 밖으로 나옵니다. 약 30분 정도 서핑을 한 후에, Jason은 물에서 나와 Angela에게 갑니다. 그는 Angela가 자신이 혼자 서핑하는 것을 도와주어서 그녀에게 고마움을 표현하고 싶어 합니다. 이런 상황에서, Jason은 Angela에게 뭐라고 말하겠습니까?

Jason: <u>네 덕분에, 내가 혼자서 서핑을 할 수 있어.</u>

▶ Topic & Situation 서핑 강습

▶ Solution
친구인 Angela 덕분에 서핑할 수 있게 되었다고 생각하는 Jason이 Angela에게 고마움을 표현하고 싶어 하는 상황이므로, Jason이 Angela에게 할 말로 가장 적절한 것은 ② '네 덕분에, 내가 혼자서 서핑을 할 수 있어.'이다.

① 만약 네가 거기에 가면, 너는 서핑을 해 봐야 해.

③ 물론이지. 네가 나보다 서핑을 훨씬 더 잘해.

④ 좋아. 네 개인 서핑 강습을 신청할게.

⑤ 맞아. 우리의 서핑 수업은 이 지역에서 최고야.

▶ Words & Phrases
encourage 격려하다 gratitude 고마움, 감사

02
정답 | ①

| Script & Translation |

M: In their second year of high school, Laura and Hank are both actively involved in different school clubs. Laura belongs to the school science club, while Hank is in the school drama club. For his club performance at the school festival last Friday, Hank borrowed a white lab coat from Laura for his costume as a doctor. Before returning the lab coat to Laura, he washes and dries it. However, while folding it, he notices the pocket is torn. Feeling sorry, Hank informs Laura about the tear and offers to buy her a new lab coat. But Laura wants to tell Hank that he doesn't need to do that because she has an extra one. In this situation, what would Laura most likely say to Hank?

Laura: <u>Don't worry about it. I have a spare lab coat.</u>

남: 고등학교 2학년에 재학하는, Laura와 Hank는 둘 다 학교의 다른 동아리에 적극적으로 참여하고 있습니다. Laura는 학교 과학 동아리에 속해 있지만, Hank는 학교 연극 동아리에 속해 있습니다. 지난 금요일 학교 축제에서 동아리 공연을 위해,

Hank는 의사 복장으로 사용하려고 Laura로부터 흰색 실험복을 빌렸습니다. Laura에게 실험복을 돌려주기 전에, 그는 그것을 세탁하고 말립니다. 하지만 그것을 개는 동안, 그는 주머니가 찢어진 것을 알아차립니다. 미안한 마음에 Hank는 Laura에게 찢어진 부분에 대해 알리고 새 실험복을 사주겠다고 제안합니다. 하지만 Laura는 자기가 여분의 실험복을 가지고 있기 때문에 Hank에게 그럴 필요가 없다고 말하고 싶어 합니다. 이런 상황에서, Laura는 Hank에게 뭐라고 말하겠습니까?

Laura: 그것은 걱정하지 마. 내게 여분의 실험복이 있어.

● Topic & Situation 실험복 돌려주기

● Solution

Hank는 동아리 연극에서 의사 복장을 하기 위해 Laura로부터 흰색 실험복을 빌렸으나 세탁 후에 옷을 개는 과정에서 주머니가 찢어진 것을 알아차린다. 미안한 마음에 Laura에게 찢어진 부분에 대해 알리고 새 실험복을 사주겠다고 제안하였으나, Laura는 자신에게 여분의 실험복이 있기 때문에 사줄 필요가 없다고 Hank에게 말하고 싶어 한다. 따라서 Laura가 Hank에게 할 말로 가장 적절한 것은 ① '그것은 걱정하지 마. 내게 여분의 실험복이 있어.'이다.

② 미안해. 그들은 이 실험복을 더 이상 팔지 않아.

③ 놀랍구나! 네 연극 공연에 행운을 빌어.

④ 와, 네게 의사로서 엑스트라 역할이 있다니 나는 믿을 수가 없어!

⑤ 아, 이런! 너는 세탁소에서 실험복을 세탁해야 해.

● Words & Phrases

borrow 빌리다   lab coat 실험복   costume 복장, 의상   notice 알아차리다, 주목하다; 공지   tear 찢다; 찢어진 부분   extra 여분의; 엑스트라, 단역 배우   dry cleaner's 세탁소

03

정답 | ②

| Script & Translation |

W: Sandra reads web novels on her computer every day to become a web novel writer. Recently, she read an article on eye health risks associated with electromagnetic waves. Worried about long-term exposure to electromagnetic waves, Sandra discusses this issue with her friend Alex, a computer programmer. He tells Sandra that he sits away from his monitor and takes frequent breaks while using the computer. He advises her to do the same. But Sandra says she believes she should do more to protect herself. Alex thinks she should install a screen filter that blocks blue light emissions from the monitor. So he wants to suggest that she apply a screen filter for her eyes. In this situation, what would Alex most likely say to Sandra?

Alex: How about using a screen filter to protect your eyes?

여: Sandra는 웹 소설 작가가 되기 위해 매일 컴퓨터로 웹 소설을 읽습니다. 최근에, 그녀는 전자파와 관련된 눈 건강 위험에 대한 기사를 읽었습니다. 전자파에 대한 장기간의 노출에 대해 걱정을 하던 Sandra는 컴퓨터 프로그래머인 친구, Alex와 이 문제에 관해 논의합니다. 그는 Sandra에게 자신은 컴퓨터를 사용하는 동안 모니터에서 멀리 떨어져 앉고, 자주 휴식을 취한다고 말합니다. 그는 그녀에게도 똑같이 해볼 것을 조언합니다. 그러나 Sandra는 자기가 스스로를 보호하기 위해 더 많은 것을 해야 한다고 믿는다고 말합니다. Alex는 그녀가 모니터로부터 나오는 청색광 방출을 차단하는 스크린 필터를 설치해야 한다고 생각합니다. 그래서 그는 그녀가 눈을 위해 스크린 필터를 사용할 것을 제안하고 싶어 합니다. 이런 상황에서, Alex가 Sandra에게 뭐라고 말하겠습니까?

Alex: 네 눈을 보호하기 위해 스크린 필터를 사용해 보는 건 어때?

● Topic & Situation 눈 건강을 지키기 위한 방법 제안

● Solution

웹 소설 작가가 되기 위해 매일 컴퓨터로 웹 소설을 읽는 Sandra가 전자파와 관련된 기사를 읽고, 전자파에 대한 장기간의 노출에 대해 걱정이 되어 친구인 Alex와 이 문제에 관해 논의한다. Alex는 자신이 눈 건강을 지키기 위해 하는 노력들을 Sandra도 똑같이 해보도록 조언하지만, 그녀는 자신을 보호하기 위해 더 많은 것을 해야 한다고 말한다. Alex는 그녀가 모니터로부터 나오는 청색광 방출을 차단하는 스크린 필터를 설치해야 한다고 생각하면서, Sandra에게 눈을 위해 스크린 필터를 사용해 보라고 제안하고 싶어 한다. 따라서 이런 상황에서, Alex가 Sandra에게 할 말로 가장 적절한 것은 ② '네 눈을 보호하기 위해 스크린 필터를 사용해 보는 건 어때?'이다.

① 다른 장르의 웹 소설을 읽어 보는 것은 어때?

③ 곧 시력 검사를 받을 계획이니?

④ 모니터와의 거리를 늘리는 게 좋을 거야.

⑤ 스크린 필터는 모니터를 긁힘으로부터 보호하는 데 정말 도움이 돼.

Words & Phrases

associated 관련된　**electromagnetic wave** 전자파　**exposure** 노출, 폭로　**frequent** 빈번한, 잦은　**filter** 필터, 여과 장치　**emission** 방출, 배출　**genre** 장르　**eye examination** 시력 검사　**distance** 거리　**scratch** 긁힘, 긁힌 자국

② 규칙적인 운동은 스트레스를 푸는 데 도움을 줘.

③ 난 네가 다음번에는 더 좋은 점수를 받을 것이라고 확신해.

④ 네가 몇 번을 실패하든 계속 시도해 봐.

⑤ 영어 수업을 포기하는 것은 좋은 생각이 아닌 것 같아.

Words & Phrases

complain 불평하다　**unnecessary** 불필요한　**look on the bright side of** ~의 긍정적인 면을 보다　**achievement** 성취, 성과　**be hard on** ~에게 심하게 굴다

04

정답 | ①

Script & Translation

M: Paul and Olivia are high school classmates who have been friends since elementary school. One day, Olivia complains to Paul about her English mid-term exam score. She made a small mistake, but she received a lower score than she expected. Paul thinks it's unnecessary for her to get so upset about her score. Paul thinks Olivia is putting too much stress on herself and that she should look on the bright side of her achievement. So he wants to say that she should be less critical of herself. In this situation, what would Paul most likely say to Olivia?

Paul: You shouldn't be hard on yourself like that.

남: Paul과 Olivia는 초등학교 때부터 친구인 고등학교 같은 반 친구입니다. 어느 날, Olivia는 Paul에게 자신의 영어 중간고사 점수에 대해 불평합니다. 그녀는 사소한 실수를 저질렀지만 그녀가 기대했던 것보다 더 낮은 점수를 받았습니다. Paul은 그녀의 점수에 대해 그녀가 그렇게 언짢아 할 필요가 없다고 생각합니다. Paul은 Olivia가 자기 자신에게 많은 스트레스를 주고 있으며, 그녀가 성취한 것의 긍정적인 면을 봐야 한다고 생각합니다. 그래서 그는 그녀가 자기 자신에게 덜 가혹해야 한다고 말하고 싶어 합니다. 이런 상황에서, Paul은 Olivia에게 뭐라고 말하겠습니까?

Paul: 너 자신에게 그렇게 심하게 굴어서는 안 돼.

○ **Topic & Situation** 자기 자신을 탓하는 친구에게 조언하기

○ **Solution**

Olivia는 사소한 실수로 자신이 기대했던 것보다 중간고사 영어 점수가 낮게 나온 것에 대해 Paul에게 불평을 하는데, Paul은 이를 듣고 Olivia가 자기 자신에게 많은 스트레스를 주고 있으며, 그녀가 성취한 것의 긍정적인 면을 보면서 자기 자신에게 덜 가혹해야 한다고 말하고 싶어 한다. 따라서 Paul이 Olivia에게 할 말로 가장 적절한 것은 ① '너 자신에게 그렇게 심하게 굴어서는 안 돼.'이다.

05

정답 | ③

Script & Translation

W: Mindy and Jason are both members of the school hip-hop dance team. Recently, their team has been preparing for a dance performance at a local festival, which is next week. They've been practicing their dance routine together three times a week. However, Jason tells Mindy that he doesn't quite like the music because he thinks it's too slow. He suggests that they change the music to something that has a faster beat. But Mindy thinks it's too late to change the music now because they have less than a week before the festival. So Mindy wants to tell Jason that she prefers they not change their music. In this situation, what would Mindy most likely say to Jason?

Mindy: I think it'd be better for our team to stick to the original music.

여: Mindy와 Jason은 둘 다 학교 힙합 댄스팀의 구성원입니다. 최근 그들의 팀은 다음 주에 열리는 지역 축제에서 펼칠 댄스 공연을 준비하고 있습니다. 그들은 일주일에 세 번, 정해진 춤 동작을 함께 연습해 왔습니다. 하지만, Jason은 Mindy에게 음악이 너무 느려서 그것이 별로 마음에 들지 않는다고 말합니다. 그는 그들이 음악을 더 빠른 비트를 가진 것으로 바꿀 것을 제안합니다. 하지만 Mindy는 축제가 일주일도 남지 않았기 때문에 지금 음악을 바꾸기에는 너무 늦었다고 생각합니다. 그래서 Mindy는 Jason에게 자신들의 음악을 바꾸지 않으면 좋겠다고 말하고 싶어합니다. 이런 상황에서, Mindy는 Jason에게 뭐라고 말하겠습니까?

Mindy: 나는 우리 팀이 원래 음악을 고수하는 것이 더 낫다고 생각해.

○ **Topic & Situation** 댄스 안무 음악 교체 제안

● Solution

같은 힙합 댄스 동아리 부원인 Jason과 Mindy는 일주일 뒤에 공연할 춤 동작을 연습하고 있는데, Jason은 그들의 음악이 너무 느리다는 이유로 마음에 들지 않아 하고, 그 음악을 조금 더 빠른 것으로 교체하고 싶다는 의사를 Mindy에게 전달한다. 하지만 Mindy는 공연이 일주일도 남지 않았기 때문에, 음악을 바꾸지 말아야 한다고 말하고 싶어하는 상황이다. 따라서 Mindy가 Jason에게 할 말로 가장 적절한 것은 ③ '나는 우리 팀이 원래 음악을 고수하는 것이 더 낫다고 생각해.'이다.

① 우리의 정해진 동작을 연습할 장소를 찾지 못하면 소용이 없어.

② 우리 공연을 향상시키기 위해 일주일에 네 번 연습하자.

④ 음악에 더 잘 맞추기 위해 우리 공연에 몇 가지 새로운 스텝이 필요해.

⑤ 공연에서 너는 더 빠르고 더 활기차게 움직일 필요가 있어.

● Words & Phrases

recently 최근 routine 정해진 동작 beat 비트, 박자 stick to ~을 고수하다

06   정답 | ⑤

| Script & Translation |

M: Shelly is considering buying a robot vacuum cleaner for her mother, who has chronic lower back pain. So, Shelly searches for reliable online user reviews of robot vacuum cleaners. She visits various websites and reads reviews for days. Thomas, Shelly's husband, notices she spends too much time without a specific purchase decision, and he asks her why she hasn't decided which robot vacuum cleaner to buy yet. She tells him there are so many reviews that it's hard to choose which review to follow. Thomas wants to tell her that she first needs to set a few standards based on her preference not to waste time. In this situation, what would Thomas most likely say to Shelly?

Thomas: You should first establish your standards to be more time-efficient.

남: Shelly는 만성 하부 요통을 앓고 있는 어머니를 위해 로봇 진공청소기 구매를 고려하고 있습니다. 그래서, Shelly는 로봇 진공청소기에 대해 신뢰할 수 있는 온라인 사용자 후기들을 검색합니다. 그녀는 다양한 웹사이트들을 방문하고 며칠 동안 리뷰들을 읽습니다. Shelly의 남편인 Thomas는 Shelly가 구체적인 구매 결정 없이 너무 많은 시간을 보내고 있는 것을 눈치채고, 그는 Shelly에게 왜 아직 어떤 로봇 진공청소기를 살지 결정하지 못했는지 묻습니다. 그녀는 그에게 후기들이 너무 많아서 어떤 후기를 따라야 할지 선택하기 어렵다고 말합니다. Thomas는 그녀에게 시간을 낭비하지 않기 위해 먼저 자신의 선호도에 따라 몇 가지 기준을 정할 필요가 있다고 말하고 싶어 합니다. 이런 상황에서, Thomas는 Shelly에게 뭐라고 말하겠습니까?

Thomas: 당신은 시간 효율성을 높이기 위해 먼저 기준을 정해야 해요.

● Topic & Situation 로봇 진공청소기 구매 결정하기

● Solution

Shelly는 어머니를 위해 로봇 진공청소기를 구매하고자 며칠 동안 웹사이트에서 사용자들의 후기들을 검색하며 읽지만, 후기들이 너무 많아서 어떤 후기를 따라야 할지 고민하고 있는 상황에서 Thomas는 그녀가 먼저 자신의 선호도에 따라 기준을 정해야 한다고 말하고 싶어 한다. 따라서 Thomas가 Shelly에게 할 말로 가장 적절한 것은 ⑤ '당신은 시간 효율성을 높이기 위해 먼저 기준을 정해야 해요.'이다.

① 당신이 후기들을 더 많이 읽으면 사실과 의견을 구별할 수 있어요.

② 당신은 로봇 진공청소기가 그 비싼 가격만큼의 가치가 있다고 생각하나요?

③ 당신이 더 많은 자세한 후기들을 읽으려면 회원 가입을 신청해야 해요.

④ 당신은 다양한 로봇 진공청소기가 있는 웹사이트를 찾아야 해요.

● Words & Phrases

vacuum cleaner 진공청소기 chronic 만성의 search for ~을 찾다 reliable 믿을[신뢰할] 수 있는 specific 구체적인, 명확한 standard 기준 preference 선호도 time-efficient 시간 효율적인

Dictations

본문 93, 96~97쪽

기출 ❶ visiting a national park
예제 ❷ taking selfies
❸ a great spot
❹ get another shot
01 ❶ taking a surfing lesson
❷ getting up on the surfboard
❸ goes out of the water
❹ express his gratitude
02 ❶ both actively involved in
❷ his costume as a doctor
❸ the pocket is torn
03 ❶ Worried about long-term exposure
❷ takes frequent breaks
❸ install a screen filter
04 ❶ made a small mistake
❷ putting too much stress
❸ less critical of herself
05 ❶ preparing for a dance performance
❷ quite like the music
❸ less than a week
06 ❶ chronic lower back pain
❷ without a specific purchase decision
❸ set a few standards

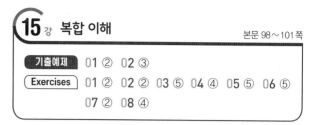

15강 복합 이해

본문 98~101쪽

기출예제 01 ② 02 ③
Exercises 01 ② 02 ② 03 ⑤ 04 ④ 05 ⑤ 06 ⑤
07 ② 08 ④

기출 예제

본문 98쪽

정답 | 01 ② 02 ③

| Script & Translation |

W: Hello, students. Last week, we learned about upcycling, the process of reusing old materials to make a new object more valuable than the original pieces. Today, I'll focus on how this eco-friendly practice is employed in architecture around the world. Our first example is a community center in Singapore, called Enabling Village. Its buildings are famous for being made from old shipping containers. Second, we have a hotel in Mexico, called Tubohotel. The capsule-style rooms of this hotel were built using huge upcycled concrete pipes. Next, Microlibrary Bima is a small local library located in Indonesia. The building was constructed by arranging 2,000 plastic ice cream buckets. Finally, there's the Circular Pavilion in France. It is known for its exterior design which consists of 180 reused wooden doors. Each of these examples shows how upcycling is applied in architecture globally to minimize our environmental footprint. Now, let's watch a video showing how these buildings were made.

여: 안녕하세요, 학생 여러분. 지난주에는 업사이클링, 즉 오래된 재료를 재사용하여 원래의 물품보다 더 가치 있는 새로운 물건을 만드는 과정에 대해 배웠습니다. 오늘 저는 이 친환경적인 실행이 세계 전역에서 건축에 어떻게 이용되는지에 중점을 두겠습니다. 우리의 첫 번째 사례는 Enabling Village라 불리는 싱가포르의 커뮤니티 센터입니다. 그곳의 건물들은 오래된 선적 컨테이너로 만들어진 것으로 유명합니다. 두 번째는 Tubohotel이라 불리는 멕시코의 호텔입니다. 이 호텔의 캡슐형 객실들은 업사이클된 대형 콘크리트 관을 이용하여 지어졌습니다. 다음으로, Microlibrary Bima는 인도네시아에 위치한 작은 지역 도서관입니다. 이 건물은 2,000개의 플라스틱 아이스크림 통을 배열하여 지어졌습니다. 마지막으로, 프랑스

의 Circular Pavilion이 있습니다. 그것은 180개의 재사용 목재 문으로 구성된 외관 디자인으로 유명합니다. 이 사례들 각각은 업사이클링이 우리의 환경 발자국을 최소화하기 위해 세계적으로 건축에 어떻게 적용되는지 보여줍니다. 이제, 이 건물들이 어떻게 만들어졌는지 보여 주는 동영상을 시청합시다.

● **Topic & Situation** 건축에서 업사이클링이 사용되는 방법

● **Solution**

01 여자는 친환경적인 업사이클링이 세계 전역에서 건축에 어떻게 이용되고 있는지에 중점을 두고 여러 사례를 소개하고 있다. 따라서 여자가 하는 말의 주제로 가장 적절한 것은 ② '세계적으로 건축에서 업사이클링이 사용되는 방법'이다.
① 건축 자재 공급원으로서의 다양한 천연 재료
③ 업사이클되는 플라스틱의 여러 나라에서의 전략적 활용
④ 건축 폐기물이 지구 환경에 미치는 영향
⑤ 국가들이 친환경 운송 방법을 이용해야 하는 이유

02 Singapore, Mexico, Indonesia, France는 언급되었지만, ③ 'Australia'는 언급되지 않았다.

● **Words & Phrases**

upcycling 업사이클링(재활용품에 디자인과 활용성을 더하는 등의 방식으로 기존의 제품보다 가치를 높이는 과정) practice 실행, 관행 employ 이용하다, 고용하다 shipping 선적, 해운업 arrange 배열하다 bucket 통, 양동이 exterior 외관의, 외부의 environmental footprint 환경 발자국(환경에 미치는 악영향)

(**Exercises**) 본문 100~101쪽

01~02 정답 | 01 ② 02 ②

| **Script & Translation** |

M: Hello, students. Have you noticed that AI is finding its way into virtually everything nowadays? It's even used in the sports industry. Let me share with you some examples of how AI is being integrated into various sports. First, AI is making its way into football. For example, one Spanish football club has implemented an AI system named Zone7. It uses medical data collected during training to prevent

injuries from occurring during a game. Another AI is in rugby. It's difficult for referees to see everything that happens during a rugby match. So if there's any confusion, referees use highly complex AI video analysis tools to make the right judgment. Also, a lot of tennis players use a range of apps built by AI experts. Using the apps enables them to get automated analyses of shot speed and accuracy and analyze their games with more precision. Lastly, to combat inaccurate decisions made during a game, AI robots have been tested in baseball. They sit above home plate and accurately read pitches. There's no doubt that AI is already having a significant impact on sports.

남: 안녕하세요, 학생 여러분. 요즘 AI(인공지능)가 거의 모든 것에 활용되고 있다는 사실을 알고 계셨나요? 심지어 스포츠 산업에서도 그것이 사용되고 있습니다. AI가 다양한 스포츠에 어떻게 융합되고 있는지 몇 가지 예를 들어 보겠습니다. 첫째, 축구에 AI가 도입되고 있습니다. 예를 들어, 스페인의 한 축구 구단은 Zone7이라는 AI 시스템을 실행했습니다. 그것은 경기 중에 부상이 발생하는 것을 방지하기 위해 훈련 중에 수집된 의료 자료를 사용합니다. 또 다른 AI는 럭비에 도입되고 있습니다. 럭비 경기 중에 일어나는 모든 상황을 심판이 모두 확인하기는 어렵습니다. 따라서 혼란스러운 상황이 발생하면, 올바른 판단을 내리기 위해 심판은 고도로 복잡한 AI 비디오 분석 도구를 사용합니다. 또한 많은 테니스 선수가 AI 전문가들이 만든 다양한 앱을 사용합니다. 이러한 앱을 사용하는 것은 그들이 샷 속도와 정확도의 자동화된 분석을 얻도록 하고 경기를 더욱 정밀하게 분석할 수 있게 합니다. 마지막으로, 경기 중 내려지는 부정확한 판정을 방지하기 위해 야구에서는 AI 로봇이 시험되고 있습니다. 그것들은 홈 플레이트 위에 앉아 투구를 정확하게 판독합니다. AI가 이미 스포츠에 상당한 영향을 미치고 있다는 것은 의심의 여지가 없습니다.

● **Topic & Situation** 스포츠에 사용되는 AI

● **Solution**

01 남자는 AI(인공지능)가 스포츠 산업에서도 사용되고 있다고 말하면서 그것이 다양한 스포츠에 융합되어 사용되고 있는 사례를 소개하고 있다. 따라서 남자가 하는 말의 주제로 가장 적절한 것은 ② '다양한 스포츠에서의 AI 적용 사례'이다.
① AI가 어떻게 스포츠를 변화시킬지에 대한 예측
③ AI 사용으로 인한 스포츠에서의 윤리적 문제
④ 스포츠 구단의 AI 기반 마케팅 전략

⑤ AI를 통한 운동 경기력 향상

02 다양한 스포츠 분야에서의 AI 적용 사례를 언급하는 과정에서 축구, 럭비, 테니스, 야구는 언급되었지만, ② '농구'는 언급되지 않았다.

❯ Words & Phrases

virtually 거의   integrate 융합시키다   implement 실행하다
referee 심판   confusion 혼란   automated 자동화된
accuracy 정확도   precision 정밀, 정확   combat 방지하다. 싸우다   pitch 투구   significant 상당한

03~04

정답 | 03 ⑤ 04 ④

| Script & Translation |

W: Good afternoon, students. The year is coming to an end. Some of you probably have a New Year's tradition. This is also true for various cultures around the world, which welcome the change of the calendar with unique traditions. Here are some more unconventional traditions you likely haven't heard of. In Spain, it's customary to eat 12 grapes. Each grape represents good fortune for each month of the coming year. Residents of Denmark greet the new year by throwing old plates and glasses against the doors of family and friends to chase away evil spirits. In Brazil, wearing special underwear on New Year's Eve is thought to bring good luck for the next year. The most popular colors are red and yellow. And citizens of Colombia walk around with an empty suitcase on New Year's Eve to bring good fortune for their upcoming travels. Now, let's watch some videos on this topic.

여: 안녕하세요, 학생 여러분. 한 해가 저물어 가고 있습니다. 여러분 중 일부는 아마도 새해 전통을 가지고 있을 것입니다. 이 것은 달력이 바뀌는 것을 독특한 전통으로 맞이하는 전 세계 다양한 문화 또한 마찬가지입니다. 여러분이 들어 보지 못했을 더 색다른 전통들을 소개합니다. 스페인에서는 열두 개의 포도를 먹는 것이 관습입니다. 각각의 포도는 다가오는 해의 각 달의 행운을 상징합니다. 덴마크의 주민들은 악령을 쫓기 위해 가족과 친구들의 문에 낡은 접시와 유리잔을 던지며 새해를 맞이합니다. 브라질에서는 새해 전날 특별한 속옷을 입는 것이 다음 해에 행운을 가져다준다고 생각합니다. 가장 인기

있는 색상은 빨간색과 노란색입니다. 그리고 콜롬비아 시민들은 다가오는 여행에 행운을 가져오기 위해 새해 전날에 빈 여행 가방을 들고 돌아다닙니다. 이제, 이 주제에 관한 동영상 몇 개를 보겠습니다.

❯ Topic & Situation   세계의 색다른 새해 전통

❯ Solution

03 여자는 전 세계 다양한 문화의 색다른 새해 전통을 소개하겠다고 말한 후, 네 나라의 사례를 그 예로 들어 설명하고 있다. 따라서 여자가 하는 말의 주제로 가장 적절한 것은 ⑤ '전 세계의 독특한 새해 풍습'이다.

① 그들만의 독특한 달력 체계를 가진 문화
② 다양한 언어로 행복한 새해를 기원하는 방법
③ 세계 최고의 가 볼 만한 새해맞이 장소
④ 나라마다 새해를 다른 날에 축하하는 이유

04 스페인, 덴마크, 브라질, 콜롬비아는 언급되었지만, ④ '그리스'는 언급되지 않았다.

❯ Words & Phrases

tradition 전통. 관습   welcome 맞이하다. 환영하다   unique 독특한. 특별한   unconventional 색다른. 독특한   customary 관습의. 관례적인   represent 상징하다. 나타내다   resident 주민. 거주자   greet 맞이하다. 환영하다   plate 접시. 그릇   chase away ~을 쫓아내다   evil spirit 악령. 귀신   citizen 시민. 주민

05~06

정답 | 05 ⑤ 06 ⑤

| Script & Translation |

M: Good afternoon, everyone! Welcome to our art lecture. Today, we'll talk about the fascinating flowers that great artists liked to paint as subjects. Vincent van Gogh's sunflowers stand out as one of the most famous examples. His use of vivid colors and bold brushstrokes in these paintings is truly striking and unforgettable. Claude Monet is famous for his beautiful paintings of water lilies. He painted these flowers in various colors and with an impressionistic style. Henri Matisse, on the other hand, loved painting roses. Throughout his career, he created numerous paintings of these flowers using bright colors and simplified forms that became his signature style. And of course, poppies, those bright red or orange flowers, have always been popular among artists. Claude Monet's *Field of Poppies* is a fantastic example. The painting features loose, impressionistic brushstrokes and bold, vivid colors that capture the essence of these beautiful flowers. Now, let's take a look at these great paintings online.

남: 안녕하세요, 여러분! 저희 예술 강좌에 오신 것을 환영합니다. 오늘, 우리는 위대한 예술가들이 주제로 그리기 좋아했던 매혹적인 꽃들에 관해 이야기하겠습니다. Vincent van Gogh의 해바라기는 가장 유명한 예시 중 하나로 두드러집니다. 이 그림들에서 그의 선명한 색과 과감한 붓놀림의 사용은 정말 놀랍고 잊을 수 없습니다. Claude Monet는 그의 아름다운 수련 그림으로 유명합니다. 그는 이 꽃을 다양한 색과 인상주의적 스타일로 그렸습니다. 그 반면, Henri Matisse는 장미를 그리는 것을 좋아했습니다. 그의 경력 내내, 그는 그의 대표적인 스타일이 된 밝은 색상과 단순화된 형태를 사용하여 이 꽃의 수많은 그림을 그렸습니다. 그리고 물론, 그 밝은 빨간색이나 주황색 꽃인 양귀비는 항상 화가들 사이에서 인기가 있었습니다. Claude Monet의 *Field of Poppies*는 멋진 예입니다. 그 그림은 이 아름다운 꽃의 본질을 담아내는 유연하고 인상주의적 붓놀림과 대담하고 선명한 색을 특징으로 합니다. 이제, 온라인에서 이 멋진 그림들을 살펴봅시다.

● **Topic & Situation** 유명 화가들이 즐겨 그린 꽃들

● **Solution**

05 남자는 위대한 예술가들이 주제로 그리기 좋아했던 매혹적인 꽃들에 관해 이야기하겠다고 하면서, 고흐, 모네, 마티스가 즐겨 그린 꽃이 무엇이며 어떻게 그렸는지를 설명하고 있다. 따라서 남자가 하는 말의 주제로 가장 적절한 것은 ⑤ '유명한 화가들에게 사랑받는 주제로 기능했던 꽃들'이다.
① 고전적인 꽃 그림 감상을 위한 조언
② 예술에서 꽃을 그리는 것의 역사적 발전
③ 인상주의 화가들이 꽃을 다양한 방식으로 그린 이유
④ 세대를 거쳐 전해진 꽃 그림 기법

06 화가들이 그리기 좋아했던 꽃으로 해바라기, 수련, 장미, 양귀비는 언급되었지만, ⑤ '데이지'는 언급되지 않았다.

● **Words & Phrases**

stand out 두드러지다, 눈에 띄다 **vivid** 선명한, 생생한 **bold** 과감한, 대담한, 용감한 **brushstroke** 붓놀림, 붓질 **striking** 놀라운, 인상적인, 눈에 띄는 **impressionistic** 인상주의의 **numerous** 수많은, 다수의 **simplified** 단순화된, 간소화된 **signature** 대표적인, 특징적인; 서명 **capture** 담다, 포착하다, 잡다 **essence** 본질, 핵심, 근본

07~08

| **Script & Translation** |

W: Hello, animal-loving viewers! Welcome to my online channel, Animal World. I'm Alice Brown. I'm going to talk about companion animals. If you're thinking about raising one, there are some important things to consider. First, you should know their personality. If you know cats are independent and not social, it'll help you coexist with them. Second, you have to think about time. For example, dogs are active and enjoy playing. So, if you don't have a lot of free time, it's not a good idea to raise one. Next, consider the cost. Parrots can be expensive to raise, just like other pets. Think about your economic situation before making any decision. Lastly, listen to what your family members think. For example, if you want to raise a hamster, but someone in your family doesn't like hamsters, it'll be difficult to keep one. Keep all these in mind and leave any questions you have in the comments below.

여: 안녕하세요, 동물을 사랑하는 시청자 여러분! 제 온라인 채널, Animal World에 오신 것을 환영합니다. 저는 Alice Brown입니다. 오늘 저는 반려동물에 대해 말하고 싶습니다. 여러분이 반려동물을 키울 생각을 하고 있다면, 고려해야 할 중요한 몇 가지가 있습니다. 맨 먼저 여러분은 반려동물의 성향을 알아야 합니다. 만약 고양이가 독립적이고 사교적이지 않다는 것을 여러분이 알고 있다면, 이것은 여러분이 고양이와 함께 사는 것을 도와줄 것입니다. 둘째, 여러분은 시간에 대해 생각해야 합니다. 예를 들어, 개는 활동적이고 노는 것을 좋아합니다. 따라서 여러분이 자유시간을 많이 가지고 있지 않다면, 개를 키우는 것은 좋은 생각이 아닙니다. 다음으로, 비용을 고려하세요. 다른 애완동물과 꼭 마찬가지로 앵무새는 키우기에 돈이 많이 들 수 있습니다. 결정을 내리기 전에 여러분의 경제 상황에 대해 생각해 보세요. 마지막으로, 여러분의 가족 구성원이 생각하는 것에 귀를 기울이세요. 예를 들어, 여러분이 햄스터를 키우고 싶은데, 가족 구성원 중 누군가가 햄스터를 좋아하지 않는다면, 이 동물을 키우는 것은 어려울 것입니다. 이 모든 것을 명심하시고 아래의 의견란에 여러분이 가지고 있는 질문을 남겨 주세요.

● **Topic & Situation** 반려동물을 키울 때의 고려 사항

● **Solution**

07 여자는 반려동물을 키우는 것과 관련해서 고려해야 할 것들

이 몇 가지 있다고 하면서, 이에 대해 구체적으로 언급하고 있으므로 여자가 하는 말의 주제로 가장 적절한 것은 ② '반려동물을 키우기 위한 고려 사항'이다.

① 야생동물을 보호해야 하는 중요한 이유
③ 야생동물이 길들여지는 서로 다른 방식
④ 반려동물을 키우는 것의 다양한 이점
⑤ 야생동물과 반려동물의 차이점

08 고양이, 개, 앵무새, 햄스터는 언급되었지만, ④ '토끼'는 언급되지 않았다.

● Words & Phrases

companion animal 반려동물 raise 키우다, 기르다 independent 독립적인 coexist 함께 살다, 공존하다 comment 의견 consideration 고려 사항 domesticate 가축화하다

Dictations

본문 99, 102~103쪽

기출 ❶ reusing old materials
예제 ❷ old shipping containers
❸ small local library
❹ exterior design
01~02 ❶ into virtually everything
❷ prevent injuries from occurring
❸ with more precision
03~04 ❶ a New Year's tradition
❷ you likely haven't heard of
❸ good fortune for each month
❹ throwing old plates and glasses
❺ with an empty suitcase
05~06 ❶ paint as subjects
❷ striking and unforgettable
❸ became his signature style
❹ capture the essence
07~08 ❶ talk about companion animals
❷ independent and not social
❸ raise one
❹ making any decision
❺ Keep all these in mind

16강 유형 심화 Ⅱ
본문 104~107쪽

Exercises 01 ③ 02 ③ 03 ③ 04 ③ 05 ⑤ 06 ④
07 ① 08 ④ 09 ④ 10 ⑤ 11 ⑤ 12 ③

Exercises
본문 104~107쪽

01
정답 | ③

| Script & Translation |

W: Honey, do you know anything about fruit and vegetable delivery services?
M: No, I don't. Why?
W: I've been thinking about trying out Sun Farms delivery service.
M: So they deliver food to us?
W: Yes. They send us a box full of fresh organic fruits and vegetables regularly.
M: Wow, that sounds nice. How often do they send us a box?
W: It depends on the plan we choose. We can have them delivered weekly, every other week, or monthly.
M: That's great. Do you know how much it costs?
W: The cost depends on the delivery frequency and the size of the box. I'll show you their plans and prices.
M: Okay. I think we should sign up. Can we just do it online?
W: Yeah. We can sign up using their mobile application. Let's figure out the plan we should go for.

여: 여보, 과일과 채소 배달 서비스에 대해 아는 게 있어요?
남: 아뇨, 몰라요. 왜요?
여: Sun Farms 배달 서비스를 이용해 볼까 생각 중이에요.
남: 그러니까 그들이 우리에게 식품을 배달해 준다고요?
여: 네. 신선한 유기농 과일과 채소로 가득 찬 상자를 정기적으로 보내줘요.
남: 와, 그거 좋네요. 그들은 얼마나 자주 우리에게 상자를 보내주나요?
여: 우리가 선택한 플랜에 따라 달라요. 매주, 격주 또는 매달 배송받을 수 있어요.
남: 좋은걸요. 비용이 얼마인지 알고 있나요?
여: 배송 빈도와 상자 크기에 따라 비용이 달라요. 그들의 플랜과

가격을 보여 줄게요.

남: 알았어요. 우리는 신청해야 할 것 같아요. 그냥 온라인으로 신청할 수 있죠?

여: 네. 그들의 모바일 애플리케이션을 사용해서 신청할 수 있어요. 우리가 어떤 플랜을 택해야 할지 알아봐요.

◉ **Topic & Situation** 과일과 채소 정기 배달 서비스

◉ **Solution**

Sun Farms 배달 서비스에 관해 배송 품목, 배송 주기, 이용료, 신청 방법은 언급이 되었으나, ③ '배송 지역'은 언급되지 않았다.

◉ **Words & Phrases**

delivery 배달   organic 유기농의   weekly 매주, 주 1회씩
every other week 격주로   monthly 매달, 한 달에 한 번   frequency 빈도, 횟수   sign up 신청하다, 가입하다   figure out ~을 알아내다

02

정답 | ③

| Script & Translation |

W: Hello, everybody. I'm Sharon Collins, the director of the community center. I'm pleased to inform you about the Special Belt-Making Class we're having on Thursday, June 13th. It's a beginners' class to introduce leather craft. The class provides participants with an experience in making leather belts totally by hand without a sewing machine. It starts at 9 a.m. and ends at 5 p.m. Due to limited space and materials, there's a six-person limit for the class. So, those who want to join must register in advance at the information desk in the main lobby. Thank you.

여: 안녕하세요, 여러분. 저는 주민센터 책임자인 Sharon Collins입니다. 6월 13일 목요일에 열리는 Special Belt-Making Class에 대해 알려 드리게 되어 기쁩니다. 그것은 가죽 공예를 소개하는 초급자 수업입니다. 그 수업은 참가자에게 재봉틀 없이 온전히 손으로만 가죽 벨트를 만드는 체험을 제공합니다. 그것은 오전 9시에 시작하여 오후 5시에 종료됩니다. 제한된 공간과 재료로 인해 수업 인원은 6명으로 제한됩니다. 따라서 참가를 원하시는 분은 중앙 현관에 있는 안내대에서 미리 등록을 하셔야 합니다. 감사합니다.

◉ **Topic & Situation** 가죽 벨트 만들기 수업

◉ **Solution**

이 수업에서는 재봉틀 없이 온전히 손으로만 가죽 벨트를 만드는

체험을 할 수 있다고 했으므로, 담화의 내용과 일치하지 않는 것은 ③ '재봉틀로 가죽 벨트를 만드는 체험을 제공한다.'이다.

◉ **Words & Phrases**

leather craft 가죽 공예   sewing machine 재봉틀   register 등록하다   in advance 미리

03

정답 | ③

| Script & Translation |

M: Honey, have you found a desk for Sean yet?

W: No. But I found a good online site. They have these five.

M: Let me see. Uhm. This one's quite pricey. We should keep it under $250.

W: Okay. That eliminates this one.

M: Oh, this one has a fixed LED light. That's pretty inconvenient because you can't move it.

W: Good point. It'd be better to have a detachable light so Sean can move it where he wants.

M: Definitely. And it's possible to adjust the height for all the desks.

W: Yeah. But a desk with an adjustable table angle will help Sean maintain a good posture.

M: I agree. Then let's get one of these two.

W: All right. What about drawers? Do you think Sean needs them?

M: No. He has his cabinet.

W: Okay. Let's order this one.

남: 여보, Sean에게 사줄 책상 아직 못 찾았어요?

여: 아니요. 하지만 좋은 온라인 사이트를 찾았어요. 여기에 이렇게 다섯 개가 있어요.

남: 어디 봐요. 음. 이건 꽤 비싸네요. 우리는 250달러 미만으로 해야 해요.

여: 네, 그러면 이것은 빠지겠네요.

남: 아, 이것은 LED 조명이 고정되어 있어요. 그러면 그것을 움직일 수 없기 때문에 꽤 불편해요.

여: 좋은 지적이에요. Sean이 원하는 곳으로 옮길 수 있도록 분리 가능한 조명이 있으면 좋겠어요.

남: 물론이죠. 그리고 모든 책상들이 높이를 조절할 수 있네요.

여: 네. 하지만 테이블 각도를 조절할 수 있는 책상은 Sean이 좋은 자세를 유지하는 데 도움이 될 거예요.

남: 동의해요. 그럼 이 두 개 중 하나로 골라요.

여: 맞아요. 서랍은 어때요? Sean에게 서랍이 필요할까요?

남: 아니요. 걔는 이미 자기 서랍장이 있잖아요.

여: 네. 이것으로 주문해요.

◑ Topic & Situation 책상 주문

◑ Solution

두 사람은 가격이 250달러 미만의, 분리 가능한 조명과 책상 높이 및 테이블 각도를 조절할 수 있는 서랍이 달려 있지 않은 책상을 선택했으므로, 두 사람이 주문할 책상은 ③이다.

◑ Words & Phrases

pricey 값비싼   eliminate 없애다   fixed 고정된   inconvenient 불편한   detachable 분리할 수 있는   adjust 조정하다, 조절하다 height 높이   angle 각도   posture 자세   drawer 서랍   cabinet 서랍장

04

정답 | ③

| Script & Translation |

W: Alex, what are you doing on your smartphone?

M: I'm trying to choose a mouthwash for our little Emma. Which one of these do you think we should add to cart?

W: Let me see.... *[Pause]* This one's only 120 ml. I guess it's the travel size.

M: Right. She needs one to use at home every day, so we should get one of the bigger ones.

W: Then how about this biggest one?

M: Well, I don't want to spend more than $20 just for mouthwash.

W: Okay. I'm surprised by all of the flavors. I think she'll like any of them except mint.

M: I agree. For some reason, she doesn't like it.

W: You're right. Then we're down to these two options. One has alcohol, and the other doesn't.

M: Alcohol is good for killing germs, but she's just a kid. I don't think it's safe for kids.

W: Then let's go with the one without alcohol.

M: Perfect. Let's order this one.

여: Alex, 스마트폰으로 뭐 하고 있어요?

남: 우리 어린 Emma를 위한 구강 청결제를 고르려고 하고 있어요. 이 중 어떤 것을 장바구니에 담으면 좋을까요?

여: 한번 볼게요…. *[잠시 후]* 이건 120ml밖에 안 돼요. 그것은 여행용 크기인 것 같아요.

남: 맞아요. 그 애에게는 집에서 매일 사용할 것이 필요하니 우리는 더 큰 것 중 하나로 사야 해요.

여: 그러면 가장 큰 이것은 어때요?

남: 음, 겨우 구강 청결제에 20달러 넘게 지출하고 싶지는 않아요.

여: 알겠어요. 여러 가지 향이 있어서 놀랐어요. 제 생각에 그 애는 박하 향만 빼고 다 좋아할 것 같아요.

남: 동의해요. 무슨 이유에서인지 그 애는 그 향을 좋아하지 않잖아요.

여: 당신 말이 맞아요. 그럼 두 가지 선택 사항으로 줄어들었네요. 하나는 알코올이 있고 다른 하나는 알코올이 없어요.

남: 알코올은 세균을 없애는 데 좋지만, 그 애는 아직 어린애잖아요. 아이에게 그것이 안전할 것 같지 않아요.

여: 그러면 알코올이 없는 것으로 해요.

남: 좋아요. 이것을 주문하도록 합시다.

◑ Topic & Situation 구강 청결제 주문하기

◑ Solution

두 사람은 120ml짜리보다 크면서 20달러 이하이고, 박하 향이 아닌 것 중에서 알코올이 없는 것으로 결정했으므로, 두 사람이 주문할 구강 청결제는 ③이다.

◑ Words & Phrases

mouthwash 구강 청결제   flavor 향   except ~을 제외하고 option 선택 사항   germ 세균

05

정답 | ⑤

| Script & Translation |

W: Robert, can I borrow your tent tomorrow?

M: Sure, no problem. So are you going camping?

W: Yes. I'm planning to go camping at Grand Forest Park. But I found out this morning that my tent had a big tear in it.

M: Don't worry. Just come to my house and take my tent.

여: Robert, 내일 네 텐트를 빌릴 수 있을까?

남: 물론이지, 문제 없어. 그래 너 캠핑 가려고?

여: 응. Grand Forest Park로 캠핑 갈 계획이야. 그런데 오늘 아침 내 텐트가 크게 찢어진 것을 발견했어.

남: 걱정 마. 그냥 우리 집에 와서 내 텐트를 가져 가.

◑ Topic & Situation 텐트 빌리기

● Solution

내일 캠핑을 갈 예정인 여자가 텐트를 빌려달라고 하면서 자신의 텐트가 크게 찢어진 것을 오늘 아침에 발견했다고 말했으므로, 이에 대한 남자의 응답으로 가장 적절한 것은 ⑤ '걱정 마. 그냥 우리 집에 와서 내 텐트를 가져 가.'이다.

① 네 덕분에, 멋진 캠핑 여행을 했어.
② 내가 너라면, 거기서 텐트를 사지 않을 거야.
③ 유감이지만 이번 주말에 할 일이 있어.
④ 좋은 생각이야. Grand Forest Park에 캠핑하러 가자.

● Words & Phrases

tear 찢어진 곳, 구멍

06

정답 | ④

| Script & Translation |

M: Lucy, are you free this Saturday? Would you like to go to the Chagall Exhibition?

W: Where is it being held? If it's not too far from here, I'd love to go with you.

M: It's at the Royal Arts Center near city hall. You know, it's only about a 10-minute subway ride from here.

W: Okay. Let's go to the exhibition this Saturday.

남: Lucy, 이번 토요일에 시간 있어요? 샤갈 전시회 보러 갈래요?

여: 그것이 어디서 열리는데요? 여기서 그리 멀지 않다면 같이 가고 싶어요.

남: 시청 근처에 있는 Royal Arts Center에서요. 알다시피, 여기서 지하철로 단지 10분 정도 걸리는 곳이에요.

여: 좋아요. 이번 토요일에 같이 그 전시회를 보러 가요.

● Topic & Situation 샤갈 전시회

● Solution

이번 토요일에 샤갈 전시회에 같이 가자는 남자의 제안에 여자가 전시회가 어디서 열리는지 물으면서 그곳이 그리 멀지 않으면 가고 싶다고 말한다. 이에 남자가 전시회 장소인 Royal Arts Center가 지하철로 단지 10분 정도 걸린다고 말했으므로, 이에 대한 여자의 응답으로 가장 적절한 것은 ④ '좋아요. 이번 토요일에 같이 그 전시회를 보러 가요.'이다.

① 아니요. 저는 아직 입장권을 예매하지 않았어요.
② 미안해요. 저는 샤갈의 작품에 관심이 없어요.
③ 물론이에요. 이 아트 센터에서 일하는 것은 상당히 좋아요.
⑤ 아니요. 저는 전에 샤갈의 작품을 결코 본 적이 없어요.

● Words & Phrases

exhibition 전시회, 전시 be held 열리다, 개최되다

07

정답 | ①

| Script & Translation |

M: Honey, can you believe our family trip to Taiwan is next month?

W: I know. It's coming up, right? We should start making a schedule.

M: Good idea. There's a canyon that I definitely want to visit.

W: I know! I want to see it, too! We also need to plan things that our daughter Betty would like.

M: For sure. Do you know what she wants to do?

W: She said she wants to have her own free time in a big city.

M: I see. She's twenty, at an age when people usually like to feel the lively atmosphere of city life.

W: Right. How about letting her have her own day in the city while you and I visit the canyon?

M: That's a good idea. She's old enough to do that.

W: Then let's ask her if she'd like to do that.

M: Okay. I'm sure she'll accept our suggestion.

남: 여보, 우리 가족 대만 여행이 다음 달이라는 게 믿어지나요?

여: 그러게요. 얼마 안 남았어요, 그렇죠? 우리 일정 짜기를 시작해야겠네요.

남: 좋은 생각이에요. 그곳에 제가 꼭 가 보고 싶은 협곡이 있어요.

여: 알고 있어요! 저도 그걸 보고 싶어요! 우리 딸 Betty가 원할 만한 것도 계획해야 해요.

남: 물론이죠. 그녀가 뭘 하고 싶어 하는지 아나요?

여: 그녀는 대도시에서 그녀만의 자유로운 시간을 갖고 싶다고 말했어요.

남: 그렇군요. 그녀는 스무 살이고, 보통 도시 생활의 활기찬 분위기를 느끼고 싶어 하는 나이죠.

여: 맞아요. 당신과 내가 협곡을 방문하는 동안 도시에서 그녀만의 하루를 보내게 하는 건 어떨까요?

남: 좋은 생각이네요. 그녀는 그렇게 할 수 있을 만큼 충분히 나이가 들었어요.

여: 그러면 그녀에게 그렇게 하고 싶은지 물어 보죠.

남: 좋아요. 그녀가 우리의 제안을 받아들일 거라 확신해요.

● **Topic & Situation** 여행지에서 딸에게 혼자만의 시간 주기

● **Solution**

대만 여행의 일정을 짜는 과정에서 여자는 딸이 대도시에서 자유로운 시간을 보내고 싶다고 했던 것을 말하면서, 딸이 여행지에서 하루를 혼자 보내게 하는 건 어떨지 남자에게 묻고 있다. 이에 남자는 좋은 생각이라고 했고, 이에 여자는 딸에게 한번 물어 보자고 한다. 따라서 여자의 마지막 말에 대한 남자의 응답으로 가장 적절한 것은 ① '좋아요. 그녀가 우리의 제안을 받아들일 거라 확신해요.'이다.

② 그럼요. 어느 나라로 갈지 정합시다.

③ 걱정하지 마세요. 그녀는 여행을 정말 즐겼어요.

④ 좋은 생각이에요. 그녀가 허락한다면 그녀와 함께합시다.

⑤ 미안해요. 그녀는 우리와 함께 여행하기에는 너무 바빠요.

● **Words & Phrases**

come up 다가오다   canyon 협곡   lively 활기찬   atmosphere 분위기   accept 받아들이다   suggestion 제안

08

정답 | ④

| **Script & Translation** |

[Telephone rings.]

W: King's Paradise Hotel. How can I help you?

M: Hi. I just checked out about an hour ago, and I think I left my wallet in the room I stayed in.

W: Okay. Can I have your name, please?

M: Sure. My name is Glenn Miller, and I stayed in Room 526.

W: Thanks. Let me check. *[Typing sound]* Okay, Mr. Miller, I found your record.

M: Would I be able to go and check the room now?

W: Actually, the housekeepers are currently cleaning the checked-out rooms.

M: Ah. Do you know if they found my wallet?

W: I'm not sure. I'll contact them and find out if they have.

M: Thank you so much for your help. Then I'll be waiting for your good news call.

W: My pleasure. I'll contact you after checking for your lost item.

[전화벨이 울린다.]

여: King's Paradise Hotel입니다. 어떻게 도와드릴까요?

남: 안녕하세요. 한 시간 전쯤에 체크아웃을 했는데, 제가 묵었던 방에 지갑을 두고 온 것 같습니다.

여: 그러시군요. 성함이 어떻게 되시죠?

남: 네. 제 이름은 Glenn Miller이고, 526호실에 묵었습니다.

여: 감사합니다. 확인해 보겠습니다. *[타자 치는 소리]* 좋아요, Miller 씨, 당신의 기록을 찾았습니다.

남: 제가 지금 가서 방을 확인해 볼 수 있을까요?

여: 사실은, 객실 청소 매니저들이 현재 체크아웃된 방들을 청소하고 있습니다.

남: 아. 당신은 그들이 제 지갑을 찾았는지를 아나요?

여: 잘 모르겠습니다. 제가 그들에게 연락해서 그들이 지갑을 가지고 있는지 알아보겠습니다.

남: 도와주셔서 정말 감사합니다. 그럼 좋은 소식 기다리겠습니다.

여: 천만에요. 손님의 분실물 확인 후 연락드리겠습니다.

● **Topic & Situation** 호텔 객실의 분실물 신고

● **Solution**

여자는 King's Paradise Hotel의 직원이고 남자는 King's Paradise Hotel에서 한 시간 전에 체크아웃을 하고 나간 투숙객이다. 남자는 전화에서 자신이 묵었던 방에 지갑을 놓고 온 것 같다고 이야기하며 자신이 방에 들어가 확인을 할 수 있는지 문의했지만, 여자는 객실 청소 매니저들이 현재 체크아웃된 방들을 청소하고 있어서 들어갈 수 없다고 답변하며 자신이 그들에게 연락해서 지갑이 있는지 알아보겠다고 응답했다. 뒤이어 남자가 감사 인사를 하고 좋은 소식을 기다리겠다고 했으므로, 이에 대한 여자의 응답으로 가장 적절한 것은 ④ '천만에요. 손님의 분실물 확인 후 연락드리겠습니다.'이다.

① 굳이 왜요? 손님의 물건을 무료로 소포로 보내 드릴 수 있습니다.

② 잠시만 기다려 주세요. 지금 손님의 기록을 찾고 있습니다.

③ 세상에! 저는 손님이 가능한 한 빨리 돌아오기를 제안합니다.

⑤ 믿어 주세요. 저희는 모든 투숙객 정보를 안전하고 확실하게 보관하고 있습니다.

● **Words & Phrases**

wallet 지갑   actually 사실, 실은   housekeeper 호텔 객실 청소 매니저   currently 현재, 지금   parcel 소포   contact 연락하다

09

정답 | ④

| Script & Translation |

W: Cindy and Greg are high school classmates and good friends. Cindy is struggling with math class and needs help. So, she asks Greg if he can help her and offers to help him with literature in exchange. Greg happily accepts her suggestion, and they meet every few days. During their third meeting, Cindy realizes that Greg sometimes skips over basic steps she doesn't understand. Cindy thinks he assumes that she already knows them. Cindy wants to request Greg not to skip even the basic steps when he explains. In this situation, what would Cindy most likely say to Greg?

Cindy: Can you please explain thoroughly without skipping basic steps?

여: Cindy와 Greg은 고등학교 동창이자 좋은 친구입니다. Cindy는 수학 수업에 어려움을 겪고 있고 도움이 필요합니다. 그래서 그녀는 Greg에게 자신을 도와줄 수 있는지 묻고 그 답례로 문학을 도와주겠다고 제안합니다. Greg은 그녀의 제안을 흔쾌히 받아들이고, 그들은 며칠마다 만납니다. 그들의 세 번째 만남에서, Cindy는 Greg가 때때로 자신이 이해하지 못하는 기본적인 단계들을 건너뛴다는 것을 깨닫습니다. Cindy는 그가 그녀는 이미 그것들을 알고 있다고 가정한다고 생각합니다. Cindy는 Greg가 설명할 때 심지어 기본적인 단계라고 해도 건너뛰지 않기를 부탁하고 싶어 합니다. 이 상황에서, Cindy는 Greg에게 뭐라고 말하겠습니까?

Cindy: 기본적인 단계들을 건너뛰지 말고 철저히 설명해 줄 수 있니?

● Topic & Situation 수학 기본 단계 설명 부탁

● Solution

Cindy에게 수학을 가르쳐 주며 상대방이 이미 알고 있다고 가정하고 기본적인 단계들을 건너뛰는 Greg에게 Cindy가 기본적인 단계들을 건너뛰지 말고 설명해 달라고 부탁하고 싶어 하는 상황이다. 따라서 Cindy가 Greg에게 할 말로 가장 적절한 것은 ④ '기본적인 단계들을 건너뛰지 말고 철저히 설명해 줄 수 있니?'이다.

① 모든 기본 단계에 세부적으로 집중하는 것은 시간 낭비야.
② 문학에 들어가기 전에 수학에 먼저 집중해야 해.
③ 수학 선생님께 그것을 차근차근 설명해 달라고 부탁드리는 것은 어떨까?
⑤ 네가 우선 기초를 배우면 수학이 훨씬 더 쉽다는 것을 알게 될

거라 생각해.

● Words & Phrases

struggle 어려움을 겪다   literature 문학   in exchange 그 답례로
every few days 며칠마다   skip over ~을 건너뛰다   assume 가정하다

10

정답 | ⑤

| Script & Translation |

M: Mr. Winston is a high school music teacher. This morning, while surfing the Internet, he reads that there's a city-wide singing competition for high school students next month. He instantly thinks that Elena, one of his students who's very good at singing, should enter the competition. He thinks singing on stage would be a highly rewarding experience for her. Later, in class, Mr. Winston tells Elena that she should enter the competition, but she's hesitant because she's not sure that she can win it. So he wants to encourage her, saying that it's worth taking part in it even if she doesn't win it. In this situation, what would Mr. Winston most likely say to Elena?

Mr. Winston: Don't worry. Just participating will be a valuable experience.

남: Winston 선생님은 고등학교 음악 교사입니다. 오늘 아침 인터넷 서핑을 하다가 그는 다음 달에 고등학생을 대상으로 하는 시 전체 노래 대회가 열린다는 것을 읽습니다. 그는 즉시 그의 학생 중 노래를 매우 잘하는 학생인 Elena가 그 대회에 참가해야 한다고 생각합니다. 무대에서 노래하는 것은 그녀에게 매우 값진 경험이 될 것이라고 그는 생각합니다. 이후 수업 시간에 Winston 선생님은 Elena에게 대회에 참가해 보라고 말하지만, 그녀는 우승할 수 있을지 확신이 서지 않아 망설입니다. 그래서 그는 그녀가 우승하지 못하더라도 그것에 참가해 볼 가치가 있다고 말하면서 그녀를 격려하고 싶어 합니다. 이런 상황에서, Winston 선생님은 Elena에게 뭐라고 말하겠습니까?

Mr. Winston: 걱정하지 마. 참가하는 것만으로도 소중한 경험이 될 거야.

● Topic & Situation 노래 대회 참가 독려

● Solution

음악 교사인 Winston 선생님은 시 전체 노래 경연 대회가 열린

다는 소식을 읽고 노래를 잘하는 Elena가 참가하는 것이 좋겠다고 생각하여 그녀에게 대회 참가를 권하지만, Elena는 우승할 수 있을지 확신이 서지 않아 망설이고 있다. Winston 선생님은 Elena가 우승하지 못해도 참가하는 것만으로도 충분한 가치가 있다고 말하면서 그녀를 격려해 주고 싶어 한다. 따라서 Winston 선생님이 Elena에게 할 말로 가장 적절한 것은 ⑤ '걱정하지 마. 참가하는 것만으로도 소중한 경험이 될 거야.'이다.

① 나를 믿어봐. 다음 노래 연습은 빠지지 않을게.
② 계속 연습해. 넌 반드시 대회에서 우승할 거야.
③ 정말 잘했어! 네가 대회에 참가해서 정말 기쁘구나!
④ 괜찮을 거야. 대회까지 아직 며칠 남아 있어.

○ Words & Phrases

competition 대회 instantly 즉시 hesitant 망설이는

11~12

정답 | 11 ⑤ 12 ③

| Script & Translation |

W: Hello, everyone! Today, we're going to talk about something really interesting—why people use special phrases and idioms associated with the body. You know, the body is a physical subject we all have. By employing expressions connected to the body, we can convey feelings and ideas in an impactful way. For example, the phrase "have butterflies in your stomach" describes feelings of nervousness or excitement. On a more literal level, the idiom "keep your chin up" can be used to encourage someone who is feeling down. In addition to expressing literal meaning, body-related expressions can convey abstract ideas. For example, the saying "get off my back" implies "stop bothering me" and also communicates the feeling of being overwhelmed or stressed. Lastly, body-related expressions can carry cultural values or beliefs. For instance, hands are seen as symbols of power, creativity, and action. This is why the saying "lend a hand" is used to ask for help. To wrap up, using these body-related expressions helps us show complex feelings and ideas, and even what our culture is like in a simple and clear way.

여: 안녕하세요, 여러분! 오늘, 우리는 정말 흥미로운 것, 즉, 사람들이 왜 신체와 관련된 특별한 어구와 관용구들을 사용하는지 이야기를 할 것입니다. 아시다시피, 신체는 우리 모두가 가진 물리적 대상입니다. 신체와 연관된 표현을 사용함으로써, 우리는 강렬한 인상을 주는 방식으로 감정과 생각을 전달할 수 있습니다. 예를 들어, "위[배] 속에 나비가 있다"라는 문구는 긴장이나 흥분의 느낌을 묘사합니다. 더 문자 그대로의 수준에서, "턱을 높이 들어"라는 관용구는 마음이 울적한 누군가를 격려하는 데 사용될 수 있습니다. 문자 그대로의 의미를 표현하는 것 외에 신체와 관련된 표현은 추상적인 생각을 전달할 수 있습니다. 예를 들어, "내 등에서 내려"라는 말은 "나를 그만 귀찮게 해"라는 것을 의미하며, 또한 압도당하거나 스트레스를 받는 느낌을 전달합니다. 마지막으로, 신체와 관련된 표현은 문화적 가치나 믿음을 전달할 수 있습니다. 예를 들어, 손은 힘, 창의성, 행동의 상징으로 여겨집니다. 이것이 도움을 요청하기 위해 "손을 빌려준다"라는 말이 사용되는 이유입니다. 마무리하자면, 신체와 관련된 이러한 표현을 사용하는 것은 우리가 복잡한 감정과 생각, 그리고 심지어 우리의 문화가 어떠한지를 간단하고 명확한 방식으로 보여 주도록 도와줍니다.

○ Topic & Situation 신체 관련 영어 표현

○ Solution

11 여자는 사람들이 왜 신체와 관련된 어구와 관용구들을 사용하는지 이야기하겠다고 하면서, 신체와 연관된 표현을 사용함으로써 강렬한 인상을 주는 방식으로 감정을 전달하고, 추상적인 생각을 전달하며, 문화적 가치나 믿음을 전달할 수 있다고 설명하고 있다. 따라서 여자가 하는 말의 주제로 가장 적절한 것은 ⑤ '의사소통에서 신체와 관련된 표현을 사용하는 이유'이다.

① 감정 변화가 신체에 미치는 영향
② 몸짓 언어에 대한 다양한 문화적 해석
③ 신체 기능을 묘사하는 비언어적 의사소통
④ 다른 언어와 문화 간의 속담의 유사성

12 언급된 신체 부위로 위, 턱, 등, 손은 언급되었지만, ③ '다리'는 언급되지 않았다.

○ Words & Phrases

phrase 어구, 구절 idiom 관용구 employ 사용하다 convey 전달하다, 나르다 impactful 강렬한 인상을 주는, 매우 효과적인 nervousness 긴장, 불안감 literal 문자 그대로의 keep one's chin up 의연한 자세를 유지하다, 용기를 잃지 않다 in addition to ~이외에 abstract 추상적인 get off one's back ~을 귀찮게 하지 않다 imply 의미하다, 암시하다 overwhelm 압도하다 wrap up ~을 마무리하다 complex 복잡한

(17)강 학업, 교육   본문 110~115쪽

기출예제 ②
Exercises   01 ④ 02 ① 03 ⑤ 04 ② 05 ④ 06 ⑤
           07 ⑤ 08 ① 09 ① 10 ② 11 ③ 12 ⑤

기출 예제   본문 110쪽
                                            정답 | ②

| Script & Translation |

W: Good morning, students. I'm Ms. Thompson, your learning consultant for today's workshop. Many of you have expressed concerns that you're having difficulty submitting your homework on time. But you know what? Making a memo is an efficient way to manage your assignments. You can't only rely on your memory. You need to make a note about what to do and when to do it so that you don't forget. Writing a memo might be annoying at first, but you'll get used to it in no time. With a memo, you can organize your assignments better. Now, we're going to see some good examples of students' memos. Let's look at the screen.

여: 좋은 아침입니다, 학생 여러분. 저는 오늘 워크숍의 학습 컨설턴트인 Ms. Thompson입니다. 여러분 중 많은 사람이 과제를 제때 제출하는 데 어려움을 겪고 있다고 걱정을 나타냈습니다. 하지만 그거 아세요? 메모를 하는 것은 과제를 관리하는 효율적인 방법입니다. 기억력에만 의존할 수는 없습니다. 잊지 않도록 해야 할 일과 그것을 언제 해야 할지를 메모할 필요가 있습니다. 처음에는 메모를 쓰는 것이 성가실 수 있지만 그것에 금방 익숙해질 것입니다. 메모를 사용하면 과제를 더 잘 정리할 수 있습니다. 이제 학생들 메모의 몇 가지 좋은 사례를 살펴보겠습니다. 화면을 보시죠.

● Topic & Situation 과제를 관리하는 효율적인 방법

● Solution

과제를 제때 제출하는 데 어려움을 겪는 학생들에게 메모하는 것이 과제를 관리하는 효율적인 방법이라는 말을 하고 있으므로, 여자가 하는 말의 요지로 가장 적절한 것은 ② '메모하는 것은 과제를 관리하는 데 효율적인 방법이다.'이다.

● Words & Phrases

concern 걱정   submit 제출하다   efficient 효율적인

---

assignment 과제   get used to ~에 익숙해지다   in no time 금방, 곧   organize 정리하다

Exercises   본문 112~115쪽

01   정답 | ④

| Script & Translation |

M: Hello, Stewart High School students. This is your principal, Mr. Ballen. This year marks our school's 30th anniversary. In celebration of this anniversary, I'm pleased to announce a school slogan contest to replace the current one. We're seeking a new slogan that powerfully reflects the mission and vision of our school. You can submit your suggestion for the school slogan from March 18th to the 22nd on the school website. The winning slogan will be used in school promotional activities and materials. Plus, awards will be given to the winning slogan and the second- and third-place slogans. I can't wait to see your creative ideas. For more details, visit the school website. Thank you.

남: 안녕하세요, Stewart 고등학교 학생 여러분. 저는 여러분의 교장 Ballen입니다. 올해는 우리 학교가 개교 30주년을 맞이하는 해입니다. 이 기념일을 축하하기 위해, 현재의 슬로건을 바꾸기 위한 학교 슬로건 공모전을 발표하게 되어 기쁘게 생각합니다. 우리는 우리 학교의 사명과 비전을 강력하게 반영하는 새 슬로건을 찾고 있습니다. 3월 18일부터 22일까지 학교 웹사이트에 학교 슬로건을 위한 여러분의 제안을 제출할 수 있습니다. 우승 슬로건은 학교 홍보 활동 및 자료에 활용될 예정입니다. 또한 우승 슬로건과 2등, 3등 슬로건에는 상이 수여될 것입니다. 여러분의 창의적인 아이디어를 기대합니다. 자세한 내용을 더 알고 싶다면 학교 웹사이트를 방문하세요. 고맙습니다.

● Topic & Situation 학교 슬로건 공모전

● Solution

개교 30주년을 맞아 학교의 새 슬로건을 마련하기 위한 공모전이 열린다는 것을 알리면서 학교 슬로건 제출 기간과 방법을 소개하

고, 당선된 슬로건은 학교 홍보 활동 및 자료에 활용될 것임을 공지하는 내용이므로, 남자가 하는 말의 목적으로 가장 적절한 것은 ④ '학교 슬로건 공모전을 공지하려고'이다.

◗ Words & Phrases

mark 기념하다   anniversary 기념일   celebration 축하
replace 바꾸다   current 현재의   seek 찾다   reflect 반영하다
submit 제출하다   suggestion 제안   promotional 홍보의

02   정답 | ①

| Script & Translation |

M: What school club are you planning on running this semester, Ms. Kim?

W: I thought maybe I'd start a club for students to read classics.

M: Do you think students will find that interesting?

W: I think some will. I just feel it's important for students to read classics to broaden their knowledge and understanding of the world.

M: But can't other types of literature achieve the same goal?

W: Sure, but classics have stood the test of time.

M: I know, but wouldn't it be difficult for students to connect their lives with characters or settings from different time periods?

W: Well, I think they can develop empathy and broaden their understanding of various perspectives by exploring different eras and cultures through classics.

M: I see your point.

W: It's important to expose students to classics across various cultures and eras.

M: I agree.

남: 이번 학기에 어떤 학교 동아리를 운영할 계획이세요, 김 선생님?

여: 저는 아마 학생들이 고전 문학을 읽는 동아리를 개설할 것 같아요.

남: 학생들이 그것을 흥미로워 할거라고 생각하시나요?

여: 어떤 학생들은 그럴 것 같아요. 저는 학생들이 세계에 대한 지식과 이해를 넓히기 위해 고전을 읽는 것이 중요하다고 생각

해요.

남: 하지만 다른 종류의 문학 작품이 같은 목표를 달성할 수 없을까요?

여: 할 수 있죠, 하지만 고전 문학은 시간의 시련을 견뎌냈어요.

남: 알아요, 하지만 학생들이 자신의 삶을 다른 시간대에서 온 등장인물이나 배경과 관련짓기는 어려울 것 같지 않나요?

여: 음, 저는 그들이 고전 문학을 통해 다른 시대와 문화를 탐구함으로써 공감을 기르고 다양한 관점에 대한 이해를 넓힐 수 있다고 생각해요.

남: 무슨 말인지 알겠어요.

여: 학생들을 다양한 문화와 시대에 걸친 고전에 노출시키는 것이 중요해요.

남: 동의해요.

◗ Topic & Situation   고전 문학 읽기 동아리 개설

◗ Solution

이번 학기에 고전 문학 읽기 동아리를 개설하려고 계획한 여자에게 남자가 동아리에 대한 학생들의 흥미나 다른 문학 작품의 역할, 그리고 고전 문학을 접하면서 느끼게 될 어려움에 관해 다양한 질문을 한다. 이에 대해 여자는 학생들이 세계에 대한 지식과 이해를 넓히기 위해 고전을 읽는 것이 중요하며, 고전은 시간의 시련을 견뎌냈고, 학생들은 이것을 통해 공감을 기르고 다양한 관점에 대한 이해를 넓힐 수 있기 때문에 학생들을 다양한 문화와 시대에 걸친 고전에 노출시키는 것이 중요하다고 답한다. 따라서 여자의 의견으로 가장 적절한 것은 ① '학생들이 고전 문학을 읽게 하는 것이 필요하다.'이다.

◗ Words & Phrases

semester 학기   broaden 넓히다, 확장하다   empathy 공감
perspective 관점   explore 탐구하다, 탐험하다   era 시대

03   정답 | ⑤

| Script & Translation |

M: Emily, how was your visit to the Science Museum with your friends?

W: Dad, it was really fun. Look at this picture I took there.

M: Wow, cool! Look at you. You're wearing star-shaped sunglasses. Where did you get them?

W: I bought them at the souvenir shop in the museum.

M: What is this round one next to you? Is it a wheel?

W: Yes, it is. It's one of the greatest human inventions.

M: I see. Why do they have a hot air balloon next to the left wall?

W: Oh, it's an exhibit that explains how hot air balloons work.

M: Ah, I get it. And is that a whale behind you?

W: That's right. It's a model whale in a glass case.

M: It looks very big and nice! And a butterfly is hanging from the ceiling next to the right wall.

W: Yes. It's a model of a beautiful butterfly.

M: Well, I'm so glad you had a great time there, honey.

남: Emily, 친구들과 함께 과학 박물관을 방문한 건 어땠니?

여: 아빠, 정말 재미있었어요. 제가 그곳에서 찍은 이 사진을 보세요.

남: 와, 멋지구나! 널 좀 봐. 너는 별 모양의 선글라스를 쓰고 있구나. 그것을 어디서 샀니?

여: 박물관에 있는 기념품 가게에서 샀어요.

남: 네 옆에 있는 이 둥근 것은 뭐니? 그것은 바퀴니?

여: 네, 그래요. 그것은 인간의 가장 위대한 발명품 중 하나죠.

남: 그렇구나. 왼쪽 벽 옆에 열기구가 왜 있는 거니?

여: 아, 그것은 열기구가 어떻게 작동하는지 설명해 주는 전시품이에요.

남: 아, 그렇구나. 그리고 네 뒤에 있는 것은 고래니?

여: 맞아요. 그것은 유리 진열장 안에 있는 모형 고래예요.

남: 그것은 매우 크고 멋져 보이는구나! 그리고 오른쪽 벽 옆에는 나비가 천장에 매달려 있구나.

여: 네. 그것은 아름다운 나비의 모형이에요.

남: 음, 네가 거기서 좋은 시간을 보냈다니 정말 기쁘구나, 얘야.

◑ **Topic & Situation** 과학 박물관 방문

◑ **Solution**

대화에서 남자는 나비가 천장에 매달려 있다고 말했는데, 그림에는 나비가 받침대 위에 놓여 있으므로, 그림에서 대화의 내용과 일치하지 않는 것은 ⑤이다.

◑ **Words & Phrases**

star-shaped 별 모양의   souvenir 기념품   hot air balloon 열기구   exhibit 전시품, 전시(회)   ceiling 천장

04

정답 | ②

| **Script & Translation** |

W: Hello, Mr. Sanders. You look busy today.

M: Yeah, Ms. Wallace. I've been busy getting ready for the school trip to Oleta National Park.

W: I remember having to do that last year.

M: And I remember you told me how much work it was.

W: Right. So, have you sent out the permission letters to the students' parents and booked everything?

M: Yes, I sent them out last week. And I've reserved the buses, but I've had some difficulty booking the resort.

W: Oh, is it already fully booked?

M: Yes. They said there aren't enough rooms.

W: Oh, I see. Well, I know another nice resort in the area. It's called Oleta Palace Resort. I'm sure they have enough rooms. Why don't you call them?

M: Oh, really? Then I'll do that right now.

W: Sounds good. I hope that works out for you.

M: Thank you, Ms. Wallace.

여: 안녕하세요, Sanders 선생님. 오늘 바빠 보이시네요.

남: 네, Wallace 선생님. Oleta 국립공원으로 가는 수학여행을 준비하느라 바빴어요.

여: 작년에 제가 그 일을 해야 했던 것이 기억나네요.

남: 그리고 저는 그것이 얼마나 많은 일인지 선생님이 제게 말했던 것을 기억해요.

여: 맞아요. 그래서 학생들의 부모님께 허가서를 보내고 모든 것을 예약하셨나요?

남: 네, 지난주에 보냈어요. 그리고 버스는 예약했는데, 저는 리조트 예약하는 데 어려움을 좀 겪고 있어요.

여: 아, 벌써 예약이 다 찼나요?

남: 네. 방이 충분히 남아있지 않대요.

여: 아, 그렇군요. 음, 저는 그 지역에 다른 좋은 리조트를 알고 있어요. 그것은 Oleta Palace 리조트라고 불려요. 저는 그곳에 충분한 방이 있다고 확신해요. 전화해 보시지 그래요?

남: 아, 그래요? 그럼 지금 바로 해볼게요.

여: 좋아요. 그것이 잘 되길 바라요.

남: 고마워요, Wallace 선생님.

◑ **Topic & Situation** 수학 여행 숙소 예약

◑ **Solution**

수학여행 업무를 담당하고 있는 남자가 숙소를 예약하는 데 어려움이 있다고 말하자, 여자는 자신이 예약이 가능할 것으로 확신하

는 좋은 리조트를 알고 있다고 하면서, 이름을 가르쳐 주고 전화해 보라고 했으며, 이에 남자는 지금 바로 해보겠다고 말했으므로, 남자가 할 일로 가장 적절한 것은 ② '리조트에 전화하기'이다.

◐ Words & Phrases
permission 허가   have difficulty -ing ~하는 데 어려움을 겪다

05
정답 | ④

| Script & Translation |

M: Hi, I'd like to enroll in an evening Korean conversation course for beginners.

W: Alright. We offer two classes for beginners.

M: What are they?

W: One is a basic class with a tuition of $50 per month, and the other is an intensive class with a tuition of $70 per month.

M: Um.... I prefer attending class every day. Does the basic class have daily lessons?

W: No, only the intensive class has daily lessons.

M: Okay, I'll take the intensive course for beginners for a month. Do I need to purchase a textbook?

W: Yes, you do. The textbook costs $5.

M: Got it. I'll buy the textbook as well. Is it true that Green University students get a 10% discount on the tuition?

W: Yes, that's correct. Please show me your student ID card.

M: Alright. Here are my ID card and credit card.

남: 안녕하세요, 초보자를 위한 저녁 한국어 회화 강좌에 등록하고 싶습니다.

여: 알겠습니다. 초보자를 위한 수업이 두 개 있습니다.

남: 그 두 수업이 무엇이죠?

여: 하나는 한 달 수업료가 50달러인 기본반이고, 다른 하나는 한 달 수업료가 70달러인 집중반입니다.

남: 음…. 저는 매일 수업에 참석하는 것을 선호합니다. 기본반에서는 수업이 매일 있나요?

여: 아니요, 집중반에서만 수업이 매일 있습니다.

남: 좋아요, 초보자를 위한 집중반을 한 달 수강할게요. 교재를 사야 하나요?

여: 예, 그렇습니다. 교재는 5달러입니다.

남: 알겠습니다. 교재도 살게요. Green 대학교 학생은 수업료에서 10% 할인 받는 것이 사실인가요?

여: 예, 맞습니다. 학생증을 보여 주세요.

남: 알겠습니다. 제 학생증이랑 신용 카드 여기 있습니다.

◐ Topic & Situation   한국어 회화 강좌 등록

◐ Solution
한 달 수업료가 70달러인 집중반 수강료와 교재 비용 5달러를 지불하기로 한 남자는 Green 대학교 학생이어서 수업료에서 10% 할인을 받았으므로, 남자가 지불할 금액은 ④ '$68'이다.

◐ Words & Phrases
enroll 등록하다   tuition 수업료   intensive 집중의, 집중적인
attend 참석하다, 다니다   purchase 구입하다

06
정답 | ⑤

| Script & Translation |

M: Hey, Jenny, I heard you won the science competition. Congratulations!

W: Thanks. It feels so good. I guess my hard work paid off.

M: I bet! So are you free these days?

W: Yeah. What's up?

M: You know our sister school from Singapore is visiting next week, right?

W: Yes. We're having a welcoming ceremony.

M: Yeah. Well, actually, I'm performing a hip-hop dance routine at the ceremony.

W: Wow, that's really cool!

M: So I'm planning to go to the Westfield Mall this Friday after school to buy some clothes for it. Would you mind going with me and helping me pick something out?

W: Oh, I'd love to, but I'm afraid I can't. I have to participate in the science club's ECO Challenge Campaign on that day. Sorry about that.

M: No worries. I'll ask Tom if he can come with me after his piano lesson.

W: Okay. I hope you find some awesome clothes.

남: 안녕, Jenny, 과학 대회에서 우승했다고 들었어. 축하해!

여: 고마워. 정말 기분이 좋아. 열심히 일한 것이 성과를 올린 것 같아.

남: 그렇겠지! 그래서 너는 요즘 한가하니?

여: 응. 무슨 일인데?

남: 싱가포르의 자매학교가 다음 주에 방문한다는 거 알고 있지, 그렇지?

여: 응. 우리는 환영식을 할 거야.

남: 그렇지. 음, 실은, 내가 그 환영식에서 힙합 댄스 동작을 공연할 거야.

여: 와, 그거 정말 멋지구나!

남: 그래서 나는 이번 주 금요일 방과 후에 Westfield Mall에 가서 그것에 맞는 옷을 살 계획이야. 나랑 같이 가서 내가 무언가 고르는 것을 도와줄래?

여: 아, 정말 그러고 싶은데, 유감스럽게도 그럴 수가 없어. 그날 과학 동아리의 ECO Challenge Campaign에 참여해야 하거든. 미안해.

남: 걱정 마. Tom에게 그의 피아노 수업이 끝난 후에 나와 함께 갈 수 있는지 물어볼게.

여: 좋아. 멋진 옷을 찾길 바라.

◑ Topic & Situation 힙합 댄스 의상 구입

◑ Solution

자매학교 학생들을 위한 환영식에서 힙합 댄스 동작을 공연하기로 되어 있는 남자가 이번 주 금요일 방과 후에 Westfield Mall에 공연을 위한 옷을 사러 갈 계획이라고 하면서, 여자에게 함께 가서 도와달라고 하자, 여자는 그날 과학 동아리 캠페인에 참여해야 한다고 하면서 부탁을 거절하고 있다. 따라서 여자가 Westfield Mall에 갈 수 없는 이유는 ⑤ '동아리 캠페인에 참여해야 해서'이다.

◑ Words & Phrases

competition 대회, 경쟁   pay off 성과를 올리다   welcoming ceremony 환영식   awesome 멋진, 굉장한

07

정답 | ⑤

| Script & Translation |

M: Hey, Natalie. What's that you're studying?

W: Hi, Jacob. I'm preparing for a Korean Proficiency Test.

M: Oh. I knew you liked Korean TV shows, but I didn't know you were studying Korean. Is the test for foreigners?

W: Yes. And that includes Koreans living abroad whose native language isn't Korean.

M: I see. Have you registered for the test?

W: Yes. I registered for the April test. It's offered six times a year.

M: It's almost April. Do you feel ready?

W: I feel pretty good. I'm taking the beginner-level test. There's an advanced-level test, too.

M: I assume that the advanced one is for people who are thinking of studying in Korea, right?

W: Yes. The beginner level test has only a listening and a reading part. But the advanced one has a writing part, too.

M: Maybe in the future, you'll take the advanced one. Keep up the studying!

남: 이봐, Natalie. 뭘 공부하고 있어?

여: 안녕, Jacob. Korean Proficiency Test를 준비하고 있어.

남: 아. 네가 한국 텔레비전 프로그램을 좋아하는 건 알고 있었지만, 한국어를 공부하는 줄은 몰랐네. 그 시험은 외국인을 대상으로 하는 거야?

여: 응. 그리고 한국어가 모국어가 아닌 해외에 사는 한국인들도 포함돼.

남: 그렇구나. 시험에 등록은 했어?

여: 응. 4월 시험에 등록했어. 일 년에 여섯 번 시행되거든.

남: 이제 곧 4월이네. 준비는 됐어?

여: 기분이 꽤 좋아. 나는 초급 레벨 시험을 볼 거야. 고급 레벨의 시험도 있어.

남: 고급 시험은 한국에서 공부할 생각을 하는 사람들을 위한 것으로 생각해, 그렇지?

여: 맞아. 초급 레벨 시험은 듣기와 읽기 파트만 있어. 하지만 고급 시험은 쓰기 파트도 있거든.

남: 언젠가는 너도 고급 시험을 볼 수 있겠네. 계속 공부해!

◑ Topic & Situation 한국어 능력 시험

◑ Solution

Korean Proficiency Test에 관해 응시 대상, 연간 시행 횟수, 시험 종류, 평가 영역은 언급이 되었으나, ⑤ '주관 기관'은 언급되지 않았다.

○ **Words & Phrases**

proficiency 숙달, 능숙   abroad 해외에   native language 모국어   register 등록하다   assume 생각하다, 추정하다   keep up ~을 계속하다

08
정답 | ①

| **Script & Translation** |

M: Nari, do you have any plans for summer vacation?

W: I'm thinking about taking a summer school science class at school. Here are the ones available.

M: Oh, I was planning on doing that too. We should take one together!

W: Great idea! What class are you interested in?

M: I've taken chemistry before, so I'd like something different.

W: Me, too. What day works for you?

M: Any weekday is fine. I work on weekends.

W: Actually, I prefer weekdays, too. Also, I'd like to take a morning class to maintain a routine during summer break.

M: I agree. Then we'll have time to do other things in the afternoon.

W: Great. Then we have only two options left. They have different class sizes.

M: Do you prefer a larger class?

W: Not really. I like smaller classes because I tend to be more actively involved in a smaller group.

M: Me, too. Then let's enroll in this class together.

W: All right.

남: Nari, 여름방학에 무슨 계획 있니?

여: 학교에서 여름방학 과학 강좌를 들을까 생각 중이야. 여기 들을 수 있는 강좌들이 있어.

남: 아, 나도 그러려고 계획 중이었어. 우리 한 강좌를 같이 듣자!

여: 좋은 생각이야! 어떤 강좌에 관심이 있니?

남: 나는 이전에 화학을 들어본 적이 있어서 다른 걸 듣고 싶어.

여: 나도 그래. 어떤 요일이 괜찮니?

남: 평일 아무 날이나 좋아. 나는 주말에 일하거든.

여: 사실, 나도 평일을 선호해. 또한 여름방학 동안 규칙적인 생활을 유지하기 위해 오전 강좌를 듣고 싶어.

남: 동의해. 그러면 오후에 다른 일을 할 시간도 있을 테니까.

여: 좋아. 그러면 이제 두 가지 선택 사항이 남았네. 두 강좌의 크기가 다르구나.

남: 더 큰 강좌를 선호하니?

여: 그렇진 않아. 난 더 작은 그룹에서 더 적극적으로 참여하는 경향이 있어서 더 작은 강좌가 좋아.

남: 나도 그래. 그러면 이 강좌에 함께 등록하자.

여: 좋아.

○ **Topic & Situation**   여름방학 과학 강좌 선택

○ **Solution**

두 사람은 화학 강좌가 아닌 것 가운데 평일 강좌를 선호하고, 오전 강좌가 좋겠다고 했으며, 크기가 더 작은 강좌를 선택했으므로, 두 사람이 수강할 강좌는 ①이다.

○ **Words & Phrases**

chemistry 화학   maintain 유지하다   be involved in ~에 참여하다   enroll 등록하다

09
정답 | ①

| **Script & Translation** |

M: Mom, I joined a morning study group. So I have to go to school early from tomorrow.

W: That's fantastic! What time do you need to be at school?

M: We meet at 7:30, so I'll have to leave home around 7. But I'm worried that I won't be able to wake up that early.

W: No problem. I'll make sure you're up early enough.

남: 엄마, 나는 아침 스터디 그룹에 가입했어요. 그래서 내일부터 학교에 일찍 가야 해요.

여: 정말 좋구나! 몇 시에 학교에 도착해야 하니?

남: 저희는 7시 30분에 모이니까, 7시쯤 집을 떠나야 할 거예요. 그런데 제가 그렇게 일찍 일어날 수 없을까 봐 걱정돼요.

여: 괜찮아. 네가 충분히 일찍 일어날 수 있도록 해 줄게.

○ **Topic & Situation**   아침 스터디 그룹 참석

○ **Solution**

아침 스터디 그룹을 위해 내일부터 7시쯤 집을 떠나야 하는데 그렇게 일찍 일어날 수 있을지 걱정된다고 하는 남자의 말에 대한 여자의 응답으로 가장 적절한 것은 ① '괜찮아. 네가 충분히 일찍

일어날 수 있도록 해 줄게.'이다.

② 알고 있어. 그래서 스터디 그룹이 일정을 변경했어.

③ 걱정하지 마. 네가 전보다 건강을 더 증진할 수 있도록 내가 도와줄게.

④ 힘내. 너는 아침 운동을 하기 위해 일찍 일어나야 할 거야.

⑤ 이해해. 네가 저녁 스터디 그룹에 들어간 것은 현명한 선택이었어.

● Words & Phrases

leave 떠나다, 출발하다   wake up 일어나다, (잠에서) 깨어나다

10
정답 | ②

| Script & Translation |

W: Shaun, have you received your biology exam results?

M: Yeah, I did. All my time and energy paid off. I got an A in the exam.

W: Wow! That's great. You must have worked really hard to prepare for the exam.

M: Right. I think the A is the result of my effort.

여: Shaun, 생물학 시험 결과 받았어?

남: 그래, 받았어. 내 모든 시간과 에너지가 결실을 맺었어. 이 시험에서 A를 받았어.

여: 와! 대단하다. 너는 이 시험을 준비하기 위해서 정말로 열심히 노력했음에 틀림없어.

남: 맞아. A는 내 노력의 결과인 것 같아.

● Topic & Situation 생물학 시험 결과

● Solution

생물학 시험에서 A 학점을 받은 남자에게 여자가 대단하다고 말하면서 시험 준비를 정말로 열심히 했음에 틀림없다고 말했으므로, 이에 대한 남자의 응답으로 가장 적절한 것은 ② '맞아. A는 내 노력의 결과인 것 같아.'이다.

① 문제는 네가 자신감이 넘친다는 거야.

③ 너랑 똑같은 생물학 수업을 수강하고 싶어.

④ 미안, 하지만 나는 너랑 함께 공부할 시간이 없어.

⑤ 맞아. 너는 생물학 수업을 수강하지 않았어야 했어.

● Words & Phrases

biology 생물학   must have p.p. ~했음에 틀림없다   overconfident 자신감이 넘치는

11
정답 | ③

| Script & Translation |

M: Hi, Ms. Jefferson.

W: Hi, Brian! It's been a while!

M: Yeah. I can't believe it's been a year since I graduated.

W: I know. How's your college life?

M: It's a lot busier than my high school life.

W: I'm sure it is. Do you like your major? It's business, right?

M: Right. Yeah, I like it. But sometimes it can be a bit challenging.

W: Do you mean the content is difficult to understand?

M: It's not about the content.

W: What do you mean by that? Can you tell me more?

M: It's the group assignments that I find challenging. I'm not used to working with others.

W: Ah, so working together can be a little uncomfortable?

M: Yes. I think I get too emotional when people disagree with me.

W: Oh, I understand. It's not easy to separate personal feelings from a heated discussion when that happens.

M: Yes, and I'm trying to get better at controlling my feelings in those situations, hoping I'll improve.

W: Good. It takes practice, but I'm sure you'll make progress.

남: 안녕하세요, Jefferson 선생님.

여: 안녕, Brian! 오랜만이야!

남: 네. 졸업한 지 1년이 지났다는 게 믿기지 않네요.

여: 그러게. 네 대학 생활은 어때?

남: 저의 고등학교 생활보다 훨씬 더 바빠요.

여: 그렇겠지. 전공은 마음에 드니? 경영학이지, 그렇지?

남: 맞아요. 네, 마음에 들어요. 하지만 가끔은 좀 어려울 때도 있어요.

여: 내용이 이해하기 어렵다는 말이니?

남: 내용에 관한 것이 아니에요.

여: 그게 무슨 의미니? 좀 더 말해 주겠니?

남: 제가 어려워하는 건 그룹 과제예요. 저는 다른 사람들과 함께 작업하는 것에 익숙하지 않아요.

여: 아, 그러니까 공동으로 작업하는 것이 좀 불편하다는 거구나?

남: 네. 제 생각에 저는 사람들이 제 의견에 동의하지 않을 때 너

무 감정적으로 되는 것 같아요.

여: 오, 이해해. 그런 일이 있을 때 개인적인 감정과 열띤 토론을 분리하는 것은 쉽지 않지.

남: 네, 그래서 그런 상황에서 감정 조절을 더 잘하려고 노력 중이고, 더 나아지기를 바라고 있어요.

여: <u>좋아. 그것엔 연습이 필요하지만, 넌 분명 발전할 거야.</u>

● **Topic & Situation** 그룹 활동에 대한 조언

● **Solution**

남자는 고등학교를 졸업한 지 1년 만에 선생님인 여자를 만나러 갔는데, 전공이 마음에 드는지 묻는 여자에게 가끔 그룹 과제 때문에 어려움을 느낀다고 말한다. 특히 사람들이 남자의 의견에 동의하지 않을 때 자신이 너무 감정적으로 되어서 불편하기도 하지만 그런 상황에서 감정을 잘 조절하기 위해 노력 중이고, 더 나아지기를 바라고 있다고 말하고 있으므로, 남자의 마지막 말에 대한 여자의 응답으로 가장 적절한 것은 ③ '좋아. 그것엔 연습이 필요하지만, 넌 분명 발전할 거야.'이다.

① 맞아. 너는 다른 사람들과 함께 일할 때 주의가 산만해질 수 있어.

② 좋아. 그 그룹이 네 의견을 좋아한다고 들으니 기쁘구나.

④ 미안해. 나는 팀에서 일을 잘하는 사람을 찾고 있어.

⑤ 물론이지. 함께 일할 때 너의 기분을 상하게 하지 않도록 노력할게.

● **Words & Phrases**

major 전공 challenging 어려운 content 내용 assignment 과제 emotional 감정적인 separate 분리하다 distract 주의를 산만하게 하다

12

정답 | ⑤

| Script & Translation |

W: Katie and Oliver are college freshmen majoring in economics. These days, Katie has been thinking she should study mathematical economics to understand economics better. When she tells this to Oliver, he tells her it's a good idea and that he's already in a mathematical economics study group that meets once a week. Katie thinks that's a great way to study mathematical economics, so she tells Oliver that she wants to be a member of the study group. Thinking it's good to study with her, Oliver wants to tell Katie

he should check with the other members if she can join the study group. In this situation, what would Oliver most likely say to Katie?

Oliver: <u>I need to ask my group members if you can join the study group.</u>

여: Katie와 Oliver는 경제학을 전공하는 대학 신입생입니다. 요즘, Katie는 경제학을 더 잘 이해하기 위해 수리 경제학을 공부해야 한다고 생각해 왔습니다. 그녀가 이것을 Oliver에게 말할 때, Oliver는 그것이 좋은 생각이며, 그는 이미 일주일에 한 번씩 만나는 수리 경제학 스터디 그룹에 속해 있다고 말합니다. Katie는 그것이 수리 경제학을 공부하는 좋은 방법이라고 생각해서, Oliver에게 자신이 그 스터디 그룹의 회원이 되고 싶다고 말합니다. Oliver는 그녀와 함께 공부하는 것이 좋다고 생각하고, 그녀가 그 스터디 그룹에 참여할 수 있는지 다른 회원들에게 확인해야 한다고 Katie에게 말하고 싶습니다. 이런 상황에서, Oliver는 Katie에게 뭐라고 말하겠습니까?

Oliver: 네가 스터디 그룹에 참여할 수 있는지 내가 그룹 회원들에게 물어봐야 해.

● **Topic & Situation** 수리 경제학 스터디 그룹

● **Solution**

수리 경제학을 공부하고 싶어 하는 Katie는 Oliver가 하고 있는 수리 경제학 스터디 그룹에 참여해 함께 공부하고 싶다고 했고, 이에 Oliver는 그것이 좋다고 생각하고, 스터디 그룹 회원들에게 그녀가 참여할 수 있을지를 물어봐야 한다고 Katie에게 말하려는 상황이다. 따라서 Oliver가 Katie에게 할 말로 가장 적절한 것은 ⑤ '네가 스터디 그룹에 참여할 수 있는지 내가 그룹 회원들에게 물어봐야 해.'이다.

① 어떻게 그렇게 훌륭한 스터디 그룹을 찾았니?

② 그 스터디 그룹에 참여할 수 있도록 나를 격려해 줘서 고마워.

③ 그 스터디 그룹을 통해서 내 수학 실력이 많이 늘었어.

④ 우리가 다른 회원이 가입하는 것을 허용해야 한다고 생각하니?

● **Words & Phrases**

major in ~을 전공하다 economics 경제학 mathematical 수리의, 수학의

Dictations

본문 111, 116~119쪽

기출 예제 ❶ submitting your homework
❷ manage your assignments
❸ organize your assignments better

01 ❶ In celebration of
❷ submit your suggestion
❸ school promotional activities

02 ❶ classics to broaden their knowledge
❷ stood the test of time
❸ can develop empathy

03 ❶ at the souvenir shop
❷ greatest human inventions
❸ hanging from the ceiling

04 ❶ remember having to do
❷ booking the resort
❸ have enough rooms

05 ❶ enroll in
❷ prefer attending class
❸ the intensive course for beginners
❹ on the tuition

06 ❶ my hard work paid off
❷ a welcoming ceremony
❸ find some awesome clothes

07 ❶ Koreans living abroad
❷ Have you registered
❸ six times a year
❹ are thinking of studying

08 ❶ taken chemistry before
❷ maintain a routine
❸ more actively involved

09 ❶ joined a morning study group
❷ wake up that early

10 ❶ paid off
❷ must have worked

11 ❶ since I graduated
❷ a bit challenging
❸ I get too emotional

12 ❶ study mathematical economics
❷ meets once a week
❸ check with the other members

18강 건강, 안전, 봉사, 환경 보호

본문 120~125쪽

기출예제 ①

Exercises 01 ① 02 ① 03 ③ 04 ⑤ 05 ② 06 ⑤
07 ④ 08 ③ 09 ⑤ 10 ④ 11 ① 12 ④

기출 예제

본문 120쪽

정답 | ①

| Script & Translation |

W: Hey, Kevin! Where are you going?

M: I'm going to take the staff fitness program.

W: Oh, is it the 25-minute lunch break workout that the company is offering?

M: That's right. I find that exercising at lunch time boosts my energy and helps me focus on my work.

W: Really? I think it would make me more tired. I usually just want to take a rest.

M: I did, too. But I actually feel more energized after the lunch break workout. It even improves my concentration.

W: You mean you have more energy and can focus better when you get back to your desk?

M: Exactly. It's been very helpful for me.

W: Okay. Maybe I'll join. Thanks for the information.

M: My pleasure.

여: 안녕하세요, Kevin! 어디 가세요?

남: 직원 피트니스 프로그램에 참여하러 가는 길이에요.

여: 아, 회사에서 제공하고 있는 점심시간 25분 운동인가요?

남: 맞아요. 점심시간에 운동하면 저의 활력을 높이고 제가 저의 업무에 집중하는 데 도움이 되더라고요.

여: 정말요? 그게 저를 더 피곤하게 만들 거라고 저는 생각해요. 저는 보통 그냥 휴식을 취하고 싶어요.

남: 저도 그랬어요. 하지만 점심시간에 운동하고 나면 실제로 저는 활력이 더 넘치는 걸 느껴요. 저의 집중력도 향상시키고요.

여: 다시 책상에 돌아왔을 때 더 많은 활력이 있고 더 잘 집중할 수 있다는 뜻인가요?

남: 맞아요. 저한테는 매우 도움이 됐어요.

여: 알았어요. 어쩌면 저도 참여할 것 같아요. 알려 줘서 고마워요.

남: 천만에요.

▶ Topic & Situation 점심시간을 활용한 직원 운동 프로그램

참여

● Solution
점심시간을 이용해 직원 운동 프로그램에 참여하러 가는 남자에게 여자는 운동은 피곤하게 만들기에 그냥 휴식을 취하고 싶다고 응답하지만 이에 남자는 여자에게 운동을 하고 나면 활력이 더 넘치고 집중력도 향상된다고 말하고 있다. 따라서 남자의 의견으로 가장 적절한 것은 ① '점심시간에 운동하는 것은 활력과 집중력을 높인다.'이다.

● Words & Phrases
staff 직원 workout 운동 concentration 집중력

Exercises

본문 122~125쪽

01
정답 | ①

| Script & Translation |

W: Hello, listeners. This is Ellie Williams with Everyday Travel. It's summer, which means it's vacation time! For some people, this includes road trips. So, let me give you some tips for things you can do to help you stay safe while on the road. First, if you're traveling in a group with multiple people who can drive, try to switch drivers occasionally. Also, remember to stop frequently to get out, walk around, and stretch. Now, here are the things not to do. Don't ever drive when you feel sleepy. Driving while tired can be dangerous. And don't drive when it's dark if you have poor night vision. Unlit highways can be especially dark. Keep these tips in mind. I'll be back right after a commercial break. Stay tuned!

여: 안녕하세요, 청취자 여러분. Everyday Travel의 Ellie Williams입니다. 여름입니다. 그 말은 즉 휴가철이라는 거죠! 어떤 사람들에게는 이것은 자동차 여행을 포함합니다. 그래서, 이동 중 안전을 유지하는 것을 돕기 위해 여러분이 할 수 있는 것들에 대한 몇 가지 조언을 알려 드리겠습니다. 먼

저, 운전을 할 수 있는 여러 사람과 함께 단체로 여행하는 경우 운전자를 가끔씩 바꿔 보세요. 또한, 자주 차를 멈추고 내려서 걷거나 스트레칭하는 것을 기억하세요. 자, 다음은 하지 말아야 할 것들입니다. 졸릴 때는 절대로 운전하지 마세요. 피곤한 상태에서 운전하는 것은 위험할 수 있습니다. 그리고 밤눈이 좋지 않은 경우 어두울 때 운전하지 마세요. 불이 켜지지 않은 고속도로는 특히 어두울 수 있습니다. 이 조언들을 명심하세요. 광고가 끝난 후 바로 돌아오겠습니다. 채널을 고정해 주세요!

● Topic & Situation 휴가철 운전 시 안전 수칙

● Solution
여자는 여름 휴가철에 자동차로 이동 시 안전을 유지하는 데 도움이 되는 조언을 제공하고 있으므로, 여자가 하는 말의 목적으로 가장 적절한 것은 ① '안전한 자동차 여행에 대해 조언하려고'이다.

● Words & Phrases
tip 조언, 정보 occasionally 가끔 frequently 자주 night vision 밤눈, 야간 시력 unlit 불이 켜지지 않은 keep ~ in mind ~을 명심하다 commercial break (라디오, TV) 광고 방송

02
정답 | ①

| Script & Translation |

M: Hi, everyone. I'm Kevin Brown, the host of One-Minute Environment. Yesterday, I watched a documentary on TV highlighting the challenging conditions our planet faces. The documentary emphasized that the primary cause of environmental destruction is the widespread use of plastic. It means that the more we reduce our plastic consumption, the greater the improvement in our environment. So, let's reduce use of single-use plastics and instead choose reusable alternatives like metal straws. Additionally, let's be mindful of our purchases by selecting products with minimal plastic packaging and choosing items made from sustainable materials such as glass. Remember, by diminishing our plastic usage, we can significantly contribute to a cleaner and healthier planet. That's all. See you next time.

남: 안녕하세요, 여러분. 저는 One-Minute Environment의 진행자 Kevin Brown입니다. 어제 저는 TV에서 지구가 직면한 어려운 상황을 강조하는 다큐멘터리를 시청했습니다. 이 다큐멘터리는 환경 파괴의 주요 원인이 플라스틱의 광범위한 사용이라는 점을 강조했습니다. 이것은 우리가 플라스틱 소비를 더 많이 줄일수록 환경이 더 크게 개선될 수 있다는 것을 의미합니다. 따라서, 일회용 플라스틱의 사용을 줄이고, 대신 금속 빨대와 같은 재사용 가능한 대안을 선택합시다. 또한, 플라스틱 포장을 최소화한 제품을 선택하고 유리와 같은 지속 가능한 소재로 만든 제품을 선택함으로써 구입 물건에도 주의를 기울이도록 합시다. 플라스틱 사용을 줄임으로써, 더 깨끗하고 더 건강한 지구를 만드는 데 크게 기여할 수 있다는 사실을 잊지 마세요. 이상입니다. 다음에 뵙겠습니다.

● **Topic & Situation** 플라스틱 사용 줄이기

● **Solution**

환경 프로그램 진행자인 남자는 환경 파괴의 주요 원인이 플라스틱 사용이라고 하면서 플라스틱 사용을 줄여서 더 깨끗하고 더 건강한 지구를 만드는 데 기여할 수 있다고 말했으므로, 남자가 하는 말의 요지로 가장 적절한 것은 ① '환경 개선을 위해 플라스틱 사용을 줄이자.'이다.

● **Words & Phrases**

highlight 강조하다 widespread 광범위한, 폭넓은 consumption 소비 metal straw 금속 빨대 sustainable 지속 가능한 diminish 줄이다

03

정답 | ③

| Script & Translation |

M: Susan, where did you get the salad you were eating for lunch? It looked delicious.

W: It indeed was delicious. I bought it from a café near my house. Let me show you a picture of it.

M: Wow, the plants hanging from the ceiling make the café look like a garden.

W: It feels like that when you're there. They also put a potted plant on each table.

M: I see that. It makes sense that they serve salads.

W: Right. The café has a nice eco-friendly interior design.

M: That's a nice touch. And I like the striped floor. It's really modern.

W: Yeah. Do you see this leaf-shaped mirror?

M: Oh, that's so pretty! It would be cool to take a picture in front of it.

W: Many people do that. And there's a bicycle in front of the counter. It matches the eco-friendly concept of the café.

M: That makes sense. I'd love to go there too.

남: Susan, 점심으로 먹던 샐러드를 어디서 샀어요? 맛있어 보였어요.

여: 정말 맛있었어요. 집 근처 카페에서 샀어요. 그곳의 사진을 보여 줄게요.

남: 와, 천장에 매달린 식물들이 카페를 정원처럼 보이게 하네요.

여: 가 보면 그렇게 느껴져요. 테이블마다 화분에 심은 식물도 놓여 있어요.

남: 그렇군요. 그들이 샐러드를 제공하는 것이 이해가 되네요.

여: 맞아요. 그 카페는 친환경적인 실내 장식이 멋지답니다.

남: 감각이 좋네요. 그리고 줄무늬 바닥도 마음에 들어요. 정말 모던하네요.

여: 네. 이 나뭇잎 모양의 거울이 보이나요?

남: 오, 너무 예뻐요! 그 앞에서 사진을 찍으면 멋질 것 같아요.

여: 많은 사람이 그렇게 하죠. 그리고 카운터 앞에 자전거가 있어요. 그것은 그 카페의 친환경적인 콘셉트와 어울린답니다.

남: 그러네요. 저도 거기 가 보고 싶어요.

● **Topic & Situation** 친환경 콘셉트의 샐러드 카페

● **Solution**

대화에서 줄무늬 바닥이 마음에 든다고 말했는데, 그림에는 바닥이 격자무늬다. 따라서 그림에서 대화의 내용과 일치하지 않는 것은 ③이다.

● **Words & Phrases**

hang 매달리다, 걸려 있다 ceiling 천장 potted 화분에 심은 make sense 이해가 되다, 말이 되다 eco-friendly 친환경적인 interior design 실내 장식

04
정답 | ⑤

| Script & Translation |

M: Hello, Ms. Henderson.

W: Hi, David. How's everything going for the club campaign? Friday is the big day!

M: We've already gathered a lot of participants and made some campaign slogans.

W: That's great. How many students are participating in the campaign?

M: Twenty five students in total.

W: Okay, that's good. So have you made the campaign banner yet?

M: Not yet. I'm going to design it tomorrow.

W: Sounds great. Is there anything else left to do?

M: We're hoping to get some water for the participants to drink. Could you help us with that?

W: No problem. There's enough money for that in the budget. I'll order some bottled water right away.

M: Thank you, Ms. Henderson.

W: My pleasure. I'll see you on Friday.

남: 안녕하세요, Henderson 선생님.

여: 안녕, David. 동아리 캠페인은 모두 어떻게 되고 있니? 금요일은 중요한 날이잖아!

남: 이미 많은 참여자들을 모았고 캠페인 슬로건을 몇 개 만들었어요.

여: 잘했구나. 얼마나 많은 학생들이 그 캠페인에 참여할 거니?

남: 총 25명이에요.

여: 좋아. 그래서 캠페인 현수막을 벌써 만들었니?

남: 아직 아니에요. 제가 내일 그것을 디자인할 거예요.

여: 좋아. 남아 있는 다른 할 일이 있니?

남: 저희는 참여자들이 마실 물을 좀 사고 싶어요. 그것을 도와주실 수 있어요?

여: 문제 없어. 예산에는 그것을 위한 충분한 돈이 있거든. 내가 지금 바로 병에 든 물을 주문할게.

남: 감사합니다, Henderson 선생님.

여: 천만에. 금요일에 보자.

▶ **Topic & Situation** 동아리 캠페인 준비

▶ **Solution**
동아리 캠페인을 준비하는 남자가 여자에게 캠페인 참가자들이 마실 물을 좀 사도록 도와달라고 부탁하자, 여자는 예산에 그것을 위한 충분한 돈이 있다고 말하면서 병에 든 물을 주문하겠다고 말했다. 따라서 여자가 할 일로 가장 적절한 것은 ⑤ '병에 든 물 주

문하기'이다.

▶ **Words & Phrases**
gather 모으다   participant 참여자   banner 현수막, 배너   budget 예산

05
정답 | ②

| Script & Translation |

W: Hi, may I help you?

M: Yes. I'm looking for Star Medicine vitamin D supplements. Do you by chance have them?

W: Sure. We carry all the Star Medicine supplements. They're right over here.

M: Oh, great. I'm glad you carry them.

W: Here's the vitamin D. This white bottle has 180 pills, and it's $30.

M: I'd like the yellow one with 360 pills.

W: Okay. It's $50.

M: All right. I'll take three of these yellow bottles.

W: That's quite a lot of vitamin D. You must be shopping for other people, too.

M: Right. I'm shopping for the whole family.

W: I got it. Oh, and because you're spending over $100, you can get 10% off the total.

M: That's nice. Here's my credit card.

여: 안녕하세요, 도와드릴까요?

남: 네. Star Medicine 브랜드의 비타민 D 보충제를 찾고 있습니다. 혹시 가지고 계신가요?

여: 물론이죠. 우리는 모든 Star Medicine 보충제를 취급하고 있습니다. 그것들이 바로 여기 있습니다.

남: 오, 좋은데요. 그것들을 취급하신다니 기쁘네요.

여: 비타민 D 여기 있습니다. 이 흰색 병에는 180정이 들어 있고 30달러예요.

남: 저는 360정이 들어 있는 노란 병이 마음에 들어요.

여: 알겠습니다. 그것은 50달러입니다.

남: 알겠습니다. 이 노란 병 세 개 주세요.

여: 그것은 상당히 많은 비타민 D인데요. 다른 분들을 위해서도 쇼핑을 하시는 것이 틀림없군요.

남: 맞아요. 온 가족을 위해 쇼핑하고 있어요.

여: 알겠습니다. 아, 그리고 손님께서 100달러 넘게 지불하시기

때문에, 총액에서 10% 할인을 받으실 수 있어요.

남: 그거 좋네요. 여기 제 신용 카드예요.

◉ Topic & Situation 비타민 D 보충제 구입

◉ Solution

한 병에 50달러인 비타민 D 보충제를 세 병 구입한 남자는 총액에서 10% 할인을 받았으므로, 남자가 지불할 금액은 ② '$135' 이다.

◉ Words & Phrases

supplement 보충제 carry 취급하다 pill 정, 알약 must be ~임에 틀림없다

06

정답 | ⑤

| Script & Translation |

M: Hi, Martha. Thank you for coming to pick me up.

W: No problem, James. How was your weekend? Did the heavy rain cause any trouble for you?

M: Actually, yes. The heavy downpour damaged the road near my house.

W: That's too bad.

M: Yeah, but it's getting repaired now.

W: That's good. By the way, this road is more crowded than usual for this time of day. Do you think there might have been an accident?

M: Well, let me check on my smartphone if any accidents happened nearby. *[Pause]* Oh, there's a marathon beginning at 10 o'clock.

W: I heard about that on the news.

M: So traffic is being redirected this way because some roads near City Hall are closed.

W: I see. Then I'm going to take a detour via Glendale Avenue to get out of this bad traffic.

M: Good idea. I don't think we'll be late for the meeting, fortunately.

남: 안녕, Martha. 저를 태우러 와줘서 고마워요.

여: 괜찮아요, James. 주말은 어땠어요? 폭우로 인해 당신에게 어떠한 어려움이라도 생겼나요?

남: 실은, 그랬어요. 심한 폭우로 저의 집 근처 도로가 훼손되었거든요.

여: 그거 정말 유감이네요.

남: 네, 하지만 그것은 지금 수리 중이에요.

여: 잘됐네요. 그런데, 이 도로가 하루 중 이 시간대의 평소보다 더 붐비네요. 사고가 있었을까요?

남: 글쎄요, 제 스마트폰으로 근처에서 어떠한 사고가 일어났는지 확인해 볼게요. *[잠시 후]* 아, 10시에 시작하는 마라톤 행사가 있어요.

여: 그것에 관해 뉴스에서 들었어요.

남: 그래서 시청 근처의 도로 몇 개가 폐쇄되었기 때문에 차량들이 이쪽으로 유도되고 있어요.

여: 알겠어요. 그럼 이 교통 혼잡에서 벗어나기 위해 Glendale Avenue를 경유해서 우회해야겠어요.

남: 좋은 생각이에요. 다행히 회의에 늦지는 않을 것 같네요.

◉ Topic & Situation 마라톤 행사로 인한 도로 폐쇄

◉ Solution

도로가 이 시간대의 평소보다 더 혼잡한 것 같다는 여자의 말에 남자가 스마트폰으로 사고가 있었는지 확인하다가 마라톤 행사로 인해 시청 근처의 도로 몇 개가 폐쇄되었고, 그 때문에 차량들이 이쪽으로 유도되고 있다고 알리자 여자가 이 교통 혼잡에서 벗어나기 위해 Glendale Avenue를 경유해서 우회해야겠다고 말한다. 따라서 여자가 Glendale Avenue로 우회하려는 이유는 ⑤ '마라톤 행사로 인한 교통 혼잡 때문에'이다.

◉ Words & Phrases

downpour 폭우 damage 훼손하다; 훼손, 피해 crowded (사람들이나 차량들로) 붐비는 traffic 차량들, 교통(량) take a detour 우회하다, 돌아서 가다

07

정답 | ④

| Script & Translation |

M: Jennifer, I heard an advertisement for the Jefferson Fire Expo on the radio. Have you?

W: No, I haven't. What's it all about?

M: It's a fire expo, where they exhibit fire equipment and technology.

W: Oh, I see. I'm curious, how many exhibitors will be there?

M: They said there will be over 400 exhibitors.

W: That's quite impressive! Where is it being held?

M: It's taking place at the Kinster Expo Center.

W: Oh, that's convenient. Are you planning to go?

M: Yes, I'm actually taking my kids along. They also have many interesting programs for children, like the junior firefighter challenges.

W: That sounds exciting! I'd love to take my kids too. Do you know the dates?

M: Sure. It's happening on May 25th and 26th, and I'm considering going on the 25th.

W: All right, thanks for sharing. I'll make a note of it.

남: Jennifer, 나는 라디오에서 Jefferson Fire Expo에 대한 광고를 들었어. 너도 들었니?

여: 아니, 못 들었어. 그게 뭐야?

남: 소방 장비와 기술을 전시하는 소방 박람회야.

여: 아, 그렇구나. 궁금한 게 있는데, 거기에 얼마나 많은 전시업체가 있을까?

남: 400개가 넘는 전시업체가 있을 거라고 했어.

여: 정말 인상적이네! 그것은 어디에서 열리는 거야?

남: Kinster Expo Center에서 열려.

여: 오, 그곳은 편리하지. 갈 계획이니?

남: 응, 사실 나는 내 아이들을 데리고 갈 거야. 주니어 소방관 챌린지와 같은 아이들을 위한 흥미로운 프로그램도 많이 있어.

여: 재밌겠네! 나도 내 아이들을 데리고 가고 싶어. 날짜는 알고 있어?

남: 물론이지. 5월 25일과 26일에 열리는데, 나는 25일에 가려고 생각 중이야.

여: 알겠어, 공유해줘서 고마워. 메모해 둘게.

◑ **Topic & Situation** Jefferson Fire Expo

◑ **Solution**

대화에서 Jefferson Fire Expo에 관해 전시업체 수, 개최 장소, 어린이 프로그램, 개최 기간은 언급되었지만, ④ '입장료'는 언급되지 않았다.

◑ **Words & Phrases**

advertisement 광고 exhibit 전시하다 equipment 장비 exhibitor 전시업체, 전시자 take place 열리다, 개최되다 convenient 편리한 make a note 메모하다

08
정답 | ③

| **Script & Translation** |

W: Hello, everybody! I'm Judy Smith, manager of the Rural Wildlife Caretaker Project. It's a pleasure to have student trainees in the animal resources department. This project serves to rescue and help wounded wild animals. And it provides opportunities to practice what you have learned in your major subjects. The whole project will last for twelve weeks. During the first week, you will have a five-day training and follow and watch instructors working before starting independent shifts. During your practice, you will prepare food, feed animals, clean cages, and keep animal records. Free shuttle bus services will be provided for your convenience. If you have any questions, see me at the management office. Thank you.

여: 안녕하세요, 여러분! 저는 Rural Wildlife Caretaker Project의 매니저인 Judy Smith입니다. 동물 자원 학과의 학생 실습생들을 받게 되어 기쁩니다. 이 프로젝트는 부상당한 야생 동물들을 구조하고 돕는 역할을 합니다. 그리고 여러분들이 전공 과목에서 배운 것을 실습할 수 있는 기회를 제공합니다. 전체 프로젝트는 12주 동안 지속될 것입니다. 첫 주에는 5일간 훈련을 받고 강사들이 일하는 것을 따라 하며 지켜보고 그 후에 독립적인 교대 근무를 시작할 것입니다. 실습 동안 여러분들은 먹이를 준비하고, 동물들에게 먹이를 주고, 우리를 청소하고 동물들에 대해 기록할 것입니다. 여러분의 편의를 위해 무료 셔틀버스 서비스가 제공될 것입니다. 궁금한 점이 있으면 관리사무소로 저를 찾아오시기 바랍니다. 감사합니다.

◑ **Topic & Situation** Rural Wildlife Caretaker Project

◑ **Solution**

실습생들은 첫 주에 5일간 훈련을 받는다고 언급하고 있으므로, 담화의 내용과 일치하지 않는 것은 ③ '실습생들은 첫 주에 7일간 훈련을 받는다.'이다.

◑ **Words & Phrases**

trainee 실습생 resource 자원 rescue 구조하다 wounded 부상을 당한 major subject 전공 과목 last 지속되다 shift 교대 근무 feed 먹이를 주다 convenience 편의

09

| Script & Translation |

M: Susan, I want to start eating healthier, but I'm not sure where to begin.

W: Why not include more vegetables in your diet?

M: That is a good idea, but I'm not a big fan of veggies. Do you have any tips on how to get more in my diet?

W: Well, you could try adding veggies to your favorite foods, like omelet.

남: Susan, 저는 더 건강하게 먹기를 시작하고 싶은데, 어디서부터 시작해야 할지 잘 모르겠어요.

여: 당신 식단에 더 많은 채소를 포함해 보는 건 어때요?

남: 그거 좋은 생각이네요. 하지만, 저는 채소를 별로 좋아하지 않거든요. 제 식단에 더 많이 넣는 방법에 대한 어떤 조언이라도 있을까요?

여: 음, 오믈렛과 같은 당신이 좋아하는 음식에 채소를 추가해 볼 수 있어요.

◉ Topic & Situation 채소 섭취

◉ Solution

더 건강하게 먹고 싶은데 어떻게 해야 할지 모르겠다는 남자의 말에 여자가 식단에 채소를 더 많이 포함시켜보라고 권한다. 이에 대해 남자가 긍정적으로 답하지만, 자신은 채소를 별로 좋아하지 않는다고 하면서 여자에게 그것들을 더 많이 포함할 수 있는 효과적인 방법을 물었으므로, 이에 대한 여자의 응답으로 가장 적절한 것은 ⑤ '음, 오믈렛과 같은 당신이 좋아하는 음식에 채소를 추가해 볼 수 있어요.'이다.

① 저는 더 많은 단백질을 먹고 있지만, 고기를 그렇게 좋아하지는 않아요.

② 조심하세요! 건강에 너무 많이 집중하는 것은 해로울 수 있어요.

③ 물론이죠. 채소 중심의 식단이 사실 항상 건강에 좋은 것은 아니에요.

④ 어떤 요리의 열량 함유량은 조리법에 따라 다를 수 있어요.

◉ Words & Phrases

include 포함하다   veggie 채소, 채식주의자   protein 단백질
content 함유량, 함량

10

| Script & Translation |

M: Cindy, I heard you recently joined a volunteer club.

W: Yes, I did. I love it. We meet up and do something for the environment.

M: Do you? What exactly do you do?

W: We go to different beaches and spend a few hours picking up trash.

M: Cool. That must be really rewarding.

W: Yeah, it is. Would you like to join? I know how much you care about the environment.

M: I'm interested in the club. How often does your club meet up?

W: Once a week. Every Saturday, we normally meet at the beach around 9 a.m.

M: Oh, I'm available at that time. How do you like everyone in the club?

W: They're all really nice. Just like you, everybody is really concerned about protecting the environment.

M: Okay! I'll join you in cleaning the beaches every Saturday.

남: Cindy, 최근에 자원봉사 동아리에 가입했다고 들었어요.

여: 네, 그랬어요. 정말 좋아요. 우리는 만나서 환경을 위해 무언가를 해요.

남: 그래요? 정확히 무엇을 하나요?

여: 우리는 여러 해변에 가서 몇 시간 동안 쓰레기를 주워요.

남: 멋지네요. 정말 보람 있겠네요.

여: 네, 그래요. 함께 하시겠어요? 저는 당신이 환경에 얼마나 관심이 많은지 알고 있어요.

남: 이 동아리에 관심이 있어요. 당신의 동아리는 얼마나 자주 모이나요?

여: 일주일에 한 번이요. 매주 토요일, 우리는 보통 오전 9시쯤 해변에서 만나요.

남: 오, 그때 시간이 돼요. 동아리에 있는 모든 사람들은 어떤가요?

여: 모두 정말 좋은 사람들이에요. 당신과 마찬가지로, 모두가 환경 보호에 관심이 정말로 많거든요.

남: 좋아요! 매주 토요일 해변 청소를 함께 할게요.

◉ Topic & Situation 자원봉사 동아리 가입

◉ Solution

환경 보호에 관심이 많은 남자가 여자로부터 동아리에 관한 다양한 정보를 들은 후에 마지막으로 동아리 회원에 대해 묻자 여자는

회원 모두가 아주 좋은 사람들이라고 말했으므로, 이에 대한 남자의 응답으로 가장 적절한 것은 ④ '좋아요! 매주 토요일 해변 청소를 함께 할게요.'이다.

① 미안해요. 하지만 나는 이 동아리를 떠날 수밖에 없어요.

② 내가 이 동아리에 가입한 지 벌써 두 달이 되었어요.

③ 걱정 마세요. 내가 이 동아리에 약간의 돈을 기부할게요.

⑤ 맞아요. 당신은 해변을 떠나기 전에 쓰레기를 주웠어야 했어요.

▶ Words & Phrases

recently 최근에 rewarding 보람 있는 care about ~에 대해 관심이 있다 normally 보통, 일반적으로 be concerned about ~에 대해 관심이 있다 have no choice but to *do* ~할 수 밖에 없다 pick up ~을 줍다

11~12

정답 | 11 ① 12 ④

| Script & Translation |

M: Good afternoon, everyone. Last class, we learned about common injuries that happen in different sports. Today, I'd like to talk about low-impact exercises which place less stress and strain on the joints, and therefore have less chance of injury. Here are several examples. First, swimming is a great low-impact exercise that is gentle on your joints. It provides a full-body workout and can help build muscle and improve flexibility. Cycling is another exercise that is easy on the joints. It provides a great workout for your heart and can help build lower-body strength. Another example is walking, a low-impact exercise that can be done almost anywhere. It can help reduce mental stress, strengthen the legs, and promote weight loss. Lastly, hiking is a low-impact exercise that can help improve strength and balance of your body without putting too much stress on your joints and muscles. Overall, there are various types of low-impact exercises, which can provide a wide range of benefits as I've just mentioned. Now let's work in pairs to talk about our experiences with them.

남: 안녕하세요, 여러분. 지난 수업에서, 우리는 다양한 스포츠에서 일어나는 흔한 부상에 대해 배웠습니다. 오늘은 제가 관절에 스트레스와 긴장을 덜 주고, 그래서 부상의 가능성이 더 적은, 충격이 적은 운동에 관해 이야기하려고 합니다. 여기 몇 가지 예가 있습니다. 첫째, 수영은 관절에 부드럽게 작용하는, 충격이 적은 훌륭한 운동입니다. 그것은 전신 운동을 제공하고 근육을 만들고 유연성을 향상시키는 데 도움을 줄 수 있습니다. 자전거 타기는 관절에 편안한 또 다른 운동입니다. 그것은 심장에 아주 좋은 운동을 제공하고 하체의 힘을 기르는 데 도움을 줄 수 있습니다. 또 다른 예는 걷기인데, 거의 모든 곳에서 할 수 있는 충격이 적은 운동입니다. 그것은 정신적인 스트레스를 줄이고, 양다리를 튼튼하게 하며, 체중 감량을 촉진하는 데 도움이 될 수 있습니다. 마지막으로, 하이킹은 여러분의 관절과 근육에 너무 많은 스트레스를 주지 않고 신체의 힘과 균형을 향상시키는 데 도움을 줄 수 있는 충격이 적은 운동입니다. 전반적으로, 다양한 유형의 충격이 적은 운동이 있으며, 이는 제가 방금 언급한 바와 같이 아주 다양한 이점을 제공할 수 있습니다. 이제 함께 짝을 지어 이러한 운동과 관련된 우리의 경험에 대해 이야기해 보겠습니다.

▶ Topic & Situation 관절에 미치는 충격이 적은 운동

▶ Solution

11 남자는 충격이 적은 운동의 정의가 무엇이고, 그러한 운동의 예시와 그것이 우리에게 신체적으로 어떤 이점이 있는지를 설명하고 있으므로, 남자가 하는 말의 주제로 가장 적절한 것은 ① '다양한 종류의 충격이 적은 운동의 이점들'이다.

② 충격이 적은 운동을 할 때 부상을 방지하는 방법

③ 충격이 적은 운동이 정신적인 스트레스를 줄이는 데 미치는 영향

④ 충격이 적은 운동을 하기에 최적의 장소와 시간

⑤ 규칙적으로 충격이 적은 운동을 하는 것의 중요성

12 수영, 자전거 타기, 걷기, 하이킹은 언급되었지만, ④ '조정'은 언급되지 않았다.

▶ Words & Phrases

low-impact 충격이 적은 strain (근육의) 긴장 joint 관절 gentle 부드러운 easy 편안한 promote 촉진하다 range 범위 optimal 최적의, 최상의 rowing 조정, 노 젓기

Dictations

본문 121, 126~129쪽

기출 예제
❶ fitness program
❷ boosts my energy
❸ lunch break workout

01 **❶** this includes road trips
❷ to help you stay safe
❸ switch drivers occasionally
❹ have poor night vision

02 **❶** our planet faces
❷ reduce our plastic consumption
❸ made from sustainable materials

03 **❶** hanging from the ceiling
❷ put a potted plant
❸ the striped floor
❹ this leaf-shaped mirror

04 **❶** some campaign slogans
❷ water for the participants
❸ some bottled water

05 **❶** by chance have them
❷ This white bottle
❸ must be shopping
❹ off the total

06 **❶** coming to pick me up
❷ more crowded than usual
❸ take a detour via

07 **❶** heard an advertisement
❷ taking my kids along
❸ a note of it

08 **❶** serves to rescue and help
❷ practice what you have learned
❸ before starting independent shifts
❹ for your convenience

09 **❶** start eating healthier
❷ a big fan of veggies

10 **❶** meet up and do something
❷ picking up trash
❸ how much you care
❹ protecting the environment

11~12 **❶** less chance of injury
❷ easy on the joints
❸ a wide range of benefits

19강 여행, 체험 활동

본문 130~135쪽

기출예제 ③

Exercises 01 ① 02 ④ 03 ⑤ 04 ② 05 ③ 06 ⑤
07 ⑤ 08 ③ 09 ① 10 ③ 11 ③ 12 ⑤

기출 예제

본문 130쪽

정답 | ③

| Script & Translation |

W: Hello, viewers! Are you looking for a fun activity for your kids to enjoy on the weekend? Then, come and join our animal camp for kids. Happy Animal Friends Camp will be held every weekend in September. We'll provide hands-on activities with a wide variety of animals such as rabbits, turtles, and parrots. Your kids will learn how to care for and interact with the animals under the guidance of experienced trainers. If your children like spending time with animals, sign them up for the Happy Animal Friends Camp! You can find more information on our website. Don't miss this great opportunity!

여: 안녕하세요, 시청자 여러분! 주말에 아이들이 즐길 수 있는 재미있는 활동을 찾고 계십니까? 그렇다면 오셔서 아이들을 위한 저희 동물 캠프에 함께 하세요. Happy Animal Friends Camp가 9월 매주 주말에 열립니다. 저희는 토끼와 거북이, 앵무새와 같은 매우 다양한 동물과 함께하는 체험 활동을 제공합니다. 아이들은 경험이 풍부한 훈련사의 지도하에 동물을 돌보고 교감하는 방법을 배울 것 입니다. 자녀가 동물과 함께 시간을 보내는 것을 좋아한다면 Happy Animal Friends Camp에 그들을 등록시키세요! 웹사이트에서 더 많은 정보를 얻을 수 있습니다. 이 좋은 기회를 놓치지 마세요!

◑ Topic & Situation Happy Animal Friends Camp 홍보

◑ Solution
여자는 9월 매주 주말에 열리는 Happy Animal Friends Camp를 소개하며 아이들이 토끼, 거북이, 앵무새와 같은 다양한 동물과 함께 체험 활동을 할 수 있다고 홍보하고 있다. 따라서 여자가 하는 말의 목적으로 가장 적절한 것은 ③ '어린이 동물 캠프를 홍보하려고'이다.

◐ Words & Phrases

hands-on activity 체험 활동   a wide variety of 매우 다양한
parrot 앵무새   guidance 지도

◐ Words & Phrases

due to ~로 인해   heavy snowfall 폭설   destination 목적지
reschedule 일정을 변경하다   original 원래의   apologize 사과하다   inconvenience 불편   disruption 혼란, 방해

Exercises 본문 132~135쪽

01 정답 | ①

| Script & Translation |

M: Good morning, everyone! I hope you're all feeling excited and ready for another day of adventure. Before we set off, I have some important news to share regarding our return flight. Unfortunately, due to heavy snowfall at our destination, we've had to reschedule our return flight to December 13th, one day later than our original plan. I truly apologize for any inconvenience this may cause and any disruption to your personal plans. Our staff is currently working on arranging your future schedule considering the flight changes. I'll be sharing all the details with you soon. Thank you for your understanding and cooperation.

남: 안녕하세요, 여러분! 여러분 모두가 신나고 또 다른 모험의 날을 위한 준비가 되어 있기를 바랍니다. 출발하기 전에, 우리의 돌아가는 항공편에 관한 중요한 소식이 있어 공유하려고 합니다. 안타깝게도, 목적지에서의 폭설로 인해, 저희는 돌아가는 항공편을 원래 계획보다 하루 늦은 12월 13일로 변경해야 했습니다. 이에 따라 발생할 수 있는 불편과 여러분 개인 일정에 생길 수 있는 혼란에 대해 진심으로 사과드립니다. 저희 직원은 현재 항공편 변경을 고려하여 여러분의 향후 일정을 정리하는 작업을 하고 있습니다. 제가 곧 모든 세부 사항을 여러분에게 알려 드리겠습니다. 이해와 협조에 감사드립니다.

◐ Topic & Situation 돌아가는 항공편 일정 변경 안내

◐ Solution

남자는 돌아가는 항공편에 관한 중요한 소식이 있다고 하면서 폭설로 인해 돌아가는 항공편 일정이 원래 계획보다 하루 뒤로 변경되었다고 안내하고 있다. 따라서 남자가 하는 말의 목적으로 가장 적절한 것은 ① '돌아가는 항공편 일정 변경을 안내하려고'이다.

02 정답 | ④

| Script & Translation |

W: Ted, have you finished packing?

M: Yes, Mom. I'm all set. I'm super excited for my trip!

W: That's great to hear! Actually, I wanted to talk to you about keeping your money safe while you're traveling.

M: Okay. What should I do?

W: Well, don't keep all of your cash in your wallet. That way, if something happens and you lose your wallet, you'll still have some money.

M: Oh, that makes sense. How much do you think I should keep out of it?

W: I recommend keeping enough to cover just one or two days' expenses.

M: Yes, Mom. I'll do that. Where should I keep the separate cash?

W: It's best to keep it in a different bag that's not easily accessible or visible to others.

M: I got it. Thanks for the advice, Mom.

W: You're welcome, dear.

여: Ted, 짐 싸기를 다 끝냈니?

남: 네, 엄마. 저는 준비가 다 됐어요. 제 여행에 너무 신이 나요!

여: 그거 정말 듣기 좋구나! 사실, 네가 여행하는 동안 돈을 안전하게 보관하는 방법에 대해 이야기하고 싶었어.

남: 좋아요. 제가 무엇을 해야 하나요?

여: 음, 지갑에 모든 현금을 다 갖고 다니지는 말아라. 그런 식으로 한다면, 만약 무슨 일이 일어나 지갑을 잃어버린다 하더라도, 너는 여전히 돈이 남아 있게 될 거야.

남: 아, 그거 말이 되네요. 얼마나 많은 돈을 지갑에서 따로 두어야 할까요?

여: 그냥 하루나 이틀 정도의 비용을 감당할 만큼의 충분한 돈을 보관하기를 추천해.

남: 네, 엄마. 그렇게 할게요. 따로 둘 돈을 어디에 보관해야 할까요?
여: 다른 사람들이 쉽게 접근 가능하거나 볼 수 없는 다른 가방에 그것을 보관하는 게 가장 좋단다.
남: 알겠어요. 충고해 주셔서 감사합니다, 엄마.
여: 천만에, 얘야.

Topic & Situation 여행 시 현금 관리 방법

Solution

여행 준비를 마친 남자에게 여자가 여행하는 동안 돈을 안전하게 보관하는 방법에 대해 이야기하고 싶다고 말하면서 지갑에 모든 현금을 다 가지고 다니지 말 것을 당부하며, 하루나 이틀 정도의 비용을 감당할 수 있을 만큼의 현금을 다른 가방에 보관하라고 충고하고 있다. 따라서 여자의 의견으로 가장 적절한 것은 ④ '여행 시 한 지갑에 모든 현금을 보관해서는 안 된다.'이다.

Words & Phrases

wallet 지갑, 가방 make sense 타당하다[말이 되다], 의미가 통하다 expense 비용, 경비 accessible 접근 가능한 visible 보이는, 가시적인

03

정답 | ⑤

| Script & Translation |

W: Honey. Look at this picture of a camper. I'd like to rent it for our camping trip next month.
M: Oh, let me see. Wow, it's nice! I love the large square ceiling light.
W: Yeah. It's almost like being in an actual house.
M: Look, the blinds on the windows are just like our living room blinds.
W: Right! Maybe they're the same brand.
M: If we end up renting this, where would we eat?
W: We could eat on the table next to the sink, which has the laptop computer on it in this picture.
M: Yeah, that should work.
W: And I love the striped rug on the floor.
M: Yeah, it's cool. And we can use the sofa on the left as a bed.
W: Right. And the two cushions on it can be our pillows.
M: Great. Let's call now to rent it.

여: 여보. 이 캠핑카 사진을 봐요. 나는 다음 달 우리의 캠핑 여행을 위해 그것을 빌리고 싶어요.
남: 아, 어디 봐요. 와, 좋아요! 나는 커다란 정사각형 모양의 천장 조명이 마음에 들어요.
여: 네. 마치 실제 집에 있는 것 같아요.
남: 봐요, 창문에 있는 블라인드는 우리 거실 블라인드와 똑같네요.
여: 맞아요! 아마 같은 브랜드일 수도 있어요.
남: 우리가 결국 이걸 빌리게 된다면 식사는 어디에서 하나요?
여: 이 사진 속 싱크대 옆의 노트북 컴퓨터가 있는 탁자에서 먹을 수 있을 것 같아요.
남: 네, 그러면 되겠네요.
여: 그리고 저는 바닥에 있는 줄무늬 양탄자가 마음에 들어요.
남: 네. 멋지네요. 그리고 우리는 왼쪽에 있는 소파를 침대로 사용할 수 있죠.
여: 맞아요. 그리고 그 위에 있는 쿠션 두 개가 우리 베개가 될 수 있어요.
남: 좋아요. 대여할 수 있게 지금 전화해요.

Topic & Situation 캠핑 여행을 위한 캠핑카 예약

Solution

여자는 소파 위에 쿠션 두 개가 있다고 말했는데, 그림에서는 쿠션 대신 곰 인형 한 개가 놓여 있다. 따라서 그림에서 대화의 내용과 일치하지 않는 것은 ⑤이다.

Words & Phrases

camper 캠핑카, 캠핑용 자동차 square 정사각형 모양의 ceiling 천장 end up -ing 결국 ~하게 되다 laptop computer 노트북 컴퓨터 striped 줄무늬의 rug 양탄자 pillow 베개

04

정답 | ②

| Script & Translation |

M: Hi, Ms. Taylor. Has it been a busy day for you?
W: Yes, Mr. Wilson. I'm getting ready for a beach trekking field trip with my students this weekend.
M: Sounds exciting! How's it going?
W: Almost done. I've planned the schedule and the route. We'll be heading to Ocean Vista Beach.
M: Great choice! Did you receive the access permit from the local department of natural resources?

W: Yes, everything's set. I've also made a bus reservation for transportation.

M: Perfect. Will the students need to bring their own lunch?

W: No, I've already ordered sandwiches and water for everyone.

M: Impressive! Just make sure not to forget a first aid kit.

W: Thanks for reminding me. I'll ask the school nurse for one later.

M: No problem. In fact, I'm on my way to see the school nurse now. Let me get it for you.

W: Wow, thanks a lot! I appreciate your help.

남: 안녕하세요, Taylor 선생님. 바쁜 하루였습니까?

여: 네, Wilson 선생님. 저는 이번 주말에 학생들과 함께 가는 해변 도보 여행 현장 체험 학습을 준비하고 있어요.

남: 재밌겠네요! 어떻게 진행되고 있나요?

여: 거의 다 끝났어요. 저는 일정과 경로를 계획했어요. 우리는 Ocean Vista Beach로 갈 거예요.

남: 좋은 선택이네요! 지역 천연자원 관리부로부터 출입 허가증을 받으셨어요?

여: 네, 모든 것이 준비됐어요. 이동 수단으로 버스 예약도 했어요.

남: 완벽하네요. 학생들이 점심을 싸 가지고 와야 하나요?

여: 아니요, 저는 이미 모두를 위해 샌드위치와 물을 주문했어요.

남: 훌륭하네요! 구급함만 잊지 않도록 하세요.

여: 상기시켜 주셔서 감사해요. 나중에 보건 선생님께 하나 요청할게요.

남: 별말씀을요. 실은 제가 지금 보건 선생님을 뵈러 가는 길이에요. 제가 그것을 선생님께 가져다드릴게요.

여: 와, 정말 고마워요! 도움에 감사드려요.

◐ **Topic & Situation** 해변 도보 여행 현장 체험 학습

◐ **Solution**
학생들과의 해변 도보 여행 현장 체험 학습을 준비하고 있는 여자가 일정과 경로를 짰고, 출입 허가증도 받았으며, 버스 예약과 점심도 준비해 놓았다고 하자, 남자는 구급함을 잊지 말라고 하고 나중에 보건 교사한테 요청하겠다는 여자의 말에 자신이 가져다주겠다고 말하고 있다. 따라서 남자가 할 일로 가장 적절한 것은 ② '구급함 가져다주기'이다.

◐ **Words & Phrases**
head to ~로 가다, ~로 향하다   access permit 출입 허가증
department of natural resources 천연자원 관리부   reservation

예약   transportation 이동 수단, 교통 수단   first aid kit 구급함, 응급 처치 세트   remind 상기시키다, (기억하도록) 다시 한 번 알려주다

05 정답 | ③

| Script & Translation |

M: Welcome to Galaxy Fun Park! How may I assist you today?

W: Hi, there. I would like to purchase tickets for two adults and two children, please. How much are they?

M: Adult tickets are $25 each, and child tickets are $10 each.

W: Okay, got it. Do you offer any discounts if I use a credit card?

M: Actually, we do. If you use a Rainbow credit card, you can get 10% off.

W: Great! I have one. Oh, and I'm interested in watching the magic show. How much is that?

M: It's an additional $5 per person. And just so you know, the credit card discount doesn't apply to the magic show.

W: No problem. I'd like to buy four tickets for that too. And what time does the magic show start?

M: It starts at 2 p.m.

W: Perfect! Here's my card.

남: Galaxy Fun Park에 오신 것을 환영합니다! 오늘은 어떻게 도와드릴까요?

여: 안녕하세요. 성인 2명과 어린이 2명의 표를 구매하려고 합니다. 얼마인가요?

남: 성인 표는 각각 25달러이고, 어린이 표는 각각 10달러입니다.

여: 네, 알겠습니다. 신용 카드를 사용하면 할인이 되나요?

남: 사실, 그렇습니다. Rainbow 신용 카드를 사용하면 10% 할인을 받을 수 있어요.

여: 좋아요! 제게 신용 카드가 있습니다. 아, 그리고 저는 마술 쇼를 보는 데 관심이 있습니다. 그것은 얼마인가요?

남: 1인당 5달러가 추가됩니다. 그리고 아시겠지만, 신용 카드 할인은 마술 쇼에는 적용되지 않습니다.

여: 괜찮아요. 저는 그것을 위한 표 네 장도 사고 싶습니다. 그리고 마술 쇼는 몇 시에 시작하나요?

남: 오후 2시에 시작합니다.

여: 완벽해요! 여기 제 카드가 있습니다.

◉ Topic & Situation Galaxy Fun Park

◉ Solution

여자는 Galaxy Fun Park를 이용하기 위해 25달러짜리 성인표 2장과 10달러짜리 어린이표 2장을 구매하고, 1인당 5달러인 마술 쇼 관람권 4장을 추가로 구매한다. Rainbow 신용 카드로 결재하면 마술 쇼를 제외한 표 구매 가격에서 10% 할인을 받을 수 있다고 했으므로 여자가 지불할 금액은 ③ '$83'이다.

◉ Words & Phrases

galaxy 은하계   assist 돕다, 도움이 되다   purchase 구입하다
additional 추가의   apply to ~에 적용되다

06
정답 | ⑤

| Script & Translation |

W: Hi, Edward. Have you received the results of your health check-up from last week?

M: Hi, Jane. Yes, I have. And the results were good. Thanks for asking.

W: Glad to hear! I think your running every day keeps you in good shape.

M: I think so too.

W: Actually, there's a charity run to raise money for local charities this weekend. How about joining together?

M: That sounds fun. Where is it held?

W: At Eastwood Park. It's close to your house.

M: Great. Oh, wait. Is it on Saturday or Sunday?

W: It's on Saturday.

M: Then, I'm afraid I can't go.

W: Why not?

M: My daughter has a talent show at her kindergarten on that day. I must be there to support her.

W: Oh, okay. You're such a lovely father!

여: 안녕하세요, Edward 씨. 지난주 건강 검진 결과는 받으셨나요?

남: 안녕하세요, Jane. 네, 받았어요. 그리고 결과는 좋았습니다. 물어봐 주셔서 감사해요.

여: 그랬다니 다행이네요! 제 생각에는 당신이 매일 달리기를 하는 것이 당신의 좋은 몸 상태를 유지시켜 주는 것 같아요.

남: 저도 그렇게 생각해요.

여: 사실은, 이번 주말에 지역 자선 단체를 위한 모금 마련 달리기 행사가 있어요. 함께 참가하는 게 어때요?

남: 재미있겠네요. 어디서 열리나요?

여: Eastwood 공원에서요. 당신 집이랑 가까워요.

남: 좋네요. 오, 잠깐만요. 행사가 토요일인가요, 일요일인가요?

여: 토요일에 있어요.

남: 그렇다면, 아무래도 저는 갈 수 없을 것 같아요.

여: 왜 안 되세요?

남: 제 딸이 그날 유치원에서 장기 자랑을 해요. 저는 그녀를 응원하기 위해 그곳에 있어야 해요.

여: 오, 알겠습니다. 당신은 정말 멋진 아빠군요!

◉ Topic & Situation 자선 달리기 행사 참가

◉ Solution

이번 주말에 있는 자선 모금 달리기 행사에 참여하려고 하는 여자가 남자에게도 같이 할 것을 권유하자, 남자는 관심을 가지고 참석하려는 의지를 보였으나, 행사 날짜가 토요일인지 일요일인지를 묻고, 여자가 토요일이라고 대답하자, 참석이 힘들 것 같다며, 그날 자기 딸이 유치원에서 장기 자랑을 하기 때문에 그곳에 응원을 하러 가야 한다고 말한다. 따라서 남자가 자선 달리기 행사에 참가하지 못하는 이유는 ⑤ '딸의 장기 자랑에 참석해야 해서'이다.

◉ Words & Phrases

check-up 검진   charity 자선 단체   talent show 장기 자랑
kindergarten 유치원

07
정답 | ⑤

| Script & Translation |

M: Lucy, check out this Skyline Broadcasting Conference leaflet.

W: Okay. Oh, it's for high school students interested in broadcasting.

M: Yeah, the theme is "Broadcasting Futures: Nurturing Young Voices in Media." Doesn't it sound fascinating?

W: It does. We should go.

M: Sure! It's from July 15th to 17th at the Skyline Convention Center. Can you make it on the 16th?

W: Yes, I'm available then. I guess we should register soon.

M: You're right. Look at the registration fee. Early bird fee is $75, but after June 30th, it's $90. So let's register before July.

W: Good idea. Oh, look here! It says the conference is limited to 300 attendees.

M: That's important to know. Let's go to their website and sign up right now.

W: Okay. I'm really excited to explore the fascinating world of broadcasting!

M: Absolutely! It's going to be awesome.

남: Lucy, 이 Skyline Broadcasting Conference 소책자를 살펴봐.

여: 알겠어. 아, 그것은 방송에 관심이 있는 고등학생들을 위한 것이네.

남: 그래, 주제는 '방송 미래: 미디어에서 젊은 목소리 육성하기'야. 매우 흥미로운 것 같지 않니?

여: 정말 그래. 우리는 가야 해.

남: 물론이지! 그것은 Skyline Convention Center에서 7월 15일부터 17일까지야. 너는 16일에 갈 수 있니?

여: 응, 나는 그때 시간이 있어. 우리는 곧 등록해야 할 것 같아.

남: 맞아. 등록비를 봐봐. 조기 등록 요금은 75달러지만, 6월 30일 이후에는 90달러야. 그러니까 7월 전에 등록하자.

여: 좋은 생각이야. 아, 여기 봐! 그 학회는 참가자가 300명으로 제한되어 있다고 쓰여 있어.

남: 그건 알아야 할 중요한 내용이네. 지금 바로 웹사이트로 가서 등록하자.

여: 좋아. 나는 매력적인 방송 세계를 탐구하게 되어 정말 신이 나!

남: 그렇고말고! 굉장할 거야.

Topic & Situation Skyline Broadcasting Conference

Solution

대화에서 Skyline Broadcasting Conference에 관해 주제, 개최 기간, 등록비, 참가 가능 인원은 언급되었지만, ⑤ '참가 신청 마감일'은 언급되지 않았다.

Words & Phrases

check out ~을 살펴보다, ~을 확인하다 broadcasting 방송 conference 학회, 학술 대회 leaflet 소책자 theme 주제 nurture 육성하다, 양육하다 convention 컨벤션, 학회 register 등록하다 early bird fee 조기 등록 요금 limited 제한된, 한정된 attendee 참가자, 출석자 fascinating 매우 흥미로운, 매력적인

08

정답 | ③

| Script & Translation |

M: Honey, don't you love staying at this resort?

W: Yeah. It's so nice! And our boys are having so much fun.

M: Yeah, they are. Hey, how about doing a water activity later today?

W: Great idea. I'll look up the water activities they offer on my cell phone. Here they are.

M: Hmm.... Oh, this one's over $100 per person. That's too much.

W: I agree. And this other one is only for adults. We need one that our boys can do.

M: Right. So we have these three options left, then.

W: How about this one? It sounds fun.

M: But they're not offering it today. Today's Monday.

W: Oh, that's right. So then let's choose one of these two activities.

M: I think we should choose this one. It has a guide, so it'll be safer and easier.

W: I was thinking the same thing. Let's choose that.

남: 여보, 이 리조트에서 지내는 게 좋지 않나요?

여: 네, 너무 좋아요! 그리고 우리 아이들도 정말 재미있게 시간을 보내고 있어요.

남: 네, 맞아요. 저기, 오늘 이따가 물놀이 활동을 하는 건 어때요?

여: 좋은 생각이에요. 내 휴대 전화로 리조트에서 제공하는 물놀이 활동들을 찾아볼게요. 여기 있어요.

남: 음…. 오, 이것은 한 사람당 100달러가 넘네요. 그것은 너무 비싸네요.

여: 동의해요. 그리고 다른 이것은 성인만을 위한 것이네요. 우리는 우리 애들도 할 수 있는 것이 필요해요.

남: 맞아요. 그러면 이 세 가지 선택 사항이 남는군요.

여: 이것은 어떨까요? 재밌을 것 같아요.

남: 하지만 그것은 오늘 제공되지 않아요. 오늘은 월요일이에요.

여: 오, 그렇네요. 그러면 이 두 활동 중에 하나를 골라 봐요.

남: 내 생각에는 이것을 선택해야 할 것 같아요. 가이드가 있으니, 더 안전하고 더 쉬울 것 같아요.

여: 나도 같은 생각을 하고 있었어요. 그것을 선택해요.

Topic & Situation 리조트에서 제공하는 물놀이 활동

Solution

남자와 여자는 리조트에서 제공하는 물놀이 활동 중 어떤 것을 선택할지 고르고 있는데, 한 사람당 비용이 100달러를 넘지 않고, 성인만 참여할 수 있는 활동은 제외하고, 월요일에 제공되는 활동이면서, 가이드가 있는 활동을 선택하려고 한다. 따라서 두 사람이 선택할 물놀이 활동은 ③이다.

Words & Phrases

resort 리조트 look up (컴퓨터 등에서 정보를) 찾아보다 offer 제공하다 guide 가이드

09
정답 | ①

| Script & Translation |

W: Hey, Ethan. You've always wanted to try bungee jumping on Tiwi Island, right?

M: Yeah, that's on my bucket list. Are you interested in that, too?

W: Absolutely! I found a special travel package deal for bungee jumping there. How do you feel about giving it a try?

M: Sounds amazing! Give me more details.

여: 안녕, Ethan. 너는 항상 Tiwi 섬에서 번지 점프를 해 보고 싶어 했잖아, 그렇지?

남: 응, 그게 내 버킷 리스트에 있지. 너도 거기에 관심이 있니?

여: 물론이지! 내가 그곳에서 번지 점프를 할 수 있는 특가 여행 패키지 상품을 찾았어. 한 번 해 보는 것에 대해서 어떻게 생각해?

남: 정말 멋지구나! 나에게 더 자세한 세부 사항을 알려 줘.

Topic & Situation Tiwi 섬 번지 점프 여행

Solution

여자는 남자에게 항상 Tiwi 섬에서 번지 점프를 해 보고 싶어 했음을 확인하는 질문을 하고, 남자는 그것이 자신의 버킷 리스트에 있다고 하면서 여자도 관심이 있는지 묻는다. 여자는 그곳에서 번

지 점프를 할 수 있는 특가 여행 패키지 상품을 찾았다고 하면서 남자에게 시도해 보는 것에 대해 어떻게 생각하는지 묻는다. 따라서 여자의 마지막 말에 대한 남자의 응답으로 가장 적절한 것은 ① '정말 멋지구나! 나에게 더 자세한 세부 사항을 알려 줘.'이다.

② 미안해. 그것은 내가 예상했던 것보다 더 비싸.

③ 그거 정말 유감이야! 특가 상품이 언제 끝났니?

④ 번지 점프보다 더 안전한 것을 시도해 보는 게 어때?

⑤ 음, 난 Tiwi 섬에서 다시 번지 점프를 하고 싶지 않아.

Words & Phrases

bucket list 버킷 리스트 give it a try 시도하다 detail 세부 사항 special deal 특가 상품 feel like ~할 마음이 나다

10
정답 | ③

| Script & Translation |

M: Mom, what do you think of the food here? This restaurant is known as the best in this area.

W: Honestly, I don't think the food is that great. Who recommended this restaurant to you?

M: I found it on the Internet. It had great customer reviews.

W: Well, I don't think we can always rely on customer reviews.

남: 엄마, 여기 음식에 대해 어떻게 생각하세요? 이 식당은 이 지역에서 최고라고 알려져 있어요.

여: 솔직히, 음식이 그렇게 훌륭한 것 같지는 않구나. 누가 너에게 이 식당을 추천했니?

남: 인터넷에서 그것을 찾았어요. 고객 후기가 아주 좋았거든요.

여: 음, 우리가 항상 고객 후기에 의존할 수는 없을 것 같구나.

Topic & Situation 온라인 고객 후기

Solution

남자가 여자에게 함께 간 식당의 음식에 대해 어떻게 생각하는지 묻자, 여자는 그다지 마음에 들어하지 않으면서 누가 이 식당을 추천했는지 묻고, 남자는 인터넷에서 찾았다고 하면서 고객 후기가 아주 좋았다고 대답한다. 따라서 남자의 마지막 말에 대한 여자의 응답으로 가장 적절한 것은 ③ '음, 우리가 항상 고객 후기에 의존할 수는 없을 것 같구나.'이다.

① 이 식당은 최근에 가 본 식당 중에서 최고구나.

② 식당 앱을 내려받아서 한번 사용해 봐!

④ 새로운 장소를 방문하기 전에 고객들의 후기를 확인하는 것이 도움이 되는구나.

⑤ 여기 근처에 좋은 식당을 추천해 줄 수 있는지 알고 싶구나.

◉ Words & Phrases

recommend 추천하다   customer review 고객 후기

11

정답 | ③

| Script & Translation |

W: Brian, how was your bike trip with Alice last weekend?

M: It was awesome! Next time we go, you should come with us. You'd love it. How was your weekend?

W: The opposite of yours. It was terrible.

M: Really? What happened?

W: My family went camping near the Ace River, but the weather was really bad. It even rained at times.

M: That's too bad. Rain can completely ruin a camping experience.

W: That wasn't even the worse part. The campground was really crowded and noisy.

M: Oh, no. I'm sorry to hear that.

W: So basically, the entire time we were there, we didn't have a relaxing moment.

M: <u>I understand why you said you had a terrible weekend.</u>

여: Brian, 지난 주말 Alice와의 자전거 여행은 어땠어?

남: 멋졌어! 다음에 갈 때는, 너도 우리와 함께 가야 해. 너도 그것을 아주 좋아할 거야. 네 주말은 어땠어?

여: 너의 주말과는 정반대였어. 끔찍했어.

남: 정말? 무슨 일이 있었는데?

여: 우리 가족이 Ace 강 근처로 캠핑하러 갔는데, 날씨가 정말로 안 좋았어. 심지어 때때로 비까지 내렸어.

남: 너무 안됐다. 비는 캠핑 경험을 완전히 망쳐 버릴 수 있잖아.

여: 그것이 심지어 더 나쁜 부분이 아니었어. 캠핑장이 정말로 붐비고 시끄러웠거든.

남: 오, 안됐네. 그 말을 듣게 되어 유감이야.

여: 그래서 결국 그곳에 있는 내내, 우리는 편안한 시간을 갖지 못했어.

남: <u>네가 왜 끔찍한 주말을 보냈다고 말했는지 이해가 돼.</u>

◉ Topic & Situation 캠핑 여행

◉ Solution

주말을 끔찍하게 보냈다고 말한 여자는 자신이 겪은 부정적인 일을 구체적으로 언급한 후에 마지막으로 캠핑하는 내내 편안한 시간을 갖지 못했다고 말했으므로, 이 말에 대한 남자의 응답으로 가장 적절한 것은 ③ '네가 왜 끔찍한 주말을 보냈다고 말했는지 이해가 돼.'이다.

① 내 자전거 여행이 네 캠핑 여행보다 비용이 더 많이 들었어.

② 나를 돌봐준 네 부모님께 정말로 감사해.

④ 네가 Alice랑 같이 여행을 가자고 주장한 사람이야.

⑤ 지난 주말 캠핑 여행을 너와 함께했어야 했는데.

◉ Words & Phrases

awesome 멋진, 굉장한   opposite 반대; 반대의   completely 완전히   ruin 망치다, 엉망으로 만들다   basically 결국, 기본적으로

12

정답 | ⑤

| Script & Translation |

W: Lena and her husband, Alex, are going to Hawaii. They're both excited to spend time together in the sun, on the beach. As they pack, they notice that one of the wheels on Alex's suitcase is broken. Alex says that he should buy a new suitcase because they will be pulling their suitcases a lot on the trip. But Lena knows they could replace the suitcase wheel quickly and easily since they know the suitcase's brand and wheel type. And she thinks they could save money by replacing the wheel. So, Lena wants to suggest to Alex that he replace the wheel rather than purchase a new suitcase. In this situation, what would Lena most likely say to Alex?

Lena: <u>Instead of buying a new suitcase, why don't you change the wheel?</u>

여: Lena와 그녀의 남편, Alex는 하와이에 갈 예정입니다. 그들은 둘 다 해변에서 햇볕을 쬐며 함께 시간을 보낼 생각에 들떠 있습니다. 짐을 꾸리던 중, 그들은 Alex의 여행 가방 바퀴 중 하나가 고장 난 것을 알아차립니다. Alex는 여행 중에 여행 가방을 많이 끌 것이기 때문에 새 여행 가방을 사야 한다고 말

합니다. 하지만 Lena는 여행 가방의 브랜드와 바퀴 유형을 알고 있기 때문에 여행 가방 바퀴를 빠르고 쉽게 교체할 수 있다는 것을 알고 있습니다. 그리고 그녀는 바퀴를 교체함으로써 비용을 절약할 수 있다고 생각합니다. 그래서 Lena는 Alex에게 새 여행 가방을 구입하는 대신 바퀴를 교체할 것을 제안하고 싶습니다. 이런 상황에서, Lena는 Alex에게 뭐라고 말하겠습니까?

Lena: 새 여행 가방을 사는 대신 그 바퀴를 바꾸는 게 어때요?

▶ **Topic & Situation** 여행용 가방 바퀴 수리

▶ **Solution**

Lena와 Alex가 하와이 여행을 준비하며 짐을 꾸리던 중에 Alex의 여행 가방 바퀴 중 하나가 고장 난 것을 알게 되고, Alex는 새 여행 가방을 사야 한다고 말하지만, Lena는 바퀴를 쉽고 빠르게 교체할 수 있고, 그렇게 해서 비용을 절약할 수 있다고 생각하여 Alex에게 새 여행 가방을 구입하는 대신 바퀴를 교체할 것을 제안하고 싶은 상황이다. 따라서 Lena가 Alex에게 할 말로 가장 적절한 것은 ⑤ '새 여행 가방을 사는 대신 그 바퀴를 바꾸는 게 어때요?'이다.

① 여행에 적합한 종류의 가방을 선택하는 것이 좋을 거예요.
② 새 여행 가방을 살 때는 크기가 중요한 요소예요.
③ 여행 가방에 공간이 더 필요하면, 옷을 돌돌 말아 넣어요.
④ 사륜구동 자동차를 빌려서 그 섬을 돌아다니는 게 어때요?

▶ **Words & Phrases**

pack (짐을) 꾸리다[싸다]   wheel 바퀴   suitcase 여행 가방
replace 교체하다, 바꾸다

03 ❶ almost like being
   ❷ end up renting this
   ❸ two cushions on it
04 ❶ the schedule and the route
   ❷ ordered sandwiches and water
   ❸ appreciate your help
05 ❶ would like to purchase tickets
   ❷ get 10% off
   ❸ watching the magic show
06 ❶ keeps you in good shape
   ❷ for local charities
   ❸ has a talent show
07 ❶ interested in broadcasting
   ❷ should register soon
   ❸ explore the fascinating world
08 ❶ doing a water activity
   ❷ these three options left
   ❸ be safer and easier
09 ❶ on my bucket list
   ❷ special travel package deal
10 ❶ known as the best
   ❷ great customer reviews
11 ❶ completely ruin
   ❷ crowded and noisy
12 ❶ As they pack
   ❷ buy a new suitcase
   ❸ replace the suitcase wheel
   ❹ rather than purchase

(Dictations)   본문 131, 136~139쪽

기출 ❶ animal camp for kids
예제 ❷ under the guidance
01 ❶ regarding our return flight
   ❷ than our original plan
   ❸ considering the flight changes
02 ❶ keeping your money safe
   ❷ recommend keeping enough to cover
   ❸ not easily accessible or visible

20강 정보 통신, 방송, 사교 활동

본문 140~145쪽

기출예제 ②

Exercises 01 ⑤ 02 ② 03 ⑤ 04 ② 05 ③ 06 ④
07 ⑤ 08 ⑤ 09 ③ 10 ① 11 ③ 12 ④

기출 예제

본문 140쪽

정답 | ②

| Script & Translation |

W: Attention, H-rail train passengers. We would like to introduce a new website called Found 211 to help you find your lost items. Found 211 provides information about items you've lost on H-rail trains. To use Found 211, you first have to be a member of the website. Then, you need to post the details of your lost items to the website. If your lost items are found, Found 211 will inform you by a text message. In addition, foreign language services are provided in various languages, including French, Spanish and Chinese. You can also use Found 211 through our mobile application. We hope you have a pleasant trip to your destination. Thank you.

여: H-rail 기차 승객 여러분, 주목해 주세요. 여러분이 분실한 물건을 찾는 것을 도와 드릴 Found 211이라는 새 웹사이트를 소개하려고 합니다. Found 211은 여러분이 H-rail 기차에서 분실한 물건에 관한 정보를 제공합니다. Found 211을 이용하기 위해서는 먼저 그 웹사이트의 회원이어야 합니다. 그다음에 여러분은 분실물의 세부 사항을 그 웹사이트에 게시해야 합니다. 여러분의 분실물이 발견되면 Found 211이 문자 메시지로 여러분에게 알려 드릴 것입니다. 게다가 프랑스어, 스페인어, 중국어를 포함한 다양한 언어로 외국어 서비스가 제공됩니다. 저희 모바일 앱을 통해서도 Found 211을 사용하실 수 있습니다. 여러분의 목적지까지 즐거운 여행을 하시기를 바랍니다. 감사합니다.

◐ Topic & Situation 웹사이트 소개

◐ Solution

Found 211을 이용하려면, 웹사이트 회원이어야 한다고 했으므로, Found 211에 관한 내용과 일치하지 않는 것은 ② '웹사이트 회원이 아니어도 사용할 수 있다.'이다.

◐ Words & Phrases

passenger 승객   inform 알리다, 통지하다   destination 목적지

Exercises

본문 142~145쪽

01

정답 | ⑤

| Script & Translation |

M: Hi, everyone! Welcome back to my online channel, *Digital World*. I'm happy to see you again. Today, I'd like to talk to you about two important things to keep in mind when communicating online. First, do not give out your personal information, such as your address or phone number, because it can be used improperly. Second, always follow basic communication manners, just like when talking in person. For example, say hello and goodbye when you start and end a chat, and avoid using language that can hurt other people's feelings. Please keep watching the monitor. I'll show you further examples of good online communication.

남: 안녕하세요, 여러분! 제 온라인 채널, *Digital World*에 다시 오신 것을 환영합니다. 여러분을 다시 만나서 기쁩니다. 오늘 저는 온라인에서 의사소통할 때 명심해야 할 중요한 두 가지에 대해 여러분에게 말씀드리겠습니다. 첫째, 주소나 전화번호와 같은 개인 정보는 부적절하게 사용될 수 있으므로 알려주지 마세요. 둘째, 직접 대화할 때와 마찬가지로 언제나 기본적인 의사소통 예절을 따르세요. 예를 들어, 대화를 시작할 때와 끝낼 때 인사말과 작별 인사를 하고, 다른 사람의 기분을 상하게 할 수 있는 언어의 사용을 피하십시오. 계속 화면을 봐 주세요. 좋은 온라인 의사소통의 사례를 더 보여 드리겠습니다.

◐ Topic & Situation 온라인 의사소통 시 유의 사항

◐ Solution

온라인 채널 *Digital World*의 진행자인 남자는 온라인에서 의사소통할 때 유의해야 할 두 가지 사항에 대해 안내하고 있으므로, 남자가 하는 말의 목적으로 가장 적절한 것은 ⑤ '온라인 의사

소통 시 유의 사항을 알려주려고'이다.

○ **Words & Phrases**
keep ~ in mind ~을 명심하다   improperly 부적절하게   avoid 피하다

02
정답 | ②

| Script & Translation |

W: Hello, parents! As an expert in child education, I know your concerns about the amount of time your kids spend on screen. While digital devices can be distracting, they hold the potential to bring your family closer. So make time each week for video calls with your child to discuss their day, listen to their thoughts, and provide guidance. Use messaging apps to share funny photos and inspiring quotes, or to simply say "I love you." Social media can also be a platform to celebrate your child's achievements and share significant family events. By using these digital tools, you can develop a deeper connection with your child. Thank you for your attention!

여: 안녕하세요, 부모님 여러분! 아동 교육 전문가로서, 저는 자녀들이 화면을 보는 데 쏟는 시간의 양에 대한 여러분의 걱정에 대해 알고 있습니다. 디지털 기기는 주의를 분산시킬 수 있지만, 가족을 더 가깝게 이어줄 수 있는 잠재력을 가지고 있습니다. 따라서 매주 자녀와 화상 통화를 할 수 있는 시간을 만들어 자녀의 하루에 대해 논의하고, 그들의 생각을 듣고, 지침을 제공해 주세요. 메시지 앱을 사용하여 재미있는 사진과 영감을 주는 인용문을 공유하거나 단순히 "나는 너를 사랑해."라고 말하세요. 소셜 미디어는 또한 자녀의 성취를 축하하고 특별한 의미가 있는 가족의 행사를 공유하는 플랫폼이 될 수 있습니다. 이러한 디지털 도구를 사용함으로써, 여러분은 자녀와 더 깊은 관계를 발전시킬 수 있습니다. 경청해 주셔서 감사합니다!

○ **Topic & Situation** 자녀와의 관계 강화를 위한 디지털 도구 활용

○ **Solution**
여자는 아이들이 화면을 보는 데 쏟는 시간 때문에 부모님들의 걱정이 많은 줄 알지만, 디지털 기기가 주의를 분산시킴에도 불구하고 가족을 더 가깝게 이어줄 수 있는 잠재력을 가지고 있다고 말하면서, 디지털 도구를 사용할 수 있는 다양한 방법을 소개하고 이를 통해 자녀와 더 깊은 관계를 발전시킬 수 있다고 말한다. 따라서, 여자가 하는 말의 요지로 가장 적절한 것은 ② '디지털 도구의 활용은 자녀와의 관계 강화에 도움이 된다.'이다.

○ **Words & Phrases**
concern 걱정, 우려   device 기기, 장치   distracting 주의를 분산시키는   potential 잠재력, 가능성   quote 인용문   celebrate 축하하다, 기념하다   achievement 성취, 업적   significant 특별한 의미가 있는, 중요한   connection 관계, 연결

03
정답 | ⑤

| Script & Translation |

M: Hi, Lisa. How was your weekend?
W: Hi, Ryan. It was super fun. I went to the filming site of the TV show *Love in Heaven*. Look at this picture.
M: Wow, it looks cool. There's a standing signboard showing a picture of the two main characters on the beach.
W: Right. That's the exact spot where the opening scene of the show was shot.
M: I remember! And look, there is a piano on the round stage!
W: Yeah. It's the actual piano the actors used in the show. And do you remember the bicycle in front of the house?
M: Sure! The main characters rode the bicycle together in the show, right?
W: Right. I think the parasol and the chairs next to the house look nice.
M: So do I. The boat floating in the sea also makes the scenery look romantic.
W: I agree. Visitors can take a boat ride there.
M: Sounds nice! After seeing this picture, I need to go there sometime.
W: I highly recommend it.

남: 안녕, Lisa. 주말은 어떻게 보냈니?
여: 안녕, Ryan. 무척 재밌었어. 나는 TV 쇼 *Love In Heaven* 촬영 현장에 갔어. 이 사진 좀 봐.

남: 와, 멋져 보인다. 해변에 두 주인공의 사진을 보여 주는 입간
판이 있네.

여: 맞아. 그곳이 그 쇼의 오프닝 장면이 촬영된 바로 그 장소야.

남: 기억나! 그리고 봐, 둥근 무대 위에 피아노가 한 대 있구나!

여: 그래. 그것은 배우들이 쇼에서 사용했던 실제 피아노야. 그리
고 집 앞에 있는 자전거를 기억하니?

남: 물론이지! 주인공들이 쇼에서 그 자전거를 함께 탔잖아, 맞지?

여: 맞아. 나는 그 집 옆에 있는 파라솔과 의자들이 멋진 것 같아.

남: 나도 그렇게 생각해. 바다에 떠 있는 배도 경치를 낭만적으로
보이게 해.

여: 동의해. 방문객들은 그곳에서 배 타기를 할 수 있어.

남: 멋진 것 같아! 이 사진을 보고 나니, 언젠가 그곳에 가봐야겠
구나.

여: 그것을 강력하게 추천해.

● **Topic & Situation** TV 쇼 촬영지 방문 여행

● **Solution**
대화에서 바다에 배가 떠 있다고 말했는데, 그림에서는 배가 해변
의 땅 위에 있으므로, 그림에서 대화의 내용과 일치하지 않는 것
은 ⑤이다.

● **Words & Phrases**
filming 촬영 standing signboard 입간판 spot 장소 parasol
파라솔 scenery 경치

04
정답 | ②

| Script & Translation |

W: Hey, Rogan, how's the preparation for the community
dance night coming along?

M: We're making good progress. The place has been
booked, and the invitations have been sent out.

W: That's great to hear. Have you finalized the menu?

M: Yes, we've settled on serving sandwiches and chips.

W: Sounds like a delicious and convenient choice. What
about the music?

M: We've hired a country band for some lively tunes.

W: That's fantastic! And how is the dance hall setup
going?

M: It's currently underway. The volunteers are busy
decorating the hall, and I'll be checking on their
progress later.

W: If you need any extra hands, I'm here to help.

M: Actually, since you have experience with sound
systems, we could really use your expertise in setting
up the speakers.

W: I can handle that. I'll head over now to take care of it.

M: Thank you so much for offering your help. We truly
appreciate it!

여: 안녕하세요, Rogan, 커뮤니티 야간 무도회 준비는 어떻게 되
어 가고 있나요?

남: 잘 진행되고 있어요. 장소를 예약했고, 초대장을 발송했어요.

여: 그 말을 들으니 좋군요. 메뉴는 확정 지었어요?

남: 네, 샌드위치와 감자 칩을 제공하기로 했어요.

여: 맛있고 편리한 선택인 것 같네요. 음악은요?

남: 우리는 활기찬 곡을 연주할 컨트리 밴드를 고용했어요.

여: 멋져요! 그리고 무도회장 설치는 어떻게 되어가고 있나요?

남: 현재 진행 중이에요. 자원봉사자들이 무도회장을 꾸미느라 바
쁘고, 저는 나중에 그들의 진행 상황을 점검할 거예요.

여: 일손이 더 필요하면, 제가 도와드릴 준비가 되어 있어요.

남: 사실, 당신이 음향 시스템에 대한 경험이 있으니까, 우리는 스
피커를 설치하는 데 당신의 전문 지식이 정말 좀 필요해요.

여: 그건 제가 다룰 수 있어요. 제가 지금 거기로 가서 그것을 처
리할게요.

남: 도움을 줘서 정말 고맙습니다. 진심으로 감사드려요!

● **Topic & Situation** 커뮤니티 야간 무도회 준비

● **Solution**
커뮤니티 야간 무도회를 준비하고 있는 남자가 일손이 필요하면
도와주겠다는 여자에게 스피커를 설치하는 데 여자의 전문 지식
이 필요하다고 말했고 여자가 지금 가서 처리하겠다고 답했으므
로, 여자가 할 일로 가장 적절한 것은 ② '스피커 설치하기'이다.

● **Words & Phrases**
preparation 준비 progress 진행, 진척 finalize 확정 짓다, 최종
적으로 결정하다 settle on ~을 결정하다, ~을 선택하다 lively 활
기찬, 생동감 있는 tune 곡, 곡조, 선율 setup 설치, 준비
underway 진행 중인 extra hand 추가적인 도움 expertise 전문
지식 handle 다루다, 처리하다 head 가다, 향하다

05

정답 | ③

| Script & Translation |

W: Hi, how may I help you?

M: Hi. I need to send two packages to Miami, one containing clothes and the other containing books.

W: All right. Let me weigh them. *[Pause]* One is 5 kg and the other 15 kg. Which shipping service would you like?

M: I need them to arrive in 3 days, so I think priority mail express would be suitable.

W: Okay. The lighter package will be $25, and the heavier one will be $35. Would you like to add any insurance to the packages?

M: No, thanks. But I'd like to purchase four sets of large bubble envelopes.

W: Okay. They're $10 per set.

M: All right. And I've heard that there's a card that offers discounts on postal fees.

W: Right. If you pay with an ABC card, you can receive a 10% discount on the postage, but not on the bubble envelopes.

M: Sounds great! Here's my ABC card.

여: 안녕하세요, 어떻게 도와드릴까요?

남: 안녕하세요. 마이애미로 두 개의 소포를 보내야 하는데, 하나 는 옷이 들어 있고, 다른 하나는 책이 들어 있어요.

여: 좋아요. 제가 무게를 달아 볼게요. *[잠시 후]* 하나는 5kg이고, 다른 하나는 15kg입니다. 어떤 배송 서비스를 이용하시겠어 요?

남: 3일 안에 도착해야 해서, 우선 취급 우편이 적절할 것 같아요.

여: 알겠습니다. 가벼운 소포는 25달러이고, 무거운 것은 35달러 가 되겠습니다. 소포에 보험을 추가하시겠어요?

남: 아니요, 괜찮습니다. 그런데 큰 버블 봉투 네 세트를 구매하고 싶습니다.

여: 알겠습니다. 한 세트당 10달러에요.

남: 좋아요. 그리고 우편 요금 할인을 제공하는 카드가 있다고 들 었어요.

여: 맞습니다. ABC 카드로 결제하시면 우편 요금에서 10% 할 인을 받을 수 있지만, 버블 봉투에는 적용되지 않습니다.

남: 잘됐네요! 여기 제 ABC 카드가 있습니다.

● Topic & Situation 우체국에서 소포 부치기

● Solution

남자는 마이애미로 두 개의 소포를 보내면서 각각 25달러와 35

달러의 우편 요금을 내야 하고, 한 세트에 10달러인 큰 버블 봉투 네 세트를 구입한다. 남자는 ABC 카드를 가지고 있고, 이 카드 로 결제하면 우편 요금에 대해서는 10% 할인을 받을 수 있다. 따 라서 남자가 지불할 금액은 ③ '$94'이다.

● Words & Phrases

package 소포   contain ~이 들어 있다. 포함하다   weigh 무게를 달다   priority mail express 우선 취급 우편, 특송 우편   suitable 적절한, 적합한   insurance 보험   purchase 구매하다   postage 우편 요금. 우송료

06

정답 | ④

| Script & Translation |

[Telephone rings.]

M: Hello. Is this Jenny Park? This is your math teacher.

W: Oh, hi, Mr. Kim.

M: Hi, Jenny. I was surprised that you missed my online math class yesterday.

W: I'm sorry, Mr. Kim. I just got confused.

M: Oh! It can be hard to learn new technologies. Do you need help with your computer?

W: No, it's okay. I know how to log on to online classes.

M: Oh? Then what happened?

W: Well, I received the text message you sent about class, but I thought the first class was on Friday.

M: Oh, I see. I guess you know now that yesterday was our first class.

W: Yes, I'm sorry. I promise I won't mix the days up again.

M: Okay, Jenny. Be sure to be present next time.

[전화벨이 울린다.]

남: 여보세요. Jenny Park이니? 난 네 수학 선생님이야.

여: 오, 안녕하세요, Kim 선생님.

남: 안녕, Jenny. 나는 어제 네가 온라인 수학 수업에 빠져서 놀랐 어.

여: 정말 죄송해요, Kim 선생님. 저는 그저 혼동을 했을 뿐이에 요.

남: 오! 새로운 기술을 배우는 것은 어려울 수 있어. 컴퓨터 관련 하여 도움이 필요하니?

여: 오, 아니에요. 온라인 수업에 접속하는 법은 알고 있어요.

남: 그래? 그러면 무슨 일이 있었던 거니?

여: 그게, 선생님이 보내주신 수업에 관한 문자 메시지를 받았는데, 첫 번째 수업이 금요일인줄 알았어요.

남: 오, 그랬구나. 이제는 어제가 첫 수업이었다는 것을 네가 알게 되었겠구나.

여: 네, 죄송해요. 다시는 날짜를 혼동하지 않겠다고 약속드릴게요.

남: 알겠다. Jenny. 다음번에는 꼭 출석하도록 하렴.

◉ **Topic & Situation** 온라인 수업에 결석한 이유

◉ **Solution**

남자는 여자에게 어제 온라인 수업에 빠진 사실을 언급하며, 무슨 일이 있었는지 묻고 있다. 남자가 여자에게 컴퓨터 관련 문제 때문인지 묻자, 여자는 아니라고 하고, 일정에 대해서도 메시지를 받았다고 말하며, 첫 번째 수업을 금요일로 혼동해서 빠진 것이라고 대답하며 사과한다. 따라서 여자가 어제 온라인 수업에 결석한 이유는 ④ '수업 일정을 혼동해서'이다.

◉ **Words & Phrases**

confused 혼동된 mix up ~을 혼동하다

07
정답 | ⑤

| Script & Translation |

M: Alice, have you heard about the new program, *Amazing World*, starting on WBS next week?

W: No, I haven't. What type of program is it?

M: It's a reality program about cool travel destinations.

W: Oh, I like reality programs about traveling. Who hosts the program?

M: Olivia Jackson!

W: Really? She's my favorite comedian. What time is the program being broadcast?

M: It starts at 7 p.m. every Friday from next week.

W: Cool. Do you know which travel destinations the program visits?

M: I heard that some Asian cities, such as Seoul and Bangkok, will appear in the first episode.

W: Sounds interesting. I'm sure it'll attract many viewers, including me.

M: I think so, too. It's going to be a popular show.

남: Alice, 다음 주에 WBS에서 시작하는 새 프로그램, *Amazing World*에 대해 들어 봤어요?

여: 아니요, 못 들었어요. 그것은 어떤 유형의 프로그램인가요?

남: 멋진 여행지에 대한 리얼리티 프로그램이에요.

여: 오, 나는 여행에 관한 리얼리티 프로그램을 좋아해요. 누가 그 프로그램을 진행하나요?

남: Olivia Jackson이요!

여: 정말이요? 그녀는 내가 제일 좋아하는 코미디언이에요. 그 프로그램은 몇 시에 방송되나요?

남: 다음 주부터 매주 금요일 저녁 7시에 시작해요.

여: 멋지네요. 프로그램에서 어떤 여행지를 방문하는지 알고 있나요?

남: 첫 회에는 서울과 방콕 같은 몇몇 아시아 도시가 나올 것이라고 들었어요.

여: 흥미롭네요. 이것은 저를 포함한 많은 시청자들의 관심을 끌 것 같아요.

남: 저도 그렇게 생각해요. 인기 있는 쇼가 될 거예요.

◉ **Topic & Situation** 여행 프로그램 *Amazing World*

◉ **Solution**

프로그램 유형, 진행자, 방영 시간, 방영 예정 도시는 언급되었지만, ⑤ '총 방영 횟수'는 언급되지 않았다.

◉ **Words & Phrases**

destination (여행의) 목적지, 행선지 host 진행하다, 주최하다 broadcast 방송하다 attract 마음을 끌다

08
정답 | ⑤

| Script & Translation |

W: Hello, listeners. I'm Sharon Parker, CEO of the Lanyard Broadcasting Company. I'm happy to announce the official opening of the Lanyard Museum of Broadcasting on May 24th. Our museum displays all sorts of radio and television technology from throughout the decades, which is sure to delight the young and old alike. We even have quite a few vintage radios and televisions made before 1950 that are still working. Also, our guides are media engineers who can't wait to take visitors around and demonstrate how broadcasting devices work. We're only open on Fridays and Saturdays, so plan your visit accordingly. Plus, on the grand opening day only, admission is free for all visitors. So come and enjoy a wonderful display of broadcasting history! Thanks for listening.

여: 안녕하세요, 청취자 여러분. 저는 Lanyard 방송사의 CEO인 Sharon Parker입니다. 5월 24일 Lanyard 방송 박물관의 공식 개관을 발표하게 되어 기쁘게 생각합니다. 우리 박물관은 수십 년 동안의 모든 종류의 라디오와 텔레비전 장비를 전시하여 젊은 사람과 나이 든 사람 모두를 틀림없이 즐겁게 해줄 것입니다. 저희는 지금도 작동하는 1950년 이전에 만들어진 지난 시대의 라디오와 텔레비전도 꽤 많이 소장하고 있습니다. 또한 저희의 가이드는 방문객을 안내하고 방송 장비가 어떻게 작동하는지 시연하기를 고대하는 미디어 엔지니어들입니다. 저희는 금요일과 토요일에만 문을 열므로 방문 일정을 그에 맞추어 계획하시기를 바랍니다. 또한 개관 행사일 당일에만 모든 방문객은 무료로 입장합니다. 그러니 오셔서 방송 역사의 멋진 전시를 즐겨보세요! 들어 주셔서 감사합니다.

○ **Topic & Situation** Lanyard 방송 박물관 개관

○ **Solution**
금요일과 토요일에만 문을 연다고 했으므로, 담화의 내용과 일치하지 않는 것은 ⑤ '매주 토요일과 일요일에만 문을 연다.'이다.

○ **Words & Phrases**
broadcasting company 방송사 opening 개관, 개장 display 전시하다; 전시 technology 장비, 기계 decade 10년 delight 즐겁게 하다 demonstrate 시연하다 accordingly 그에 맞추어

09
정답 | ③

| Script & Translation |

W: David, I sent you an email regarding the details of our upcoming presentation. Did you get it?

M: I checked my email last night, but I didn't see it. When did you send it?

W: I sent it this morning. I'm sorry I sent it a little late. Can you make sure you got it?

M: No problem. I'll check my email right away.

여: David, 곧 있을 우리 발표의 세부 사항에 관하여 이메일을 당신에게 보냈습니다. 그것을 받으셨나요?

남: 어젯밤에 제 이메일을 확인했지만, 보지 못했습니다. 언제 그것을 보내셨나요?

여: 오늘 아침에 보냈습니다. 조금 늦게 보내서 죄송합니다. 당신이 그것을 받았는지 확인해 줄 수 있을까요?

남: 문제없습니다. 제 이메일을 바로 확인해 볼게요.

○ **Topic & Situation** 이메일 수신 확인 요청

○ **Solution**
여자가 남자에게 곧 있을 발표의 세부 사항에 관하여 이메일을 보냈는데 이를 확인했는지 묻자, 남자가 어젯밤에 자신의 이메일을 확인했지만 보지 못했다고 한다. 이에 여자가 자신이 오늘 아침에 보냈다고 하면서, 이메일을 받았는지 확인해 줄 수 있는지를 묻고 있으므로, 남자의 응답으로 가장 적절한 것은 ③ '문제없습니다. 제 이메일을 바로 확인해 볼게요.'이다.

① 오, 안 돼! 그것에 파일을 첨부하는 것을 잊었어요.
② 맞아요. 제 발표를 끝냈습니다.
④ 걱정 마세요. 당신은 노트북을 사용할 수 있습니다.
⑤ 물론이죠. 당신 이메일 주소를 제게 알려주세요.

○ **Words & Phrases**
regarding ~에 관하여 upcoming 곧 있을, 다가오는 attach 첨부하다

10
정답 | ①

| Script & Translation |

M: Ms. Hoffman, how do you feel about the art museum?

W: I love it. It's wonderful. I love seeing all the different forms of art.

M: Me, too. I'm surprised to see so many people here. I didn't expect it to be so popular.

W: I know! More and more people seem to be taking an interest in art these days.

M: Yes. I noticed young people are especially interested in the Jeremy Cooper exhibit.

W: He's really popular on social media nowadays.

M: Oh, really? What do you think of his paintings then?

W: I think they're really creative. I like the way he uses shadows. How about you?

M: To be honest, they're unfamiliar and a bit strange to me.

W: I can understand that. They're pretty abstract, which some people don't like.

M: Oh, is that so? Maybe that's why I'm not much of a fan.

W: That's okay. It's all a matter of personal taste.

남: Hoffman 씨, 미술관에 대해 어떻게 생각하세요?

여: 아주 마음에 듭니다. 멋져요. 저는 모든 다양한 형태의 예술을 보는 것을 좋아하거든요.

남: 저도요. 여기서 그렇게 많은 사람들을 보게 되어 놀랐어요. 이렇게 인기가 많을 거라고는 예상 못 했거든요.

여: 그러게요! 요즘 예술에 관심을 갖는 사람들이 점점 더 많아지고 있는 것 같아요.

남: 맞아요. 젊은 사람들이 특히 Jeremy Cooper 전시회에 특별히 관심이 있더라고요.

여: 요즘은 그가 소셜 미디어에서 정말 인기가 많아요.

남: 아, 정말요? 그럼 당신은 그의 그림들에 대해 어떻게 생각하세요?

여: 저는 아주 창의적이라고 생각해요. 저는 그가 그림자를 이용하는 방식이 마음에 들어요. 당신은 어떻게 생각하세요?

남: 솔직히, 그것들이 저에게는 낯설고 조금 이상해요.

여: 이해할 수 있어요. 그것들은 꽤 추상적이라서 어떤 사람들은 좋아하지 않아요.

남: 아, 그런가요? 아마 그래서 제가 그다지 팬은 아닌가 봐요.

여: 괜찮아요. 그것은 모두 개인적인 취향의 문제예요.

◑ Topic & Situation 미술관 관람

◑ Solution

Jeremy Cooper의 그림이 아주 창의적이라고 생각하는 여자가 남자에게 그의 그림에 대해 어떻게 생각하는지 묻자, 남자는 자신에게는 그의 그림들이 낯설고 조금 이상하다고 하자 여자는 그것들이 꽤 추상적이라서 어떤 사람들은 좋아하지 않는다는 의견을 전해준다. 여자의 말을 듣고 남자가 아마 그래서 자신이 그다지 팬은 아닌 것 같다고 부정적인 대답을 했으므로, 남자의 마지막 말에 대한 여자의 응답으로 가장 적절한 것은 ① '괜찮아요. 그것은 모두 개인적인 취향의 문제예요.'이다.

② 음, 당신 말뜻은 이해하지만, 나는 여전히 그것들을 좋아하지 않아요.

③ 미안해요. 저는 당신과 함께 사진 전시회에 갈 수 없어요.

④ 예술에 관해서라면, 저는 미술관에 오는 걸 좋아해요.

⑤ 그래서 젊은 사람들이 그의 전시회에 무관심해요.

◑ Words & Phrases

exhibit 전시회, 전시품   creative 창의적인   shadow 그림자, 그늘
unfamiliar 낯선, 익숙지 않은   abstract 추상적인   not much of a

그다지[그렇게] ~는 아닌   **when it comes to** ~에 관해서라면
indifferent 무관심한, 냉담한

11~12

정답 | 11 ③ 12 ④

| Script & Translation |

W: Hello, everybody. I'm Kerry McDonnell, the activity director here at Greenville Senior Center. We really enjoy providing our community's seniors with fun activities, but today I'd like to recommend some social activities to help you stay healthy. Just going for a walk with friends is one of the best activities. With only a pair of walking shoes, you can combine fitness and socializing at the same time. Gardening with others is also an enjoyable social activity. Digging, planting and weeding with someone while you talk about plants provide you with not only exercise but also opportunities for pleasant socialization. Or if you love to sing, singing regularly in a group a few times a week is perfect. Singing with others helps improve mental health and boosts self-confidence. Dancing is another social activity since it normally requires a partner. It's not only a lot of fun, but it's also a great mind and body workout. If you're interested in these activities, why don't you get started today?

여: 안녕하세요, 여러분. 저는 여기 Greenville Senior Center의 활동 책임자인 Kerry McDonnell입니다. 우리는 우리 지역 사회의 어르신들에게 재미있는 활동을 제공하는 것을 정말 좋아하는데, 오늘 저는 여러분이 건강을 유지하는 데 도움이 되는 사교 활동 몇 가지를 추천하고 싶습니다. 친구들과 산책만 하는 것도 최고의 활동 중 하나입니다. 단 한 켤레의 워킹화만 있으면, 여러분은 신체 건강과 사교를 동시에 결합할 수 있습니다. 다른 사람들과 정원을 가꾸는 것도 즐거운 사교 활동입니다. 식물에 대해 이야기하면서 누군가와 함께 땅을 파고, 심고, 잡초를 뽑는 것은 여러분에게 운동뿐만 아니라 즐거운 사교의 기회를 줍니다. 또는 만약 여러분이 노래하는 것을 좋아한다면, 일주일에 몇 번씩 정기적으로 모임에서 노래하는 것은 더할 나위 없이 좋습니다. 다른 사람들과 함께 노래하는 것은 정신 건강을 향상시키고 자신감을 증진시키는 데 도움이

됩니다. 춤추기는 보통 파트너를 필요로 하기 때문에 또 다른 사교 활동입니다. 그것은 매우 재미있을 뿐만 아니라, 훌륭한 심신 운동입니다. 이런 활동들에 관심이 있으시다면, 오늘 당장 시작해 보시는 것은 어떨까요?

● **Topic & Situation** 노인들이 참여할 수 있는 건강에 이로운 사교 활동

● **Solution**

11 여자는 노인들이 건강을 유지하는 데 도움이 되면서 다른 사람과 함께할 수 있는 사교 활동을 소개하고 있다. 그러므로 여자가 하는 말의 목적으로 가장 적절한 것은 ③ '노인들에게 건강에 이로운 사교 활동들을 소개하려고'이다.

12 산책하기, 정원 가꾸기, 노래 부르기, 춤추기는 언급되었지만 ④ '그림 그리기'는 언급되지 않았다.

● **Words & Phrases**

senior 어르신, 연장자 recommend 추천하다 combine 결합하다 socializing 사교 dig 땅을 파다 weed 잡초를 뽑다 boost 증진시키다, 북돋다 self-confidence 자신감

05 ❶ the other containing books
   ❷ priority mail express
   ❸ discounts on postal fees
06 ❶ missed my online math class
   ❷ to learn new technologies
   ❸ mix the days up
07 ❶ cool travel destinations
   ❷ being broadcast
   ❸ attract many viewers
08 ❶ throughout the decades
   ❷ that are still working
   ❸ plan your visit accordingly
09 ❶ regarding the details of
   ❷ make sure you got it
10 ❶ taking an interest in
   ❷ unfamiliar and a bit strange
   ❸ not much of a fan
11~12 ❶ recommend some social activities
   ❷ stay healthy
   ❸ Gardening
   ❹ pleasant socialization
   ❺ requires a partner

Dictations   본문 141, 146~149쪽

기출 ❶ find your lost items
예제 ❷ post the details
     ❸ through our mobile application
01 ❶ communicating online
   ❷ be used improperly
   ❸ avoid using language
02 ❶ hold the potential
   ❷ provide guidance
   ❸ using these digital tools
03 ❶ two main characters
   ❷ rode the bicycle
   ❸ floating in the sea
04 ❶ finalized the menu
   ❷ busy decorating the hall
   ❸ use your expertise

21강 가사, 쇼핑, 직장 업무

본문 150~155쪽

기출예제 ①

Exercises 01 ⑤ 02 ① 03 ⑤ 04 ⑤ 05 ② 06 ②
07 ④ 08 ③ 09 ⑤ 10 ② 11 ① 12 ④

기출 예제

본문 150쪽

정답 | ①

| Script & Translation |

W: Honey, our moving day is coming up in two weeks.

M: Yeah. I think we need to check our to-do list again.

W: Okay. We got the confirmation from the moving company for the date, right?

M: Yes, we did. Did you sign up for the Internet at our new place?

W: Uh-huh, I did. It should be connected by the move-in date. And I already put stickers on the chairs we will throw away.

M: Great. Oh, I still have to wrap the crystal vases.

W: That's okay. You have time. Did you call our son's new school? Did they tell you what he needs to take with him on his first day?

M: Yes, he has to bring the uniform for his gym class. Oh, we forgot to make a reservation with the cleaning company.

W: No worries. I'll do it right now.

M: Thanks.

여: 여보, 우리의 이삿날이 2주 앞으로 다가왔어요.

남: 네. 우리는 우리의 할 일 목록을 다시 확인해야 할 것 같아요.

여: 알겠어요. 우리는 이삿짐을 운송하는 회사에서 날짜를 확인받았지요, 그렇죠?

남: 네, 그랬어요. 우리의 새집에서 인터넷에 가입했나요?

여: 아, 했어요. 입주일까지는 인터넷이 연결될 거예요. 그리고 버릴 의자들에 내가 이미 스티커를 붙였어요.

남: 좋군요. 오, 나는 아직 크리스털 꽃병들을 포장해야 해요.

여: 괜찮아요. 그걸 하세요. 우리 아들의 새 학교에 전화했나요? 학교에서 그 애가 첫날 무엇을 가져가야 하는지 말했나요?

남: 네, 그 애는 체육 수업에 입을 유니폼을 가져가야 해요. 오, 우리는 청소 회사에

예약하는 걸 잊었어요.

여: 걱정하지 말아요. 내가 지금 바로 할게요.

남: 고마워요.

○ Topic & Situation 이사를 위해 할 일 확인

○ Solution

두 사람은 이사를 위해 할 일들을 확인하고 있는데, 남자가 청소 업체에 예약하는 것을 잊었다고 하자 여자가 그것을 하겠다고 말했으므로, 여자가 할 일로 가장 적절한 것은 ① '청소 업체 예약하기'이다.

○ Words & Phrases

to-do list 할 일 목록   crystal 크리스털(유리의 일종)   reservation 예약

Exercises

본문 152~155쪽

01

정답 | ⑤

| Script & Translation |

W: Honey, I think we need to clean out the fridge. There are so many things that we're never going to eat.

M: Totally. I'm sure there are also a bunch of things that are expired.

W: For sure there are.

M: We always buy more than we need, which is a waste of food and money. Let's try to stop doing that from now on.

W: Okay. How should we try to do that?

M: I think we should make a list before we go shopping.

W: What do you mean?

M: We can go through the fridge and see what we're running out of, and then write down what we need.

W: So, you mean keep a grocery list?

M: Exactly. If we stick to the list, we won't buy things that we don't really need just because they're on sale.

W: Sounds like a good plan. Let's start doing that.

M: I'm sure that'll help us control our spending.

여: 여보, 냉장고를 청소해야 할 것 같아요. 우리가 절대 먹지 않을 것들이 아주 많이 있어요.

남: 전적으로 동의해요. 유통 기한이 지난 것들도 많이 있을 거라 확신해요.

여: 물론 있죠.

남: 우리는 항상 우리가 필요한 것보다 더 많이 구매하는데, 이것은 음식과 돈을 낭비하는 것이에요. 이제부터 이런 일은 그만하도록 노력해봐요.

여: 그래요. 어떻게 우리가 그것을 위해 노력해야 할까요?

남: 내 생각에는 쇼핑하러 가기 전에 목록을 작성해야 할 것 같아요.

여: 그게 무슨 뜻이에요?

남: 우리는 냉장고를 뒤져서, 무엇이 부족한지 보고, 그리고 나서 우리가 필요한 것을 적을 수 있어요.

여: 그러니까, 식료품 목록을 만들자는 이야기인가요?

남: 맞아요. 만약 그 목록을 고수한다면, 우리가 정말 필요로 하지 않은 물건을 단지 할인한다는 이유로 사지는 않을 거예요.

여: 좋은 계획으로 들리네요. 그렇게 하도록 시작해 봐요.

남: 그것이 우리가 소비를 조절하는 데 도움이 될 거라 확신해요.

○ Topic & Situation 쇼핑 전 구매 목록 작성하기

○ Solution

냉장고 청소를 해야 할 것 같다는 여자의 말에, 남자는 동의를 하면서 자신들이 불필요한 것을 너무 많이 구매하는 것 같다는 의견을 제시하며, 앞으로는 그러지 않기 위해 노력해야 할 것 같다고 말한다. 이에 여자가 어떻게 하면 좋을까 고민하자, 남자는 쇼핑 전에 사야 할 물건을 정확히 파악한 뒤 구매 목록을 미리 작성해 두면 불필요한 물건의 구매를 피할 수 있을 거라 말한다. 따라서 남자의 의견으로 가장 적절한 것은 ⑤ '쇼핑 전 구매 목록을 작성하면 불필요한 물건의 구매를 막을 수 있다.'이다.

○ Words & Phrases

fridge 냉장고 a bunch of 다수의 ~ expired 유통 기한이 지난 go through ~을 살펴보다 run out of ~이 떨어지다 stick to ~을 고수하다

02

정답 | ①

| Script & Translation |

W: Hello, Bargain Hunter listeners! There is one thing you should keep in mind to keep your money and your data secure when shopping online. While buying something online comfortably at your favorite coffee shop may seem appealing, it comes with a few hidden risks. Public Wi-Fi networks are vulnerable to abuse, allowing hackers to steal all kinds of personal data, including your searching history, and access to your email and your passwords. What's more, if you decide to shop online while using a public Wi-Fi connection, you risk giving away your credit card details and your name. So next time you want to do online shopping, make sure to do it safely by using a secure Internet connection rather than public Wi-Fi networks.

여: 안녕하세요, Bargain Hunter 청취자 여러분! 여러분이 온라인 쇼핑을 할 때 여러분의 돈과 정보를 안전하게 보호하기 위해 명심해야 할 한 가지가 있습니다. 여러분이 가장 좋아하는 커피숍에서 편안하게 온라인으로 무언가를 사는 것이 매력적으로 보일 수 있지만, 그것은 몇 가지 숨겨진 위험과 함께 옵니다. 공용 와이파이 네트워크는 악용에 취약하여 해커가 검색 기록을 포함한 모든 종류의 개인 정보를 가로채고 이메일 및 암호에 접근하는 것을 허용할 수 있습니다. 게다가, 만약 여러분이 공공 와이파이에 접속한 채 온라인 쇼핑을 하기로 결정하면, 여러분은 여러분의 신용 카드 정보와 이름을 누설할 위험이 있습니다. 그러므로 다음 번에 온라인 쇼핑을 하고 싶으시면, 공공 와이파이 네트워크보다는 반드시 안전한 인터넷 연결을 사용하여 안전하게 쇼핑하도록 하세요.

○ Topic & Situation 온라인 쇼핑 시 공공 와이파이 사용의 위험성

○ Solution

여자는 온라인 쇼핑 시 돈과 정보를 안전하게 보호하기 위해 기억해야 할 중요한 한 가지가 있다고 말하면서, 공공 와이파이 네트워크는 악용에 취약하고 해커가 개인 정보에 접근할 수 있다고 경고하며, 온라인 쇼핑은 안전한 인터넷 연결이 가능한 곳에서 할 것을 권고하고 있다. 따라서 여자가 하는 말의 요지로 가장 적절한 것은 ① '공공 와이파이에 접속하여 온라인 쇼핑을 하는 것은 안전하지 않다.'이다.

○ Words & Phrases

keep ~ in mind ~을 명심하다 secure 안전한 appealing 매력적인 vulnerable 취약한 abuse 악용 steal 가로채다, 훔치다 give away ~을 누설하다

03

정답 | ⑤

| Script & Translation |

M: What are you looking at, honey?

W: A picture of my sister Anna's baby's room she sent me. Take a look.

M: Oh, yeah. Anna has a baby on the way. She said it's a boy, right?

W: Yes. Don't you love this round rug with stars on it on the floor?

M: Yeah. The baby's room has an outer space theme. Look at the spaceship on the wall.

W: Oh, you're right! Maybe she wants her boy to grow up to be an astronaut!

M: Haha! And the sun-shaped clock on the wall is really cool.

W: Yeah. The plant in the corner of the room is really nice, too.

M: And it should help purify the air.

W: Right. And she installed blinds instead of curtains because she can clean them frequently. She told me she was doing that.

M: That's a good idea. I can't wait to meet her baby boy.

W: Me, too!

남: 뭘 보고 있어요, 여보?

여: 내 동생 Anna가 보내준 아기방 사진이요. 한번 봐요.

남: 아, 그래요. Anna가 곧 아기를 낳는다고 했지요. 아들이라고 했죠?

여: 네. 바닥에 별이 그려진 이 둥근 깔개가 마음에 들지 않나요?

남: 그래요. 아기방이 우주를 테마로 했네요. 벽에 우주선을 봐요.

여: 오, 당신 말이 맞아요! 아마도 그녀는 아들이 우주 비행사로 자라기를 원하나 봐요!

남: 하하! 그리고 벽에 있는 태양 모양의 시계가 정말 멋지네요.

여: 그래요. 방 구석에 있는 식물도 정말 좋아요.

남: 그리고 그것은 공기를 정화하는 데 도움이 되겠어요.

여: 맞아요. 그리고 그녀는 자주 청소할 수 있기 때문에 커튼 대신 블라인드를 설치했대요. 그녀가 나에게 그렇게 하겠다고 말했어요.

남: 좋은 생각이에요. 그녀의 아들을 빨리 만나고 싶네요.

여: 나도 그래요!

◉ Topic & Situation 아기방 꾸미기

◉ Solution

대화에서 자주 청소할 수 있기 때문에 커튼 대신 블라인드를 설치

했다고 말했는데, 그림에는 창문에 커튼이 걸려 있다. 따라서 그림에서 대화의 내용과 일치하지 않는 것은 ⑤이다.

◉ Words & Phrases

have a baby on the way 곧 아기를 낳다 rug 깔개 spaceship 우주선 astronaut 우주 비행사 purify 정화하다 install 설치하다

04

정답 | ⑤

| Script & Translation |

W: Eric, is the conference room all ready? Our promotional event for the new wireless earphones is just around the corner now.

M: Right. Only three days left now.

W: I can't overstress how important this is. We're targeting reporters.

M: About that... I now have 60 reporters confirmed as attending the event.

W: That's great. I can't wait to see their reactions to the new earphones.

M: I'm sure they'll be extremely impressed with them.

W: I hope so. Ah, have you checked the audio system in the conference room? I heard that the microphone had some problems at a meeting yesterday.

M: Really? I'll go there now and check it.

W: Sounds good. It would be a disaster if the microphone didn't work during the event.

M: Definitely. All our hard work would be wasted.

W: Let's do our best to prevent any troubles.

여: Eric, 회의실 준비가 다 되었나요? 새 무선 이어폰을 위한 우리의 홍보 행사가 이제 코 앞으로 다가왔어요.

남: 그래요. 이제 3일밖에 남지 않았어요.

여: 이 행사가 얼마나 중요한 일인지는 아무리 강조해도 지나치지 않아요. 기자들을 대상으로 하고 있으니까요.

남: 그와 관련해서 말인데요… 지금 60명의 기자들이 행사에 참석하는 것으로 확인되었습니다.

여: 잘됐네요. 이어폰에 대한 그들의 반응을 어서 빨리 보고 싶어요.

남: 그들이 새 이어폰에 대해 굉장히 좋은 인상을 받을 것이라고 확신해요.

여: 그러길 바라요. 아, 회의실에 있는 오디오 시스템을 확인했나요? 어제 어떤 회의에서 마이크에 문제가 있었다는 이야기를 들었거든요.

남: 정말이요? 지금 거기에 가서 그것을 확인할게요.

여: 좋아요. 행사 동안에 마이크가 작동되지 않으면 재앙일 거예요.

남: 그렇죠. 우리의 모든 노력이 허사가 될 거예요.

여: 그 어떠한 문제라도 예방하기 위해서 최선을 다합시다.

● Topic & Situation 무선 이어폰 홍보 행사

● Solution

3일 후에 열릴 예정인 새 무선 이어폰 홍보 행사를 위해 남자는 회의실에 있는 마이크 상태를 지금 점검하겠다고 말했으므로, 남자가 할 일로 가장 적절한 것은 ⑤ '마이크 상태 점검하기'이다.

● Words & Phrases

conference room 회의실 promotional event 홍보 행사 wireless 무선의 overstress 지나치게 강조하다 attend 참석하다 extremely 매우, 굉장히 disaster 재앙, 재난 prevent 막다, 금지하다

05
정답 | ②

| Script & Translation |

W: Welcome to Clear View Optics. How can I help you?

M: Hi, I'd like to get a new pair of glasses.

W: All right. Do you have a prescription?

M: Yes, here it is. Could you help me choose the frames and lenses?

W: I'd be glad to help. Here are our newest frames.

M: Hmm.... Ooh, I really like this rectangular one. How much is it?

W: It's $50.

M: Wow, that's cheap. I'll take it.

W: All right. Now let's look at the lenses. Do you need any special type of lens?

M: No. Just regular ones.

W: Okay. Then the lenses you need are $20 each, so $40 for your glasses. Would you like anti-reflective coating added? It's an extra $10 for the pair.

M: Yeah. I definitely need the coating. Oh, by the way, I have this 10%-off coupon. Can I use it?

W: Sure. You can get a 10 percent discount off the total price.

M: Great. Here's my credit card.

여: Clear View Optics에 오신 것을 환영합니다. 어떻게 도와드릴까요?

남: 안녕하세요. 저는 새 안경 하나를 사고 싶습니다.

여: 알겠습니다. 처방전을 갖고 계신가요?

남: 네, 여기 있습니다. 안경테와 렌즈를 고르는 것을 도와주실 수 있나요?

여: 기꺼이 도와드리겠습니다. 여기 저희 가게의 최신의 안경테들이 있습니다.

남: 음…. 오, 저는 이 직사각형 안경테가 정말 마음에 들어요. 얼마인가요?

여: 50달러입니다.

남: 와, 싸네요. 그걸로 할게요.

여: 알겠습니다. 이제 렌즈를 볼게요. 특별한 종류의 렌즈가 필요하신가요?

남: 아니요. 그냥 일반적인 것으로 할게요.

여: 네. 그렇다면 고객님이 필요로 하는 렌즈는 하나에 20달러이니까, 고객님의 안경에는 40달러입니다. 반사 방지 코팅을 추가하시겠어요? 안경 하나에 10달러의 추가 요금이 붙습니다.

남: 네. 코팅이 정말 필요해요. 오, 그런데 저한테 이 10% 할인 쿠폰이 있습니다. 사용 가능한가요?

여: 물론이죠. 총 금액에서 10%의 할인을 받으실 수 있습니다.

남: 잘됐네요. 여기 제 신용 카드가 있습니다.

● Topic & Situation 안경 사기

● Solution

남자는 새 안경을 사려고 안경테와 렌즈를 고르는데, 50달러짜리 안경테와 하나에 20달러인 렌즈 한 쌍을($50+$20×2=$90) 선택하고, 추가로 10달러가 드는 반사 방지 코팅도 선택한다. 또한 총 금액의 10% 할인 쿠폰을 적용받게 되므로, 남자가 지불할 금액은 ② '$90'이다.

● Words & Phrases

glasses 안경 frame 안경테 rectangular 직사각형 모양의 anti-reflective 반사 방지의

06
정답 | ②

| Script & Translation |

[Cell phone rings.]

M: Hi, honey.

W: Hi, honey. Did you pick up Jason at the gym?

M: I'm on my way now. Where are you?

W: I just finished meeting Jason's homeroom teacher. Oh, and I'll be home late today.

M: Do you have to stop by your parents' house?

W: No. I need to go to the bookstore downtown.

M: Why is that?

W: Do you remember Jason said he needs a book for his school assignment?

M: Yeah. Didn't he check it out from the library?

W: No, he said there aren't any available copies at the library right now. So he asked me to buy it for him.

M: I see. Are you sure the bookstore downtown has it?

W: Yes. I called, and they told me they have a few copies. So, I'm going to get it and head straight home.

M: Okay. Then I'll make dinner when I get home.

[휴대 전화가 울린다.]

남: 안녕, 여보.

여: 안녕, 여보. 체육관으로 Jason을 데리러 갔어요?

남: 지금 가는 중이에요. 당신은 어디에 있어요?

여: 방금 Jason의 담임 선생님과 만남이 끝났어요. 아, 그리고 오늘 늦게 귀가할 거예요.

남: 당신의 부모님 댁에 들러야 하나요?

여: 아니요. 시내에 있는 서점에 가야 해요.

남: 그건 왜죠?

여: Jason이 학교 과제를 위해 책이 필요하다고 했던 거 기억나요?

남: 네. 그 애가 도서관에서 책을 대출하지 않았나요?

여: 아니요. 그 애는 지금 당장 도서관에 이용 가능한 책이 없다고 했어요. 그래서 그 애는 나에게 그것을 사다 달라고 부탁했어요.

남: 그렇군요. 시내에 있는 서점에 그것이 있는 게 확실한가요?

여: 네. 전화했더니 몇 권 있다고 하더군요. 그래서, 저는 그것을 사서 바로 집으로 가려고요.

남: 네. 그럼 나는 집에 가서 저녁을 준비할게요.

◎ Topic & Situation 여자가 오늘 늦게 귀가하는 이유

◎ Solution

여자는 아들의 부탁으로 학교 과제를 위해 필요한 책을 시내의 서점에서 구매한 후에 귀가하겠다고 말하고 있으므로 여자가 오늘 늦게 귀가하는 이유는 ② '서점에서 책을 구매해야 해서'이다.

◎ Words & Phrases

gym 체육관   stop by ~에 들르다   assignment 과제   copy (책 등의) 한 권   head 가다

07
정답 | ④

| Script & Translation |

W: Hey, Nick, have you heard about the Golden Plaza Shopping Mall opening next month?

M: I think I saw a banner about it, but I'm not sure. When does it open?

W: It opens on August 31st, the last Saturday of the month.

M: Oh, yes. Isn't it located downtown?

W: Yes, it is. The shopping mall is right in the heart of downtown, close to the subway station.

M: That's cool!

W: I heard they're having a special opening event with live music performances.

M: That sounds like fun. Do you know what stores or facilities it will have?

W: Well, it'll have popular fashion brands, electronics shops, and a large food court with various dining options.

M: Sounds like a one-stop destination for shopping and dining. I can't wait to check it out.

W: Me, neither. Let's go together on the opening day.

M: Okay!

여: 이봐, Nick, Golden Plaza 쇼핑몰이 다음 달에 문을 연다는 것에 대해 들었어?

남: 그것에 관한 현수막을 본 것 같은데, 확실하지는 않아. 언제 개장하니?

여: 그것은 그달의 마지막 토요일인 8월 31일에 개장해.

남: 아, 그렇구나. 그것은 시내에 위치해 있지 않니?

여: 응, 맞아. 그 쇼핑몰은 지하철역에서 가까운 시내 중심부에 있어.

남: 그거 멋지구나!

여: 라이브 음악 공연이 있는 특별한 개장 행사를 할 거라고 들었어.

남: 재밌겠다. 너는 쇼핑몰에 어떤 상점이나 시설이 있을지 아니?

여: 음, 거기에는 인기 있는 패션 브랜드, 전자 제품 매장, 그리고 다양한 식사 옵션이 있는 대형 푸드코트가 있을 거야.

남: 쇼핑과 식사를 한 곳에서 다할 수 있는 장소인 것 같아. 빨리 확인하고 싶어.

여: 나도 그래. 개장일에 같이 가자.

남: 좋아!

◑ Topic & Situation Golden Plaza Shopping Mall

◑ Solution

Golden Plaza Shopping Mall에 관해 개장일, 위치, 개장 행사, 푸드코트 시설은 언급되었으나, ④ '영업 시간'은 언급되지 않았다.

◑ Words & Phrases

be located 위치하다 facilities 시설, 설비 electronics 전자 기기 dining 식사, 정찬 destination 목적지 can't wait to 빨리 ~하고 싶다

08
정답 | ③

| Script & Translation |

W: Daniel, it's lunchtime.

M: Sorry, Rachel. I just need a few more minutes. I need to order a new planner board for the office wall. I'm trying to choose one of these from this online store.

W: Oh, let me help. Do you know how large the space is?

M: Yes. It's 120 cm wide and 80 cm high.

W: Then we can't buy this one because it's too wide. Is there a price limit?

M: Yes. I can spend up to $70. Oh, then that means this one is out, too.

W: Right. And I assume that it should be a monthly planner, not a weekly one.

M: Yeah, you're right. We need it so we can easily see all of the deadlines for the month.

W: Then we should get one of these two monthly ones.

M: How about the board color? I think black would be better than white.

W: I agree. It can be more readable if we use bright-colored markers. Then order this one, Daniel.

M: Okay, I will. Thanks, Rachel. Let's go to lunch right after this.

여: Daniel, 점심시간이에요.

남: 미안해요, Rachel. 저는 단지 몇 분이 더 필요해요. 저는 사무실 벽에 걸 새로운 플래너 보드를 주문해야 하거든요. 이 온라인 상점에서 이것들 중 하나를 고르려고 해요.

여: 아, 제가 도와드릴게요. 그 공간이 얼마나 넓은지 아세요?

남: 네, 그것은 너비가 120cm이고 높이가 80cm예요.

여: 그러면 이건 너비가 너무 넓어서 살 수 없겠어요. 가격 제한이 있어요?

남: 네, 70달러까지 쓸 수 있어요. 아, 그럼 이것도 제외한다는 뜻이군요.

여: 맞아요. 그리고 저는 주간이 아닌 월간 플래너여야 한다고 생각해요.

남: 네, 맞아요. 그달의 마감일을 모두 쉽게 볼 수 있으려면 우리는 그것이 필요하죠.

여: 그럼, 이 두 개의 월간 플래너 중의 하나를 사야겠네요.

남: 보드의 색은 어때요? 흰색보다는 검은색이 나을 것 같아요.

여: 동의해요. 밝은 색의 마커펜을 사용하면 더 잘 읽힐 수 있을 거예요. 그럼 이것을 주문해요, Daniel.

남: 네, 그럴게요. 고마워요, Rachel. 이걸 끝내고 바로 점심 먹으러 가요.

◑ Topic & Situation 플래너 보드 주문

◑ Solution

사무실 벽에 걸 플래너 보드를 주문하는 남자는 여자와 상의하면서 폭이 120cm보다 넓은 것과 가격이 70달러가 넘는 것은 제외시키고, 월간 플래너이면서, 보드의 색이 검은색인 것을 주문하겠다고 했다. 따라서 남자가 주문할 플래너 보드는 ③이다.

◑ Words & Phrases

assume 생각하다, 추측하다 deadline 마감일, 마감 기한 bright-colored 밝은 색의 marker (형광펜 등의) 마커펜

09
정답 | ⑤

| Script & Translation |

W: Mr. Thompson. The printer is out of paper. Should I bring some from the supply room?

M: I'm afraid there's no paper left in the supply room, either. Could you call the office manager and order boxes of paper right away?

W: Okay. How many boxes do you think we need?

M: I think we need at least five considering our recent use.

여: Thompson 씨. 프린터에 용지가 다 떨어졌어요. 비품실에서 좀 가지고 올까요?

남: 비품실에도 남아있는 용지가 없을 것 같아요. 사무실 관리자에게 전화해서 종이 몇 박스를 바로 주문해 주시겠어요?

여: 네. 저희는 몇 박스나 필요할까요?

남: 최근에 우리가 사용한 것을 고려할 때, 적어도 다섯 개는 필요할 것 같아요.

◉ **Topic & Situation** 복사 용지 주문

◉ **Solution**

여자가 프린터기에 용지가 다 떨어졌다고 말하고, 비품실에서 용지를 가져와야 할지 남자에게 물어 보자, 남자는 비품실에도 용지가 없을 거라 말하며, 사무실 관리자에게 종이를 주문할 것을 요청하고 있다. 이에 여자가 몇 박스를 주문해야 할지 물었으므로, 여자의 마지막 말에 대한 남자의 응답으로 가장 적절한 것은 ⑤ '최근에 우리가 사용한 것을 고려할 때, 적어도 다섯 개는 필요할 것 같아요.'이다.

① 프린터기가 지난주 이후로 작동하지 않았어요.
② 아무래도 오늘은 사무실 관리자가 근무하지 않는 것 같아요.
③ 사무용품을 위한 더 큰 예산이 정말 필요해요.
④ 비품실의 맨 아래 선반에 한 박스가 있어요.

◉ **Words & Phrases**

out of ~가 떨어진   supply room 비품실   office manager 사무실 관리자   office supplies 사무용품   shelf 선반

10

정답 | ②

| Script & Translation |

M: Excuse me, do you know how I can get to the Central Shopping Mall?

W: I'm sorry, but I'm a stranger here, too. Why don't you ask the information center?

M: Oh, thank you. But I can't see the information center.

W: Oh, it's really close. It's right over there next to the bank.

남: 실례합니다. Central Shopping Mall로 가려면 어떻게 가야 하는지 아시나요?

여: 죄송합니다만, 저도 이곳에 처음 왔어요. 안내 센터에 가서 물어 보시는 게 어때요?

남: 오, 감사합니다. 하지만 안내 센터가 보이질 않네요.

여: 아, 매우 가깝습니다. 저기 은행 바로 옆에 있어요.

◉ **Topic & Situation** 쇼핑몰로 가는 길 묻기

◉ **Solution**

남자가 여자에게 Central Shopping Mall로 가는 길을 물었고, 여자는 자신도 그곳에 처음 와서 잘 모르니, 안내 센터에 가서 물어볼 것을 권한다. 남자가 안내 센터의 위치를 모르겠다고 했으므로, 남자의 마지막 말에 대한 여자의 응답으로 가장 적절한 것은 ② '아, 매우 가깝습니다. 저기 은행 바로 옆에 있어요.'이다.

① 동의해요. 저도 그 지도가 너무 혼동된다고 생각했어요.
③ 괜찮습니다. 원하시는 만큼 많은 질문을 하셔도 돼요.
④ 감사합니다만, 전 괜찮아요. 저는 어제 쇼핑을 벌써 끝냈습니다.
⑤ 맞아요. Central Shopping Mall은 여기서 걸어서 5분 거리에 있어요.

◉ **Words & Phrases**

information center 안내 센터   confusing 혼동시키는

11

정답 | ①

| Script & Translation |

M: Hi, Ms. Baker. Can we talk about my grass cutter you borrowed last week?

W: Of course. Is there something wrong?

M: Well, after you returned it, the engine was making strange noises, like it was about to cut out.

W: Really? I'm so sorry.

M: Did you notice anything wrong with the grass cutter when you used it?

W: No, it was working fine. I didn't notice any problems with it.

M: Hmm... maybe something happened while you were bringing it back.

W: Yeah, I guess so, too.

M: I actually had to get it repaired, and it cost me $80. I hope you can share some of the repair costs.

W: Of course I can. I'm so sorry about that.

M: Thanks for understanding. Let's each pay half.

남: 안녕하세요, Baker 씨. 지난주에 당신이 빌려간 내 잔디 깎는 기계에 대해 얘기할 수 있을까요?

여: 물론이죠. 뭔가 잘못된 거라도 있나요?

남: 음, 당신이 그것을 돌려준 후에, 마치 작동을 멈출 것처럼 엔진이 이상한 소리를 내고 있었어요.

여: 진짜요? 정말 죄송합니다.

남: 잔디 깎는 기계를 사용했을 때 뭔가 이상한 점을 알아챘나요?

여: 아니요. 그것은 잘 작동하고 있었어요. 저는 그것과 관련해서 어떤 문제도 알아차리지 못했거든요.

남: 흠… 그럼 아마도 당신이 그것을 다시 가져다주는 동안에 무슨 일이 생긴 것 같아요.

여: 네, 저도 그렇게 생각합니다.

남: 사실 그것을 수리해야 했는데, 비용이 80달러가 들었어요. 수리 비용의 일부를 나눠 부담해 주시면 좋겠어요.

여: 물론 부담할게요. 그것에 관해서 정말 죄송해요.

남: 이해해 주셔서 감사합니다. 우리 각자 반씩 냅시다.

● **Topic & Situation** 빌린 물건의 손상에 대한 배상

● **Solution**

남자는 여자에게 잔디 깎는 기계를 빌려주었다가 돌려받은 이후 엔진이 이상한 소리를 냈다고 말하면서 여자에게 사용할 때 이상한 점을 알아챘는지 물었다. 여자가 잘 작동하고 있었다고 답하자 남자는 잔디깎는 기계를 가져다 주는 동안에 문제가 생긴 것 같다고 말하며 수리비로 80달러가 들었으니 수리 비용의 일부를 나눠 부담해 주면 좋겠다고 말했고, 이에 대해 여자는 부담하겠다고 하면서 미안하다고 사과했다. 따라서 여자의 마지막 말에 대한 남자의 응답으로 가장 적절한 것은 ① '이해해 주셔서 감사합니다. 우리 각자 반씩 냅시다.'이다.

② 글쎄요. 수리 비용이 정확하지 않을 수 있어요.

③ 미안해요. 지난주에 잔디 깎는 기계를 이웃에게 빌려주었어요.

④ 좋아요! 당신의 잔디 깎는 기계를 사용할 때는 정말 조심할게요.

⑤ 그렇고말고요. 잔디 깎는 기계를 수리점에 가져가는 게 좋겠어요.

● **Words & Phrases**

grass cutter 잔디 깎는 기계, 잔디깎이   borrow 빌리다, 차용하다
be about to *do* 막 ~하려고 하다   notice 알아차리다   repair 수리하다
inaccurate 부정확한

12

| **Script & Translation** |

W: Paul walks into his grandmother's house while she is about to cook pumpkin soup. He asks her to teach him how to make the soup. His grandmother smiles and says she would be happy to teach him. She begins to explain the recipe step by step. She shows Paul how to chop the pumpkin and cook it in butter, and how to add other ingredients to create a smooth, creamy soup. After making the soup, they sit down and enjoy it together. Paul is proud that he learned how to make such a delicious food. He wants to express his gratitude to his grandmother. In this situation, what would Paul most likely say to his grandmother?

Paul: Thanks a lot for teaching me how to make this amazing soup.

여: Paul은 할머니가 호박 수프를 막 요리하려고 하는 중에 할머니의 집으로 걸어 들어갑니다. 그는 그녀에게 그 수프를 만드는 방법을 가르쳐 달라고 부탁합니다. 그의 할머니는 미소를 짓고 그에게 가르쳐 주면 기쁠 것이라고 말합니다. 그녀는 요리법을 차근차근 설명하기 시작합니다. 그녀는 Paul에게 호박을 썰어 버터에 익히는 방법과 다른 재료를 추가하여 부드러운 크림 같은 수프를 만드는 방법을 보여줍니다. 수프를 만든 후, 그들은 앉아 그것을 함께 즐깁니다. Paul은 그렇게 맛있는 음식을 만드는 방법을 배웠다는 것이 자랑스럽습니다. 그는 할머니에게 감사하는 마음을 표현하고 싶어 합니다. 이런 상황에서, Paul이 그의 할머니에게 뭐라고 말하겠습니까?

Paul: 이 굉장한 수프를 만드는 방법을 가르쳐 주셔서 정말 고마워요.

● **Topic & Situation** 할머니에게 호박 수프 요리 배우기

● **Solution**

할머니에게 호박 수프 만드는 방법을 배운 Paul은 그렇게 맛있는 음식을 만드는 방법을 배웠다는 것에 대해 자랑스러워하고, 할머니에게 감사의 마음을 전하고 싶어 하는 상황이다. 따라서 이런 상황에서 Paul이 할머니에게 할 말로 가장 적절한 것은 ④ '이 굉장한 수프를 만드는 방법을 가르쳐 주셔서 정말 고마워요.'이다.

① 할머니가 제 요리 실력을 칭찬해 주시다니 정말 자상하세요.

② 할머니가 제 호박 수프 요리법을 좋아하셔서 정말 기뻐요.

③ 제게 호박 수프를 만들어 주실 수 있다면 정말 고맙겠어요.

⑤ 이 굉장한 요리책을 선물해 주셔서 정말 고마워요.

● Words & Phrases

recipe 요리법 step by step 차근차근 chop 썰다 ingredient
재료 smooth 부드러운 creamy 크림 같은 proud 자랑스러운
gratitude 감사(하는) 마음 praise 칭찬하다 grateful 고마워하는

12 ❶ how to make the soup
   ❷ add other ingredients
   ❸ to express his gratitude

Dictations

본문 151, 156~159쪽

기출 ❶ got the confirmation
예제 ❷ throw away
     ❸ make a reservation
01 ❶ a bunch of things
   ❷ go through the fridge
   ❸ stick to the list
02 ❶ should keep in mind
   ❷ a few hidden risks
   ❸ risk giving away
03 ❶ this round rug with stars on it
   ❷ the spaceship on the wall
   ❸ the sun-shaped clock
   ❹ instead of curtains
04 ❶ is just around the corner
   ❷ impressed with them
   ❸ the microphone had some problems
   ❹ prevent any troubles
05 ❶ a new pair of glasses
   ❷ like this rectangular one
   ❸ anti-reflective coating added
06 ❶ pick up Jason at the gym
   ❷ for his school assignment
   ❸ have a few copies
07 ❶ saw a banner
   ❷ in the heart of downtown
   ❸ can't wait to check
08 ❶ order a new planner board
   ❷ all of the deadlines
   ❸ can be more readable
09 ❶ out of paper
   ❷ order boxes of paper
10 ❶ how I can get to
   ❷ a stranger here
11 ❶ was about to cut out
   ❷ were bringing it back
   ❸ get it repaired

22강 실전 모의고사 1회

본문 162~167쪽

01 ⑤	02 ⑤	03 ①	04 ⑤	05 ⑤	06 ④
07 ②	08 ④	09 ④	10 ①	11 ⑤	12 ②
13 ①	14 ②	15 ③	16 ③	17 ④	

01

정답 | ⑤

| Script & Translation |

W: Hello, Westridge High School students. This is your vice principal, Ms. Collins. The main stove in our school cafeteria broke down this afternoon, and we had a repairperson look at it. The repairperson said a part in the stove needs to be replaced, and it won't be available until tomorrow. We tried to provide the planned food, but we won't be able to serve tomorrow's original lunch meal plan. So we will be serving sandwiches and orange juice for lunch instead of the original meal. I apologize for any inconvenience this may cause. Thank you for your understanding and cooperation!

여: 안녕하세요, Westridge 고등학교 학생 여러분. 저는 여러분의 교감인 Collins 선생님입니다. 오늘 오후에 학교 구내식당의 메인 스토브가 고장이 나서 수리 기사에게 점검받았습니다. 수리 기사가 스토브의 부품을 교체해야 한다고 해서 내일까지 사용할 수 없을 것 같습니다. 우리는 예정된 음식을 제공하려고 노력했지만, 내일 원래의 점심 식사를 계획대로 제공할 수 없을 것 같습니다. 그래서 원래 식사 대신 샌드위치와 오렌지 주스를 점심으로 제공할 예정입니다. 이로 인해 불편을 끼쳐 죄송합니다. 여러분의 이해와 협조에 감사드립니다!

○ **Topic & Situation** 학교 구내식당 메인 스토브 고장

○ **Solution**
여자는 학생들에게 구내식당 메인 스토브가 고장이 나서 내일 점심으로 예정되어 있던 음식을 제공하지 못하게 되었음을 알리면서, 대신 샌드위치와 오렌지 주스가 제공될 것임을 공지하고 있다. 따라서 여자가 하는 말의 목적으로 가장 적절한 것은 ⑤ '예정된 음식 대신 다른 음식이 제공됨을 공지하려고'이다.

○ **Words & Phrases**
vice principal 교감   cafeteria 구내식당   break down 고장이 나다   repairperson 수리 기사   replace 교체하다   apologize 사과하다   inconvenience 불편   cooperation 협조, 협동

02

정답 | ⑤

| Script & Translation |

W: Good morning, Sam. How are you?

M: I'm good, Jenny. How about you?

W: I'm pretty tired. I stayed up really late, surfing the Internet on my smartphone for about three hours.

M: Again? Don't you think you should manage your screen time?

W: What do you mean?

M: I mean, you should control the amount of time you spend in front of the screen. Long screen time can be really bad for your eyes.

W: Oh, is it that bad?

M: It's not just the eyes. Too much screen time can have a variety of negative health effects including disrupted sleep patterns and a lack of exercise.

W: Hmm.... Maybe that's why I always feel tired in the afternoon.

M: That's right. You should really think about controlling your screen time for your health.

W: Okay. Thanks for your advice. I'll try to do that.

M: I'm sure you'll start feeling less tired.

여: 안녕, Sam. 어떻게 지내니?

남: 잘 지내, Jenny. 너는 어때?

여: 난 꽤 피곤해. 내 스마트폰으로 세 시간 정도 인터넷을 검색하느라, 정말 늦게까지 깨어 있었어.

남: 또? 너의 화면 보는 시간을 관리해야 한다고 생각하지 않니?

여: 그게 무슨 말이야?

남: 내 말은 네가 (전자 기기의) 화면 앞에서 보내는 시간을 조절해야 한다는 거야. 긴 화면 노출 시간은 네 눈에 정말 나쁠 수 있어.

여: 오, 그게 그렇게 나쁜 것이니?

남: 눈에만 그런 것이 아니야. 지나친 화면 노출 시간은 수면 패턴의 방해와 운동 부족을 포함해서, 건강에 다양하게 부정적 영향을 끼치게 돼.

여: 음…. 아마도 그래서 내가 항상 오후에 피곤함을 느끼는 것 같아.

남: 맞아. 너의 건강을 위해서 화면 노출 시간을 조절하는 것에 대해 너는 정말 생각해 봐야 해.

여: 알겠어. 조언해 줘서 고마워. 그러기 위해 노력할게.

남: 네가 피곤함을 덜 느끼기 시작할 거라고 확신해.

○ **Topic & Situation** 전자 기기 화면에 노출되는 시간 조절하기

Solution

여자가 늦게까지 스마트폰을 보느라 피곤하다고 말하자 남자는 화면을 보는 시간을 조절할 필요가 있다고 말하면서, 전자 기기 화면에 노출되는 시간이 너무 많으면 건강에 안 좋은 영향을 끼칠 수 있다고 경고한다. 따라서 남자의 의견으로 가장 적절한 것은 ⑤ '건강을 위해 전자 기기 화면에 노출되는 시간을 조절해야 한다.'이다.

Words & Phrases

surf the Internet 인터넷을 검색하다 manage 관리하다 screen (전자 기기의) 화면 a variety of 다양한 disrupt 방해하다

03

정답 | ①

| Script & Translation |

W: Good morning, listeners! Thanks for tuning in to my channel. In this episode, I'll discuss a consideration when talking with others. Suppose you have a friend who unintentionally annoys people. She continuously talks about things that no one knows anything about. Your group of friends feels exhausted from listening to her long personal stories. What do you think this friend should do? I think it's best to always try to talk about topics that everyone in the group is familiar with. This way, everybody can feel they're a part of the conversation and enjoy themselves more.

여: 안녕하세요, 청취자 여러분! 제 채널에 맞춰 주셔서 감사합니다. 이번 방송분에서, 저는 다른 사람들과 대화할 때 고려할 사항을 논의할 것입니다. 의도치 않게 사람들을 짜증나게 하는 친구가 있다고 가정해 봅시다. 그녀는 아무도 모르는 것들에 대해 계속 이야기합니다. 당신이 속한 친구 모임은 그녀의 긴 개인적인 이야기들을 듣는 것에 지쳤다고 느낍니다. 여러분은 이 친구가 어떻게 해야 한다고 생각하세요? 저는 모임의 모든 사람들에게 친숙한 주제에 대해 이야기하려고 항상 노력하는 것이 가장 좋다고 생각합니다. 이렇게 하면 모든 사람이 자신이 대화의 일부라고 느낄 수 있고 더 즐길 수 있습니다.

Topic & Situation 사람들과 함께 있을 때의 대화 주제

Solution

여자는 친구들과 있을 때 남들이 알지 못하는 것들에 대해 계속 이야기해서 의도치 않게 사람들을 짜증나게 하는 친구를 예로 들면서, 다른 사람들과 대화할 때 모두에게 친숙한 주제에 관해 말하는 것이 좋다고 말했다. 따라서 여자가 하는 말의 요지로 가장 적절한 것은 ① '사람들과 대화할 때 모두에게 친숙한 주제로 말하는 것이 좋다.'이다.

Words & Phrases

tune in to (라디오 · 텔레비전의 채널을) ~에 맞추다 episode (라디오 · 텔레비전 연속 프로의) 1회 방송분 unintentionally 의도치 않게 annoy 짜증이 나게 하다 exhausted 지친, 고갈된 familiar 친숙한

04

정답 | ⑤

| Script & Translation |

W: Honey, I think it's about time that we remodel our garage.

M: I completely agree. We should get it remodeled like my brother's garage. Let me show you a picture of it. Here.

W: Wow, it looks great! He even has a treadmill in it.

M: Yeah. That's where he works out.

W: That's a great idea. I also like the storage rack along the right wall.

M: Definitely. And the rack has wheels, so it's easy to move around. And look, there's a rectangular sink under the window.

W: That'd be really nice to wash up there after gardening.

M: For sure. And my brother put a refrigerator in the left corner.

W: That's nice, but I don't think we need one. That would be a waste of electricity.

M: Good point.

W: I like the landscape painting on the left wall. You should ask him where he got it.

M: Okay, I will.

여: 여보, 우리 차고를 개조할 때가 된 것 같아요.

남: 전적으로 동의해요. 그것을 내 동생의 차고처럼 개조해야 해요. 사진을 보여 줄게요. 여기요.

여: 와, 그것은 아주 멋지군요! 그는 심지어 그 안에 러닝 머신도 가지고 있군요.

남: 네. 그것이 그가 운동하는 곳이거든요.

여: 아주 좋은 생각이네요. 나는 오른쪽 벽에 있는 보관 선반도 마음에 들어요.

남: 물론이에요. 그리고 그 선반은 바퀴가 달려 있어서 이동하기 쉬워요. 그리고 보세요, 창문 아래에 직사각형의 싱크대가 있어요.

여: 정원 가꾸기를 하고 나서 거기서 씻으면 정말 좋을 것 같아요.

남: 물론이죠. 그리고 내 남동생은 왼쪽 코너에 냉장고를 두었어요.

여: 그거 좋은데, 우리는 그것이 필요 없을 것 같아요. 그것은 전기 낭비가 될 거예요.

남: 좋은 지적이에요.

여: 저는 왼쪽 벽에 있는 풍경화가 마음에 들어요. 어디에서 그것을 구했는지 물어 보세요.

남: 네, 그럴게요.

● **Topic & Situation** 차고 리모델링 구상

● **Solution**
대화에서 왼쪽 벽에 풍경화가 있다고 했는데, 그림에서는 가족의 사진으로 보이는 그림이 붙어 있으므로, 그림에서 대화의 내용과 일치하지 않는 것은 ⑤이다.

● **Words & Phrases**
garage 차고   treadmill 러닝 머신   storage rack 보관 선반
rectangular 직사각형의   gardening 정원 가꾸기   refrigerator
냉장고   electricity 전기   landscape 풍경

05
정답 | ⑤

| Script & Translation |

W: Hi, James. I heard you're organizing a high school reunion for Friday next week.

M: Yes, Mom. We invited Mr. Anderson. He retired last month.

W: Oh, I didn't know that. Do you have any gift for him?

M: Yes. I ordered a thank-you cake for him.

W: That's really thoughtful. Where's the reunion going to be at?

M: At the Italian restaurant, Dino. I reserved a table for 20.

W: I see. So that many people have told you that they're attending?

M: No. That's how many people were invited.

W: Then you should probably confirm who's going to be able to attend. You might have to adjust the reservation if not everybody can join.

M: Good idea. Then I'll text everybody and find out.

W: Sounds good.

M: Thanks for the advice, Mom.

여: 안녕, James. 다음 주 금요일에 고등학교 동창회를 네가 준비 중이라고 들었어.

남: 네, 엄마. 저희는 Anderson 선생님을 초대했어요. 그분은 지난달에 퇴임하셨거든요.

여: 아, 나는 그걸 몰랐어. 너는 그분을 위한 선물이 있니?

남: 네. 저는 그분을 위해 감사 케이크를 주문했어요.

여: 그건 정말 사려 깊구나. 동창회가 어디에서 있을 예정이니?

남: 이탈리아 식당인 Dino에서요. 20명을 위한 테이블을 예약했어요.

여: 그렇구나. 그래서 그 많은 사람들이 다 참석한다고 네게 말했니?

남: 아니요. 그만큼의 사람이 초대되었지요.

여: 그럼 누가 참석할 수 있는지를 아마도 네가 확인해야 할 것 같구나. 모두 참석할 수 있는 것이 아니면, 네가 예약을 조정해야 할 수도 있어.

남: 좋은 생각이에요. 그럼 제가 모두에게 문자를 보내서 알아볼게요.

여: 좋을 것 같아.

남: 조언해 주셔서 고마워요, 엄마.

● **Topic & Situation** 동창회 모임 준비

● **Solution**
고등학교 동창회를 준비하고 있는 남자에게 여자가 모두 참석할 수 있는 것이 아니면, 예약을 조정해야 할 수도 있다고 충고하자, 남자는 모두에게 문자를 보내서 알아보겠다고 대답했다. 따라서 남자가 할 일로 가장 적절한 것은 ⑤ '문자 메시지 보내기'이다.

● **Words & Phrases**
organize 준비하다, 조직하다   reunion 동창회   retire 은퇴하다
thoughtful 사려 깊은   confirm 확인하다   adjust 조정하다

06

| Script & Translation |

M: Welcome to Daniel's Doughnuts. How may I help you?

W: Hi. How much are the family doughnut boxes?

M: They're normally $30, but we're having a special promotional event right now, so they're $25. The promotional event ends tomorrow.

W: Perfect timing! So it's $5 off. I'll take one family doughnut box.

M: All right. Is there anything else you'd like? Just so you know, if you spend more than $30, you can get a 10-dollar mug for free.

W: Really? Then I'll buy some chocolate chip cookies too. How much are they?

M: They're $1 each. How many would you like?

W: I'll take 10 of them. So I get a mug then, right?

M: Yeah. I'll get that for you.

W: Thanks. And I have a Happy Buy credit card. Do I get 10% off with it?

M: I'm sorry, but we no longer have a partnership with that credit card company.

W: Oh, I see. No problem. Here's my credit card.

남: Daniel's Doughnuts에 오신 것을 환영합니다. 어떻게 도와 드릴까요?

여: 안녕하세요. 패밀리 도넛 상자는 얼마예요?

남: 보통 30달러인데, 지금 특별 판촉 행사 중이어서 25달러예요. 판촉 행사는 내일 종료돼요.

여: 매우 좋은 타이밍이네요! 그래서 5달러 할인하는군요. 패밀리 도넛 한 상자를 살게요.

남: 알겠습니다. 더 필요하신 것이 있나요? 참고로 말씀드리자면, 30달러 넘게 쓰시면 10달러짜리 머그잔을 무료로 받으실 수 있거든요.

여: 그래요? 그럼 초콜릿 칩 쿠키도 좀 살게요. 그것들은 얼마예요?

남: 개당 1달러예요. 몇 개 드릴까요?

여: 10개 살게요. 그럼 그 머그잔 하나를 받는 거지요, 맞죠?

남: 네. 제가 그것을 가져다드릴게요.

여: 고마워요. 그리고 저는 Happy Buy 신용 카드를 가지고 있어요. 그것으로 10% 할인을 받을 수 있나요?

남: 죄송하지만, 저희는 그 신용 카드 회사와 더 이상 제휴하지 않아요.

여: 아, 그렇군요. 괜찮아요. 여기 제 신용 카드가 있어요.

▶ Topic & Situation   도넛과 초콜릿 칩 쿠키 구매

▶ Solution

여자는 도넛 가게에서 원래 30달러인데 특별 판촉 행사 중이어서 25달러에 팔고 있는 패밀리 도넛 한 상자와 하나에 1달러인 초콜릿 칩 쿠키를 10개 사면서, Happy Buy 신용 카드로 할인을 받을 수 있는지 물었고, 이에 남자가 그 신용 카드 회사와 더 이상 제휴를 맺고 있지 않아서 할인해 줄 수 없다고 했으므로, 여자가 지불할 금액은 ④ '$35'이다.

▶ Words & Phrases

promotional event 판촉 행사   partnership 제휴

07

| Script & Translation |

W: Hello, Mr. Davidson. How is your elbow today?

M: Hello, Ms. Smith. My elbow is okay now. I actually just finished playing a game of badminton.

W: That's great. Oh, your racket is a new one, right?

M: Yes. I bought a new racket yesterday. It's a little lighter than the old one.

W: It's really nice! Would you like to play badminton with me now?

M: Sorry, I can't play any more today.

W: Oh! I didn't think you're still recovering and must be tired.

M: No, I only played for an hour. I'm good, but I have dinner plans with my friend now.

W: I see. Then can we play together tomorrow?

M: Sure. I'll be back tomorrow evening. Does that work for you?

W: Yes. Badminton tomorrow then!

M: See you.

여: 안녕하세요, Davidson 씨. 오늘 팔꿈치는 어떠세요?

남: 안녕하세요, Smith 씨. 제 팔꿈치는 이제 괜찮아요. 저는 사실 방금 배드민턴 한 경기를 마쳤어요.

여: 잘됐네요. 아, 당신의 라켓이 새것이지요, 맞죠?

남: 네. 어제 새 라켓을 샀어요. 그것은 예전 것보다 조금 더 가벼워요.

여: 그거 정말 좋군요! 지금 저와 배드민턴을 치실래요?

남: 죄송합니다. 오늘은 더 이상 칠 수 없어요.

여: 아! 아직도 회복 중이라 피곤하실 거라고 생각하지 못했어요.

남: 아니요, 저는 한 시간밖에 안 했어요. 괜찮아요, 하지만 지금은 친구와 저녁 식사 약속이 있거든요.

여: 그렇군요. 그럼 내일 같이 칠 수 있을까요?

남: 물론이죠. 내일 저녁에 다시 올게요. 그게 괜찮으세요?

여: 네. 그럼 내일 배드민턴을 쳐요!

남: 나중에 봐요.

◐ **Topic & Situation** 배드민턴 함께 치기

◐ **Solution**

여자가 자신과 지금 배드민턴을 칠 수 있는지를 남자에게 묻자, 남자는 친구와 저녁 식사 약속이 있어서 오늘 배드민턴을 더 이상 칠 수 없다고 대답했으므로, 남자가 오늘 배드민턴을 그만 치려는 이유는 ② '저녁 식사 약속이 있어서'이다.

◐ **Words & Phrases**

elbow 팔꿈치 recover 회복하다

08
정답 | ④

| Script & Translation |

M: Hi, Rachel. Do you have any plans this weekend?

W: Hi, Kevin. I'm going to the Green Energy Festival.

M: Oh, what's that about?

W: Its main events are workshops and discussions about sustainable living. And in the evening, they have some live music performances.

M: Sounds like fun. When is it?

W: It starts at 10 a.m. tomorrow and ends on Sunday at 5 p.m.

M: I see. Who is hosting the festival?

W: It's held by Eco People, a big environmental group. They started holding the festival 10 years ago.

M: I've heard of that group. How can I sign up for the festival?

W: If you go to the Eco People website, there's a registration form to fill out. It's pretty easy.

M: I see. I'll probably go on Saturday.

W: That's when I'm going! We can go together.

남: 안녕, Rachel. 이번 주말에 무슨 계획이 있니?

여: 안녕, Kevin. 나는 Green Energy Festival에 갈 거야.

남: 아, 그것은 무슨 축제니?

여: 그것의 주요 행사는 지속 가능한 생활에 관한 워크숍과 토론이야. 그리고 저녁에는, 라이브 음악 공연을 해.

남: 재미있겠다. 그게 언제니?

여: 내일 오전 10시에 시작해서 일요일 오후 5시에 끝나.

남: 그렇구나. 누가 그 축제를 주최하는 거니?

여: 그것은 큰 환경 단체인 Eco People이 개최하는 거야. 그들은 10년 전에 그 축제를 개최하기 시작했어.

남: 그 단체에 대해 들어 본 적이 있어. 그 축제를 어떻게 신청할 수 있니?

여: Eco People 웹사이트에 가면 작성할 신청서가 있어. 그것은 아주 쉬워.

남: 알겠어. 나는 아마도 토요일에 갈 것 같아.

여: 나도 그때 갈 거야! 우리 같이 갈 수 있겠구나.

◐ **Topic & Situation** Green Energy Festival

◐ **Solution**

두 사람의 Green Energy Festival에 관한 대화에서 주요 행사, 축제 기간, 주최 기관, 신청 방법은 언급되었지만, ④ '참여 단체의 수'는 언급되지 않았다.

◐ **Words & Phrases**

sustainable 지속 가능한 performance 공연 sign up for ~을 신청하다 registration form 신청서 fill out ~을 작성하다

09
정답 | ④

| Script & Translation |

M: Hello, listeners! I'm Eric Peterson. Are you looking for an educational TV show to watch with your children? Orange Edu TV has launched a new science educational series called *Future Science Brain*. The program covers various science fields with fun approaches. The first three episodes about animals, computers, and the universe were broadcast and the reviews have been great. The series features popular child actors Jessica Davis, Ben Colbert, and Edward Duncan. To watch this series, you must subscribe to the channel, which is $10 per month.

Future Science Brain airs every Friday evening from 7 p.m. to 8 p.m. Don't miss out on this fun educational program that you can enjoy with your children!

남: 안녕하세요, 청취자 여러분! 저는 Eric Peterson입니다. 아이들과 함께 볼 수 있는 교육적인 TV 쇼를 찾고 계신가요? Orange Edu TV가 *Future Science Brain*이라는 새로운 과학 교육 시리즈를 출시했습니다. 그 프로그램은 다양한 과학 분야를 재밌는 접근 방식으로 다루고 있습니다. 동물, 컴퓨터, 우주에 관한 처음 세 편이 방송되었고 평이 매우 좋았습니다. 그 시리즈에는 인기 있는 어린이 배우인 Jessica Davis, Ben Colbert, 그리고 Edward Duncan이 출연합니다. 이 시리즈를 시청하시려면 채널을 구독하셔야 하는데, 구독료는 월 10달러입니다. *Future Science Brain*은 매주 금요일 저녁 7시부터 8시까지 방송됩니다. 아이들과 함께 즐길 수 있는 이 재미있는 교육 프로그램을 놓치지 마세요!

◐ Topic & Situation *Future Science Brain*

◐ Solution

구독료는 월 10달러라고 했으므로, 담화의 내용과 일치하지 않는 것은 ④ '구독료를 따로 낼 필요는 없다.'이다.

◐ Words & Phrases

launch 출시하다   educational 교육적인   episode 편, (라디오·텔레비전 연속 프로의) 1회 방송분   review (비)평, 평론   subscribe to ~을 구독하다   air 방송되다

10
정답 | ①

| Script & Translation |

M: Kate! What are you looking at?

W: Hi, Eric. I'm looking at a website to sign up for a group tennis lesson for beginners. I'm not sure which one to take, though.

M: Oh, that's cool. Let me see. *[Pause]* Are there any days you're not free?

W: Yeah. I have to babysit my brother every Tuesday.

M: Okay. They're all in the evening. Is that okay?

W: That's good, but I don't want to finish after 9 p.m. That seems pretty late.

M: I agree. Oh, I think it'd be better if you learned how to play tennis on an indoor court.

W: Good point. Then I won't have to worry about the weather.

M: That's right. You can play indoors rain or shine.

W: Well then, I guess it's down to these two.

M: Look. This group lesson already has four people. I think it'd be better for you to choose a smaller group.

W: Right. Then I'll sign up for this lesson. Thank you, Eric.

남: Kate! 무엇을 보고 있어?

여: 안녕, Eric. 초보자를 위한 그룹 테니스 수업을 신청하려고 웹사이트를 보고 있어. 그런데 어떤 것을 수강해야 할지 잘 모르겠어.

남: 아, 멋지구나. 어디 봐. *[잠시 후]* 네가 한가하지 않은 날이라도 있니?

여: 응. 나는 매주 화요일마다 남동생을 돌봐야 해.

남: 좋아. 그것들은 모두 저녁에 있어. 괜찮겠어?

여: 그건 좋아, 하지만 저녁 9시 이후에 마치고 싶지 않아. 그것은 꽤 늦은 것 같아.

남: 동의해. 아, 실내 코트에서 테니스 치는 법을 배우는 게 더 좋을 것 같아.

여: 좋은 지적이야. 그럼 날씨 걱정을 안 해도 되겠구나.

남: 맞아. 날씨와 관계없이 실내에서 칠 수 있어.

여: 그렇다면, 이 두 가지만 남은 것 같아.

남: 봐. 이 그룹 수업에는 이미 네 명이 있어. 더 작은 수업을 선택하는 게 더 좋을 것 같아.

여: 맞아. 그럼 나는 이 수업에 등록할게. 고마워, Eric.

◐ Topic & Situation 그룹 테니스 수업 신청하기

◐ Solution

여자는 남자의 조언을 들어 화요일이 아니고, 저녁 9시 이전에 끝나고, 실내 코트에서 진행되며, 남은 두 가지 중에 인원이 더 적은 수업을 신청하겠다고 말했다. 따라서 여자가 신청할 그룹 테니스 수업은 ①이다.

◐ Words & Phrases

babysit (아기를) 돌보다   indoor 실내의   rain or shine 날씨와 관계없이   be down to ~만 남다

11

정답 | ⑤

| Script & Translation |

M: Hey, Emma. Did you notice Judy's leg today? She had a cast on it.

W: Yeah, I saw that. She said she sprained her ankle pretty badly while playing soccer yesterday.

M: It must be tough for her to walk home with her bag. We should help her out.

W: Good idea. Let's offer to carry her bag when she goes home.

남: 안녕, Emma. 오늘 Judy의 다리를 봤니? 그녀는 깁스했어.

여: 응, 봤어. 그녀는 어제 축구를 하다가 발목을 아주 심하게 삐었다고 말했어.

남: 그 애가 가방을 가지고 집으로 걸어가는 것은 분명 힘들 거야. 우리가 그 애를 도와야 해.

여: 좋은 생각이야. 그 애가 집에 갈 때 가방을 들어 주겠다고 제안하자.

● **Topic & Situation** 다리를 다친 친구 돕기

● **Solution**

Judy가 축구를 하다가 발목을 삐었다고 여자가 말하자, 남자는 그녀가 가방을 가지고 집으로 걸어가는 것이 힘들 것 같다면서 그녀를 도와야 한다고 말했다. 따라서 이에 대한 여자의 응답으로 가장 적절한 것은 ⑤ '좋은 생각이야. 그 애가 집에 갈 때 가방을 들어 주겠다고 제안하자.'이다.

① 그렇게 말해 줘서 고맙지만, 내가 직접 할 수 있어.

② 맞아. 그 애는 우리와 함께 축구하는 것을 정말 좋아해.

③ 좋아! 그 애가 깁스를 풀어서 정말 기뻐.

④ 잘됐구나. 그 애는 네 도움 덕분에 집에 안전하게 도착했어.

● **Words & Phrases**

notice 보다, 알아차리다   cast 깁스   sprain 삐다

12

정답 | ②

| Script & Translation |

[Cell phone rings.]

W: Daniel, don't forget that we're supposed to go to your grandparents' house for dinner today.

M: I know, Mom. I need to return a book to the library after school, but it won't take long.

W: Okay. Remember that we're leaving at 5 p.m. So you should be here before then.

M: Don't worry. I'll make sure to get home on time.

[휴대 전화가 울린다.]

여: Daniel, 우리 오늘 조부모님 댁에 저녁 먹으러 가기로 한 거 잊지 마.

남: 알아요, 엄마. 방과 후에 도서관에 책을 반납해야 하지만, 그것은 오래 걸리지 않을 거예요.

여: 알겠어. 우리가 오후 5시에 떠나는 것을 기억하렴. 그러니까 그 전에 여기에 와야 해.

남: 걱정하지 마세요. 꼭 제시간에 집에 도착하도록 할게요.

● **Topic & Situation** 조부모님과의 저녁 식사

● **Solution**

저녁 먹으러 조부모님 댁에 가기로 한 것을 잊지 말라고 당부하는 여자의 말을 듣고, 남자가 방과 후에 책을 반납해야 하지만, 그것은 오래 걸리지 않을 거라고 대답했고, 이에 여자는 오후 5시에 떠날 테니 그 전에 오라고 말했다. 따라서 이에 대한 남자의 응답으로 가장 적절한 것은 ② '걱정하지 마세요. 꼭 제시간에 집에 도착하도록 할게요.'이다.

① 알겠어요. 지금 당장 우리 자리를 예약하기 위해 전화할게요.

③ 아, 안 돼요! 그들이 벌써 집에 간다니 아쉬워요.

④ 알겠어요. 다시는 학교에 늦지 않도록 노력할게요.

⑤ 물론이죠. 조부모님과 함께 한 저녁 식사는 정말 좋았어요.

● **Words & Phrases**

be supposed to *do* ~하기로 되어 있다   on time 제시간에

13

정답 | ①

| Script & Translation |

M: Chloe, what are you doing after school?

W: I have no plans. Do you want to go see a movie?

M: Yeah, that sounds fun. What time are you free?

W: I'm free from 3 o'clock, right after class. How about you?

M: Well, I'll be free around 3:30. I need to go see Mr. Davis after class.

W: Okay. Then I'll wait for you at the library. By the way, did you hand in your literature assignment today? You said it was due today.

M: You're right. I was going to hand it in after class.

W: Then you should take care of it before we go to the movies.

M: Right. But I haven't printed it out yet.

W: Well, then I can do it for you after class since I have nothing to do.

M: Really? Thank you, Chloe. Here's my USB drive. The file is in the assignment folder.

W: All right. I'll print out your assignment while I wait.

남: Chloe, 방과 후에 뭐 할 거니?

여: 계획이 없는데. 영화 보러 갈래?

남: 응, 재미있겠다. 너는 몇 시에 시간이 있어?

여: 나는 수업 직후인 3시부터 한가해. 너는 어떠니?

남: 음, 나는 3시 30분쯤에 시간이 나. 수업이 끝난 후 Davis 선생님을 뵈러 가야 하거든.

여: 알겠어. 그럼 나는 도서관에서 너를 기다릴게. 그런데, 오늘 문학 과제를 제출했니? 오늘까지라고 말했었잖아.

남: 맞아. 나는 수업이 끝나고 그것을 제출하려고 했어.

여: 그럼 영화 보러 가기 전에 너는 그것을 처리해야 해.

남: 맞아. 하지만 그것을 아직 출력하지 않았어.

여: 음, 그럼 내가 할 일이 없으니 수업이 끝난 후에 그것을 해 줄 수 있어.

남: 정말이니? 고마워, Chloe. 여기 내 USB 드라이브가 있어. 파일은 과제 폴더에 있어.

여: 알겠어. 내가 기다리는 동안에 네 과제를 출력할게.

◑ **Topic & Situation** 친구의 과제물 출력해 주기

◑ **Solution**

수업이 끝나고 영화를 보러 가기 전에 남자를 기다려 주기로 한 여자가 남자에게 문학 과제에 관해 묻자, 남자는 수업이 끝나고 그것을 제출해야 하는데 아직 출력하지 않았다고 대답했고, 이에 여자는 자신이 그것을 대신해 줄 수 있다고 했다. 이에 남자는 고맙다며 자신의 USB 드라이브를 주면서 파일의 위치를 알려 주었다. 따라서 이에 대한 여자의 응답으로 가장 적절한 것은 ① '알겠어. 내가 기다리는 동안에 네 과제를 출력할게.'이다.

② 나는 오늘 방과 후에 영화를 보러 갈 수 없을 것 같아.

③ 우리가 떠나기 전에 네 과제를 끝내는 게 좋을 것 같아.

④ 좋아. 나는 문학 과제를 위한 자료를 수집할 거야.

⑤ 물론이지. 나는 우리가 영화를 보러 가기 전에 과제를 끝낼 수 있어.

◑ **Words & Phrases**

hand in ~을 제출하다   literature 문학   assignment 과제   take care of ~을 처리하다, ~을 돌보다   print out ~을 출력하다

14

| Script & Translation |

W: Honey, you haven't looked up from your phone for about an hour.

M: Sorry, sweetie. I'm shopping for a secondhand tent on an online flea market. I'm thinking about getting this one. Take a look.

W: Oh, that's the exact tent you wanted to buy. How much is it?

M: It's $150. That's less than half the original price.

W: Great. How many years has it been used?

M: The seller said it's been two years since he bought it and used it only five times.

W: That sounds good, but you still should see it in person before buying it.

M: But look at this picture. It looks like it's in great condition.

W: Sure, but it's a picture. There may be tears that you can't see in the picture.

M: Well, that makes sense. I need to be more careful.

W: That's right. I think you'd better decide after you check it out yourself.

M: Okay. I'll ask the seller if I can see the tent first.

여: 여보, 당신은 약 한 시간 동안 전화기에서 눈을 떼지 않았어요.

남: 미안해요, 여보. 온라인 벼룩시장에서 중고 텐트를 쇼핑하고 있어요. 이것을 살까 생각 중이에요. 한번 봐요.

여: 아, 그것은 당신이 사고 싶어 했던 바로 그 텐트잖아요. 그게 얼마예요?

남: 150달러예요. 그것은 원래 가격의 절반도 안 되는 가격이에요.

여: 좋군요. 그건 몇 년이나 사용되었나요?

남: 판매자는 그것을 산 이후로 2년이 지났고, 다섯 번밖에 사용하지 않았다고 말했어요.

여: 좋은 것 같은데, 그래도 사기 전에 그것을 직접 봐야 해요.

남: 하지만 이 사진을 봐요. 상태가 아주 좋아 보여요.

여: 물론이죠, 하지만 이건 사진이에요. 사진에서 볼 수 없는 찢어진 부분이 있을 수 있어요.

남: 흠, 그것은 일리 있는 말이에요. 제가 좀 더 신중할 필요가 있겠군요.

여: 맞아요. 당신이 직접 확인한 후에 결정하는 게 더 좋을 거예요.

남: 알겠어요. 판매자에게 텐트를 먼저 볼 수 있는지 물어볼게요.

● Topic & Situation 중고 텐트 구매

● Solution

남자가 온라인 벼룩시장에 나와 있는 중고 텐트를 사려고 하자, 여자는 사진으로 볼 수 없는 찢어진 부분이 있을 수 있다면서 사기 전에 직접 봐야 한다고 말했고, 이에 남자는 일리가 있는 말이라면서 좀 더 신중하겠다고 했다. 이어서 여자가 직접 확인한 후에 결정하는 것이 더 좋을 거라고 조언했으므로, 이에 대한 남자의 응답으로 가장 적절한 것은 ② '알겠어요. 판매자에게 텐트를 먼저 볼 수 있는지 물어볼게요.'이다.

① 물론이죠. 제가 그 텐트를 직접 확인해 보고 구매했어요.

③ 맞아요. 우리는 그 텐트를 너무 오래 사용한 것 같아요.

④ 괜찮아요. 내가 혼자서 그에게 그 중고 텐트를 가져다줄게요.

⑤ 나는 그렇게 생각하지 않아요. 그는 텐트를 가지고 제시간에 오기로 약속했어요.

● Words & Phrases

secondhand 중고의   flea market 벼룩시장   tear 찢어진 부분; 찢다

15

정답 | ③

| Script & Translation |

W: Mr. Wilson has been working as an apartment manager for a year. He does a lot of things to keep the environment of the apartment clean and safe for the residents. Today, he notices that one of the swings in the children's playground is not balanced, making it dangerous. He goes to his office and writes "Do Not Use" in large letters on a piece of paper. Then he goes back to the playground to attach it to the swing. However, when he gets to the playground, a little girl is using the swing. He thinks the girl should use a safer swing. In this situation, what would Mr. Wilson most likely say to the little girl?

Mr. Wilson: This swing is not safe to ride, so please use another one.

여: Wilson 씨는 아파트 관리인으로 1년째 일하고 있습니다. 그는 거주민들을 위해 아파트의 환경을 깨끗하고 안전하게 유지하기 위해 많은 일을 합니다. 오늘, 그는 어린이 놀이터의 그

네 중 하나가 균형이 맞지 않아 위험하다는 것을 알아차립니다. 그는 사무실에 가서 종이 위에 '사용하지 마시오.'라고 큰 글씨로 씁니다. 그러고 나서 그것을 그네에 붙이기 위해 놀이터로 돌아갑니다. 하지만, 그가 놀이터에 도착하니, 한 어린 여자아이가 그 그네를 사용하고 있습니다. 그는 그 여자아이가 더 안전한 그네를 사용해야 한다고 생각합니다. 이런 상황에서, Wilson 씨는 그 여자아이에게 뭐라고 말하겠습니까?

Wilson 씨: 이 그네는 타기에 안전하지 않으니까, 다른 것을 사용하렴.

● Topic & Situation 균형이 맞지 않는 그네

● Solution

아파트 관리인인 Wilson 씨가 어린이 놀이터 그네 중 하나가 균형이 맞지 않아 사용하지 말라는 문구를 쓰려고 사무실에 다녀오는 사이에 한 어린 여자아이가 그 그네를 사용하고 있는 것을 발견하고, 그 아이가 더 안전한 그네를 사용해야 한다고 말하고 싶은 상황이다. 따라서 Wilson 씨가 여자아이에게 할 말로 가장 적절한 것은 ③ '이 그네는 타기에 안전하지 않으니까, 다른 것을 사용하렴.'이다.

① 놀이터에 있는 그네 위에서 서지 말아라.

② 그네를 타려면 균형을 잘 잡아야 하니?

④ 기다리고 있는 다른 아이들이 그네를 타게 해 줄 수 있겠니?

⑤ 그네를 타는 동안 줄을 꽉 잡아라.

● Words & Phrases

resident 거주민   swing 그네   attach 붙이다

16~17

정답 | 16 ③ 17 ④

| Script & Translation |

M: Hello, students! Last class, we talked about a variety of modern computer technologies. Today we're going to focus on how VR technology, which means virtual reality technology, is used in various fields. It has become increasingly popular in a wide range of fields because of its ability to involve users in a simulated environment. First of all, in gaming, VR technology allows players to feel as if they are inside the game, creating a more realistic and engaging experience. In education, VR can be used to provide engaging learning experiences that help students better understand complex concepts. Moreover, in healthcare, VR technology can be used for pain management, physical therapy, and even as a tool for diagnosing and treating mental health conditions. Lastly, in tourism, VR technology can let people travel to different countries, visit world-famous landmarks, and experience a glimpse into another culture. It's very useful because we can try a holiday before we decide where to go. Overall, VR technology has proven to be a valuable tool for various fields. Now, let's talk more about the uses of VR technology after watching a short video.

○ Words & Phrases

a variety of 다양한 **focus on** ~을 집중적으로 알아보다, ~에 집중하다 **virtual reality** 가상 현실 **a wide range of** 광범위한 **simulated** 모의실험의, 모조의 **engaging** 매력적인 **healthcare** 의료, 건강 관리 **management** 관리 **physical therapy** 물리치료 **diagnose** 진단하다 **glimpse** 짧은 경험 **valuable** 귀중한

남: 안녕하세요, 학생 여러분! 지난 수업에서, 우리는 다양한 현대 컴퓨터 기술에 관해 이야기했습니다. 오늘은 가상 현실 기술을 의미하는 VR 기술이 다양한 분야에서 어떻게 활용되고 있는지 집중적으로 알아보겠습니다. 그것은 모의 환경에 사용자를 참여시킬 수 있다는 것 때문에 광범위한 분야에서 점점 더 인기를 끌고 있습니다. 우선, 게임하기에서 VR 기술은 플레이어가 게임 안에 있는 것처럼 느낄 수 있게 하여 더 현실적이고 매력적인 경험을 만듭니다. 교육에서, VR은 학생들이 복잡한 개념을 더 잘 이해하도록 돕는 매력적인 학습 경험을 제공하는 데 사용될 수 있습니다. 더욱이, 의료 분야에서 VR 기술은 통증 관리, 물리치료, 그리고 심지어 정신 건강 상태를 진단하고 치료하는 도구로 사용될 수 있습니다. 마지막으로, 관광에서, VR 기술은 사람들이 다른 나라로 여행하고, 세계적으로 유명한 명소를 방문하고, 다른 문화를 짧게 경험할 수 있게 해 줍니다. 우리가 어디로 갈지 결정하기 전에 휴가를 시도할 수 있어서 그것은 매우 유용합니다. 전반적으로, VR 기술은 다양한 분야를 위한 귀중한 도구인 것으로 입증되었습니다. 이제, 짧은 비디오를 본 후에 VR 기술의 사용에 대해 더 이야기해 봅시다.

○ Topic & Situation 현대 사회에서 VR 기술의 쓰임

○ Solution

16 남자는 현대 사회에서 VR 기술이 유용하게 쓰이고 있는 분야에 관해서 설명하고 있으므로, 남자가 하는 말의 주제로 가장 적절한 것은 ③ 'VR 기술의 다양한 현대적 쓰임'이다.

① VR 기술의 기본 원리
② VR 기술과 관련된 새로운 직업
④ VR 기술로 유발된 사회 문제
⑤ VR 기술 사용의 경제적 이익

17 VR 기술이 유용하게 쓰이고 있는 분야들로 게임하기, 교육, 의료, 관광은 언급되었지만, ④ '건축'은 언급되지 않았다.

23강 실전 모의고사 2회

본문 168~173쪽

01 ①	02 ⑤	03 ③	04 ④	05 ④	06 ②
07 ⑤	08 ④	09 ⑤	10 ④	11 ④	12 ②
13 ⑤	14 ②	15 ③	16 ③	17 ④	

01

정답 | ①

| Script & Translation |

W: All right, everyone. Now that you've got your flippers on, let's go to the next step, which is how to use the snorkel. First, put your mask on, and adjust the small rubber strap so that the snorkel passes just above your left ear. Then, take a deep breath, bite down on the mouthpiece, and put your head in the water. Breathe out sharply once to clear any water in the snorkel. This is called "blasting." Then try swimming and breathing at the same time. But move gently so your snorkel doesn't fill up with water. And remember to blast whenever water gets in the snorkel.

여: 좋아요, 여러분. 이제 오리발을 착용했으니 다음 단계인 스노클 사용법으로 넘어가 보겠습니다. 먼저, 마스크를 착용하고 스노클이 왼쪽 귀 바로 위를 지나가도록 작은 고무끈을 조절하세요. 그런 다음 심호흡을 하고, 마우스피스를 물고, 머리를 물속에 넣습니다. 한 번 세게 숨을 내쉬어 스노클 안의 물을 모두 제거하세요. 이것을 '불어 내기(바람을 불어 물을 강제로 빼내기)'라고 합니다. 그런 다음 수영과 호흡을 동시에 해 보세요. 하지만 스노클에 물이 가득 차지 않도록 부드럽게 움직이세요. 그리고 스노클에 물이 들어올 때마다 불어 내기를 기억하세요.

● **Topic & Situation** 스노클 사용 방법

● **Solution**
오리발 착용 후 다음 단계로 스노클을 착용하고, 호흡하는 방법 및 스노클에 물이 들어올 때 바람을 불어 물을 빼내는 방법을 설명하고 있으므로, 여자가 하는 말의 목적으로 가장 적절한 것은 ① '스노클을 사용하는 방법을 알려 주려고'이다.

● **Words & Phrases**
flipper 오리발   snorkel 스노클(잠수 중에 물 밖으로 연결하여 숨을 쉬는 데 쓰는 관)   rubber strap 고무끈   take a breath 숨을 쉬다

mouthpiece 마우스피스, 입을 대는 부분   breathe out 숨을 내쉬다
sharply 세게, 격렬하게

02

정답 | ⑤

| Script & Translation |

M: Clara, have you been burning candles in your room?

W: Yeah. Have you smelled the lavender? It's nice, right?

M: Yes, but do you know that burning candles in a small room can pollute the air?

W: Really? I had no idea.

M: Yes. It's because burning candles release tiny chemical particles into the air, which collect in really small spaces.

W: That doesn't sound good.

M: It's not. If you breathe in that air for a long time, you can get some health problems.

W: I see. I didn't know that burning candles could be harmful.

M: I don't think many people do. But it's important to be aware of this, especially if you burn candles in a small, enclosed space like your room.

W: Thanks for telling me. I'll stop burning candles.

남: Clara, 네 방에서 양초를 켜고 있었니?

여: 응. 라벤더 향 맡아 봤지? 그건 좋아, 그렇지?

남: 응, 하지만 좁은 방에서 양초를 켜면 공기를 오염시킬 수 있다는 것 알아?

여: 정말? 전혀 몰랐어.

남: 맞아. 양초를 켜면 작은 화학 입자들이 공기 중으로 방출되어, 아주 좁은 공간에서는 모이기 때문이야.

여: 좋지 않은 것 같은데.

남: 좋지 않아. 그 공기를 오랫동안 들이마시면, 건강에 문제가 생길 수 있어.

여: 알겠어. 나는 양초를 켜는 것이 해로울 수 있다는 것을 몰랐어.

남: 많은 사람이 모르고 있을 거라고 생각해. 하지만 특히 네 방처럼 좁고 밀폐된 공간에서 양초를 켤 때는 이것을 알고 있는 것이 중요해.

여: 알려 줘서 고마워. 양초를 그만 켜야겠다.

◐ **Topic & Situation** 양초 켜기와 공기 오염

◐ **Solution**

여자가 방 안에 양초를 켜 둔 것을 알고 남자는 여자에게 좁은 방에서 양초를 켜면 공기가 오염되고 그 공기를 오랫동안 들이마시면 건강에 해로울 수 있다고 말하고 있다. 따라서 남자의 의견으로 가장 적절한 것은 ⑤ '좁은 공간에서 양초를 켜면 실내 공기가 오염돼 건강에 해로울 수 있다.'이다.

◐ **Words & Phrases**

candle 양초 lavender 라벤더 pollute 오염시키다 release 방출하다 chemical 화학의, 화학적인 particle (아주 작은) 입자 breathe in ~을 들이마시다 enclosed 밀폐된

여기고 작은 것에서 행복을 찾아봅시다.

◐ **Topic & Situation** 일상에서 찾는 작은 행복

◐ **Solution**

'바로 이 순간에도 경험할 수 있는 소소한 기쁨이 너무나 많다.'는 말을 인용하며, 일상 속 소소한 기쁨에 감사하며 행복을 찾아보자는 내용이므로, 여자가 하는 말의 요지로 가장 적절한 것은 ③ '일상의 작은 즐거움에 감사하며 행복을 느끼자.'이다.

◐ **Words & Phrases**

take a moment (잠깐) 시간을 내다 appreciate 감사하다 gratitude 감사 stroll 산책, (한가로이) 거닐기 hike 하이킹 immense 엄청난 laughter 웃음소리, 웃음 take a look (한번) 보다 countless 수많은, 셀 수 없이 많은 consistent 변함없는 cherish 소중히 여기다

03

정답 | ③

| **Script & Translation** |

W: Welcome to Lazy Afternoon with your host, Olivia. We should always take moments throughout our day to appreciate the simple joys of life and express our gratitude. Oprah Winfrey once said, "There are so many simple joys to be experienced in this very moment." From a relaxing stroll alone to an energizing hike with friends, these moments bring us immense happiness. The blue sky, the laughter of children, and the smile of a loved one — each holds its own magic. Take a closer look, and you'll find countless reasons to be thankful: something to do, a place to rest, and consistent support from those around us. Let's cherish these blessings and find happiness in the little things.

여: Olivia가 진행하는 Lazy Afternoon에 오신 것을 환영합니다. 우리는 항상 온종일 삶의 소소한 기쁨에 감사하며 감사를 표현하는 시간을 가져야 합니다. Oprah Winfrey는 '바로 이 순간에도 경험할 수 있는 소소한 기쁨이 너무나 많다.'고 말한 적이 있습니다. 혼자만의 여유로운 산책부터 친구들과 함께하는 활기찬 하이킹까지, 이러한 순간은 우리에게 엄청난 행복을 가져다줍니다. 푸른 하늘, 아이들의 웃음, 사랑하는 사람의 미소는 각각 고유한 마법을 담고 있습니다. 더 자세히 살펴보면, 할 일, 쉴 곳, 주변 사람들의 변함없는 지지와 같은 감사해야 할 수많은 이유를 찾을 수 있습니다. 이러한 축복을 소중히

04

정답 | ④

| **Script & Translation** |

M: Maria, why are you smiling?

W: Hi, Michael. I'm looking at a photo of my niece, Lily. She's my sister's daughter. They had a little photo shoot at home.

M: Let me see. Wow, she's so cute. Lily must've turned 100 days old since her jumpsuit says '100 Days' on it.

W: Right. She turned 100 days two days ago.

M: She's wearing a crown on her head!

W: I know! Her parents wanted to make her 100th day a special occasion.

M: The stuffed animal next to her is so cute. I love giraffes!

W: Thanks. The stuffed giraffe was a gift from me.

M: It's perfect for the photo. The giraffe even matches Lily's striped socks.

W: Oh yeah! I hadn't noticed. My favorite part is the star-shaped cushion under her legs.

M: Yeah, it's cool too.

W: I can't wait to see Lily this weekend!

남: Maria, 왜 웃고 있어요?

여: 안녕하세요, Michael. 제 조카 Lily의 사진을 보고 있어요. 그녀는 제 여동생의 딸이에요. 그들이 집에서 소규모로 사진

촬영을 했어요.

남: 어디 봐요. 와, 너무 귀여워요. Lily의 점프 슈트에 '100 Days'라고 적혀 있는 걸 보니 백일이 된 게 분명하군요.

여: 맞아요. 이틀 전에 백일이 되었어요.

남: 그녀가 머리에 왕관을 쓰고 있네요!

여: 맞아요! 그녀의 부모님이 그녀의 백일을 특별한 날로 만들어 주고 싶었나 봐요.

남: 그녀 옆에 있는 봉제 동물 인형이 너무 귀엽네요. 저는 기린을 좋아해요!

여: 고마워요. 그 봉제 기린 인형은 제가 선물한 거예요.

남: 사진에 꼭 알맞네요. 기린은 Lily의 줄무늬 양말과도 잘 어울려요.

여: 오 맞아요! 몰랐네요. 제가 좋아하는 부분은 그녀의 다리 밑에 있는 별 모양 쿠션이에요.

남: 네, 그것도 멋지네요.

여: 이번 주말에 Lily를 빨리 보고 싶네요!

● **Topic & Situation** 조카 사진

● **Solution**

대화에서 Lily는 줄무늬 양말을 신고 있다고 했는데, 그림에는 물방울 무늬 양말이다. 따라서 그림에서 대화의 내용과 일치하지 않는 것은 ④이다.

● **Words & Phrases**

niece 조카(딸)   photo shoot 사진 촬영   jumpsuit 점프 슈트
stuffed animal 봉제 동물 인형   giraffe 기린   match 어울리다

05

정답 | ④

| Script & Translation |

M: Katie, I'm looking forward to handing out snacks before the midterm exam tomorrow.

W: Me, too. It's one of my favorite student council events. I think we're almost ready.

M: Right. I updated the message on the LED display board.

W: I saw it. I like the encouraging message you added.

M: I hope it helps the students. Did you place the order for the snacks?

W: Yes, I did. However, I received a text message saying the delivery would be delayed.

M: Oh, no. Will it still arrive today, though? Can you track the order?

W: Yeah, it's supposed to arrive today. I'll track it to see its current location.

M: Okay. And I texted the other student council members to inform them about when and where to meet tomorrow morning.

W: Great. It's going to be a fun day tomorrow.

남: Katie, 내일 중간고사 전에 간식 나눠 주기(행사)를 기대하고 있어.

여: 나도. 그것은 내가 가장 좋아하는 학생회 행사 중 하나야. 거의 다 준비된 것 같아.

남: 맞아. 내가 LED 전광판의 메시지를 업데이트했어.

여: 봤어. 네가 추가한 격려의 메시지가 마음에 들어.

남: 학생들에게 도움이 되길 바라. 네가 간식 주문을 했지?

여: 응, 그래. 그런데 배송이 지연된다는 문자 메시지를 받았어.

남: 오, 안 돼. 그래도 오늘 도착하겠지? 주문을 추적할 수 있어?

여: 응, 오늘 도착할 예정이야. 내가 현재 위치를 추적해 볼게.

남: 알겠어. 그리고 다른 학생회 위원들에게 문자를 보내 내일 아침 언제 어디서 만날지 알렸어.

여: 잘했네. 내일 즐거운 하루가 될 거야.

● **Topic & Situation** 학생회 행사 준비

● **Solution**

내일 학생회의 간식 나눠 주기 행사 준비를 점검하면서 여자는 간식 주문을 했는데 배송 지연 문자 메시지를 받았다고 하자 남자가 주문을 추적할 수 있냐고 묻고, 여자가 현재 위치를 추적해 보겠다고 말했다. 따라서 여자가 할 일로 가장 적절한 것은 ④ '물품 배송 추적하기'이다.

● **Words & Phrases**

look forward to ~을 기대하다   midterm exam 중간고사
student council 학생회   encouraging 격려의   delivery 배송, 배달   track 추적하다   text 문자를 보내다

06

정답 | ②

| Script & Translation |

W: Welcome to Chef's Paradise. May I help you?

M: Yes. Can you point me to your measuring spoon sets?

W: Sure. *[Pause]* Right here. We have a plastic set with four spoons and a metal set with seven spoons.

M: How much are they?

W: The plastic set is $5, and the metal one is $13.

M: I'll take a metal set.

W: Okay. Currently, we have a special offer. If you purchase a measuring spoon set and a measuring cup set together, you'll get a discount.

M: Oh, great. I could use some new measuring cups.

W: Here's our metal measuring cup set. It comes with five cups and costs $17. But since you're getting the measuring spoon set, you get 10% off the total.

M: Great. I'll buy both sets.

W: Okay. One metal measuring spoon set and one metal measuring cup set, right?

M: Yes. Here's my credit card.

여: Chef's Paradise에 오신 것을 환영합니다. 도와드릴까요?

남: 네. 계량스푼 세트가 있는 곳을 좀 알려 주시겠어요?

여: 물론이죠. [잠시 후] 여기 있습니다. 스푼이 네 개 들어 있는 플라스틱 세트와 스푼이 일곱 개 들어 있는 금속 세트가 있습니다.

남: 그것들은 얼마인가요?

여: 플라스틱 세트는 5달러이고, 금속 세트는 13달러입니다.

남: 금속 세트 하나로 하겠습니다.

여: 알겠습니다. 지금 특별 할인을 하고 있습니다. 계량스푼 세트와 계량컵 세트를 함께 구매하면 할인을 받으실 거예요.

남: 오, 좋아요. 새 계량컵이 좀 필요할 것 같습니다.

여: 여기 금속 계량컵 세트가 있습니다. 계량컵 다섯 개가 들어 있고 가격은 17달러입니다. 하지만 계량스푼 세트를 구매하시기 때문에 총금액에서 10% 할인이 됩니다.

남: 좋아요. 세트 둘 다 살게요.

여: 네. 금속 계량스푼 세트 하나와 금속 계량컵 세트 하나 맞으시죠?

남: 네. 여기 제 신용 카드입니다.

○ Topic & Situation 계량스푼 세트와 계량컵 세트 구입

○ Solution
계량스푼 일곱 개가 들어 있는 금속 계량스푼 세트 하나는 13달러이고, 계량컵 다섯 개가 들어 있는 금속 계량컵 세트 하나는 17달러로 총 30달러인데 계량스푼과 계량컵을 함께 구매하면 총금액에서 10% 할인이 된다고 했으므로, 남자가 지불할 금액은 ② '$27'이다.

○ Words & Phrases
measuring spoon 계량스푼   measuring cup 계량컵   get a discount 할인을 받다

07

| Script & Translation |

M: Diana, another salad for lunch? That's all you've had all week.

W: Hi, David. I started a new diet this week.

M: Oh, I see. And have you stopped working out in the evening? I haven't seen you at the gym recently.

W: No. I've just changed gyms.

M: Really? I thought you liked our gym because it's so close to the office and it has a lot of machines.

W: That's true. But my friend recommended a personal trainer at her gym.

M: Oh, I see. So how's your new trainer?

W: She's awesome. She doesn't push me too hard like my previous trainer. And the program she has me on is better than the last one.

M: Sounds perfect.

W: Yes. I'm much happier.

남: Diana, 점심으로 또 샐러드인가요? 일주일 내내 샐러드만 먹고 있네요.

여: 안녕하세요, David. 제가 이번 주에 새로 다이어트를 시작했거든요.

남: 아, 그렇군요. 그리고 저녁에 운동하는 것은 그만뒀어요? 최근에 체육관에서 당신을 본 적이 없어요.

여: 아니요. 체육관을 옮겼어요.

남: 정말요? 우리 체육관이 사무실과 가깝고 운동 기구가 많아서 좋아하는 줄 알았는데요.

여: 맞아요. 하지만 제 친구가 자신의 체육관에 있는 개인 트레이너를 추천해 줬어요.

남: 아, 그렇군요. 그래서 새로운 트레이너는 어때요?

여: 그녀는 정말 대단해요. 그녀는 이전 트레이너처럼 나를 너무 힘들게 몰아붙이지 않아요. 그리고 그녀가 제게 제공하는 프로그램은 지난번 프로그램보다 더 좋아요.

남: 완벽하네요.

여: 네. 훨씬 더 좋아요.

○ Topic & Situation 체육관과 개인 트레이너

○ Solution
여자는 친구가 자신이 다니는 체육관의 개인 트레이너를 추천해 줘서 체육관을 옮겼다고 말했다. 따라서 여자가 체육관을 옮긴 이유는 ⑤ '새로운 개인 트레이너를 추천받아서'이다.

Words & Phrases

work out 운동하다   recommend 추천하다   personal trainer 개인 트레이너   push 몰아붙이다

08

정답 | ④

Script & Translation

M: Honey, I was thinking that while we're in Osaka on our trip, we should go to a hot spring.

W: I was thinking that, too! Do you know of a good place?

M: Yeah. There's a place called Hara Hot Springs, just a few stops away from Osaka Station.

W: Cool. Do you have their hours? I'd love to spend a whole day there.

M: Let me check. *[Pause]* They're open from 10 a.m. to 10 p.m.

W: Great. Do you know if they have different themed hot spring pools?

M: Yeah. They have a Japanese garden-themed pool, a natural rock pool, and an outdoor hot spring pool.

W: Perfect! Do we need to bring anything there?

M: We should bring our own bathing suits.

W: Okay. And do they sell snacks there?

M: Actually, there's a restaurant on-site that serves traditional Japanese cuisine.

W: Awesome, let's go there!

남: 여보, 나는 우리가 여행 중 오사카에 있는 동안 온천에 가는 것을 생각했어요.

여: 나도 그 생각을 했어요! 좋은 곳을 알고 있어요?

남: 네. 오사카역에서 몇 정거장만 가면 Hara Hot Springs라는 곳이 있어요.

여: 좋아요. 영업시간은 알아요? 그곳에서 온종일 보내고 싶네요.

남: 확인해 볼게요. *[잠시 후]* 오전 10시부터 오후 10시까지 영업하네요.

여: 좋아요. 특정한 테마를 살린 다양한 온천 수영장이 있는지 알고 있나요?

남: 네. 일본식 정원을 테마로 한 수영장, 천연 암반 수영장, 그리고 야외 온천 수영장이 있어요.

여: 완벽해요! 우리가 거기에 가져가야 할 것이 있어요?

남: 수영복은 각자 챙겨야 해요.

여: 알았어요. 거기서 간식도 팔아요?

남: 실은, 현장에 전통 일본 요리를 제공하는 식당이 있어요.

여: 굉장해요. 거기로 가요!

Topic & Situation   Hara Hot Springs

Solution

Hara Hot Springs에 관해 위치, 영업시간, 수영장 종류, 식당은 언급이 되었으나, ④ '예약 방법'은 언급되지 않았다.

Words & Phrases

hot spring 온천   stop 정거장   themed 특정한 테마를 살린   outdoor 야외의   bathing suit 수영복   on-site 현장에

09

정답 | ⑤

Script & Translation

W: Hello, everyone. Welcome to Tasabay Winery. The Tasabay Winery Tour starts in the garden right over there, and it takes about an hour. A guide will show you around the main building and teach you about the wine-making process. Then he will take you inside the production area to see where our dedicated team crafts our original wine from Bali. After experiencing our unique wine-making process, the guide will accompany you to the tasting room. And there, you can try tasting three of our wines. With your taste buds stimulated, you can visit the retail shop, where you can buy wine at a discounted price. Thank you for joining us today.

여: 안녕하세요, 여러분. Tasabay Winery에 오신 것을 환영합니다. Tasabay Winery Tour는 바로 저쪽 정원에서 시작되며, 대략 한 시간 정도 소요됩니다. 가이드가 본관을 안내하고 와인 제조 과정에 관해 가르쳐 줄 것입니다. 그런 다음 그는 여러분을 생산 구역 안으로 안내하여 전담 팀이 발리의 오리지널 와인을 공들여 만드는 곳을 보여 드릴 것입니다. 독특한 와인 제조 과정을 체험한 후에 가이드가 여러분과 함께 시음실까지 동행할 것입니다. 그리고 그곳에서 여러분은 저희 와인 중 세 가지를 시음하실 겁니다. 여러분의 미뢰를 자극한 후에, 여러분은 할인된 가격에 와인을 구입할 수 있는 소매점을 방문할 수 있습니다. 오늘 함께해 주셔서 감사합니다.

○ Topic & Situation Tasabay Winery Tour

○ Solution

시음실에서 세 가지 와인을 시음할 것이라고 했으므로, 담화의 내용과 일치하지 않는 것은 ⑤ '다섯 가지 와인을 시음할 것이다.'이다.

○ Words & Phrases

winery 와이너리, 포도주 양조장   dedicated 전담의, 오직 특정한 목적을 위한   craft 공들여 만들다   accompany 동행하다, 동반하다   tasting room 시음실   taste bud 미뢰(혀의 미각 기관)   stimulate 자극하다   retail shop 소매점

10
정답 | ④

| Script & Translation |

W: Mr. White. Do you know much about USB hubs? I need to buy one for the teachers' office.

M: Yeah, I know a little bit. Do you need help choosing one?

W: Yes, thanks. I found these five models on this website.

M: Well, first off, this one only has three ports. That's not enough.

W: Okay. Oh, I just noticed that this one is out of the budget range.

M: How much is the budget?

W: It's $20. How about this one? It has the longest cable.

M: I think it's actually too long. When the cable is over 25 centimeters, it tends to get twisted.

W: Ah, that's a good point. So then it's down to these two.

M: Most of the other computer accessories are black, right?

W: Yeah. I'll go with the same color. I'll order this one.

여: White 선생님. USB 허브에 대해 잘 아세요? 교무실용으로 하나 사야 해서요.

남: 네, 조금 압니다. 고르는 데 도움이 필요하세요?

여: 네, 감사합니다. 제가 이 웹사이트에서 이 다섯 가지 모델을 찾았어요.

남: 음, 우선, 이것은 포트가 세 개밖에 없네요. 그걸로는 충분하

지 않아요.

여: 네. 아, 방금 이것이 예산 범위를 벗어난다는 것을 알았네요.

남: 예산이 얼마인가요?

여: 20달러요. 이것은 어때요? 케이블이 가장 길어요.

남: 사실 너무 긴 것 같아요. 케이블이 25cm가 넘으면 꼬일 수 있어요.

여: 아, 좋은 지적이에요. 그럼 이 두 개만 남네요.

남: 다른 컴퓨터 액세서리가 대부분 검은색이죠, 그렇죠?

여: 네. 같은 색으로 할게요. 저는 이것을 주문할게요.

○ Topic & Situation USB 허브 주문

○ Solution

세 개의 포트로는 충분하지 않다는 남자의 말에 동의하며, 20달러 예산 내에서 케이블 길이가 25cm를 넘지 않는 검은색으로 주문하기로 했으므로, 여자가 주문할 USB 허브는 ④이다.

○ Words & Phrases

port 포트(컴퓨터의 주변 기기 접속 단자)   cable 케이블, 전선   first off 우선, 먼저   budget 예산   get twisted 꼬이다   accessory 액세서리, 부대 용품

11
정답 | ④

| Script & Translation |

M: Lydia, how's your Italian class at the language school?

W: Great! I feel like I'm learning a lot though my teacher teaches even without a textbook.

M: Really? How does the teacher do that?

W: He uses interactive activities like games and role plays.

남: Lydia, 어학원의 이탈리아어 수업은 어때요?

여: 좋아요! 선생님이 교과서 없이 가르치는 데도 많은 것을 배우고 있는 것 같아요.

남: 정말요? 그 선생님은 어떻게 그럴 수 있어요?

여: 그는 게임이나 역할극과 같은 상호적인 활동을 사용해요.

○ Topic & Situation 외국어 수업

○ Solution

여자가 어학원 선생님이 수업에서 교과서를 사용하지 않는 데도 많은 것을 배우고 있다고 하자 남자가 어떻게 교과서 없이 가르칠

수 있는지 묻고 있으므로, 이에 대한 여자의 응답으로 가장 적절한 것은 ④ '그는 게임이나 역할극과 같은 상호적인 활동을 사용해요.'이다.

① 그는 우리 모두에게 이탈리아로 유학을 가라고 했어요.
② 그는 교과서에 있는 연습 문제를 풀도록 강요해요.
③ 그는 내가 이탈리아어를 가르친 최고의 학생 중 한 명이에요.
⑤ 그는 내가 어학원에서 이탈리아어 수업을 듣도록 제안했어요.

● **Words & Phrases**

Italian 이탈리아어   language school 어학원   textbook 교과서

12
정답 | ②

| **Script & Translation** |

W: Excuse me. Is this elevator working?

M: No, it's not. We're doing some maintenance on it right now. Sorry for the inconvenience.

W: No problem. I'm trying to get to the shoe department on the sixth floor. Do you know how I can get there?

M: There's an escalator over there you can use to arrive there.

여: 실례합니다. 이 엘리베이터는 작동하나요?

남: 아니요, 작동하지 않습니다. 저희가 지금 그것을 정비 중입니다. 불편을 드려 죄송합니다.

여: 괜찮아요. 6층에 있는 신발 매장에 가려고 하는데요. 어떻게 갈 수 있는지 아세요?

남: 그곳으로 가기 위해 이용하실 수 있는 에스컬레이터가 저쪽에 있습니다.

● **Topic & Situation**   엘리베이터 정비

● **Solution**

남자가 엘리베이터를 정비 중이라고 말하자, 여자가 6층에 있는 신발 매장을 가려면 어떻게 가야 하는지 묻고 있으므로, 여자의 마지막 말에 대한 남자의 응답으로 가장 적절한 것은 ② '그곳으로 가기 위해 이용하실 수 있는 에스컬레이터가 저쪽에 있습니다.'이다.

① 저희에게 완벽한 유지 보수 서비스를 받으실 수 있습니다.
③ 이 양식을 작성해 주세요. 6일 후에 신발 수선을 완료할 수 있습니다.
④ 신발 매장을 찾으신다면, 그것은 6층에 있습니다.
⑤ 이 층에서 내리시면 됩니다. 신발 매장은 오른쪽에 있습니다.

● **Words & Phrases**

maintenance 정비, 유지 보수   inconvenience 불편   department (백화점, 시장 따위의) 매장, 코너

13
정답 | ⑤

| **Script & Translation** |

M: Tina, what is that strange smell?

W: Hey, Kevin. It's this fruit called durian. Have you heard of it?

M: Oh, yeah. I've heard it smells bad. I've never seen one, though.

W: Well, trust me. It tastes better than it smells. Do you want to try it?

M: No, thanks. Just the smell makes me feel sick.

W: It's considered a delicacy in some Asian countries. They call it the "king of fruits."

M: No way! You're pulling my leg.

W: It's true!

M: All right. What does it taste like, then?

W: It's a little bit hard to describe. It's neither sweet nor bitter.

M: Whatever! I still can't get rid of the smell in my nose. How can you eat something that smells so bad?

W: Just try it! I think you'll be pleasantly surprised by the taste.

남: Tina, 이 이상한 냄새는 뭐야?

여: 어, Kevin. 두리안이라는 과일이야. 들어 본 적 있어?

남: 오, 그래. 냄새가 고약하다고 들었어. 하지만 한 번도 본 적은 없어.

여: 음, 날 믿어 봐. 냄새보다 맛이 더 좋을 거야. 먹어 볼래?

남: 아니, 괜찮아. 냄새만 맡아도 속이 메슥거려.

여: 일부 아시아 국가에서는 별미로 여겨져. 그들은 그것을 '과일의 왕'이라고 불러.

남: 말도 안 돼! 날 놀리고 있구나.

여: 사실이야!

남: 알았어. 그럼, 어떤 맛이 나는데?

여: 설명하기가 좀 어려워. 달지도 않고 쓰지도 않아.

남: 뭐든! 아직도 코에서 나는 냄새를 없앨 수가 없어. 어떻게 그렇게 냄새가 심한 걸 먹을 수가 있지?

여: 그냥 먹어 봐! 넌 그 맛에 기분 좋게 놀랄 거라고 생각해.

○ **Topic & Situation** 과일의 왕, 두리안

○ **Solution**

두리안이라는 과일의 이상한 냄새를 맡고 속이 메슥거린다는 남자에게 여자는 냄새보다 맛은 더 좋고, 일부 아시아 국가에서는 '과일의 왕'이라고도 불린다고 말하며 남자에게 먹어 볼 것을 계속 권하고 있다. 따라서 남자의 마지막 말에 대한 여자의 응답으로 가장 적절한 것은 ⑤ '그냥 먹어 봐! 넌 그 맛에 기분 좋게 놀랄 거라고 생각해.'이다.

① 왜 안 돼? 네가 두리안을 좋아한다니 정말 기뻐.
② 맞아. 너의 코가 막힌 것처럼 들려.
③ 잘 모르겠어. 하지만 그것은 두리안과 맛이 아주 똑같아.
④ 간단해. 냄새로 음식이 상했는지 알 수 있어.

○ **Words & Phrases**

hear of ~에 대해 듣다 feel sick 메슥거리다. 토할 것 같다 delicacy 별미, 진미 pull one's leg ~을 놀리다. 농담을 던지다 neither ~ nor ... ~도 아니고 …도 아니다

14
정답 | ②

| **Script & Translation** |

W: Jake, that's quite a bruise you have on your leg.

M: I know. It's huge. I got it while playing soccer last weekend.

W: I didn't know you played soccer. Are you on a team?

M: No. Just my friends and I play futsal every weekend, just for fun.

W: That's cool. I used to play soccer in high school.

M: Really? Maybe you should join us. It's a mix of men and women.

W: Yeah, I'll think about that. I've been doing yoga for a while, but I feel like playing a team sport again.

M: Then come this upcoming Saturday. At least check it out. And if it seems good, just hop in a game and play.

W: Maybe I will. But it's been so long since I've played. I don't know if I'll still be any good.

M: Don't worry! It's all about having fun and staying active.

여: Jake, 다리에 멍이 많이 들었네요.
남: 알아요. 엄청나게 크죠. 지난 주말에 축구를 하다가 그랬어요.
여: 당신이 축구하는 줄 몰랐네요. 팀에 속해 있나요?
남: 아니요. 그냥 친구들과 주말마다 그저 재미로 풋살을 해요.
여: 멋지네요. 나도 고등학교 때 축구를 했어요.
남: 정말요? 우리와 같이해야겠네요. 남자와 여자가 섞여 있어요.
여: 네, 생각해 볼게요. 한동안 요가를 했었는데, 다시 팀 운동을 하고 싶네요.
남: 그러면 이번 주 토요일에 오세요. 최소한 확인만이라도 해 보세요. 그리고 괜찮아 보이면, 바로 들어와서 경기를 하세요.
여: 그럴 수도 있을 것 같아요. 하지만 경기를 한 지 너무 오랜만이라서요. 내가 아직도 잘할 수 있을지 모르겠어요.
남: 걱정하지 마요! 다 재미있게 즐기고 활동적으로 지내자는 거니까요.

○ **Topic & Situation** 축구 경기 초대

○ **Solution**

주말마다 친구들과 풋살을 한다는 남자에게 여자가 자신도 고등학교 때 축구를 했다고 말하자 남자가 이번 주 토요일에 와서 함께하자고 권하는데, 여자는 아직도 잘할 수 있을지 모르겠다고 한다. 따라서 여자의 마지막 말에 대한 남자의 응답으로 가장 적절한 것은 ② '걱정하지 마요! 다 재미있게 즐기고 활동적으로 지내자는 거니까요.'이다.

① 고등학교 때 축구를 하다가 다리가 부러졌던 기억이 나네요.
③ 멍이 사라지지 않으면 병원에 가 봐야 해요.
④ 팀 운동은 별로 관심이 없지만, 요가는 정말 좋아해요.
⑤ 당신만 그런 게 아니에요. 나도 스포츠에 별로 관심이 없어요.

○ **Words & Phrases**

bruise 멍, 타박상 futsal 풋살. 5인제 미니 축구 for a while 한동안 team sport 팀 운동 upcoming 다가오는

15
정답 | ③

| **Script & Translation** |

M: Max is helping his mother, Maria, clean out their medicine cabinet. While sorting through the medications, Maria throws an expired container of pills into the garbage and pours a bottle of expired liquid medicine down the sink. Remembering what he learned in health class, Max tells Maria that she should not throw medication in the trash because it's bad for the environment. Maria says she never thought about that and thanks Max for telling her. Then she asks him what they should do instead. Max knows some pharmacies accept and dispose of expired and unused medications. So Max wants to suggest to Maria that they find a pharmacy near them that does that. In this situation, what would Max most likely say to Maria?

Max: <u>Let's locate a nearby pharmacy that will take our old medications.</u>

남: Max는 어머니 Maria가 약장을 정리하는 것을 돕고 있습니다. 약을 분류하는 동안 Maria는 기한이 지난 약이 담긴 용기를 쓰레기통에 버리고, 기한이 지난 액체 약 한 병을 싱크대에 쏟아 버립니다. 보건 시간에 배운 내용을 기억한 Max는 Maria에게 약은 환경에 나쁘기 때문에 쓰레기로 버리면 안 된다고 말합니다. Maria는 그것에 대해 생각해 본 적이 없다며 자신에게 말해 준 것에 대해 Max에게 고맙다고 합니다. 그러고 나서 대신 어떻게 해야 하는지를 그에게 물어봅니다. Max는 일부 약국에서 기한이 지난 약이나 사용하지 않은 약을 받아 처리한다는 것을 알고 있습니다. 그래서 Max는 Maria에게 그들 근처에 그렇게 하는 약국을 찾아보자고 제안하고 싶습니다. 이런 상황에서, Max는 Maria에게 뭐라고 말하겠습니까?

Max: <u>우리의 오래된 약을 받아 줄 가까운 약국을 찾아봐요.</u>

▶ Topic & Situation 폐의약품 안전하게 버리기

▶ Solution

Max는 어머니 Maria가 약장을 정리하면서 기한이 지난 약이 담긴 용기를 쓰레기통에 버리고, 기한이 지난 액체 약 한 병을 싱크대에 쏟는 것을 보고, 약은 환경에 나쁘기 때문에 쓰레기로 버리면 안 된다고 말하며 대신 기한이 지난 약이나 사용하지 않은 약을 받아 처리하는 약국을 찾아보자고 제안하고 싶어 한다. 따라서 Max가 Maria에게 할 말로 가장 적절한 것은 ③ '우리의 오래된 약을 받아 줄 가까운 약국을 찾아봐요.'이다.

① 우리는 서로 처방약을 공유해서는 안 돼요.
② 우리는 용기에서 모든 개인 정보를 제거해야 해요.
④ 담당 약사와 약에 대해 상담하는 것이 어떨까요?
⑤ 가까운 약국에서 처방전 없이 살 수 있는 약을 사는 것은 어떨까요?

▶ Words & Phrases

medicine cabinet 약장, 약품 수납장 sort 분류하다 medication 약, 약물 expired 기한이 지난 garbage 쓰레기(통) pour 쏟다, 붓다 sink 싱크대, 개수대 trash 쓰레기 pharmacy 약국 dispose of

~을 처리하다 prescription medication 처방약 over-the-counter 처방전 없이 살 수 있는

16~17

정답 | 16 ③ 17 ④

| Script & Translation |

W: Hello, students. This week we've been talking about the five types of musical instruments: percussion, string, brass, woodwind, and keyboard instruments. These categories are based on how the instruments produce sounds. Today, we'll focus on string instruments, which produce sound by vibrating strings. There are three ways of doing this. One way is to rub a bow against the strings. You've all seen people playing the violin this way. The cello is also normally played with a bow as well. Another way to vibrate the strings is to pull them with your fingers. This is called plucking, and it's how people play the guitar. They pluck the strings with their fingers or some other device. The third common method is to strike the strings. For example, piano strings vibrate by hammers hitting them. So, the piano is unique because it's considered both a string and a percussion instrument. Now let's listen to how these instruments sound.

여: 안녕하세요, 학생 여러분. 이번 주에 우리는 타악기, 현악기, 금관 악기, 목관 악기, 건반 악기의 다섯 가지 유형의 악기에 관해 이야기했습니다. 이러한 범주는 악기가 소리를 내는 방식에 근거한 것입니다. 오늘은 현을 진동시켜 소리를 내는 현악기에 대해 집중적으로 알아보겠습니다. 이렇게 하는(현을 진동시키는) 방법에는 세 가지가 있습니다. 한 가지 방법은 활을 현에 문지르는 것입니다. 여러분은 모두 이런 식으로 바이올린을 연주하는 사람들을 본 적이 있을 겁니다. 첼로도 보통 활로 연주합니다. 현을 진동시키는 또 다른 방법은 손가락으로 현을 당기는 것입니다. 이것은 퉁기기라고 불리며, 이것은 사람들이 기타를 연주하는 방식입니다. 그들은 손가락이나 다른 기구로 현을 퉁깁니다. 세 번째 일반적인 방법은 현을 치는 것입니다. 예를 들어, 피아노 현은 그것을 치는 망치에 의해 진동합니다. 그래서 피아노는 현악기이자 타악기로 여겨지기 때문에 독특합니다. 이제 이 악기들이 어떻게 소리를 내는지

들어 보겠습니다.

◉ Topic & Situation 현악기의 현을 진동시키는 방법

◉ Solution

16 여자는 오늘 현을 진동시켜 소리를 내는 현악기에 대해 집중적으로 알아보겠다고 말한 후, 현을 진동시키는 세 가지 방법에 관해 설명하고 있다. 따라서 여자가 하는 말의 주제로 가장 적절한 것은 ③ '현악기가 소리를 내는 다양한 방법'이다.

① 악기를 분류하는 몇 가지 방법
② 연주하기 가장 어려운 현악기
④ 다양한 현악기의 음역 수준
⑤ 현대 음악에서 가장 인기 있는 악기

17 바이올린, 첼로, 기타, 피아노는 언급되었지만, ④ '하프'는 언급되지 않았다.

◉ Words & Phrases

percussion 타악기 string 현악기, (악기의) 현 brass 금관 악기 woodwind 목관 악기 category 범주 vibrate 진동시키다 rub 문지르다 bow 활 pluck 퉁기다 strike 치다 hammer 망치

24강 실전 모의고사 3회

본문 174~179쪽

01 ③	02 ⑤	03 ③	04 ⑤	05 ①	06 ④
07 ⑤	08 ④	09 ③	10 ④	11 ①	12 ③
13 ②	14 ④	15 ③	16 ②	17 ④	

01

정답 | ③

| Script & Translation |

W: Good morning, Woodside High School students! This is Ms. Parker, your school librarian, and I have fantastic news to share. Over the weekend, a remarkable group of college student volunteers visited our library and brought about incredible improvements! They transformed our bulletin board, giving it a fresh and organized look. Additionally, they decorated our walls with beautifully crafted posters featuring illustrations and quotes from famous authors. They even created a cozy reading area in the corner, complete with comfortable cushions. Thanks to these dedicated volunteers, our library has become a more inviting and enriching space for all of us. Come and witness these incredible changes for yourselves. See you at the library soon!

여: 안녕하세요, Woodside 고등학교 학생 여러분! 저는 학교 도서관 사서 Parker 선생님이고, 여러분에게 전해 드릴 멋진 소식이 있습니다. 지난 주말에 특별한 대학생 자원봉사자 단체가 우리 도서관을 방문하여 놀라운 개선을 이뤄 냈습니다! 그들은 우리 게시판을 새롭고 정돈된 모습으로 변화시켰습니다. 게다가, 유명 작가들의 그림과 명언을 특별히 담은 아름답게 공들여 만든 포스터들로 우리 벽을 장식했습니다. 그들은 심지어 코너에 편안한 쿠션들을 갖춘 아늑한 독서 공간까지 만들었습니다. 이러한 헌신적인 자원봉사자들 덕분에, 우리 도서관은 우리 모두에게 더 매력적이고 풍요로운 공간이 되었습니다. 오셔서 이 놀라운 변화들을 직접 목격해 보세요. 곧 도서관에서 만나요!

◉ Topic & Situation 대학생 자원봉사자들의 도서관 개선 작업 결과 홍보

◉ Solution

고등학교 사서 교사인 여자는 지난 주말에 대학생 자원봉사자들이 도서관에 와서 놀라운 개선 작업을 했다고 하면서 그 내용을

안내하고, 헌신적인 자원봉사자들 덕분에 도서관이 더 매력적이고 풍요로운 공간이 되었으니 직접 와서 변화를 목격하라고 홍보하고 있다. 따라서 여자가 하는 말의 목적으로 가장 적절한 것은 ③ '자원봉사자들의 도서관 개선 작업 결과를 홍보하려고'이다.

◉ Words & Phrases

remarkable 특별한, 주목할 만한, 놀라운 bring about ~을 초래하다, 가져오다 incredible 놀라운, 믿기 어려운 improvement 개선, 향상 transform 변화시키다 bulletin board 게시판 organized 정돈된, 체계적인, 조직적인 crafted 공들여 만든, 정성스럽게 만들어진 feature 특별히 포함하다 illustration 그림, 삽화 quote 명언, 인용구 complete with ~을 갖춘, ~로 완성된 dedicated 헌신적인, 전념하는 enriching 풍요롭게 하는, (더욱) 풍부하게 하는 witness 목격하다, 증인이 되다

02

정답 | ⑤

| Script & Translation |

W: Hi there, Ben! What are you reading?

M: Hey, Sally! I'm reading a book about Edgar Allan Poe.

W: Oh, are you interested in Poe?

M: Actually, we've been studying his poems in class, and I've been struggling to fully understand their meanings. So, I decided to read this book for a better understanding.

W: How can that help?

M: Well, this book provides a lot of information about the cultural context of Poe's era. Knowing the cultural background of a poet can give us valuable insights into their poems, helping us comprehend them better.

W: Ah, I see.

M: Poetry is not just a collection of words. It reflects the experiences and values of its time.

W: That's a great point, Ben.

M: Absolutely. Understanding a poet's cultural background helps us connect with their work on a deeper level.

W: I couldn't agree more. Thanks for sharing your insights!

여: 안녕, Ben! 지금 뭘 읽고 있니?

남: 안녕, Sally! 나는 Edgar Allan Poe에 관한 책을 읽고 있어.

여: 오, 너는 Poe에 관심 있니?

남: 사실, 우리는 수업 시간에 그의 시를 공부하고 있는데, 나는 그 의미를 완전히 이해하는 데 어려움을 겪고 있어. 그래서 나는 더 잘 이해하기 위해 이 책을 읽기로 결정했어.

여: 그게 어떻게 도움이 될까?

남: 음, 이 책은 Poe의 시대의 문화적 맥락에 대한 많은 정보를 제공해. 시인의 문화적 배경을 알면 그들의 시에 관한 소중한 통찰력을 얻을 수 있고, 그것이 시를 더 잘 이해하는 데 도움이 돼.

여: 아, 그렇구나.

남: 시는 단순히 단어들의 모음이 아니야. 그것은 그 시대의 경험과 가치를 반영해.

여: 좋은 지적이야, Ben.

남: 물론이지. 시인의 문화적 배경을 이해하는 것은 우리가 시인의 작품과 더 깊은 수준에서 연결되도록 도와줘.

여: 전적으로 동의해. 너의 통찰력을 공유해 줘서 고마워!

◉ Topic & Situation 시인의 문화적 배경 이해의 중요성

◉ Solution

남자는 수업 시간에 배우고 있는 Edgar Allan Poe의 시를 더 잘 이해하기 위해 그에 관한 책을 읽고 있다고 하면서 시인의 문화적 배경을 이해하는 것이 그 시인의 작품을 더 잘 이해하는 데 도움이 된다고 말하고 있다. 따라서 남자의 의견으로 가장 적절한 것은 ⑤ '시인의 문화적 배경을 아는 것은 시를 더 잘 이해하는 데 도움이 된다.'이다.

◉ Words & Phrases

struggle 고군분투하다, 투쟁하다 fully 완전히, 전적으로 valuable 귀중한, 가치 있는 insight 통찰력, 통찰 comprehend 이해하다 collection 모음, 집합 reflect 반영하다, 나타내다

03
정답 | ③

| Script & Translation |

W: Good evening, parents! I'm Dr. Geraldine Moore from Little Angels Medical Center. Are you concerned about your child's sleep habits? Tonight, I'd like to highlight the importance of establishing a consistent bedtime routine to promote healthy sleep for your kid. This can involve activities such as taking a warm bath, reading a book together, or engaging in calming play. By consistently following this routine, your child develops a sense of predictability and signals their body that it's time to relax and prepare for sleep. Numerous studies have shown that children who maintain a consistent bedtime routine fall asleep more easily and experience better quality sleep. Now, I'm happy to answer any questions you may have before we move on.

여: 안녕하세요, 부모님 여러분! 저는 Little Angels Medical Center의 Geraldine Moore 박사입니다. 자녀의 수면 습관이 걱정되십니까? 오늘 밤, 저는 여러분 자녀의 건강한 수면을 촉진하기 위해 일관된 잠자리 준비 습관을 형성하는 것의 중요성을 강조하고자 합니다. 이것은 따뜻한 목욕을 하거나, 함께 책을 읽거나, 차분한 놀이에 참여하는 것과 같은 활동을 포함할 수 있습니다. 일관되게 이 습관을 따름으로써, 여러분의 자녀는 예측 가능성의 감각을 발달시키고 휴식을 취하고 잠을 잘 준비할 시간이라는 신호를 자기 몸에 보내게 됩니다. 다수의 연구는 일관된 잠자리 준비 습관을 유지하는 아이들이 더 쉽게 잠들고 더 좋은 질의 수면을 경험한다는 것을 보여 주었습니다. 자, 다음으로 넘어가기 전에 질문이 있으시면 기꺼이 답변 드리겠습니다.

◉ Topic & Situation 자녀의 숙면을 위한 일관된 잠자리 준비 습관 형성의 중요성

◉ Solution
여자는 자녀의 수면 습관이 걱정되는 부모들에게 자녀가 일관된 잠자리 준비 습관을 형성하게 되면 더 쉽게 잠들고 수면의 질이 좋아진다고 설명하고 있으므로, 여자가 하는 말의 요지로 가장 적절한 것은 ③ '자녀의 건강한 수면을 위해 일관된 잠자리 준비 습관을 형성해야 한다.'이다.

◉ Words & Phrases
be concerned about ~에 대해 걱정하다   highlight 강조하다
establish 형성하다, 수립하다   consistent 일관된, 일정한   bedtime

routine 잠자리 준비 습관(잠자리 들기 전에 정해진 활동을 따르는 것)
promote 촉진하다, 증진하다   involve 포함하다   engage in ~에 참여하다   calming 차분한, 침착한   consistently 일관되게, 계속해서
predictability 예측 가능성   signal 신호하다   numerous 다수의, 많은   study 연구, 조사   maintain 유지하다, 지속하다   move on 다음으로 넘어가다, 진행하다

04
정답 | ⑤

| Script & Translation |

M: Honey, what are you looking at?

W: It's a photo that my friend Miranda just sent from Seoul. She's on vacation there right now.

M: Oh, let me see. *[Pause]* She's wearing *hanbok*. It looks good on her. And it appears she's in a traditional house.

W: Actually, she mentioned that it's a café.

M: Ah, I see. The round table next to her looks quite charming.

W: Yes, and the view of the mountain behind the café is simply breathtaking.

M: It's truly beautiful. And look at that lovely garden! There's a pond in the center.

W: Oh, wow! They even have stepping stones across the pond. How cool!

M: I bet it'd look even more amazing at night when the lantern hanging from the tree is lit up.

W: Absolutely. This photo really makes me want to visit Seoul.

M: I feel the same.

남: 여보, 뭘 보고 있어요?

여: 내 친구 Miranda가 방금 서울에서 보낸 사진이에요. 그녀는 지금 그곳에서 휴가 중이거든요.

남: 오, 보여 줘 봐요. *[잠시 후]* 그녀는 한복을 입고 있네요. 그녀에게 잘 어울려요. 그리고 그녀는 전통 가옥에 있는 것 같아요.

여: 사실, 그녀는 그곳이 카페라고 했어요.

남: 아, 그렇군요. 그녀 옆에 있는 둥근 테이블이 정말 매력적으로 보여요.

여: 네, 그리고 카페 뒤에 있는 산의 경치는 그냥 숨이 멎을 정도예요.

남: 정말 아름답네요. 그리고 저 아름다운 정원을 보세요! 가운데에 연못이 있어요.

여: 오, 와! 심지어 연못을 가로지르는 징검다리도 있어요. 정말 멋지네요!

남: 나무에 매달린 등이 켜지는 밤에는 틀림없이 훨씬 더 멋져 보일 거예요.

여: 물론이에요. 이 사진을 보니 서울을 방문하고 싶어져요.

남: 나도 그래요.

● **Topic & Situation** 서울의 한옥 카페

● **Solution**

남자가 나무에 매달린 등이 켜지는 밤에 훨씬 더 멋져 보일 것이라고 했는데, 그림에서는 등이 나무 아래에 세워져 있으므로, 그림에서 대화의 내용과 일치하지 않는 것은 ⑤이다.

● **Words & Phrases**

traditional 전통적인, 전통의   mention 말하다, 언급하다   charming 매력적인, 사랑스러운   breathtaking 숨 막히는   pond 연못   stepping stone 징검다리   lantern 등   light (불을) 켜다, 밝히다 (lit –lit)

05

정답 | ①

| **Script & Translation** |

[Cell phone rings.]

M: Honey, how's it going?

W: Just finished my department meeting and taking a break with some refreshments. How about you?

M: Working from home is nice. I had lunch with my parents today.

W: That's nice. Unfortunately, I'll be working late tonight. I'm not fully prepared for tomorrow's presentation.

M: But you said you were almost ready.

W: I was, but I couldn't find an important file with statistics and graphs, so I have to recreate it.

M: That's too bad. It'll take up a lot of your time.

W: Yeah, I printed out some relevant data, but I can't find it either. I might have left it at home.

M: I remember seeing a similar printout in the bedroom. I'll go and check. *[Pause]* Ah, I found it. It has graphs and images.

W: Oh, that's it! I'll go and pick it up now.

M: Actually, I can bring it to your office in an hour. I'm almost done with my work.

W: That'd be great. Thanks a lot.

[휴대 전화가 울린다.]

남: 여보, 어떻게 되어 가고 있어요?

여: 방금 부서 회의를 마치고 다과를 들면서 휴식을 취하고 있어요. 당신은요?

남: 집에서 일하는 게 좋아요. 오늘은 부모님과 점심을 먹었어요.

여: 잘했네요. 안타깝게도, 나는 오늘 밤 늦게까지 일을 할 거예요. 내일 발표 준비가 완전히 끝나지 않았어요.

남: 하지만 거의 준비가 되었다고 말했잖아요.

여: 그랬죠, 하지만 통계 자료와 그래프가 있는 중요한 파일을 찾을 수 없어서, 다시 만들어야 해요.

남: 정말 안됐네요. 그것은 많은 시간이 걸릴 거예요.

여: 네, 관련된 자료를 출력했는데, 그것도 찾을 수가 없어요. 집에 두고 왔을지도 몰라요.

남: 침실에서 비슷한 출력물을 본 기억이 나요. 내가 가서 확인해 볼게요. *[잠시 후]* 아, 찾았어요. 그래프와 이미지가 들어 있네요.

여: 오, 바로 그거예요! 내가 지금 가지러 갈게요.

남: 사실, 한 시간 뒤에 당신 사무실로 가져다줄 수 있어요. 내 일이 거의 끝났거든요.

여: 그거 좋겠어요. 정말 고마워요.

● **Topic & Situation** 집에 놓고 간 출력물 가져다주기

● **Solution**

여자는 내일 있을 발표에 필요한 중요한 파일을 다시 만들어야 해서 오늘 밤 늦게까지 일해야 하는데 관련 자료 출력물을 집에 두고 온 것 같다고 했고, 집에서 근무 중인 남자는 침실에서 그것을 찾았고 한 시간 뒤에 사무실로 가져다주겠다고 했으므로, 남자가 할 일로 가장 적절한 것은 ① '출력물 가져다주기'이다.

● **Words & Phrases**

refreshment (가벼운) 다과, 음식물   presentation 발표, 프레젠테이션   statistics 통계 (자료)   recreate 다시 만들다   take up (시간을) 차지하다[쓰다]   relevant 관련된, 적절한   similar 비슷한, 유사한   printout 출력물

06
정답 | ④

| Script & Translation |

M: Hello, how can I help you today?

W: Hi, what's the price for your apples?

M: The smaller ones are $2 each, while the larger ones go for $3. They're all very tasty.

W: I'll take 10 of the larger ones, please.

M: Actually, if you add an extra $10, you can get a box containing 15 larger apples.

W: That sounds like a great deal. Alright, I'll go for one box.

M: Okay. Is there anything else I can assist you with?

W: How much are your avocados?

M: They're $3 each, but a pack of 6 avocados is $15.

W: I'll just take 2 avocados. Here's my credit card.

M: Great. Let me pack up your apples and avocados for you.

W: Thank you.

남: 안녕하세요, 오늘은 어떻게 도와드릴까요?

여: 안녕하세요, 사과 가격이 어떻게 돼요?

남: 작은 것은 개당 2달러이지만, 큰 것은 3달러입니다. 모두 매우 맛있습니다.

여: 큰 것 10개 주세요.

남: 사실, 10달러를 더 추가하시면, 큰 사과 15개가 들어 있는 한 상자를 살 수 있습니다.

여: 그건 좋은 거래처럼 들리네요. 알겠어요, 한 상자로 할게요.

남: 알겠습니다. 더 도와드릴 일이 있을까요?

여: 아보카도는 얼마예요?

남: 개당 3달러인데, 아보카도 6개짜리 한 팩이 15달러예요.

여: 그냥 아보카도 2개만 살게요. 여기 제 신용 카드입니다.

남: 좋습니다. 사과와 아보카도를 포장해 드리겠습니다.

여: 감사합니다.

🔘 **Topic & Situation** 사과와 아보카도 구매

🔘 **Solution**
여자는 3달러짜리 사과 10개 금액에 10달러를 추가하여 15개짜리 사과 한 상자($40)와 3달러짜리 아보카도를 2개($6) 샀으므로, 여자가 지불할 금액은 ④ '$46'이다.

🔘 **Words & Phrases**
tasty 맛있는 extra 추가의, 여분의 a great deal 좋은 거래 assist 도와주다 pack up ~을 포장하다, 싸다

07
정답 | ⑤

| Script & Translation |

W: Mr. Anderson, are you busy?

M: Hey, Ms. Parker. No, come on in.

W: Are you still preparing for the English speaking contest?

M: Yeah, but I'm almost ready. Thanks for agreeing to be the judge.

W: No problem. Do you still have the files for the teaching materials we worked on together for the novel *Pride and Prejudice*?

M: Sure. Are you planning to use them next semester?

W: I'm considering it, but I can't open the files. I suspect it's because of a virus. Can I copy them from you?

M: Unfortunately, I can't provide the files right now.

W: Don't you have them on your PC?

M: No, they're on my laptop, which my elder brother borrowed during his business trip. His laptop is currently broken.

W: I see. I'll come pick it up later then. No rush.

M: Okay. I'll let you know when he returns.

여: Anderson 선생님, 바쁘세요?

남: 안녕하세요, Parker 선생님. 아니요, 들어오세요.

여: 아직도 영어 말하기 대회 준비 중이신가요?

남: 네, 하지만 거의 다 됐어요. 심사 위원을 하는 데 동의해 주셔서 감사합니다.

여: 괜찮습니다. 소설 '오만과 편견'을 위해 저희가 함께 작업했던 수업 자료 파일을 아직도 가지고 있으신가요?

남: 물론이죠. 다음 학기에 그것을 사용할 계획이세요?

여: 고려 중인데, 파일을 열 수가 없어요. 바이러스 때문인 것 같아요. 선생님에게서 그것을 복사해도 될까요?

남: 아쉽게도, 지금은 파일을 드릴 수가 없네요.

여: 그것이 선생님 PC에 있지 않나요?

남: 아뇨, 제 노트북에 있는데, 그것을 제 형이 출장 중에 빌려 갔어요. 그의 노트북이 현재 고장 났거든요.

여: 그렇군요. 그럼 제가 나중에 와서 가져갈게요. 급하지는 않아요.

남: 알겠어요. 그가 돌아오면 선생님께 알려 드릴게요.

🔘 **Topic & Situation** 수업 자료 파일을 줄 수 없는 이유

🔘 **Solution**
여자는 두 사람이 함께 작업했던 소설 수업 자료 파일을 열 수가 없어서 남자의 파일을 복사할 수 있는지 물었고, 남자는 지금은

파일을 줄 수가 없다고 하면서 파일이 들어 있는 노트북을 형이 빌려 갔기 때문이라고 설명하고 있다. 따라서 남자가 지금 수업 자료 파일을 줄 수 없는 이유는 ⑤ '파일이 들어 있는 노트북을 형에게 빌려 줘서'이다.

○ **Words & Phrases**

agree to *do* ~하기로 동의하다 judge 심사 위원, 판사 teaching material 수업 자료, 교재 semester 학기 consider 고려하다 suspect 의심하다 copy 복사하다, 사본을 만들다 (There's) no rush 급할 것이 없다

08

정답 | ④

| Script & Translation |

M: Hey, Lydia, have you heard about the Moonlight Walk happening this weekend?

W: No, I haven't. What's it all about?

M: It's an organized nighttime group walk. It seems like a wonderful way to explore and enjoy the city during the night.

W: That sounds interesting! When is it taking place?

M: It's scheduled for this Saturday, starting at 7 p.m.

W: Oh, that'll work for me. Can you tell me about the route?

M: Sure! It begins at Central Square and then goes through downtown, passing through some neighborhoods on the east side.

W: So, it's a bit lengthy, right?

M: Yeah, it covers approximately 8 kilometers, so it should take around two hours to complete.

W: Is there a fee to participate?

M: Yes, there's a participation fee of $20 per person, which includes a complimentary T-shirt.

W: That's great! Thanks for informing me. I'm considering joining.

M: Awesome! It'd be fantastic to walk together at the event.

남: 안녕, Lydia, 이번 주말에 열리는 Moonlight Walk에 대해 들었어?

여: 아니, 듣지 못했어. 그게 다 뭔데?

남: 그건 조직된 야간 단체 산책이야. 밤에 도시를 탐험하고 즐기는 멋진 방법인 것 같아.

여: 흥미롭게 들리네! 언제 열리는 거야?

남: 이번 주 토요일 오후 7시에 시작될 예정이야.

여: 오, 그것은 나에게 맞을 거야. 경로에 대해 말해 줄 수 있니?

남: 물론이지! 그것은 Central Square에서 시작해서 시내를 지나 동쪽의 몇몇 동네를 지나가.

여: 그래서, 좀 길지, 맞지?

남: 그래, 대략 8km 정도를 가니까, 끝마치는 데 약 2시간 정도 걸릴 거야.

여: 참가비가 있어?

남: 응, 1인당 20달러의 참가비가 있는데, 무료 티셔츠가 포함돼 있어.

여: 좋네! 알려 줘서 고마워. 참가를 고려 중이야.

남: 정말 잘됐다! 그 행사에서 함께 걸으면 정말 좋을 거야.

○ **Topic & Situation** Moonlight Walk

○ **Solution**

Moonlight Walk에 관해 개최 일시, 출발 장소, 소요 시간, 참가비는 언급되었으나, ④ '신청 마감일'은 언급되지 않았다.

○ **Words & Phrases**

organized 조직된, 체계적인 schedule 예정하다 neighborhood 동네, 이웃 지역 lengthy 긴, 길게 이어지는 cover (거리를) 가다, 이동하다 approximately 대략 complete 끝마치다, 완료하다, 끝내다 participate 참가하다, 참여하다 complimentary 무료의, 서비스로 제공되는 inform 알리다, 정보를 주다

09

정답 | ③

| Script & Translation |

M: Are you looking to add some greenery to your home in a fun, unique way? Then join our Bottle Terrarium Workshop to learn how to create your very own mini garden inside a glass bottle! The workshop takes place on Saturday, May 4th, from 6 p.m. to 8 p.m. at the Briswick Community Center. The cost is $50 per person. This includes all the necessary materials, such as a bottle, plants, soil, sand, and rocks. And the best part is that the bottle garden you make will be yours to take home and watch grow. The workshop is only open to people aged 18 or older. Finally, there's a 10-person class size limit, so don't wait long to register. This is a great chance to add a personal touch of nature to your home!

남: 여러분은 재미있고 독특한 방법으로 여러분의 집에 녹색 식물을 좀 추가하려고 하십니까? 그렇다면 저희 Bottle Terrarium Workshop에 참여하여 유리병 안에 여러분만의 미니 정원을 만드는 방법을 배워 보십시오! 워크숍은 5월 4일 토요일 오후 6시부터 오후 8시까지 Briswick Community Center에서 개최됩니다. 비용은 1인당 50달러입니다. 여기에는 병, 식물, 흙, 모래, 그리고 돌멩이와 같은 필요한 모든 재료가 포함되어 있습니다. 그리고 가장 좋은 점은 여러분이 만든 병 정원은 여러분의 것이 되어 집으로 가져가 성장하는 것을 지켜볼 수 있을 거라는 것입니다. 워크숍은 18세 이상의 사람들만 참여할 수 있습니다. 마지막으로, 수강 인원이 10명으로 제한되어 있으니, 등록하기 위해 오래 기다리지 마세요. 이것은 여러분의 집에 개인적인 자연의 손길을 더할 수 있는 기회입니다!

◑ **Topic & Situation** Bottle Terrarium Workshop

◑ **Solution**

남자가 비용에 모든 재료가 포함되어 있다고 안내하고 있으므로, 담화의 내용과 일치하지 않는 것은 ③ '참가비 외에 재료비를 별도로 내야 한다.'이다.

◑ **Words & Phrases**

look to *do* ~을 의도하다, ~을 기대하다   greenery 녹색 식물   unique 독특한, 유일한   cost 비용, 가격   material 재료   soil 흙, 토양   limit 제한, 한계   personal 개인적인, 개인의

10

| **Script & Translation** |

M: Mom, could you help me with something?

W: Of course, Kevin. What is it?

M: I want to purchase a clothing hanger set from this website, but I'm not sure which one to choose. Could you help me decide?

W: Sure, let me have a look. Do you have any specific material preference?

M: Not really. But I don't want wooden hangers because they're too bulky.

W: Then we can eliminate this one. What's your budget?

M: I'd like to keep it under $40.

W: In that price range, you have these three options. It's definitely a good idea to go for non-slip hangers.

M: Okay, I'll consider one of these two then.

W: How about this set? It comes with more hangers.

M: Well, I don't think I need that many. I'll go for the other set.

W: That's a wise choice!

남: 엄마, 저 좀 도와주시겠어요?

여: 물론이지, Kevin. 무슨 일인데?

남: 이 웹사이트에서 옷걸이 세트를 사고 싶은데, 어떤 걸 골라야 할지 잘 모르겠어요. 제가 결정하는 것을 도와주시겠어요?

여: 그럼, 내가 한번 볼게. 좋아하는 특정한 재료가 있니?

남: 그렇지는 않아요. 하지만 나무 옷걸이는 부피가 너무 커서 원하지 않아요.

여: 그러면 이것을 제외하면 되겠네. 예산이 어떻게 되니?

남: 40달러 아래로 유지하고 싶어요.

여: 그 가격대에서는 이 세 가지 옵션이 있네. 미끄럼 방지 옷걸이로 고르는 것은 분명히 좋은 생각이야.

남: 알겠어요, 그럼 이 두 개 중 하나를 고려해 볼게요.

여: 이 세트는 어때? 옷걸이가 더 많이 딸려 오네.

남: 음, 그렇게 많이 필요하지 않을 것 같아요. 다른 세트로 할게요.

여: 현명한 선택이야!

◑ **Topic & Situation** 옷걸이 세트 구매하기

◑ **Solution**

남자는 나무 옷걸이를 제외한 옷걸이 세트 중에서 40달러보다 저렴하면서 미끄럼 방지가 되는 것 중 옷걸이 개수가 더 적은 세트로 골랐으므로, 남자가 구입할 옷걸이 세트는 ④이다.

◑ **Words & Phrases**

purchase 사다, 구매하다   specific 특정한, 구체적인   preference 선호, 우선순위   bulky 부피가 큰   eliminate 제외하다, 없애다   budget 예산, 자금 계획   price range 가격대, 가격 범위   non-slip 미끄러짐을 방지하는

11

M: Honey, have you taken a look at how worn out the fence in the backyard looks recently? We should repaint it.

PART III 실전편

W: Yes, I have, and I was just thinking the same thing.

M: Then I'll go to the paint store to buy some new paint later today. When should we start painting it?

W: I think next weekend would be ideal.

남: 여보, 요즘 뒤뜰에 있는 울타리가 얼마나 낡아 보이는지 봤어요? 다시 페인트칠해야 해요.

여: 네, 봤어요. 그리고 나도 바로 같은 생각을 하고 있었어요.

남: 그럼 오늘 이따 페인트 가게에 가서 새 페인트를 좀 사 올게요. 언제 그것을 페인트칠하기 시작해야 할까요?

여: 다음 주말이 가장 좋을 것 같아요.

○ **Topic & Situation** 뒤뜰 울타리 페인트칠하기

○ **Solution**

두 사람은 뒤뜰 울타리가 너무 낡아 다시 페인트칠해야 한다는 생각을 같이하고 있고, 남자가 오늘 이따 새 페인트를 사러 가게에 간다고 하면서 언제 페인트칠해야 할지 묻고 있으므로, 이에 대한 여자의 응답으로 가장 적절한 것은 ① '다음 주말이 가장 좋을 것 같아요.'이다.

② 지금 그 새 페인트로 그것을 시작해 봐요.

③ 우리가 언제 울타리를 페인트칠했는지 기억이 안 나요.

④ 우리가 다시 울타리를 페인트칠해야 하는지 잘 모르겠어요.

⑤ 우리는 즉시 그림 수업에 등록해야 해요.

○ **Words & Phrases**

worn out 낡은, 닳아 해진   backyard 뒤뜰, 뒷마당   ideal 가장 좋은, 이상적인

12
정답 | ③

W: John, take a look at my cell phone. Doesn't the screen look really dark?

M: Yeah, Grandma. You should adjust the brightness. I'll show you how. *[Pause]* How does it look now?

W: Oh, it's much better now. Thanks! I thought it was dark because my phone battery was getting weak.

M: Actually, the brightness setting was simply set too low.

여: John, 내 휴대 전화 좀 보렴. 화면이 정말 어두워 보이지 않니?

남: 그래요, 할머니. 밝기를 조절하셔야 해요. 방법을 알려 드릴게요. *[잠시 후]* 지금은 어때 보여요?

여: 오, 이제 훨씬 더 좋구나. 고마워! 나는 내 전화기 배터리가 약해지고 있어서 어둡다고 생각했단다.

남: 사실, 밝기 설정이 너무 낮게 설정되어 있었을 뿐이에요.

○ **Topic & Situation** 휴대 전화 화면 밝기 조정

○ **Solution**

자신의 휴대 전화 화면이 어두워 보인다는 여자의 말을 듣고 남자는 밝기를 조절해야 한다고 하면서 방법을 알려 주고, 여자는 이제 훨씬 좋아졌다고 하면서 전화기 배터리가 약해지고 있어서 어둡다고 생각했다고 말하고 있다. 따라서 여자의 마지막 말에 대한 남자의 응답으로 가장 적절한 것은 ③ '사실, 밝기 설정이 너무 낮게 설정되어 있었을 뿐이에요.'이다.

① 정확히 그래요. 문제는 배터리가 다 되어 가고 있어서 발생한 것뿐이었어요.

② 맞아요. 화면과 배터리가 지금 바로 교체되어야 해요.

④ 그래요. 할머니는 휴대 전화를 사용하는 시간을 줄이셔야 해요.

⑤ 좋아요. 제가 밝기 문제를 처리하기 위해 그것을 수리 센터에 가져갈게요.

○ **Words & Phrases**

adjust 조정하다   brightness 밝기   setting 설정   address (문제 등을) 처리하다, 다루다

13
정답 | ②

| Script & Translation |

M: Honey, have you thought about our summer vacation destination?

W: Yes! I think we should go somewhere focused on eco-tourism. I read about it online.

M: What does eco-tourism mean exactly?

W: It means choosing a destination that actively preserves nature and promotes sustainable living.

M: That sounds great! Any specific places in mind known for eco-tourism?

W: Yes, I found an amazing eco-friendly resort in Costa Rica that has received excellent reviews.

M: Wonderful! Tell me more about it.

W: The resort is surrounded by breathtaking natural beauty. They are dedicated to sustainability, relying heavily on solar power, growing their own food, and implementing various green programs.

M: Perfect! Let's make a reservation now.

W: Alright. I'll check if they have available rooms for our travel dates.

M: Great. I hope we can secure our booking. I don't want to miss out on this incredible experience.

W: Me, too. It'll be wonderful to enjoy an eco-friendly summer vacation.

남: 여보, 우리 여름휴가 여행지에 대해 생각해 봤어요?

여: 네! 환경 관광에 초점을 맞춘 어딘가로 가는 게 좋을 것 같아요. 나는 인터넷에서 그것에 관해 읽었어요.

남: 환경 관광이 정확히 무슨 의미예요?

여: 그것은 적극적으로 자연을 보존하고 지속 가능한 삶을 촉진하는 여행지를 선택하는 것을 의미해요.

남: 좋은 것 같네요! 마음에 두고 있는 환경 관광으로 알려진 특정한 곳이 있어요?

여: 네, 뛰어난 평가를 받은 코스타리카에 있는 굉장한 친환경 리조트를 찾았어요.

남: 멋져요! 그곳에 대해 좀 더 얘기해 줘요.

여: 그 리조트는 숨이 멎을 듯한 자연의 아름다움에 둘러싸여 있어요. 그들은 지속 가능성에 헌신해서, 태양열에 많이 의존하고, 식량을 자체 생산하고, 다양한 환경 보호 프로그램을 시행하고 있어요.

남: 완벽해요! 지금 예약해요.

여: 알았어요. 우리의 여행 날짜에 이용 가능한 방이 있는지 확인해 볼게요.

남: 좋아요. 우리가 예약을 확보할 수 있기를 바라요. 이 놀라운 경험을 놓치고 싶지 않거든요.

여: 나도 그래요. 친환경적인 여름휴가를 즐기는 것은 정말 멋질 거예요.

◉ Topic & Situation 친환경적인 여름휴가 즐기기

◉ Solution

여름휴가 여행지에 대해 생각해 봤느냐는 남자의 말에 여자는 환경 관광에 초점을 둔 휴가지로 가고 싶다고 하면서 코스타리카에 있는 친환경 리조트가 그런 곳이라고 남자에게 설명하고, 지금 예약하자는 남자의 말에 이용 가능한 방이 있는지 확인해 보겠다고 말했다. 남자가 예약을 확보할 수 있기를 바란다고 하면서 그런 놀라운 경험을 놓치고 싶지 않다고 했으므로, 남자의 마지막 말에 대한 여자의 응답으로 가장 적절한 것은 ② '나도 그래요. 친환경적인 여름휴가를 즐기는 것은 정말 멋질 거예요.'이다.

① 멋져요! 머물 수 있는 이렇게 좋은 친환경 리조트를 찾아 줘서 고마워요.

③ 걱정하지 마요. 내가 이미 리조트에 전화를 걸어서 예약했어요.

④ 네. 나는 환경을 보존하기 위해 당신과 함께 자원봉사를 하게 되어 기뻐요.

⑤ 물론이죠. 하지만 지속 가능한 여행을 경험하러 어디로 가야 할지 모르겠어요.

◉ Words & Phrases

destination 여행지, 목적지   eco-tourism 환경 관광   preserve 보존하다, 보호하다   sustainable 지속 가능한   be dedicated to ~에 헌신하다   rely on ~에 의존하다   heavily 많이, 대단히   implement 시행하다, 실행하다   secure 확보하다

14
정답 | ④

| Script & Translation |

M: Amelia, can I talk to you for a moment?

W: Sure, little brother. Oh, why the long face? Is something wrong?

M: Yeah. I have a science project due in a couple of weeks, but I don't know where to start.

W: What's the project about?

M: I have to create a model of the solar system and describe the different planets and their characteristics.

W: Okay, I think I can help you with that. What do you already know about the solar system?

M: We learned about the eight planets in science class, but I want to know more about them.

W: Then I can show you some websites where you can research and gather important details.

M: That'd be great. Thanks, Amelia.

W: No problem. I also have some science journals that may give you some ideas for creating your model. I'll lend them to you.

M: You're a life saver! Now I think I can start working on the science project.

남: Amelia 누나, 잠깐 얘기할 수 있어?

여: 물론이지, 동생아. 오, 왜 그렇게 우울해? 무슨 힘든 일이 있니?

남: 응. 두어 주 있으면 과학 프로젝트가 마감인데, 어디서부터 시작해야 할지 모르겠어.

여: 프로젝트가 무엇에 관한 거야?

남: 태양계 모형을 만들고 각 행성과 그것들의 특징을 설명해야 해.

여: 알겠어, 내가 그것을 도와줄 수 있을 것 같아. 태양계에 대해 이미 얼마나 알고 있어?

남: 과학 수업에서 여덟 개의 행성에 대해 배웠는데, 그것들에 대해 더 알고 싶어.

여: 그러면 네가 중요한 세부 사항을 조사하고 수집할 수 있는 웹사이트를 몇 개 알려 줄 수 있어.

남: 그게 좋겠다. 고마워, Amelia 누나.

여: 별말을. 나한테는 또 너에게 네 모형을 만들기 위한 아이디어를 줄 수 있는 과학 저널이 몇 권 있어. 그것들을 네게 빌려줄게.

남: <u>누나는 생명의 은인이야! 나는 이제 과학 프로젝트를 시작할 수 있을 것 같아.</u>

◐ **Topic & Situation** 남동생 과학 프로젝트 도와주기

◐ **Solution**

태양계의 모형을 만들고 각 행성에 관해 설명해야 하는 과학 프로젝트를 하는 데 어려움을 겪고 있는 남자가 여자에게 도움을 청하고, 여자는 중요한 세부 사항을 조사하고 수집할 수 있는 웹사이트를 알려 주고, 모형을 만드는 데 도움이 될 만한 과학 잡지를 빌려주겠다고 말하고 있다. 따라서 여자의 마지막 말에 대한 남자의 응답으로 가장 적절한 것은 ④ '누나는 생명의 은인이야! 나는 이제 과학 프로젝트를 시작할 수 있을 것 같아.'이다.

① 그거 좋겠다. 누나가 나를 위해 그 모형을 만들어 줘서 정말로 고마워.

② 진짜? 누나가 나한테 그 과학 저널들을 사 주고 싶다니 정말 고마워.

③ 좋은 생각이야! 나는 지금 그 과학 저널들을 주문하기 위해 그 웹사이트들을 확인해 볼게.

⑤ 고마워. 하지만 나는 이미 과학 프로젝트를 끝마쳐서 그것들이 필요 없어.

◐ **Words & Phrases**

due 마감인, 기한이 도래한   solar system 태양계   describe 설명하다, 묘사하다   characteristic 특징, 특성   research 조사하다, 연구하다   detail 세부 사항, 상세한 내용   lend 빌려주다   life saver 생명의 은인, 구원자, 구세주

15

정답 | ③

| Script & Translation |

W: Emma is getting ready to go to her friend's piano concert, but she's having a difficult time deciding what to wear. So she asks her brother Jack for his opinion since he has a good sense of fashion. When Emma shows him the outfits, Jack suggests that she wear the floral dress. Emma says that she thinks it might be too casual for the concert. However, Jack tells her that with the right accessories, it'll be appropriate. She trusts him and wears the floral dress to the concert, and she receives numerous compliments from her friends. Emma wants to express her gratitude to Jack for his suggestion when she returns home. In this situation, what would Emma most likely say to Jack?

Emma: <u>I'm grateful that you recommended me to wear the floral dress.</u>

여: Emma는 친구의 피아노 연주회에 가기 위해 준비 중이지만, 무엇을 입을지 결정하는 데 어려움을 겪고 있습니다. 그래서 그녀는 오빠 Jack이 패션 감각이 뛰어나므로 그에게 의견을 구합니다. Emma가 그에게 의상들을 보여 주자, Jack은 그녀가 꽃무늬 원피스를 입을 것을 제안합니다. Emma는 그것이 연주회에 너무 격식 없는 차림인 것 같다고 말합니다. 그러나 Jack은 그녀에게 적절한 액세서리를 착용하면 그것이 적합할 것이라고 말합니다. Emma는 그를 믿고 연주회에 꽃무늬 원피스를 입고 가서, 친구들로부터 많은 칭찬을 받습니다. Emma는 집에 돌아와서 Jack에게 그의 제안에 대해 고마움을 표현하고 싶어 합니다. 이런 상황에서, Emma는 Jack에게 뭐라고 말하겠습니까?

Emma: 나에게 그 꽃무늬 원피스를 입으라고 추천해 줘서 고마워.

◐ **Topic & Situation** 연주회 참석 복장

◐ **Solution**

패션 감각이 뛰어난 오빠 Jack은 Emma에게 친구 피아노 연주회에 입고 갈 옷으로 꽃무늬 원피스를 제안하고, Emma는 그 옷이 너무 격식 없는 것 같다고 생각했지만 적절한 액세서리를 착용하면 적합할 거라는 Jack의 말을 듣고 꽃무늬 원피스를 입고 연주회에 가서 많은 칭찬을 받고 집에 와서 그런 제안을 해 준 Jack에게 고마움을 표현하고 싶어 하는 상황이다. 따라서 Emma가 Jack에게 할 말로 가장 적절한 것은 ③ '나에게 그 꽃무늬 원피스를 입으라고 추천해 줘서 고마워.'이다.

① 오빠가 내 제안을 따라 주어서 오빠를 칭찬하고 싶어.

② 나에게 아름다운 꽃과 선물을 보내 줘서 고마워.

④ 연주회에 꽃을 가지고 가라고 나에게 조언해 주다니 오빠는 사려 깊어.

⑤ 나에게 그 원피스를 위한 이 예쁜 꽃 모양 액세서리를 사 줘서 고마워.

Words & Phrases

outfit 의상, 복장   floral 꽃무늬의, 꽃의   casual 격식을 차리지 않는, 평상시의   appropriate 적절한, 알맞은   trust 믿다, 신뢰하다   numerous 많은, 다수의   compliment 칭찬, 찬사: 칭찬하다   gratitude 고마움, 감사

16~17

정답 | 16 ② 17 ④

| Script & Translation |

M: Welcome to *Senior Insights*! Today, we're going to explore how life can get even better as we age. While we often think of aging in terms of physical changes, there are actually many aspects of life that can improve with time. One of these aspects is our relationships. As we grow older, our long-term connections with family and friends can become deeper and more meaningful. Another area that improves with age is our expertise. Throughout our lives, we learn and gain skills in various areas. As we age, we have the opportunity to further develop and refine our expertise, becoming true masters in our fields. Emotional intelligence also tends to improve with age. As we go through life, we become better at understanding our own emotions and the feelings of others. Lastly, enjoyment is something that can increase with age. As we gain wisdom and experience, we learn to appreciate the simple pleasures in life. We find joy in the little things and contentment in the present. We'll be back after a short commercial break, so stay tuned!

남: *Senior Insights*에 오신 것을 환영합니다! 오늘은 나이가 들면서 어떻게 삶이 더욱 더 좋아질 수 있는지 알아보려 합니다. 우리는 종종 노화를 신체적 변화의 관점에서 생각하지만, 실제로 시간이 지남에 따라 개선될 수 있는 삶의 많은 측면이 있습니다. 이러한 측면 중 하나는 우리의 관계입니다. 우리가 나이 들어감에 따라, 가족과 친구들과의 장기적인 관계는 더 깊어지고 더 의미 있게 될 수 있습니다. 나이가 들수록 향상되는 또 다른 분야는 우리의 전문성입니다. 우리는 일생을 통해 다양한 분야에서 배우고 기술을 습득합니다. 나이가 들면서 우리는 전문성을 더욱 발전시키고 숙달할 기회를 얻게 되어 우리의 분야에서 진정한 대가가 됩니다. 감정 지능도 나이가 들수

록 향상되는 경향이 있습니다. 삶을 살아가면서, 우리는 우리 자신의 감정과 다른 사람들의 감정을 더 잘 이해하게 됩니다. 마지막으로, 즐거움은 나이가 들수록 커질 수 있는 것입니다. 우리가 지혜와 경험을 얻으면서, 우리는 삶의 소소한 즐거움에 감사하는 것을 배웁니다. 우리는 작은 것에서 기쁨을 찾고 현재에서 만족을 찾습니다. 짧은 광고 휴식 후에 돌아오겠으니, 채널 고정해 주세요!

Topic & Situation 나이가 들면서 더 좋아질 수 있는 것들

Solution

16 남자는 나이가 들면서 어떻게 삶이 더욱 좋아질 수 있는지 알아보려고 한다면서 실제로 시간이 지남에 따라 개선될 수 있는 삶의 측면에 관해 설명하고 있다. 따라서 남자가 하는 말의 주제로 가장 적절한 것은 ② '나이가 들면서 더 좋아질 수 있는 것들'이다.
① 노화로 인한 스트레스를 풀기 위한 조언
③ 더 행복한 노년 생활을 위해 중요한 측면들
④ 우아한 노화를 위한 생활 방식 변화 채택하기
⑤ 노인들이 신체와 정신의 균형을 필요로 하는 이유

17 나이가 들면서 더 좋아질 수 있는 것들로 관계, 전문성, 감정 지능, 즐거움은 언급되었지만, ④ '자신감'은 언급되지 않았다.

Words & Phrases

aging 노화   in terms of ~의 관점에서, ~에 관하여   aspect 측면   long-term 장기적인   connection 관계, 연결   expertise 전문성, 전문 지식   refine 숙달하다, 개선하다   master 대가, 장인   emotional intelligence 감정 지능   enjoyment 즐거움   appreciate 감사하다, 감상하다   pleasure 기쁨   contentment 만족   commercial break 광고 시간   relieve stress 스트레스를 풀다[해소하다]   crucial 중요한   adopt 채택하다

PART III
실전편

25강 실전 모의고사 4회

본문 180~185쪽

01 ③	02 ④	03 ③	04 ④	05 ②	06 ②
07 ①	08 ④	09 ④	10 ②	11 ②	12 ③
13 ④	14 ⑤	15 ③	16 ③	17 ⑤	

01

정답 | ③

| Script & Translation |

M: Hi, everyone! Before we start today's class, I have something important to share with you. Yesterday, I received news from the Spring Department Store culture center that they're having an Asian food cooking contest next month. All of you have been here learning how to cook various Asian dishes for the past six months, so this contest is a perfect opportunity to showcase your cooking skills! I believe you're all good enough to be competitive and even win the contest. You can register for it on the Spring Department Store website. I really hope all of you will participate in this contest and show off your cooking skills.

남: 안녕하세요, 여러분! 오늘 수업을 시작하기 전에, 여러분과 공유할 중요한 것이 있습니다. 어제 저는 Spring 백화점 문화 센터로부터 그들이 다음 달에 아시아 음식 요리 대회를 개최할 것이라는 소식을 들었습니다. 여러분 모두 지난 6개월 동안 이곳에서 다양한 아시아 음식을 요리하는 법을 배웠으므로, 이 대회는 여러분의 요리 실력을 보여 줄 수 있는 완벽한 기회입니다! 저는 여러분 모두 이 대회에서 경쟁력이 있고 심지어 우승을 하기에 충분히 실력이 있다고 믿습니다. 여러분은 Spring 백화점 웹사이트에서 이 대회에 등록할 수 있습니다. 저는 정말로 여러분 모두가 이 대회에 참가해서 여러분의 요리 실력을 자랑하기를 바랍니다.

○ **Topic & Situation** 아시아 음식 요리 대회

○ **Solution**
남자는 요리를 배우는 수강생들의 요리 실력이 아시아 음식 요리 대회에 참가하기에 충분하다고 말하면서 수강생들에게 이 대회에 참가할 것을 권장하고 있으므로, 남자가 하는 말의 목적으로 가장 적절한 것은 ③ '요리 대회에 참가할 것을 권유하려고'이다.

○ **Words & Phrases**
various 다양한   showcase 보여 주다, 진열하다   competitive 경

쟁력 있는, 경쟁의   participate in ~에 참가하다   show off ~을 자랑하다

02

정답 | ④

| Script & Translation |

W: Hey, Jason! Have you decided on how you're going to travel around Australia on your trip?

M: Well, I'm thinking about getting my international driver's license and renting a car.

W: That sounds fun, but Australia is huge, so you may get tired driving by yourself. While traveling there, I found it easy to get around by bus.

M: Really? I never considered buses.

W: Traveling Australia by bus has a lot of benefits. First, you won't have to worry about driving long distances.

M: That sounds good to me.

W: And it's a lot cheaper than having to constantly fill up a car with gas.

M: That's a great point, especially with the cost of gas nowadays.

W: And who knows? Maybe you can make friends with other people traveling on the bus.

M: That's exactly what I want. I'll seriously consider your suggestion.

여: 안녕, Jason! 너의 여행에서 호주를 어떻게 여행할지 결정했니?

남: 그게, 나는 국제 운전 면허증을 발급받아서 차를 빌릴까 생각 중이야.

여: 재미있을 것 같긴 한데, 호주는 땅이 넓어서, 혼자 운전하면 피곤할 수도 있어. 거기서 여행을 하면서, 나는 버스로 돌아다니는 것이 쉽다는 것을 알았어.

남: 정말? 버스는 한 번도 생각해 본 적이 없어.

여: 버스로 호주 여행을 하는 것은 많은 장점이 있어. 첫째, 너는 장거리 운전에 대해 걱정할 필요가 없어.

남: 그것은 나에게 좋은 것 같아.

여: 그리고 그것은 차에 계속 기름을 넣어야 하는 것보다 훨씬 더 저렴해.

남: 특히 요즘의 유류 비용을 생각하면 그것은 정말 좋은 점이구나.

여: 그리고 누가 알아? 어쩌면 너는 버스를 타고 여행하는 다른 사람들과 친구가 될 수 있어.

남: 내가 원하는 것이 바로 그거야. 네 제안을 진지하게 생각해 볼게.

○ Topic & Situation 호주 버스 여행

○ Solution
자동차를 운전해서 호주를 여행하려고 생각했던 남자에게 여자는 버스를 타고 여행하는 것이 많은 장점이 있다고 하면서 이에 대해 구체적으로 언급하고 있으므로, 여자의 의견으로 가장 적절한 것은 ④ '호주 버스 여행은 여행자에게 다양한 이점을 제공한다.'이다.

○ Words & Phrases
international driver's license 국제 운전 면허증 get around 돌아다니다 distance 거리 seriously 진지하게

03

정답 | ③

| Script & Translation |

M: Hi, everyone! I'm Alex Kim, and I am currently a sophomore majoring in economics. Thank you for inviting me to the on-campus broadcasting program. As you know, I have won the writing contests for the past two years. Many people have wondered what contributed to my success in these contests. Now, I'm going to share with you how I improved my writing skills. It's quite simple: write in a diary every day. I firmly believe that the more you write, the better your writing skills will become. Keeping a diary is an effective way to encourage yourself to write as often as possible. So, if you truly want to enhance your writing skills, write in a diary at anytime convenient for you before going to bed. You'll see a significant difference in no time. For more tips, join me again tomorrow. Now back to some music.

남: 안녕하세요, 여러분! 저는 현재 경제학을 전공하고 있는 대학 2학년생인 Alex Kim이라고 합니다. 교내 방송 프로그램에 저를 초대해 주셔서 감사합니다. 아시다시피, 저는 지난 2년간 글쓰기 대회에서 우승을 했습니다. 많은 분들이 이 대회에서의 무엇이 제 성공의 원인이 되었는지에 대해 궁금해 하셨습니다. 이제 제가 어떻게 글쓰기 실력을 향상했는지 여러분과 공유해 보려고 합니다. 아주 간단합니다. 매일 일기를 쓰세요. 저는 글을 많이 쓸수록 글쓰기 실력이 더 좋아질 것이라고 굳게 믿습니다. 일기를 쓰는 것은 가능한 한 자주 글을 쓰도록 스스로를 격려하는 효과적인 방법입니다. 따라서 진정으로 글쓰기 실력을 향상시키고 싶다면 잠자리에 들기 전, 언제라도 편한 시간에 일기를 쓰세요. 여러분은 곧 상당한 차이를 알아차리게 될 것입니다. 더 많은 조언을 원하시면, 내일 다시 저와 함께해 주세요. 이제 음악으로 돌아가겠습니다.

○ Topic & Situation 글쓰기 실력을 향상시키는 방법

○ Solution
글쓰기 대회에서 2년간 우승한 남자는 매일 일기를 쓰는 것이 글쓰기 실력을 향상하는 간단한 방법이라고 말했으므로, 남자가 하는 말의 요지로 가장 적절한 것은 ③ '일기 쓰기는 글쓰기 실력 향상에 큰 도움이 된다.'이다.

○ Words & Phrases
currently 현재 sophomore (대학) 2학년 contribute to ～의 원인이 되다, ～에 기여하다 firmly 굳게, 단호하게 enhance 향상시키다 convenient 편리한 in no time 곧

04

정답 | ④

| Script & Translation |

W: Honey, did you finish rearranging Jenny's room?

M: Yeah, I finally finished it. What do you think about it?

W: Oh, you placed Jenny's bed in the center of the room.

M: And I put her penguin doll on the table beside the bed.

W: That's nice. The elephant-shaped pencil holder on the desk is very unique. Jenny is sure to like it.

M: I hope so.

W: Oh, I've never seen that heart-shaped clock on the wall. When did you get it?

M: On my way home from work yesterday. See the flowerpot in the left corner of the room?

W: Yeah. It's great. It makes the room cozier.

M: That's the nice thing about plants.

W: You did a great job, honey.

여: 여보, Jenny의 방을 재배치하는 것을 끝냈나요?

남: 네, 드디어 끝냈어요. 어떻게 생각해요?

여: 오, 당신은 방 가운데에 Jenny의 침대를 놓았군요.

남: 그리고 Jenny의 펭귄 인형을 침대 옆에 있는 탁자 위에 놓았어요.

여: 잘했어요. 책상 위에 있는 코끼리 모양의 연필꽂이가 매우 독특해요. Jenny가 그것을 분명히 좋아할 거예요.

남: 그러길 바라요.

여: 오, 벽에 걸린 저 하트 모양의 시계는 본 적이 없어요. 그것을 언제 샀나요?

남: 어제 퇴근하고 집에 오는 길에요. 방의 왼쪽 구석에 화분이 보이나요?

여: 네, 아주 멋져요! 화분이 방을 더 아늑하게 만들어 주고 있어요.

남: 그것이 식물에 대한 좋은 점이죠.

여: 아주 잘했어요, 여보.

○ **Topic & Situation** 방 재배치

○ **Solution**
여자가 벽에 걸린 하트 모양의 시계를 처음 보았다고 하면서 그것을 언제 샀는지 물었으므로, 그림의 내용과 일치하지 않는 것은 ④이다.

○ **Words & Phrases**
rearrange 재배치하다　cozy 아늑한

05
정답 | ②

| Script & Translation |

W: Brian, I'm getting a little nervous. Our magic club's performance is almost here.

M: I know. It's just two weeks away. I finally finished designing the flyer for it. Here it is on my computer.

W: Wow, great job! You're really talented at graphic design.

M: Thanks. Why don't we make 100 copies and pass them around to students at lunch time?

W: Good idea. So will you make the copies?

M: Yeah. I'll take care of it.

W: Great. I'll make the schedule for the magic performers.

M: All right. You know Stella really wants to go first, right?

W: Yeah. And other members told me their preferences too. Everybody should be able to get the order they want.

M: That's good. I hope many people come to see our performance.

W: I hope so, too.

여: Brian, 나 좀 긴장돼. 우리 마술 동아리의 공연이 거의 다가왔어.

남: 알아. 2주밖에 안 남았어. 내가 드디어 공연 전단 디자인을 끝냈어. 여기 내 컴퓨터에 있어.

여: 와, 아주 잘했어! 넌 정말로 그래픽 디자인에 재능이 있어.

남: 고마워. 100부를 복사해서 점심시간에 학생들에게 나누어 주는 것은 어때?

여: 좋은 생각이야. 그럼 네가 복사를 할래?

남: 그래. 내가 그것을 맡을게.

여: 좋아. 나는 마술 공연자들을 위한 순서를 짤게.

남: 알았어. Stella가 정말로 제일 먼저 공연하고 싶어 하는 것을 알고 있지, 그렇지?

여: 그래. 그리고 다른 부원들도 나한테 자신들이 선호하는 순서를 말해 줬어. 모두가 원하는 순서를 받을 수 있어야 해.

남: 잘됐네. 많은 사람들이 우리 공연을 보러 오기를 바라.

여: 나도 그러길 바라.

○ **Topic & Situation** 마술 공연 준비

○ **Solution**
마술 공연 전단을 복사하겠다는 남자의 말에 이어 여자는 자신이 공연자들을 위해 순서를 짤 것이라고 했으므로, 여자가 할 일로 가장 적절한 것은 ② '공연 순서 짜기'이다.

○ **Words & Phrases**
flyer 전단　copy 복사본, 한 부　preference 선호(하는 것)

06
정답 | ②

| Script & Translation |

M: Hi, I'd like to buy cat food made with tuna.

W: I see. How about this 2 kg bag? It's $10.

M: Hmm. That would last probably about a month?

W: Yeah, for one adult cat, that's about right.

M: Do you have one bigger than this?

W: Sure! This is a 5 kg bag. And it's $20, so you save a little money.

M: Great. I'll take two 5 kg bags.

W: Okay. And since you're buying two, you get 10% off the total price of the cat food.

M: That's great. And I also need a bottle of cat shampoo.

W: All right, it's right over here. It's $12 a bottle. You can also get a 10% discount if you buy two bottles of cat shampoo.

M: No thanks. I'll take one bottle. That's all. Here's my credit card.

W: Thank you.

남: 안녕하세요, 참치로 만들어진 고양이 사료를 사고 싶은데요.

여: 알겠습니다. 이 2kg 자루는 어떠세요? 10달러입니다.

남: 음. 그것은 대략 한 달 정도 가나요?

여: 네, 다 큰 고양이의 경우 대략 맞습니다.

남: 이것보다 더 큰 것이 있나요?

여: 물론이죠! 이것은 5kg 자루입니다. 그리고 이것은 20달러여서, 손님께서는 약간 돈을 절약하는 겁니다.

남: 좋은데요. 5kg 자루를 두 개 살게요.

여: 알겠습니다. 그리고 고객님께서 두 개를 구입하시니까, 이 고양이 사료의 총액에서 10% 할인을 받습니다.

남: 좋군요. 그리고 저는 고양이 샴푸 한 통도 필요해요.

여: 알겠습니다, 그건 이쪽에 있습니다. 한 통에 12달러입니다. 고양이 샴푸를 두 통 구입하시면, 이것 또한 10% 할인 받을 수 있습니다.

남: 아니요, 괜찮습니다. 한 통 살게요. 이게 다예요. 제 신용 카드가 여기 있습니다.

여: 고맙습니다.

● **Topic & Situation** 고양이 사료와 샴푸 구입

● **Solution**

5kg 한 자루에 가격이 20달러인 고양이 사료를 두 자루 구입한 남자는 총액에서 10% 할인을 받았고($40−$4), 추가로 12달러짜리 고양이 샴푸를 한 통 구입했으므로, 남자가 지불할 금액은 ② '$48'이다.

● **Words & Phrases**

tuna 참치   last 지속되다   bottle 통, 병

07

정답 | ①

| **Script & Translation** |

W: John, you went to Tata Island last year, didn't you?

M: Yeah, with my wife. Why? Are you planning to go there too?

W: Yes, I am. Can you recommend a good hotel to me?

M: Oh, I highly recommend the Tata View Hotel. I stayed there and it was so nice.

W: Cool. Is it near the beach?

M: Absolutely! It's only a one-minute walk from the hotel to the beach. And it's only a couple of years old.

W: That sounds great. How much is a room?

M: Around $200 a day. It's a five-star hotel.

W: Oh, that's more expensive than I want. I'm travelling alone, so I'd prefer a more reasonably priced hotel.

M: But it serves free breakfast and it has a really nice swimming pool.

W: It does sound really nice, but it's beyond my budget. I'll look for another place.

M: I understand.

여: John, 작년에 Tata 섬에 갔었지, 그렇지 않니?

남: 맞아, 아내와 함께 갔었어. 왜? 너도 거기에 갈 계획이니?

여: 그래. 나에게 좋은 호텔을 추천해 줄 수 있어?

남: 오, Tata View 호텔을 강력하게 추천해. 내가 거기서 묵었는데 아주 좋았어.

여: 좋아. 그것이 해변 가까이에 있니?

남: 물론이지! 호텔에서 해변까지 걸어서 1분밖에 걸리지 않아. 그리고 호텔은 생긴 지 2년 정도밖에 되지 않았어.

여: 아주 마음에 들어. 객실은 얼마야?

남: 하루에 대략 200달러 정도. 5성급 호텔이야.

여: 오, 내가 원하는 것보다 더 비싸구나. 나는 혼자 여행을 하니까, 더 적정하게 가격이 매겨진 호텔을 선호해.

남: 하지만 이 호텔은 무료 아침 식사를 제공하고 정말로 멋진 수영장을 가지고 있어.

여: 진짜 좋게 들리기는 하지만, 내 예산을 넘어서. 나는 다른 곳을 알아봐야겠어.

남: 이해해.

● **Topic & Situation** 호텔 예약

● **Solution**

5성급 호텔이어서 하루에 객실 요금이 200달러 정도라는 말을 듣자, 여자는 자신이 혼자 여행을 할 것이어서 더 적정한 가격의

호텔을 찾아야겠다고 말했으므로, 여자가 Tata View Hotel에 투숙하기를 원하지 않는 이유는 ① '객실료가 비싸서'이다.

◉ Words & Phrases

recommend 추천하다   reasonably 적당하게, 타당하게   budget 예산

08

정답 | ④

| Script & Translation |

W: Albert, have you heard about the Green Auto Show coming up?

M: Yeah. I try to go there every year. Have you ever been there?

W: No, but I'd like to go this time. It's June 3rd to June 13th at the Midvale Convention Center.

M: Let's go together. Do you know how much the tickets are?

W: They're $20 for an adult, and free for children under 14.

M: Oh, it was the same last year. The show always displays the coolest, newest eco-friendly cars.

W: I heard there are going to be more than 200 models this year.

M: Cool. I can't wait to see them.

W: The newspaper article about the show I read said around 600,000 people are expected to attend this year.

M: Wow, it keeps on getting more popular.

W: Yeah. I think it may become the most popular event in the city someday.

여: Albert, 다가오는 Green Auto Show에 대해 들었어?

남: 그래. 나는 해마다 거기에 가려고 해. 너는 거기에 가 본 적 있어?

여: 아니, 하지만 이번에 가 보고 싶어. 그것은 6월 3일부터 6월 13일까지 Midvale 컨벤션 센터에서 열려.

남: 우리 같이 가자. 티켓이 얼마인지 알아?

여: 성인은 20달러이고 14세 미만 어린이는 무료야.

남: 오, 작년에도 똑같았어. 그 쇼는 언제나 가장 멋진, 최신의 친환경 자동차를 전시해.

여: 올해는 200개가 넘는 모델이 있을 거라고 들었어.

남: 멋져. 그것들을 빨리 보고 싶어.

여: 내가 읽은 그 쇼에 관한 신문 기사에서 약 60만 명이 올해 참석할 것으로 예상된다고 했어.

남: 와, 그 쇼는 계속 인기가 더 많아지는군.

여: 그래. 그것이 언젠가 우리 도시에서 가장 인기 있는 행사가 될 것 같아.

◉ Topic & Situation Green Auto Show

◉ Solution

Green Auto Show에 관해 개최 기간, 티켓 가격, 전시 모델 수, 예상 방문객 수는 언급되었으나, ④ '주관 단체'는 언급되지 않았다.

◉ Words & Phrases

adult 성인, 어른   display 전시하다, 보여 주다   eco-friendly 친환경적인   article 기사   attend 참석하다

09

정답 | ④

| Script & Translation |

W: Okay, students. Before wrapping up today's class, I have an important announcement. Lexington College's Korean Education Center is holding a Korean speech contest to celebrate Visit Korea Year. The contest is open to all students at Lexington College. The contest theme is "Korean Traditional Culture." The script must be written by the participant, and its length should be between 800 and 1,000 words. The first-place winner will receive a gold medal and a tablet PC. A silver medal and wireless earphones will be given to the second-place winner. Starting tomorrow, registration will be available on the center website until September 20th. I hope many of you participate in the contest.

여: 자, 학생 여러분. 오늘 수업을 마무리하기 전에, 중요한 공지가 있습니다. Lexington 대학의 한국어 교육 센터는 한국 방문의 해를 기념하기 위해 한국어 말하기 대회를 개최합니다. 이 대회는 Lexington 대학의 모든 학생들에게 열려 있습니다. 대회 주제는 '한국의 전통문화'입니다. 원고는 참가자가 작성해야 하며, 원고의 길이는 800 단어에서 1,000 단어 사이

여야 합니다. 1등 수상자는 금메달과 태블릿 PC를 받을 것입니다. 2등 수상자에게는 은메달과 무선 이어폰이 주어질 것입니다. 내일부터 9월 20일까지 센터 웹사이트에서 등록할 수 있을 것입니다. 여러분 중에서 많은 학생이 대회에 참가하기를 바랍니다.

Topic & Situation 한국어 말하기 대회

Solution

1등 수상자는 금메달과 태블릿 PC를 받을 것이라고 했으므로, 담화의 내용과 일치하지 않는 것은 ④ '1등 수상자는 무선 이어폰을 받을 것이다.'이다.

Words & Phrases

wrap up ~을 마무리하다, 끝내다 announcement 공지, 발표 participant 참가자 wireless 무선의 registration 등록

10

정답 | ②

| Script & Translation |

W: Hi, can I help you?

M: Yes, please. I'm looking to rent a copy machine for my business.

W: Okay, I'd be glad to help you out. Could you tell me your budget?

M: I'd like to keep it under $80 a month if possible.

W: Got it. How long do you need the copy machine?

M: Um... I need it for 12 months.

W: How about Wi-Fi? Do you need one with Wi-Fi access?

M: Yes, I do. Without that function, it's quite inconvenient to use a copy machine.

W: Yeah, right. Um... there are two copy machines left that fit what you've said so far. Now you only have to think about color copying.

M: I'll rent the one with color copying.

W: Okay. Wait a minute, please. I'll get you the contract.

여: 안녕하세요, 도와드릴까요?

남: 네, 그래요. 제 사업을 위해서 복사기를 대여하려고 생각 중인데요.

여: 알겠습니다, 기꺼이 도와드리겠습니다. 예산을 말씀해 주시겠어요?

남: 가능하다면 한 달에 80달러 미만으로 유지하고 싶습니다.

여: 알겠습니다. 복사기는 얼마나 오래 필요하죠?

남: 음… 12개월 동안 필요합니다.

여: 와이파이는 어떤가요? 와이파이 접속 기능이 있는 복사기가 필요한가요?

남: 네, 그래요. 그 기능이 없으면, 복사기를 사용하는 것이 상당히 불편하거든요.

여: 네, 맞습니다. 음… 지금까지 손님께서 말씀하신 것에 맞는 복사기가 두 대 남았네요. 이제 컬러 복사에 대해서만 생각하면 됩니다.

남: 컬러 복사를 할 수 있는 것으로 대여할게요.

여: 알겠습니다. 잠시만 기다려 주십시오. 계약서를 가져다드리겠습니다.

Topic & Situation 복사기 대여

Solution

남자는 한 달에 80달러 미만의 비용으로 12개월 동안 와이파이 접속 기능이 있으면서 컬러 복사를 할 수 있는 복사기를 대여하겠다고 말했으므로, 남자가 대여할 복사기는 ②이다.

Words & Phrases

copy machine 복사기 Wi-Fi 와이파이, 무선 데이터 전송 시스템 inconvenient 불편한 contract 계약서, 계약

11

정답 | ②

| Script & Translation |

M: My Korean teacher told me that there are grammar errors in my report.

W: Well, how about using a Korean grammar checker online? They check for grammar errors and they're free.

M: Oh, why didn't I think of that? Do you know of a good Korean grammar checker online?

W: Sure, I'll text you the website address right now.

남: 한국어 선생님께서 내 보고서에 문법 오류가 있다고 말씀하셨어.

여: 음, 온라인에서 한국어 문법 검색 프로그램을 사용하는 것은 어때? 그것은 문법 오류를 점검하고, 무료야.

남: 오, 왜 내가 그것을 생각하지 못했지? 온라인에서 좋은 한국어 문법 검색 프로그램을 알고 있니?

여: 물론이지. 바로 지금 네게 웹사이트 주소를 문자로 보내 줄게.

○ Topic & Situation 한국어 문법 오류 검색 프로그램

○ Solution

여자가 온라인에서 한국어 문법 검색 프로그램을 사용할 것을 제안하자 남자는 온라인에서 좋은 검색 프로그램을 알고 있는지 물었으므로, 이에 대한 여자의 응답으로 가장 적절한 것은 ② '물론이지. 바로 지금 네게 웹사이트 주소를 문자로 보내 줄게.'이다.

① 좋아. 그 보고서를 같이 읽자.

③ 나도 그래. 나도 문법 오류를 수정하고 싶어.

④ 좋아. 그 프로그램을 삭제하는 방법을 네게 말해 줄게.

⑤ 물론이야. 그 보고서를 쓰는 것은 상당히 힘들었어.

○ Words & Phrases

checker (철자나 문법 사항 등의 오류를 확인하는) 검색 프로그램 correct 수정하다 remove 삭제하다, 지우다 demanding 힘든, 어려운

12

정답 | ③

| Script & Translation |

W: Dad, I'm hungry. Is there something to eat?

M: Look in the fridge. There should be some leftover pizza from last night.

W: Oh, I forgot about that. I'll eat that. It'll be so cold and hard, though.

M: Don't worry. Just heat it up in the microwave.

여: 아빠, 배가 고파요. 먹을 것이 있나요?

남: 냉장고 안을 보렴. 지난밤에 먹다 남은 피자가 있을 거야.

여: 아, 그것을 깜박 잊었어요. 그것을 먹을게요. 그런데 그것이 너무 차갑고 딱딱할 거예요.

남: 걱정 마라. 그냥 전자레인지에 그것을 데우렴.

○ Topic & Situation 남은 피자 먹기

○ Solution

여자는 냉장고에 있는 피자를 먹겠다고 말하면서, 피자가 너무 차갑고 딱딱할 것이라는 말을 덧붙였으므로, 이에 대한 남자의 응답으로 가장 적절한 것은 ③ '걱정 마라. 그냥 전자레인지에 그것을 데우렴.'이다.

① 알았어. 내가 지금 바로 냉장고를 청소할게.

② 좋아. 이제 네게 피자 만드는 법을 가르쳐 줄게.

④ 오, 정말 배불러. 도저히 다른 것을 먹을 수 없어.

⑤ 정말 맛있어. 네가 만든 피자가 식당에서 파는 피자보다 더 나아.

○ Words & Phrases

fridge 냉장고 leftover 남은 heat up ~을 데우다 microwave 전자레인지

13

정답 | ④

| Script & Translation |

M: Cathy, are you planning on watching the *Women's Figure Skating World Championship* tonight?

W: Yeah, I can't wait. Who do you think will win?

M: I'm expecting Lucy Kim to win.

W: She's currently ranked number 1 in the world, right?

M: Yeah. She's been performing so well recently.

W: How about Jennifer Brown? She's ranked number 2 and won the competition last year.

M: Right. But I read an article that said she hasn't fully recovered from her ankle injury.

W: Oh, if that's the case, she probably won't be able to perform her most difficult moves.

M: Exactly. And she lost to Lucy Kim this year.

W: Then as you said, Lucy Kim is most likely to win the competition.

남: Cathy, 오늘 밤 세계 여자 피겨 스케이팅 선수권 대회 볼 계획이야?

여: 그래, 빨리 보고 싶어. 너는 누가 우승할 것 같아?

남: 나는 Lucy Kim이 우승할 것 같아.

여: 그녀는 현재 세계 랭킹 1위지, 맞지?

남: 그래. 최근에 그녀가 정말로 잘하고 있어.

여: Jennifer Brown은 어때? 그녀는 세계 랭킹 2위이고 작년에 대회에서 우승했잖아.

남: 맞아. 하지만 그녀가 발목 부상에서 완전히 회복하지 못했다고 하는 기사를 읽었어.

여: 오, 그것이 사실이라면, 그녀는 아마 자신의 가장 어려운 동작을 수행할 수 없을 거야.

남: 그렇지. 그리고 그녀는 올해 Lucy Kim에게 졌어.

여: 그러면 네가 말한 대로, Lucy Kim이 대회에서 우승할 가능성이 가장 높네.

○ Topic & Situation 세계 여자 피겨 스케이팅 선수권 대회

○ Solution

남자는 세계 여자 피겨 스케이팅 선수권 대회에서 세계 랭킹 1위인 Lucy Kim이 우승할 것이라고 말하며 세계 랭킹 2위인 선수가 부상에서 완전히 회복하지 못했다는 기사를 읽고 올해 Lucy Kim에게 졌다고 말했으므로, 남자의 마지막 말에 대한 여자의 응답으로 가장 적절한 것은 ④ '그러면 네가 말한 대로, Lucy Kim이 대회에서 우승할 가능성이 가장 높네.'이다.

① 걱정 마. 지금 바로 온라인으로 우리 입장권을 예매할게.
② 맞아. 나는 실시간으로 선수권 대회를 봤어야 했어.
③ 걱정 마. 지금부터 내가 네게 스케이트 타는 법을 가르쳐 줄게.
⑤ 물론! Jennifer Brown의 동작이 다른 사람들의 동작보다 훨씬 더 예술적이었어.

○ Words & Phrases

currently 현재   rank (순위 등을) 차지하다   article 기사   recover 회복하다   ankle injury 발목 부상

14

정답 | ⑤

| Script & Translation |

W: Excuse me. I bought this laptop here, and it's having problems. I was wondering if you could repair it.

M: Of course, I'd be happy to help. What problem is it having?

W: It sometimes makes an unusual noise while I'm using it.

M: I see. When did you purchase it? You can get free repair service for the first two years.

W: I bought it last year. Here's my membership card.

M: Let me check. *[Pause]* Okay, I see it here. The repair will be free.

W: Good. How long do you think the repair will take to complete?

M: It depends on the degree of the problem.

W: I see. Can I leave my laptop with you now?

M: Sure. As soon as the repair is done, I'll let you know.

여: 실례합니다. 제가 여기서 이 노트북을 구입했는데, 문제가 있어서요. 수리할 수 있는지 궁금했습니다.
남: 물론이죠, 기꺼이 도와드리겠습니다. 어떤 문제가 있나요?
여: 제가 사용하는 동안에 가끔 이상한 소리가 나요.
남: 알겠습니다. 언제 구입하셨죠? 처음 2년 동안은 무상 수리 서

비스를 받을 수 있습니다.
여: 작년에 구입했습니다. 제 회원 카드가 여기 있습니다.
남: 확인해 볼게요. *[잠시 후]* 네, 여기 있네요. 수리는 무료로 이루어질 것입니다.
여: 좋아요. 수리가 끝나는 데 얼마나 오래 걸릴까요?
남: 그것은 문제의 정도에 따라 다릅니다.
여: 알겠습니다. 제가 지금 노트북을 맡겨도 될까요?
남: 물론이죠. 수리가 완료되는 대로, 알려 드리겠습니다.

○ Topic & Situation   노트북 수리하기

○ Solution

노트북 수리를 맡기려는 여자가 남자에게 수리하는 데 얼마나 걸리는지 묻자, 남자는 고장 정도에 따라 다르다고 말한다. 이에 여자가 알았다고 하면서 지금 노트북을 맡겨도 되는지 물었다. 따라서 여자의 마지막 말에 대한 남자의 응답으로 가장 적절한 것은 ⑤ '물론이죠. 수리가 완료되는 대로, 알려 드리겠습니다.'이다.

① 네, 나는 컴퓨터를 살 돈을 당신에게 빌려 줄 수 있어요.
② 네, 당신이 원하면 언제든지 내 노트북을 사용할 수 있어요.
③ 아니요, 나는 지금 당장은 컴퓨터 가게에 갈 수 없어요.
④ 아니요, 당신은 무료로 수리를 받을 수 없어요.

○ Words & Phrases

laptop 노트북, 휴대용 컴퓨터   repair 수리(하다)   unusual 이상한   purchase 구입하다   complete 완료하다, 끝마치다   free of charge 무료로

15

정답 | ③

| Script & Translation |

M: Kate, a casting director at a movie studio, is holding auditions to find an actor to play the lead role in an upcoming film. Daniel is auditioning for the main character role. Kate asks him to perform a scene where the main character reflects on a past failure. Daniel does a pretty good job, and Kate thinks he may be the person to play the main character in the film. So she gives him a chance to attend the final audition. However, Daniel does a poor job in the final audition, and Kate realizes that he's not a good fit for this film. So Kate decides not to cast Daniel in this film. In this situation, what would Kate most likely say to Daniel?

Kate: I'm sorry, but you're not exactly what I want for this film.

남: 영화 스튜디오의 배역 담당 책임자인 Kate는 다가오는 영화에서 주연을 맡을 배우를 찾기 위해 오디션을 개최하고 있습니다. Daniel은 주인공 역할 오디션에 참가하고 있습니다. Kate는 그에게 주인공이 과거의 실패에 대해 곰곰이 생각하는 장면을 연기해 달라고 요청합니다. Daniel은 꽤 잘 해내고, Kate는 그가 영화에서 주인공을 연기할 사람일 수도 있다고 생각합니다. 그래서 그녀는 그에게 최종 오디션에 참가할 기회를 줍니다. 하지만 Daniel은 최종 오디션에서 잘하지 못하고, Kate는 그가 이 영화에 적합하지 않다는 것을 깨닫습니다. 그래서 Kate는 Daniel을 이 영화에 캐스팅하지 않기로 결심합니다. 이런 상황에서, Kate가 Daniel에게 뭐라고 말하겠습니까?

Kate: 미안하지만, 당신은 이 영화를 위해 내가 원하는 바로 그 사람이 아니에요.

● **Topic & Situation** 배우 캐스팅

● **Solution**
배역 담당 책임자인 Kate가 최종 오디션에서 연기를 제대로 하지 못한 Daniel을 영화에 캐스팅하지 않기로 결심한 상황이므로, Kate가 Daniel에게 할 말로 가장 적절한 것은 ③ '미안하지만, 당신은 이 영화를 위해 내가 원하는 바로 그 사람이 아니에요.'이다.
① 맞아요. 내가 원하는 것은 배역 담당 책임자가 되는 거예요.
② 물론이죠. 영화를 위해 적절한 배우들을 뽑는 것은 그렇게 쉽지 않아요.
④ 좋았어요, 그래서 당신에게 다음 오디션을 볼 기회를 주고 싶어요.
⑤ 정말 좋은 영화였기 때문에 추천해 주어서 고마워요.

● **Words & Phrases**
casting 배역 선정, 캐스팅 audition 오디션; 오디션을 보다 reflect on ~에 대해 곰곰이 생각하다, 숙고하다 attend 참가하다 fit 꼭 맞는 것 follow-up 다음의, 후속의

16~17

정답 | 16 ③ 17 ⑤

| Script & Translation |

W: Hi, everyone. Welcome to Sarah's online video channel, *Wonderful Animals*. Today I'd like to talk about how animals defend themselves from their predators. It's not easy to survive in the wild, so good defense is extremely important. One common method is disguise. Animals such as octopuses can change the color of their skin to make it difficult for predators to spot them. Another way is by simply using their speed. For example, kangaroos are incredibly fast, so they can just outrun their predators. A third way animals defend themselves is through the use of warning signals. African grey parrots make loud calls to warn other parrots nearby when they face danger. Thanks to the warning signals, the parrots in the area can be alerted and take necessary action. Finally, some animals like skunks emit a strong odor that can prevent predators from attacking them. Now let me show you videos of these animals.

여: 안녕하세요, 여러분. Sarah의 온라인 동영상 채널, *Wonderful Animals*에 오신 것을 환영합니다. 오늘 저는 동물들이 포식자로부터 스스로를 어떻게 방어하는지에 관해 이야기를 하고 싶습니다. 야생에서 살아남는 것은 쉽지 않아서, 좋은 방어 능력이 매우 중요합니다. 한 가지 일반적인 방법은 변장입니다. 문어 같은 동물은 포식자가 자신을 발견하기 어렵게 하기 위해 피부 색을 바꿀 수 있습니다. 또 다른 방법은 단순히 속도를 이용하는 것입니다. 예를 들어, 캥거루는 엄청나게 빨라서, 포식자보다 더 빨리 달릴 수 있습니다. 동물이 자신을 방어하는 세 번째 방법은 경고 신호를 사용하는 것입니다. 아프리카 회색 앵무새는 위험에 직면하면 근처에 있는 다른 앵무새에게 경고하기 위해 커다란 소리를 냅니다. 그 경고 신호 덕분에 그 지역에 있는 앵무새는 경계심을 가져서 필요한 조치를 취할 수 있습니다. 마지막으로, 스컹크와 같은 일부 동물은 포식자가 자신을 공격하지 못하게 할 수 있는 강한 악취를 방출합니다. 이제 이러한 동물들의 영상을 여러분에게 보여 드리겠습니다.

● **Topic & Situation** 야생 동물의 생존 방법

● **Solution**
16 온라인 동영상 채널, *Wonderful Animals*의 운영자인 여자는 동물들이 포식자로부터 자신을 보호하는 다양한 방법을 소개하고 있으므로, 여자가 하는 말의 주제로 가장 적절한 것은 ③ '동물이 포식자로부터 자신을 보호하는 방법들'이다.
① 먹이를 잡기 위해 포식자가 사용하는 기술
② 야생 동물이 야생에서 직면할 수 있는 어려움
④ 식물과 동물의 생물학적 차이
⑤ 환경 파괴가 동물 서식지에 미치는 영향

17 문어, 캥거루, 앵무새, 스컹크는 언급되었지만, ⑤ '돌고래'는 언급되지 않았다.

○ **Words & Phrases**

predator 포식자   defense 방어   extremely 매우, 몹시
disguise 변장, 가장   outrun ~보다 빨리 달리다   alert 경계심을 가지게 하다, 경보를 발하다   emit 내뿜다, 발산하다   odor 악취, 냄새
attack 공격하다

26강 실전 모의고사 5회   본문 186~191쪽

01 ①	02 ④	03 ④	04 ③	05 ③	06 ②
07 ①	08 ④	09 ④	10 ⑤	11 ③	12 ④
13 ⑤	14 ⑤	15 ⑤	16 ②	17 ③	

01   정답 | ①

| Script & Translation |

M: Attention, students! This is your principal, Mr. Thompson. I regret to inform you that the midterm exam period, originally scheduled for April 17th to the 19th, has been postponed due to unexpected circumstances. Several classrooms have experienced flood damage from the recent heavy rain, and they won't be repaired and suitable for use in time for the exam period. The new exam period date will be announced as soon as the classrooms are safe for use. I apologize for the inconvenience. Please keep an eye out for further updates regarding the revised date. Thank you for your understanding and cooperation.

남: 주목해 주세요, 학생 여러분! 저는 Thompson 교장 선생님입니다. 원래 4월 17일부터 19일까지 예정되어 있던 중간고사 기간이 예기치 못한 상황 때문에 연기되었음을 알리게 되어 유감입니다. 최근의 폭우로 인해 몇 개의 교실이 수해를 입어 시험 기간에 맞추어 수리되어 사용하기에 적합한 상태가 되지 못할 것입니다. 새로운 시험 기간 날짜는 교실이 안전하게 사용될 수 있게 되는 대로 발표될 것입니다. 불편을 주어 미안합니다. 수정된 날짜에 대한 추가 업데이트를 지켜봐 주세요. 여러분의 이해와 협조에 감사드립니다.

○ **Topic & Situation** 중간고사 일정 연기

○ **Solution**

남자는 최근의 폭우로 몇 개의 교실이 수해를 입어 시험 기간에 맞추어 수리되어 사용하기에 적합한 상태가 되지 못할 것이며, 새로운 시험 기간 날짜는 교실이 안전하게 사용될 수 있게 되는 대로 발표될 것이라고 말하고 있다. 따라서 남자가 하는 말의 목적으로 가장 적절한 것은 ① '중간고사 일정 연기를 공지하려고'이다.

○ **Words & Phrases**

principal 교장; 주요한, 주된   regret to *do* ~하게 되어 유감이다
period 기간, 시기   postpone 연기하다, 미루다   circumstance 상

황, 환경 damage 피해, 손상 suitable 적합한, 적절한 apologize
for ~에 대해 사과하다 inconvenience 불편 keep an eye out
지켜보다, 주시하다 revised 수정된

02

정답 | ④

| Script & Translation |

M: Hi, Jin! How's your French study going?

W: Hi, Steven. I feel like my grammar and reading are getting better, but it's hard to improve my listening and speaking. I'm not sure what to do.

M: Have you thought about watching French TV shows? Watching TV shows can help you improve your foreign language communication skills.

W: I haven't considered that.

M: TV shows often have a lot of good real-life conversations. You can imitate the speech patterns of the characters.

W: Sounds terrific. But don't you think they may be too hard for a beginner like me?

M: Then just watch them with subtitles. As your listening skills improve, you won't have to rely on subtitles as much.

W: Good idea. Is that how you became so good at Korean?

M: Yes. Watching TV shows has been really helpful for me. It's a great way to learn a new language!

W: Okay. I'll give it a try!

남: 안녕하세요, Jin! 당신의 프랑스어 공부는 잘 되어 가고 있나요?

여: 안녕하세요, Steven. 문법과 독해는 점점 나아지는 것 같지만, 듣기와 말하기를 향상시키는 것은 어려워요. 어떻게 해야 할지 모르겠어요.

남: 프랑스 TV 드라마를 시청하는 것에 대해 생각해 본 적이 있어요? TV 드라마를 시청하는 것은 당신이 외국어 의사소통 능력을 향상하도록 도울 수 있어요.

여: 그것을 고려해 보지는 않았어요.

남: TV 드라마에는 자주 실생활의 좋은 대화가 많이 나옵니다. 당신은 등장인물의 대화 패턴을 따라 할 수 있어요.

여: 아주 좋네요. 하지만 저와 같은 초보자한테는 그것들이 너무 어려울 수 있다고 생각하지 않나요?

남: 그럼 그냥 자막과 함께 보세요. 듣기 능력이 향상되면 자막에 그렇게 많이 의존할 필요가 없게 될 거예요.

여: 좋은 생각이군요. 당신은 그런 식으로 한국어를 아주 잘하게 된 건가요?

남: 네. TV 드라마를 시청하는 것은 제게 정말 도움이 되었어요. 그것은 새로운 언어를 배우는 좋은 방법이에요!

여: 좋아요. 한번 해 볼게요!

● Topic & Situation TV 드라마 시청을 통한 외국어 의사소통능력 함양

● Solution

남자는 듣기와 말하기 실력을 개선하고자 하는 여자에게 프랑스 TV 드라마를 시청하라고 권하면서 그것이 외국어 의사소통 능력의 향상을 도울 수 있다고 말한다. 그런 것을 고려해 보지 않았다는 여자에게 남자는 TV 드라마에는 실생활의 좋은 대화가 많이 나오며, 등장인물의 대화 패턴을 따라 할 수 있다고 말하면서, 초보자에게 너무 어렵지 않겠냐고 반문하는 여자에게 자막을 함께 보라고 권하고, TV 드라마 시청이 자신이 한국어를 배우는 데 정말 도움이 되었으며, 그것은 새로운 언어를 배우는 좋은 방법이라고 말했다. 따라서 남자의 의견으로 가장 적절한 것은 ④ 'TV 드라마 시청을 통해 외국어 의사소통 능력을 향상할 수 있다.'이다.

● Words & Phrases

grammar 문법 foreign 외국의 language 언어 imitate 따라 하다, 모방하다 character 등장인물 terrific 아주 좋은, 멋진 subtitle 자막 give it a try 한번 해 보다, 시도하다

03

정답 | ④

| Script & Translation |

M: Hello, listeners! Welcome to *Parenting Power Hour*! As parents, you've probably felt the desire to lend a hand when your kids face challenges like tying their shoelaces. It's completely normal to want to help and show support. However, you shouldn't take over and perform the tasks for them. Instead, encourage them to handle the tasks they are capable of, like dressing themselves or packing their school bag. Allowing your kids to do things within their abilities is essential for their growth. It's a way for them to feel accomplished and become more independent. On today's episode of *Parenting Power Hour*, we'll explore this empowering approach further. Stay tuned!

남: 안녕하세요, 청취자 여러분! *Parenting Power Hour*에 오신 것을 환영합니다! 부모로서, 여러분은 아마 자녀들이 신발 끈을 묶는 것과 같은 어려움에 직면했을 때 도움을 주고 싶은 욕구를 느끼셨을 것입니다. 돕고 싶고 지지를 보여 주고 싶은 것은 완전히 정상적인 일입니다. 그러나 여러분은 그들을 위해 일을 넘겨받아 수행해서는 안 됩니다. 대신, 옷을 입거나 학교 가방을 싸는 일처럼 아이들이 할 수 있는 일들을 처리할 수 있도록 격려하세요. 여러분의 자녀들이 자신의 능력 안에서 일을 하도록 허용하는 것은 그들의 성장에 매우 중요합니다. 그것은 아이들이 성취감을 느끼고 더 독립적이 될 수 있는 방법입니다. 오늘의 *Parenting Power Hour* 방송(분)에서는 이러한 권한 부여 접근 방식에 대해 더 자세히 알아보겠습니다. 채널 고정해 주세요!

◑ Topic & Situation 자녀의 성취감과 독립심을 키우기 위한 부모의 양육 태도

◑ Solution
남자는 아이들이 신발 끈을 묶는 것과 같은 어려움에 직면했을 때 도와주고 싶더라도 그들의 일을 넘겨받아 수행해서는 안 된다고 하면서, 아이들이 자신의 능력 안에서 일을 하도록 하는 것이 그들의 성장에 매우 중요하며, 그로 인해 아이들이 성취감을 느끼고 더 독립적이 될 수 있다고 말한다. 따라서 남자가 하는 말의 요지로 가장 적절한 것은 ④ '아이들이 할 수 있는 일을 스스로 하게 하는 것이 성장에 중요하다.'이다.

◑ Words & Phrases
parenting 육아 desire 욕구 tie (끈을) 매다 shoelace 신발끈, 구두끈 take over ~을 넘겨받다. 인수하다 be capable of ~할 수 있다 essential 매우 중요한, 필수의 accomplished 성취된, 완성된 independent 독립적인 explore 알아보다. 탐험하다 empower 권한을 부여하다

04
정답 | ③

| Script & Translation |
M: What are you doing on the computer?
W: I made an invitation for Mom and Dad's 30th wedding anniversary party. Take a look!

M: Wow! I like how you put the number '30' under the crown.
W: Thanks! Do you think I should change the phrase 'Years of Love, Laughter & Togetherness' in the banner?
M: No. It perfectly describes their marriage.
W: It took me a while to think of the right phrase. And I put our favorite picture of Mom and Dad on the far right. It's the one where they're facing each other.
M: That's such a good picture. And I like the heart in the middle with the party date and place.
W: Thanks. See this QR code in the bottom left corner. If you scan it, it takes you to a photo album with more photos of Mom and Dad.
M: That's amazing! Everybody's going to love your invitation!
M: I hope so!

남: 컴퓨터에서 뭐 하고 있니?
여: 엄마와 아빠의 30주년 결혼 기념일 파티 초대장을 만들었어. 한번 봐봐!
남: 와! 왕관 아래에 숫자 '30'을 넣은 것이 마음에 들어.
여: 고마워! 배너에 있는 '사랑, 웃음, 단란함의 세월' 문구를 바꿔야 한다고 생각하니?
남: 아니. 그것은 그분들의 결혼 생활을 완벽하게 묘사하고 있어.
여: 적절한 문구를 생각하는 데 시간이 좀 걸렸어. 그리고 맨 오른쪽에 우리가 가장 좋아하는 엄마와 아빠 사진을 넣었어. 그분들이 서로를 마주보고 있는 그 사진이야.
남: 그건 진짜 좋은 사진이지. 그리고 파티 날짜와 장소가 있고 가운데 있는 하트가 마음에 들어.
여: 고마워. 왼쪽 아래 구석에 있는 이 QR 코드 좀 봐봐. 그것을 스캔하면 엄마와 아빠의 사진이 더 많이 있는 앨범으로 이동해.
남: 정말 놀랍구나! 모두가 너의 초대장을 좋아할 거야!
여: 그러기를 바라!

◑ Topic & Situation 부모님의 30주년 결혼기념일 파티 초대장

◑ Solution
대화에서는 엄마와 아빠가 서로 마주보고 있는 사진이라고 했는데, 그림에서는 두 명 모두 정면을 보고 있으므로, 그림에서 대화의 내용과 일치하지 않는 것은 ③이다.

◑ Words & Phrases
invitation 초대장, 초대 wedding anniversary 결혼기념일 crown

왕관 phrase 문구, 구절 laughter 웃음 describe 묘사하다 face 마주 보다

05

| Script & Translation |

M: Linda, I can't believe the School Family Reading Night is today.

W: Me, neither. Do you think we have everything ready?

M: I think so. Earlier today I put posters up along the school hallways to introduce new books.

W: I noticed a lot of students looking at them. Did you inform the guest speaker about the schedule after her speech?

M: Yes, I did. I've been in touch with her via email about that.

W: Great. I finished setting up the tables in the auditorium a little while ago.

M: Awesome. And did you put the snacks and drinks out?

W: Yes, I did. But I think we might need more. Last year, more people showed up than we had anticipated.

M: Oh, I see. I'll go to the supermarket to get more.

W: Okay, thanks. And I'll pick up the schedules from the printing room so we can pass them out later.

M: All right. I think we're about ready.

남: Linda, School Family Reading Night이 오늘이라니 믿을 수가 없어요.

여: 저도요. 우리가 모든 준비를 다 마쳤다고 생각해요?

남: 그런 것 같아요. 오늘 일찍 제가 학교 복도를 따라 새 책을 소개하는 포스터를 붙였어요.

여: 많은 학생이 그것들을 보고 있는 것을 목격했어요. 선생님은 초청 연사에게 연설 이후의 일정에 대해 알려 주셨나요?

남: 네, 했어요. 저는 그것에 관해 그녀와 계속 이메일을 통해 연락하고 있었어요.

여: 잘했네요. 저는 조금 전에 강당에 테이블을 설치하는 것을 마쳤어요.

남: 멋지네요. 그리고 간식과 음료를 밖으로 꺼내 놓았나요?

여: 네, 꺼내 놓았습니다. 하지만 좀 더 필요할 것 같아요. 작년에는 우리가 예상했던 것보다 더 많은 사람이 참석했거든요.

남: 아, 알겠어요. 제가 슈퍼마켓에 가서 좀 더 사올게요.

여: 좋아요, 고마워요. 그럼 저는 우리가 나중에 나누어 줄 수 있도록 인쇄실에서 일정표를 가지고 올게요.

남: 알겠습니다. 준비가 거의 다 된 것 같아요.

◉ **Topic & Situation** School Family Reading Night

◉ **Solution**

School Family Reading Night을 준비하면서 여자가 작년에는 예상보다 더 많은 사람이 참석했다고 말하면서 간식과 음료가 좀 더 필요할 것 같다고 하자, 남자가 슈퍼마켓에 가서 좀 더 사오겠다고 말했다. 따라서 남자가 할 일로 가장 적절한 것은 ③ '간식과 음료 더 사 오기'이다.

◉ **Words & Phrases**

put up ~을 붙이다. 게시하다 hallway 복도 be in touch with ~과 연락하다 via 통하여, 경유하여 set up ~을 설치하다 auditorium 강당 show up 참석하다. 나타나다 anticipate 예상하다. 예측하다 pass ~ out ~을 나눠주다

06

| Script & Translation |

W: Hi. Can I get two large cappuccinos to go?

M: Sure. Would you like any toppings?

W: No, just regular cappuccinos, please.

M: Okay. That will be $10 total.

W: All right. And I noticed a sign at the entrance of the coffee shop that all the tumblers are currently on sale. How much is this teddy bear tumbler?

M: It's regularly $30, but it's 20% off right now.

W: Oh, that's great! I'll take it.

M: Okay. Anything else for you?

W: Yes, actually, I want to buy a gift card for a friend's birthday. What amounts do they come in?

M: Our gift cards come in $10, $20, and $50 amounts.

W: Perfect! I'll take a $20 one, please.

M: Okay. Would you like to pay for everything now?

W: Yes, please. Here's my card.

여: 안녕하세요. 라지 카푸치노 두 잔 포장해 주시겠어요?

남: 알겠습니다. 토핑을 원하시나요?

여: 아니요, 그냥 일반 카푸치노로 주세요.

남: 알겠습니다. 총 10달러입니다.

여: 좋아요. 그리고 커피숍 입구에서 현재 모든 텀블러가 할인 중이라는 표지판을 보았는데요. 이 테디 베어 텀블러는 얼마인가요?

남: 정상가는 30달러인데, 지금은 20% 할인 중입니다.

여: 아, 잘됐네요! 그걸로 살게요.

남: 좋아요. 더 필요한 게 있으신가요?

여: 네, 실은, 친구의 생일 선물로 기프트 카드를 사고 싶어요. 어떤 금액으로 나오나요?

남: 저희 기프트 카드는 10달러, 20달러, 50달러짜리로 나옵니다.

여: 완벽해요! 20달러짜리 하나 주세요.

남: 알겠습니다. 지금 다 결제하시겠어요?

여: 네, 부탁드려요. 여기에 제 카드가 있습니다.

▶ Topic & Situation 커피 및 커피 관련 상품 구매하기

▶ Solution

여자는 일반 카푸치노 라지 사이즈 2잔을 10달러에 사고, 정상가 30달러인 테디 베어 텀블러를 20% 할인된 가격으로 구입하였으며, 20달러짜리 기프트 카드를 추가로 구입하였으므로, 여자가 지불할 금액은 ② '$54'이다.

▶ Words & Phrases

topping 토핑, 고명   regular 일반적인, 보통의   total 총, 전체의   tumbler 텀블러(굽이나 손잡이가 없고 바닥이 납작한 큰 잔)   gift card 기프트 카드

07

정답 | ①

| Script & Translation |

[Cell phone rings.]

M: Honey, how did the conference go today?

W: It was really informative. I learned a lot about the latest AI research.

M: That's great to hear. Did you end up going to the Harbor Robotics Center after the seminar?

W: No. Unfortunately it was canceled due to unexpected maintenance.

M: I'm sorry to hear that. So, what's your plan now? Are you coming straight home?

W: No. I'm going to have lunch with Professor Miller before I head back.

M: All right. What time will you arrive at the station?

W: My train is supposed to get there at 4 p.m. Can you pick me up from there?

M: I'm sorry, but I have a meeting with a client then.

W: No problem. I'll take a taxi. How about Patrick? What is he doing?

M: He's at his swimming lesson right now.

W: Ah, that's right. See you later then.

[휴대 전화가 울린다.]

남: 여보, 오늘 학회는 어땠어요?

여: 정말 유익했어요. 저는 가장 최근의 AI 연구에 대해 많은 것을 배웠어요.

남: 정말 잘됐네요. 세미나가 끝나고 Harbor Robotics Center에 가게 되었나요?

여: 아니요. 안타깝게도 예상치 못한 정비 때문에 취소되었어요.

남: 유감이네요. 그래서, 이제 당신의 계획은 뭔가요? 곧바로 집에 올 건가요?

여: 아니요. 돌아가기 전에 Miller 교수님과 점심을 먹을 거예요.

남: 알겠어요. 몇 시에 역에 도착할 예정이에요?

여: 내 기차는 오후 4시에 거기에 도착하기로 되어 있어요. 거기로 나를 태우러 올 수 있어요?

남: 미안하지만, 그때 고객과 회의가 있어요.

여: 괜찮아요. 택시를 탈게요. Patrick은요? 뭐 하고 있어요?

남: 걔는 지금 수영 강습을 받고 있어요.

여: 아, 맞네요. 그럼 나중에 봐요.

▶ Topic & Situation 기차역으로 마중 나갈 수 없는 이유

▶ Solution

여자가 자신의 기차가 오후 4시에 역에 도착한다고 말하면서 남자에게 자신을 태우러 역으로 나올 수 있는지 묻자, 남자는 고객과 회의가 있다고 말하면서 미안하다고 말했다. 따라서 남자가 기차역으로 마중 나갈 수 없는 이유는 ① '고객과 회의가 있어서'이다.

▶ Words & Phrases

conference 학회, 회의   latest (가장) 최근의, 바로 앞의   harbor 항구, 항만, 피난처   cancel 취소하다   maintenance 정비, 관리   be supposed to *do* ~하기로 되어 있다   client 고객

08

정답 | ④

| Script & Translation |

M: Hey, Jenny! Have you heard about the 2024 Vision Scholarship?

W: No. What is it about?

M: It's a scholarship for students who do volunteer work. I know you volunteer a lot, so I thought you'd be interested in it.

W: Oh, I definitely am! What are the requirements?

M: To apply for the scholarship, you need to have completed 100 hours of community service in the previous year.

W: I've done that. How do I apply?

M: You just need to fill out a form online, upload your grades, and write a 500-word essay about your community service experience.

W: Thanks for letting me know. Do you know when the deadline is?

M: It's April 30th.

W: Oh, next week. I'd better get started on my application right away. How much is the scholarship?

M: It's $1,500! It can be used for tuition, books, or other education-related expenses.

W: That's a lot! Thanks for the information!

남: 이봐, Jenny! 2024 비전 장학금에 대해서 들어 봤니?

여: 아니. 그게 뭔데?

남: 자원봉사를 하는 학생들을 위한 장학금이야. 네가 자원봉사를 많이 하는 것을 알고 있어서, 네가 관심을 가질 거라고 생각했어.

여: 아, 확실히 그렇지! 자격 요건은 뭐야?

남: 장학금 신청을 하려면 전년도에 100시간의 지역 사회 봉사를 마쳤어야 해.

여: 그건 했지. 어떻게 신청하는 거야?

남: 온라인으로 양식을 작성하고 성적표를 업로드하고, 지역 사회 봉사 경험에 대해 500단어짜리 에세이를 쓰기만 하면 돼.

여: 알려 줘서 고마워. 마감일이 언제인지 아니?

남: 4월 30일이야.

여: 아, 다음 주네. 지금 당장 신청을 시작하는 것이 좋겠어. 장학금은 얼마니?

남: 1,500달러야! 그것은 등록금, 책 또는 기타 교육 관련 경비로 사용할 수 있어.

여: 정말 많구나! 정보를 알려 줘서 고마워!

> **Topic & Situation** 2024 Vision Scholarship

> **Solution**

2024 Vision Scholarship에 관해 신청 자격 요건, 신청 방법, 신청 마감일, 장학금 액수는 언급되었지만, ④ '추천서 필요 여부'는 언급되지 않았다.

> **Words & Phrases**

scholarship 장학금, 학문 requirement 자격 요건 apply for ~을 신청하다 previous 바로 앞의, 이전의 fill out ~을 작성하다, 기입하다 expense 경비, 비용

09

정답 | ④

| Script & Translation |

W: Hello, Oakville residents! The 2024 Winter Family Fun Day is right around the corner! It's on December 18th from 11 a.m. to 4 p.m. at Bridgeview Park. This is one of the most fun local community-hosted events of the year, bringing Oakville together to celebrate the winter season. Tickets are $15 per person, and kids under five are free. Bring the whole family for ice skating, sledding, snowman building, and face painting. Light snacks and beverages are included in the price of admission! Be sure to bring your ice skates and sleds for a day of winter fun. You can buy admission tickets online at the community center website. We hope to see you there!

여: 안녕하세요, Oakville 주민 여러분! 2024년 Winter Family Fun Day가 코앞으로 다가왔습니다! 그것은 12월 18일 오전 11시부터 오후 4시까지 Bridgeview 공원에서 열립니다. 이것은 올해 가장 재미있는 지역 사회 주최 행사 중 하나로, Oakville을 하나로 모아 겨울철을 축하하는 자리입니다. 표는 개인당 15달러이며, 5세 미만의 어린이는 무료입니다. 아이스 스케이팅, 썰매 타기, 눈사람 만들기, 그리고 페이스 페인팅에 가족 모두를 데리고 오세요. 입장료 가격에는 가벼운 간식과 음료가 포함되어 있습니다! 겨울 놀이를 즐길 수 있는 하루를 위해 여러분의 아이스 스케이트와 썰매를 꼭 가져오세요. 여러분은 우리 커뮤니티 센터 웹사이트에서 온라인으로 입장권을 구매할 수 있습니다. 그곳에서 여러분을 만나길 바랍니다!

> **Topic & Situation** 2024 Winter Family Fun Day

◐ Solution

여자는 입장료 가격에 가벼운 간식과 음료가 포함되어 있다고 했으므로, 담화의 내용과 일치하지 않는 것은 ④ '간식을 위해 별도의 비용을 지불해야 한다.'이다.

◐ Words & Phrases

around the corner 코앞에, 곧 community-hosted 지역 사회에 의해 주최된 celebrate 축하하다, 기념하다 sled 썰매를 타다; 썰매 beverage 음료 admission 입장(료)

10 정답 | ⑤

| Script & Translation |

M: Hi. I'd like to buy a summer blanket. Can you tell me where they are?

W: Well, they're currently in the storeroom. We haven't put them out yet. Let me get a catalog for you though. [Pause] Here you are. Take a look.

M: Great. Well, I definitely don't want cotton. It'd be too hot for the summer.

W: Right. The other two materials are better for summer. What size do you need?

M: Either a queen or double would work.

W: Then for those sizes, the prices range from $85 to $110.

M: Hmm, I like these two models, but they're both over $100.

W: No worries. This week, we're actually offering a 10% discount on all products over $100.

M: That's fantastic!

W: So, what color are you interested in?

M: I don't think brown is a good summer color, so I'll get this other one.

W: Okay. I'll get it for you.

M: Great. Thanks.

남: 안녕하세요. 여름 담요를 사고 싶은데요. 그것들이 어디에 있는지 말씀해 주시겠어요?

여: 음, 그것들은 지금 창고에 있습니다. 아직 꺼내 놓지 않았어요. 하지만, 손님께 카탈로그를 가져다드릴게요. [잠시 후] 여기 있어요. 한번 보세요.

남: 멋지네요. 그런데, 확실히 면은 원하지 않아요. 여름에는 그것

이 너무 더울 것 같아요.

여: 맞아요. 다른 두 소재가 여름에는 더 낫지요. 어떤 사이즈가 필요하세요?

남: 퀸이나 더블 사이즈면 괜찮아요.

여: 그렇다면 그런 사이즈들은 가격이 85달러부터 110달러까지 다양합니다.

남: 흠, 저는 이 두 가지 모델이 마음에 드는데, 둘 다 100달러가 넘네요.

여: 걱정하지 마세요. 이번 주에는, 사실 100달러가 넘는 모든 제품에 10% 할인을 제공하고 있어요.

남: 환상적이네요!

여: 그럼, 어떤 색상에 관심이 있으신가요?

남: 갈색은 여름 색상으로는 좋지 않을 것 같아서, 다른 걸로 할게요.

여: 알겠습니다. 당신께 그걸로 가져다드릴게요.

남: 좋아요. 감사합니다.

◐ Topic & Situation 여름 담요 구매하기

◐ Solution

남자는 담요를 구매하면서, 면 소재가 아니고 퀸이나 더블 사이즈 크기이며, 100달러가 넘지만 갈색이 아닌 것을 선택했다. 따라서 남자가 구입할 담요는 ⑤이다.

◐ Words & Phrases

blanket 담요 cotton 면 material 소재, 재료 range from ~ to ... (범위가) ~에서 …에 이르다 linen 리넨, 아마 섬유

11 정답 | ③

| Script & Translation |

M: Hi, Ms. Sandler. How's your heating bill nowadays? Mine has been extremely high because of the cold weather.

W: Hi, Mr. Baker. Mine is about the same as last year. I always keep the temperature at 18 degrees.

M: Really? I would give that a try, but that sounds quite cold.

W: Don't worry. It's not so bad once you get used to it.

남: 안녕하세요, Sandler 씨. 요즘 난방비는 어떠세요? 저의 난방비는 추운 날씨 때문에 굉장히 많이 나왔어요.

여: 안녕하세요, Baker 씨. 제 것은 작년과 거의 같아요. 저는 항

상 온도를 18도로 유지하거든요.

남: 정말이요? 저도 한번 해 보고 싶지만, 그것은 꽤 추울 것 같네요.

여: 걱정 마세요. 일단 그것에 익숙해지면 그렇게 나쁘지 않아요.

◎ Topic & Situation 난방비 줄이기

◎ Solution

추운 날씨 때문에 난방비가 많이 나왔다며 난방비가 어떤지 묻는 남자에게 여자가 자신의 난방비는 작년과 거의 같고 항상 온도를 18도로 유지한다고 하자, 남자는 자신도 시도해 보고 싶지만, 그것이 꽤 추울 것 같다고 말했다. 따라서 남자의 마지막 말에 대한 여자의 응답으로 가장 적절한 것은 ③ '걱정 마세요. 일단 그것에 익숙해지면 그렇게 나쁘지 않아요.'이다.

① 저도 마찬가지예요. 저는 그런 온도에서 살 수 없었어요.

② 이렇게 추운 날씨에는 히터가 충분히 따뜻하지 않아요.

④ 온도를 18도보다 높게 유지하는 것이 더 낫습니다.

⑤ 이번 달 저의 난방비가 평소보다 훨씬 더 많아요.

◎ Words & Phrases

heating bill 난방비   extremely 굉장히, 극도로   get used to ~에 익숙해지다

12
정답 | ④

| Script & Translation |

W: Honey, the plant in the living room is doing very well. But I think it might be outgrowing the pot.

M: Yeah, right. Since you changed the soil mix, it's grown a lot.

W: It has. What do you think about changing the pot?

M: Okay. It'd be a good idea to get a larger pot for the plant.

여: 여보, 거실에 있는 식물이 아주 잘 자라고 있어요. 하지만 그것은 너무 자라서 화분에 안 맞는 것 같아요.

남: 네, 맞아요. 당신이 배합토를 바꾼 이후로, 식물이 많이 자랐지요.

여: 그래요. 화분을 바꾸는 것에 대해서 어떻게 생각하세요?

남: 좋아요. 식물을 위해 더 큰 화분을 구하는 게 좋을 것 같아요.

◎ Topic & Situation 분갈이

◎ Solution

여자가 거실에 있는 식물이 너무 자라서 화분에 안 맞는 것 같다

고 하자, 남자는 여자가 배합토를 바꾼 이후로 식물이 많이 자랐다고 말했다. 이 말을 듣고 여자가 남자에게 화분을 바꾸는 것에 대해서 어떻게 생각하는지 물었으므로, 여자의 마지막 말에 대한 남자의 응답으로 가장 적절한 것은 ④ '좋아요. 식물을 위해 더 큰 화분을 구하는 게 좋을 것 같아요.'이다.

① 내 말이 그말이에요. 저는 당신이 그것에 비료를 좀 줘야 한다고 생각해요.

② 어머, 세상에! 당신은 일주일에 두 번 이상 물을 주면 안 돼요.

③ 물론이에요. 저는 그 식물을 위해 사용할 최고의 배합토를 조사했어요.

⑤ 왜 안 되겠어요? 그 식물을 빨리 거실로 옮깁시다.

◎ Words & Phrases

outgrow 너무 커져 맞지 않게 되다, ~보다 더 커지다   pot 화분, 냄비
soil mix 배합토   fertilizer 비료

13
정답 | ⑤

| Script & Translation |

M: Hi, Susan, you look serious. What's going on?

W: Oh, hi! I'm just thinking whether I should go to the library. I'm not sure if I can make it there before they close.

M: It's already 5:30. You're never going to make it. Is there a book you want to check out?

W: Yeah. It's a book on running a business. I think it'd be really helpful for my new business project.

M: Then, why don't you use the library's nighttime check-out service?

W: What's that?

M: It's a service that allows you to check out books after the library closes.

W: Really? That's great! How does it work?

M: First, you need to reserve a book online. Then, you pick it up from the self-checkout machine outside the library using your library card.

W: Wow, that's awesome. I'd like to try that service today.

M: Hurry! You need to reserve your book before the library closes.

남: 안녕하세요, Susan. 당신 심각해 보여요. 무슨 일인가요?

여: 아, 안녕하세요! 그냥 도서관에 가야 할지 생각하고 있는 중이에요. 그들이 문을 닫기 전에 거기에 시간 맞춰 갈 수 있을지 모르겠어요.

남: 벌써 5시 30분이에요. 당신은 결코 시간 맞춰 갈 수 없을 거예요. 대출하고 싶은 책이 있나요?

여: 네. 그것은 사업 운영에 관한 책이에요. 저의 새로운 사업 프로젝트에 정말 도움이 될 것 같아요.

남: 그럼, 도서관 야간 대출 서비스를 이용해 보는 건 어때요?

여: 그게 뭐예요?

남: 도서관이 문을 닫은 후에 책을 대출할 수 있게 해 주는 서비스예요.

여: 그래요? 잘됐네요! 어떻게 운영되죠?

남: 먼저, 온라인으로 책을 예약해야 해요. 그런 다음 도서관 밖에 있는 셀프 대출 기계에서 도서관 카드를 이용해 책을 수령하면 돼요.

여: 와, 정말 멋지네요. 오늘 그 서비스를 이용해 보고 싶어요.

남: 서둘러요! 도서관이 문을 닫기 전에 책을 예약해야 해요.

● **Topic & Situation** 야간 도서 대출 서비스

● **Solution**

책을 대출받고 싶지만 도서관이 문을 닫기 전에 시간 맞춰 갈 수 있을지 몰라 망설이는 여자에게 남자가 야간 대출 서비스를 이용해 보라고 제안하면서 이용법에 관해 설명하자, 여자가 오늘 그 서비스를 이용해 보고 싶다고 말한다. 따라서 여자의 마지막 말에 대한 남자의 응답으로 가장 적절한 것은 ⑤ '서둘러요! 도서관이 문을 닫기 전에 책을 예약해야 해요.'이다.

① 잘됐네요! 당신은 폐관 시간 전에 거기에 도착할 수 있어요.
② 확실하지 않아요. 하지만 밤에는 그 서비스를 이용할 수 없다고 알고 있어요.
③ 아, 이런! 셀프 대출 기계가 고장난 것 같아요.
④ 물론이죠. 사업에 대한 아이디어를 얻는 것이 도움이 될 수도 있어요.

● **Words & Phrases**

make it 시간 맞춰 가다   check out ~을 대출하다   reserve 예약하다   awesome 굉장한, 기막히게 좋은   out of order 고장난   beneficial 유익한, 이로운

14
정답 | ⑤

| Script & Translation |

M: Hey, Corey, you've seemed a bit down lately. Is everything okay?

W: I've been worried about something.

M: What is it?

W: Well, my dad has been pressuring me into studying business, but I want to study art.

M: Hmm, have you told him that?

W: Yes, but my dad is stubborn and won't listen to me.

M: Have you tried having an honest conversation with him? I mean a heart-to-heart talk where you express how unhappy you are.

W: I wish I could, but I'm scared to disappoint him.

M: Remember, it's your life and your happiness that matters. Your dad will love and support you no matter what.

W: You're right. I think it's about time I gather the courage to tell him how unhappy I would be studying business.

M: Good. If you're just honest about your feelings with your dad, it'll work out.

W: Right. He'll probably finally stop pressuring me to study business.

남: 안녕, Corey, 최근에 네 기분이 조금 안 좋아 보이던데. 모든 일이 괜찮은 거니?

여: 걱정되는 것이 있어.

남: 뭔데?

여: 음, 아빠는 나더러 비즈니스를 공부하라고 압박하고 계시는데, 나는 미술을 공부하고 싶거든.

남: 음, 그걸 아버지께 말씀드려 봤니?

여: 응, 하지만 아빠는 완고하셔서 내 말을 듣지 않으실 거야.

남: 아버지와 솔직한 대화를 시도해 봤니? 내 말은, 네가 얼마나 불행한지 표현하는 마음을 터놓고 하는 대화 말이야.

여: 나도 그러고 싶지만, 아빠를 실망시킬까 봐 두려워.

남: 기억해, 중요한 것은 너의 인생과 너의 행복이야. 너의 아버지는 무슨 일이 있어도 널 사랑하고 지원하실 거야.

여: 네 말이 맞아. 이제는 내가 비즈니스를 공부하는 것이 얼마나 불행할지 아빠한테 말씀드릴 용기를 낼 때가 되었다고 생각해.

남: 좋아. 아버지한테 네 감정을 솔직하게 표현한다면, 그것은 효과가 있을 거야.

여: 맞아. 아빠는 아마도 나에게 비즈니스를 공부하라고 압박하는 것을 결국 그만두실 거야.

● **Topic & Situation** 진로 문제로 인한 갈등

Solution

진로 문제에 관해 아버지와 갈등을 겪고 있는 여자에게 남자가 아버지와 솔직한 대화를 나눠 볼 것을 권유하며, 아버지는 무슨 일이 있어도 여자를 사랑하고 지원할 것이며, 여자가 아버지에게 감정을 솔직하게 표현한다면 효과가 있을 거라고 격려해 주고 있다. 따라서 남자의 마지막 말에 대한 여자의 응답으로 가장 적절한 것은 ⑤ '맞아. 아빠는 아마도 나에게 비즈니스를 공부하라고 압박하는 것을 결국 그만두실 거야.'이다.
① 물론이야. 나는 아빠의 기대에 부응하도록 노력할 거야.
② 안타깝지만, 나에겐 예술가가 될 소질이 없어.
③ 신경 쓰지 마. 아빠를 설득할 그밖에 다른 방법은 없어.
④ 용기를 내 봐. 너의 아버지와 진심 어린 대화를 나누려고 노력해 봐.

Words & Phrases

pressure 압력을 가하다   stubborn 완고한, 고집이 센   conversation 대화   scare 두려워하다   disappoint 실망시키다   live up to (기대 등)에 부응하다   expectation 기대, 예상   aptitude 소질, 적성   convince 설득하다, 납득시키다   heartfelt 진심 어린

15
정답 | ⑤

| Script & Translation |

W: Roger and Chloe meet again at their high school reunion after ten years since graduation. Roger is surprised to see Chloe with short hair because she always had long hair throughout high school. Chloe tells him that she donated her hair to help sick children and suggests that Roger do the same. He's encouraged by her suggestion, so he asks her about the required length of his hair for donation. Chloe says it should be at least eight inches long and gives him information about the organization she donated her hair through. Roger wants to express his gratitude to Chloe for motivating him to donate his hair to help children suffering from illnesses. In this situation, what would Roger most likely say to Chloe?

Roger: Thank you for inspiring me to donate my hair for sick children.

여: Roger와 Chloe는 졸업 후 10년 만에 고등학교 동창회에서 다시 만납니다. Roger는 Chloe가 고등학교 시절 내내 항상 긴 머리를 하고 있었기 때문에 짧은 머리를 한 Chloe를 보고 놀랍니다. Chloe는 그에게 자신의 머리카락을 아픈 아이들을 돕기 위해 기부했다고 말하며 Roger도 같은 일을 할 것을 제안합니다. 그는 그녀의 제안에 고무되어 기부를 위해 요구되는 머리카락 길이에 대해 묻습니다. Chloe는 적어도 8인치는 되어야 한다고 말하며 자신이 머리카락을 기부해 온 단체에 관한 정보를 알려 줍니다. Roger는 Chloe가 병을 앓고 있는 아이들을 돕기 위해 그의 머리카락을 기부하도록 동기를 부여한 것에 대해 감사를 표현하고 싶어 합니다. 이런 상황에서, Roger는 Chloe에게 뭐라고 말하겠습니까?

Roger: 아픈 아이들을 위해 내가 머리카락을 기부하도록 격려해 주어서 고마워.

Topic & Situation 머리카락 기부

Solution

Roger는 고등학교 시절 내내 긴 머리를 하고 있다가 10년 만에 고등학교 동창회에 머리를 짧게 자르고 나타난 Chloe로부터 그녀가 아픈 아이들을 돕기 위해 머리카락을 기부했다는 말을 듣고 같은 일을 해 볼 것을 제안받는다. 그녀의 제안에 고무된 Roger는 기부에 필요한 머리카락의 길이를 묻고, 그녀가 기부한 단체에 관한 정보도 알게 되면서, 그가 머리카락을 기부하도록 동기부여를 한 Chloe에게 감사함을 느끼는 상황이다. 따라서 Roger가 Chloe에게 할 말로 가장 적절한 것은 ⑤ '아픈 아이들을 위해 내가 머리카락을 기부하도록 격려해 주어서 고마워.'이다.
① 아픈 아이들을 위해 머리카락을 기부하는 것에 대해 알고 싶어.
② 나는 고등학교 동창회에서 너를 더 자주 만나고 싶어.
③ 고등학교를 졸업한 이후로 너는 너무나 많이 변했어.
④ 긴 머리 스타일은 네가 고려하기에 좋은 선택이 될 수 있어.

Words & Phrases

reunion 동창회   length 길이   at least 적어도   organization 단체, 조직   gratitude 감사, 고마움   graduate 졸업하다   inspire 격려[고무]하다

16~17
정답 | 16 ② 17 ③

| Script & Translation |

M: Hello, students! I'm Brian Humphrey, director of Green Earth. Today, I want to share with you how buildings with amazing designs contribute to environmental preservation. These buildings not only look incredible but also help protect our environment.

One great example is the Bosco Verticale in Italy, which has trees and plants inside to maintain a comfortable temperature all year round. Agbar Tower in Spain is shaped like a fountain and employs special design elements to control temperature and make the most of natural light. It also has energy-efficient lighting systems and a water recycling system to save resources and use less energy. The Rock restaurant in Tanzania is built on a big rock in the ocean and is only accessible by boat during high tide. It uses solar panels to generate electricity, which is a clean and renewable energy source. Lastly, the Bullitt Center in the US boasts of a rainwater collection system and a garden that provides a home for birds and insects. These eco-friendly buildings showcase how nature can inspire sustainable structures that benefit us and the planet. I hope you found them interesting!

남: 안녕하세요, 학생 여러분! 저는 Green Earth의 책임자, Brian Humphrey입니다. 오늘, 저는 놀라운 디자인의 건물들이 어떻게 환경 보존에 기여하는지 여러분과 공유하고 싶습니다. 이 건물들은 믿기 어려울 만큼 훌륭하게 보일 뿐 아니라 우리의 환경을 보호하는 데 도움을 줍니다. 한 가지 훌륭한 예는 이탈리아의 Bosco Verticale로, 이 건물 안에는 나무와 식물이 있어 일년 내내 편안한 온도를 유지합니다. 스페인의 Agbar Tower는 분수처럼 생겼고 온도를 조절하고 자연광을 최대한 활용하기 위해 특별한 디자인 요소를 사용합니다. 또한 에너지 효율적인 조명 시스템과 물 재활용 시스템을 갖추고 있어 자원을 절약하고 에너지를 덜 사용합니다. 탄자니아의 Rock 식당은 바다의 큰 바위 위에 지어져서 만조 때에만 배로 접근할 수 있습니다. 그것은 태양 전지판을 사용하여 전기를 만들어 내는데, 이것은 깨끗하고 재생 가능한 에너지원입니다. 마지막으로, 미국의 Bullitt Center는 빗물 수집 시스템과 새와 곤충들에게 집을 제공하는 정원을 자랑합니다. 이러한 친환경 건물들은 자연이 우리와 지구에 이익이 되는 지속 가능한 구조물들에 어떻게 영감을 줄 수 있는지 보여 줍니다. 여러분이 그것들을 흥미롭게 느꼈기를 바랍니다!

❍ **Topic & Situation** 환경 보존에 영향을 미치는 친환경 건물들

❍ **Solution**

16 남자는 놀라운 디자인의 건물들이 어떻게 환경 보존에 기여하는지 학생들과 공유하고 싶다고 말하면서 다양한 방식으로 환경 보호에 도움이 되고 있는 여러 건축물에 대해서 언급하고 있

다. 따라서 남자가 하는 말의 주제로 가장 적절한 것은 ② '놀랍게 설계된 구조물이 환경 보호에 기여하는 방법'이다.

① 친환경 건물 설계 시 어려움
③ 자연 환경을 재창조할 때 기술 혁신의 역할
④ 일년 내내 건물의 온도를 일관되게 유지하기 위한 조언
⑤ 친환경 건물이 건축의 미래를 위해 만들고 있는 변화들

17 이탈리아, 스페인, 탄자니아, 미국은 언급되었지만, ③ '프랑스'는 언급되지 않았다.

❍ **Words & Phrases**

director 책임자, 감독   contribute 기여하다, 이바지하다   preservation 보존, 보호   incredible (믿기 어려울 만큼) 훌륭한, 믿기 힘든   temperature 온도, 기온   all year round 일년 내내   fountain 분수   element 요소, 성분   energy-efficient 에너지 효율적인, 연료 효율이 좋은   accessible 접근 가능한, 이해하기 쉬운   high tide 만조   solar panel 태양 전지판   generate 만들어 내다, 발생시키다   boast 자랑하다, 뽐내다   eco-friendly 친환경의, 친환경적인   sustainable 지속 가능한   innovation 혁신, 쇄신   consistent 일관된, 변함없는   architecture 건축

27강 실전 모의고사 6회

본문 192~197쪽

01 ④	02 ③	03 ①	04 ③	05 ⑤	06 ⑤
07 ④	08 ③	09 ②	10 ①	11 ⑤	12 ②
13 ④	14 ②	15 ④	16 ③	17 ③	

01

정답 | ④

| Script & Translation |

M: Good evening, residents. This is the apartment management office. Recently, we have received multiple complaints about people not throwing out their garbage appropriately. This has led to unpleasant odors and unsanitary conditions. To ensure a clean and healthy environment for everybody, we kindly request that you throw away your trash in the designated containers. First, be sure to separate recyclables from non-recyclables. Remember the red container is for plastics and the yellow one is for glass. For items that are too large to fit in the normal containers, please use the big black container next to the maintenance office. By working together to properly dispose of our trash, we can improve our apartment environment. Thank you for your cooperation.

남: 안녕하세요, 주민 여러분. 여기는 아파트 관리 사무실입니다. 최근에, 저희는 사람들이 쓰레기를 적절하게 버리지 않는다는 다수의 불만을 접수했습니다. 이로 인해 불쾌한 냄새와 비위생적인 환경이 발생했습니다. 모든 이들의 깨끗하고 건강한 환경을 보장하기 위해, 지정된 용기에 여러분의 쓰레기를 버리도록 정중히 요청합니다. 먼저 재활용할 수 없는 것과 재활용품을 반드시 분리해 주세요. 빨간색 용기는 플라스틱, 노란색 용기는 유리를 버리는 곳이라는 것을 기억해 주십시오. 일반 용기에 집어넣기에 너무 큰 품목은 관리 사무소 옆에 있는 큰 검은색 용기를 사용해 주세요. 쓰레기를 적절하게 처리하기 위해 함께 노력함으로써, 우리는 아파트 환경을 개선할 수 있습니다. 협조해 주셔서 감사합니다.

◐ Topic & Situation 쓰레기를 지정된 용기에 버리도록 요청하는 안내 방송

◐ Solution

남자는 최근 아파트에 쓰레기를 적절하지 않은 방식으로 버리는

것에 대해 다수의 불만이 접수되고 있다고 말하며, 쓰레기를 종류에 따라 지정된 용기에 버리도록 주민들에게 요청하고 있다. 따라서 남자가 하는 말의 목적으로 가장 적절한 것은 ④ '쓰레기를 종류에 따라 지정된 용기에 버리도록 요청하려고'이다.

◐ Words & Phrases

resident 주민 management 관리 appropriately 적절하게
odor 냄새, 악취 designated 지정된 recyclables 재활용품
dispose 처리하다, 폐기하다

02

정답 | ③

| Script & Translation |

W: Honey, did you throw away coffee grounds?

M: Yes, I did. Why's that?

W: I'd like to put some in our flowerpots.

M: Why? Is that good for plants?

W: Yes. Coffee grounds have some good oils and nutrients for plants. And they protect against bugs.

M: Oh, I've never guessed that.

W: You can also put coffee grounds in a shoe closet to help remove the smell.

M: That's really helpful to know. Do you know of any other uses?

W: Yes. They can also remove bad smells in sinks and refrigerators.

M: I see. From now on, I won't throw out the coffee grounds after I make coffee.

W: Great. We can use them in our daily lives.

M: Thanks for letting me know.

여: 여보, 커피 찌꺼기를 버렸어요?

남: 네, 그랬어요. 왜 그래요?

여: 화분에 좀 넣고 싶거든요.

남: 왜요? 그게 식물에 좋은가요?

여: 네. 커피 찌꺼기는 식물에 좋은 기름과 영양분을 가지고 있거든요. 그리고 벌레들로부터 보호해 줘요.

남: 아, 나는 그걸 전혀 생각도 못 했어요.

여: 커피 찌꺼기를 신발장에 넣으면 냄새를 제거하는 데 도움이 되기도 해요.

남: 그것을 알면 정말 도움이 되겠군요. 다른 어떤 용도도 알고 있어요?

여: 네. 싱크대와 냉장고의 나쁜 냄새도 제거할 수 있어요.

남: 그렇군요. 이제부터는 커피를 내리고 나서 커피 찌꺼기를 버리지 않을게요.

여: 좋아요. 우리는 그것을 우리의 일상생활에서 사용할 수 있어요.

남: 알려 줘서 고마워요.

● **Topic & Situation** 커피 찌꺼기의 유용성

● **Solution**

여자는 사용하고 남은 커피 찌꺼기가 식물에 영양을 공급하고 벌레를 막아 주기 때문에 커피 찌꺼기를 화분에 넣고 싶다고 말했고, 또한 커피 찌꺼기를 신발장이나 싱크대, 냉장고에 두어 냄새를 제거하는 등 일상생활에서 활용할 수 있다고 말했으므로, 여자의 의견으로 가장 적절한 것은 ③ '커피 찌꺼기는 일상에서 유용하게 쓰일 수 있다.'이다.

● **Words & Phrases**

coffee grounds 커피 찌꺼기   flowerpot 화분   nutrient 영양분
shoe closet 신발장   refrigerator 냉장고

03

정답 | ①

| Script & Translation |

M: Good morning, listeners. This is Dr. Robinson from *The Medical Minute*. A cell phone is something that many people use on a daily basis. It's a personal device that we keep close to us and always touch with our hands, which means it can easily become covered in germs. And what is especially unsanitary about it is how close you put it to your face and mouth. That's why it's important to clean your cell phone regularly. To clean your cell phone, you can use a damp cloth or an alcohol-based cleaner. By taking a few minutes to clean your cell phone on a regular basis, you can help keep it free of germs. This will help to keep you healthy and prevent the spread of illness.

남: 안녕하세요, 청취자 여러분. 저는 *The Medical Minute*의 Robinson 박사입니다. 휴대 전화는 많은 사람들이 매일 사용하는 것입니다. 이것은 우리가 가까이에 두고 항상 손으로 만지는 개인용 기기인데, 이는 세균으로 쉽게 뒤덮일 수 있다는

것을 의미합니다. 그리고 특히 그것에 대한 비위생적인 것은 그것을 우리가 얼굴과 입에 얼마나 가깝게 대느냐 하는 점입니다. 그렇기 때문에 정기적으로 휴대 전화를 소독하는 것이 중요합니다. 휴대 전화를 소독하기 위해, 여러분은 물기가 있는 천이나 알코올계 세정제를 사용할 수 있습니다. 정기적으로 휴대 전화를 소독하는 데 몇 분의 시간을 들임으로써, 여러분은 그것을 세균이 없는 상태로 유지하는 데 도움을 줄 수 있습니다. 이것은 여러분의 건강을 유지하고 질병의 확산을 막는 데 도움이 될 것입니다.

● **Topic & Situation** 건강을 위한 휴대 전화 소독의 중요성

● **Solution**

남자가 휴대 전화는 우리가 매일 사용하는 것이기에 세균에 감염되기 쉬우며, 얼굴과 입에 가까이 대는 개인적인 물건이기 때문에 소독을 꼭 해 줘야 한다고 강조하고 있다. 따라서 남자가 하는 말의 요지로 가장 적절한 것은 ① '건강을 위해 휴대 전화를 정기적으로 소독할 필요가 있다.'이다.

● **Words & Phrases**

daily 매일   device 기기, 장치   germ 세균   unsanitary 비위생적인   regularly 정기적으로   damp 물기가 있는, 축축한   alcohol-based 알코올계의, 알코올을 바탕으로 하는   free of ~가 없는   illness 질병

04

정답 | ③

| Script & Translation |

M: Hey, Molly. Have you seen the students' lounge since it was renovated?

W: Not yet. How is it?

M: It's way better than before. Here, I took a picture of it.

W: Let me see. *[Pause]* Wow! I like the plants hanging from the bar above the table.

M: They really make the atmosphere fresher. And aren't these ball-shaped lights on the ceiling really cool?

W: Definitely! Oh, those two chairs near the round table look comfortable.

M: Yeah, we can sit there and study together.

W: They installed a vending machine on the right wall! Awesome! Students are going to love that.

M: For sure. It has a good selection of snacks in it.

W: What do you think this TV screen next to the vending machine is for?

M: Maybe they'll use it as a bulletin board for important announcements.

W: You're probably right. Let's go to the lounge after school today.

남: 저기, Molly. 학생 휴게실을 새롭게 수리하고 난 뒤 본 적 있니?

여: 아직 못 봤어. 어때?

남: 그전보다 훨씬 더 좋아. 여기, 내가 그곳 사진을 찍어 왔어.

여: 어디 한번 보자. *[잠시 후]* 와! 탁자 위 막대 모양의 가로대에 걸려 있는 식물들이 마음에 들어.

남: 그것이 정말 분위기를 더 새롭게 만들고 있어. 그리고 천장에 있는 저 공 모양의 조명들이 정말 멋지지 않니?

여: 정말 그래! 오, 둥근 탁자 주변의 저 두 의자는 정말 편안해 보인다.

남: 맞아, 우리가 거기 앉아서 같이 공부할 수 있겠다.

여: 오른쪽 벽에 자판기를 설치했네! 멋진 걸! 학생들은 그것을 정말 좋아할 거야.

남: 분명히 그럴 거야. 그 안에 다양한 종류의 간식이 있어.

여: 자판기 옆의 이 TV 화면은 무엇을 위해 있는 걸까?

남: 아마도 중요한 공지 사항을 보여 줄 게시판으로 사용할 것 같아.

여: 네 말이 아마도 맞을 거야. 오늘 학교 끝나고 휴게실에 가 보자.

◐ Topic & Situation 새롭게 꾸며진 학생 휴게실

◐ Solution

여자가 둥근 탁자 주변의 의자에 앉아 공부해야겠다고 했으나, 그림 속 탁자는 네모난 모양을 하고 있다. 따라서 그림에서 대화의 내용과 일치하지 않는 것은 ③이다.

◐ Words & Phrases

lounge 휴게실   renovate 새롭게 단장하다   vending machine 자판기   bulletin board 게시판   announcement 공지 사항

05 정답 | ⑤

| Script & Translation |

W: Mr. Choi, how's the preparing for next Monday's parent-teacher night conference going?

M: Hi, Ms. White. I'm almost done. I only have a few more things to check.

W: I can give you a hand if you want.

M: That'd be great. Here's the checklist of things to prepare.

W: Let me see. *[Pause]* Hmm.... I'm sure you've already contacted all the parents.

M: Yes. I did that last week.

W: What about the handouts?

M: I've printed them out and put them on the desk in the conference room.

W: Great. Did you also prepare some paper and pencils for the parents to use when taking notes?

M: Oh, I did prepare the paper, but I forgot to buy some pencils.

W: Don't worry. I'll go and buy some.

M: Thanks. I'll go over the other things on the checklist.

여: 최 선생님, 다음 주 월요일 학부모 교사 저녁 간담회 준비는 어떻게 되어 가세요?

남: 안녕하세요, White 선생님. 거의 끝나가요. 몇 가지 더 확인해 볼 것만 남았어요.

여: 원하신다면 제가 도와 드릴게요.

남: 그러면 좋죠. 여기 준비해야 할 일들의 확인 목록이에요.

여: 한번 보죠. *[잠시 후]* 음…. 모든 부모님께 연락하는 것은 선생님이 이미 하셨을 게 분명해요.

남: 네. 지난주에 했어요.

여: 유인물은 어떻게 하셨어요?

남: 제가 출력해서 회의실 책상 위에 올려 두었어요.

여: 잘됐네요. 학부모님들이 필기할 때 쓸 종이와 연필도 좀 준비하셨나요?

남: 아, 종이는 준비했는데, 연필을 좀 사는 것을 잊어버렸네요.

여: 걱정하지 마세요. 제가 가서 몇 개 사 올게요.

남: 감사합니다. 저는 확인 목록에 있는 다른 것들을 살펴볼게요.

◐ Topic & Situation 학부모 교사 저녁 간담회 준비하기

◐ Solution

여자는 남자에게 다음 주에 있을 학부모 교사 저녁 간담회 준비가 잘 되어 가고 있는지 물었고, 남자가 거의 다 끝나간다고 대답하자, 여자가 더 도울 일이 없는지 재차 물었고, 남자는 그러면 준비된 것에 대해 확인을 해 달라고 한다. 여자가 참가자 명단과 유인물 준비에 대해 묻자, 남자는 모두 준비가 완료되었다고 했고, 여자가 다시 학부모들이 사용할 종이와 연필을 준비했는지 묻자, 남자는 종이는 준비했는데, 연필은 준비가 되지 않았다고 말한다. 이에 여자가 자신이 연필을 사 오겠다고 했으므로, 여자가 할 일

로 가장 적절한 것은 ⑤ '연필 사 오기'이다.

● **Words & Phrases**

parent-teacher night conference 학부모 교사 저녁 간담회 give a hand 돕다 checklist 확인 목록 contact 연락하다 take notes 필기하다, 메모하다

06

| **Script & Translation** |

W: Welcome to Wheelworks Bicycle Shop! How can I help you?

M: Hi, there are some bike accessories I'd like to get. The first one is a helmet.

W: Okay. Here are our helmets.

M: Hmm.... How much is this white one?

W: It's $60.

M: I'll take it. And I also need a bicycle light.

W: They are over here. These two models are the most popular. This one is $20, and this one is $10.

M: Hmm.... I'll take the cheaper one. And lastly, I need a pair of gloves.

W: I'd recommend these ones. They're originally $20 a pair, but they're on sale for 50% off.

M: Wow, I'll take a pair of those gloves, too.

W: Is there anything else you need?

M: No, that's all. Here's my credit card.

여: Wheelworks 자전거 판매점에 오신 것을 환영합니다! 어떻게 도와드릴까요?

남: 안녕하세요, 구입하고 싶은 자전거 부대 용품이 몇 가지 있어요. 첫 번째 물건은 헬멧입니다.

여: 알겠습니다. 여기 저희 가게의 헬멧들이 있어요.

남: 음…. 이 하얀색 헬멧은 얼마인가요?

여: 60달러입니다.

남: 그것으로 할게요. 저는 또한 자전거용 조명이 하나 필요해요.

여: 그것들은 저쪽에 있어요. 이 두 모델이 가장 인기가 있어요. 이것은 20달러이고, 이것은 10달러예요.

남: 음…. 더 싼 것으로 할게요. 그리고 마지막으로 장갑 한 켤레가 필요해요.

여: 이것들을 추천해요. 원래는 한 켤레에 20달러인데, 50% 할인하여 판매하고 있어요.

남: 와, 그 장갑도 살게요.

여: 다른 필요하신 것이 있나요?

남: 아니요, 그게 다입니다. 여기 제 신용 카드가 있어요.

● **Topic & Situation** 자전거 용품 구입하기

● **Solution**

남자가 60달러인 헬멧 한 개와, 10달러인 자전거용 조명 한 개, 그리고 50% 할인되어 10달러인 장갑을 한 켤레 구입하였으므로, 남자가 지불할 금액은 ⑤ '$80'이다.

● **Words & Phrases**

accessory 부대 용품 originally 원래 on sale 할인 판매 중인

07

| **Script & Translation** |

M: Good to see you again, Ms. Robinson. How have you been?

W: Hi, Mr. Kim. Good to see you, too.

M: How's your back feeling today?

W: Great. The poses that you taught me last week helped ease my back pain.

M: That's good to know. By the way, I was surprised you missed last Friday's yoga class. You didn't forget there was a class, did you?

W: No, I didn't forget. I even set a reminder on my phone.

M: Then, were you on the business trip you told me about?

W: Actually, I came back last Thursday, so that's not the reason.

M: Well, I hope it wasn't anything bad.

W: It was a challenging day from the start. My son suddenly got sick that day, so I had to take him to the doctor.

M: Oh, no. Is he okay?

W: Yes, he's much better now. Thanks for asking.

남: 다시 뵙게 되어 반갑습니다. Robinson 씨. 어떻게 지내셨나요?

여: 안녕하세요, Kim 선생님. 저도 다시 뵙게 되어 반갑네요.

남: 오늘 등은 좀 어떠세요?

여: 좋아요. 지난주 선생님께서 가르쳐주신 자세가 등 통증을 완화시키는 데 도움이 되었어요.

남: 알게 되어 기쁘네요. 그나저나, 지난주 금요일 요가 수업을 빠지셔서 놀랐습니다. 수업이 있다는 것을 잊으신 것은 아니겠지요, 그렇지요?

여: 아뇨, 잊어버리지 않았습니다. 심지어 제 전화기에 상기시켜 주는 것을 설정해 놓았어요.

남: 그러면 저에게 말씀하셨던 출장을 가셨던 건가요?

여: 사실, 지난주 목요일 돌아왔기 때문에, 그게 이유는 아니었습니다.

남: 음, 나쁜 일 때문이 아니었기를 바랍니다.

여: 처음부터 힘든 하루였어요. 제 아들이 갑자기 그날 아프게 되어서 제가 그를 병원에 데리고 갔어야 했습니다.

남: 오, 저런. 그는 괜찮나요?

여: 네, 지금은 많이 좋아졌습니다. 물어봐 주셔서 감사해요.

◐ Topic & Situation 요가 수업에 빠진 이유

◐ Solution

남자는 여자가 지난주 금요일 요가 수업을 빠진 이유를 궁금해 하며, 요가 수업 날짜를 잊어버렸거나 출장 때문인 건지 묻자, 여자는 자신의 아들이 아파서 병원에 데리고 가야 해서 수업에 빠졌다고 말한다. 따라서 여자가 지난주 금요일 요가 수업을 빠진 이유는 ④ '아들을 병원에 데려가야 해서'이다.

◐ Words & Phrases

back 등, 허리 pose 자세 ease 완화하다 reminder 상기시켜 주는 것 business trip 출장

08   정답 | ③

| Script & Translation |

W: Jim, have you heard about the new ice rink that just opened up in town?

M: No, I haven't. I really like ice skating. I'd love to visit there. Where is it located?

W: It's located near Central Park. It's a great location, and I heard that the rink is really nice. We should go there sometime.

M: Let's do it. When is it open?

W: It's open from 10 a.m. to 9 p.m. every day.

M: Cool. How much is admission?

W: It's $10 for adults and $8 for kids.

M: That's not bad. Is there a limit on how many people can skate at once? I don't feel comfortable when it's really crowded.

W: Yes. They have a 100-person limit.

M: That's good to hear. Then, how about going there tomorrow afternoon?

W: Great! I'm excited to check it out!

여: Jim, 시내에 막 문을 연 새로운 아이스 링크에 대해 들어 봤니?

남: 아니, 듣지 못했어. 나는 아이스 스케이팅을 정말 좋아해. 그곳을 방문하고 싶어. 그곳은 어디에 위치해 있니?

여: Central Park 근처에 있어. 위치가 좋고, 링크가 정말 좋다고 들었어. 우리 언제 가 보면 좋겠어.

남: 그러자. 언제 문을 여니?

여: 매일 오전 10시에서 오후 9시까지 문을 열어.

남: 좋아. 입장료는 얼마야?

여: 성인은 10달러, 어린이는 8달러야.

남: 나쁘지 않네. 동시에 얼마나 많은 사람이 스케이트를 탈 수 있는지에 대한 제한이 있니? 나는 사람이 너무 많아 붐빌 때는 편하지가 않거든.

여: 응. 100명의 제한 인원이 있어.

남: 그거 반가운 소리네. 그러면 내일 오후에 그곳에 가 보는 게 어때?

여: 좋아! 그곳을 살펴보게 되어 신이 나!

◐ Topic & Situation 새로 문을 연 아이스 링크

◐ Solution

새로 문을 연 아이스 링크에 관해 위치, 개장 시간, 입장료, 입장 제한 인원은 언급되었으나, ③ '교통편'은 언급되지 않았다.

◐ Words & Phrases

ice rink 아이스 링크 admission 입장료 crowded 사람이 많아 붐비는 check out 살펴보다

09   정답 | ②

| Script & Translation |

W: Hello, listeners! Today, I'd like to tell you about one of the most unique festivals in the world, the Whale Festival! It's an annual event held in the coastal town of Greenville. The festival celebrates the yearly arrival of whales in the waters off the coast. It typically takes place over a weekend in late September or early October and features a variety of events and activities for visitors of all ages. Visitors can take boat tours or walk along the cliffs to watch the whales as they swim and play in the ocean. And local vendors sell a wide variety of foods and drinks, as well as crafts and souvenirs. The festival also includes a range of workshops on environmental issues, including marine life conservation. It sounds like fun, doesn't it?

여: 안녕하세요, 청취자 여러분! 오늘, 저는 세계에서 가장 독특한 축제 중 하나인 고래 축제에 대해 말씀드리려고 합니다! 이 축제는 해안가 마을 Greenville에서 매년 열리는 행사입니다. 이 축제는 매년 고래들이 해안가 해역에 도착하는 것을 기념합니다. 그것은 일반적으로 9월 말이나 10월 초 주말 동안에 열리며 모든 연령의 방문객들을 위한 다양한 행사와 활동을 특별히 포함하고 있습니다. 방문객들은 보트 투어를 하거나 절벽을 따라 걸으며 고래들이 바다에서 수영하고 노는 것을 볼 수 있습니다. 그리고 지역 노점상들은 공예품과 기념품뿐만 아니라 매우 다양한 음식과 음료를 판매합니다. 그 축제는 또한 해양 생물 보존을 포함한 환경 문제에 관한 다양한 워크숍을 포함합니다. 재밌게 들리네요, 그렇죠?

◐ Topic & Situation Whale Festival

◐ Solution
여자는 축제가 일반적으로 9월 말이나 10월 초 주말 동안에 열린다고 했으므로, 담화의 내용과 일치하지 않는 것은 ② '보통 10월 말이나 11월 초에 주말 동안 열린다.'이다.

◐ Words & Phrases
unique 독특한 annual 매년의, 해마다의 coastal 해안의 take place 열리다 cliff 절벽 local vendor 지역 노점상 craft 공예품 souvenir 기념품 marine 해양의 conservation 보존

10 　　　　　　　　　　정답 | ①

| Script & Translation |

M: Welcome to Rolling Wheels Skate Shop. How can I help you?

W: Hi, I'm looking for a skateboard for my teenage son. He's a complete beginner.

M: A new skateboarder! Awesome! Let me show you what we have. I recommend one of these five. How tall is your son?

W: He's about 168 cm.

M: Then you should get a deck width smaller than 8 inches.

W: Okay. What about the material?

M: For a beginner, I recommend a wood deck. It's more stable than plastic.

W: That makes sense. What about the wheels?

M: I recommend soft wheels, which are better for beginners.

W: Okay. So it's down to these two. Hmm.... I'll take this. It's more expensive, but my son will love the design.

M: It's a great choice. How would you like to pay?

W: With a credit card. Here you go.

남: Rolling Wheels Skate Shop에 오신 것을 환영합니다. 어떻게 도와드릴까요?

여: 안녕하세요, 저는 제 십 대 아들을 위한 스케이트보드를 찾고 있어요. 그는 완전히 초보자예요.

남: 새로운 스케이트보더네요! 멋집니다! 저희가 가진 것들을 보여 드릴게요. 저는 이 다섯 가지 중에 하나를 추천해 드립니다. 아드님의 키가 어떻게 되나요?

여: 대략 168cm 정도 됩니다.

남: 그렇다면 덱의 폭이 8인치보다 더 작은 것을 사셔야 합니다.

여: 알겠어요. 재료는요?

남: 초보자에게는, 저는 나무 덱을 추천해 드립니다. 플라스틱보다 더 안정적이에요.

여: 일리가 있네요. 바퀴는 어떻나요?

남: 저는 부드러운 바퀴를 추천해 드리는데, 그게 초보자들에게 더 좋거든요.

여: 알겠어요. 그러면 이 두 가지로 좁혀지네요. 음…. 이것으로 하겠습니다. 더 비싸기는 하지만, 제 아들이 디자인을 정말 좋아할 것 같아요.

남: 좋은 선택이십니다. 어떻게 지불하시겠습니까?

여: 신용 카드로 할게요. 여기 있습니다.

◐ Topic & Situation 스케이트보드 구입하기

◐ Solution
스케이트보드 초보자인 아들을 위한 보드를 구입하기 위해 여자가 남자에게 조언을 구하고 있는데, 덱 폭은 8인치 미만이고,

재료는 나무이며, 바퀴는 부드러운 것을 남자가 추천했고, 남은 두 개 중 더 비싼 것을 여자가 선택했으므로, 여자가 구입할 스케이트보드는 ①이다.

● **Words & Phrases**

beginner 초보자   width 폭   stable 안정적인

11
정답 | ⑤

| **Script & Translation** |

M: Honey, have you seen my watch? I put it on the desk, but it's not there.

W: Are you sure? I cleaned up the desk a few hours ago, and nothing was on it.

M: Hmm.... Maybe I put it somewhere else, but I can't remember. Where could it be?

W: Why don't you look on the dining table in the kitchen?

남: 여보, 제 시계 봤어요? 책상 위에 두었는데, 거기에 없네요.

여: 분명해요? 몇 시간 전에 책상을 청소했는데, 그곳에 아무것도 없었어요.

남: 음…. 아마 다른 곳에다 두었나 본데, 기억이 나질 않네요. 어디에 있을까요?

여: 부엌에 있는 식탁 위를 살펴보지 그래요?

● **Topic & Situation** 남편이 잃어버린 시계를 찾는 것을 도와주는 아내

● **Solution**

남자는 여자에게 책상 위에 둔 자신의 시계를 본 적이 있는지 물었고, 여자는 몇 시간 전에 그곳을 청소할 때 보지 못했다고 했다. 남자가 아마도 다른 곳에 둔 것 같은데 기억이 나질 않는다며, 어디에 있을지 묻고 있으므로, 남자의 마지막 말에 대한 여자의 응답으로 가장 적절한 것은 ⑤ '부엌에 있는 식탁 위를 살펴보지 그래요?'이다.

① 다음 주까지 제 시계를 고치는 것이 가능할까요?

② 탁자 근처 아무 데서나 제 시계를 본 적 있나요?

③ 제가 지금 바로 방을 청소하기를 원하시나요?

④ 당신 시계를 찾는 데 얼마나 걸릴 것 같나요?

● **Words & Phrases**

fix 고치다, 수리하다   dining table 식탁

12
정답 | ②

| **Script & Translation** |

W: Hi, Mr. Smith. Did you want me to check your computer?

M: Oh, hi, Ms. Lewis. Yes. My Internet browser keeps shutting down, and I don't know why.

W: Let me take a quick look. *[Typing sounds]* Hmm.... This will take some time. I hope that's okay with you.

M: No problem. I don't need to use it for a while.

여: 안녕하세요, Smith 씨. 제가 선생님의 컴퓨터를 점검해 주기를 원하셨나요?

남: 오, 안녕하세요, Lewis 선생님. 네. 제 인터넷 브라우저가 계속 멈추는데, 저는 그 이유를 모르겠어요.

여: 제가 빠르게 살펴볼게요. *[타자 치는 소리]* 음…. 시간이 좀 걸릴 것 같아요. 그게 선생님에게 괜찮기를 바랍니다.

남: 문제없습니다. 한동안은 저는 그것을 사용할 필요가 없어요.

● **Topic & Situation** 컴퓨터 고치기

● **Solution**

여자가 남자에게 컴퓨터 점검 때문에 자신을 보기를 원했는지 물었고, 남자가 그렇다고 대답하며 자신의 컴퓨터에 이상 증상이 있음을 여자에게 말한다. 여자는 잠시 남자의 컴퓨터를 살펴본 뒤, 고치는 데 시간이 좀 걸릴 것 같다며, 남자가 그것에 대해 괜찮은지 물어본다. 따라서 여자의 마지막 말에 대한 남자의 응답으로 가장 적절한 것은 ② '문제없습니다. 한동안은 저는 그것을 사용할 필요가 없어요.'이다.

① 음, 제 생각에는 제 컴퓨터가 잘 작동하는 것 같아요.

③ 죄송합니다만, 제가 지금 바로 인터넷에 접속할 수가 없어요.

④ 괜찮아요. 이미 어제 제가 기술적 지원을 요청해 두었어요.

⑤ 신경 쓰지 마세요. 제가 당신 컴퓨터를 수리점에 그냥 보낼게요.

● **Words & Phrases**

browser 브라우저(인터넷의 자료들을 읽을 수 있게 해 주는 프로그램)

shut down 멈추다, 정지하다   technical 기술적인

13

정답 | ④

| Script & Translation |

[Telephone rings.]

M: Thank you for calling The Hungry Table. How can I help you?

W: Hi, I have a reservation for four tonight at 7 p.m., but I'd like to change the time. Is that possible?

M: Of course. Can I have the name for the reservation?

W: Yes, it's under Emily Bennett.

M: Thank you. What time would you like to change your reservation to?

W: I'd like to change it to 8 p.m.

M: Okay. I'll make that change for you right now. Is there anything else I can help you with?

W: Oh, one more thing. I asked for a booth when I made the initial reservation. Is that still possible?

M: I'm sorry, but all the booths are reserved for 8 p.m. However, I can give you a table near the window.

W: Is that area quiet?

M: Yes. It is as quiet as a booth.

W: In that case, sitting near the window sounds great.

[전화벨이 울린다.]

남: The Hungry Table에 전화해 주셔서 감사합니다. 어떻게 도와드릴까요?

여: 안녕하세요, 그곳에 오늘 저녁 7시에 4명 자리를 예약했는데, 시간을 바꾸고 싶어서요. 가능할까요?

남: 물론입니다. 예약하신 성함을 말씀해 주시겠어요?

여: 네, Emily Bennett이라는 이름으로 예약했습니다.

남: 감사해요. 예약을 몇 시로 바꿔 드릴까요?

여: 오후 8시로 바꾸고 싶습니다.

남: 알겠습니다. 제가 지금 바로 바꿔 드리도록 하겠습니다. 다른 도와드릴 일이 있을까요?

여: 오, 한 가지 더 있습니다. 처음 예약할 때 칸막이가 있는 자리를 요청드렸습니다. 여전히 가능한가요?

남: 죄송합니다만, 모든 칸막이 자리의 저녁 8시 예약은 꽉 찼습니다. 하지만 창가 자리는 드릴 수 있습니다.

여: 그 구역은 조용한가요?

남: 네 그렇습니다. 칸막이가 있는 자리만큼 조용합니다.

여: 그런 경우라면, 창문 근처에 앉는 것이 좋겠네요.

◐ Topic & Situation 식당 예약 시간 변경하기

◐ Solution

여자는 자신이 예약한 식당의 예약 시간을 변경하고자 식당에 전화를 걸었고, 전화에 응대한 남자는 예약 시간을 조정하는 것이 가능하다며 곧바로 여자가 원하는 시간으로 변경해 준다. 곧이어 남자가 또 다른 요구 사항이 있는지 물었고, 여자가 원래 예약했던 대로 칸막이가 있는 좌석이 가능하냐고 묻자, 남자는 이는 불가하지만 칸막이 자리만큼 조용한 창가 자리는 가능하다고 대답한다. 따라서 남자의 마지막 말에 대한 여자의 응답으로 가장 적절한 것은 ④ '그런 경우라면, 창문 근처에 앉는 것이 좋겠네요.'이다.

① 칸막이가 있는 자리에 앉게 해 주셔서 감사해요.

② 그것이 제가 예약을 취소하고 싶은 이유입니다.

③ 당신과 함께 이곳에서 저녁을 먹게 되어 정말 신나요.

⑤ 우리는 그 시간에 맞춰 갈 수 없을 것 같아요.

◐ Words & Phrases

reservation 예약   booth 칸막이가 있는 자리   initial 최초의
reserved 예약이 되어 있는

14

정답 | ②

| Script & Translation |

W: Grandpa, do you have a minute? I have something to tell you.

M: Of course, my dear. What is it?

W: I think I made my friend Susan angry at school. I don't know what to do.

M: Oh, what happened?

W: She asked me to help her with her homework, but I was really busy doing my own. So I angrily told her to leave me alone.

M: Oh, that's a pretty harsh thing to say to your friend.

W: I know. I was just so focused on my own work, and her request really annoyed me.

M: I understand. But you should've thought more carefully about your words. It sounds like you may have hurt Susan's feelings.

W: You're right. When I think about it again, I was too mean to her.

M: Well, I think you should say sorry to her.

W: But I think I missed the right timing. I wonder she'll be even more upset if I apologize late.

M: Don't worry. It's never too late to say sorry.

여: 할아버지, 잠깐 시간 있으세요? 말씀드릴 것이 있어요.

남: 물론이지, 애야. 무슨 일이니?

여: 제가 학교에서 제 친구 Susan을 화나게 만든 것 같아요. 어떻게 해야 할지 모르겠어요.

남: 오, 무슨 일이 있었니?

여: 그녀가 자기의 숙제를 도와달라고 부탁했는데, 제가 제 숙제를 하느라 정말 바빴어요. 그래서 저는 그녀에게 화를 내며 저를 혼자 내버려 두라고 말했어요.

남: 오, 친구에게 하기에는 매우 가혹한 말이구나.

여: 알아요. 저는 그저 제 일에 너무 몰두해 있었고, 그녀의 요청이 저를 정말 짜증나게 했어요.

남: 이해해. 하지만 네 말에 대해 더 세심하게 생각했어야 해. 네가 Susan의 감정에 상처를 준 것 같이 들리는구나.

여: 맞아요. 다시 생각해 보면, 그녀에게 너무 못되게 군 것 같아요.

남: 음, 그녀에게 미안하다고 말해야 할 것 같구나.

여: 하지만 제가 적당한 때를 놓친 것 같아요. 제가 늦게 사과하면 그녀가 훨씬 더 언짢아하지 않을까 모르겠어요.

남: 걱정 말거라. 미안하다고 말하는 것은 언제 해도 늦지 않단다.

○ Topic & Situation 할아버지에게 조언을 구하는 손녀

○ Solution

여자가 남자에게 고민이 있다고 말하고, 남자가 무슨 일이냐고 묻자, 여자는 숙제를 도와 달라는 친구에게 화를 내며 자신을 혼자 내버려 두라고 말했다고 했고, 남자는 그것은 친구에게 너무 가혹한 말이며, 여자가 친구의 마음에 상처를 준 것이라고 말한다. 남자는 여자가 친구에게 사과해야 한다고 말했고, 여자는 너무 늦은 사과 때문에 친구가 훨씬 더 언짢아할지 모르겠다고 한다. 따라서 여자의 마지막 말에 대한 남자의 응답으로 가장 적절한 것은 ② '걱정 말거라. 미안하다고 말하는 것은 언제 해도 늦지 않단다.'이다.

① 힘내! 너는 다음번에 더 좋은 점수를 받을 거야.

③ 맞아. 그녀는 너를 만나 행복할 거야.

④ 문제 없어. 내가 도움이 될 수 있어 기쁘구나.

⑤ 동의해. 너는 그녀에게 화가 날 만해.

○ Words & Phrases

harsh 가혹한   annoy 짜증나게 하다   mean 못된   apologize 사과하다

15

| Script & Translation |

M: Amy and Peter have been dating for a few months and they are looking for new ways to spend time together. They usually have dinner dates, movie nights and they often go on long walks, but they are both looking to do something they've never done together before. One day, Peter suggests they go on a hiking trip, since they both like outdoor activities. On the other hand, Amy finds out about a cooking class for couples at a nearby community center. Peter says he would be glad to try both, and asks Amy what she would like to do. Amy also thinks that both are great plans, but she wants to take the cooking class first. In this situation, what would Amy most likely say to Peter?

Amy: <u>Both sound good to me, but let's try the cooking class first.</u>

남: Amy와 Peter는 몇 달 동안 데이트해 오고 있는데, 그들은 함께 시간을 보낼 새로운 방법을 찾고 있습니다. 그들은 보통 같이 저녁 먹기, 밤에 영화 보기를 하고, 종종 오래 산책하기를 하지만, 둘 다 그전에는 함께해 본 적이 없는 것을 찾고 있습니다. 어느 날, Peter는 하이킹 여행을 가자고 제안하는데, 이는 둘 다 야외 활동을 좋아하기 때문입니다. 반면 Amy는 인근 지역 주민 센터에서 하는 커플을 위한 요리 교실에 대해 알게 되었습니다. Peter는 기꺼이 두 가지를 모두 해보겠다고 말하고 Amy에게 무엇을 하고 싶은지 물어봅니다. Amy도 둘 다 좋은 계획이라고 생각하지만, 그녀는 먼저 요리 수업을 듣고 싶어 합니다. 이런 상황에서, Amy는 Peter에게 뭐라고 말하겠습니까?

Amy: <u>내겐 둘 다 좋은 것 같지만, 먼저 요리 수업을 수강하자.</u>

○ Topic & Situation 새로운 데이트 계획하기

○ Solution

데이트를 해 온 Amy와 Peter는 새로운 형태의 데이트 활동을 물색 중인데, Peter는 하이킹을, Amy는 요리 교실에 참여하는 것을 해보고 싶어 한다. Peter가 둘 다 괜찮은데 어떻게 하겠냐고 Amy에게 물어 보고, Amy는 요리 교실에 참여하는 것을 먼저 해보고 싶다고 말하려는 상황이다. 따라서 Amy가 Peter에게 할 말로 가장 적절한 것은 ④ '내겐 둘 다 좋은 것 같지만, 먼저 요리 수업을 수강하자.'이다.

① 네가 전문 요리사처럼 요리를 할 수 있다는 것이 안 믿어져.

② 그렇게 멋진 데이트를 나를 위해 계획해 줘서 고마워.

③ 우리 친구들과 함께 모두 다 같이 여행을 간다면 재미있을 거야.

⑤ 너는 야외 활동을 좋아하니까 캠핑을 정말 좋아할 것이 분명해.

● Words & Phrases

walk 산책, 걷기   outdoor 야외의, 바깥의   community center 지역 주민 센터   professional 전문적인

16~17

정답 | 16 ③ 17 ③

| Script & Translation |

W: Welcome back to class, everyone. Last class we talked about how important it is to keep a well-balanced diet. Today, I'd like to tell you about some seasonal fruits and why adding them to our diet is helpful to our health. Here are some examples. First, strawberries are a great spring fruit. Strawberries are rich in vitamins A and K, which will help you overcome spring fatigue. Also, eating watermelons is perfect for summer because it can help keep you hydrated and cool in the summer heat. Another example is apples for the fall. They're rich in fiber and antioxidants, which can help boost your immune system. This can help you adjust to the change in weather. Lastly, oranges are a good choice for winter. They are rich in vitamin C, which helps prevent the common cold. Overall, eating seasonal fruit is a good way to keep you healthy. Now, let's try these seasonal fruits that I brought in for you today.

여: 수업에 다시 오신 것을 환영합니다, 여러분. 지난 수업에서 우리는 균형 잡힌 식단을 유지하는 것이 얼마나 중요한지에 대해 이야기했습니다. 오늘, 저는 여러분에게 계절 과일과 그것을 우리의 식단에 첨가하는 것이 왜 우리의 건강에 도움이 되는지 말해 주려고 합니다. 여기 몇 가지 예가 있습니다. 첫째, 딸기는 좋은 봄철 과일입니다. 딸기에는 비타민 A와 K가 풍부한데, 그것들은 여러분이 봄에 느끼는 피로감을 극복하는 데 도움을 줄 것입니다. 또한, 여러분에게 수분을 공급하고 여름의 열기 속에 여러분을 시원하게 유지시켜 주는 데 도움을 줄 수 있기 때문에 수박을 먹는 것은 여름에 매우 좋습니다. 또 다른 예는 가을에 먹는 사과입니다. 그것들은 섬유질과 산화 방지제가 풍부해서 면역 체계를 강화하는 데 도움을 줄 수 있습니다. 이것은 여러분이 날씨 변화에 적응하는 것을 도울 수 있습니다. 마지막으로, 오렌지는 겨울에 좋은 선택입니다. 그것들에는 감기를 예방하는 데 도움이 되는 비타민 C가 풍부합니다. 일반적으로, 계절 과일을 먹는 것은 여러분 자신을 건강하게 유지하는 좋은 방법입니다. 이제 제가 오늘 여러분들을 위해 가지고 온 제철 과일을 먹어 봅시다.

● Topic & Situation 계절별로 먹으면 좋은 과일들과 그 이점

● Solution

16 여자는 계절 과일을 섭취하는 것이 계절별로 어떻게 건강에 도움을 줄 수 있는지 예를 들어 설명하고 있다. 따라서 여자가 하는 말의 주제로 가장 적절한 것은 ③ '계절 과일을 먹는 것이 어떻게 우리가 건강을 유지하도록 도울 수 있는가'이다.

① 건강하고 균형 잡힌 음식을 먹는 것의 중요성
② 지역 시장에서 계절 과일을 사는 최상의 방법
④ 각각 다른 계절에 신선한 과일을 찾아내는 것의 어려움
⑤ 과일에서 흔하게 발견되는 다양한 종류의 비타민

17 계절 과일의 예시로 딸기, 수박, 사과, 오렌지는 언급되었지만, ③ '포도'는 언급되지 않았다.

● Words & Phrases

well-balanced 균형 잡힌   diet 식단, 음식   seasonal 계절적인   rich 풍부한   hydrated 수분이 공급된   fiber 섬유질   antioxidant 산화 방지제, 항산화제   immune system 면역 체계   adjust to ~에 적응하다

고1~2 내신 중점 로드맵

과목	고교 입문		기초	기본	특화		+	단기
국어	고등 예비 과정	내 등급은?	윤혜정의 개념의 나비효과 입문편/워크북	**기본서** 올림포스	**국어 특화** 국어 독해의 원리 / 국어 문법의 원리			단기 특강
			어휘가 독해다!	올림포스 전국연합 학력평가 기출문제집				
영어			정승익의 수능 개념 잡는 대박구문		**영어 특화** Grammar POWER / Reading POWER / Listening POWER / Voca POWER			
			주혜연의 해석공식 논리 구조편					
수학			**기초** 50일 수학	**유형서** 올림포스 유형편	**고급** 올림포스 고난도			
			매쓰 디렉터의 고1 수학 개념 끝장내기	**수학 특화** 수학의 왕도				
한국사 사회		**인공지능** 수학과 함께하는 고교 AI 입문 수학과 함께하는 AI 기초		**기본서** 개념완성 / 개념완성 문항편	고등학생을 위한 多담은 한국사 연표			
과학								

과목	시리즈명	특징	수준	권장 학년
전과목	고등예비과정	예비 고등학생을 위한 과목별 단기 완성	●	예비 고1
	내 등급은?	고1 첫 학력평가+반 배치고사 대비 모의고사	●	예비 고1
국/수/영	올림포스	내신과 수능 대비 EBS 대표 국어·수학·영어 기본서	●	고1~2
	올림포스 전국연합학력평가 기출문제집	전국연합학력평가 문제+개념 기본서	●	고1~2
	단기 특강	단기간에 끝내는 유형별 문항 연습	●	고1~2
한/사/과	개념완성 & 개념완성 문항편	개념 한 권+문항 한 권으로 끝내는 한국사·탐구 기본서	●	고1~2
국어	윤혜정의 개념의 나비효과 입문편/워크북	윤혜정 선생님과 함께 시작하는 국어 공부의 첫걸음	●	예비 고1~고2
	어휘가 독해다!	학평·모평·수능 출제 필수 어휘 학습	●	예비 고1~고2
	국어 독해의 원리	내신과 수능 대비 문학·독서(비문학) 특화서	●	고1~2
	국어 문법의 원리	필수 개념과 필수 문항의 언어(문법) 특화서	●	고1~2
영어	정승익의 수능 개념 잡는 대박구문	정승익 선생님과 CODE로 이해하는 영어 구문	●	예비 고1~고2
	주혜연의 해석공식 논리 구조편	주혜연 선생님과 함께하는 유형별 지문 독해	●	예비 고1~고2
	Grammar POWER	구문 분석 트리로 이해하는 영어 문법 특화서	●	고1~2
	Reading POWER	수준과 학습 목적에 따라 선택하는 영어 독해 특화서	●	고1~2
	Listening POWER	수준별 수능형 영어듣기 모의고사	●	고1~2
	Voca POWER	영어 교육과정 필수 어휘와 어원별 어휘 학습	●	고1~2
수학	50일 수학	50일 만에 완성하는 중학~고교 수학의 맥	●	예비 고1~고2
	매쓰 디렉터의 고1 수학 개념 끝장내기	스타강사 강의, 손글씨 풀이와 함께 고1 수학 개념 정복	●	예비 고1~고1
	올림포스 유형편	유형별 반복 학습을 통해 실력 잡는 수학 유형서	●	고1~2
	올림포스 고난도	1등급을 위한 고난도 유형 집중 연습	●	고1~2
	수학의 왕도	직관적 개념 설명과 세분화된 문항 수록 수학 특화서	●	고1~2
한국사	고등학생을 위한 多담은 한국사 연표	연표로 흐름을 잡는 한국사 학습	●	예비 고1~고2
기타	수학과 함께하는 고교 AI 입문/AI 기초	파이선 프로그래밍, AI 알고리즘에 필요한 수학 개념 학습	●	예비 고1~고2

고2~N수 수능 집중 로드맵

수능 입문			기출 / 연습		연계+연계 보완		심화 / 발전	모의고사

수능 입문
- 윤혜정의 개념/ 패턴의 나비효과
- 하루 6개 1등급 영어독해
- 수능 감(感)잡기
- 수능특강 Light

강의노트
- 수능개념

기출 / 연습
- 윤혜정의 기출의 나비효과
- 수능 기출의 미래
- 수능 기출의 미래 미니모의고사
- 수능특강Q 미니모의고사

연계+연계 보완
- 수능연계교재의 VOCA 1800
- 수능연계 기출 Vaccine VOCA 2200

연계
- 감수 수능특강
- 감수 수능완성

- 수능특강 사용설명서
- 수능특강 연계 기출
- 수능 영어 간접연계 서치라이트
- 수능완성 사용설명서

심화 / 발전
- 수능연계완성 3주 특강
- 박봄의 사회 · 문화 표 분석의 패턴

모의고사
- FINAL 실전모의고사
- 만점마무리 봉투모의고사
- 만점마무리 봉투모의고사 시즌2

구분	시리즈명	특징	수준	영역
수능 입문	윤혜정의 개념/패턴의 나비효과	윤혜정 선생님과 함께하는 수능 국어 개념/패턴 학습		국어
	하루 6개 1등급 영어독해	매일 꾸준한 기출문제 학습으로 완성하는 1등급 영어 독해		영어
	수능 감(感) 잡기	동일 소재 · 유형의 내신과 수능 문항 비교로 수능 입문		국/수/영
	수능특강 Light	수능 연계교재 학습 전 연계교재 입문서		영어
	수능개념	EBSi 대표 강사들과 함께하는 수능 개념 다지기		전 영역
기출/연습	윤혜정의 기출의 나비효과	윤혜정 선생님과 함께하는 까다로운 국어 기출 완전 정복		국어
	수능 기출의 미래	올해 수능에 딱 필요한 문제만 선별한 기출문제집		전 영역
	수능 기출의 미래 미니모의고사	부담없는 실전 훈련, 고품질 기출 미니모의고사		국/수/영
	수능특강Q 미니모의고사	매일 15분으로 연습하는 고품격 미니모의고사		전 영역
연계 + 연계 보완	수능특강	최신 수능 경향과 기출 유형을 분석한 종합 개념서		전 영역
	수능특강 사용설명서	수능 연계교재 수능특강의 지문 · 자료 · 문항 분석		국/영
	수능특강 연계 기출	수능특강 수록 작품 · 지문과 연결된 기출문제 학습		국어
	수능완성	유형 분석과 실전모의고사로 단련하는 문항 연습		전 영역
	수능완성 사용설명서	수능 연계교재 수능완성의 국어 · 영어 지문 분석		국/영
	수능 영어 간접연계 서치라이트	출제 가능성이 높은 핵심만 모아 구성한 간접연계 대비 교재		영어
	수능연계교재의 VOCA 1800	수능특강과 수능완성의 필수 중요 어휘 1800개 수록		영어
	수능연계 기출 Vaccine VOCA 2200	수능-EBS 연계 및 평가원 최다 빈출 어휘 선별 수록		영어
심화/발전	수능연계완성 3주 특강	단기간에 끝내는 수능 1등급 변별 문항 대비서		국/수/영
	박봄의 사회·문화 표 분석의 패턴	박봄 선생님과 사회·문화 표 분석 문항의 패턴 연습		사회탐구
모의고사	FINAL 실전모의고사	EBS 모의고사 중 최다 분량, 최다 과목 모의고사		전 영역
	만점마무리 봉투모의고사	실제 시험지 형태와 OMR 카드로 실전 훈련 모의고사		전 영역
	만점마무리 봉투모의고사 시즌2	수능 완벽대비 최종 봉투모의고사		국/수/영

memo

총신대학교
CHONGSHIN UNIVERSITY

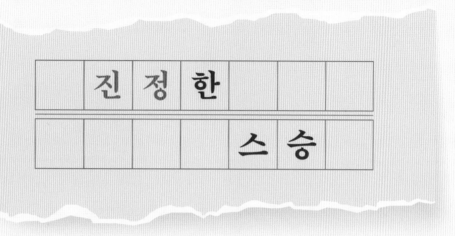

진정한
스승

지식을 전달하는 스승이 있습니다.
기술을 전수하는 스승이 있습니다.
삶으로 가르치는 스승이 있습니다.
모두가 우리의 인생에 필요한 분들입니다.

**그러나 무엇보다도 진정한 스승은
생명을 살리는 스승입니다.**

또 비유로 말씀하시되 소경이 소경을 인도할 수 있느냐 둘이 다 구덩이에 빠지지 아니하겠느냐
— 누가복음 6장 39절 —

11159 경기도 포천시 호국로 1007(선단동)
입학 문의 및 상담 : 031-539-1234
대진대학교 홈페이지 : http://www.daejin.ac.kr

미래를 향한 항해가 시작되었습니다.
대진대학교는 당신의 **등대**입니다.

본 교재 광고의 수익금은 콘텐츠 품질 개선과 공익사업에 사용됩니다.
모두의 요강(mdipsi.com)을 통해 대진대학교의 입시정보를 확인할 수 있습니다.

대진대학교
DAEJIN UNIVERSITY

고2~N수 수능 집중 로드맵

수능 입문 → 기출 / 연습 → 연계+연계 보완 → 심화 / 발전 → 모의고사

수능 입문
- 윤혜정의 개념/패턴의 나비효과
- 하루 6개 1등급 영어독해
- 수능 감(感)잡기
- 수능특강 Light

강의노트 수능개념

기출 / 연습
- 윤혜정의 기출의 나비효과
- 수능 기출의 미래
- 수능 기출의 미래 미니모의고사
- 수능특강Q 미니모의고사

수능연계교재의 VOCA 1800
수능연계 기출 Vaccine VOCA 2200

연계
- 수능특강
- 수능완성

연계+연계 보완
- 수능특강 사용설명서
- 수능특강 연계 기출
- 수능 영어 간접연계 서치라이트
- 수능완성 사용설명서

심화 / 발전
- 수능연계완성 3주 특강
- 박봄의 사회·문화 표 분석의 패턴

모의고사
- FINAL 실전모의고사
- 만점마무리 봉투모의고사
- 만점마무리 봉투모의고사 시즌2
- 만점마무리 봉투모의고사 BLACK Edition
- 수능 직전보강 클리어 봉투모의고사

구분	시리즈명	특징	수준	영역
수능 입문	윤혜정의 개념/패턴의 나비효과	윤혜정 선생님과 함께하는 수능 국어 개념/패턴 학습	●	국어
	하루 6개 1등급 영어독해	매일 꾸준한 기출문제 학습으로 완성하는 1등급 영어 독해	●	영어
	수능 감(感) 잡기	동일 소재·유형의 내신과 수능 문항 비교로 수능 입문	●	국/수/영
	수능특강 Light	수능 연계교재 학습 전 연계교재 입문서	●	영어
	수능개념	EBSi 대표 강사들과 함께하는 수능 개념 다지기	●	전 영역
기출/연습	윤혜정의 기출의 나비효과	윤혜정 선생님과 함께하는 까다로운 국어 기출 완전 정복	●	국어
	수능 기출의 미래	올해 수능에 딱 필요한 문제만 선별한 기출문제집	●	전 영역
	수능 기출의 미래 미니모의고사	부담없는 실전 훈련, 고품질 기출 미니모의고사	●	국/수/영
	수능특강Q 미니모의고사	매일 15분으로 연습하는 고품격 미니모의고사	●	전 영역
연계 + 연계 보완	수능특강	최신 수능 경향과 기출 유형을 분석한 종합 개념서	●	전 영역
	수능특강 사용설명서	수능 연계교재 수능특강의 지문·자료·문항 분석	●	국/영
	수능특강 연계 기출	수능특강 수록 작품·지문과 연결된 기출문제 학습	●	국어
	수능완성	유형 분석과 실전모의고사로 단련하는 문항 연습	●	전 영역
	수능완성 사용설명서	수능 연계교재 수능완성의 국어·영어 지문 분석	●	국/영
	수능 영어 간접연계 서치라이트	출제 가능성이 높은 핵심만 모아 구성한 간접연계 대비 교재	●	영어
	수능연계교재의 VOCA 1800	수능특강과 수능완성의 필수 중요 어휘 1800개 수록	●	영어
	수능연계 기출 Vaccine VOCA 2200	수능-EBS 연계 및 평가원 최다 빈출 어휘 선별 수록	●	영어
심화/발전	수능연계완성 3주 특강	단기간에 끝내는 수능 1등급 변별 문항 대비서	●	국/수/영
	박봄의 사회·문화 표 분석의 패턴	박봄 선생님과 사회·문화 표 분석 문항의 패턴 연습	●	사회탐구
모의고사	FINAL 실전모의고사	EBS 모의고사 중 최다 분량, 최다 과목 모의고사	●	전 영역
	만점마무리 봉투모의고사	실제 시험지 형태와 OMR 카드로 실전 훈련 모의고사	●	전 영역
	만점마무리 봉투모의고사 시즌2	수능 직전 실전 훈련 봉투모의고사	●	국/수/영
	만점마무리 봉투모의고사 BLACK Edition	수능 직전 최종 마무리용 실전 훈련 봉투모의고사	●	국·수·영
	수능 직전보강 클리어 봉투모의고사	수능 직전(D-60) 보강 학습용 실전 훈련 봉투모의고사	●	전 영역